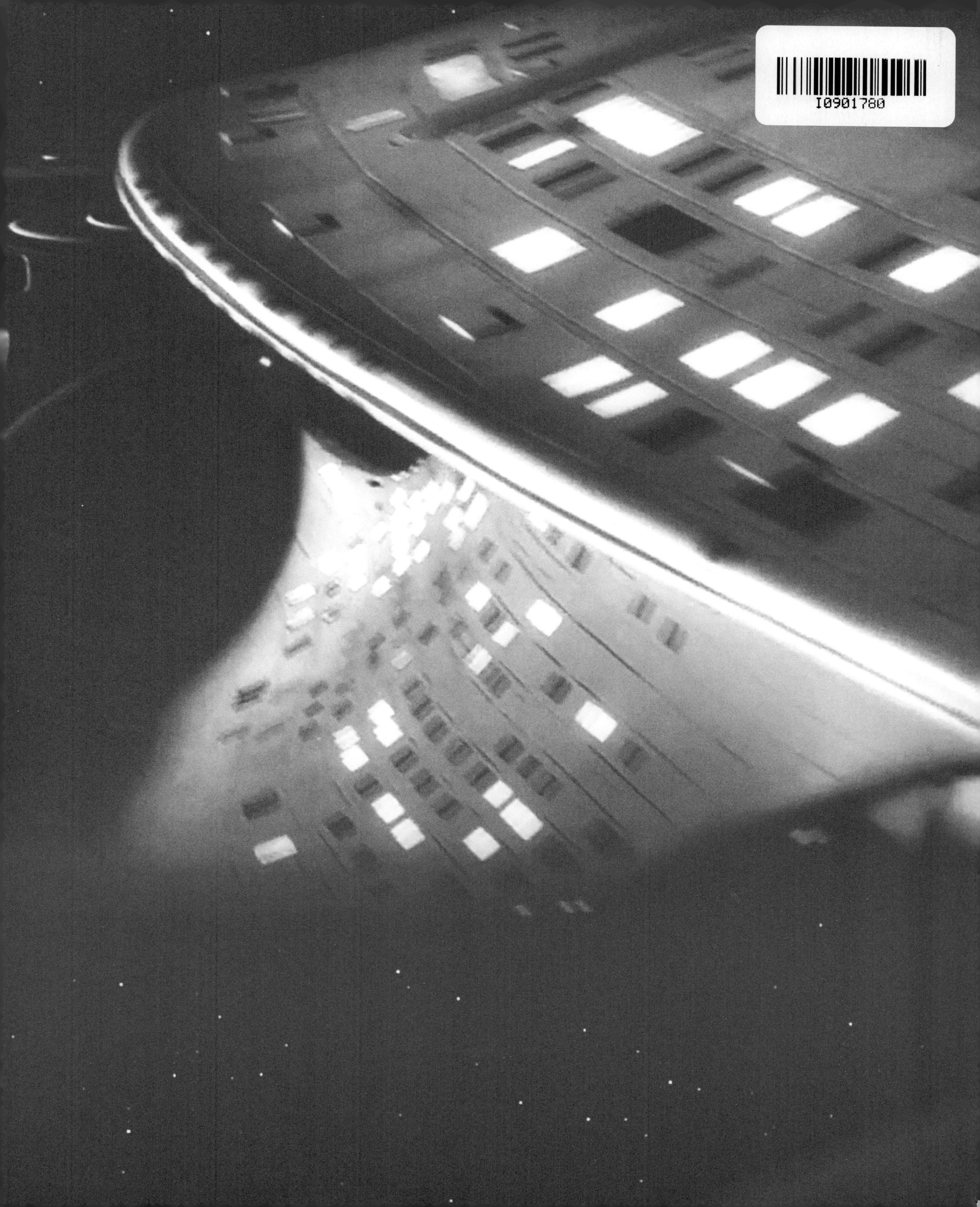

STAR TREK:
THE ARTISTRY OF DAN CURRY

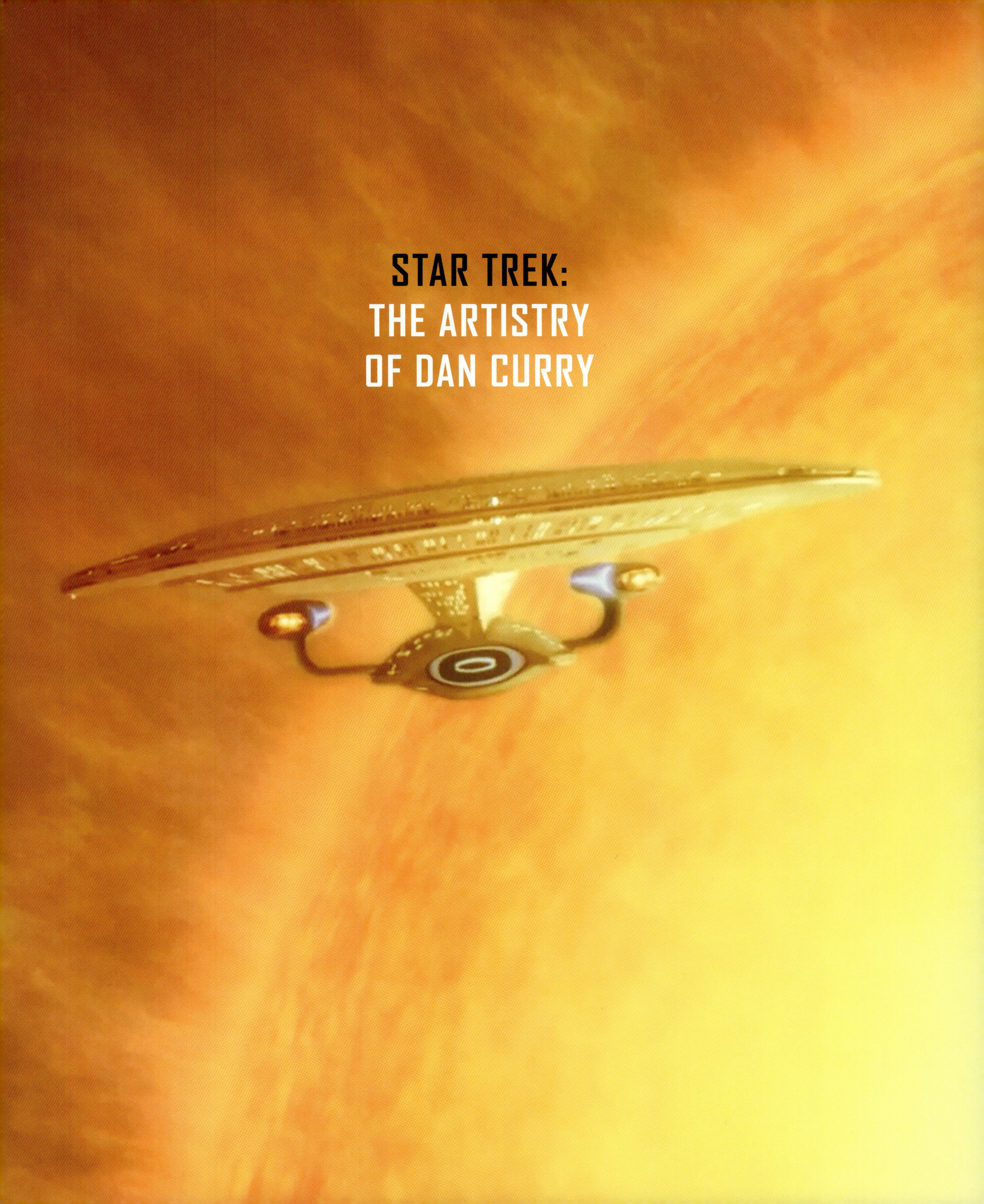

STAR TREK:
THE ARTISTRY OF DAN CURRY

ISBN: 9781785659348

Published by
Titan Books
A division of Titan Publishing Group Ltd
144 Southwark Street
London
SE1 0UP

First edition: November 2020

2 4 6 8 10 9 7 5 3 1

A CIP catalogue record for this title is available from the
British Library.

Printed and bound in China.

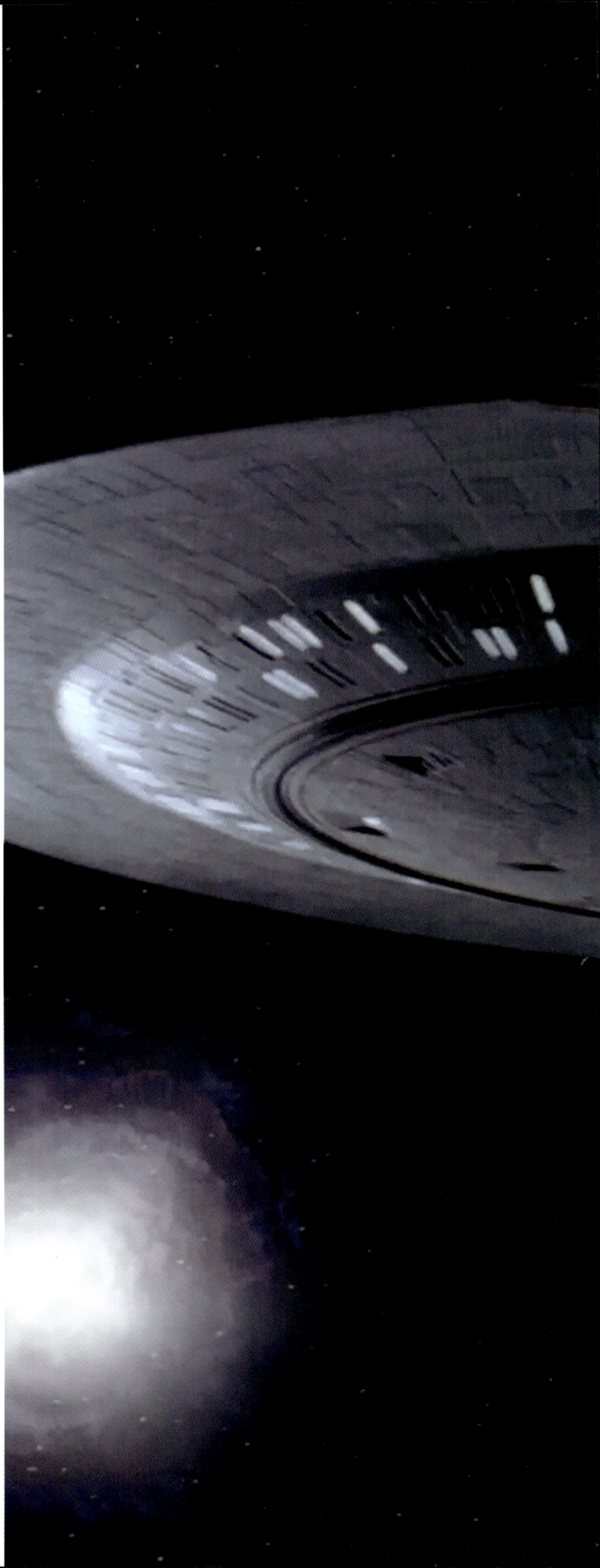

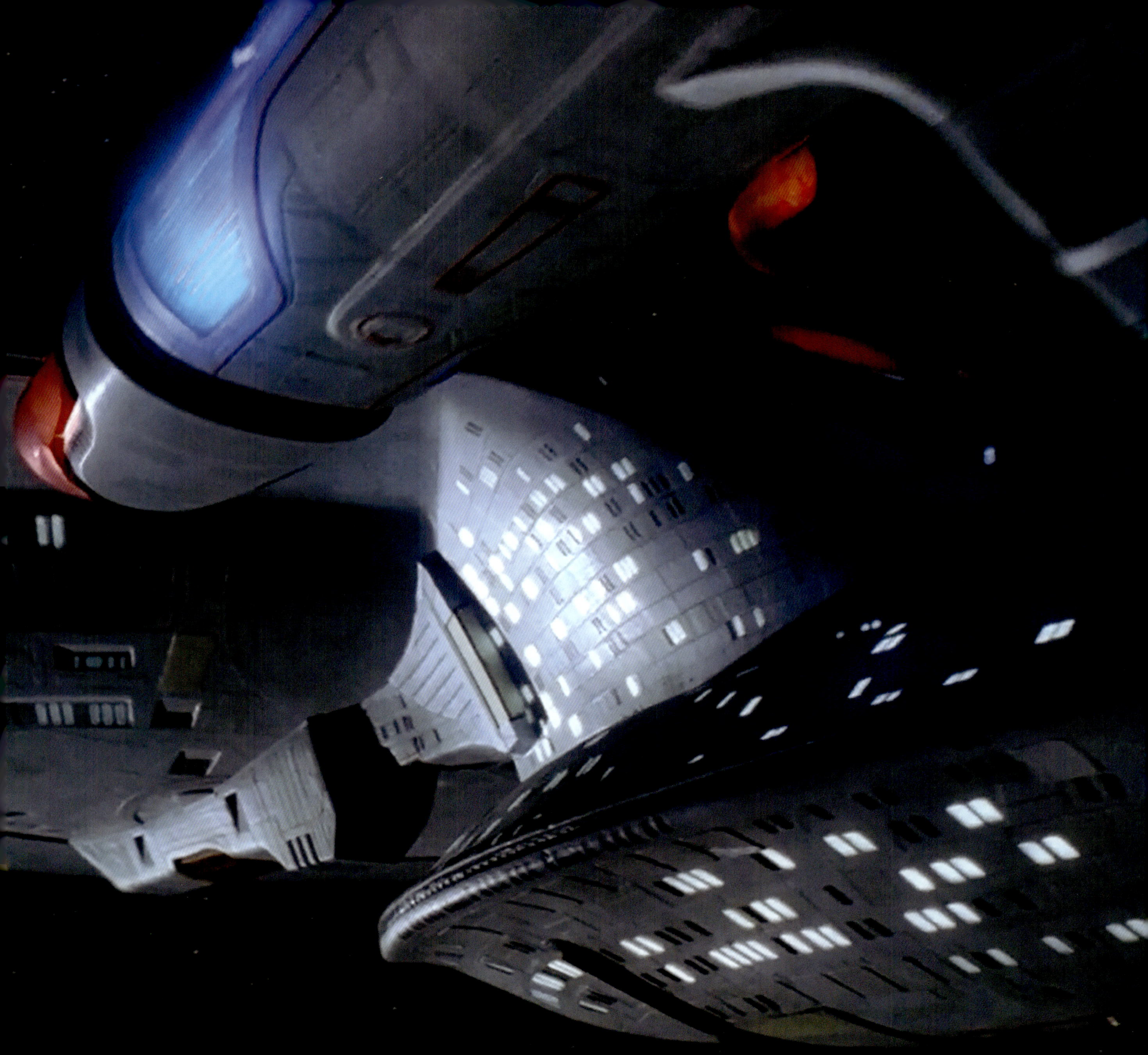

STAR TREK:

THE ARTISTRY OF DAN CURRY

DAN CURRY, VES & BEN ROBINSON

TITAN BOOKS

CONTENTS

(Nebula airbrushed painting by Dan Curry for 'All Good Things...' *TNG* finale.)

DAN

To Hua and Devin, pillars of my life,
and to the memory of my parents, Florence and John,
without whose unwavering support and encouragement there never
would have been a reason to write this book

A special personal thanks to all the teachers and professors that contributed to the education that made my career possible. Teachers at Floral Park Bellerose School and Floral Park Memorial High School instilled the foundations that a great liberal arts education at Middlebury College built upon. The focus on film and theatre and creative opportunities in grad school at Humboldt State University were essential in developing skill sets that served me well throughout my career. The wisdom shared by people from other cultures helped me imagine alien cultures for *Star Trek*.

The storytellers and image makers of *Star Trek* are deeply indebted to the real heroes of space exploration, the scientists whose passion for learning the secrets of the cosmos broadens human understanding and inspires speculative storytellers. "Now that we know this, what if that?" Amazing technical achievements enable scientists to look ever deeper into the mysteries of creation, capturing images that spark the imaginations of sci-fi artists to envision phenomena and depict unexplored regions of the universe with previously unimaginable realism.

To our friends at NASA, JPL, and scientists everywhere we owe thanks for their generous dissemination of knowledge, and hope that our imaginary voyages into the realm of what-ifs may inspire real journeys to go "where no one has gone before."

BEN

This book wouldn't have been possible without help from many people, who generously provided their time, their pictures and their stories.

From the VFX team we'd like to thank Peter Lauritson, David Stipes, John Teska, Fred Raimondi, Paul Hill, Eric Alba, Image G's Tom Barron and Dennis Hoerter, and in particular Ron Moore, who remembered many things that Dan didn't. Syd Dutton and Bill Taylor provided their beautiful art and insights on working with Dan. Brandon MacDougall provided images of the alien Night ship and his work with Dan on guitars.

We can't thank Scott Bakula, Ira Behr, Michael Dorn, Robert Duncan McNeill, Kate Mulgrew and Armin Shimerman enough for finding time in their incredibly busy schedules to talk and to share their stories about Dan.

Fabio Passaro pitched in to help out with new renders of CG creatures.

Dan's wife Hua has tirelessly sorted through boxes, uncovering long-lost artwork.

Finally, we'd like to thank our friends at CBS, in particular Risa Kessler, who started it all when she heard Dan speak at San Diego Comic-Con, and made it her mission to make sure he produced a book.

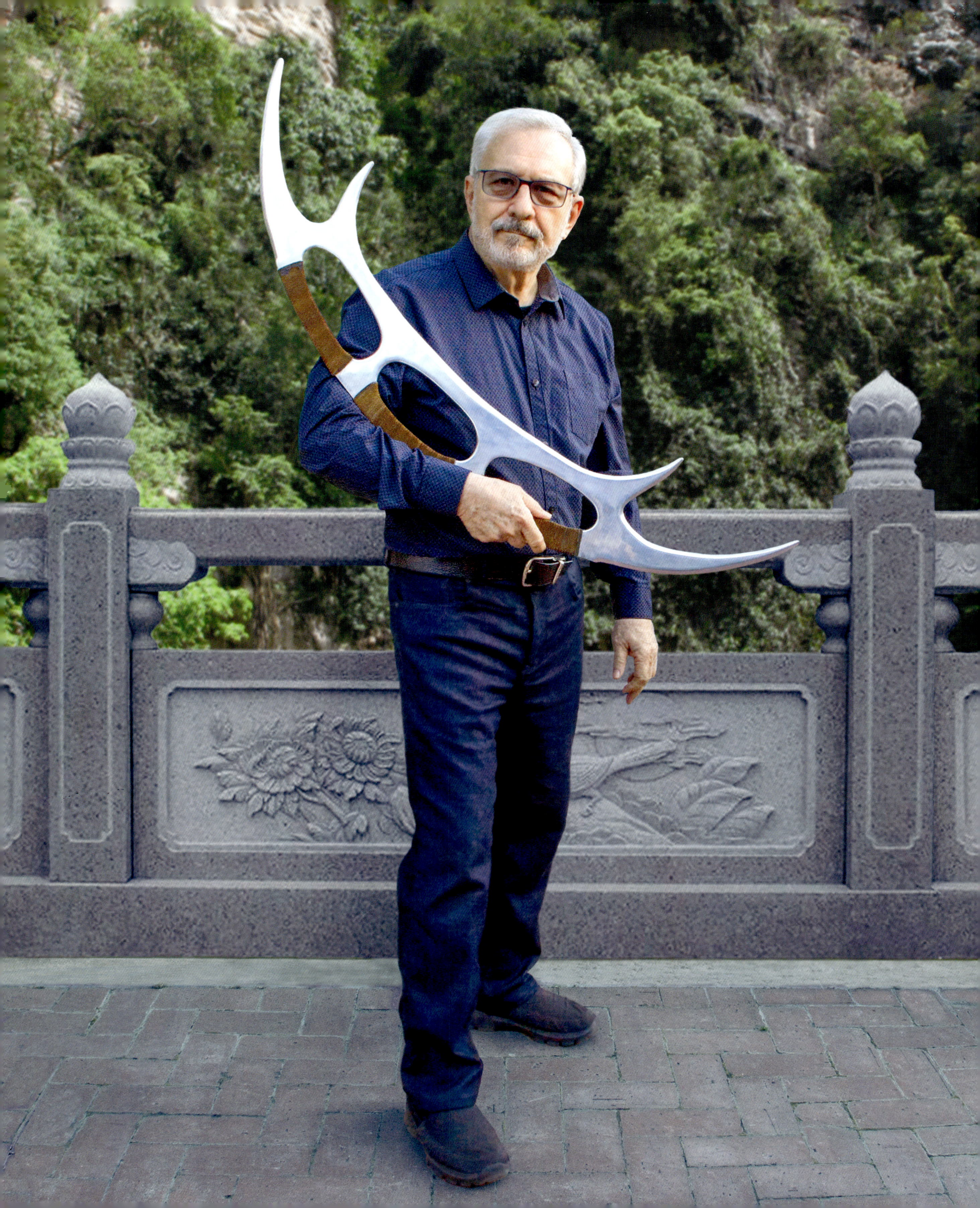

FOREWORD

I look back on my years as part of the *Star Trek* family with wonder. At the time I didn't always appreciate what an incredible cultural phenomenon we were part of—we were all so busy making *Star Trek* and dealing with the daily challenges posed by the daunting schedules that we didn't have time to think about the millions of people around the world who saw our collective work and were stirred by it.

The purpose of this book is not to presumptuously speak for every member of the *Star Trek* visual-effects department or to discuss their individual approaches to creating visual effects, nor is it to claim credit for or overshadow my colleagues' brilliant pioneering individual achievements. The quality of their work speaks for itself. This volume is meant to give the reader one individual's perspective on the experience of being part of *Star Trek*.

I will always appreciate the trust *Star Trek* creator Gene Roddenberry, executive producer Rick Berman and his colleagues, and supervising producer Peter Lauritson placed in me to create for the franchise. Our goal in VFX was always to support the stories, and to visualize a universe for those stories to unfold in. During my 18 years on *Star Trek* we saw amazing strides made in all aspects of filmmaking, especially in the art and technology of special visual effects that, along with other industry pioneers, we helped to evolve. The technological leap forward was extraordinary; when we started on *The Next Generation* visual effects were akin to medieval alchemy. Eighteen years later, when we shot the final episode of *Star Trek: Enterprise* it was all about computer algorithms.

All filmmaking is collaborative. The range of skills required to bring a film or television show into existence is like a military operation. Each individual, no matter what level of responsibility, contributes an essential part of the complex whole. *Star Trek* was blessed by having an army of dedicated, talented, and knowledgeable people in every department who went above and beyond the call of duty. Please note the liberal use of the word 'we' throughout this book—the boundary between 'I' and 'we' is often impossible to discern. Those of us in leadership positions relied on colleagues in the visual-effects department, brilliant artists at vendor companies, and the support of the cast and crew on stage. We benefited from collaboration with the camera, art, stunt, makeup, special-effects, costume, and editorial departments. There were so many people who contributed to our work that it is impossible to mention everyone in this volume, but I hope they all understand how much their support was valued and appreciated. Special recognition must be given to my friend and colleague Ronald B. Moore, whose talents as coordinator made it possible for me to focus on creative endeavors. When I started overseeing VFX on simultaneous series, Ron became an excellent VFX supervisor in his own right.

My goal with this book is to share my personal experiences, and reveal some of the ways *Star Trek* visual effects were created. With the support of the producers I was also lucky enough to contribute outside the confines of visual effects. Production designers Herman Zimmerman and Richard James recognized my background in fine arts and production design, and were open to my taking on design responsibilities that are normally the strict purview of the art department. Stunt coordinators Dennis Madalone and Vince Deadrick, Jr. also welcomed my contributions in martial arts.

In the first seasons of *The Next Generation* we had significant budgetary challenges, so I took to designing 'guest' spaceships and building them using found objects. When we moved over to CG on *DS9*, *Voyager*, and *Enterprise*, I would provide sketches of ship designs to excellent digital modelers like Pierre Drolet, Rob Bonchune, Brandon MacDougall, and Koji Kuramura.

Before the advent of computer animation, almost all our creatures were designed by legendary makeup artist Michael Westmore. CG meant we no longer had to rely on actors in prosthetic suits and as a result, aliens became visual effects. From early childhood I loved drawing weird creatures, so when a script called for a new alien species I was given the opportunity to try my hand. Elsewhere in this book readers will see sketches of my designs that were brilliantly executed by 3D artists like John Teska, David Morton, and Eric Hance.

While living in Asia I had the opportunity to study a variety of martial arts. That background found its way into *Star Trek*, beginning with a *TNG* episode about Worf inheriting a traditional Klingon weapon. I felt the Klingons should have something never seen before but practical. I made a foam core mock-up of an ergonomically sound weapon I had been imagining that became known as the bat'leth.

Prior to joining *Star Trek* I had designed over 100 title sequences for features and TV, so I also got to design the *DS9* and *Voyager* main titles. An especially enjoyable aspect of my job was directing second unit; we borrowed crewmembers from the main unit, and shot unfinished or added scenes, inserts, stunts, and time-consuming, technically difficult shots that involved visual and special effects.

This book is dedicated to the army of people who contributed in their own ways to the creation of *Star Trek*'s visual effects. There is not enough room to list them all, but please know that without their tireless dedication and artistry the universe of *Star Trek* would not have been quite so glorious.

Dan Curry

INTRODUCTION FROM BEN ROBINSON

Dan's spirit is infused in so many aspects of *Star Trek* that it's impossible to imagine it without him. The contribution he made to the effects had a huge influence on the look of the show, but that's just the beginning. Without Dan there would be no *bat'leth* or Klingon martial arts, and Species 8472 would probably have had two legs. It goes even further than that: as Michael Dorn reveals, Dan was a very real influence on his portrayal of Worf. Take Dan away and the show would be radically different. And that's just what we see on screen; Dan was one of the show's leaders, and a massive influence on everyone who worked for or with him.

I wanted to talk to other people about Dan because I knew he doesn't understand quite how unusual he is. Everyone I talked to laughed when I said that and replied, "No, he doesn't!" They'd go on to tell me how talented and kind and patient and enthusiastic he is, and more than one person told me that he was their hero. That's something I'll tell you too—somehow Dan combines an understanding of his own abilities with a very real modesty. If we can be a little more like him, the world will be a better place.

That modesty and generosity is essential to who he is. Whenever we talked he was keen to emphasize that he was part of a team and that he worked with talented people, so much so that I had to cut out much of that praise in order to make the text flow. What Dan also has—that is much harder to emulate—is an extraordinary amount of talent. He seems to be really good at almost everything (apart, perhaps, from being tidy). He's a master of several martial arts, he is musical—he even designs his own guitars—and, of course, he's an incredible sculptor and painter.

Star Trek benefited massively from that talent, and it's not an exaggeration to say that the visual-effects industry did too, something the Visual Effect Society recognised when they gave him the honor of making him a Fellow. His 18 years on *Star Trek* were an era of incredible change in the visual-effects industry.

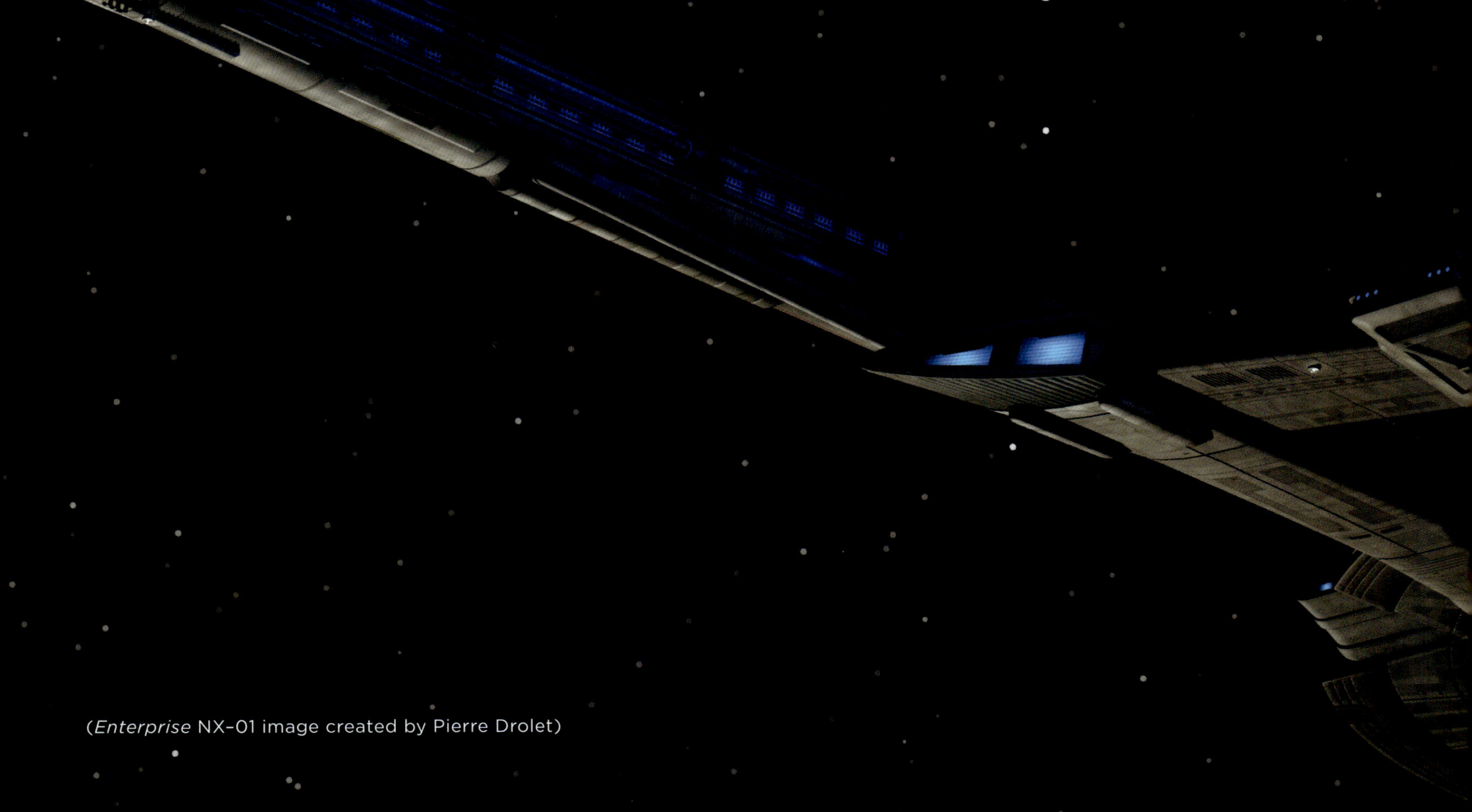

(*Enterprise* NX-01 image created by Pierre Drolet)

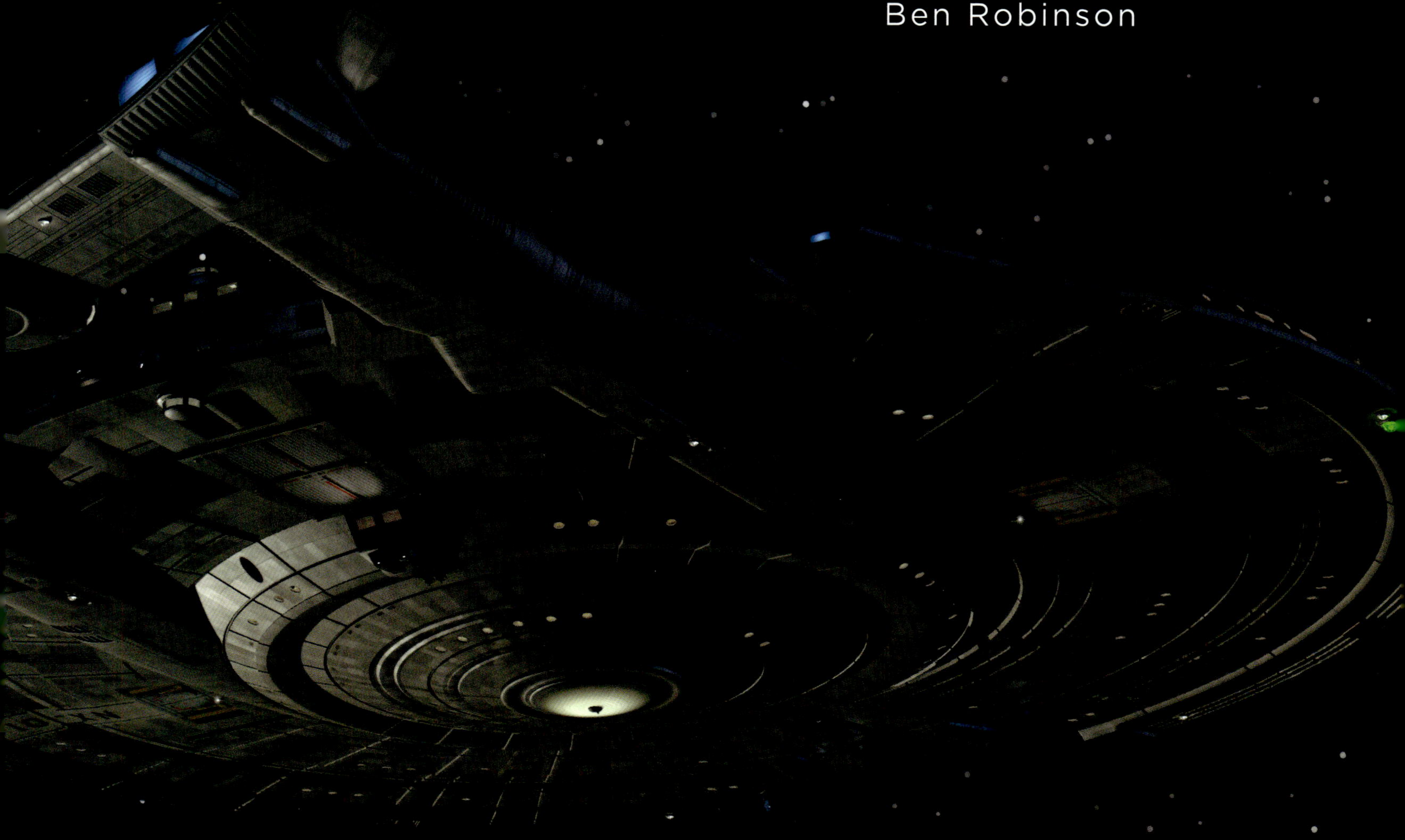

As Dan puts it, when they started on *TNG*, effects were like medieval alchemy, where they would try things without ever being certain what they would get. But by the end it was all about algorithms, and almost everything was created in a computer. The *Star Trek* VFX team was instrumental in that revolution. They were turning out hundreds of effects every year, often using techniques that were in their infancy. The way they chose to do things showed everyone how it could be done. I'd ask Dan about this and he'd shrug, saying they were too busy making the show to think about it.

It's clear to me that he didn't do things the way anyone else would have done. Every time a new technology became available he would bring an artist's eye to it, and when something needed an innovative solution, he often brought leftfield, low-tech approaches to the table. When I say that *Star Trek* would be different without Dan, what I mean is that he came up with genuinely unique ideas that nobody else would have thought of.

This book just scratches the surface of who Dan is, and I know it doesn't do him justice. When you talk to him he is full of stories about his time in the Peace Corps, about the extraordinary people he has worked with, and about the history of visual effects. Writing it with him and getting to know him has been a real privilege, and I am going to miss those weekly calls. The best thing of all is that I now count this exceptional man as a friend.

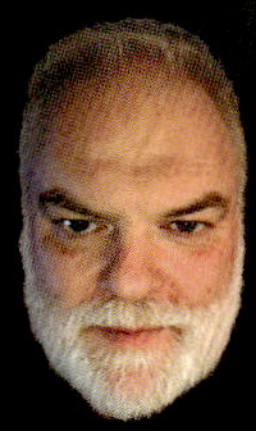

Ben Robinson

DAN CURRY: A TIMELINE

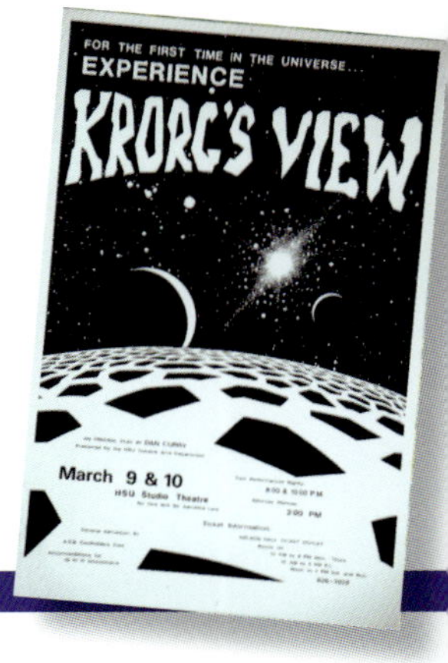

1946
- Spew forth from amniotic fluid and commence breathing air

1953
- See *The Beast From 20,000 Fathoms*, perceive that there are different levels of reality within a film image

1956
- See *Forbidden Planet*, perceive that a film image is comprised of live action, painting, animation, and models
- See *Earth vs The Flying Saucers*
- Build 8mm rear-projection system

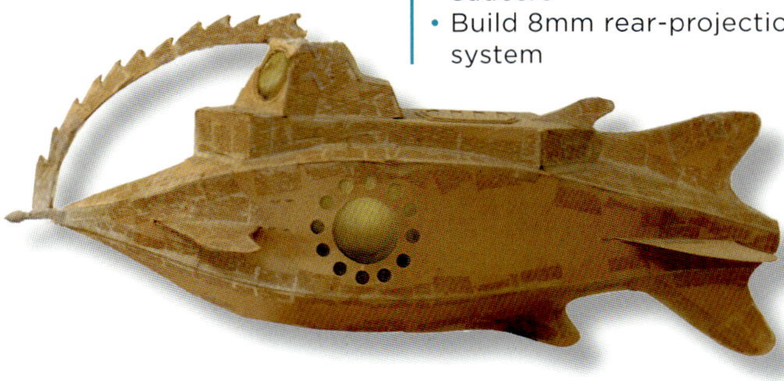

1957
- See *Gunfight At The O.K. Corral*, Kirk Douglas inspires me to start throwing knives

1958
- See *The Seventh Voyage Of Sinbad*, display in the theater lobby opens my eyes to the possibilities of visual effects
- See *The Vikings*, depiction of warrior culture lays seeds that will later influence the Klingons. Kirk Douglas inspires ax throwing

1960
- See *Spartacus*, noting the power of the Saul Bass title sequence
- Begin storyboarding imaginary movies

1962
- First oil painting, 'Opus Africanus' (self-taught)

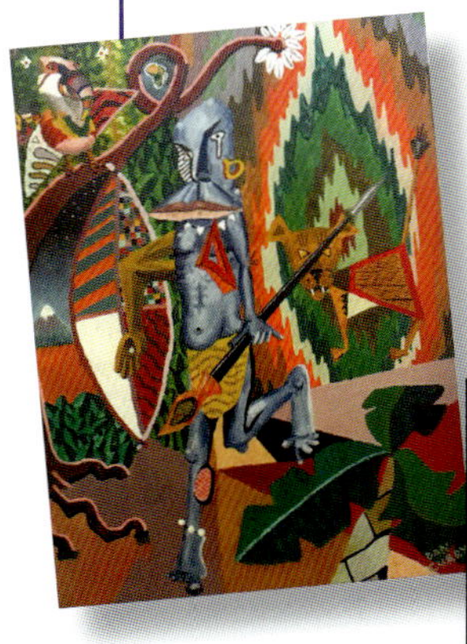

1964
- Graduate from high school
- Start at Middlebury College, Middlebury, VT: Fine Arts major, Theatre minor study with production designer Chandler Potter, direct student film set in medieval Iceland
- Lots of drawing, painting and skiing

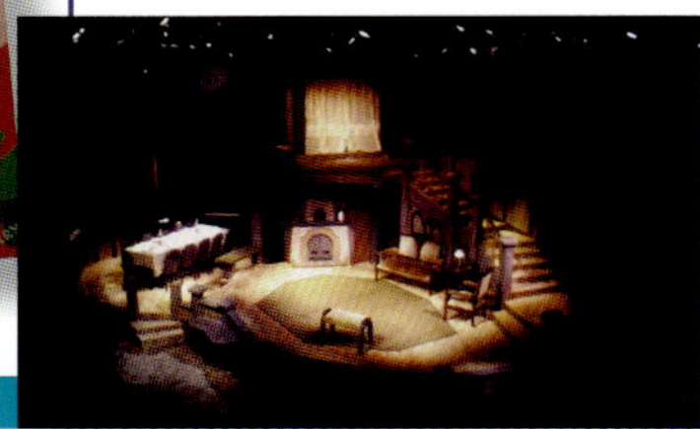

1979
- Start as a matte artist at Universal Hartland on *Buck Rogers In The 25th Century* and *Battlestar Galactica*, mentored by Peter Anderson and David Stipes. Learn about motion-control miniature photography, visual-effects animation, model building, and optical printing
- Also work on *The Incredible Shrinking Woman* and *Cheech & Chong's Next Movie*

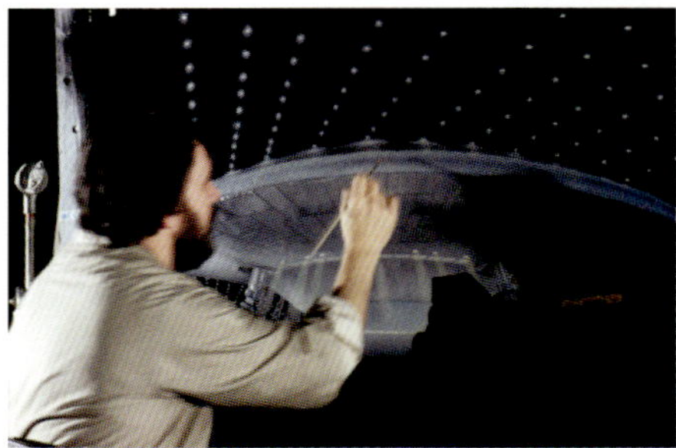

1983–1985
- Art director, title designer, and in-house VFX supervisor at Modern Film Effects in Hollywood
- Work on numerous features and television productions, including *Raiders Of The Lost Ark, Indiana Jones And The Temple Of Doom, Dead Men Don't Wear Plaid, Pennies From Heaven, Amadeus, Wolfen, Hill Street Blues, St. Elsewhere, Staying Alive, The Man With Two Brains, The Right Stuff, Tootsie,* and *The Natural*, among others

1985–1987
- Vice President, Director of Creative Services at Cinema Research Corp., Hollywood: client relations and creative supervision
- Title design, in-house VFX supervisor, second-unit director. Notable feature productions: *Top Gun*; *Days of Thunder*; *Star Trek IV: The Voyage Home*; *Back to School*; *The Golden Child*; *Big Trouble in Little China*; *Three Amigos* and *Fatal Attraction*, among others

1987–2005
- Visual-effects supervisor/producer, director, second-unit director, title designer and conceptual designer for *Star Trek: The Next Generation*, *Deep Space Nine*, *Voyager*, and *Enterprise*
- Win 7 Emmys, Visual Effects Society Award, inaugural Hollywood Digital Award, 3 International Monitor Awards

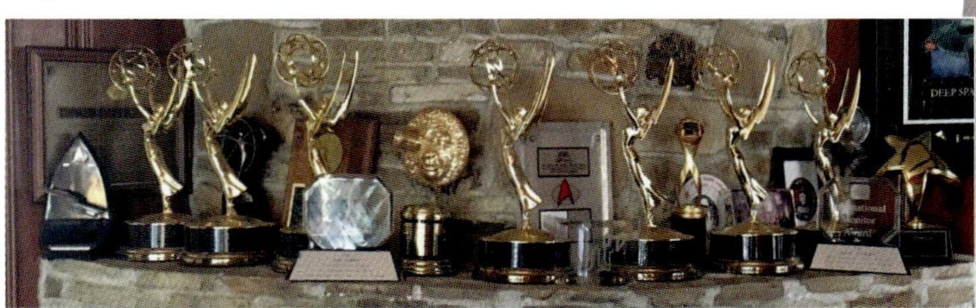

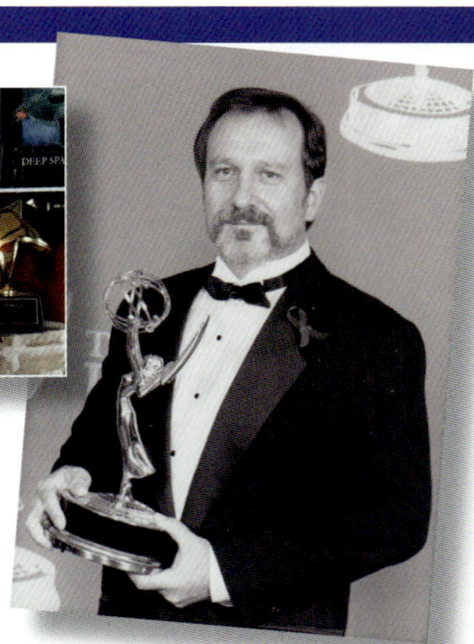

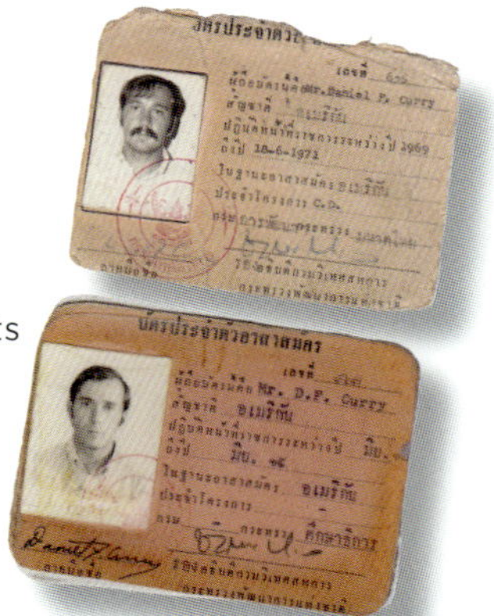

1968

- See *2001: A Space Odyssey*, Doug Trumbull's amazing work redefines my ideas of what is possible in visual effects
- Graduate from Middlebury College, Middlebury, VT
- Volunteer for Peace Corps
- Temp job: ski pro Macy's NYC while waiting for Peace Corps training to begin

1971

- Writer/producer/director/animator/puppeteer for educational children's TV series *Maitre And The Magic Chopsticks* at Ministry of Education, Bangkok, Thailand
- Win commission as production designer for King Bhumibol Adulyadej of Thailand's Royal Charity Ball held on the palace grounds

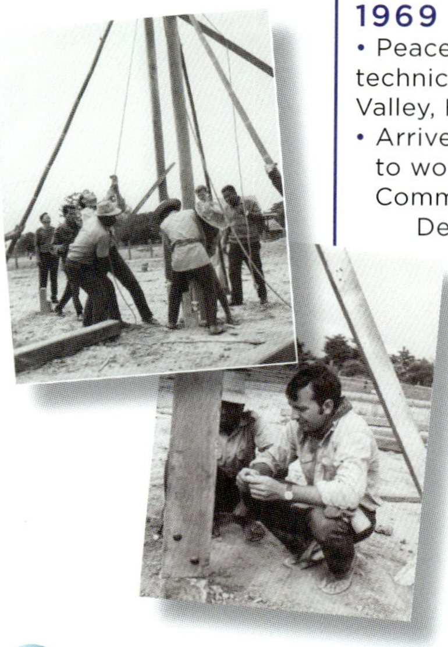

1969

- Peace Corps language and technical training in Waipio Valley, Hawaii
- Arrive in Khon Kaen, Thailand to work for Royal Thai Community Development Department, designing and supervising construction of small dams and bridges in remote rural villages; first introduction to traditional village martial arts
- Monsoon season: teach architectural drafting at Khon Kaen University

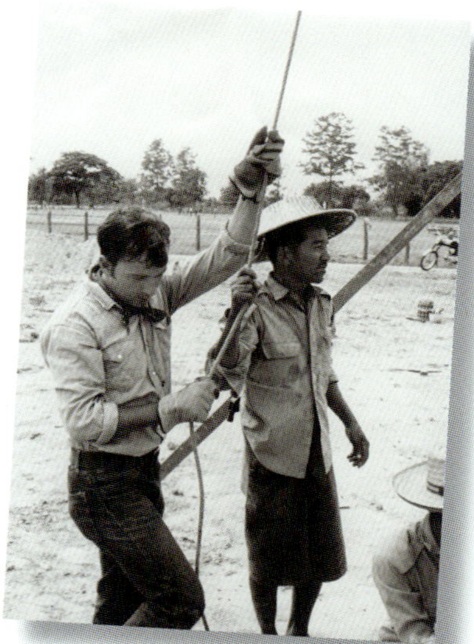

1972–1974

- Freelance filmmaker/production designer/artist; art, architecture, and production design for various clients, ranging from designing a library and sculpture garden for the United States Information Service to sets for the Bangkok Opera and designing the An-An Nightclub for the Montien International Hotel. During this time I take the opportunity to visit and/or do projects in surrounding countries Laos, Cambodia, Myanmar, Malaysia, Indonesia, Bangladesh, India, Pakistan, Afghanistan, and a very long trek in Nepal

1974

- Return to New York, USA; work as bio-medical illustrator for Vantage Art

1975

- Accept a teaching position in Fine Arts at Cape Cod Community College, Centerville, Massachusetts

1977–1979

- Attend grad school, Film & Theatre, Humboldt State University, Arcata, California. Teach part-time, write, design, and direct student films and award-winning sci-fi play with unique audience/cast/set relationship set in an alien prison, where the audience portrays beds of sentient hydroponic plants, and the prisoners are from a variety of sentient species including an insectoid, a reptilian, a tripod creature, a mineral creature, and humanoids
- Marcia Lucas visits campus to give seminar on editing, sees my paintings in one-man show, and suggests I look into matte painting. Introduces Dennis Muren, Alan Maley, and Mike Pangrazio at Industrial Light and Magic, who mentor about the art form
- Graduate with MFA in Film & Theatre

2005–

- Form Evergreen Productions to develop film and television properties, and do visual-effects supervision and directing. Clients include Sony Imageworks/Sony Computer Entertainment Europe; Warner Bros VFX Dept. Head (*Moonlight*, *Chuck*, *Cult*); AD Whitaker Entertainment (direct *The Chronicles Of Elijah Sincere*); 20th Century Fox (*The Witches Of East End*, *Crisis*, *Clan Of The Cave Bear*, *Marvel's The Gifted*, *This Is Us*); Paramount Pictures/CBS (supervise VFX for *TNG* Season 2 re-release in Blu-ray)
- During this time also consult with NASA's Vision Team and co-present with NASA scientists at several venues on the symbiotic relationship between science fiction and real science

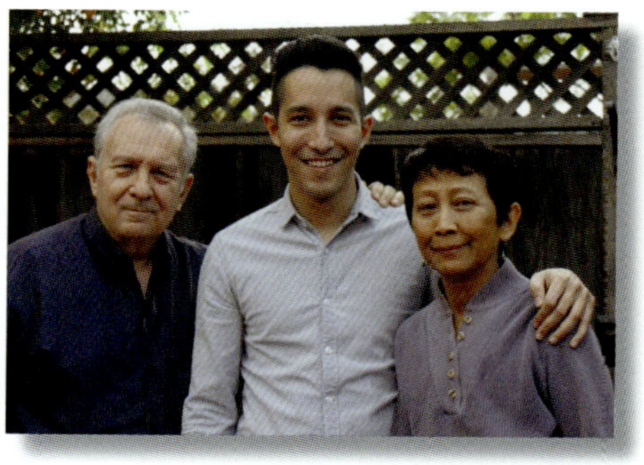

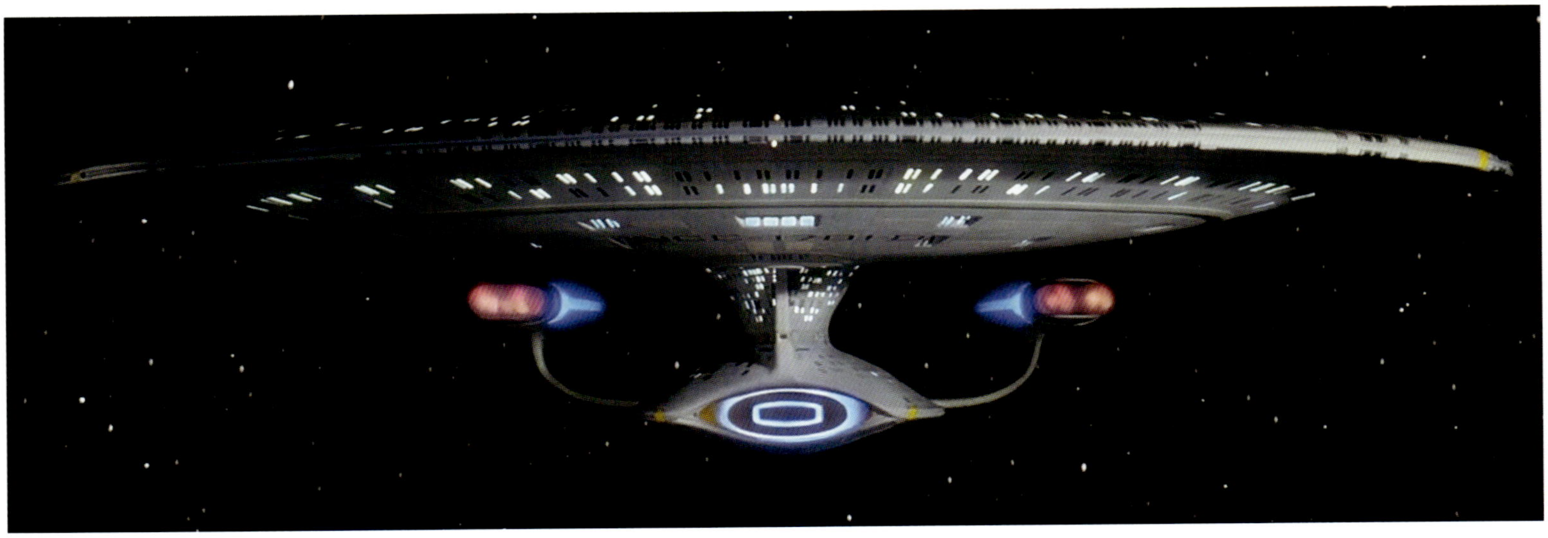

WHERE NO ONE HAS GONE BEFORE...

BREAKTHROUGH FILMING TECHNIQUES ON *THE NEXT GENERATION*

I handed the hard drive over to Peter Lauritson for the last time, and walked across the Paramount lot to my office. The drive contained the last visual-effects shot for *Enterprise*. After 18 years, an important chapter of my life, and what had been the focus of my creative endeavors, was going away. My son Devin had turned from a toddler to a grown man during those years. I'd watched my friends and colleagues grow older, and the color fade from my hair and beard. As I walked across the back lot, I felt great pride with what we had accomplished, and a great sadness, knowing that our lives would never be the same again.

My office was legendarily messy. At the beginning of *TNG* I didn't have a computer, just a drawing table and a flat file. In nearly two decades of work, I'd accumulated lots of stuff—stacks of drawings and blueprints from the art department, and drawings and storyboards of my own. The organized chaos included art supplies, random model parts, and piles of outlines, memos and scripts, along with prop weapons, reference materials, light meters, still cameras, and home-made angle-measuring devices. It was all piled up around a cluttered desk with a computer, monitor, and drawing tablet. I enjoyed doing hands-on work.

Originally, I was only going to do a few days work for *Star Trek*. I was working at Cinema Research Corporation as VP, Director of Creative Services, designing main title sequences and supervising in-house visual effects for features and television. Through CRC I had done a lot of projects with Peter Lauritson, when he was at Paramount Television's post-production department. Peter left that position to take over post-production for *Star Trek: The Next Generation*. Early in the planning phase he called and asked me if I'd be willing to meet with him and Gene Roddenberry to discuss doing some storyboards as a side job. Sounded interesting...

The plan was to create a library of stock shots of the *Enterprise*-D flying in a variety of directions that could be added to different backgrounds. They would be used in every episode, much the way they did in the original series. There would be 40 stock shots in all: the *Enterprise* coming at camera, going away, a panning 'fly by', entering orbit, exiting orbit, in orbit, and so on.

For reference, Peter gave me a handful of polaroid photos of the prototype *Enterprise*-D model that had been designed by Andy Probert. I thought it was just going to be a little freelance job to help them out. The plan was that the ship effects were going to be done by ILM. Then they'd be transferred from film to video, and put everything together with the backgrounds down in LA, where they would also do the animation effects. Rob Legato had extensive video experience and was supervising the *TNG* pilot. Rob brought in Gary Hutzel to help him with the effects, and I recommended my

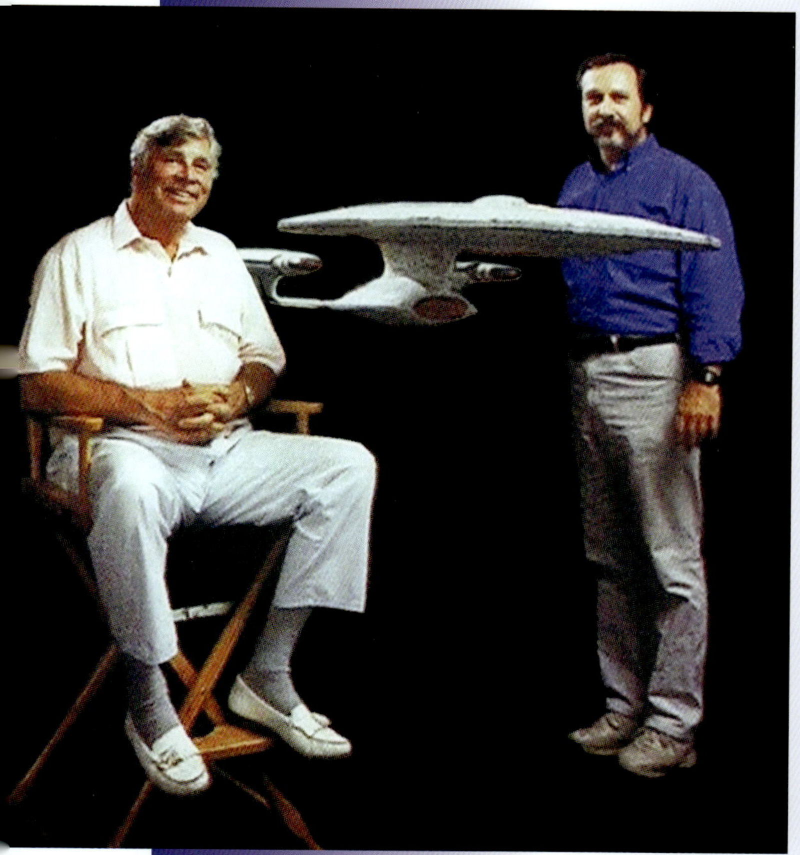

We didn't really interact with Gene Roddenberry that directly on visual-effects issues. When we did I found my interactions with Gene quite enjoyable. We got along really well. Our personalities seemed to mesh, and we would talk about things other than work. Gene's comments about VFX work were pretty general and supportive.

During the end of the second season, as Gene's health suffered, he became more of a distant presence. Rick Berman was our main go-to guy to discuss conceptual work and final approval on shots.

Dan on *Star Trek*'s creator

old friend Ron Moore as visual-effects editor.

A few weeks into the pilot, the VFX team realized they needed more help, so Peter called and asked if I would like to join the *Star Trek* team as an additional visual-effects coordinator alongside Rob (Rob and I were given the credit 'coordinator,' but we functioned as supervisors. That credit was later corrected, and Ron and Gary were credited as coordinators).

I was ready to leave Cinema Research. It was a wonderful company, and I worked with great people, but I really wanted to focus on visual effects. I had not been a major *Star Trek* fan because I was in college when it was on, so I didn't really see much of it. In those days it was unheard of for a college student to have a television. *Star Trek* seemed to offer me a home where my range of goofy skills had value, and I was excited about being able to work on a cultural icon, so of course I said yes. At the time I could never have imagined how big a part of my life *Star Trek* would become. What at first seemed a chance to do some cool space stuff evolved into something more profound.

The first time I walked on the set, I was overwhelmed. Everything was so big and grand. Herman Zimmerman's production design, the uniforms, the busy crew... everything was amazing. They had been working together for a couple of weeks, and I was like the new draftee in a platoon. I felt a little out of place, and hoped that I could rise to the occasion.

I remember saying to Rob, "Who's the captain?" He said, "That bald guy over there." I was still thinking in terms of William Shatner and Captain Kirk, so I admit my response was, "Really? The bald guy is the captain?" They were just prepping for a shot, then Patrick Stewart came out and performed his lines and I thought, "Yeah, he's the captain!" He just had that incredible sense of authority and gravitas. I admit to being a little star-struck. I didn't recognize the actors—they weren't household names yet—but they were very impressive.

By the time I became part of the *Star Trek* VFX team, the original plan of using 40 stock shots had been thrown out the window. Once they had the scripts, the producers realized a library of stock shots could never work. It rapidly became apparent that *TNG* wasn't going to be like the old series, where the crew would beam down to a planet and interact with the inhabitants. Audiences had now seen *Star Wars* and Doug Trumbull's brilliant work on *Star Trek: The Motion Picture*, both of which had raised their expectations. It became obvious that we were going to have to step up and expand the operation to deliver the volume of effects work required to tell the *TNG* stories.

Delivering such a high volume of quality visual effects became possible because Paramount broke with tradition and made a courageous decision: instead of doing all postproduction for *The Next Generation* on film using optical printers for compositing, they were going to use a hybrid of film and video technology. We shot everything on film, the way you would have done for any feature, but then we transferred our film to video and did all compositing in state-of-the-art video edit bays. Coming from the world of rows of optical printers, motion-control matte stands, on-site black-and-white processing labs, and judging color on a large light table

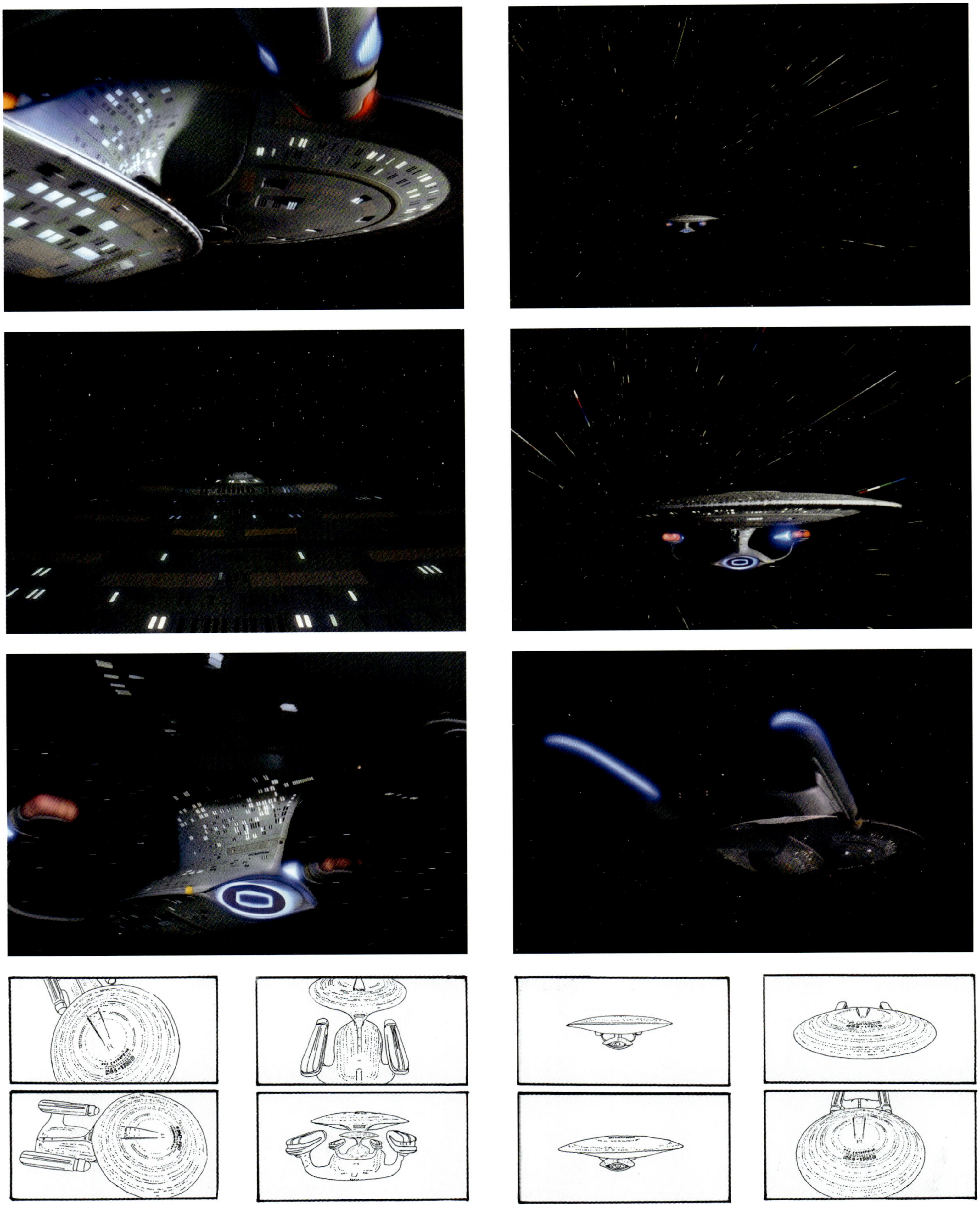

ABOVE: I was brought in to design 40 or so stock shots of the *Enterprise* that were intended to cover everything future episodes would need. I imagined what those shots could be, and drew up storyboards showing what needed to be shot. The series required fly-bys, toward and away from us, orbiting, and going to warp.

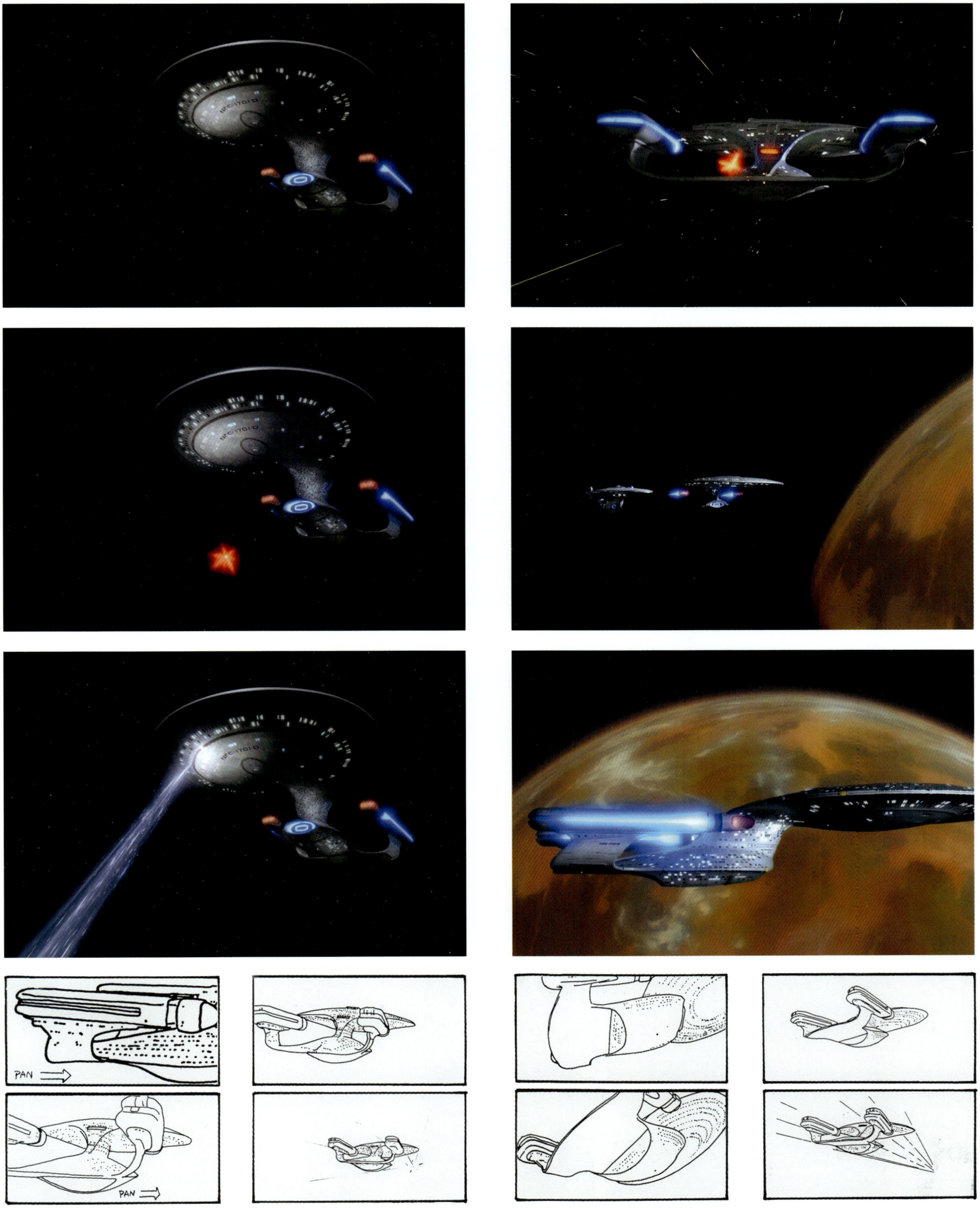

ABOVE: Many ship shots were used for different episodes. For example, the same *Enterprise* would fire phasers in one scene and photon torpedoes in another. Orbit shots could be used with different planets. *TNG* turned out to be much more ambitious, and 40 shots would prove to be inadequate.

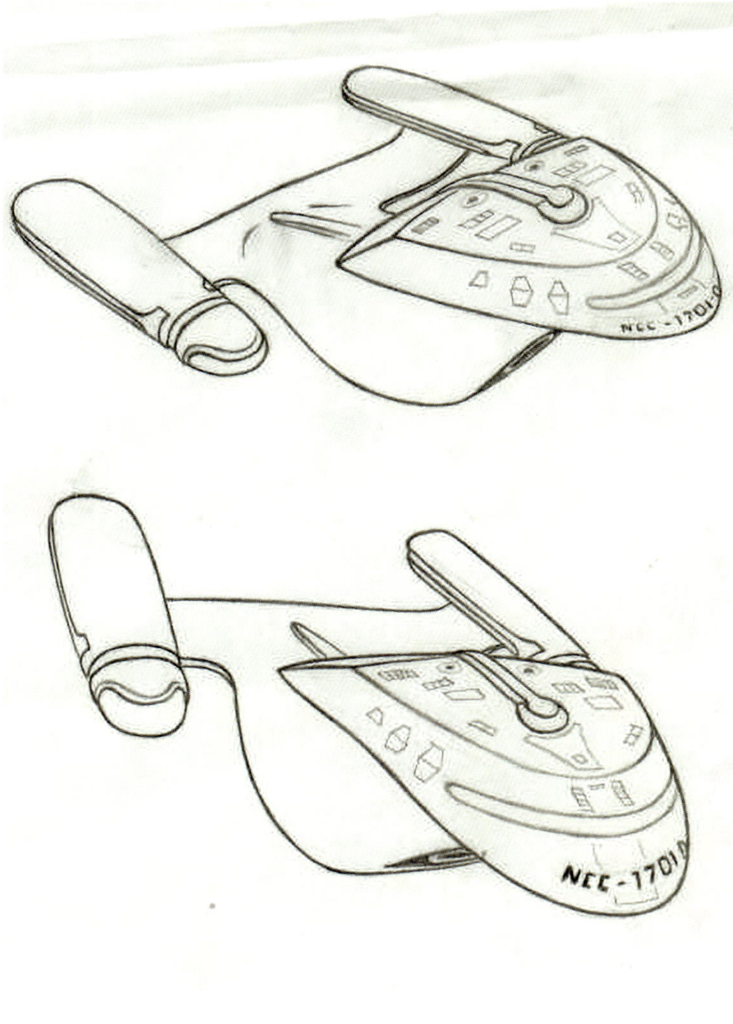

ABOVE: I drew quick study drawings of the *Enterprise* to get a feel for the ship's elegant proportions.

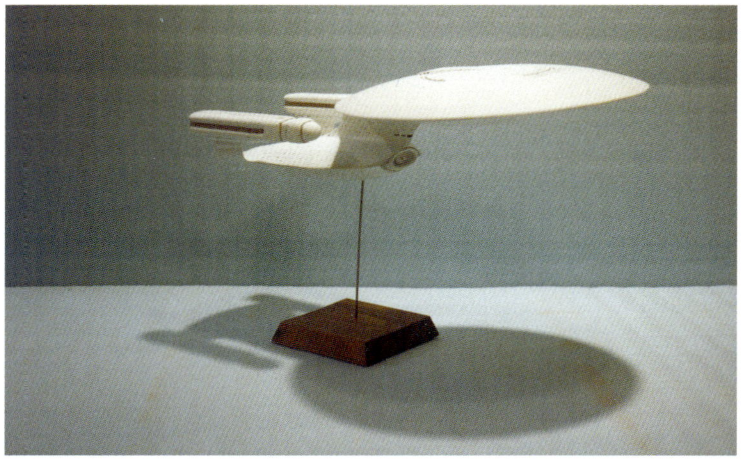

ABOVE: Gene and Peter showed me an early study model of Andy Probert's design for the *Enterprise* so knew what it would look like.

looking at test prints through a magnifying glass, entering a video edit bay for the first time was almost as astonishing as walking onto the bridge of the *Enterprise*.

The process began with transferring our film to video at CIS (Composite Image Systems) in Hollywood, using their proprietary pin registered transfer system necessary for accurate compositing. 2D compositing of transferred video was split between CIS and nearby The Post Group. CIS's Price Pethel and Don Lee, and The Post Group's Fred Raimondi were among the many guides in transitioning to the world of video technology. At first, we struggled to understand each other as film and video terminology differs as much as the technology. My friend and colleague Ron Moore also came from the world of film opticals, but had worked in video long enough to know the parlance. Immersion into the world of electronic image making was like immersion into another culture.

Working on video had huge advantages. Everything was much faster than working with film, and therefore cheaper. For example, using film technology it was necessary to draw a phaser beam on white paper by hand, one frame at a time, and photograph it with hi-con film stock on an animation stand (a camera fixed to a movable light table). Next, a line-up person prepared each piece of film for use on a printer, and wrote 'count sheets' for the printer operator to put it together on an optical printer (a camera and projector pointed at each other in a system that lets you line up multiple layers of film to combine them), after days of testing with various filters. Every time you made a change, it would be another trip to the lab and another day lost to see the results. Video? Instant gratification. You could 'draw' a phaser blast directly onto a video image and it would be there at once. Done. You could isolate different parts of an image and manipulate them as if they were in 3D space. For example, you could make a planet by taking a photograph, or even another piece of moving video, and wrapping it around a virtual sphere. You could also separate out a particular color, a technique called keying or matting, and replace it with something else, or you could keep layering images on top of one another.

For me, video technology offered the promise of unfettered artistic expression where trips to the film labs to review tests were replaced by a truly painterly experience. That was made possible by collaboration with some great compositors. Fred Raimondi, Price Pethel, Don Lee, Paul Hill, Peter Moyer, Steve Fong, Don Greenberg, Scott Rader, Peter Sternlicht and Pat Clancey are among other great compositing editors who contributed to *Star Trek*. Talented effects animators included Helen Davis, Steve Price, Joni Jacobsen, Steve Scott, Adam Howard and Greg Rainoff.

The video technology available to us had been used before, but not on this scale. It was something used on a lot on commercials, and there had been some attempts to use it for TV shows, but *Star Trek* was taking it much further. Before long we were shooting our own ship shots. Despite the incredible quality of their work, Industrial Light and Magic was just too expensive for the budget of a weekly series. They were used to working on major feature schedules too, not to the pace of TV. Rob already had a relationship with a motion-control facility in Hollywood, not far from Paramount, Image G, where we could do almost everything we needed to photograph motion-control models and elements like liquid nitrogen, and could tank images.

Star Trek forced us to invent new ways of doing things; we didn't really know what was possible, or even what it would cost. We were asked to create things that no-one had ever seen before. We would take a good guess at what might work, but nobody really knew how it would come out until we had done it.

We weren't working with huge budgets. What we put on screen might have looked like it belonged in a feature, but we were not a big operation. By comparison, years earlier when I was at Universal Hartland working on the original *Battlestar Galactica* and *Buck Rogers in the 25th Century*, we had a really big room with rows of optical printers, and people operating them for 12 to 16 hours a day, and we had multiple motion-control stages with nifty self-

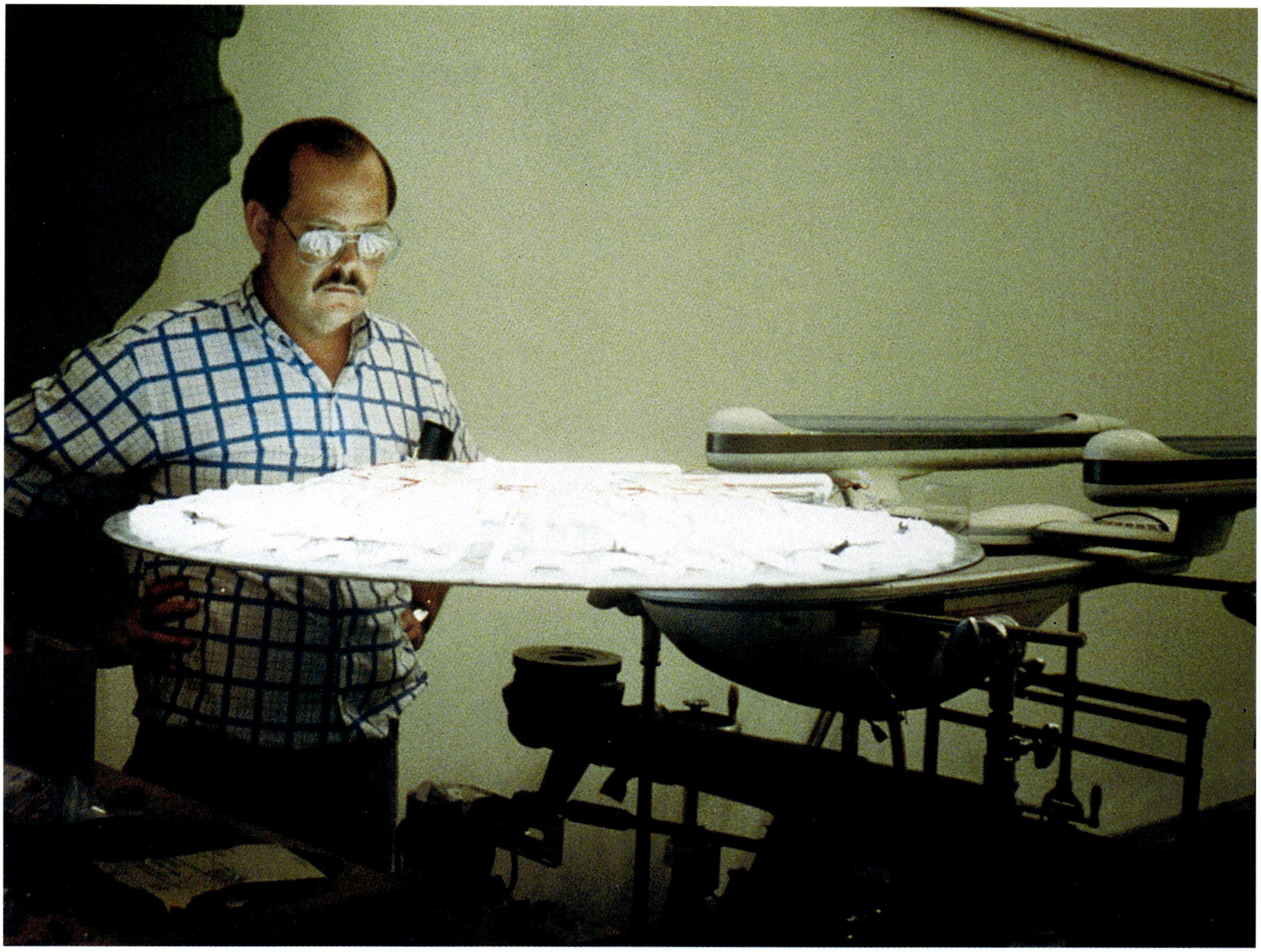

ABOVE: My good friend and colleague Ron Moore with the shooting model of the *Excelsior*, which we used often. Ron and I worked together throughout our time on *Star Trek*; Ron is one of the most organized people in the world. Our different skills complemented each other.

illuminated blue-screen sleeves that could cover the model mounts, and wall-sized backlit blue screens. We probably had about 80 to 85 people cranking out those shots.

When we began *The Next Generation* we had one motion-control stage and relied on Image G's small but excellent crew, hiring extra help when needed. Then we had the people at CIS, which would be an editor and assistant, and support personnel. We kept two edit bays going at The Post Group, and a couple of artists doing phasers and hand-animated effects. It was a fraction of the team required to do *Buck Rogers*. Then we had our two supervisors (Rob Legato and myself) and two coordinators (Gary Hutzel with Rob, and Ron Moore with me). We had a visual-effects associate, the eminently organized David Takemura, who worked with both teams and kept them informed of each other's activities.

We were fearless as we didn't know what we couldn't do. We were confident that we would just figure it out somehow. One of my great joys was using physical objects and materials, which we could make behave in unexpected ways and look like things far removed from what they really were.

We rarely said we couldn't do something. The writers just wrote what they thought worked for a story, and we did the best we could to present their vision and delight the audience. Sometimes we succeeded gloriously, sometimes we succeeded less satisfactorily—there are shots that still make me grimace when I see them. Creating *Trek* VFX was a learning curve for all of us, the demands were so intense I don't think any of us realized how much we were loving what we were doing, and how much we were learning by doing it.

In the beginning we didn't really know the best way to divide the workload, but once we got through the pilot, Rob and I came up with the 'two teams' system, where we would alternate episodes so that he and Gary would do even-numbered shows and Ron and I odd-numbered ones. That way, one supervisor/coordinator team could focus on supervising the compositing and shooting models and elements for one show, while the other team could be on stage for the episode being filmed, and to start prepping for the next one. This way each team would know why things were shot in a certain way and eliminate guesswork in compositing. That system was one of the keys to being able to deliver so much work in such a quick time.

The workload was pretty crazy. There were a lot of expectations that were not grounded in reality and the limits of available technology, budgets, and especially the time constraints. We all

PETER LAURITSON

STAR TREK SUPERVISING PRODUCER

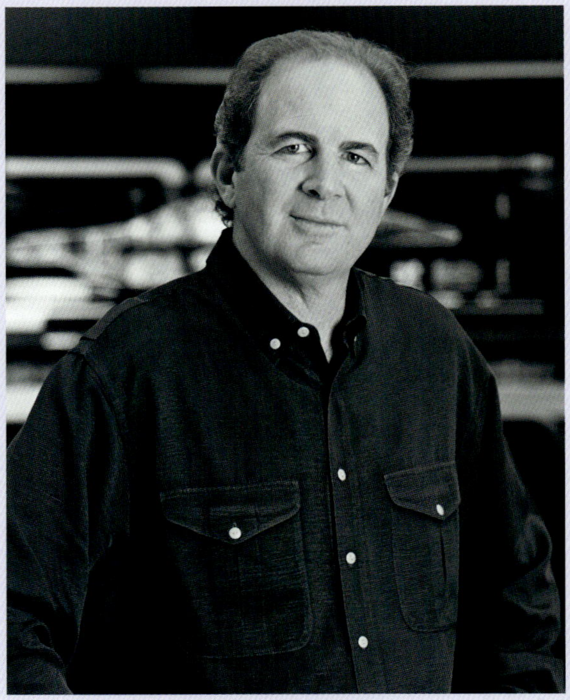

Peter Lauritson was in charge of postproduction on *Star Trek*, and was Dan's boss. It was his job to make sure that the shows produced the best possible effects on time, and on budget. They worked together for 18 years.

"Dan's an amazing guy, and always surprises you. I first got to know him when I was in charge of the TV postproduction department at Paramount—he was a title designer, and worked at an optical house. We liked his work, and used him on a number of projects. I got to know that he was truly an artist.

"When they put me in charge of the postproduction end of *Star Trek*, I was charged with finding people to do the visual-effects work. I found Rob Legato, who had experience of working in video, and we hired him and Gary Hutzel. We engaged ILM to build the ship model, and to shoot the effects; we had talked to them about shooting an initial library of shots, but they didn't know what those shots were going to be, so I engaged Dan to do storyboards. He came in and brainstormed the type of shots that would be most beneficial and reusable. Originally, that was going to be it.

"'Encounter at Farpoint' was pretty huge in terms of the number of effects shots we had to do. ILM was doing a lot of the ship stuff, but Rob and Gary were doing a lot of work. At that point it became clear that they were not going to be able to manage this by themselves—that's when I brought on Dan full-time. He was a great resource for our team. He knew visual effects, but he was a treble threat: he was an artist; he could sketch and do a full-on matte painting; he had experience in martial arts and music, and he loved *Star Trek*. He was fun to work with because he has quite a vocabulary. Whenever he's telling a story—which he has plenty of—he uses a lot of very flowery descriptions, and a lot of it is very amusing.

"A lot of those stories were about the history of visual effects, which he had studied. In the early visual-effects days, in the original *Star Trek*, there were a lot of low-tech solutions. Dan was enamored by that. He was good at saying, 'What if we just put this bit of cardboard right over here?' And all of a sudden it was done. It was a simple solution to what could have been hours of the crew standing around. That kind of thinking was the most cost-effective way of doing things, and it looked just as good as the more expensive way. I loved that about Dan, because we were always fighting to put the most we could on the screen. Whenever we did something that was cheap, but still looked great, then we were ahead of the game.

"The same thing was true of ships. Those models were expensive to build. If it was a hero ship, and it was going to be in a number of shots, we would build something for that, but if it was only going to be in two shots we would look in our catalogue of models to see if there was something we could recycle. I remember a number of times we would pick one out, and Dan would say, 'Okay, I'll do something with that.' He would take the model, and flip it over and stick a couple of pieces on here and there that could easily be taken off again, so he wouldn't ruin anything. Suddenly it could be a different ship.

"He was always ready to go the extra hour, or the extra mile, for the show. If we needed something like a background, Dan would go home and paint it at night. Suddenly we'd have a cool background, or a new element that we could add to a shot. That was great. Any artist is going to get carried away and lose track of the schedule at times, and that happened plenty at times, but Ron was always there with him, and sometimes would rein him in and remind him about the budget and the schedule. I was always confident that we could go to Dan to sort something out. In any meeting where we reached a point where words failed, Dan could illustrate it to the room. We'd just say, 'Dan's going to draw it for us,' and it would suddenly be crystal clear to everybody.

"It wasn't all low-tech by any means. I was always looking for new technology—new boxes were being created and brought into the mix all the time. But Dan would always be able to see further into it than the rest of us because he would bring his art eye into it. He was very helpful and critical to helping the CG vendors understand what we needed from them.

"The best word I can come up with to describe Dan is 'multi-faceted.' He was perfect for *Star Trek*."

felt a great responsibility to deliver the best work we could. We used to have a sign up in our office that said, 'Good enough is the enemy of excellence.' That was our working motto. Sometimes we would make wrong decisions—at least I know *I* did—and sometimes we would make great decisions, but we had to live with decisions made because there was no time to go back and redo anything.

We didn't sleep much; a light week would have been 60 hours. I would crash on the couch at Image G when we were doing a light pass because it took a couple of hours to shoot, and watching the rig eke through its path had all the visceral thrills of watching cattle graze. Long passes gave us chances to get catnaps and grab something to eat. The same was true on set—we might have a visual-effects shot in the morning, and then one later in the day, and another late at night, so you could go back to the office and catch up on paperwork, design shots, work on a model, or even just sit in a chair and meditate for 10 minutes.

We did whatever it took to get the shots done. Sometimes that meant slapping models together out of whatever we could find, or filming any weird substance we could manipulate later in compositing. We were lucky enough to work with brilliant people; Greg Jein and Tony Meininger were making models for us, and Syd Dutton, a truly great artist, was doing matte paintings for us. The crew at Image G were super, and our compositing editors and animators brought skill and creativity to the process.

We certainly benefited from a lot of favors around town. In the Hollywood visual-effects world there's a lot of mutual support and shared knowledge. People would come forward and help us out selflessly—they had nothing to gain by sharing their hard-earned knowledge, but there's a professional camaraderie that came to the fore with surprising frequency. Love of what *Star Trek* stood for was certainly a factor.

We were working so hard that we didn't have time to think about anything beyond our immediate challenges, so a lot of us working on the show were surprised at its instant popularity. I'd say a lot of that was due to Gene Roddenberry's genius in insisting upon depth of meaning in the stories and creating really engaging characters. Audiences instantly embraced the cast, especially Patrick Stewart as Captain Picard, with his incredible gravitas and charisma. So by the end of Season 1 we were pretty confident that we'd be coming back.

Ron Moore and David Takemura got us organized. Animators Helen Davis and Steve Price got really fast and created the elements we needed for phasers, force fields, photon torpedoes and other often-used elements, and kept them available whenever needed. Later, animators Steve Scott, Gregg Rainoff, and Adam Howard continued and built upon *Star Trek*'s level of excellence.

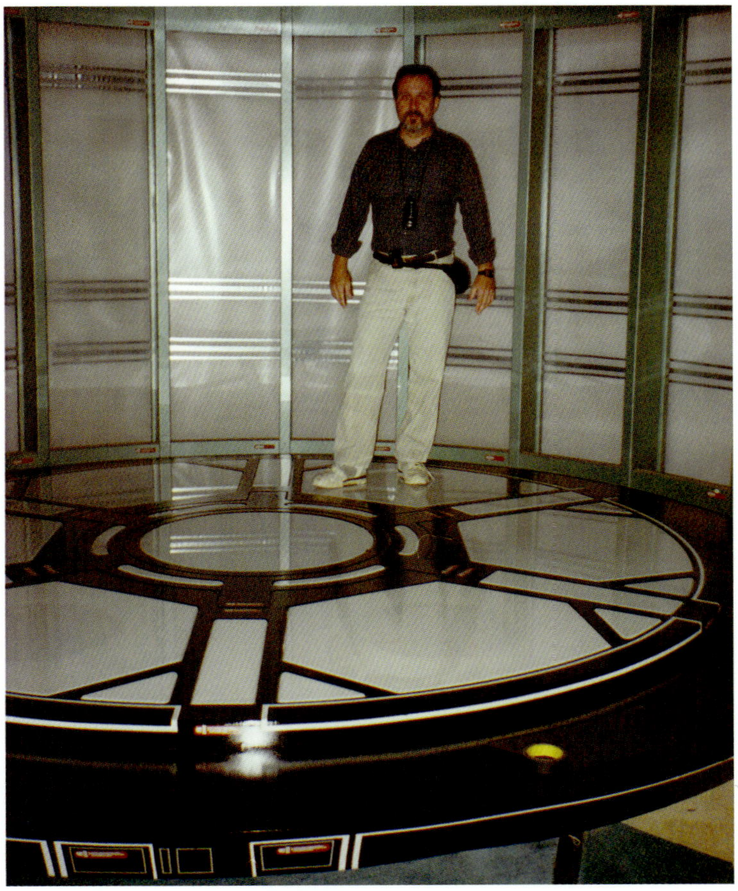

ABOVE: The VFX team spent a lot of time on set collaborating with directors, cast and crew to make sure we could work with what was filmed. Herman Zimmerman's sets for *TNG* were extraordinary—it was like stepping into the 24th century.

When we came back for Season 2, we all had our opinions about how to make things better. It was primarily changes in the work pipeline, but one of the main things was getting a smaller model of the *Enterprise*. The one ILM built was so big that it was difficult for us to work with on the stage at Image G. We hired legendary model maker Greg Jein to make a new, 4-ft model for us—not only was it smaller, but it also had raised panels on it so

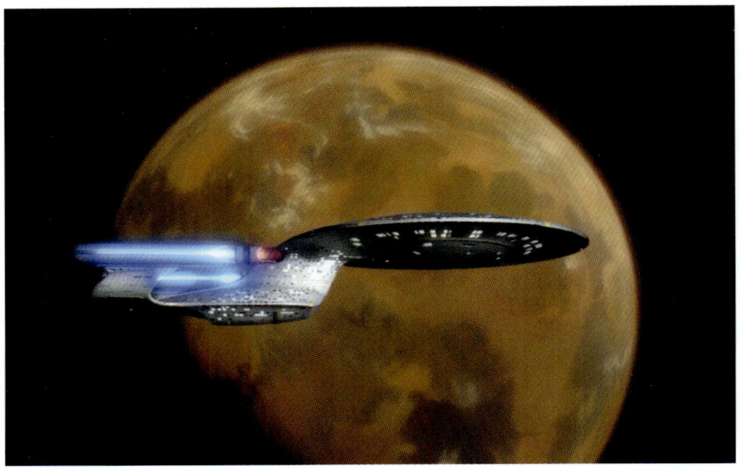

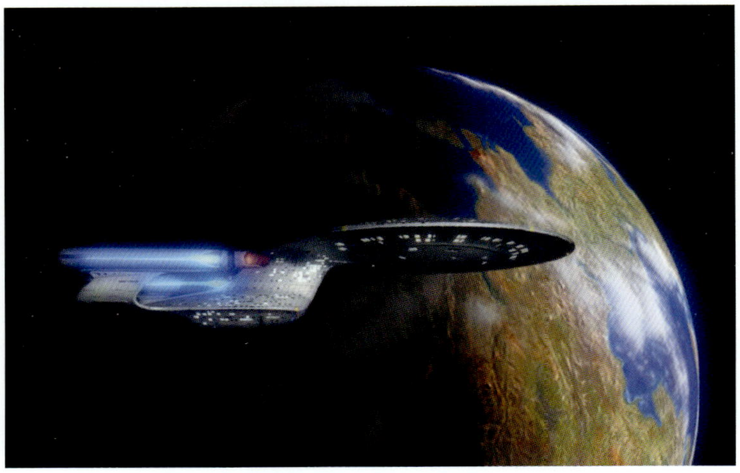

ABOVE: One of the great advantages of video technology was that you could swap out elements very quickly and easily. For example, we could change the planet in the background and see what that would look like without having to do a full comp on an optical printer and go back to the lab for processing, as with a film composite.

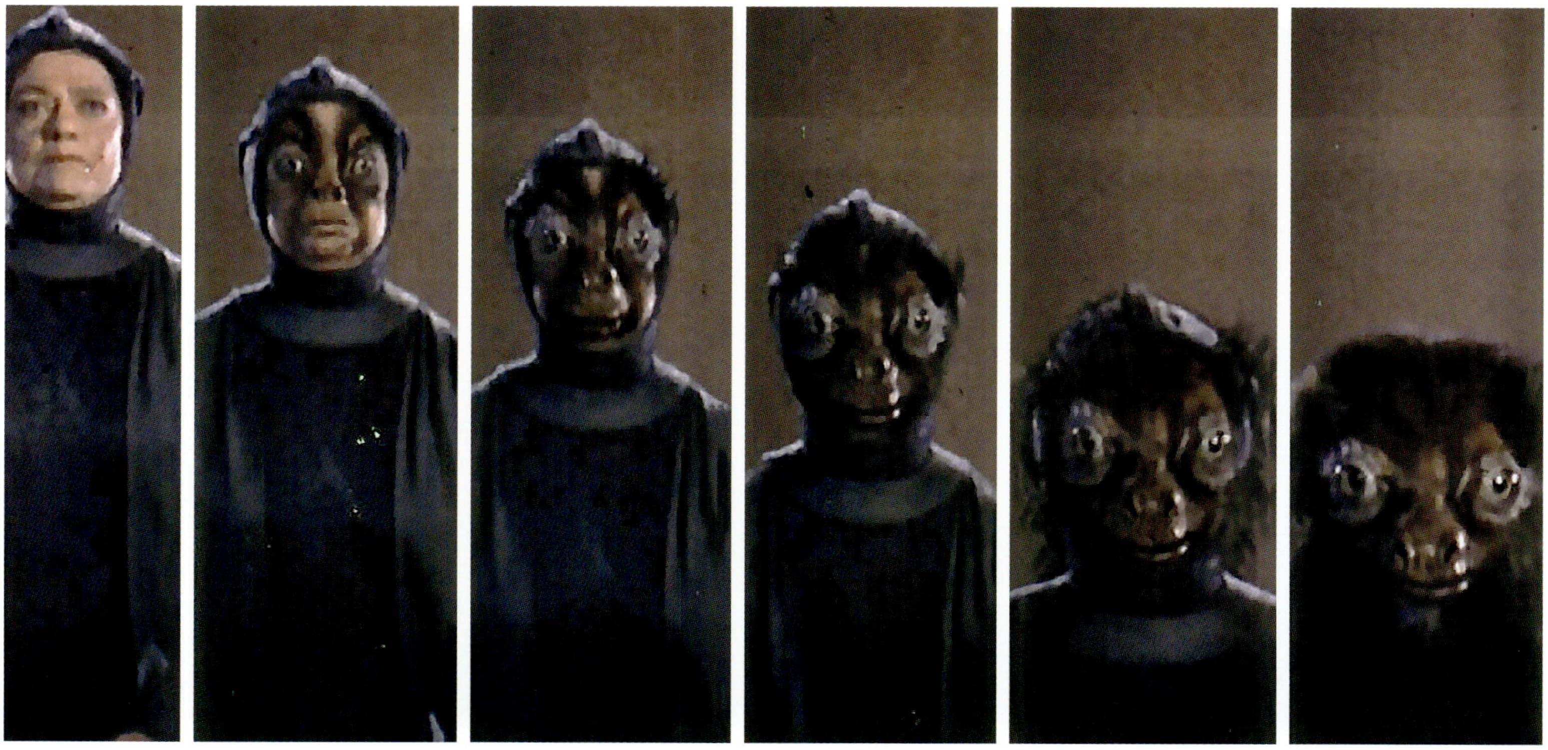

ABOVE: We often used traditional techniques alongside video technology. For example, this morph was painted by hand directly in video by artist Steve Price. Today, of course, it would be done on a computer in a fraction of the time.

that there were more surfaces to catch light and cast shadows to give a bigger sense of scale on screen.

We started to develop a library of elements we could use for effects, as well as a library of stock shots, the way we'd always planned. Because we were working in video we could use the same *Enterprise* in an orbit shot and just change the planet beneath it. That really helped in terms of time and budget because we would only have to shoot new episode-specific shots and not waste time

BELOW: Directing second unit for a morph sequence, where we transformed a beautiful princess and her nurse into monstrous aliens.

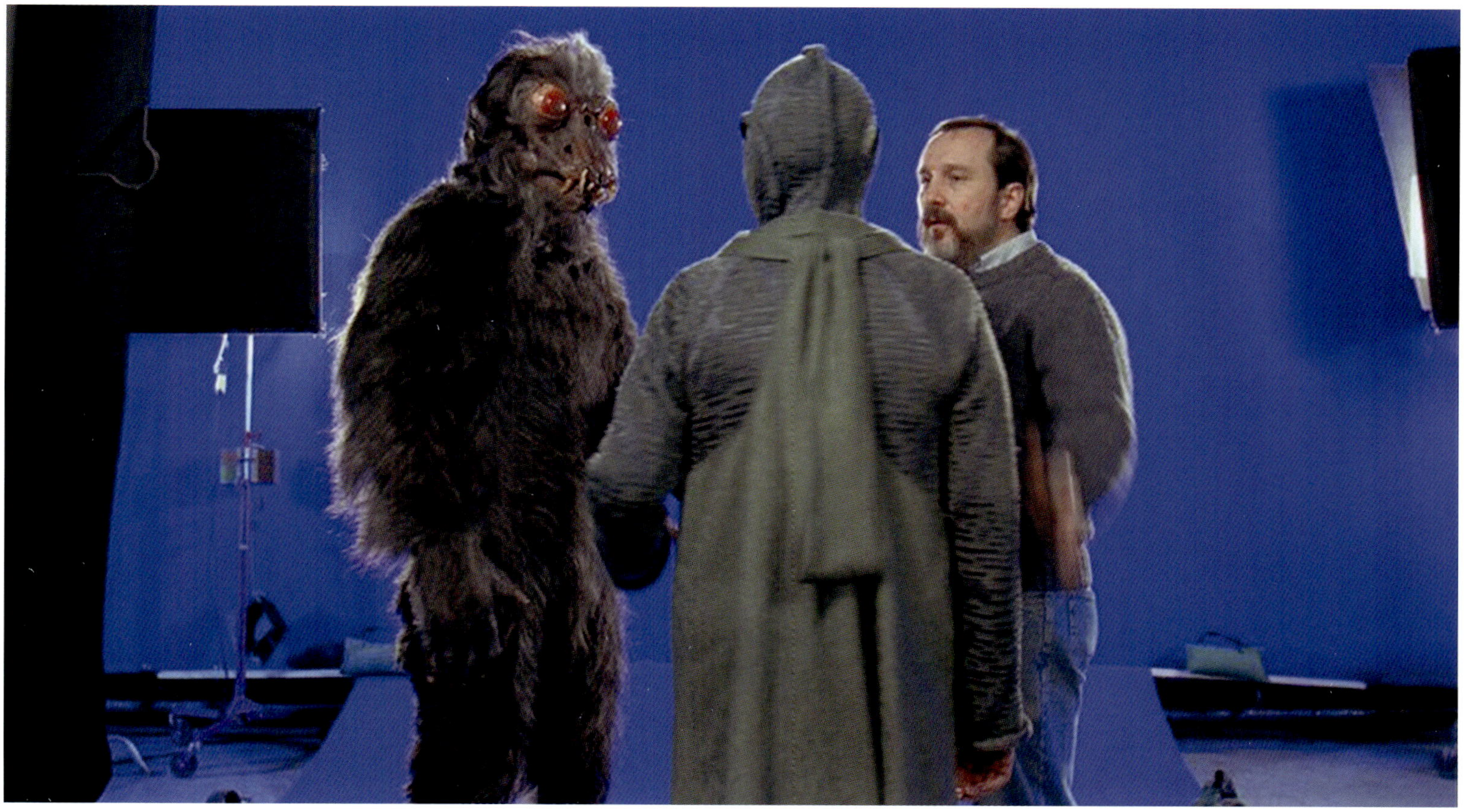

FRED RAIMONDI

TNG FIRST SEASON VIDEO COMPOSITOR

Fred Raimondi was the principal compositor on the first season of *Star Trek: The Next Generation.* He and Dan worked closely, putting the visual-effects shots together using video editing and manipulating technology—something that was new territory in 1987. He is recognized as one of the preeminent digital artists in the world. As a visual-effects supervisor he has partnered on projects with David Lynch, Michael Bay, David Fincher, Mark Pellington, Gus Van Sant, Lance Acord, and Alex Proyas.

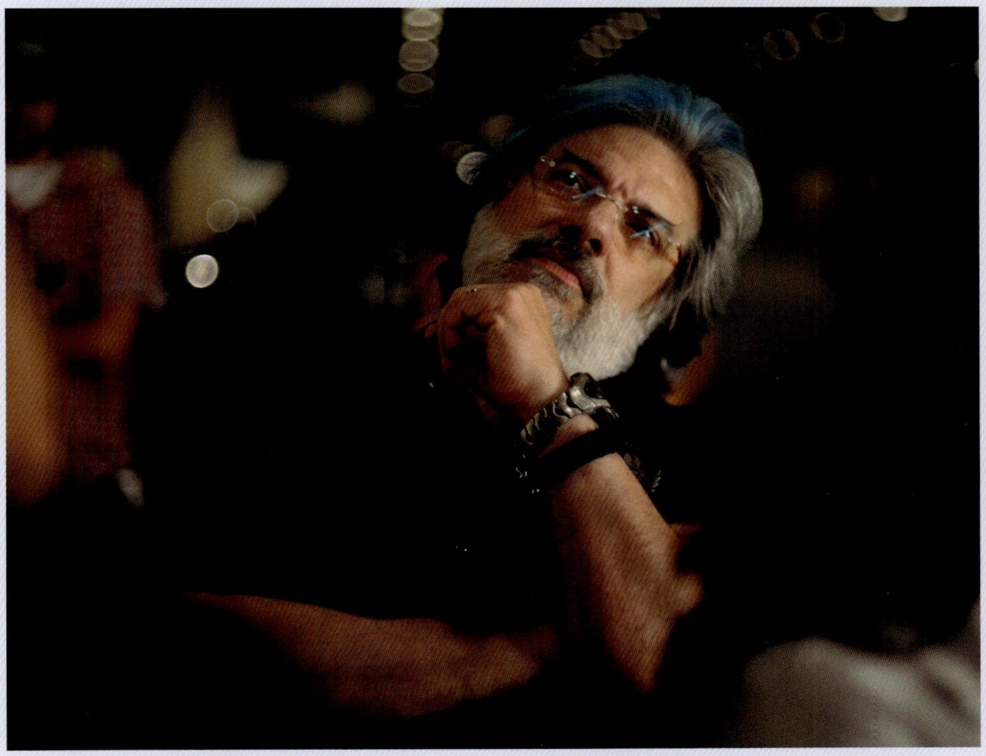

ABOVE: Fred Raimondi was one of the first video compositors I worked with, and one of the most talented people I have ever met. In the beginning it was as if we were talking different languages: he introduced me to new technology, and I worked with him to explain how I would use film technology to create the image we were looking for.

"Dan was this soft-spoken guy who was really quite unremarkable in terms of his looks—short hair and a close-cropped beard with the tiniest tinge of gray—but in his demeanor and actions you could see right off the bat that this was someone who had nothing to prove. What I didn't know was that he was a 'devil may care' prankster wrapped in a gentle soul, who had the heart of an artist. He would regale me for hours with his stories about his time as a professor, and his time in the Peace Corps.

"He always made you feel as if you were working with him, not for him. Our relationship was quite symbiotic. He was filling in for me what I didn't know about art, and I was filling in for him what he didn't know about compositing in the video/electronic medium.

"Dan would do everything he could to make sure we were spending 90% of the time in compositing making the work look cool, and 10% of the time fixing production mistakes rather than the other way around, which seemed to be the case on other shows. The main reason for that was the prepping that was done before shooting. For example, there's an episode with a robot flying through a jungle; Dan had the foresight to take a piece of blue-screen material, and photograph multiple plates with different pieces of foliage. A little thing, but it allowed us to put the robot inside the foliage with very little work. This sounds simple now, but in 1987 it was some pretty heads-up visual-effects supervision.

"Dan was one of the first VFX designers that I worked with who actually had fine-art chops in drawing and painting. He is an artist's artist. That is to say, he approaches the work from an artistic perspective first, and then works out the technical details. He was a quick study, and had a real understanding of the compositing tools. I believe he approached designing the visual-effects scenes by sketching them out in his brain, and then using the various tools and disciplines of the filmmaking process to bring them to fruition. He sees objects the way most of us don't, especially in terms of artistic applications.

"I was just an Italian guy from NJ who had wanted to make films since I was a little boy. I had no formal art training, so to be working with someone like Dan was really an education for me. He was very influential in the way that I looked at my work in visual effects, and even more influential in my decision to actually get some fine-art training. I saw that his eye as a fine artist made his work as a visual-effects artist so much better."

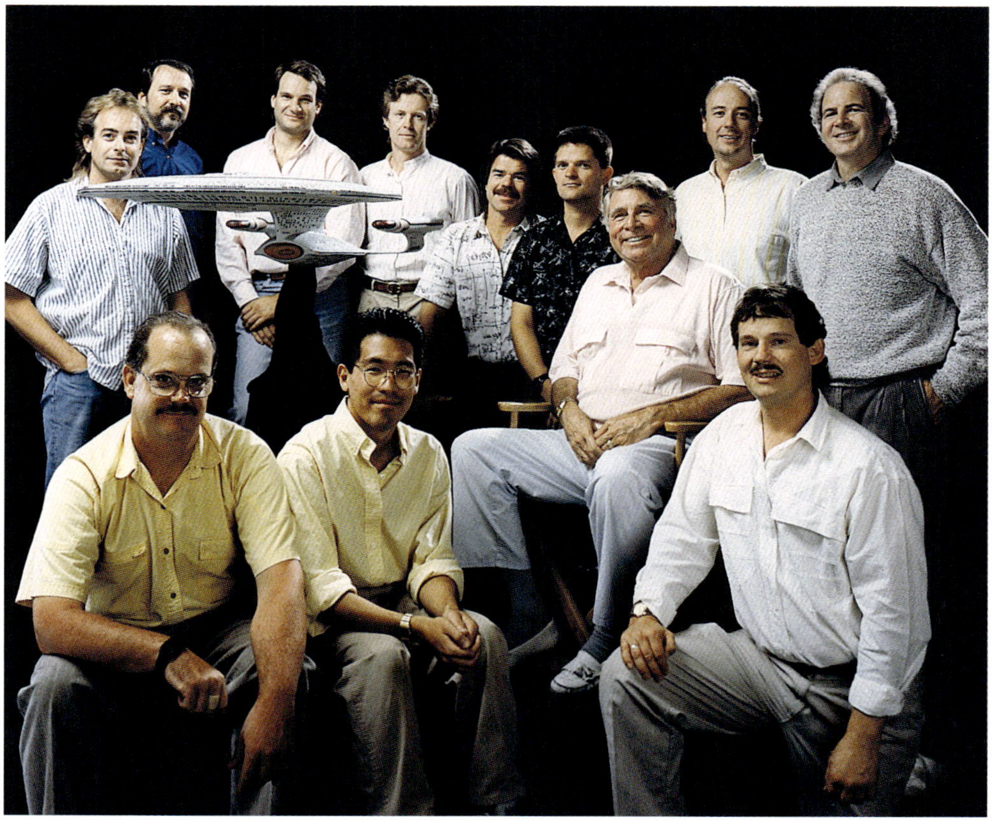

LEFT: Top row, left to right: Adrian Hurley, Dan Curry, Rob Legato, Walter Hart, Dennis Hoerter, Eric Nash, Tom Barron, Peter Lauritson. Middle row: *Enterprise*-D model, Gene Roddenberry. Bottom row: Ron B. Moore, David Takemura, Gary Hutzel.

reshooting the same standard shots.

By now we had started to get an idea of what things would cost, so when the producers saw the budgets we'd hack away at them by making adjustments in the script to get the costs down to something acceptable. Also, the writers and producers started to understand what was within our means, and wrote scripts we could handle, but always on the edge of what was doable. The VFX team was always ambitious, wanting to break new ground. We learned from our mistakes, but as hard as we tried, we couldn't always avoid making new ones during our explorations into the unknown.

In the third season, Marvin Rush joined *Star Trek* as the new director of photography, replacing Eddie Brown. Marvin was eager to be an ally of visual effects, and helped us out whenever possible. He would be active in discussions on how VFX shots would be approached, and offered valuable suggestions. After Marvin moved over to *DS9*, Jonathan West became DP for *The Next Generation*, and brought that same level of skill, artistry, and enthusiasm. The camera crews were supportive, and trusted our judgement on VFX shots.

One of the things that really made a difference for the success of *Star Trek* was the way everyone worked together. Michael Westmore and the makeup team, Herman Zimmerman and the art department, the grips and construction crew, and Dennis Madalone and the stunt performers always worked together with us in visual effects. Every episode involved a series of meetings. We started with a general production meeting; I always thought of them as medieval banquets. The executive producers and director of the episode sat at the head of the table, and then there was an unspoken hierarchy in seating order, with people from each department sitting next to each other to discuss relevant issues. Occasionally there would be a monitor to show something for discussion.

At production meetings, the first assistant director would go through the script, bringing up the needs and logistical challenges of each scene and what each department had to contend with, and agree on an approach. Subsequently there were separate stunt meetings, art department and construction meetings, makeup and hair meetings, costume meetings, tone meetings with the directors, and the 'optical' meetings (using the older term for visual effects) where our first budget was presented to the producers, who, after recovering from cardiac arrest at the big numbers, would work with us to figure out what was doable within our budgetary and time limitations and still tell the story.

Technically, things were constantly improving. Every year we'd get a new device in the edit bay that was better, faster, and had a wider range of capabilities than the one we had the year before. Whenever a new tool become available, we would find new things we could do with it. Artistic potentials expanded.

With the arrival of the digital D5 format we were able to abandon 1-inch analog compositing technology that had been tying our hands in a significant way. The major problem with 1-inch analog was that every time you duped a layer there would be a noticeable image quality loss. This meant you could only work a shot so much until its degradation became unacceptable. With D5 the images are digital and mathematically reproducible, so you can have unlimited duplication without quality loss.

At the same time, the writers, actors, and directors were getting to know the characters better, and to understand what drives them. The characters evolved. One of my favorite characters, Worf, portrayed by the great Michael Dorn, evolved from somebody who stood around growling to to a thoughtful noble warrior from a generations-old respected Klingon family. That is a testament to Michael's screen presence and talent.

Those seven years on *The Next Generation* were a stressful experience, but though I might not have been aware of it at the time, I loved almost every minute of it. The scripts brought challenges like "This has to look like something we've never seen before." I thought that was brilliant because it gave us the opportunity to just make it up. Among my favorites were time-space continuum anomalies, or gaps into another dimension. "How are you going to do that?" "Let's try pouring some liquid nitrogen over black velvet and put a vacuum cleaner next to a light to suck the vapors into a light source, then we can composite it into a star field." "Cool!" It was a lot of fun.

We actually got paid to play and do cool stuff that any kid would love. I hope our joy in creating visual effects for *Star Trek* was a factor in not only supporting the stories, but in delivering delight and inspiring the imaginations of our audience.

RON B. MOORE

VFX SUPERVISOR

Ron B. Moore was one of the few members of the *Star Trek* team who was with the production for 18 years. He was the third person to join the VFX team (after Rob Legato and Gary Hutzel), and was given the job because Dan recommended him to Peter Lauritson. His credits outside *Star Trek* include *Ghostbusters*, *2010*, and the *Twilight* saga. After Dan joined *Star Trek*, the two men worked incredibly closely throughout their time on the various shows. Ron's work on the franchise earned him 13 Emmy nominations with five wins, and a prestigious VES award.

"Dan is not in the least like other people. I don't think he understands that. He sees the world differently, and he has such a unique perspective on life. We worked together for all 18 years of *Star Trek*, and even before that. He's one of my oldest friends. We were a very good team, we were just so opposite that it really worked. What I could do best and what he could do best was what we needed to do together. He was strange, but I loved him like a brother.

"When we started out everything was new. We made it up because nobody had ever done this stuff before. Dan excelled at that; he would constantly come up with solutions I would never have thought of. I've never seen anything like it, but it was absolute genius. There were endless times when we thought he was crazy. Low tech was his thing—some of the things he'd come up with, you'd just shake your head and think, 'It can't possibly work,' but it did. He brought in this pom-pom that ended up in virtually every show as forcefields, or different kinds of energy. I can't tell you how many times I used it. Or he'd say things like, "We'll fill a tray with water and make it vibrate, and turn it into a forcefield." We learned so much from that.

"I think *Star Trek* was the right place for him at the right time. There was so little time you could do whatever you wanted, and there wasn't enough time for anyone to come back and throw your stuff away. You could be creative. There were times when you were in the edit bay, and you've got nothing. Dan loved that. He thrived on it. He's got this unique perspective, but he needs the freedom to do his own thing. You have to understand when he makes this right turn, never underestimate him. It might not sound right—you don't go down to go up—but that's what he's saying. You have to listen to him because odds on you are missing something.

"I think he was good when he was desperate, [although] you'd never know it. He had a vision of stuff that I've never seen from anyone else. He will always keep working at something, making it better. If he was left alone to do anything it could cost us thousands, and we'd be over budget, but on the other hand we'd win an Emmy. He and I had an understanding, and we agreed that there were certain shots where he could go wild, and other shots where we would kind of watch ourselves a little bit. He became pretty good at that.

"For Dan it was all about the art, and the tools were just a means to an end. When he started using Photoshop it was difficult for him. Little things, like the pressure of a paintbrush, [were] a whole different process. He'd be frustrated, and ring up John Knoll (who invented Photoshop) and say "What the hell is this?" When he grew into it, suddenly it was going the other way around, and John was ringing him and asking his advice about things like how to name tools.

"Once he started to get the hang of it, it changed everything. We all knew when we were sitting there in the edit bay watching him do that, that this was going to change our lives. We had watched him create something revolutionary."

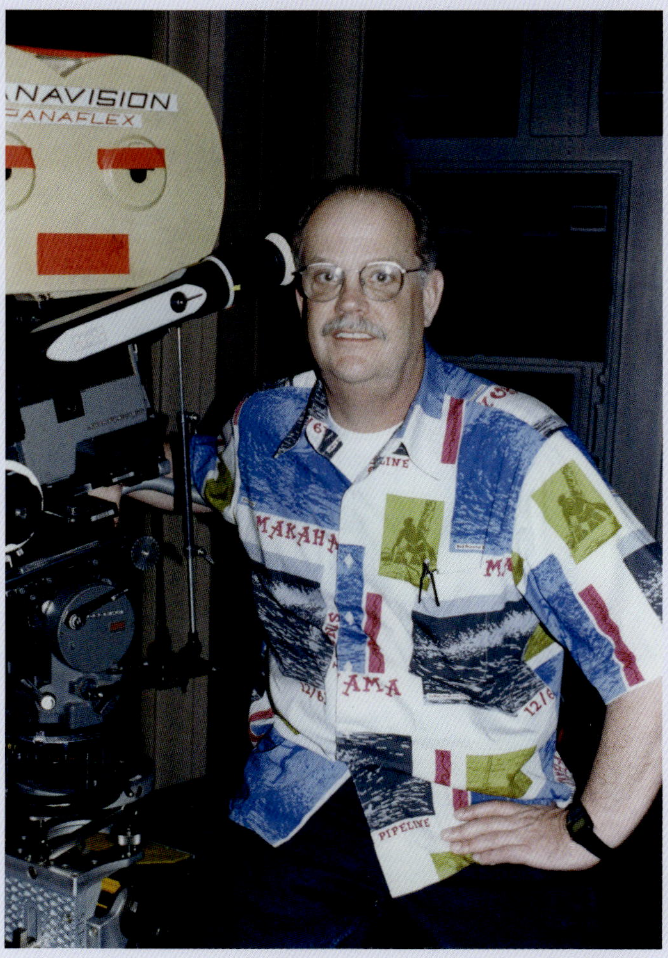

RIGHT: Ron is a great friend, and a mainstay of the *Star Trek* VFX team. He played a significant role in getting our workflow efficient; *Star Trek* wouldn't have been the same without him.

BELOW: The *Enterprise* fires a photon torpedo. This effect was created using a pre-built animated element that cculd be applied to shots as needed. The animator would move it along correct lines of perspective.

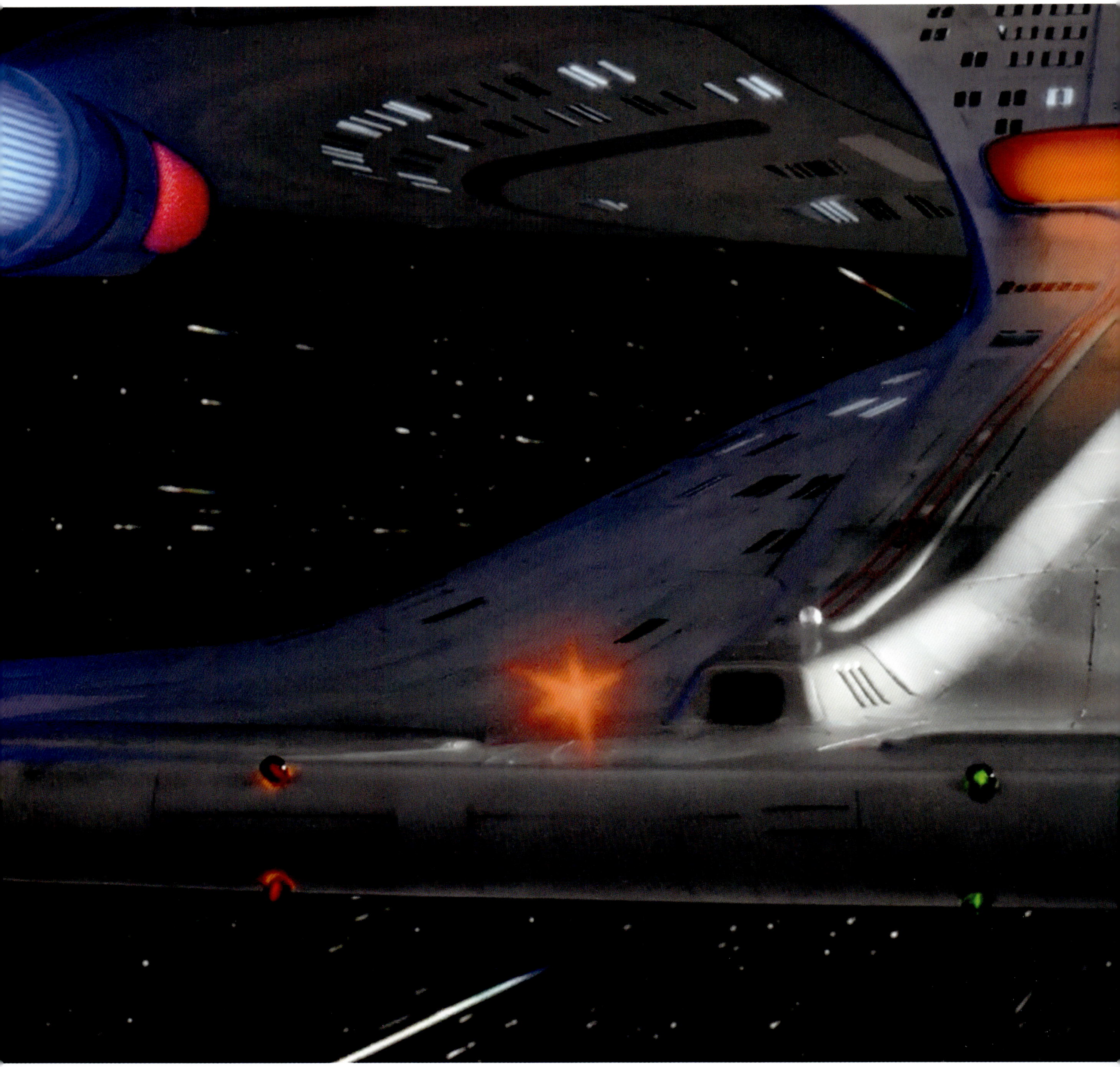

VIDEO COMPOSITING

LEARNING NEW SKILLS IN A NEW AGE OF COMPOSITING TECHNOLOGY

When I joined *Star Trek* I was new to video. I had always worked with film using traditional optical printers to do the compositing. When I realized the artistic potential and the speed that things could be done with video technology it was like somebody pulled up the window shades and the light came in—it transformed compositing from a highly technical time-consuming process to something more like painting. You could see the elements of an image build layer upon layer as you were working. It wasn't just cheaper and faster, it was artistically liberating. Things literally happened in front of you.

The *TNG* VFX supervisors and coordinators had varying degrees of experience in video. Rob and Gary had worked with video before. Ron and I both came from a traditional film background, where we were reliant on optical printers for compositing the type of effects *Star Trek* needed, from motion-control miniatures to matte shots painted in oils. We were well versed in techniques that dated back to legendary pioneer George Méliés, who made the first science-fiction films at the turn of the twentieth century and to whom all visual-effects artists owe a great debt. The guys who worked at CIS and The Post Group came from the world of electronics and its rapidly evolving technology. We were using a different set of tools to accomplish the same goals. Video compositing still entailed combining the same range of elements into new cinematic realities, just in different ways. I knew how to capture and combine those elements, but had to learn the technology and culture of the edit bay. It was a symbiotic relationship; the editors brought their depth of knowledge of video technology, and I brought film-compositing thinking and a painter's eye. Together we invented new approaches, creating a hybrid of thinking drawn from both the film and video worlds.

When we started out on *TNG* we filmed physical models for all our spaceships. We used the same motion-control techniques that we would have used on film, but compositing was much faster and easier on video. At the same time, we discovered things you could do on video that you couldn't accomplish with an optical printer. You could tweak color, brightness, focus, and see how all elements look in relationship to one another. "The warp drive looks a little dim, let's brighten that up." We could also change perspective on video, which was not readily possible on film.

There were moments when we literally didn't understand one another, so we had to learn each other's language. We quickly realized that we just had different terms for the same things. My first experience with a compositing editor was with the brilliantly creative Fred Raimondi at The Post Group. "DDR? What the hell is a DDR?" (Digital Disk Recorder). Watching Fred spin those

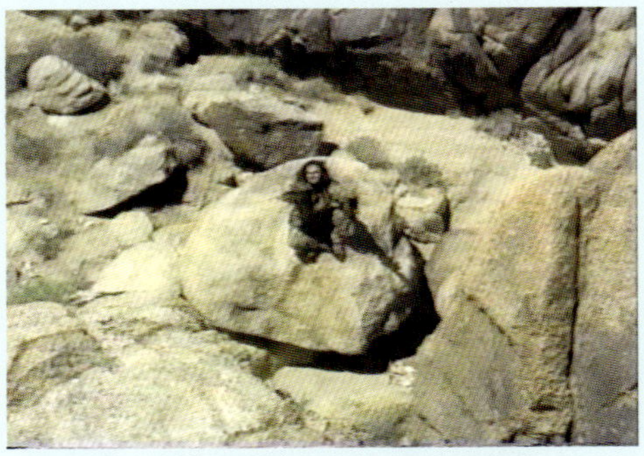

ABOVE: We filmed stunt actor Linda Colucci Madalone in a dry riverbed on location in the Alabama Hills, Lone Pine, California.

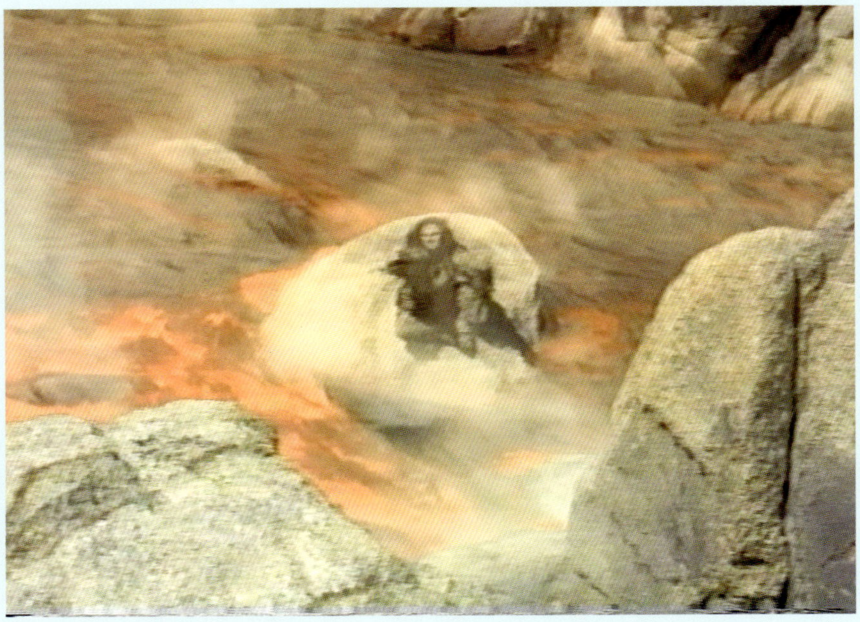

ABOVE: A shot like this is made up of many different elements that are combined in the video-compositing bay. It is essential to make sure that everything looks as if it belongs together—it is a balance between art and science.

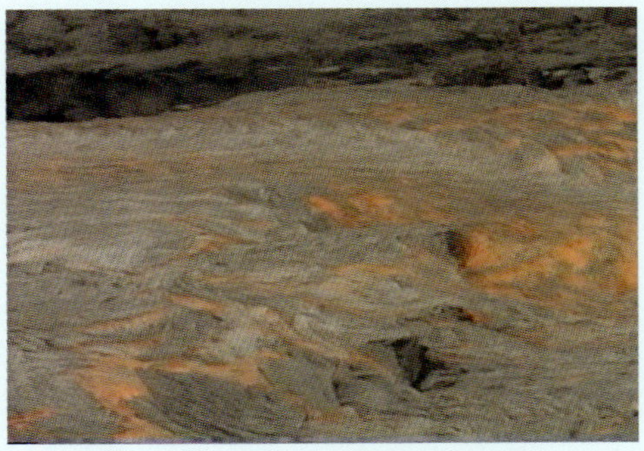

ABOVE: The lava we used in this shot was stock footage of a volcano in Hawaii.

INSIDE STORY

LAVA FLOW IN 'BASICS'

In the *Voyager* episode 'Basics' we had to show one of the primitive inhabitants of the planet trapped on a rock surrounded by lava, before Chakotay leaps in and rescues her. To do that we filmed a stunt actor—who was actually our stunt coordinator Dennis Madalone's wife, Linda—in a dry streambed in the Alabama Hills near Lone Pine, CA, where we shot most of the episode.

Phony movie lava looks like phony movie lava, and I really wanted to avoid that. We always say that nothing is more real than real, so I found some stock footage of lava from Hawaii, and composited the lava over the dry streambed. I cut around the perimeter of the lava flow to make an alpha channel, or 'window,' to contain the molten rock. To make it look right, I asked the compositing editor to twist the perspective a little bit so it looked like it was flowing in that terrain. Then we added a little color to make it look as if the lava was really hot, and finally composited in some liquid nitrogen vapors that we had shot separately to look like steam.

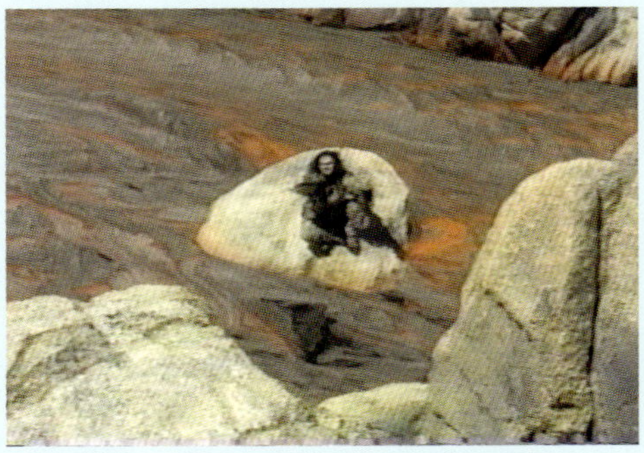

ABOVE: We made a matte, or silhouette, to make a space where the lava would be. Lava from the stock shot was skewed into proper perspective, and on a paint box I added an interactive heat glow on the surrounding rocks.

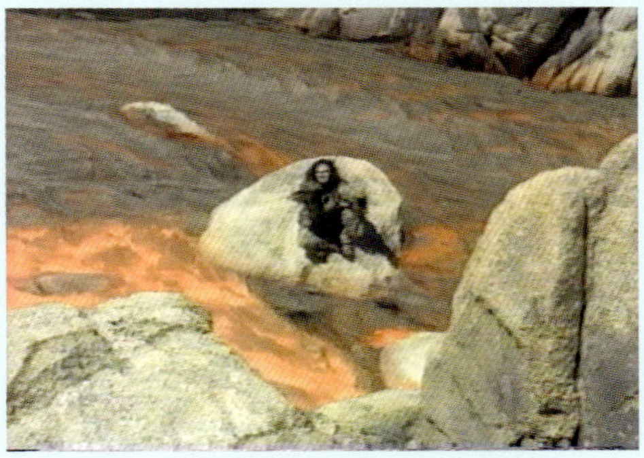

LEFT: We blended in additional hot lava to add a little heat intensity. Finally we added liquid nitrogen vapors for steam.

trackballs surrounded by rows of screens, small scopes and big monitors was quite different from looking through microscope-like bore scopes on optical printers. Color in video was eminently adjustable in real time. That was not true in an optical house, where you had to examine rows of film prints made with subtle variations on a wide light table as you peered through a magnifying loupe. I was entering a new world, and I smelled the future. On video a shot could be put together in a few hours that would have taken days on

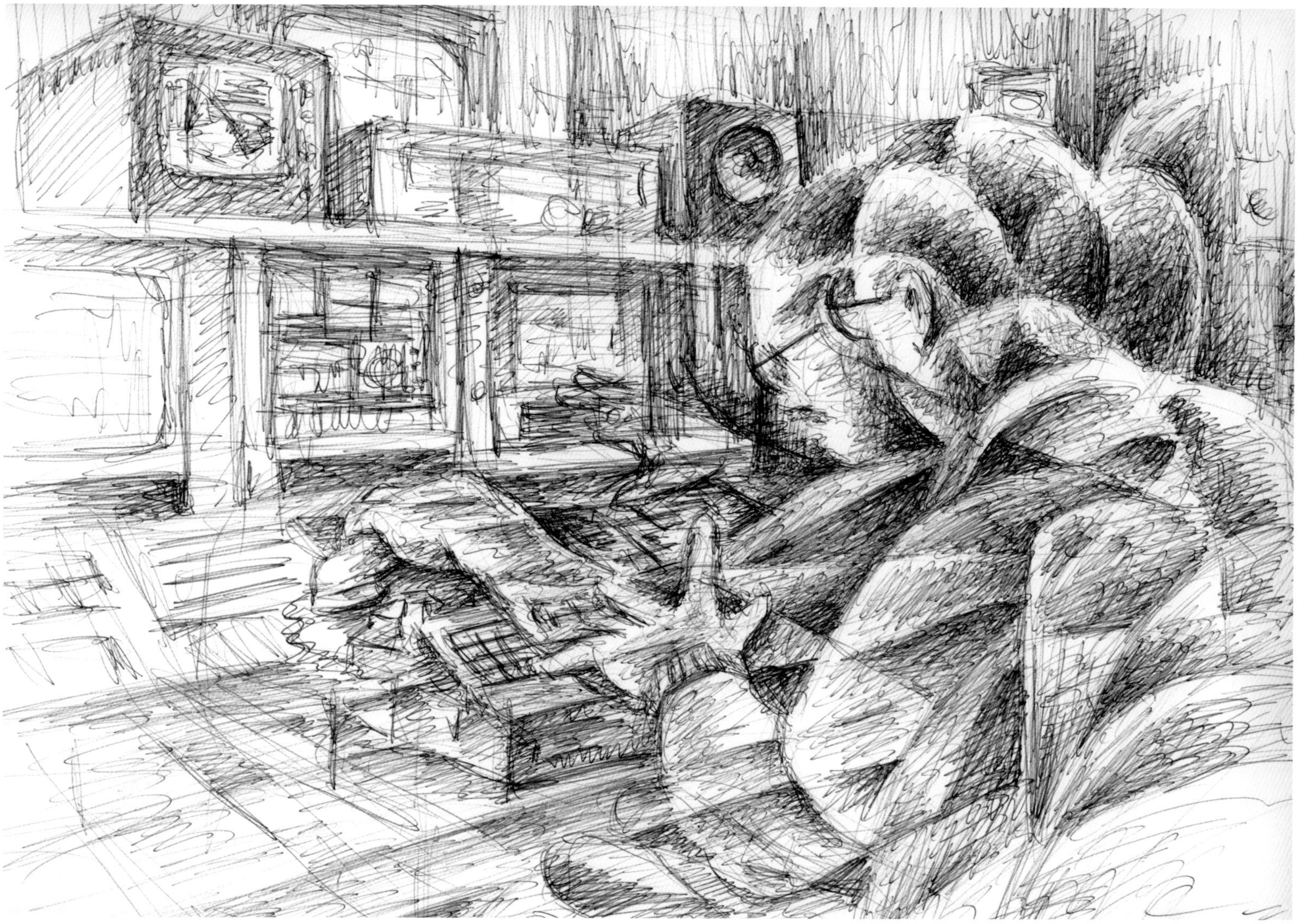

ABOVE: Working in The Post Group's Edit Bay 8 I tried to capture master VFX editor Peter Moyer's movements in a cubist pen-and-ink drawing.

an optical printer when each test and adjustment meant another trip to the lab and another day lost Compositing electronically became very painterly. "Here's my underpainting, here's this, here's that." You can actually see a shot evolve as you are working on it. In an edit bay you could take a shot from start to final product in a series of steps in one session. It was so incredibly efficient, and so much more satisfying.

Occasionally, we would run out of time and have to accept less than perfection. We would call those shots 'CBBs' ('Could Be Betters'), and would revisit them if time allowed before delivery date. In film technology, blue-screen exposure has to be perfect. When you make mattes for compositing you have to measure the black and white hi-con film with a densitometer to make sure the density is absolutely correct so there will be no light leak. There's very little tolerance for error. Even in the early days of one-inch analog video tape compositing the process was way more forgiving. As a shot evolves, artistic collaboration with the compositing editor is essential. We were most fortunate working with some great talents. As a shot progressed, we could experiment in finding ways to improve it and make adjustments in the visual relationships between the various elements. "Well, let's try this." "Can we change that over there?" Working in edit bays became like conducting an orchestra of virtuoso musicians, or like being the coach of a team rather than a player on the field. When paint systems became available, I had my own workstation in the edit bay. While working with the VFX compositing editor on the main shots, I could also be creating elements for matte shots and set extensions, and elements for animation to be comped later.

Even though our animators and compositing editors worked for different vendor companies, they were as dedicated to *Star Trek* as any member of the cast and crew at Paramount. *Star Trek* was their full-time job. Even the edit bays were configured to serve *Star Trek*'s specific needs. When not being used by *Star Trek*, the vendor company could make its hi-tech bays available to other clients.

Another thing we could do with video was to have our animators draw directly onto a video frame. This was great for effects like phasers as we could see perspective and interactive light. Even that wasn't as simple as it sounds; a phaser would be made up of three different elements. There would be the hot core, then there would be the kinetic outer orange surrounding glow, the barrel glow, the impact hit, and, if time allowed, we would add a little heat distortion to the air. To save time and avoid having to do each shot from scratch, the animators kept a library of elements that could be skewed into the various perspectives required by different shots.

We could also paint directly onto the frame. For example, in 'The Dauphin' we saw an old nurse and the beautiful princess morph into other things. Those morphs were hand-painted one frame at a time by the brilliant Steve Price. There was no morph software.

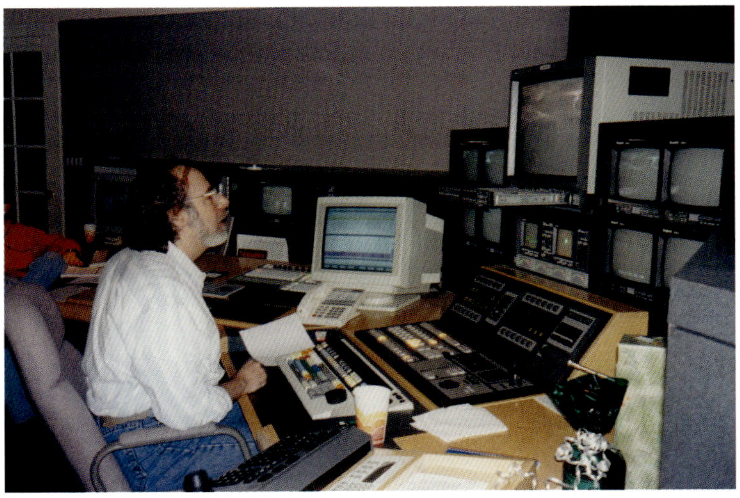

LEFT: Veteran VFX editor Don Greenberg working in an edit bay at Digital Magic. Digital technology evolved at an astonishing rate, giving us more and better tools every season.

Drawing something onto a video frame wasn't exactly like drawing or painting in traditional media because you are working with moving images. You can distort an image, change its color and make it into something else. Over the years we filmed countless things we could use as elements to build our effects.

Working in the edit bay was always fun. Despite the long hours we were always in high spirits. The bays were equipped with superlative sound systems required for professional work. Ron and Fred, both excellent guitarists, had large collections of music so I would frequently hear something new and exciting. Having lived overseas for so long, there was a gap in my exposure to contemporary musical culture. All our subsequent editors had great

PAUL HILL

VFX COMPOSITOR

Paul joined *Star Trek* as an assistant to the visual-effects compositor in *TNG*'s fourth season, and rose to become the lead compositor, working on *DS9*, *Voyager*, and *Enterprise*. He earned 12 Emmy nominations for his work on *Star Trek*, with three wins.

"The fact that I was sitting in a room with Dan Curry at this particular time in visual-effects history is not lost on me. I had to pinch myself so many times. *Star Trek* was a pioneer in taking film-based effects, and doing them digitally. They were writing the book on how to do this. When I started, my job was to provide painted elements for the VFX compositor, so I was responsible for a graphics workstation at the side of the bay where all of the painting had to be done. That meant I worked closely with Dan.

"Dan is an extremely gracious individual who shares everything he knows. He has never been possessive about any of it. He sat with me, and showed me the best way to do things. This is in addition to all his other responsibilities on the show. By the time I walked in, they had already figured out how to do things, but there was so much more to come. Eventually the workstation I was on was going to become the workstation at the center of the operation, and the other stuff was going to go away.

"I was absolutely aware that I was part of something that was changing, that was birthing. I could instantly see what Dan's part in that was—the merging of fine art and electronic digital visual effects. He was bringing things in that he had painted in Photoshop at home. We were then porting them in on my box, and putting them together with other elements.

"He would say, 'Try this,' 'Make this,' 'Do that.' Occasionally, he would just take the pen himself and say, 'Let me try. I'm going to paint this thing on the graphics workstation. We'll give it to the VFX compositor, and we're just going to see how it works.' That had to be a unique situation for *Star Trek*—to have this fine artist working in the room with us who, at a moment's notice, could create a matte painting from scratch, or alter the one he'd brought from home, or give us an element that would make a shot better.

"Dan made me laugh. He's a wonderful storyteller. He's a wonderful person. He never treated you like you're an idiot; he respected you. He's just a very generous man, a great teacher, and a fabulous artist. He kept things light. The only time there was ever any tension was because of a deadline or something like that, but it was as good as it gets. Even today I ask myself, 'What would Dan do? How would Dan make this shot better?'"

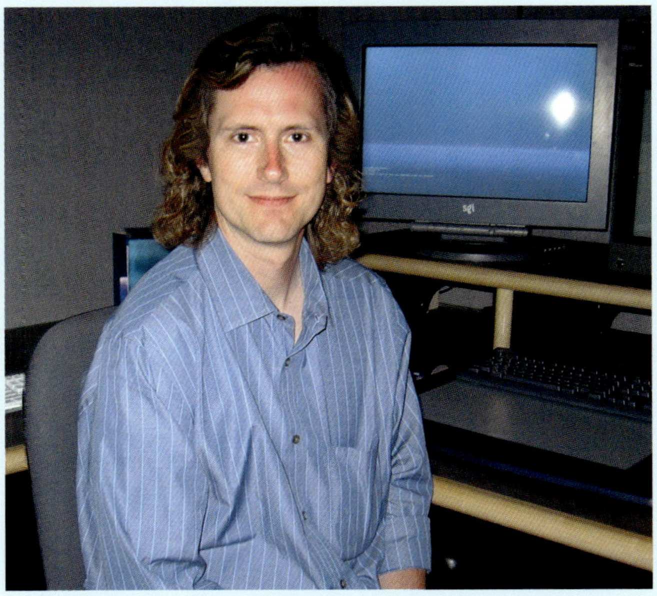

ABOVE: Paul is a highly talented compositor, combining artistic judgment, technical mastery, and a willingness to try new approaches to VFX.

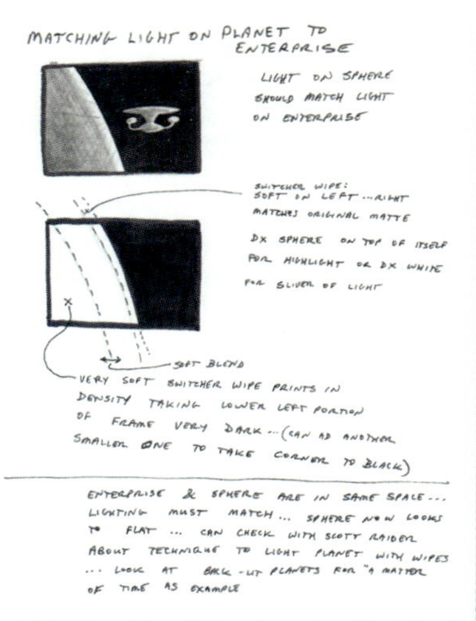

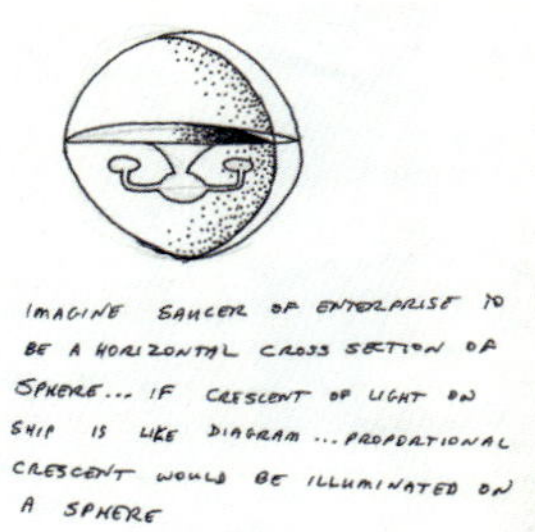

Note to compositors to help understand how to accurately create planet shadows.

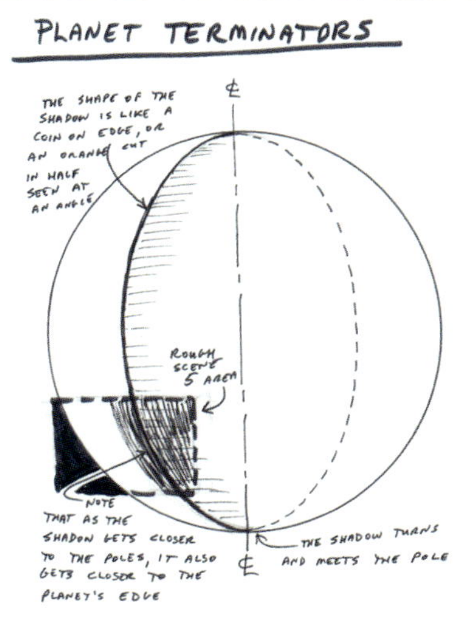

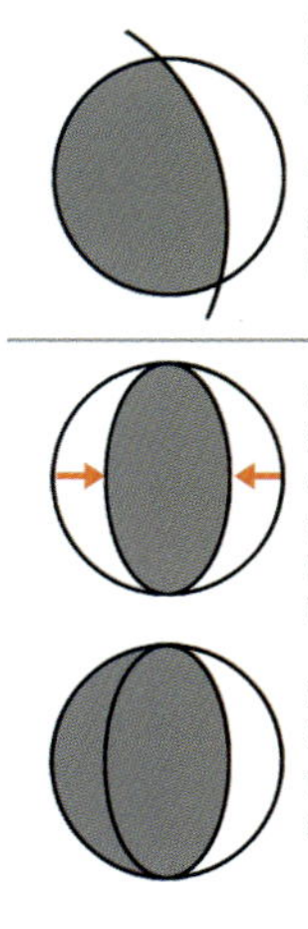

Incorrect method to create a planet terminor shadow: drawing an arc across the planet.

The problem: the shape of the shadow does not properly relate to a sphere.

Correct method: Step 1 - Squeeze the matte (alpha channel) of the planet into an elipse that perfectly fits inside the planet's circumference yielding a true cross-section of the planet.

Step 2 - Fill in the rest of the shadow and rotate the planet to match the angle of the light source in the scene.

INSIDE STORY

MAKING PLANETS

When you look at a planet from orbit, you can see its atmosphere. In order for it to look correct, the atmosphere should sit above the planet, and should move independently. On *Star Trek* we used a variety of techniques to create planets. Only once did I use a physical model planet (for the *TNG* episode 'Home Soil'), because we already had a 4-ft-diameter model that was used as part of the set for the colony station in the story. Rob and Gary tried projecting images onto a white sphere so they could use motion-control data from ship shots when photographing the planet. For greater verisimilitude, I preferred 'wrapping' images onto virtual spheres, or sometimes I would do photo-real 2D oil paintings, as seen in the *Voyager* title sequence.

When we made our planets digitally we had a device that could generate a virtual sphere, and we could wrap part of a photograph around it so it looked a solid surface. Sometimes we used satellite photographs, macro shots of rocks in my garden, or undisclosed organic substances. A lot of the time we used talcum powder to create a weather system; we would sprinkle the talcum powder, and film it against a black background so we could isolate it, then we just wrapped it around the planet. The white powder looked like clouds. We used our compositing system to put it on another layer that was moving in a slightly different way than the planet's surface, so it looked like the clouds were moving independently. We could even offset the cloud pattern to make another layer that cast a shadow from the clouds on the planet's surface.

If we wanted to make the atmosphere look turbulent, we used one of the liquid nitrogen elements, and printed into the clouds so it looked like weird stuff was happening below. One of the elements used was a glass tray about 2 ft x 16 in, filled with hot water, and with little particles of dry ice sprinkled into it so that it boiled and churned.

Our goal was always to present to the audience as much verisimilitude as possible, but it doesn't matter what technology you've got if you don't understand how something works. When we started making CG planets, some compositors needed help with terminators—the point on the planet where light and dark meet. Some of the artists would just put an over-sized arc there, and I always got really picky about it. They would complain, but if they just put an arc in, it never looked like it perfectly fitted to the planet. What I would have them do is take the circle representing the circumference of the planet, and then compress it into an ellipse and make a matte out of that. Then we drew a line from one top to bottom, and filled in the rest of the planet's shadow. That way it made the shape of the terminator shadow fit the sphere perfectly.

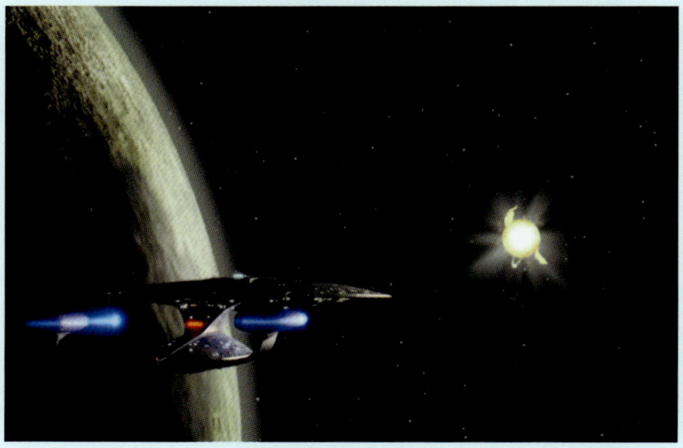

LEFT: It's important to understand the way light falls on spheres. Charts like these helped our compositors and CG teams to use the right techniques to create light and shadows around a planet.

RIGHT: In a shot like this the lighting on the planet and the ship has to match and to look as if it is being cast by a distant sun, in this case, with active flares.

music collections and carried on the tradition of great music. Of course, we would kill the tunes when concentration was required.

I will always recall with great fondness the camaraderie we shared in the countless hours spent putting shots together. I met people for whom I developed profound respect and built abiding friendships. I am also proud of all that we were able to accomplish. The *Star Trek* VFX team produced an incredible amount of work despite daunting schedules and budget limitations. I am proud that we, in our humble way, were catalysts contributing to the evolution from film to the limitless possibilities of digital technologies.

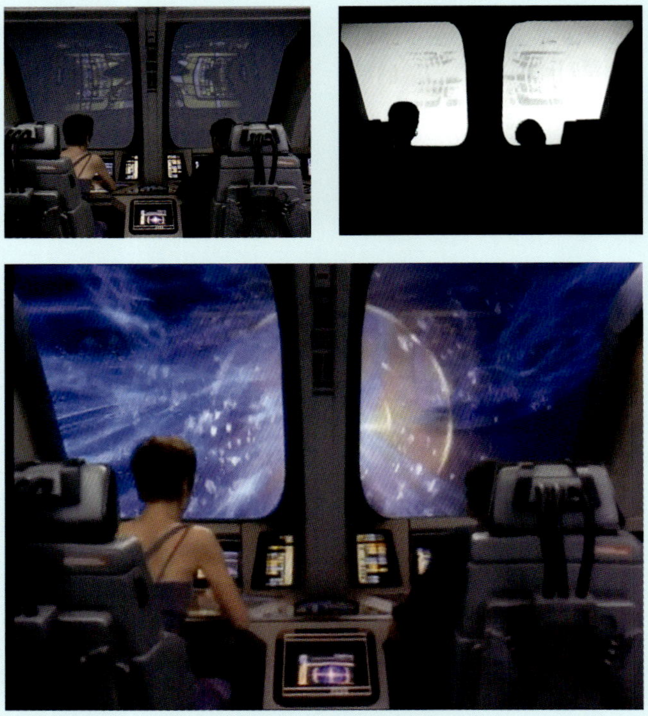

ABOVE: One of the most common shots involved replacing a blue or green screen window with a visual effect to show what is outside.

INSIDE STORY

WINDOW SHOTS

Every episode of *Star Trek* involved us adding something that wasn't there to a computer screen or a window. It's one of the most basic gags you can do, and it was something that was a lot faster with video compositing than traditional optical printing. The VFX compositor would isolate the area you wanted to replace—sometimes pulling a matte from a blue screen shot, but if no one moved in front of the window or screen you could trace the shape of the area to be replaced to create a matte. Before the development of tracking software the camera couldn't move. The compositor would remove that part of the original image and replace it with something we'd created elsewhere, in this case from *DS9* a piece of CG footage showing the inside of the wormhole.

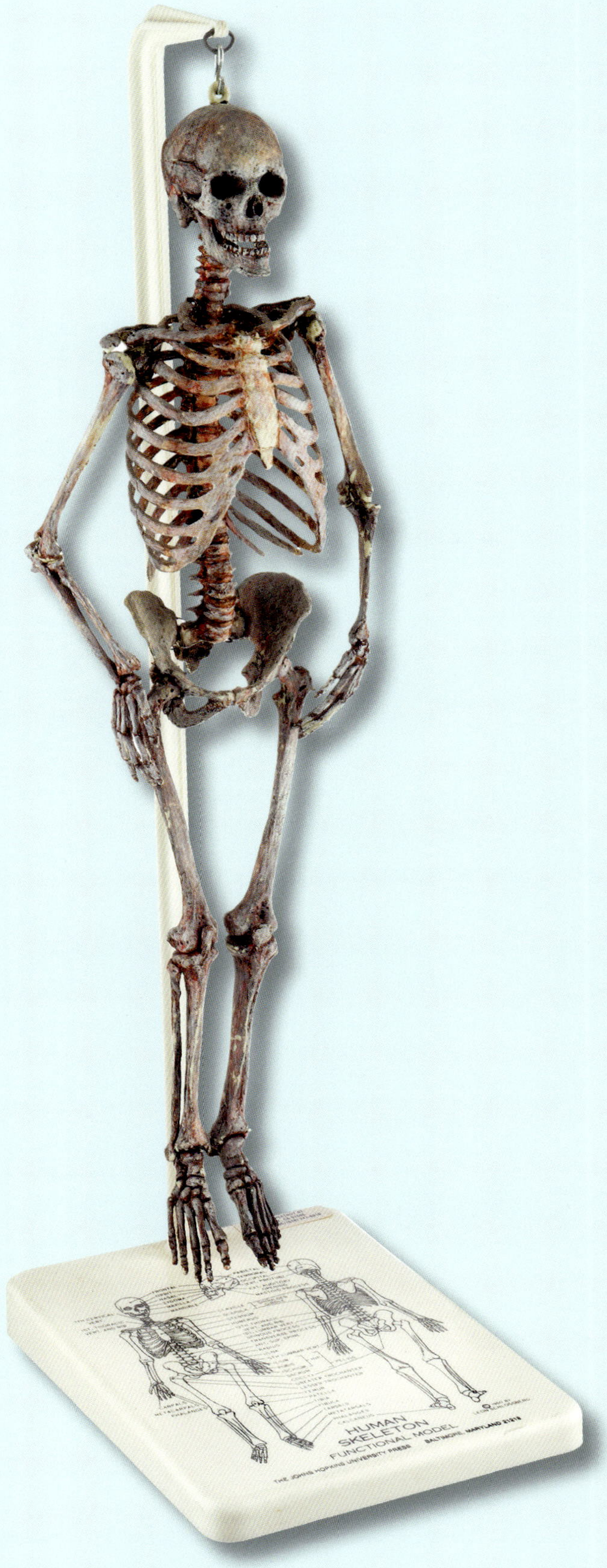

ABOVE: We posed an anatomically accurate 18" skeleton to match each actor's position. I painted it to look more fresh and grisly.

INSIDE STORY

UNDER THE SKIN

You could use video compositing to mix between two different images, so you could remove one image and replace it with something else. For *TNG*'s 'Loud As A Whisper' I wanted to disintegrate characters in a different way. It was my homage to George Pal's *War of the Worlds* where we see a glimpse of a sizzling skeleton when an army officer is dematerialized by an alien ray. As a child I thought that was cool.

I bought a 2-ft miniature skeleton that was anatomically accurate. It was just white plastic, so I hand-painted it so it was grisly looking and fresh. We filmed the actors on the stage, shot a clean background plate, then we lined the skeleton up so it was in the same position, and filmed that. In the editing bay, the characters' soft tissue was erased a frame at a time to reveal disintegrating bones as they vanished.

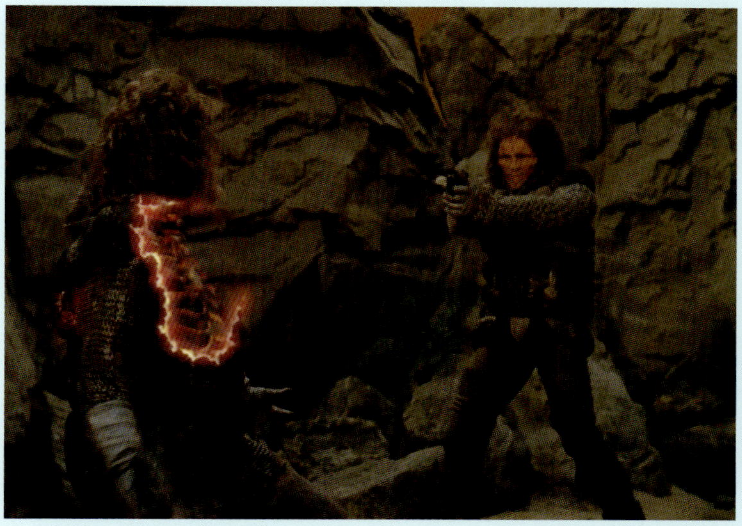

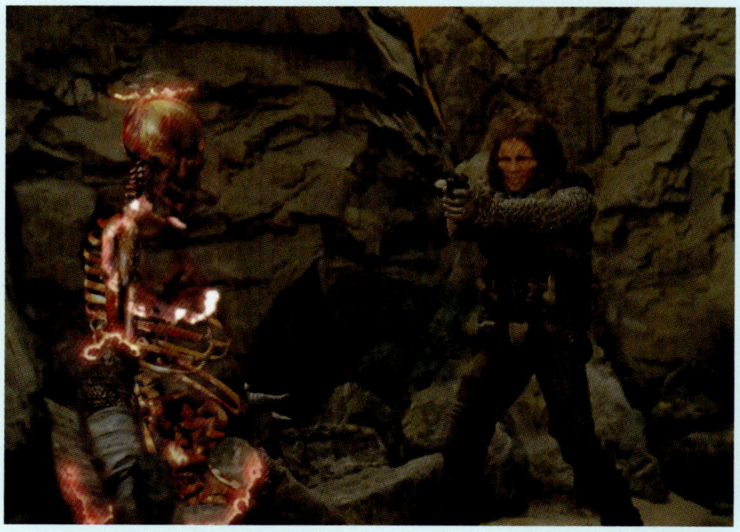

ABOVE: Video compositing enables lining up two different images as layers and animating one layer away to reveal the one below, in this case to reveal the skeleton as the body is disintegrated.

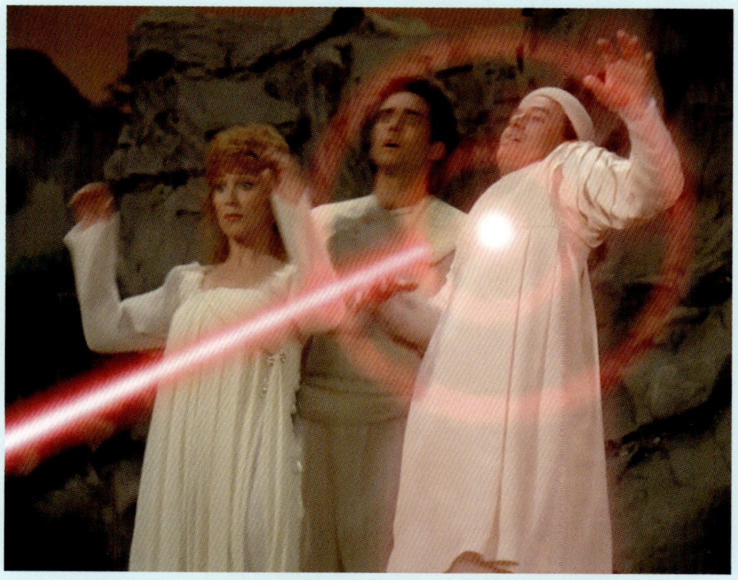

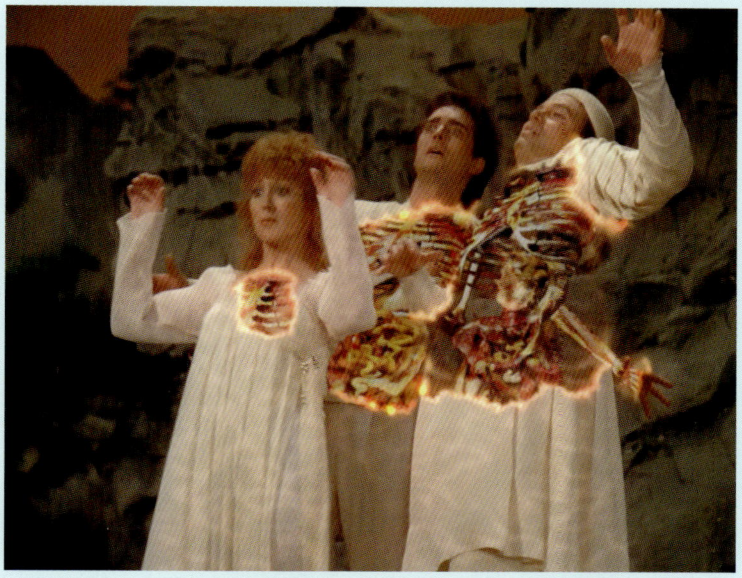

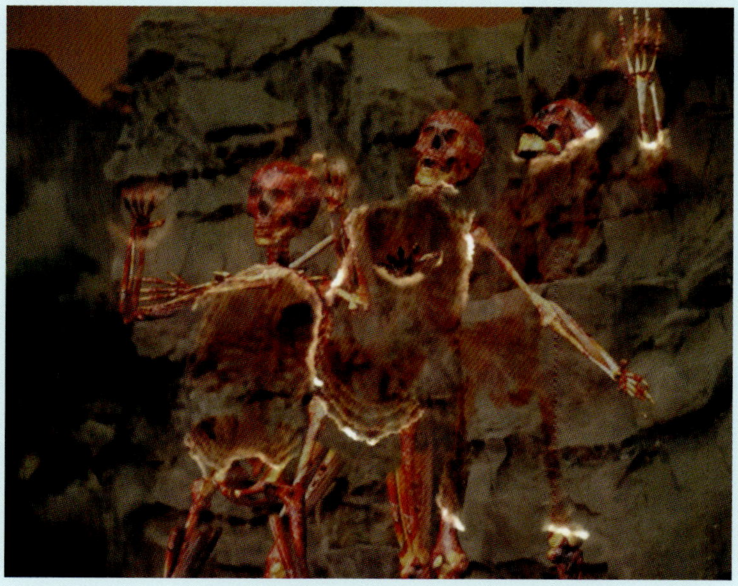

ABOVE: We used the same skeleton for all three people in this shot. We just put it in a matching position for each actor and then filmed it again and again, before compositing it with the live-action footage.

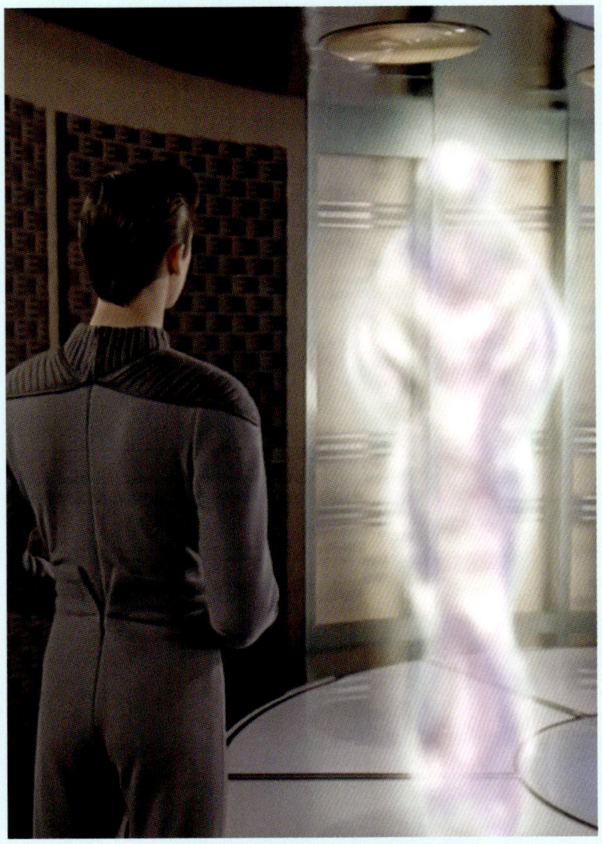

INSIDE STORY

THE DAUPHIN'S TRUE FORM

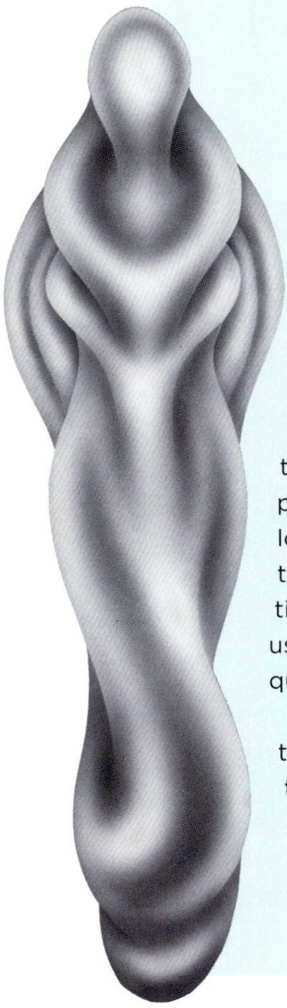

At the end of 'The Dauphin' the alien princess Salia, who Wesley has been falling for, reveals her true form: a being of pure light. We filmed the actress, Jaime Hubbard, on the transporter, and I created a painting of her final alien shape. In the editing bay, we changed her proportions to match the painting, and then made it undulate to give the image a little more life. I airbrushed the painting on shiny black paper so that we would have lots of contrast, and in compositing we animated the painting by playing with glows, highlights and tinted shadows so that it seemed to move. We only used the highlights, which gave Salia the ephemeral quality we were looking for.

Audience reaction was mixed. Some people thought it was really goofy, and some people thought it was elegant. You can't please everybody.

ABOVE: Salia's true form was created using a piece of hand-drawn art (left) and animation techniques in the edit bay.

INSIDE STORY

BEAMING IN AND OUT

When we did a transporter effect the first step was to film the place the person was going to beam in to or out of. We shot it twice: once with the person in place, and once without (called a clean plate). You can dissolve between these two takes, making it look as if someone appears or disappears, but the transporter effect was more involved than that.

The next thing we did was to cut (rotoscope) the character out to create a matte, or alpha channel. Once we'd done that, we could treat it as a separate element. We could add elements inside the matte. I used to airbrush a more 3D-looking matte so that the sparkle elements would be concentrated and brighter in the middle.

Next, we added the additional layers that made up the transporter effect done for *Star Trek* by Stokes Kohne Associates, Inc. For a beam out, we first added the 'shower curtain,' which 'falls' from the top and covers the person being transported. If we could see the person operating the transporter, we'd make sure this happened when the transporter chief touched the controls.

Then we added in the sparkle pass, which faded in under

BELOW: On the transporter platform, Riker and his companions prepare to beam out. I have isolated Riker to more easily show the process (opposite).

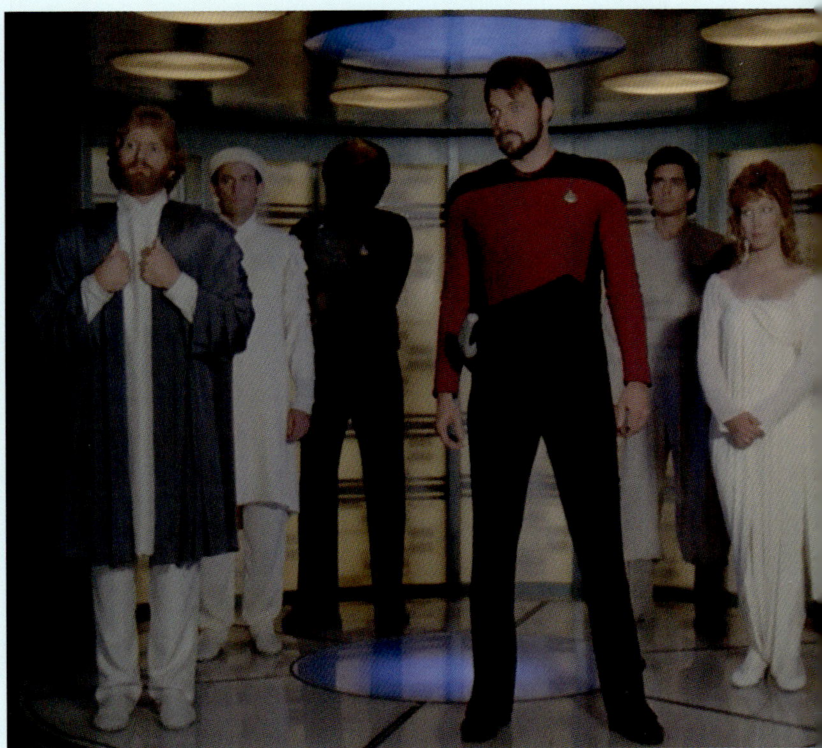

the shower curtain, and covered up the person as they disappeared. Finally, after the actor has disappeared, we'd leave a 'power pellet.' For a beam in, the shower curtain would start first, followed by the sparkles and power pellet as the character fades in.

We used the same transporter effect for *DS9*, but for *Voyager* and *Enterprise* we redesigned them as if different manufacturers' transporters had a slightly different technology and thus a different look. Alien transporters, such as Klingons and Ferengis, all had a unique design but worked on the same basic principle that began with the original series.

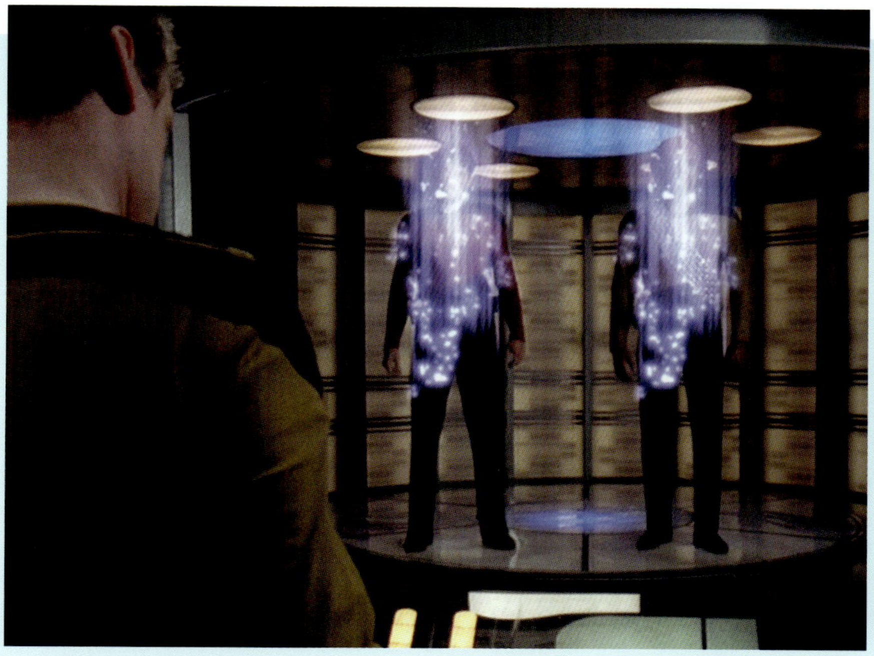

LEFT: Shower curtain falls and covers the actors in sync with the transporter operator's action on the controls.

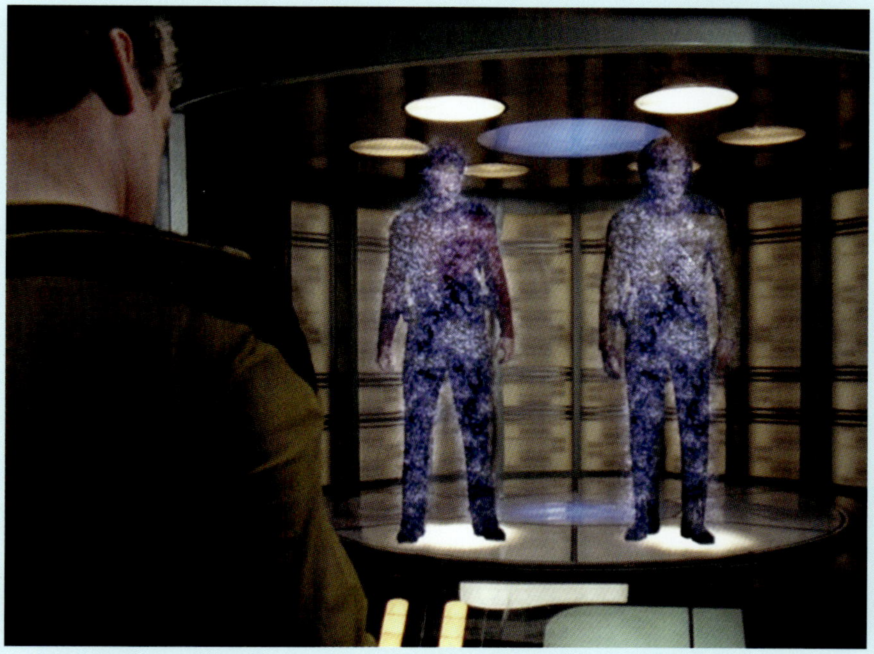

LEFT: Sparkle pass fades in under the shower curtain and covers the actors as they dissolve out.

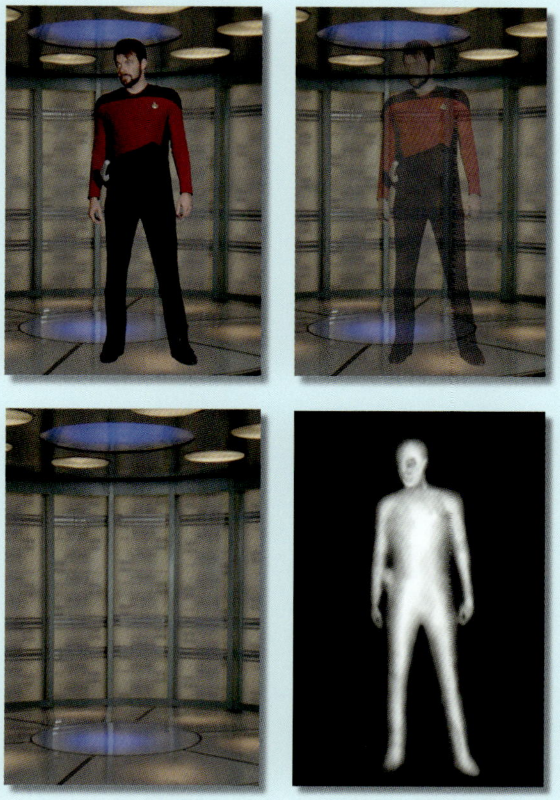

ABOVE: We shot two versions of the shot, one with the actor and one without. Then we create a dissolve in the edit bay to make the actor disappear. We created an air brush to contain the sparkles.

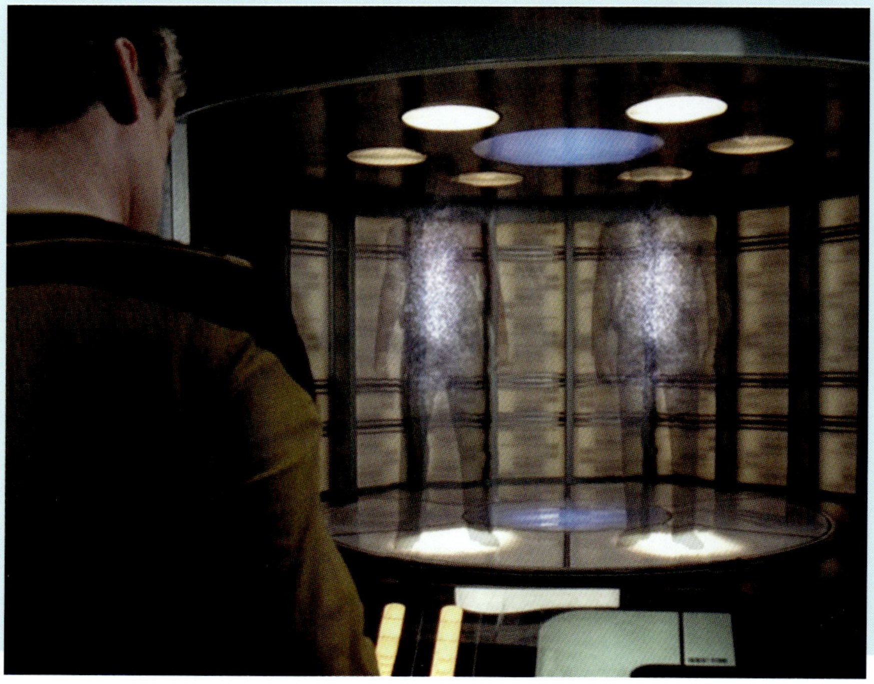

LEFT: Power pellet is a residual layer after the actors have faded out.

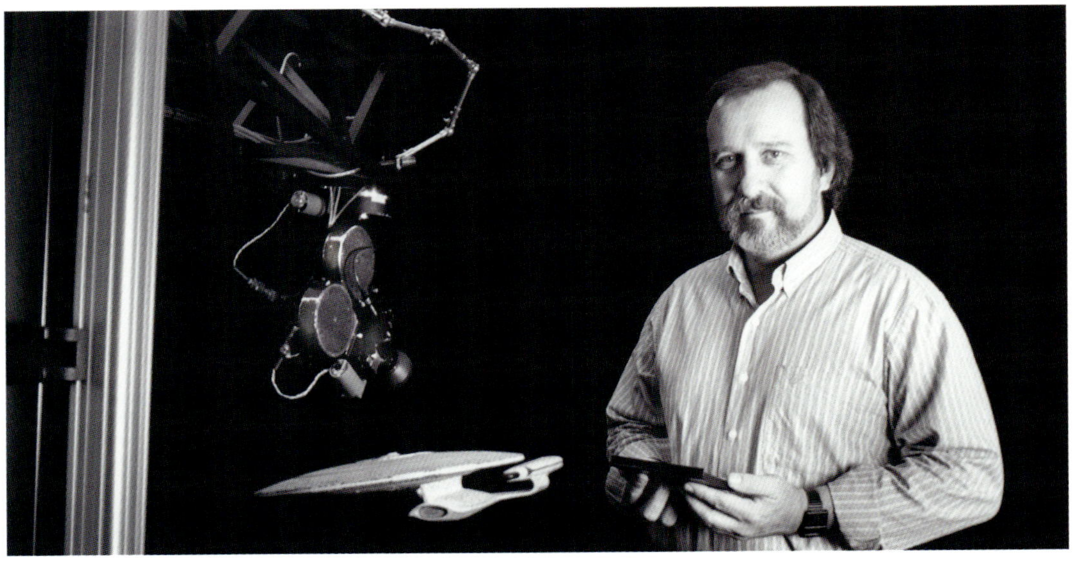

MOTION CONTROL

LINING IT ALL UP

In 1987, if you were filming a spaceship you used a technique called motion control. You couldn't shoot everything you needed in one go—if you wanted a ship with lights and glowing nacelles and stars, all those things had to be shot in a different way, and you had to be able to remove the model stands and so on. So what you did was film each different element, or pass, separately and then combine them into a single new cinematic reality.

Each element required a different exposure. Window lights, for example, are not bright enough to be seen when shooting a beauty pass, and the warp nacelles and deflector dish needed special diffusion filtration to create the illusion that they were glowing.

A standard shot of the *Enterprise* involved a minimum of seven passes: matte pass; beauty pass; windows; running lights; warp drive; deflector shield, and impulse drive. Then if there was interactive light, say from a nearby explosion, that would require an additional pass. All of that takes time, and in order to make the lights bright enough and to make them look real, you had to shoot those passes with long exposure times, so a shot that may only last a few seconds on screen may take many hours to film.

Another issue is that the elements from each pass must line up absolutely perfectly with the others or the windows would ride up and down on the hull, and the warp drive lights would bounce around. Motion control makes that possible because the computer-controlled system repeats the same movement precisely every time.

In motion control, the model is mounted on a modified gear head that allows the ship to roll, pitch and yaw. The illusion of all forward, backward or up-and-down motion is created by the motion of the camera moving back and forth on the track, east and west or up and down on the tower. This way we only had to light the place where the model was mounted, saving time and effort instead of having to light a corridor through which the ship passed.

For *The Next Generation, Deep Space Nine*, and *Voyager*, we shot most of our motion control with the excellent crew at Image G, a facility in Hollywood not far from the Paramount lot. The tracks at the heart of their motion-control system were actually made for *Star Trek: The Motion Picture*, and Image G's business depended on it. The polished cylindrical tracks had to be maintained in pristine condition and divot free, or there would be bumps in the ship movement. Every once in a while somebody would get yelled at for stepping on it; one time there was a new guy who was adjusting something next to the track with a wrench. On every turn the handle of the wrench would hit the rail with a loud clang. I thought he was going to be disembowelled by the rest of the crew.

Shooting motion control for *TNG* employed the same techniques as a feature. The pioneering difference at the time was that although we shot all elements on 35mm motion picture film, instead of compositing the elements on an optical printer we did ours electronically on video.

Once all the elements for a ship shot had been photographed, they had to be transferred to video to make compositing possible. When transferring the film to video, all the elements had to line up perfectly. There was only one place, I think, on the planet at the time that could transfer film to video accurately enough, and that was CIS (Composite Image Systems) in Hollywood. They had a pin registered transfer technology, using a mechanical movement from an optical printer built into a video transfer machine so that each element would perfectly register with every other element. The people at CIS don't get the credit they deserve, and should be recognized for that major contribution, because without them we could never have done what we did.

Years later, when we redid the *Next Generation* VFX for the Blu-ray edition, those mechanical pin registered transfer devices were no longer available, and even laser scanning the sprocket holes wasn't as accurate. We had to go back and re-tweak every element to make it fit properly by hand.

When we started on *The Next Generation* nobody knew how much miniature photography we were going to shoot. In the beginning the idea was that the show would just reuse a limited number of stock visual-effects ship shots, and only create a few new shots for certain episodes like they did on the original series. The writers were unfettered by the limitations of stock shots, though. They just wrote what they thought would be good, as they should have. Paramount recognized that after *Star Trek: The Motion Picture*, the audience expected a high quality of effects. We had to deliver or we wouldn't have an audience at all. Because we were doing things so differently, nobody knew how much we'd be able to accomplish, or even what it would cost, as there were no

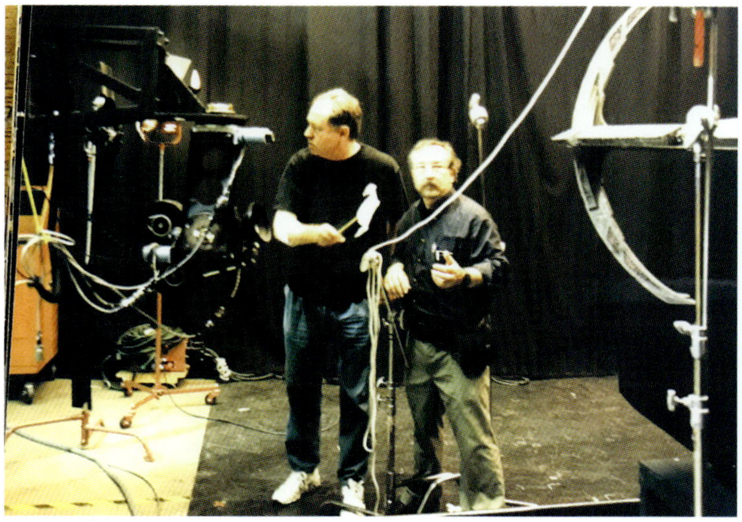

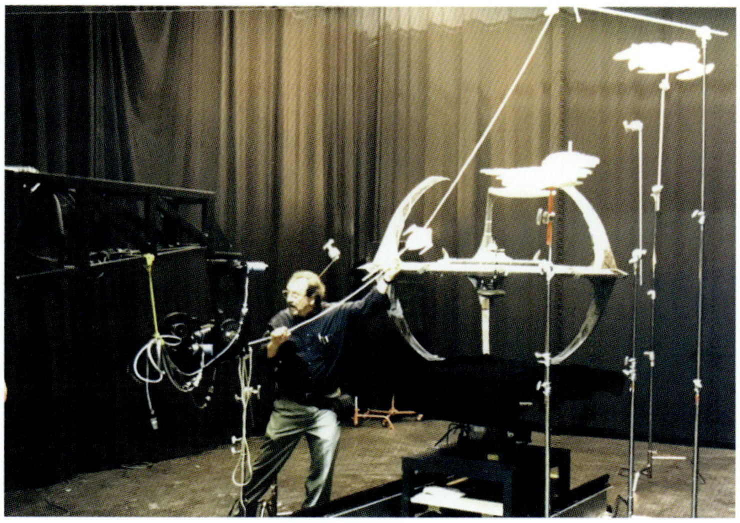

ABOVE: VFX supervisor David Stipes and I set up a motion-control shot. One of the challenges is combining models of different scales so their size relationship and camera moves are correct in the final shot, requiring lots of math.

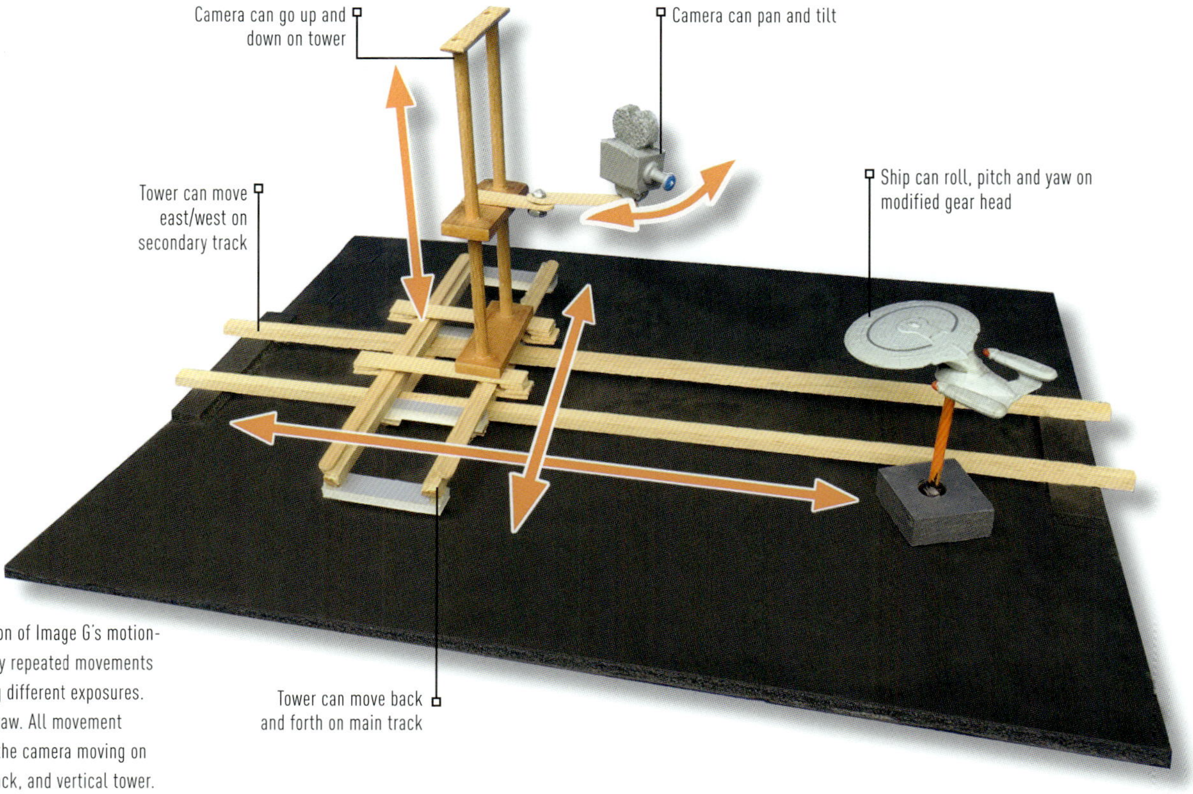

ABOVE: Crude illustration of Image G's motion-control rig, allowing precisely repeated movements for different passes requiring different exposures. The ship can roll, pitch and yaw. All movement through space is created by the camera moving on the main track, east/west track, and vertical tower.

real precedents for our work pipeline.

We had no idea what was coming. We would get a script, or sometimes just a story treatment in the form of a 'beat sheet,' and we would work out what we could do. The average episode would involve somewhere from no new motion-control shots to over 30. It just depended on the script. By the time we got to some of the big space battle shows on *DS9* there could be well over 100.

We had about three weeks to finish VFX for an episode after getting a cut from the editors. This schedule included shooting the ships and finishing the compositing. Usually we would try to get our motion control done in a week, but that wouldn't always be possible. We were shooting models for 60, sometimes 80 hours a week, just to keep up with our delivery dates.

Shooting motion control is a slow process. When you shoot miniatures you tend to use wider lenses that help to give a sense of scale. You have to avoid shooting with a wide aperture since that would result in a very shallow depth of field, and the focus would fall off very quickly. That makes the models look like toys, and destroys any sense of scale and verisimilitude.

Motion control allows for long exposures, so you can use narrow apertures that transmit adequate light to the film, giving you greater depth of focus and allowing the entire model to be in focus and look like something much bigger. Since the model and camera are in constant motion, there is natural motion blur that contributes to the illusion of reality.

Motion control also allows for streak and slit scan photography. Streak photography involves moving the camera and model a specific distance for each frame while the shutter remains open, resulting in a stretched image. Slit scan involves photographing a model through a computer-controlled moving slit in black

BELOW: When compositing models, it is necessary to make a silhouette of the ship to make a space for it in the background. By making the area behind the model a single color it can be digitally 'keyed' out. We stopped using white cards when Gary Hutzel had the idea to use Day-Glo orange and ultraviolet light to give the background a more even exposure, thus matte density.

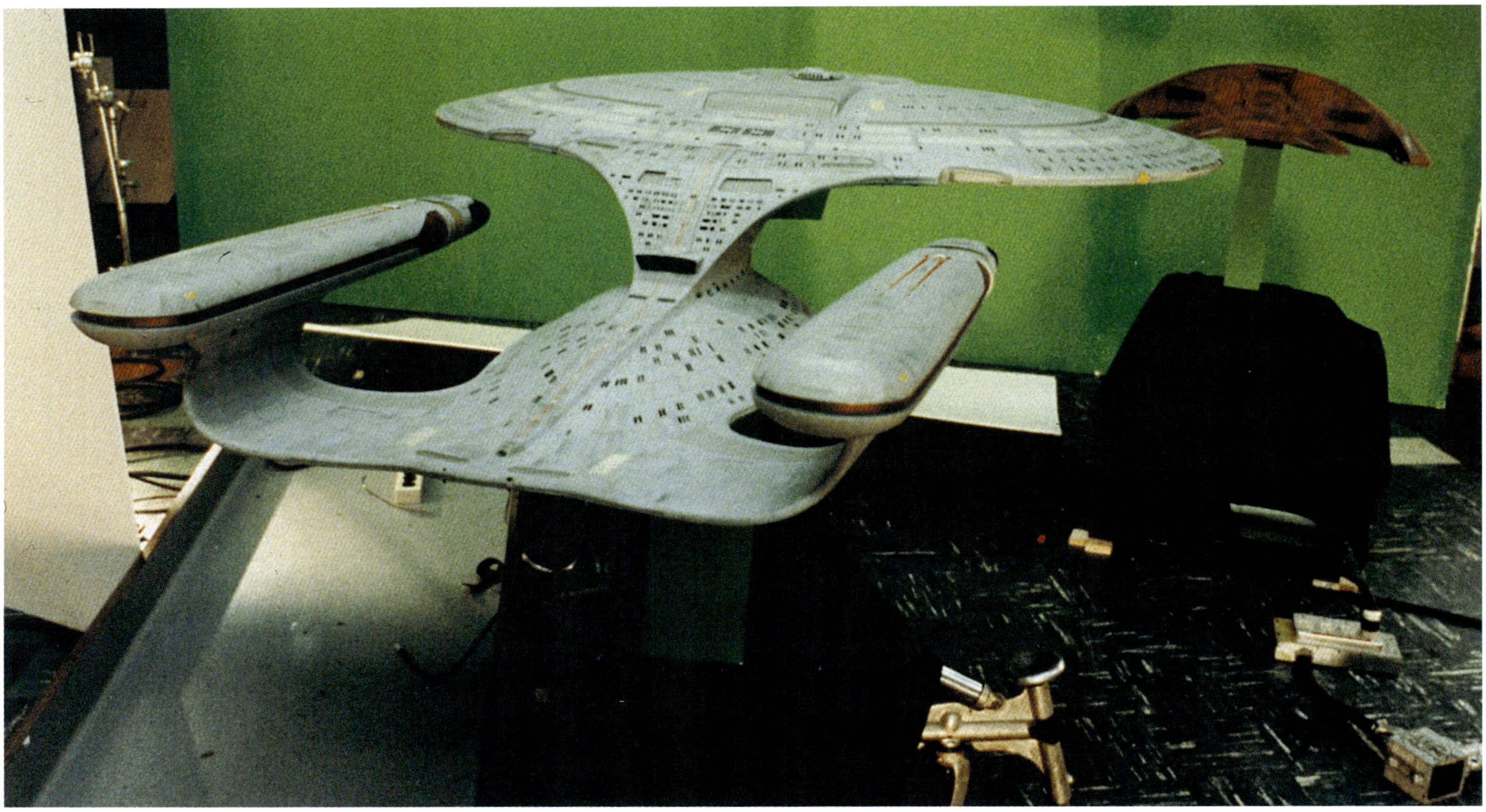

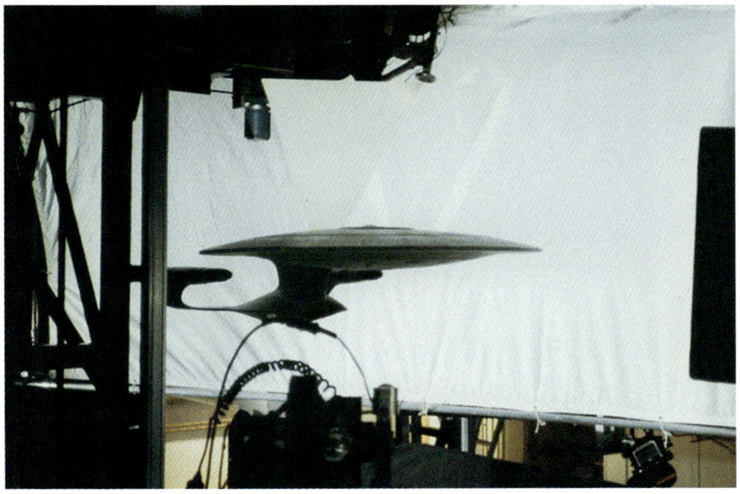

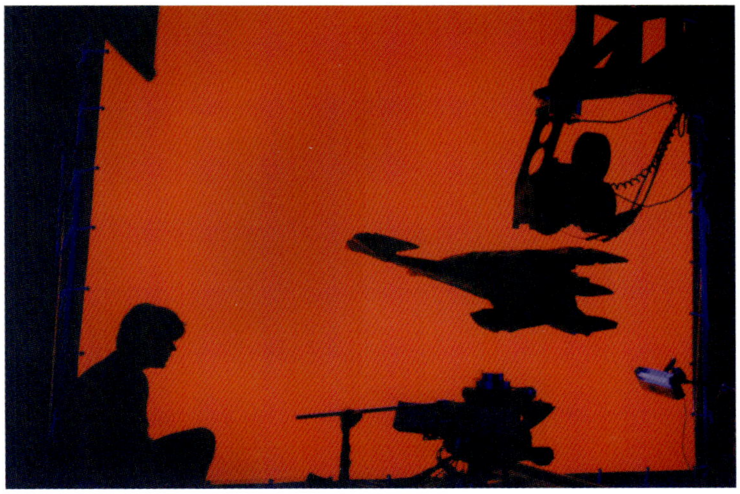

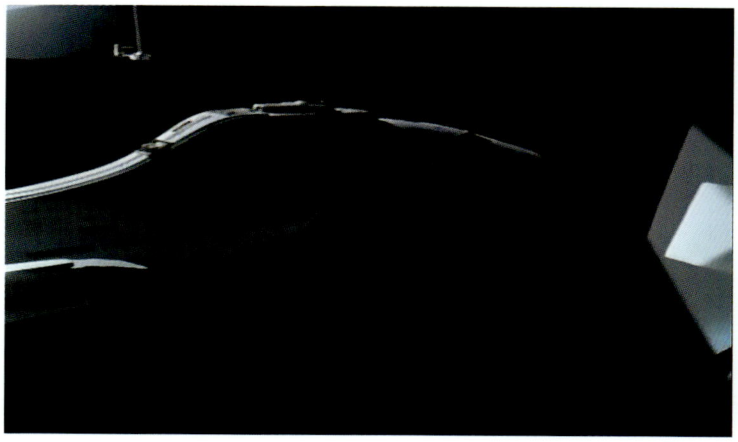

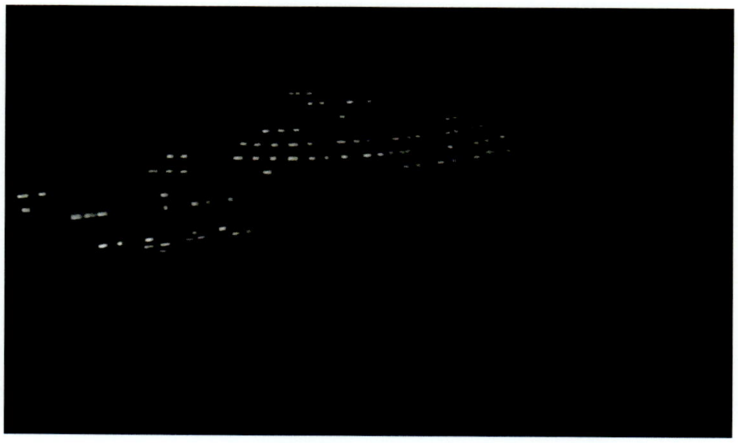

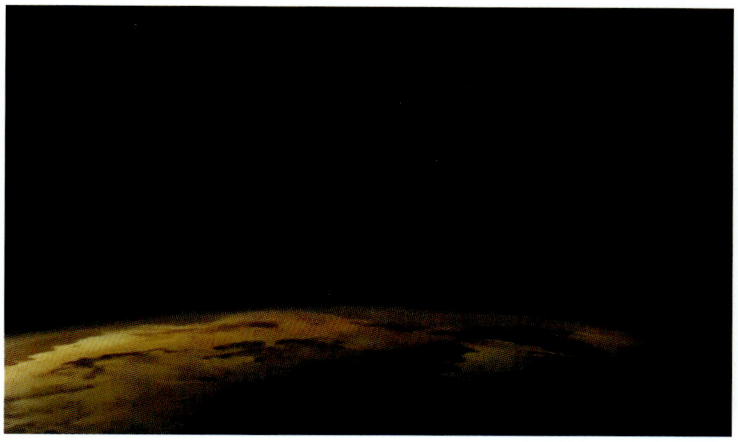

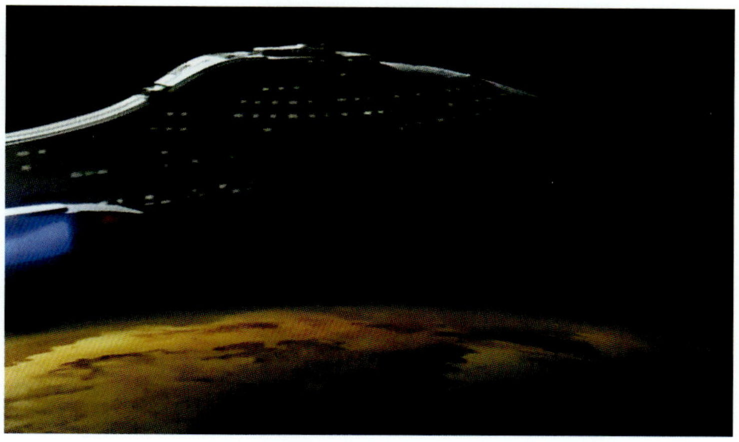

ABOVE: A finished shot of a spaceship involves filming several passes of various elements of a model, each requiring a different exposure. On *Star Trek* they were composited in video to create a complete image.

cardboard or metal that is mounted in front of the lens. It wipes an exposure onto the negative as the camera is also moving. This allows an image to be stretched and distorted while remaining in focus. These techniques were used when the *Enterprise* leaps to warp speed. (This is complicated, and there's a lot more to say about how it works, but this book isn't the place.)

Shooting a typical fly-by would take us a long day. By feature standards that was lightning fast. One of the luxuries one has on a feature is time, and that's one thing we didn't have. If ILM was shooting something, they could do it a first time, then analyse the shot and go back, relight it, shoot it again and so on until it was perfect. We didn't have time to do lighting tests, so we would rely on our spot light meters to measure highlights and shadows to create dramatic lighting. We had an advantage, though—in one season we did many more shots than there would be in many features. Because we did so much, we would learn ways of making our work faster and better.

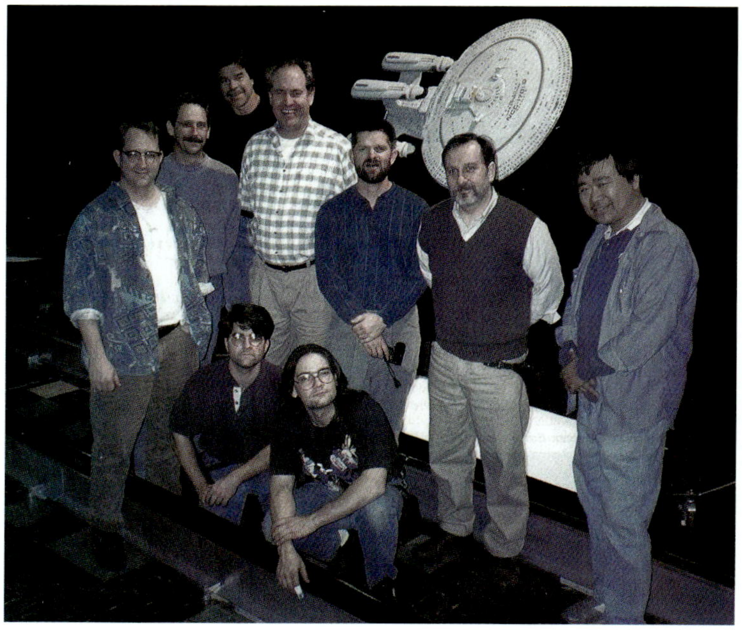

The crew at Image G were really wonderful, and gave us incredible support. Our motion-control camera operators like Erik Nash, Adrian Hurley, Josh Kushner, Jim Rider and Les Bernstein among others, and riggers like Dennis Hoerter and Chris Schnitzer were real heroes in their dedication to working on *Star Trek*. We were friends and colleagues working on something we knew was bigger than the sum of its parts.

When shooting motion control there are a lot of things to think about. You need to be able to isolate the ship's silhouette so that you can add it to another image such as a planet or a spatial anomaly. That is accomplished by filming what's called a matte pass. You just need the shape of the ship against a single color. The color area becomes a hold-out matte that makes a place in the frame for the ship by preventing that area from being exposed. The area with the ship in is called the clear center, the silhouette. On some big-budget features they use a blue-screen background with no light on the model so its silhouette is completely black and you get a matte pass with the even density best for compositing. When we started out on *TNG*, we used white cards behind the models to

LEFT: The VFX crew on Image G's motion-control stage: Back row (left to right): Joe Bauer, Tim Stel, Dennis Hoerter, David Stipes, Eric Nash, Dan Curry, Greg Jein. Kneeling: AJ Voitano, Chris Schnitzer.

IMAGE G

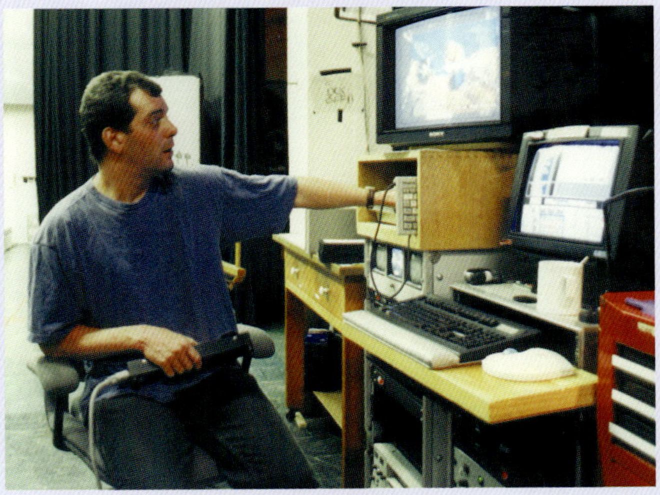

As in every other aspect of *Star Trek*, the people made the difference. Image G's staff, led by owner Tom Barron, were as utterly dedicated to *Star Trek* as any of us directly employed by the production company. The value of their contribution to the franchise cannot be understated. Despite the long hours, I always looked forward to working at Image G, not only because we were working with some of the coolest models in the world, but because of the quality of the people. It was a privilege to work with them.

LEFT: Working with mo-co operators like Jim Rider, we could preview camera moves and make adjustments as they evolved into final versions.

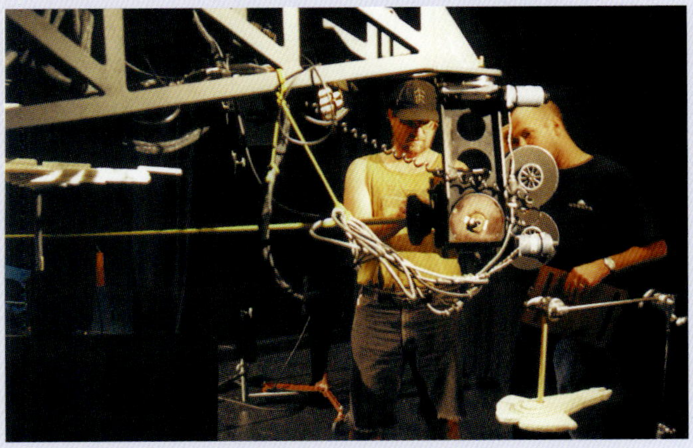

ABOVE: When filming miniatures it's important to maintain focus, so careful measurements of the changing distance between model and camera are required.

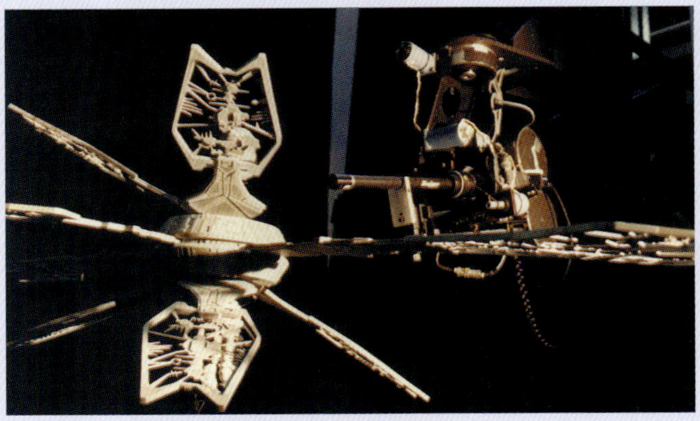

LEFT: Model shots are done at slow shutter speeds, so a single pass can take hours.

get the silhouette. We couldn't afford large, self-illuminated blue screens. One of the problems we ran into using that technique was that each card was at a slightly different angle to the light, so it would have a slightly different brightness, thus a slightly different density, making it very difficult to get an even, high-contrast matte and clear center. The extra steps involved made compositing more difficult and time consuming.

That's when Gary Hutzel came up with the idea of shooting matte passes with ultraviolet light to illuminate Day-Glo orange foam core panels. That made our lives a lot easier because it didn't matter what angle the Day-Glo orange was to the light source, it always had the same luminosity. That was a big breakthrough for us.

Another challenge with motion control is that the model ships were not in scale with one another. Working out mo-co moves was complicated when you had to shoot two or more models that would be combined in a single shot. Even if you could do a big move on one model, you might not be able to do a matching move on the other one because of the limitations of the mo-co rig. We had to determine the relative scales of the models and which one most limited the amount of motion possible, then design around that. It was necessary to use the same lens for every model within a given shot otherwise the perspective on the various models would be different and viewers would instinctively feel that something is unnatural. For example, we did a shot when the *Enterprise*-D docks at Deep Space 9. The Deep Space 9 model was 6 ft in diameter, and the hero *Enterprise*-D was 4 ft long. Together in the final shot, the *Enterprise* had to be many times smaller than the station. We designed shots artistically so that the audience was never aware that we were constrained by technical limitations. Luckily, our motion-control camera operators were mathematically brilliant, and they were able to do all the calculations required to scale things up and down so that everything looked like it belonged together.

The way objects are visually balanced in frame needs to be artistically satisfying. The size of the model and the dimensions of the mo-co rig limited what camera moves were possible. Most of the movement was generated by the camera. The audience can't tell whether it's the camera or the ship that's moving because the scale changes and the perspective shifts are the same either way. The ship could roll and yaw on its mount, but it couldn't go back and forth or up or down. If the movement was created by a model on a track, you would have to make a corridor of perfectly even light to cover the move, which is not practical. Most models could be mounted from various points: top, bottom, front and back. The design of the shot determined which mount would be used. We could only show so much of any ship in the same shot because we couldn't reveal the support rod holding up the model. When we saw the bottom of

INSIDE STORY

CUTTING UP THE *ENTERPRISE*

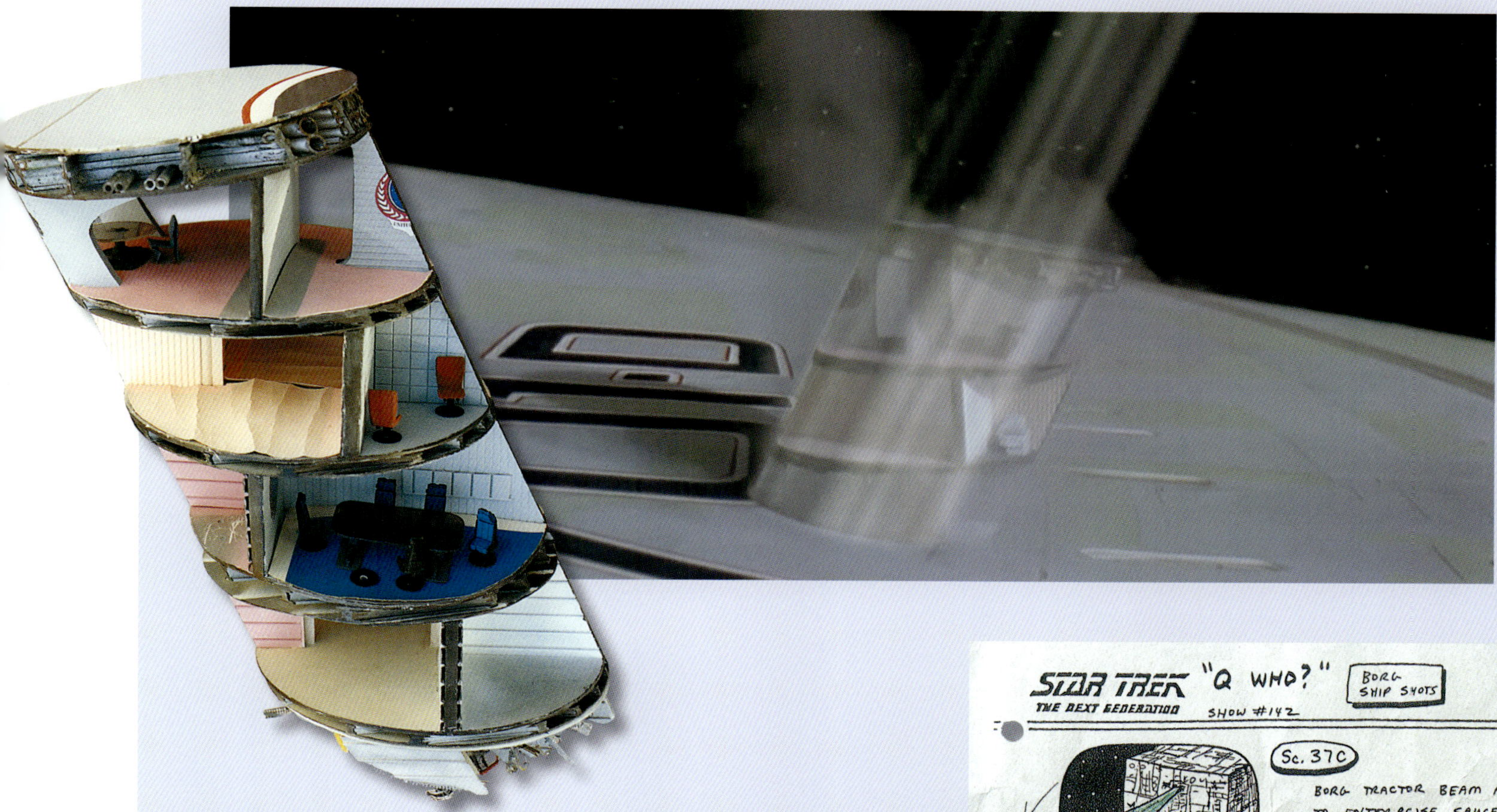

ABOVE: This shot was done by making special models: a forced-perspective part of the saucer, and a core that was cut out of it (left).

In 'Q Who?' the Borg want to find out more about the *Enterprise*, so they cut a tubular section of decks out of the hull—like a core sample. We couldn't shoot any of our regular models that close up. They were too small and didn't have enough detail. We needed a large enough core section model to show interior decks. We hired model maker Kim Bailey to build a 2-ft core section and a 15-ft forced-perspective section of the *Enterprise* saucer in scale with it. There was a hole in the large model of the saucer section with an angled tube beneath it that acted as a guide; we slid the core section into it, and then raised it with a motorized lever, adding a tuft of smoke to simulate escaping atmosphere. We shot with David Stipes at his mo-co stage before he joined *Star Trek* full time.

In the edit bay we blended the seam between the core section and the hull. Then we animated a Borg cutting beam, and a tractor beam that looked as if it was pulling the section out of the saucer. If we'd had all the time and money in the world, we would have had little people on those decks, who would have drifted off into space. We couldn't put a matching hole in our *Enterprise* model, so we were careful to avoid showing that part of the saucer for the rest of the episode. I always theorized they went back to spacedock and got it repaired before the next show.

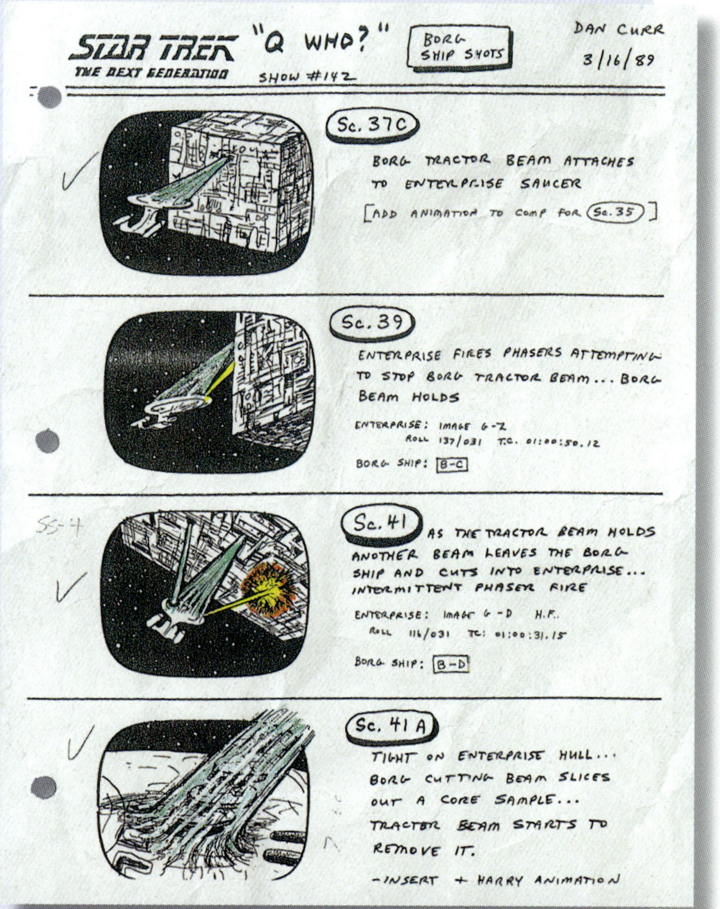

ABOVE: Storyboarding sequences help keep track of the elements needed, and show the cast and crew the flow of images and what they will look like.

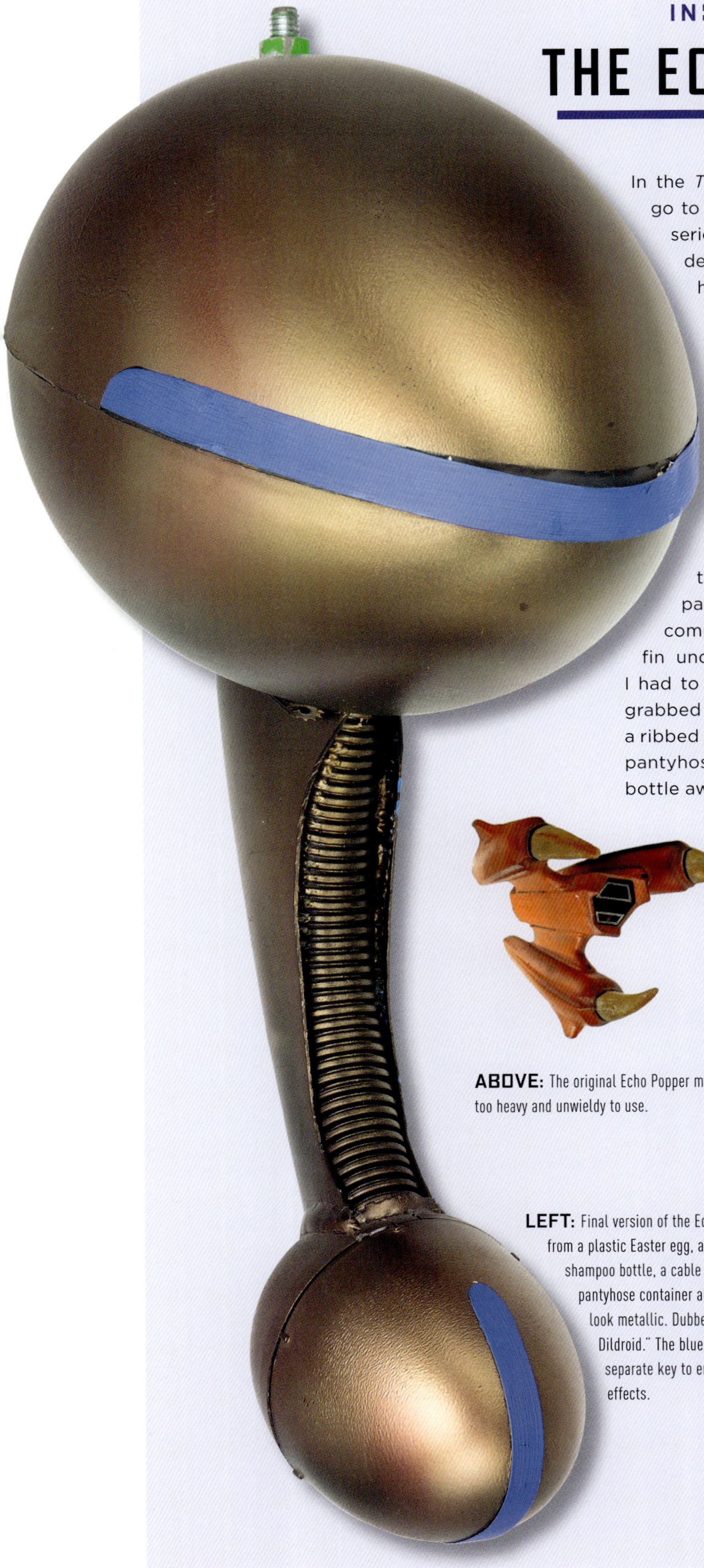

INSIDE STORY

THE ECHO POPPER

In the *TNG* episode 'Arsenal of Freedom,' the crew go to a planet where the people had developed a series of powerful weapons that had ended up destroying them. The weapons are still active, however, and start attacking our crew.

Someone had designed a huge claw-like robot for the Echo Popper. It was so heavy we couldn't fly it on wires on the set as planned, and, being a claw, it kept snagging on the jungle foliage. We had to ditch it. Instead, I decided to shoot silhouettes of the foliage on stage so we could shoot our drone later.

We were running out of time, so I realized I'd better come up with something fast for the drone. I had the idea of a sleek, two-part shape, with an upper part containing its computer brain and weapons, and a stabilizing fin underneath that could emit energy beams. I had to build it with whatever I could find, so I grabbed a plastic Easter egg, a shampoo bottle, a ribbed cover for computer cables, and a L'eggs pantyhose container. I cut part of the shampoo bottle away, and glued the other parts together.

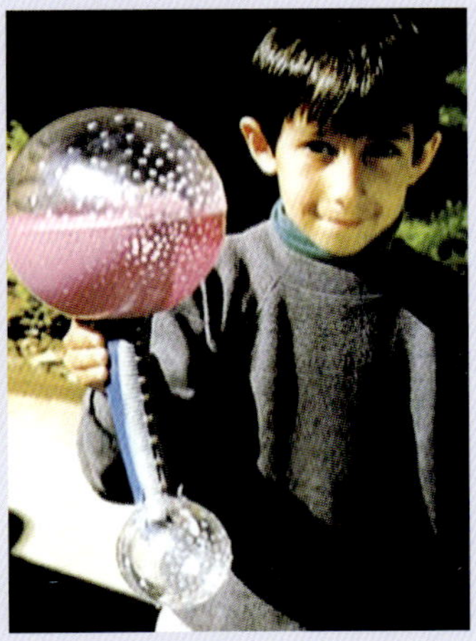

ABOVE: My six-year-old son Devin with the unpainted Echo Popper.

BELOW: The model used for the re-entry sequence was covered with slivers of plastic bag to flap in electric fan wind to create gaseous motion blur resulting from long exposures per frame.

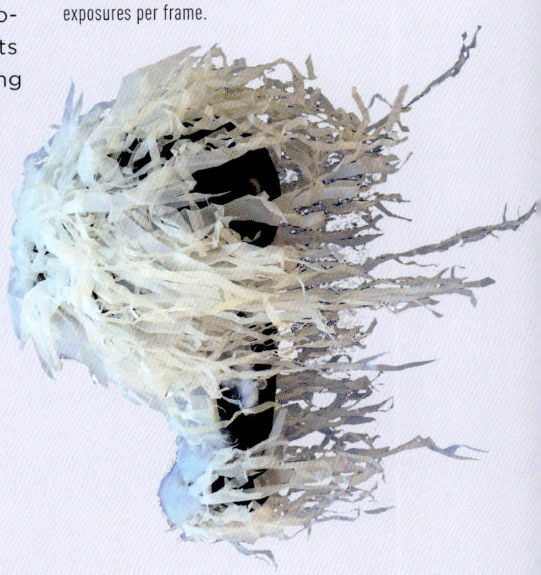

ABOVE: The original Echo Popper model that was too heavy and unwieldy to use.

LEFT: Final version of the Echo Popper made from a plastic Easter egg, a portion of a shampoo bottle, a cable sleeve, and a pantyhose container airbrushed to look metallic. Dubbed by Ron, "The Dildroid." The blue tape allowed a separate key to enable lighting effects.

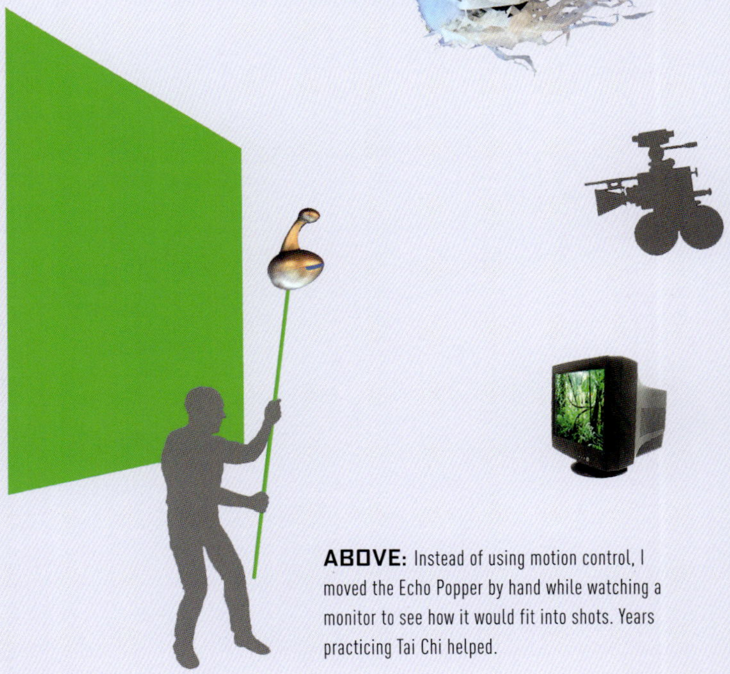

ABOVE: Instead of using motion control, I moved the Echo Popper by hand while watching a monitor to see how it would fit into shots. Years practicing Tai Chi helped.

Then I airbrushed it with subtly different, iridescent paint—mostly metallic gold, but with hints of magenta, green and blue. Then I put some bright blue labelling tape on it so we could pull a matte to add some animated light, and have an origin point for the phaser beams. Rather than using the motion-control rig, I decided to move it around by hand so that it had a more organic and nimble sense of motion. Because I had been doing Tai Chi for years, I was able to make the movements very smooth, and as we'd already shot the live-action footage I was able to eyeball exactly where it should go. But, watching me, my colleagues thought I was crazy and couldn't stop laughing.

We also needed to show a bigger version of the same model in orbit, where it is attacking the *Enterprise*. A cloaking device made it invisible, so the *Enterprise* couldn't target it to fight back. Geordi, who is in command of the ship, lures it into the planet's atmosphere, where the friction caused by re-entry into the atmosphere makes the ship visible.

To create the illusion of hot gasses around the giant Echo Popper, I covered the model with black flocking. Then I cut up a white plastic bag and glued the shredded pieces to the model. We surrounded the model with fans to make the plastic move, and filmed it against black on the motion-control stage at three seconds per frame to get motion blur that looked gaseous. In the edit bay we mixed in some fire and added in the space background to make it look as if atmosphere was heating up around the ship.

BELOW: The invisible ship is revealed by its hot re-entry gasses.

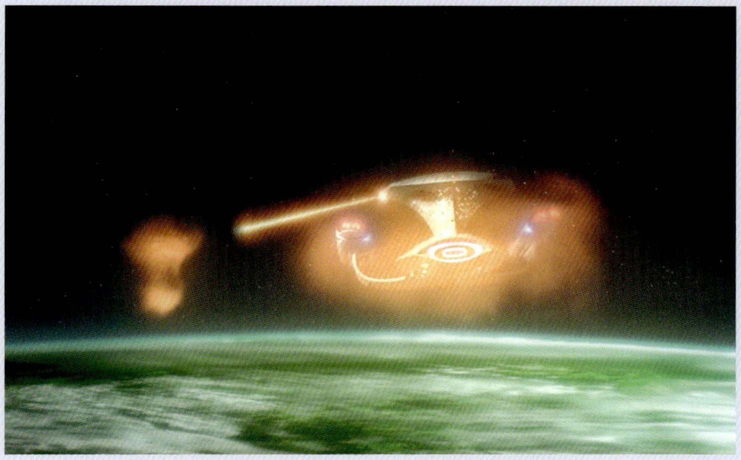

BELOW: Comp of the Echo Popper hovering in the forest.

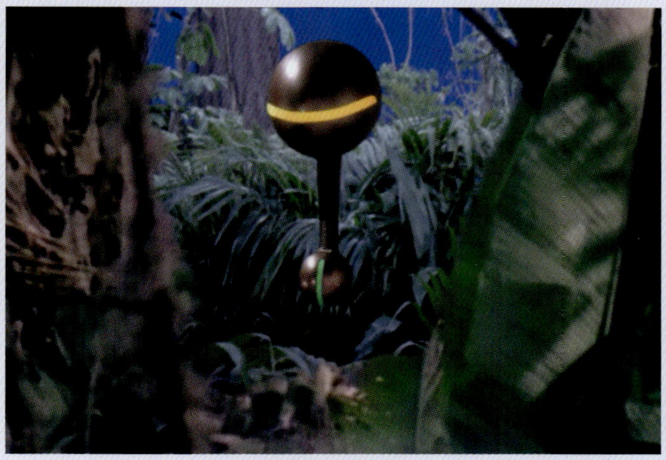

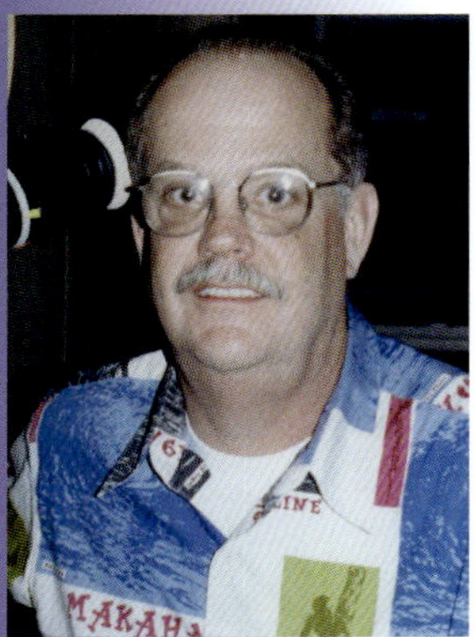

"Dan is a master at pulling things out of nothing. We went over to motion control with this stupid-looking thing; Rob and Gary just went nuts, and kept saying that this was just the worst. Dan's got it stuck on a stick, and he was just bouncing it up and down. We were sitting there laughing and saying, 'We're going to take TV back 20 years.' So we shoot this thing, but Dan's not happy with it, so he takes the plastic bag that all this stuff had come in, and cuts it into strips and glues it together, making something out of it to shoot! It just blew us away.

We finally got a look at the teasers for the show. There were four of them, and they kept getting shorter and shorter. When it got down to the five-second teaser, the only shot they put into it was this one shot of Dan's model!"

Ron B. Moore, VFX supervisor

INSIDE STORY

THE DIRECTION OF THE STARS

When audiences saw a star field through windows on the *Enterprise*, it was actually a velvet drape mounted on a commercial laundry's circulating conveyor belt to create movement. The rig was rolled into position as needed for camera. Random shiny flakes reflected light to look like stars. If the ship was at warp we'd composite animated warp stars into the windows to show them streaking. We soon realized that sometimes we'd be in the same chamber, but the stars would be going in a different direction than the last time we saw them. Our audience was very perceptive about continuity, so we determined where each compartment would be on the ship, and I made a chart showing which way the stars should be moving.

RIGHT: This chart was to help the VFX team be consistent in how the stars moved outside the windows of various compartments on the *Enterprise*.

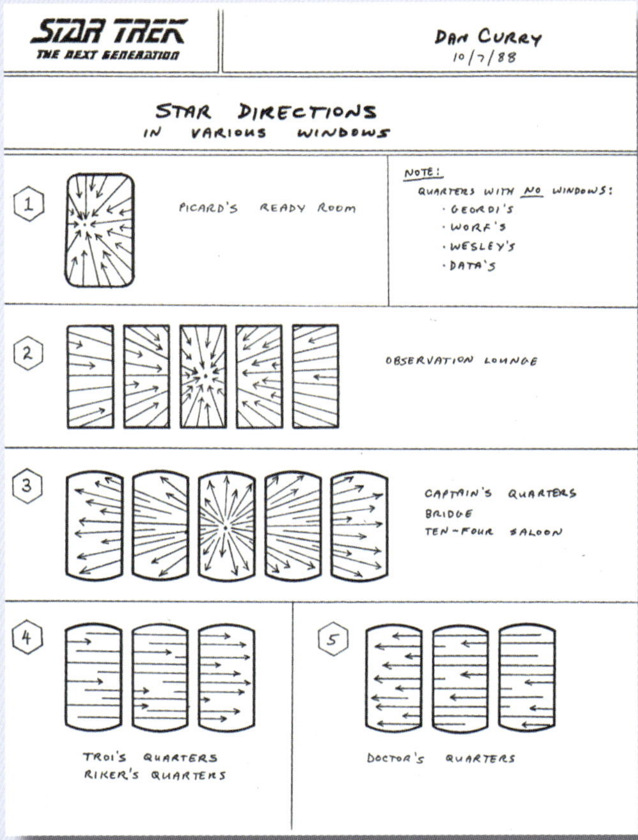

the *Enterprise*, we mounted it upside down so the camera could run over it. We would either mount the camera upside down or just flip the image over when transferring to video.

There were stylistic conventions on *Star Trek* too. To save money using stock ships from our library, we needed to be able to combine as many different ships as possible. As a result, many ships were photographed on the same plane, almost as if they were sitting on parallel panes of glass, but it was something that we were always trying to break away from.

Whenever possible I would storyboard space sequences, but sometimes we just didn't have time, or if it was a simple shot we didn't bother. On the finale of *The Next Generation*, 'All Good Things...,' there were almost no storyboards. Toy *Star Trek* models were available by then, and we'd fly them around with our hands to demonstrate what we wanted. We'd mime a move and say, "Okay, I want the *Enterprise* to do this."

On the Image G stage we had primitive black and white monitors that showed us what the ships would be doing in frame as we programmed a shot. When we designed a shot we could look at it to make certain it served the story and make adjustments. You'd look at it and say, "Well, maybe the Klingon bird-of-prey should bank a little sooner," or "I don't like how it hugs the edge of frame and then flies off into the corner." I remember one time I wanted to cut to a Klingon bird-of-prey right after a shot of Patrick delivering a line. I said, "Okay, here's where Patrick's face is. I want to have a powerful impact when we cut to the Klingon ship, so let's put it in exactly the same place where the audience is looking at Captain Picard."

We shot spaceships this way for all of *The Next Generation*. The bulk of *Deep Space Nine* and *Voyager* were technical hybrid shows combining motion-control models and computer-generated images. That's 526 episodes. I have no idea how many feet of film we shot, but I do know that during that during those years, the *Enterprise*-D, DS9, and *Voyager* models was probably among the most photographed objects in the world.

As in every other aspect of *Star Trek*, the people made the difference. Image G's staff, led by owner Tom Barron, were as utterly dedicated to *Star Trek* as any of us. The value of their contributions to the franchise cannot be understated. Despite the long hours, I always looked forward to working at Image G, not only because we were working with some of the coolest models in the world, but because we had the privilege of working with terrific people.

BELOW: The 'star drum' was used to shoot background star fields for mo-co shots using the same pan/tilt data without the track move to make sure the background correctly matched the ship moves.

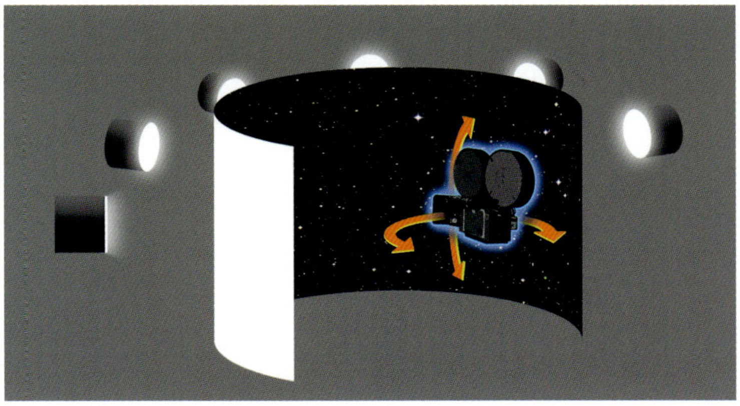

INSIDE STORY

A SENSE OF SCALE

When it came to filming shots where *Voyager* was supposed to have landed on the surface of a planet, we needed some kind of reference so that cast and crew would know how big the ship would be in frame, so I asked the art department to make me some simple foam core models that we could take on location. We could use those models as lighting and scale reference for when we were shooting the hero model back in the studio.

On location, the foam core mock-ups helped us work out the true size of the ship, and the best composition for the shot. The art department made two versions for us—one 25 inches long, and the other 15 inches long. On location, we measured out the actual size of the ship on the ground—I remember we were surprised at just how big it was. Then we lined up the foam core mock-up in front of the camera, positioning it as a forced-perspective foreground miniature so it looked full size in frame. We also took careful note of the angle of the sun. Back at the studio, we did a temp comp, removing the support stand from the shot, and drew in the shadow it would have cast on the ground. This provided the editors with temp comps to cut in until the final shot was available.

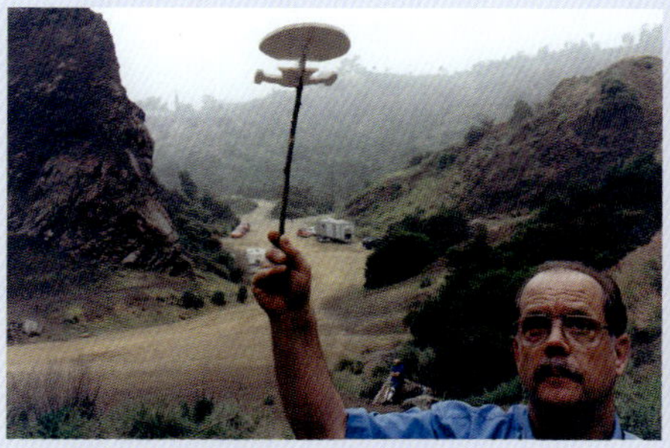

ABOVE: Ron shows the path *Voyager* will take.

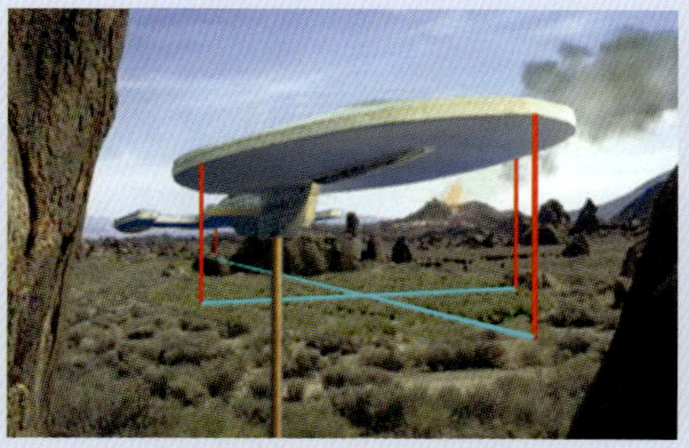

ABOVE: Measurements show the actual size of *Voyager*.

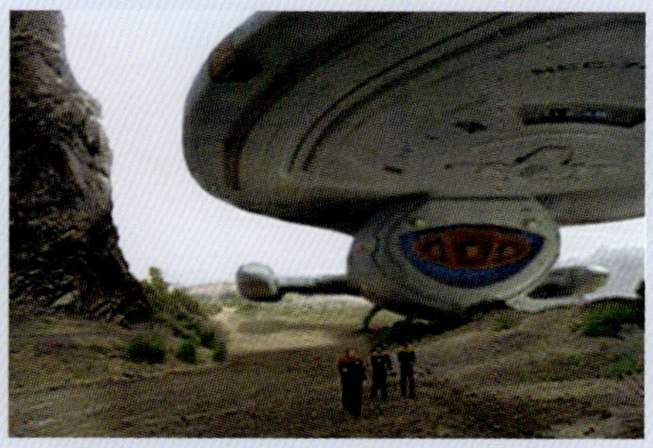

ABOVE: Finished shot of *Voyager* landed, background hills painted out.

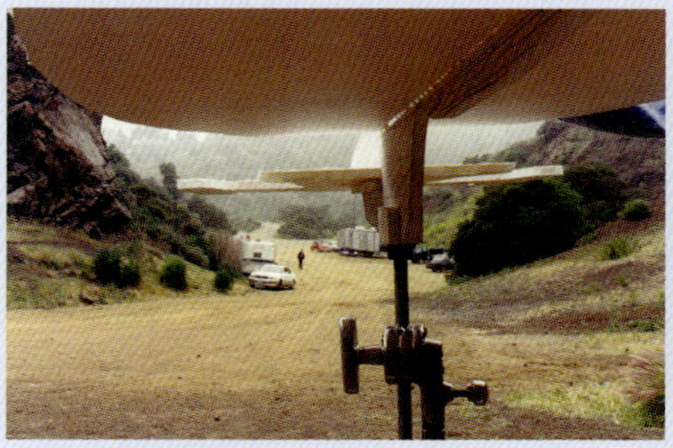

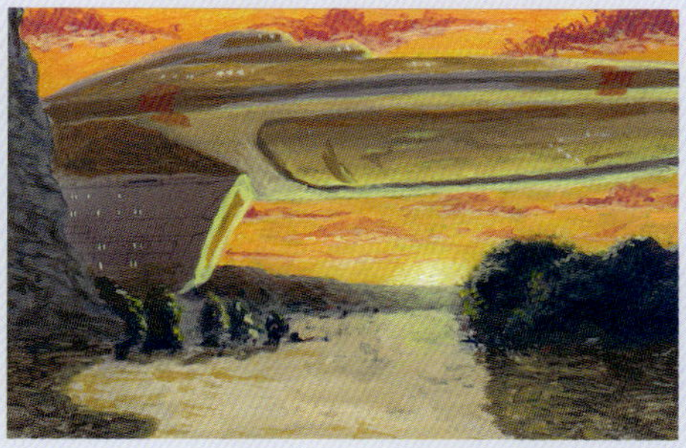

FAR LEFT: Foam core mock-up shot to show scale of *Voyager* from this perspective.

LEFT: This rough concept painting done on a Polaroid taken on location shows what the finished shot will look like, and helps to determine the relative sizes of the various elements.

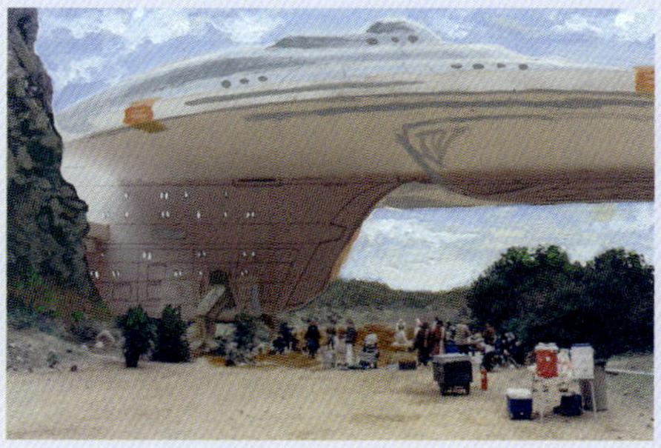

LEFT: Rough concept painting showing a more dramatic silhouette of *Voyager* when the background hills are painted out.

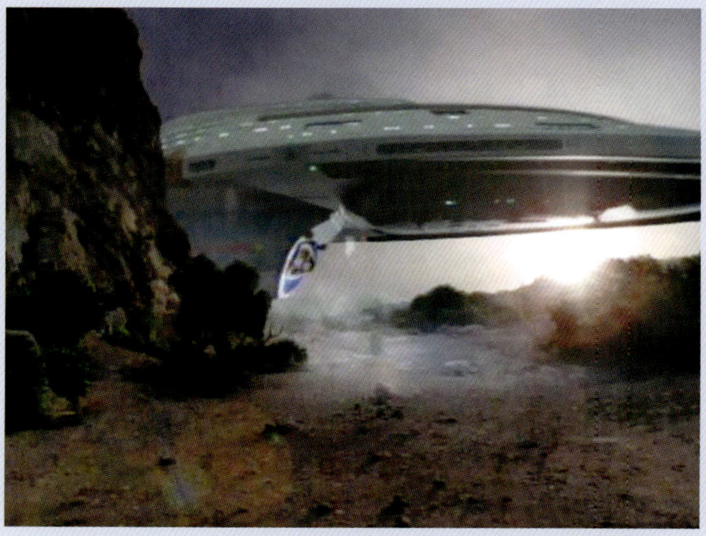

RIGHT: In the finished shot, photography of the model is combined with live-action footage of the actors on location. The shadow cast by the ship is an important part of selling the illusion.

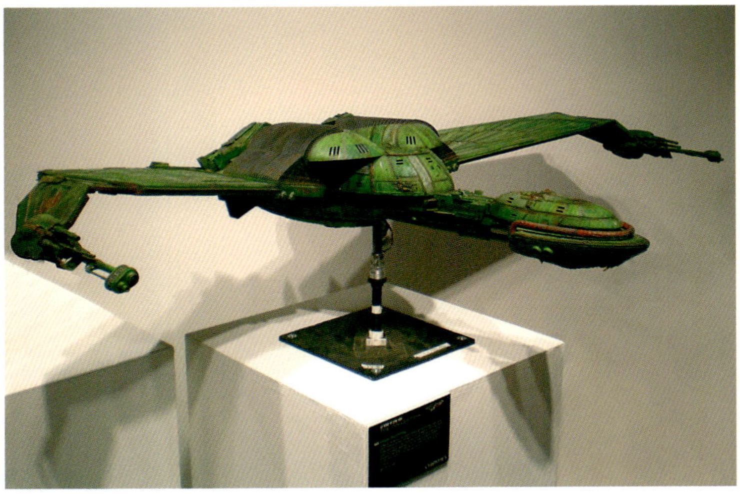

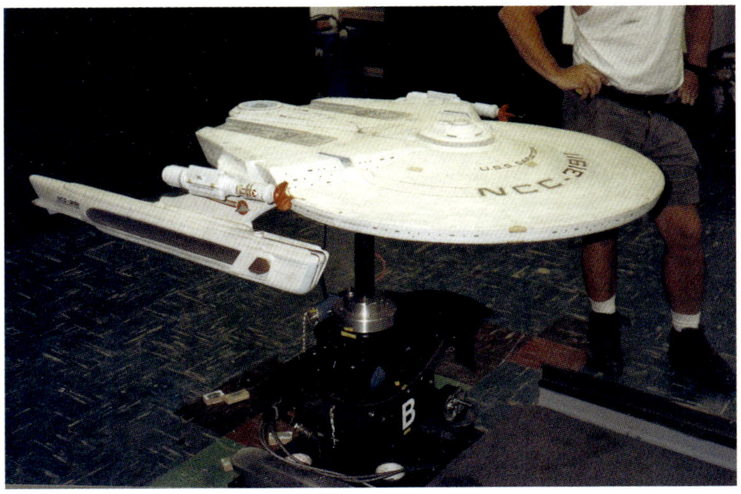

ABOVE: When we started on *TNG* we relied on some of ILM's models that had been built for *Trek* features.

MODELS

BEAUTIFUL AND COMPLEX WORKS OF CRAFTSMANSHIP, THESE WERE THE REAL HEROES OF *STAR TREK*

When we started on *The Next Generation* we had large physical models of the *Enterprise*-D and several other ships that ILM had built for the *Star Trek* features—the *Reliant*, the Klingon battlecruiser and bird-of-prey, a freighter that had been used in *Star Trek III*, the *Oberth* class, and the *Excelsior*. They were all beautiful models that had been made to the highest possible standard. I particularly loved working with the exquisitely crafted bird-of-prey, which had movable wings.

In the beginning we didn't have much of a budget for building new ships. A highly detailed hero ship model with internal electric circuits for window, running and engine lights could easily cost more than fifty or sixty thousand dollars, so we only invested in a model of that quality when it played a big part in an episode, and was likely to be seen in future shows. In the first season of *TNG*, Greg Jein built the Ferengi Marauder, Picard's old ship the *Stargazer*, and the Romulan Warbird. I don't think there was another season where we built as many high-end ships, but over the years we got the budget to build more high-quality ships, and our fleet grew.

'Guest ships of the week' tended to use existing models that had been built for something else—maybe another episode, some other TV show, or a movie—that we could borrow, rent and adapt. We had a couple of model freighters that we used a lot. We would repurpose them by sticking some extra pieces on them, turning them upside down, repainting them—doing whatever we could to make them look different. For example, with the *Reliant*, we'd take the 'roll bar' off the top and add pieces on the side to make it look like a different ship. Sometimes we'd send the models back to the modelmakers to make the revisions, but other times we'd just do it ourselves in the shop at Image G.

The models were designed so they could be mounted in different ways on the motion-control rig. They could be photographed from different angles. The mounting points were strong enough to support the heavy models, and were hidden under removable panels that were built into the hull.

Typically, you could mount a model from underneath, from either side, and from the front or back, depending on the design of the model and where mounts could fit. Most of the spaceship models had complicated lighting inside that could be used to illuminate the windows, engine lights and so forth, but sometimes, if the model was in the background and we wouldn't see it too closely, we could paint where the windows would be with colorless fluorescent paint and shoot a window pass with ultraviolet light.

We had the good fortune to work with some brilliant modelmakers. Primarily we relied on master modellers Greg Jein and Tony Meininger, who built and modified many ships for *Star Trek*.

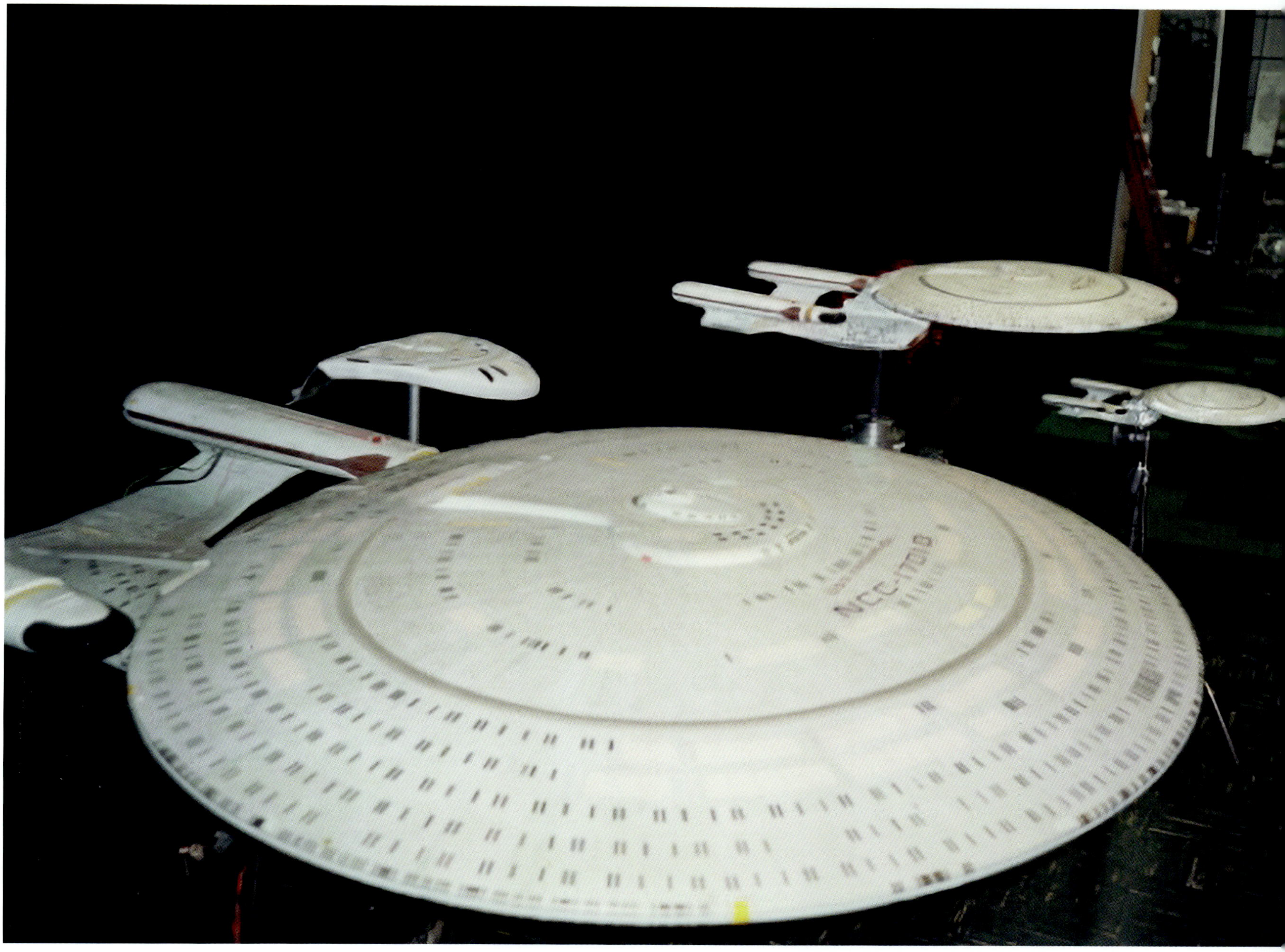

ABOVE: There were several different models of the *Enterprise*-D that varied slightly in detail and proportions. A particular sized model was chosen depending on how big it would appear in shot.

After working with it for a while, our VFX team decided that the difficulties of using a model as large as ILM's 7-ft *Enterprise*-D were costing us too much time. The production company engaged Greg Jein to build a 4-ft version with raised panelling to catch light and lend a sense of scale. Considering the number of frames we shot on all the different passes at slow speeds, this model may have been one of the most photographed objects in the world.

Tony Meininger built the spectacular 6-ft-diameter Deep Space 9 model at his company Brazil Fabrication. He built a second version without a center hub structure and only one side so we could shoot from the center looking outwards to composite into shots where the camera would see out the windows of the full-size sets.

Greg and Tony are master craftsmen. The quality of their work speaks for itself—precision, fit and finish, engineering, and design sense. They were always super cooperative, and would take notes without complaint. Steven Spielberg once referred to Greg as the greatest modelmaker in Hollywood after he built the Santa Monica Pier miniature for *1941*. I hold that level of respect for Tony too. Both were such supporters of *Star Trek*, they gave us way more than we ever paid them for.

Occasionally we farmed out a special model to an individual builder such as Kim Bailey, who made the Borg Cube, the forced-perspective *Enterprise*-D hull for 'Q Who?,' and the core section of decks the Borg cut from it. Don Pennington built the new Klingon cruiser for us. Brick Price at Wonderworks built the Kazon ships and a miniature of the interior of the turbolift for *TNG*.

I loved going to all our model makers' shops because they reminded me of my grandfather's workshop when I was a little boy. Grandpa was the one who taught me to use tools, and fostered a love and pride in working with one's hands. Each model shop was very different, and reflected the owner's personality. Tony's was spartan, filled with all sorts of stuff, including the large-scale radio-controlled model airplanes he loved to fly. You had to be really careful how you walked around in Greg's shop; there were mountains of seemingly disorganized stuff on the floor, but he could still find anything immediately. Kim's was well organized, and

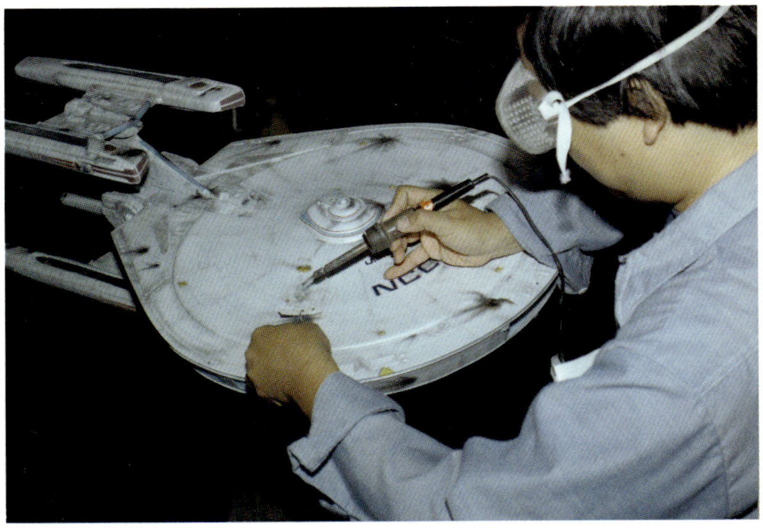

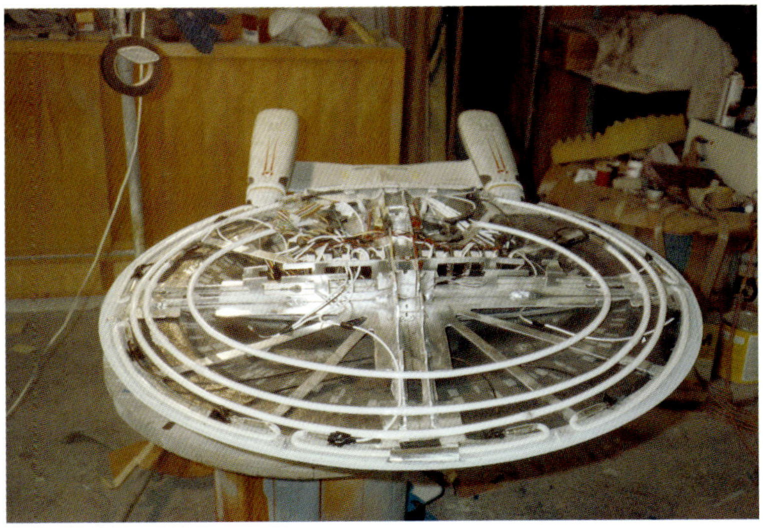

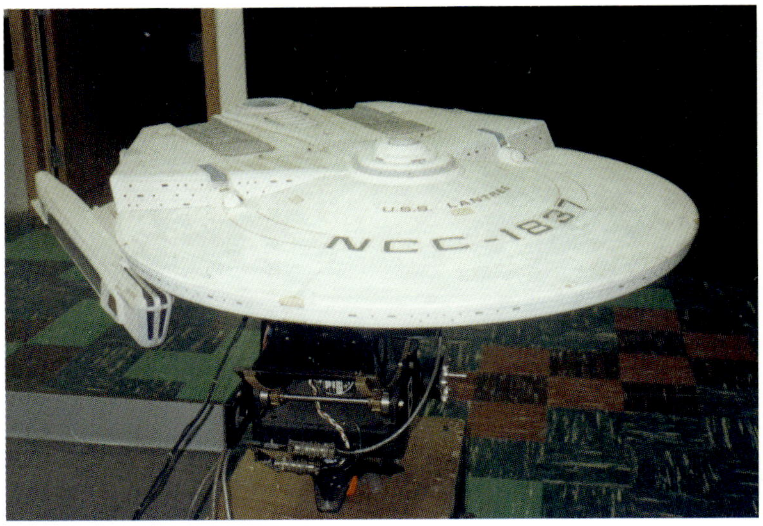

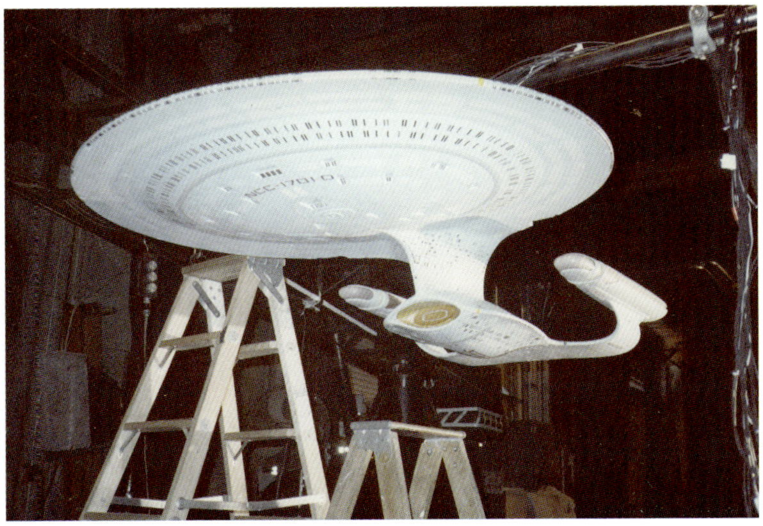

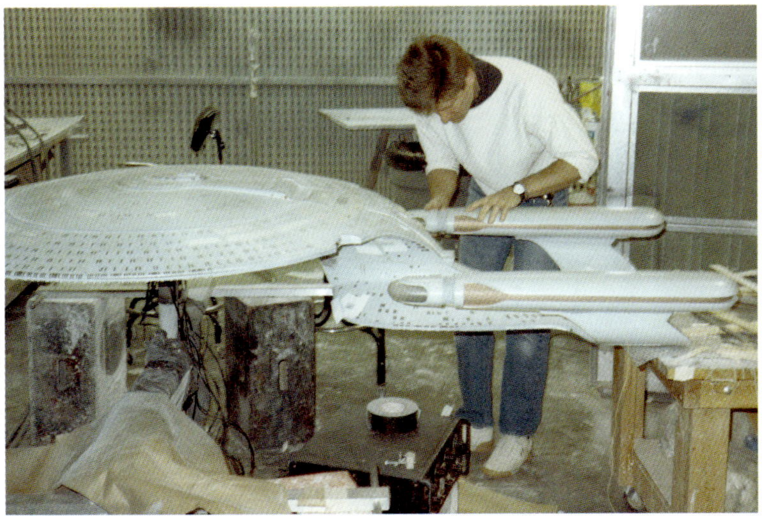

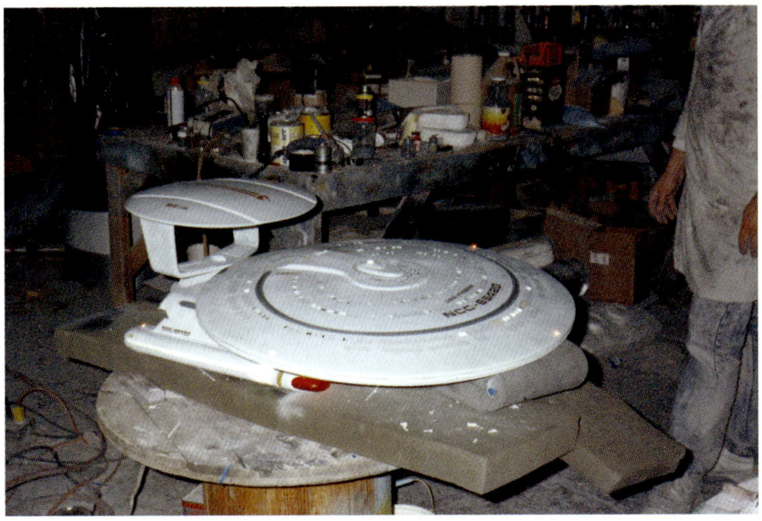

ABOVE: Our models were works of art made by highly skilled master craftsmen. They were often cast from fiberglass molds with internal light circuits (as seen upper right).

had lots of safety features. Don's shop was a museum, with models from numerous productions. Brick's Wonderworks was a warren of shop rooms and storage yards filled with large-scale constructions for amusement parks.

For the finale of *The Next Generation*, 'All Good Things...,' we needed a medical ship for Dr. Crusher. Bill George, a master model maker at ILM, built a beautiful, fully functional Starfleet ship of his own design for himself with a sphere instead of a saucer for the main crew habitat. He was generous to let us use it, and it appeared in a number of shots.

There were times when we needed to add small background spacecraft to a shot when we really couldn't afford to construct something new. We would then build models ourselves. I really enjoyed using found objects, plumbing pieces, purloined bits from model kits, broken toys, shampoo bottles, deodorant bottles and even office supplies. It was great fun to see discarded objects become dramatically lit vessels flying through the *Star Trek* universe. When I would visit a hardware store I viewed things independently of their scale and original purpose. What I saw was potential spaceship parts. For example, a sleeve to repair damaged sprinkler systems had a high-tech look, and became the main hull of an Angosian escape pod. Adding a stock plastic dome, some handles from disposable razors, and a few small random parts known as 'nurnies' or 'griebels' for light-catching details finished the craft.

In one episode we needed to show a large fleet of damaged Starfleet ships returning from a space battle in *Deep Space Nine*, so everybody on the VFX team decided to make their own ship. We used *Star Trek* model kits so they all looked like they employed the same technology and had the Starfleet aesthetic. We pillaged parts from different boxes, assembled them in ways never intended—'kit bashing'—and created original starships to fill out the fleet.

Eventually, that kind of miniature work was replaced by computer-generated images. The challenges are the same for physical models and CG, they just provide different tools to approach them with. CG brought me the opportunity to work with a new team of brilliant digital model makers like Pierre Drolet, John Teska, Brandon MacDougall, Rob Bonchune, David Morton, Koji Kuramura, and others whose talent, skill sets, and artistic judgement became indispensable parts of the *Star Trek* universe.

CG technology has undeniable advantages, but I do miss playing with the coolest toys in the world. The artistry and craftsmanship of physical modelmakers like Tony and Greg earned a place in *Star Trek* history.

INSIDE STORY

WORKER BEE

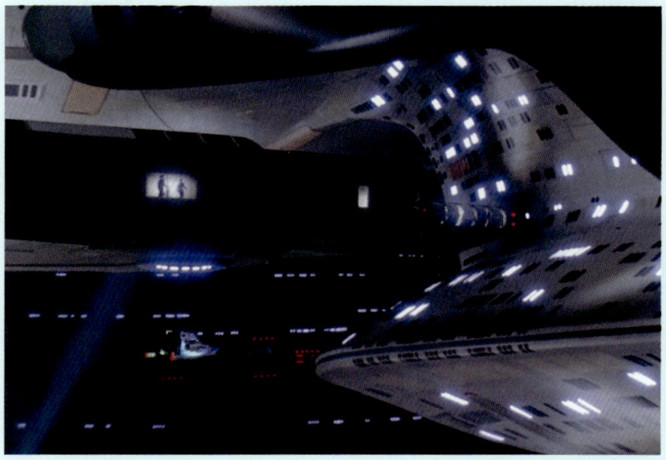

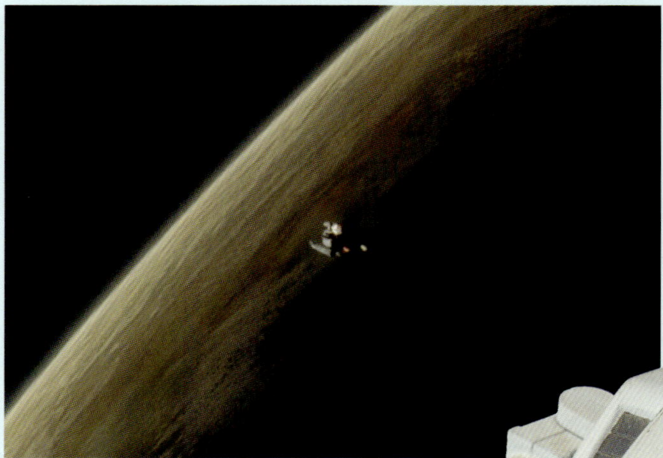

This was something I put in the background of space shots when the *Enterprise* is in Starfleet drydock. It was just a tiny utility craft flying around to make things look more busy. It really didn't have to be detailed, just tech-looking highlights and shadows. My son Devin had a broken toy robot, so I took its foot and turned it into a spacecraft. Gary Hutzel wired lights inside it. In addition to the robot's foot, there are other items I found around the house, including a pencil eraser and disposable razor handles for the nacelles.

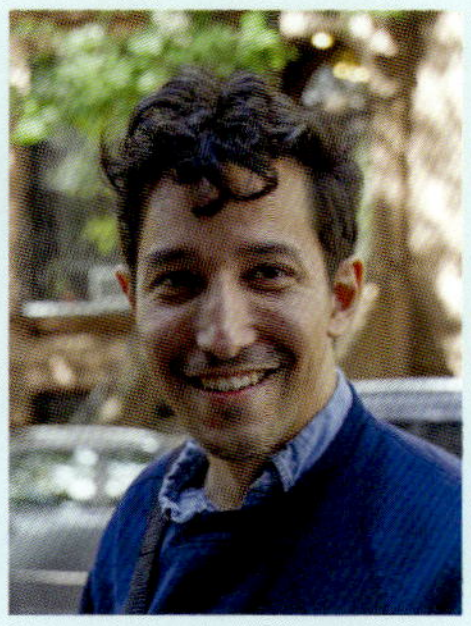

Devin Curry: "When I was a kid my father requisitioned—without my consent—the foot of one of my robots, and turned it into a model for the show. It just disappeared, and I didn't know what happened to it. When I asked him about it, he said, 'Oh, I had to take that because we needed a model. I'll get you something else.' At first, I was kind of displeased. I remember very distinctly that he glued disposable razors on the side, and it was bright blue before he repainted it. I was really excited when they installed the LEDs, it was magical to see it all light up. After he'd used it on the show, it sat in a glass cabinet, and I liked to turn the little switches and to see it light up. I thought that was pretty cool."

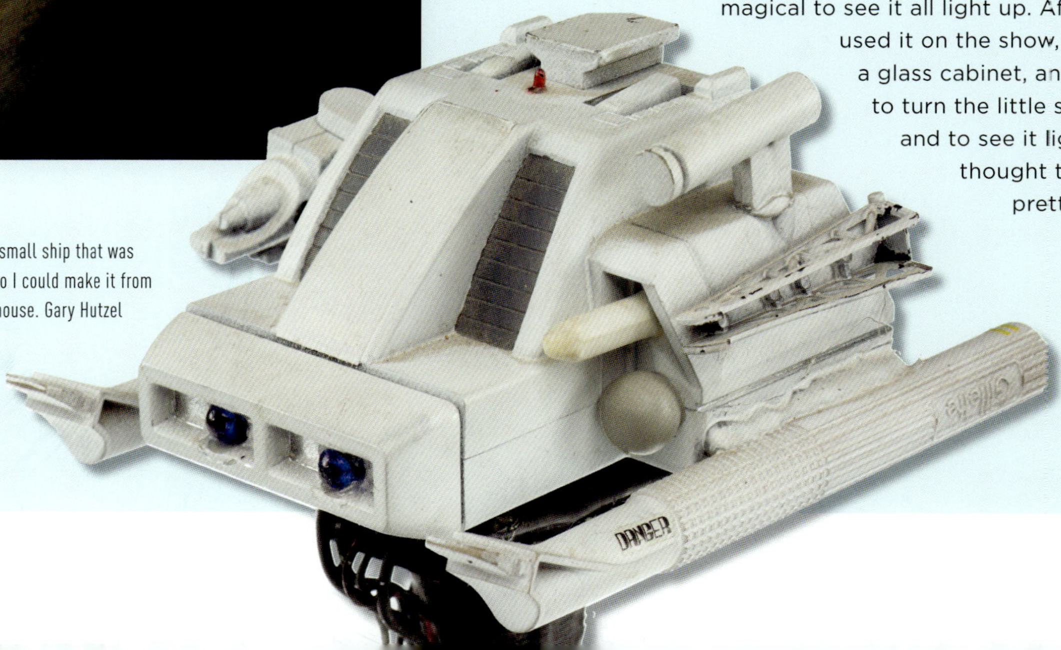

RIGHT: The worker bee was a small ship that was never going to be seen close up, so I could make it from simple things I found around the house. Gary Hutzel added battery-powered lights.

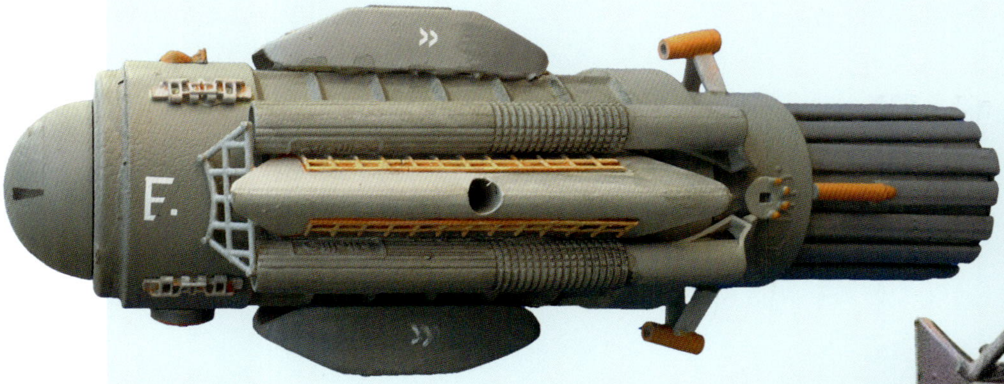

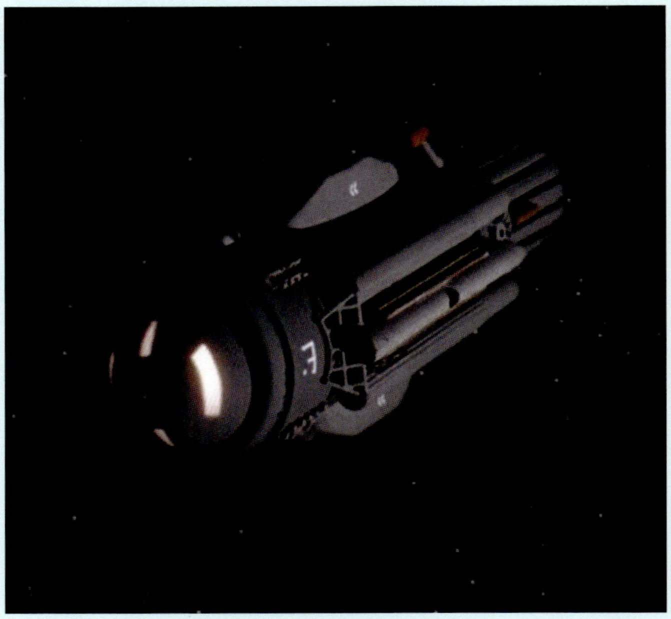

KIT BASHES

ANGOSIAN ESCAPE POD

There's an episode of *TNG* ('The Hunted') where the crew encounters a genetically engineered special forces soldier. At one point he tries to get away in an escape pod. We could have shown it far away, just a dot on the screen, but I had the time to build something.

I had a bucket of stock domes glued together as balls left over from the 1988 remake of *The Blob*. The creature was a bunch of plastic balls in a gauze bag, filled with a slimy substance called methylcel. For the escape pod I snapped a ball in half and glued it to a sleeve used to repair sprinkler pipes, added some disposable razors, anchors for aquarium plants, some spare model parts, and some coffee stirrers. Paramount even issued a trading card of it.

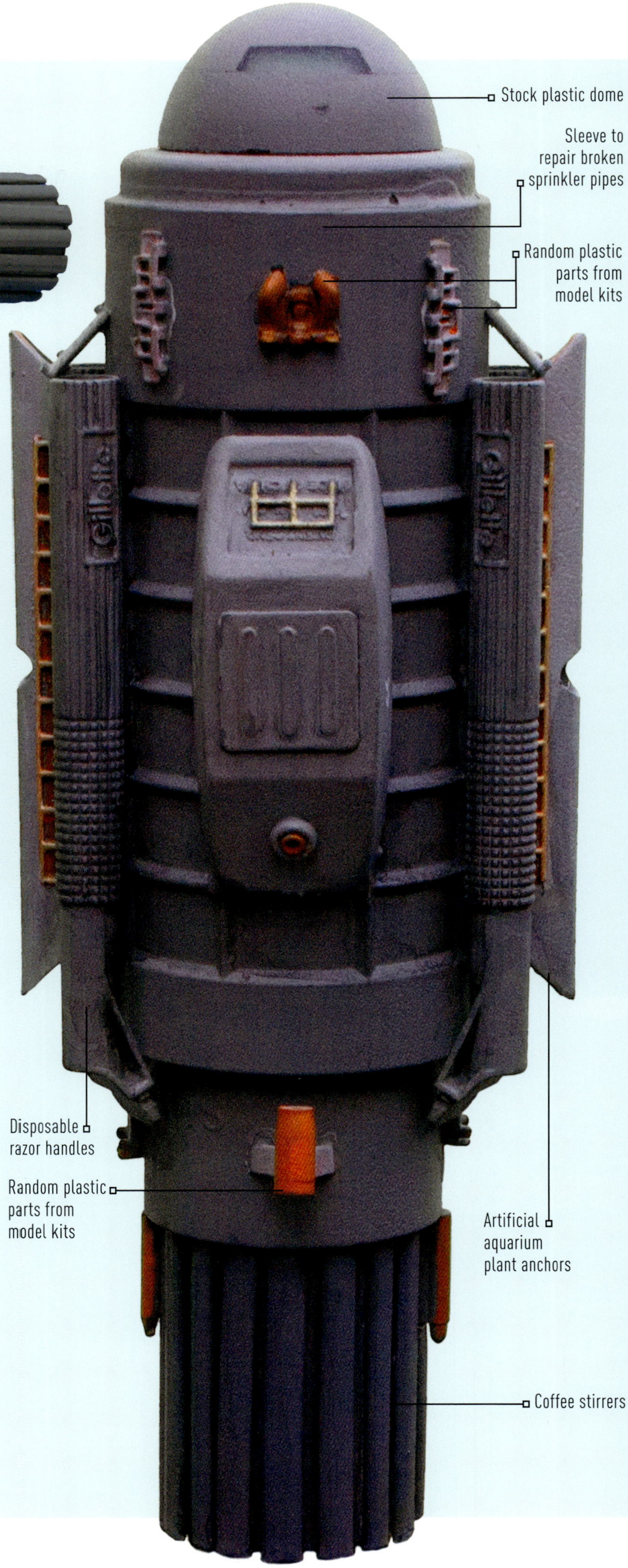

U.S.S. CURRY

This ship was made out of model kits for an episode of *DS9* where a battle-damaged Federation fleet limps home. A lot of people in the VFX team made a ship. I made it one day while we were shooting motion control at Image G. We had a bunch of boxes we pillaged for parts. We didn't put that much detail in, though, because we knew they would just be background ships.

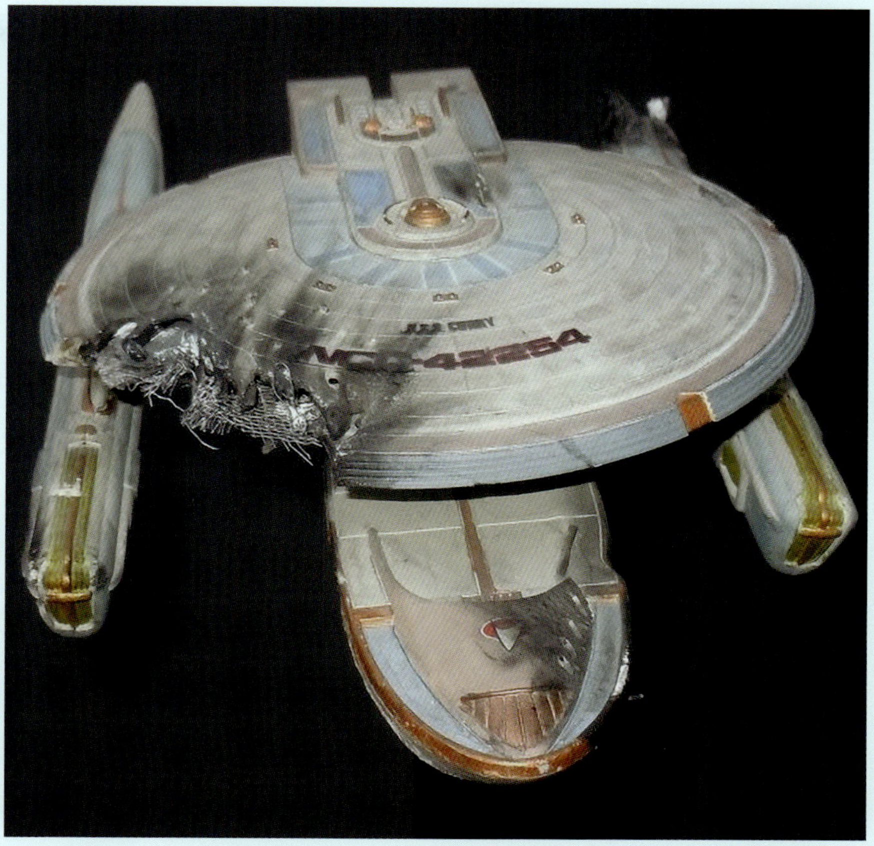

RIGHT AND BELOW: The *U.S.S. Curry* was made of parts from existing model kits bashed together to make a new ship.

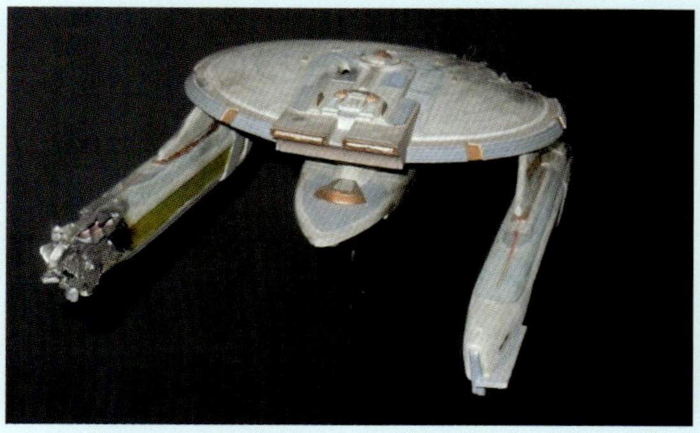

SPACE DEBRIS

These pieces were fabricated from random items like broken toys, hair curlers, fast food sauce cups, flower pots, model trees, etc., partially melted over a candle to simulate the effect of heat from a phaser blast. The pieces were mounted on our motion-control rig at Image G, and photographed as if they were drifting through the void of space in various episodes.

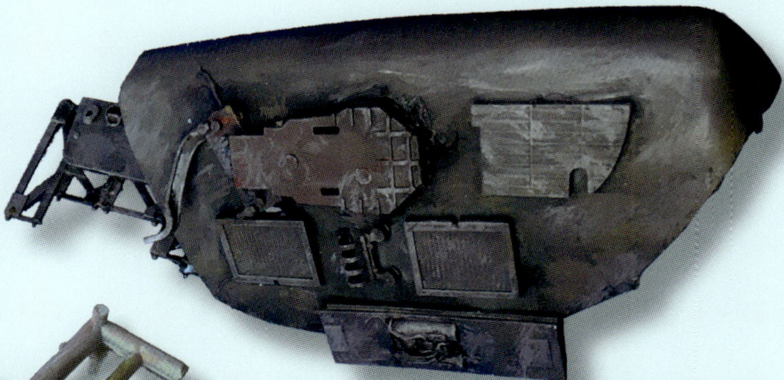

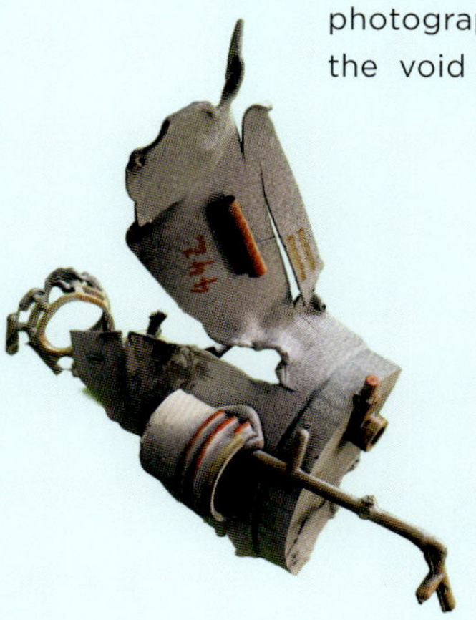

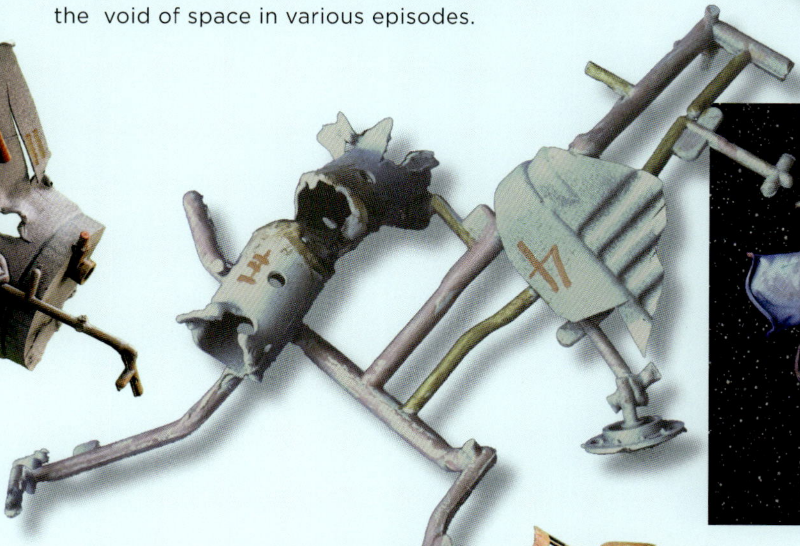

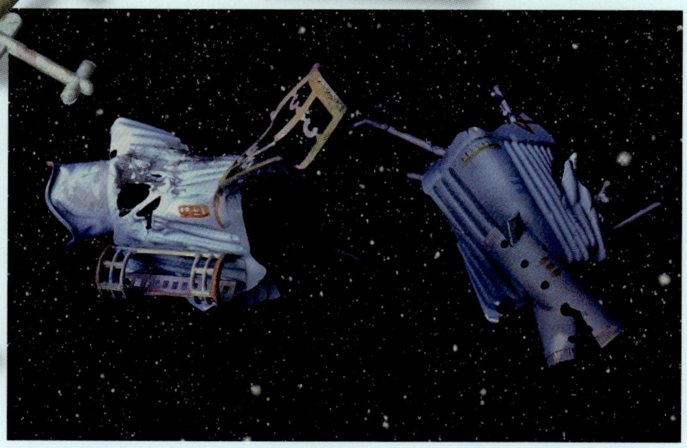

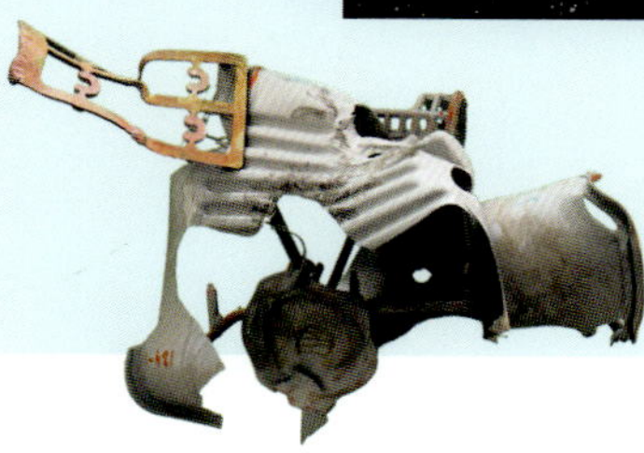

RIGHT: Debris from exploded starships was made from random plastic parts and cut-up found objects partially melted over a candle. These were never intended to be seen close up.

INSIDE STORY

SELF-HEALING BORG CUBE

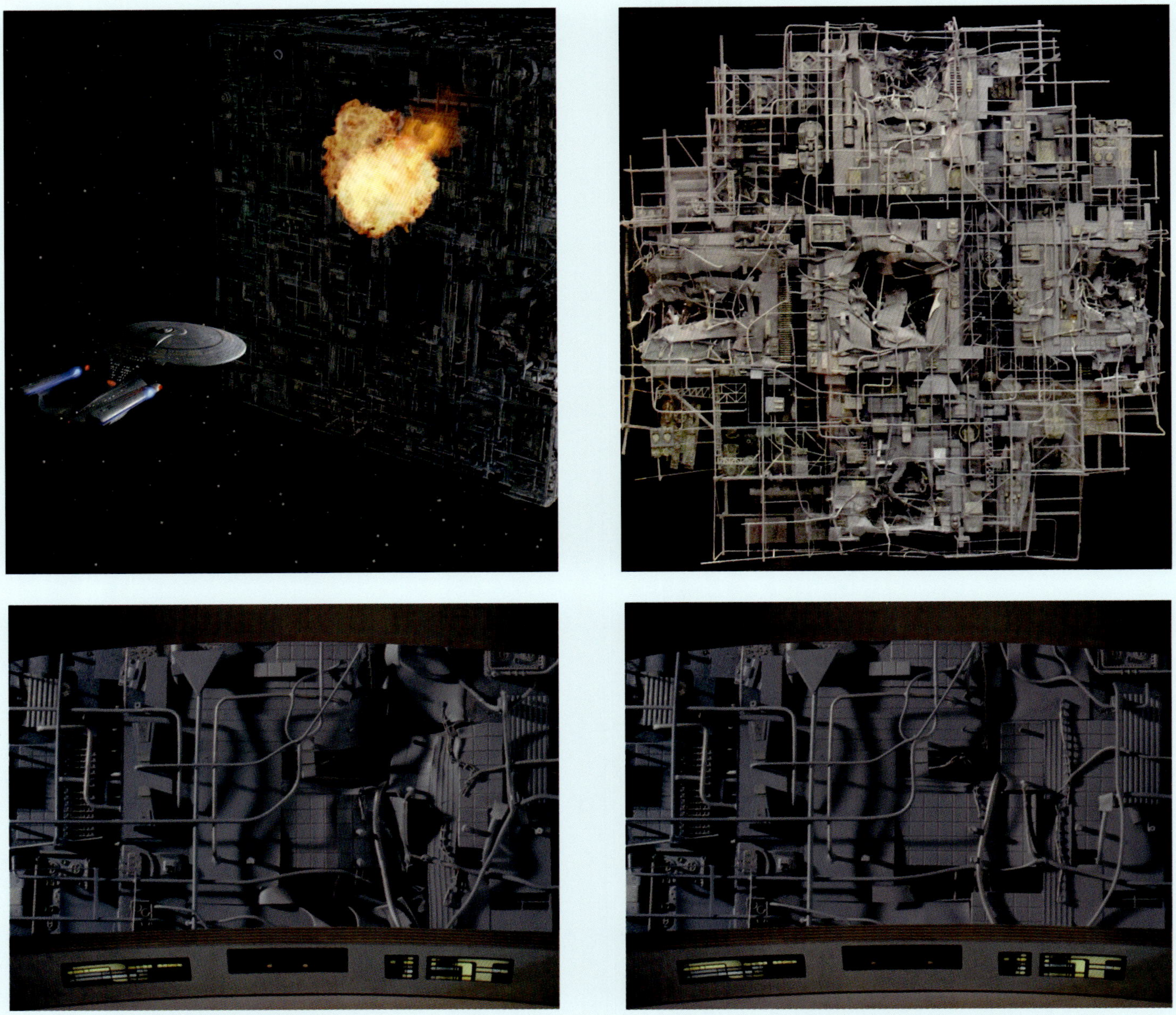

ABOVE: In 'Q Who?' the *Enterprise* attacks a Borg Cube, but as soon as it is damaged it starts to inexplicably repair itself.

In the episode 'Q Who?' when Picard firsts meets the Borg, the *Enterprise* fires on the cube. We can see the damage, but then the Borg Cube heals itself, so we had to work out a way of showing that process convincingly.

I asked Kim Bailey, who made the original model of the Borg Cube, to also make a close-up model. He made something that was about 4 ft x 4 ft and looked like the detail on the surface of the Borg ship on a much larger scale.

We put the model on a platform on the floor, and put the camera directly above it, so we were shooting straight down, making gravity our ally so the whole thing would look like it was taking place in zero G. I had two blowtorches, one on either side of the lens, pointing down at the plastic model. The blowtorches melted the plastic and, because we were shooting down, all the plastic parts melted directly away from the lens. Then, in the edit bay we played it back in reverse, so instead of looking as if it was melting, it looked like the Borg Cube was healing itself from a destructive phaser blast.

INSIDE STORY

THE *VOYAGER* MODEL

The model of the *U.S.S. Voyager* was the last physical version of one of our hero ships. It was built by Tony Meininger, an incredible artist and craftsman. Rick Sternbach prepared detailed schematic diagrams of every detail on the ship. Tony fabricated a sculptural model of each piece, which his crew used to make molds. Then they cast fiberglass shells that they put around a metal skeleton and the internal light circuits. Tony even made detachable scale legs that we could fix to the hero model when we wanted to show the ship landed on the surface of a planet.

One of the biggest challenges was that the producers wanted the warp nacelles to fold upwards when the ship leapt to warp. Today, with a CG model, that would be no trouble, but at the time it was a really big deal. The nacelles had to be able to repeat their movements with absolute precision or we wouldn't be able to combine the various passes that were needed for motion-control photography. Tony found some incredible, super high-tech mini chain belts that he could fit inside the wings. They worked with miniature gear mechanisms driven by small computer-controlled stepper motors that he also put inside the model. One thing I asked Tony to do was to put little bits of slide film showing the sets inside the windows. When shooting the window light pass, the back-lit transparancies meant the audience could see the rooms inside the ship and the perspective would change as *Voyager* flew by.

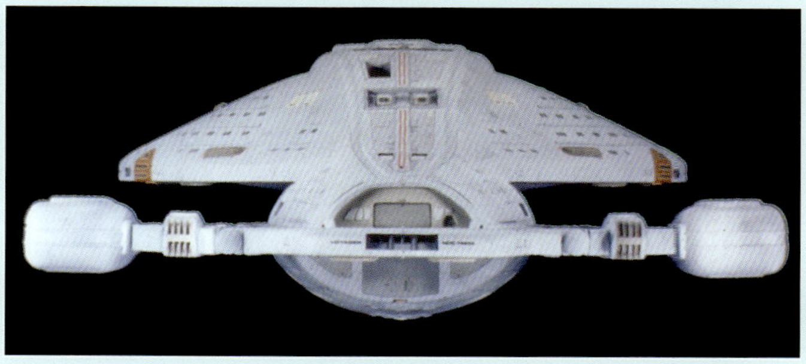

ABOVE: One of the major innovations on the model was the inclusion of tiny motors and high-tech precision chains in the nacelles so they could move when it jumps to warp.

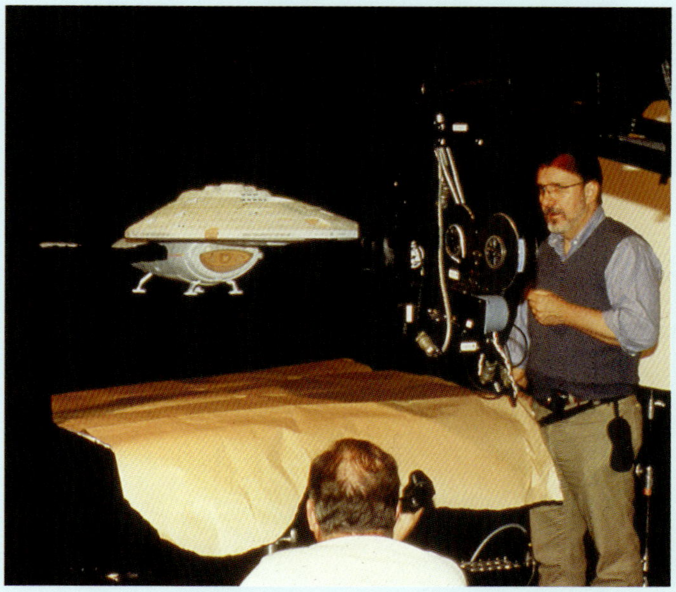

RIGHT: David Stipes and I prep *Voyager* with added legs to land on a planet. Brown paper reflects the color of interactive light from the planet surface.

BELOW: Examining the almost-finished *Voyager* with brilliant master model maker Tony Meininger at his shop.

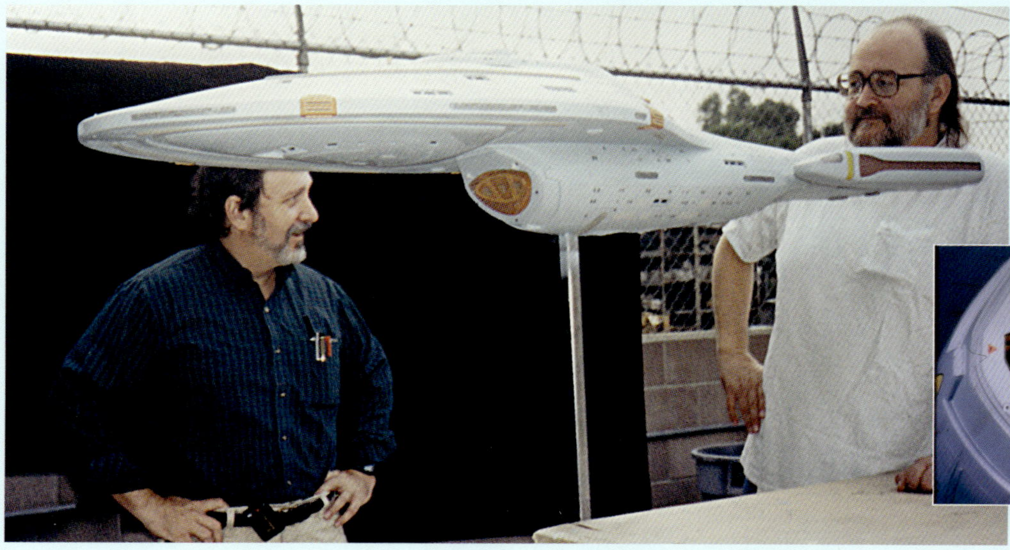

BELOW: Tony's model was beautifully detailed, enabling us to shoot very close to it.

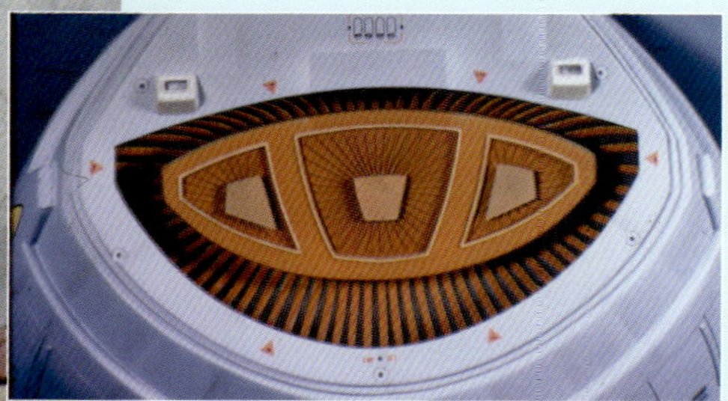

STARSHIP GALLERY

BORG UNICOMPLEX

When we were doing complex designs, the CG modelers found it easier to understand my vision if I gave them a physical 3D mock-up so they could see it from every direction. The Borg Unicomplex was a vast city floating in space—the Borg just attached new modules whenever needed without any aesthetic sense. In my home shop, I assembled bits of wood and bamboo trying to think like a Borg using thin connecting rods, as in zero gravity tether strength would be adequate to hold the modules together. I gave the rough model to CG artist Koji Kuramura, explaining that the cube would be a kilometer on a side and structures would grow out from it like a geometric cancer. Koji added his own creative genius to give us a great final product.

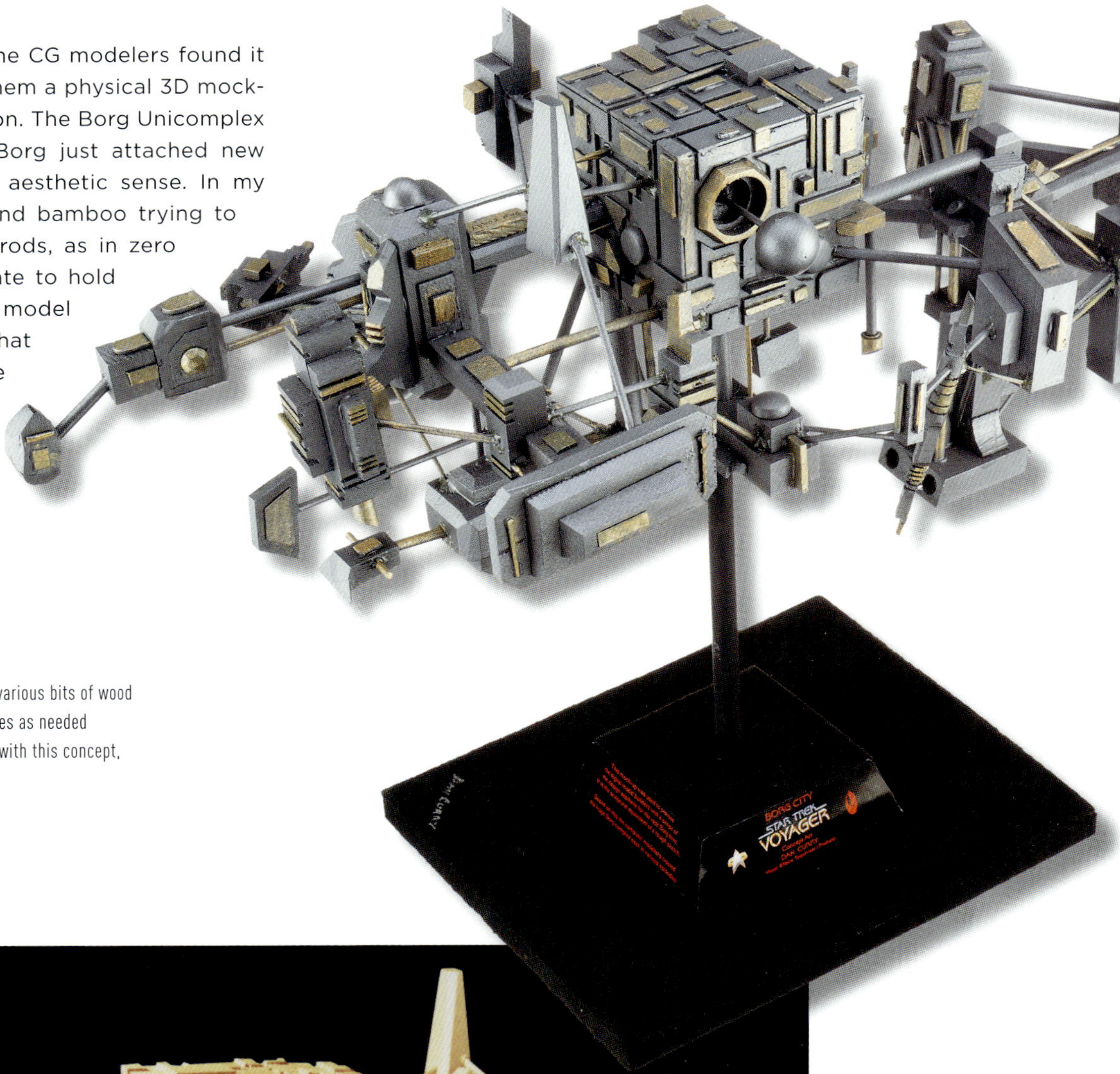

RIGHT: I built the study model for the Borg Unicomplex from various bits of wood in my home shop, reflecting the Borg aesthetic of adding structures as needed without regard to artistic beauty. Digital artist Koji Kuramura ran with this concept, adding his own brilliant creative touches to the vast Borg Unicomplex.

BELOW: The original wooden model of the Unicomplex before it was painted.

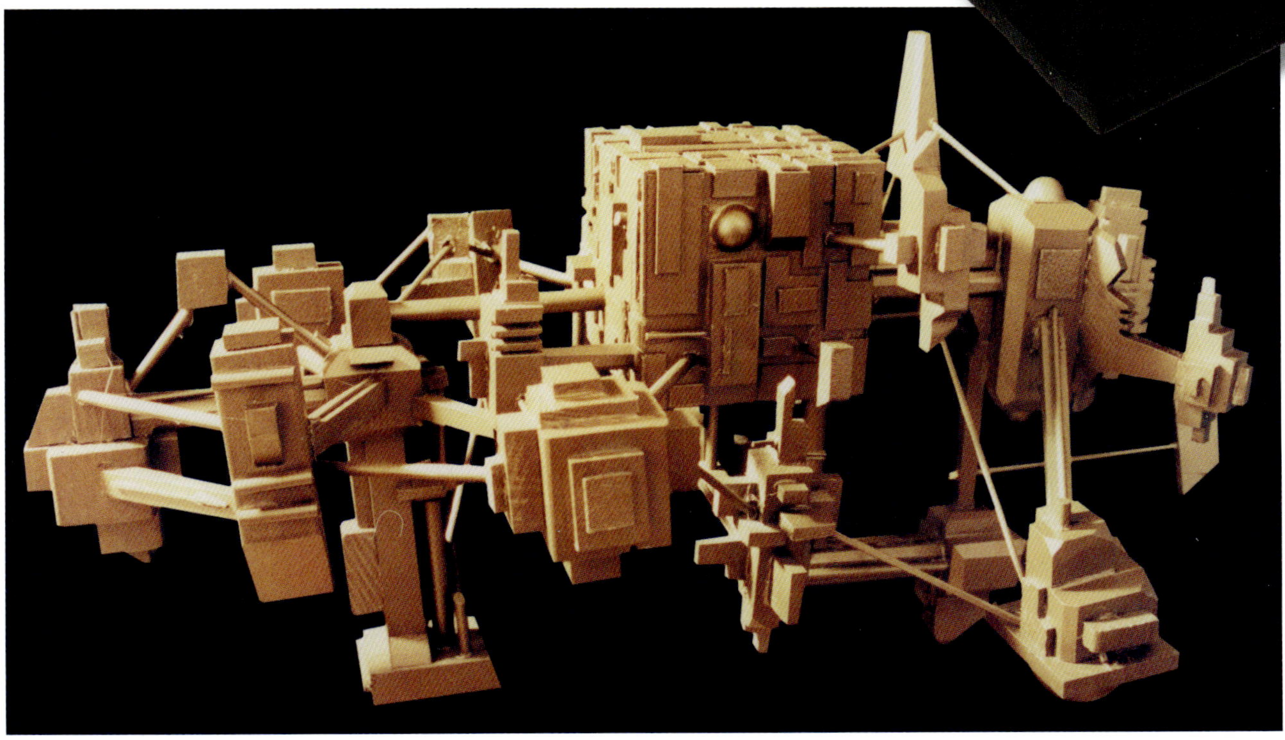

BORG RENEGADE SHIP

In 'Descent' the crew encounters a group of Borg who have been severed from the collective. They have gone rogue and are following Data's evil brother Lore, who is like a cult leader. I wanted something asymmetrical but with balanced masses in keeping with the Borg aesthetic of form following function with elements added on as needed. I made a study model that I carved from Styrofoam and covered with black photographer's tape and acrylic paint to suggest details, leaving room for Greg Jein's creative interpretation when he built the final model.

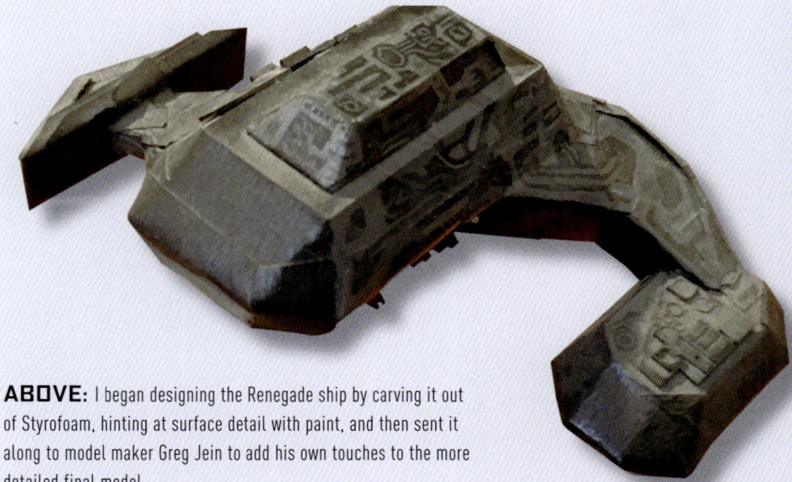

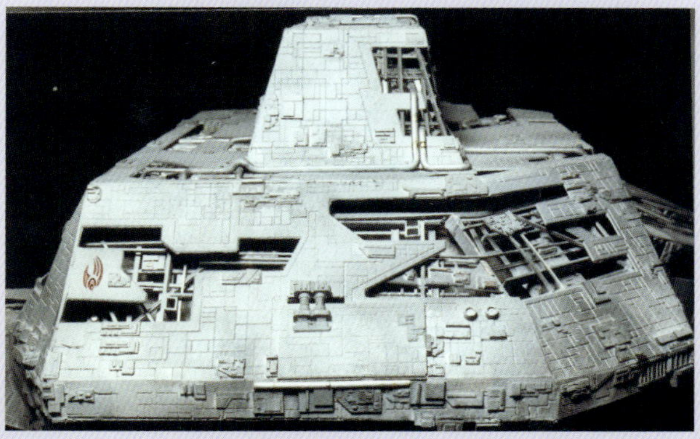

ABOVE: I began designing the Renegade ship by carving it out of Styrofoam, hinting at surface detail with paint, and then sent it along to model maker Greg Jein to add his own touches to the more detailed final model.

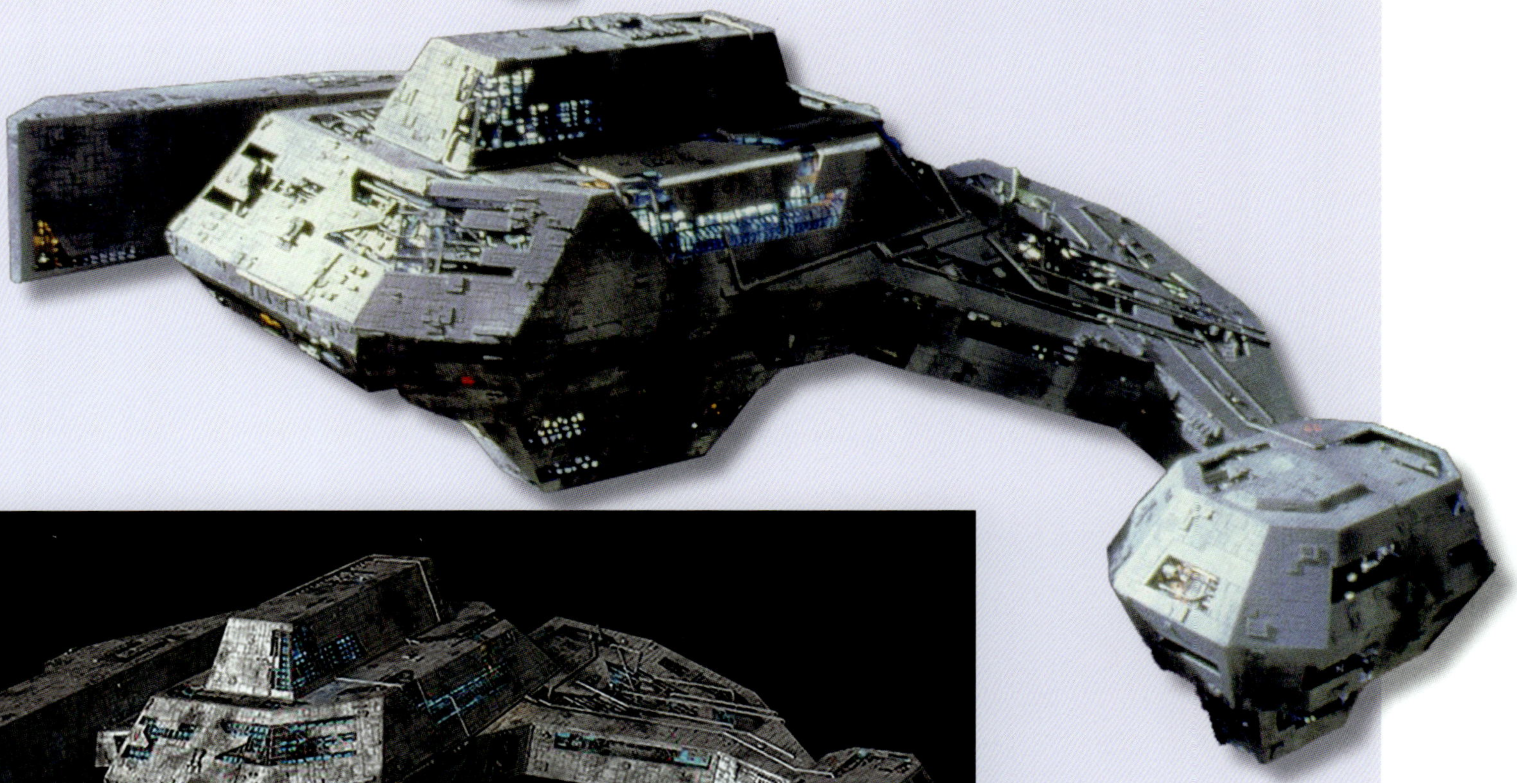

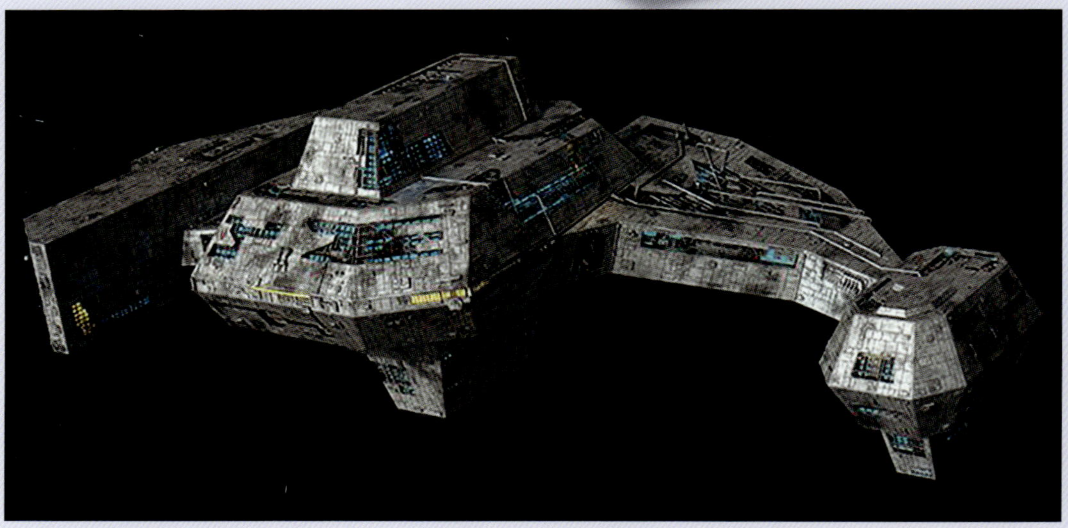

LEFT AND ABOVE: I wanted the Renegade ship to be asymmetrical to reflect the ruthlessly pragmatic minds of the Borg who built it, and to show the irrelevance of aerodynamics in the vacuum of space.

CAPTAIN PROTON'S ROCKET SHIP

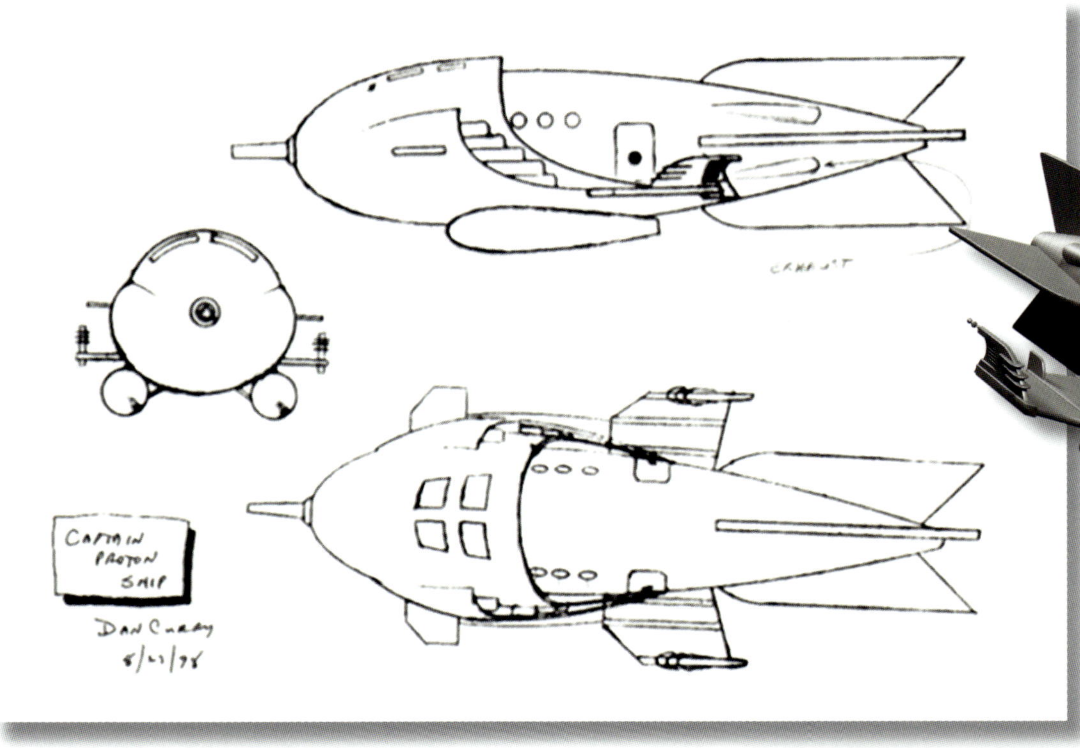

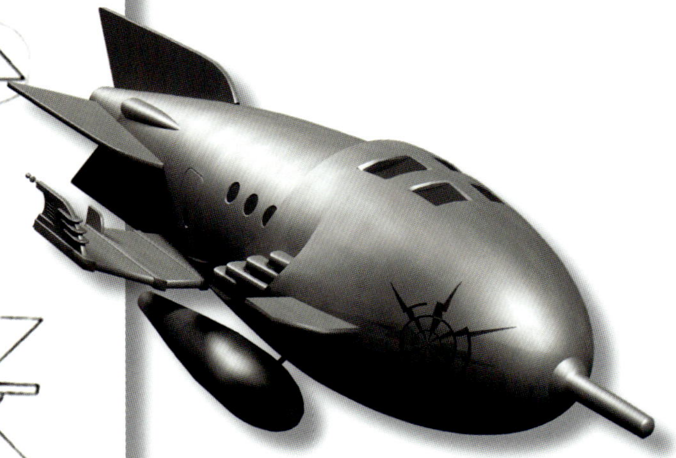

LEFT AND BELOW: Captain Proton's rocket ship was inspired by my memories of watching the wonderful Republic serial *Flash Gordon* when I was a kid.

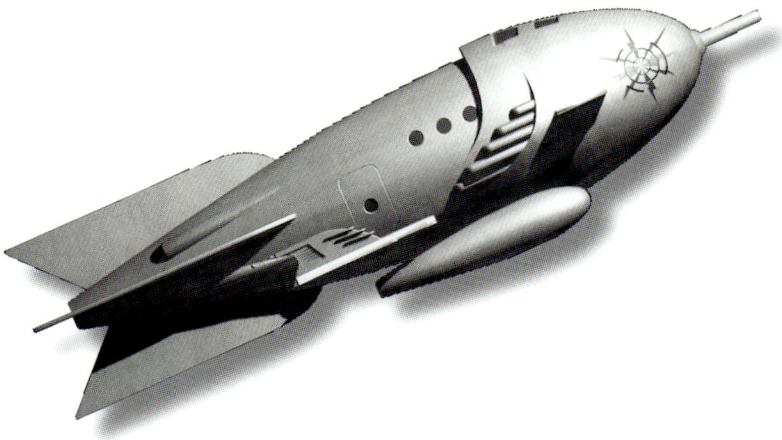

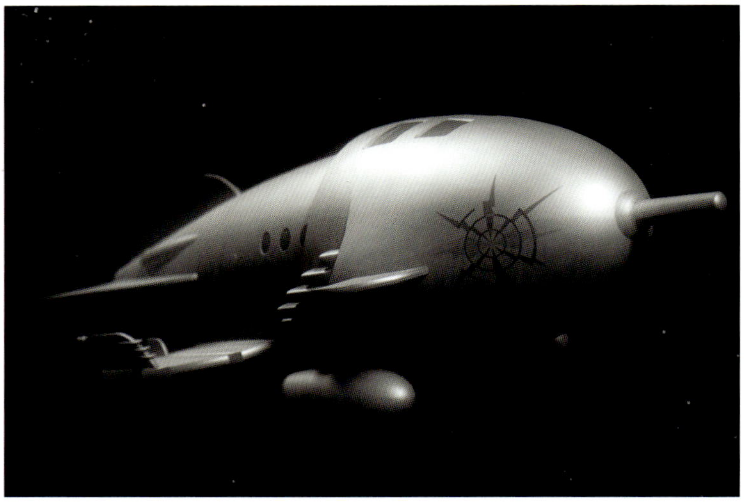

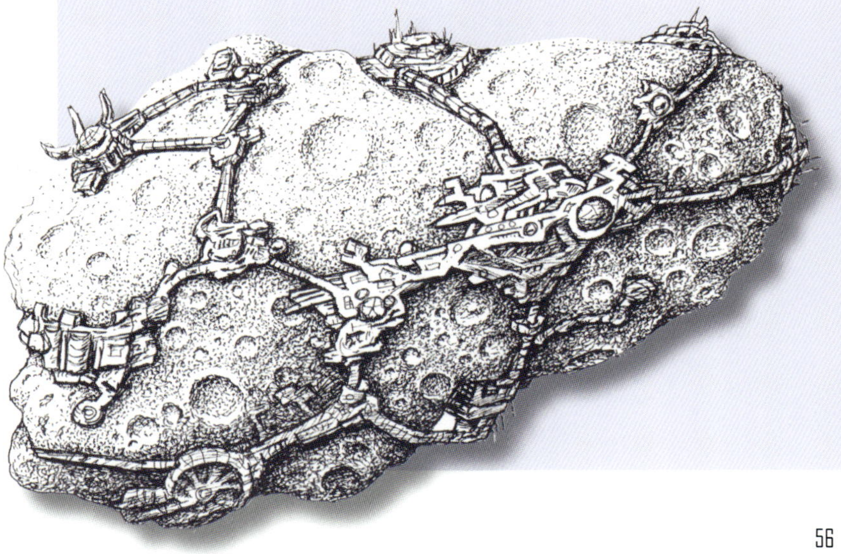

CARDASSIAN MOON

During the Battle of Chintoka the Cardassian weapons platform drew its power from a nearby moon. I've long been fascinated by the idea of using hollowed-out asteroids as living habitats. The idea is that most of the structures would be inside the asteroid.

LEFT: This concept showed how the Cardassians had taken a small asteroid and turned it into a power station with interconnected structures on its surface.

THE CARETAKER'S ARRAY

I came up with several designs for the Caretaker's array for *Voyager*'s pilot. I thought that since we were going into a strange part of the Galaxy, things could be very different, and much more organic. I did some paintings and also made a model out of foam core, painted with a stone texture. Rick Berman felt the arms on the front looked too much like Deep Space 9. He was right. The producers chose a much more technical design by Daren R. Dochterman with refinements by Rick Sternbach, built by Tony Meininger—lovingly nicknamed the 'Casablanca ceiling fan.'

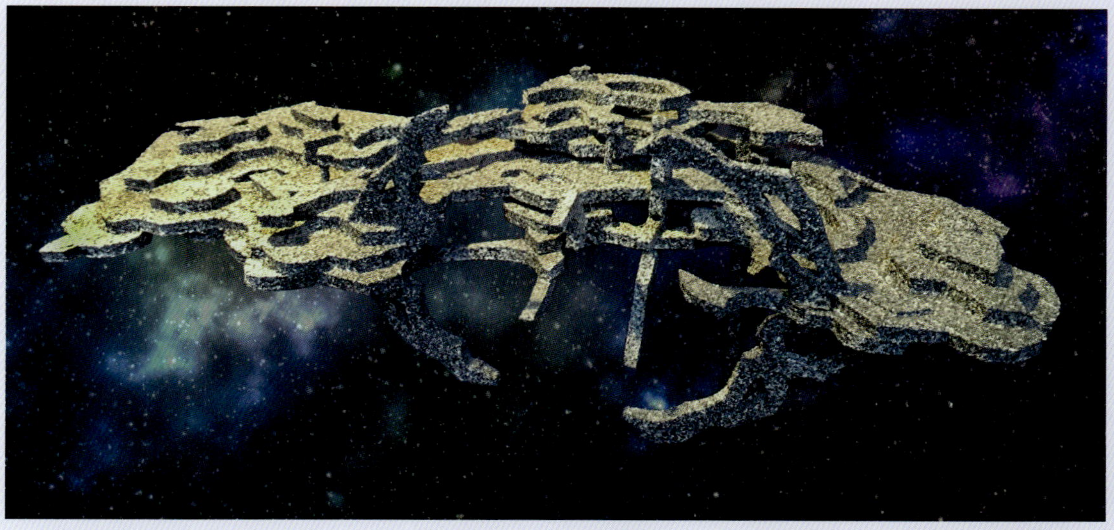

LEFT: I was imagining a habitat grown like coral, and built this out of layers of foam core. The producers wanted something more technical, and objected to the arcing shapes as they resemble the arms on Deep Space 9.

BELOW: Things could look very different in the Delta Quadrant, so I experimented with some designs that were much more organic than we were used to on *TNG*, not really expecting they would be approved but you never know.

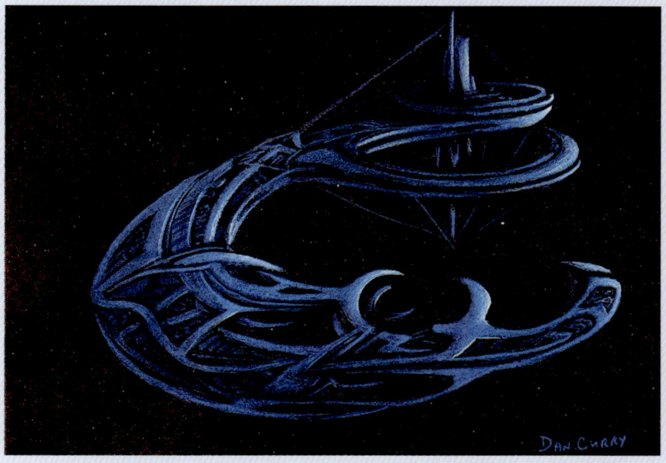

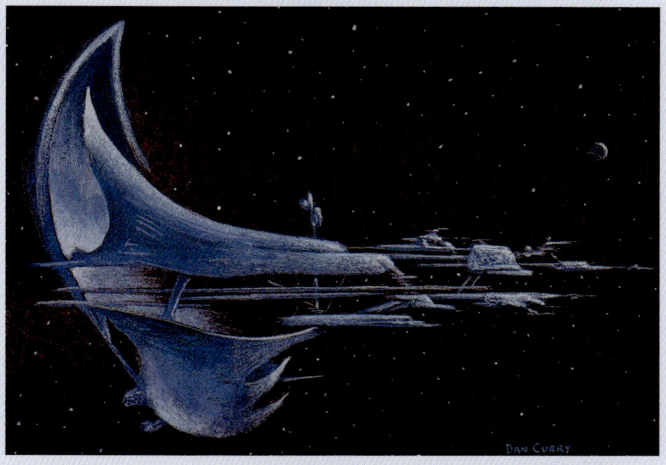

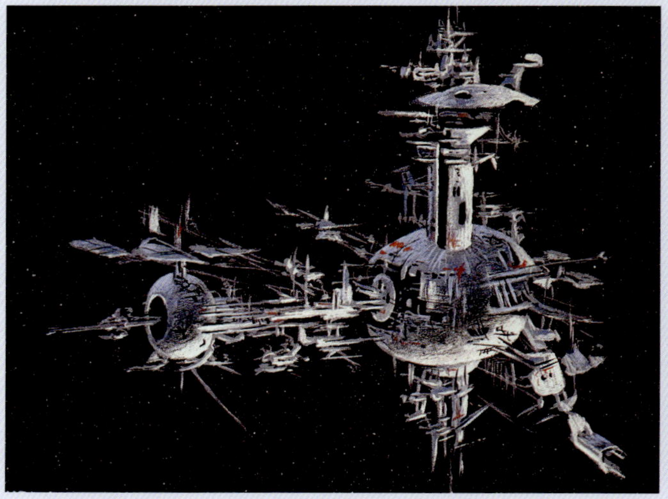

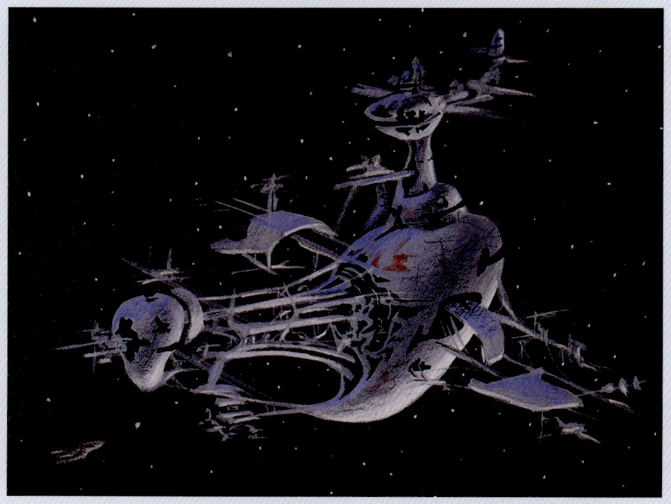

D'ARSAY ARCHIVE

This is an alien library from 'Masks' in *TNG*'s final season, and is one of our earlier experiments with CG. We went down that route because when the *Enterprise* first encounters it, it's frozen inside a comet. Captain Picard decides to melt the ice around it. We needed a technology that would allow us to do that. If we'd used a physical model it would have taken forever chipping away whatever material we used for the 'ice' frame by frame using stop-motion animation. I wanted the library to have a little Frank Lloyd-Wright, Mayan quality. I began with a core, and started adding to it like any piece of art. I was looking for a shape with balanced masses.

RIGHT: Constructing a rough study model allowed the digital modelers to see what the alien archive looked like from different angles. It was designed to be built in CG.

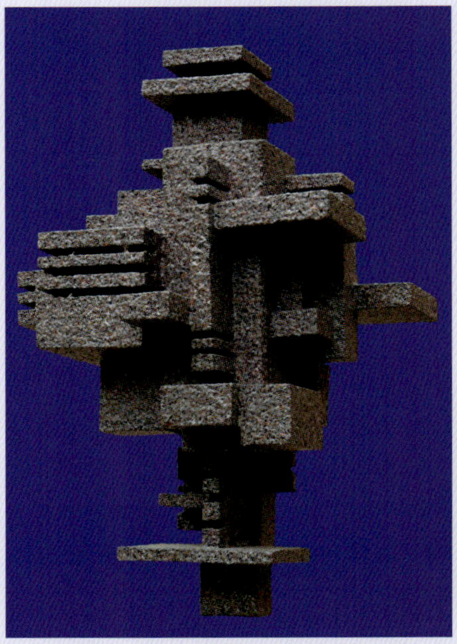

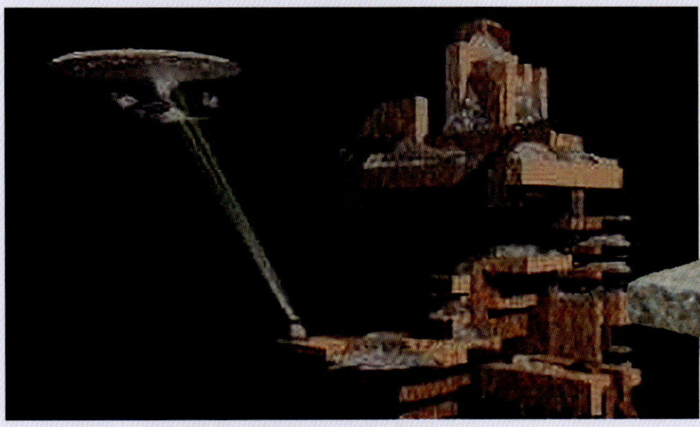

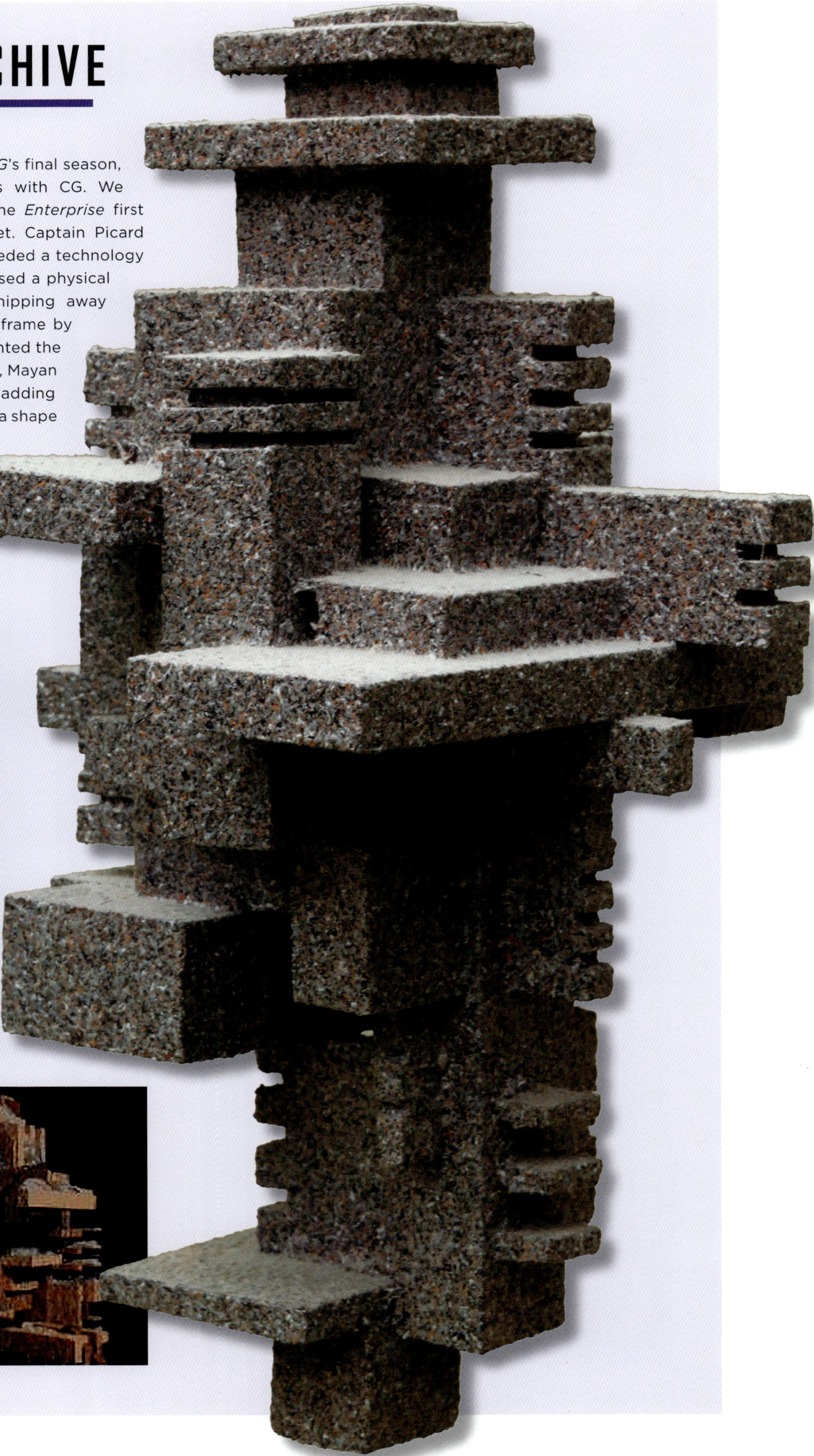

KAZON SHIPS

The Kazon ships were loosely inspired by the architecture of Lebbeus Woods because of its bizarre aesthetic. It had hints of steampunk, a weird Jules Verne-like quality, with a little *Mad Max* thrown in. I thought that look would be perfect for the barbarous Kazons.

A jet plane has a stern rudder that goes up, but for this fighter I decided to put the rudder in the nose, pointing down to look outlandish. Rick Berman thought the nose rudder looked too long, so he had me come into his office and trim it. The large ship remained in the vacuum of space, so aerodynamic features were unnecessary.

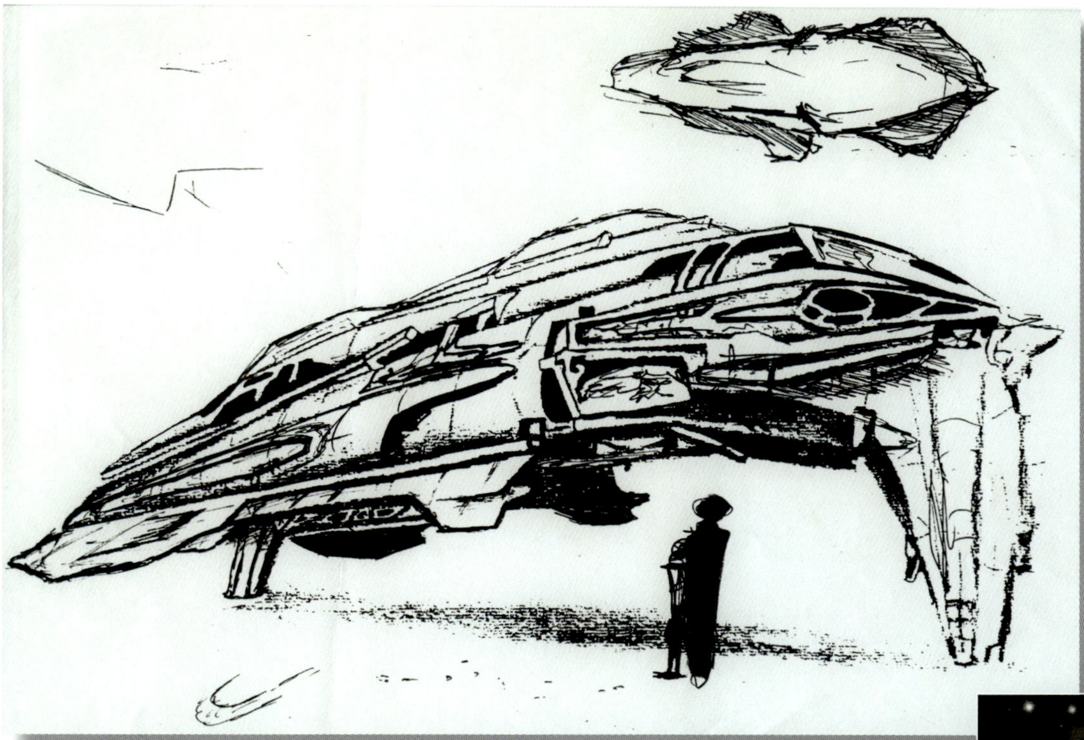

LEFT: Taking the opportunity to design some of the ships for *Voyager*'s pilot episode, I wanted the Kazon ships to look very different to anything we had seen before—in keeping with the crass aesthetic of their species.

BELOW: The finished model by Brick Price at Wonderworks follows my design closely.

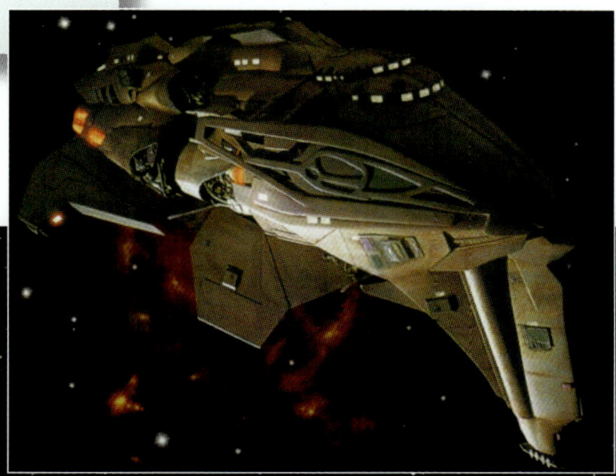

BELOW: I also designed a larger version of the Kazon ship that we called the Mother Ship. Chakotay rams it with his Maquis ship in a kamikaze attack in the *Voyager* pilot, 'Caretaker.'

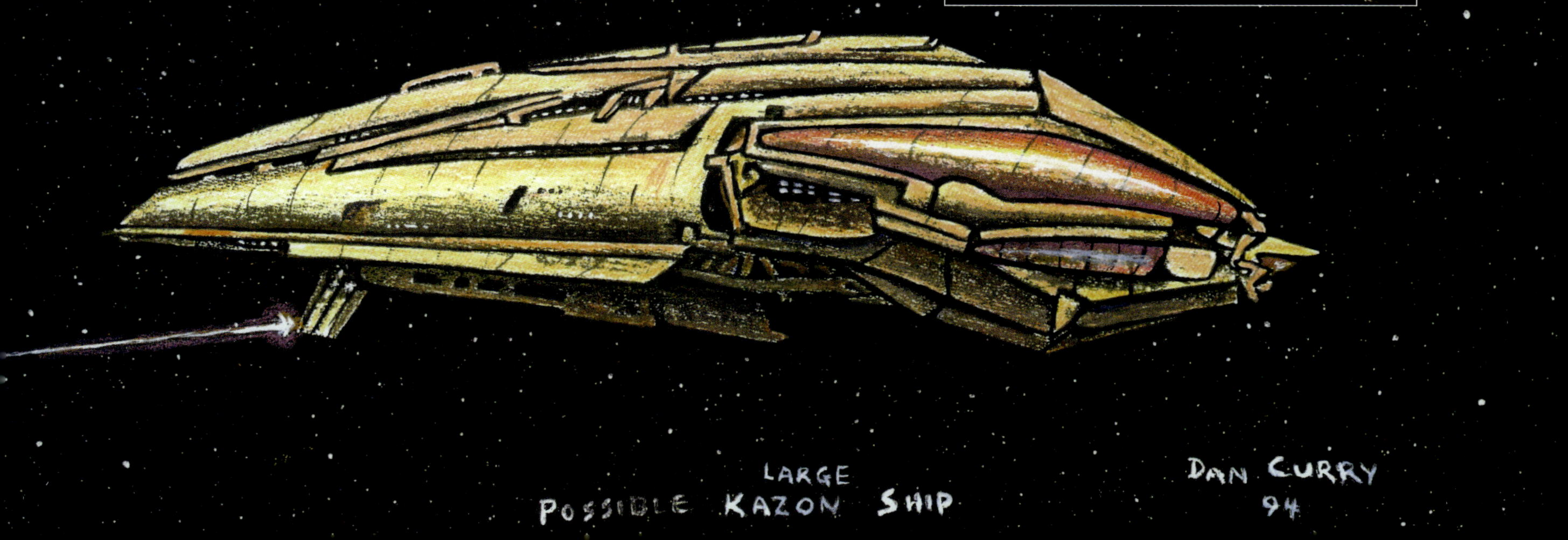

NIGHT SH

This was a mysterious ship that *Voyag* a lightless region of space without st for something really different; an o ship. I often consider subconsci audiences make that I can tap into. of a deep-water sea creature genera and having a symbiotic relationship fitted it with technology and lives in s within. Brandon MacDougall's digit Night ship was brilliant.

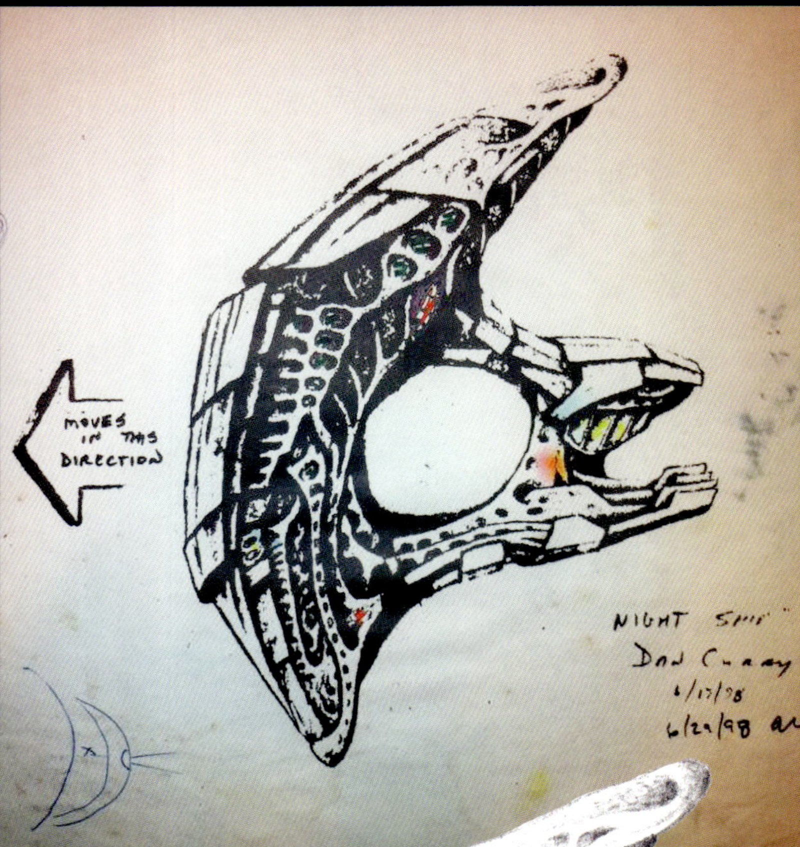

ABOVE: My initial rough sketch.

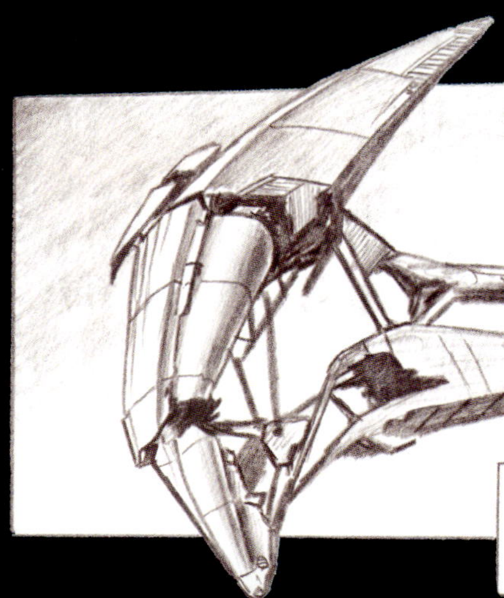

ABOVE: Unused alternate design.

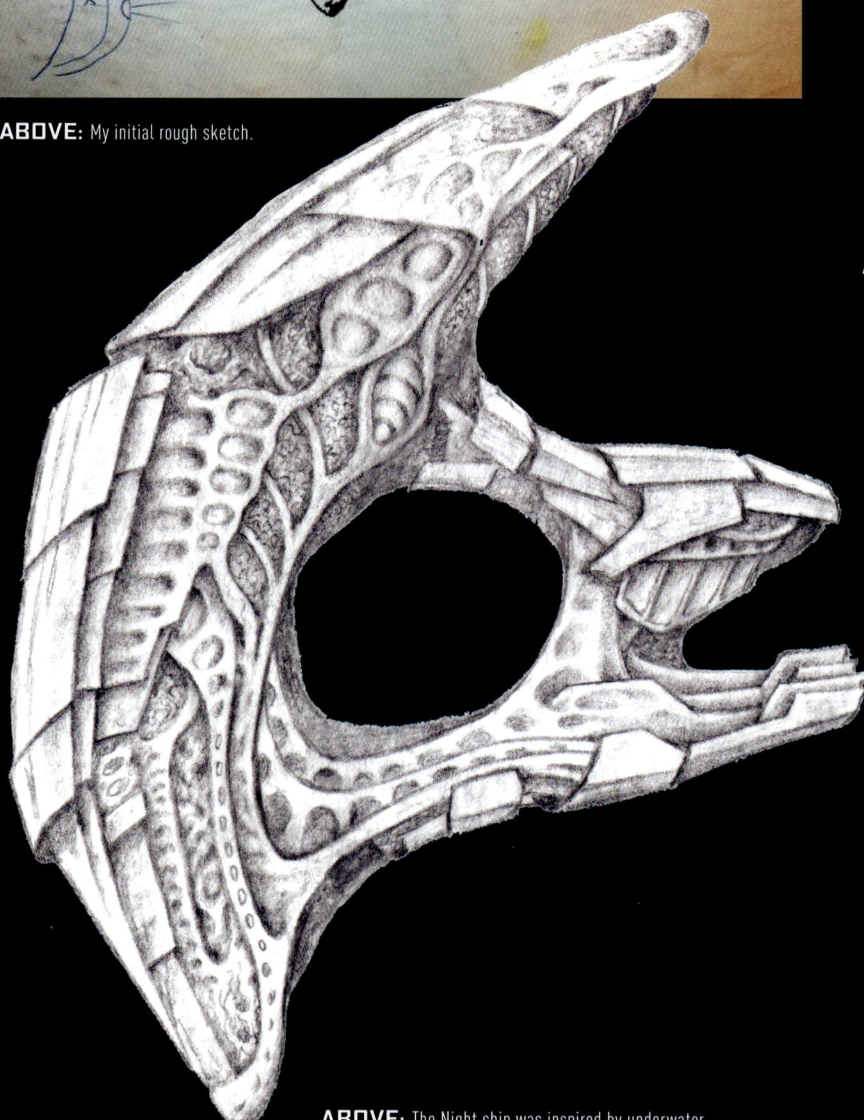

ABOVE: The Night ship was inspired by underwater sea creatures that glow in the dark. I wanted it to feel like it could have been organically grown and fitted with armor.

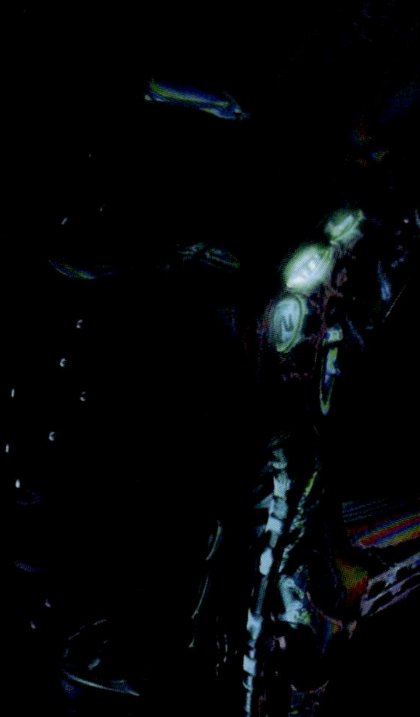

LEFT: was buil MacDoug creativity making i

HIERARCHY SHIP

I designed this ship for the *Voyager* episode 'Tinker Tenor Doctor Spy.' The look of the ship reflected the race that operated it—the Hierarchy. My thinking was that it would have been built by putting a flexible material inside a metal framework and inflating it, much like a blown-glass Mexican lamp. The material would harden over time to form the hull.

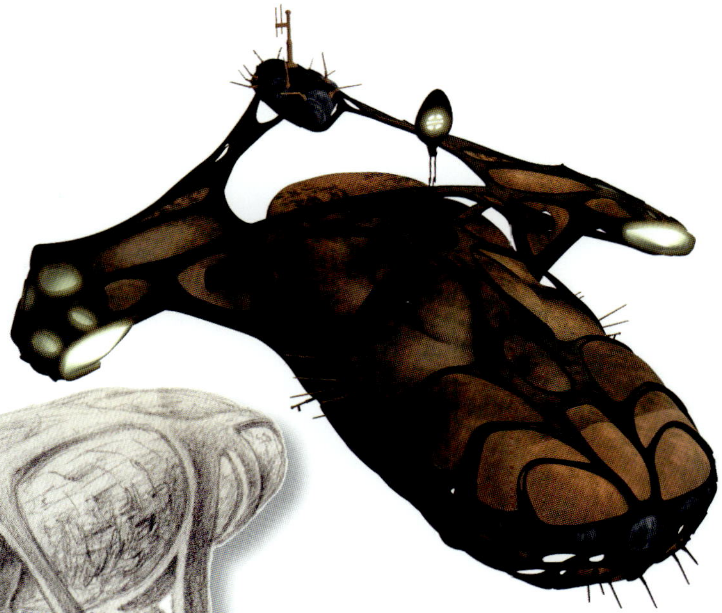

ABOVE: The CG version of the Hierarchy ship shows the digital modeler's own creative touches.

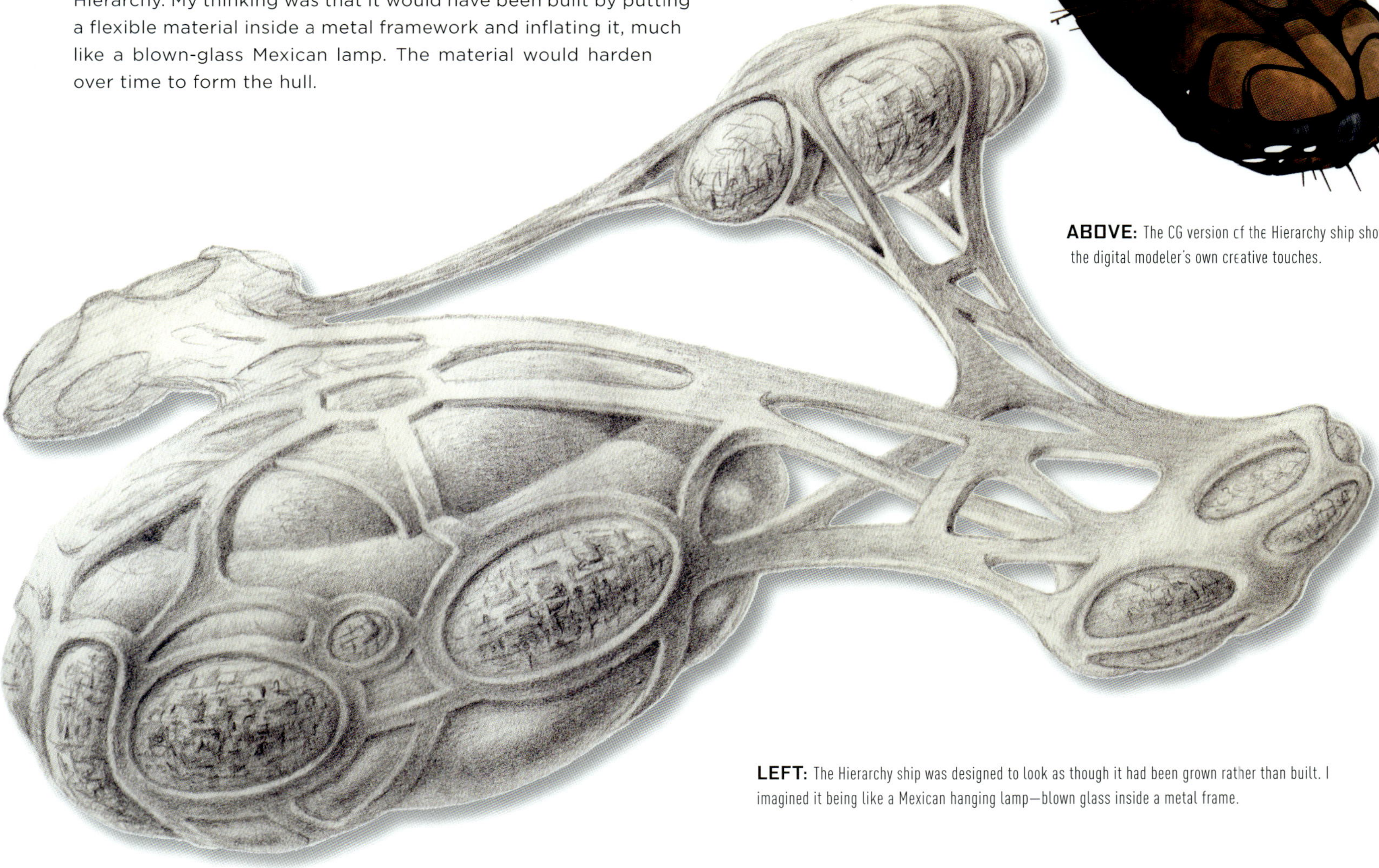

LEFT: The Hierarchy ship was designed to look as though it had been grown rather than built. I imagined it being like a Mexican hanging lamp—blown glass inside a metal frame.

DOMINION SHIP

This sketch was done very hastily and the ship was assumed to be axially symmetrical, so there was no need for a lot of detail to be indicated on its far side.

RIGHT: This was a concept for a Dominion ship that was never used. It may have been an idea for a Jem'Hadar fighter.

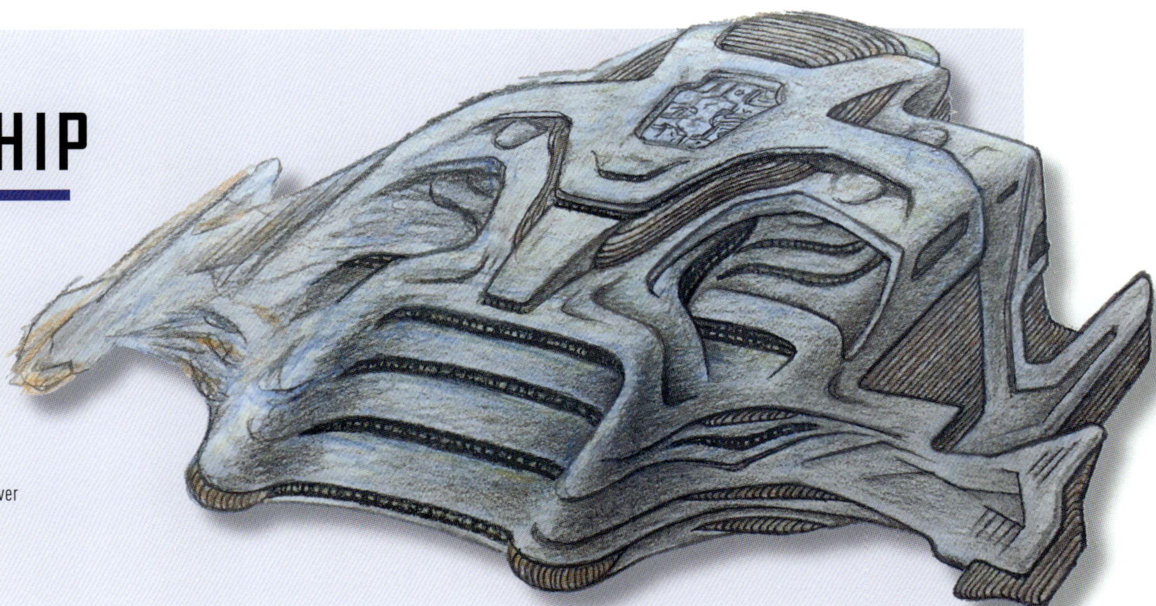

VIDIIAN SHIP

I remember doing different drawings of this ship. We were on the other side of the Galaxy, but I wanted to create recognizable warp and impulse drive technology to imply that different spacefaring species ultimately developed similar propulsion systems, so the orange parts on the front and the back were the equivalent of warp nacelles.

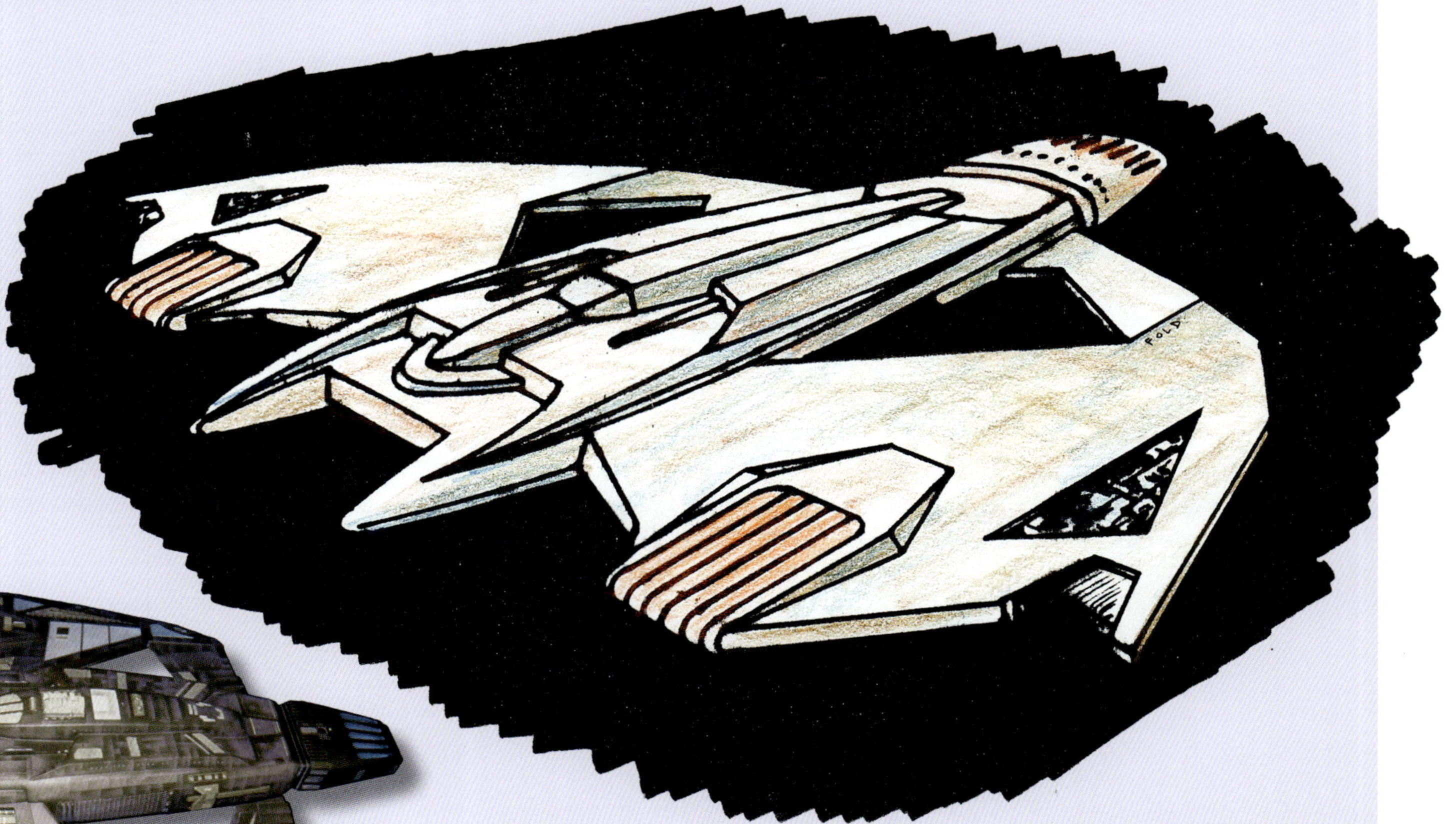

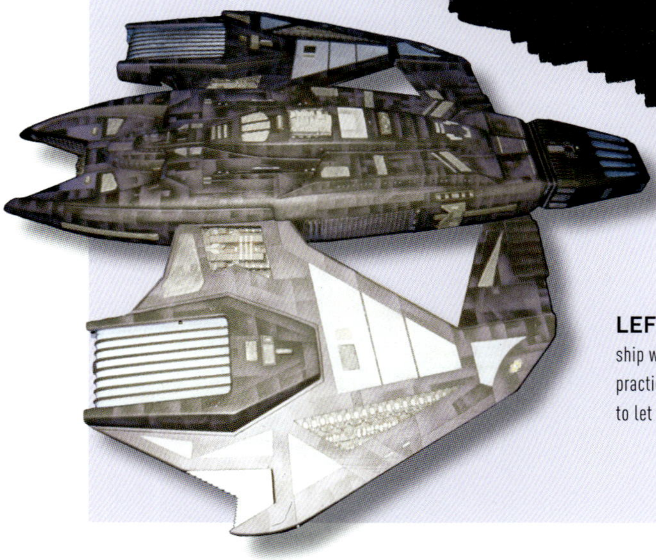

LEFT: The finished model of the Vidi an ship was one of the last vessels we built practically. By this time, we were almost ready to let CG take over.

ABOVE: I wanted the Vidiian ship to have strange proportions to distinguish it from the Starfleet aesthetic. I intentionally didn't include too much detail in the sketch so the model maker could add his own creative touches.

FIXED WING

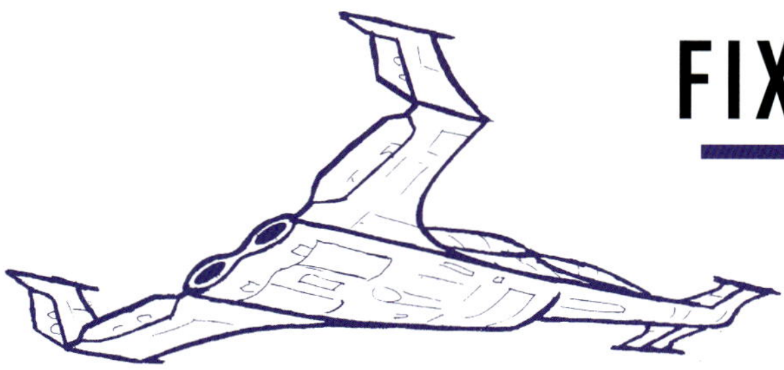

We needed a ship that could believably fly in an atmosphere. In homage to the Wright brothers I put the small wing (cunard) in front.

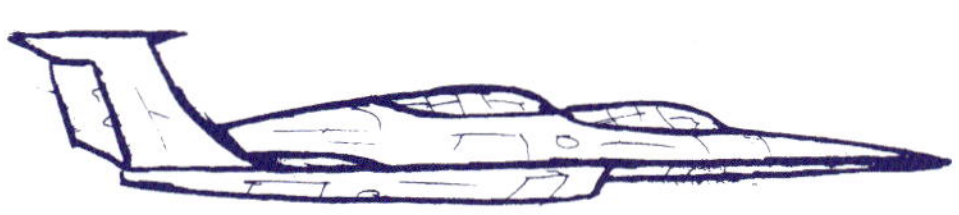

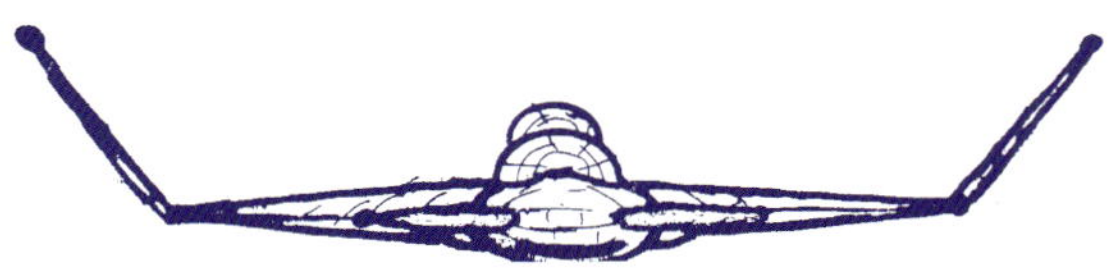

VAHKLAS

I designed this Vulcan ship for the first season of *Enterprise*. I wanted something in keeping with Vulcan ships seen before, so I kept part of the ring featured on earlier Vulcan ships to imply a consistent technology, but because the *Vahklas* was a smaller ship I decided to break the ring, suggesting that it wasn't as powerful. I kept the sketch devoid of details so the model maker could add his own creative vision.

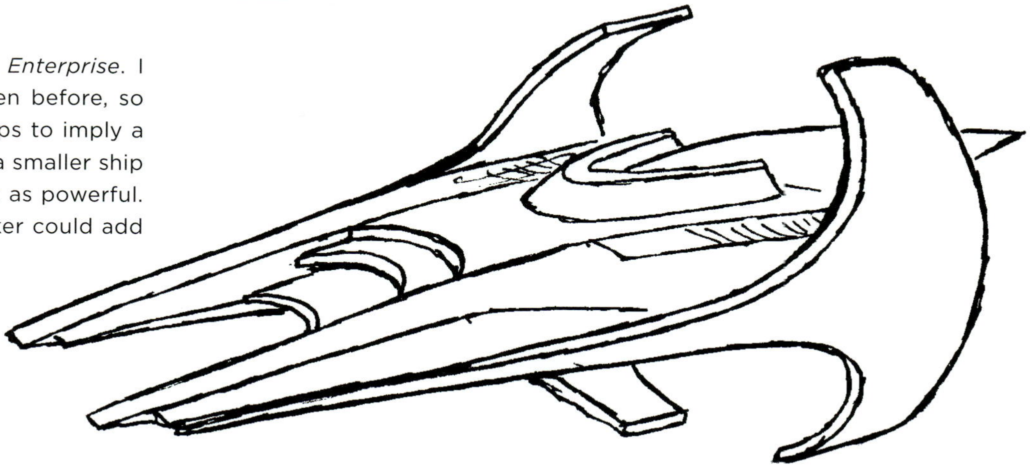

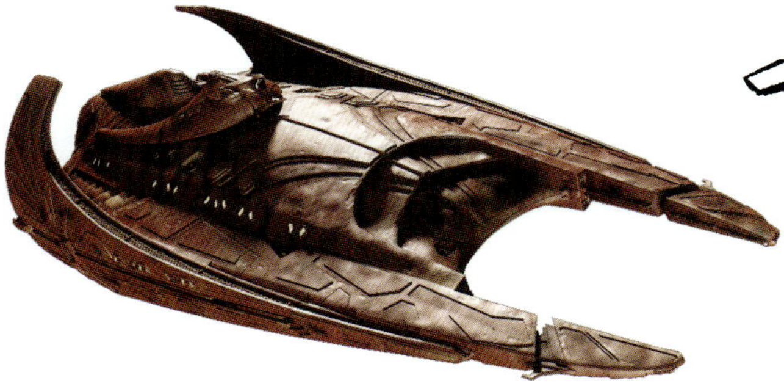

ABOVE: Most of the ships for *Enterprise* were designed by brilliant conceptual artist John Eaves, but when circumstances allowed I enjoyed helping out.

LEFT: The model of the *Vahklas* was built digitally at EdenFX, where they gave it a texture to make it look as if it was an older ship.

TNG STATION

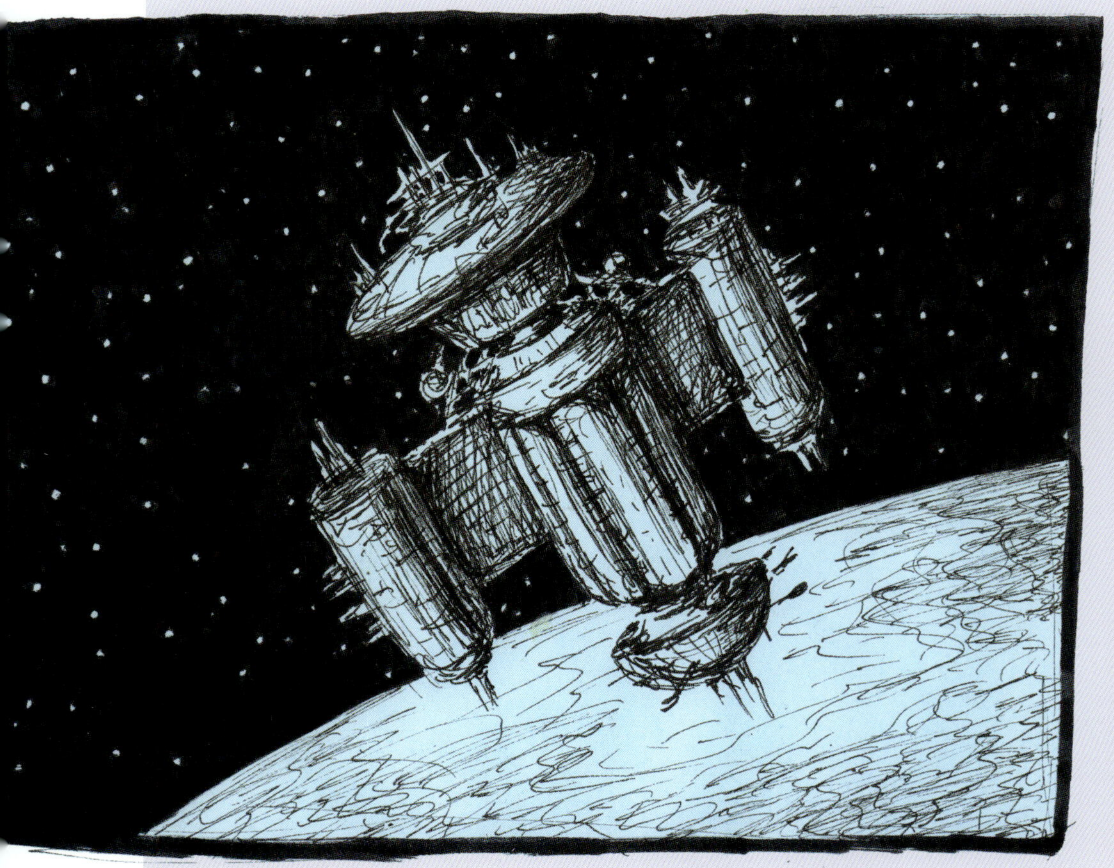

This was a very rough sketch done in a production meeting. I can't be 100% certain, but I think it was for the particle fountain in 'The Quality of Life.'

LEFT: I'd often produce rough sketches during production meetings when we first heard about the producers' vision. Sometimes they were literally sketched on a page of the script.

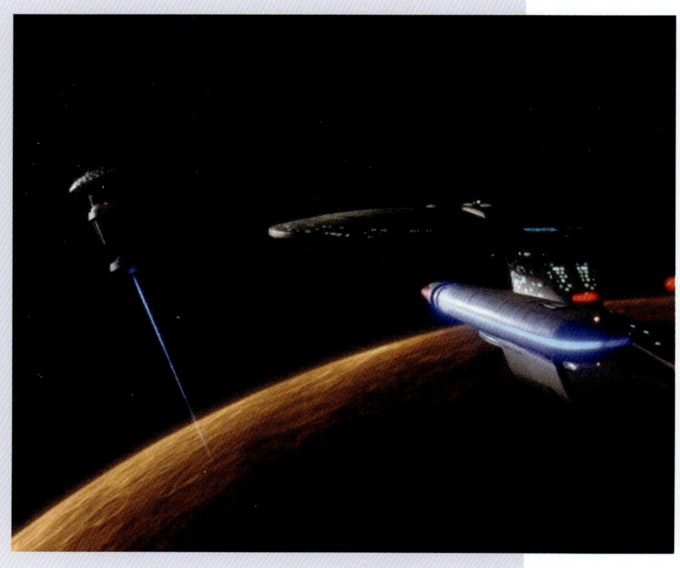

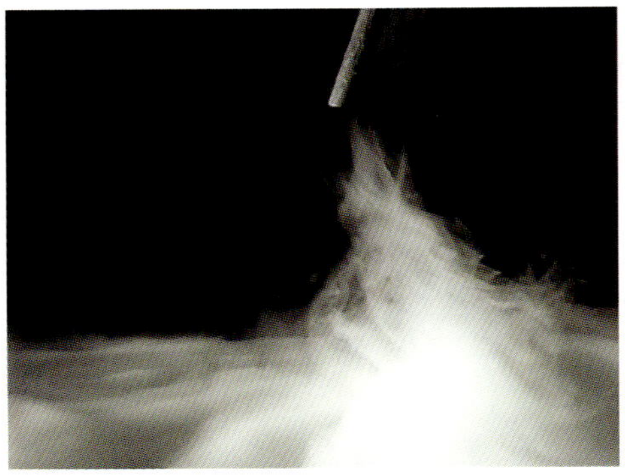

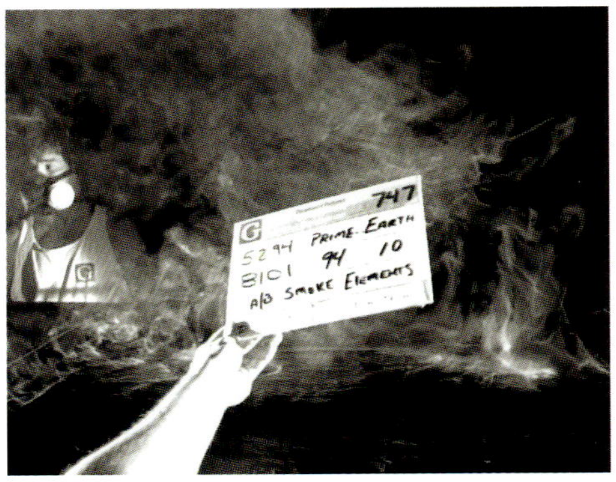

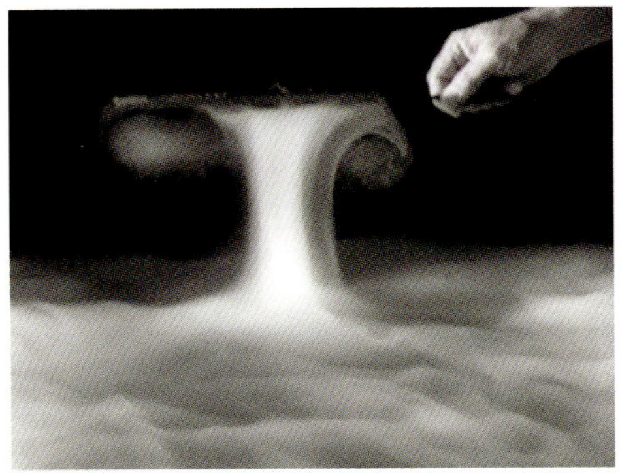

EXTRAORDINARY ELEMENTS

CREATING THE STRANGEST PHENOMENA FROM THE MOST MUNDANE RESOURCES

Before CG, visual effects were like medieval alchemy, taking one thing and making it something it's not—lead into gold. The nature of *Star Trek* is that it asks for the impossible—things that simply cannot be filmed in the real world. We had to create rifts in the space-time continuum, strange spatial phenomena, plasma fires, mysterious light beings... anything the writers could think of. Often as not, we'd create those illusions with very ordinary things—by the time we filmed them, scaled, stretched them, colorized and composited them, they looked like something completely different.

Today, most visual effects are created with a computer. When *TNG* started that wasn't an option, but we were eager to explore ways of combining traditional movie techniques with video technology. With video you can select a shape or a color, manipulate it, or use it as a matte to replace it with something else. You can literally paint new elements directly into your picture. Say we needed a volcano with erupting lava plumes. This could be accomplished by using baking soda tossed upwards and filmed at a high frame rate, separating it from the background, colorizing it and adding it to a different image. The trick is determining what you can use. That kind of old-school approach requires a different type of thinking. It's very creative, and a lot of fun. The materials used can be unexpected and very low tech. We used all sorts of things—a Mylar pom-pom, powdered walnuts, DayGlo gloves, ash, water, liquid nitrogen, vermiculite, whatever we could think of. We all had different ways of doing things. My approaches were probably the most low-tech—sometimes the rest of the team would look at me like I was nuts.

Over the years, we filmed lots of things to use for different effects. They'd rarely get used on their own, but became parts of an image, which is why they are called 'elements.' On *TNG* the two VFX teams—Rob Legato and Gary Hutzel comprising one team, and Ronald B. Moore and me the other—were constantly shooting episode-specifc elements, and built a library we could repurpose. We called ours DRE reels, for 'Dan and Ron Element' reels. Rob and Gary had their own element reels too, and we'd borrow things from one another to avoid wasting time and energy shooting the same thing twice. The range of elements would vary, as new episodes called for new phenomena. We invented techniques as we went along, trying anything that might work. The tight schedules of episodic TV rarely allowed a chance to do anything twice, so we crossed our fingers and hoped it would work. We frequently looked for things that could be used as energy patterns. Creating convincing random kinetic motion was always a challenge, but you can find it in all sorts of places in nature.

There is an inherent randomness about organic elements that

LEFT: The natural randomness of 'organic' elements enables them to look like something they are not. Liquid nitrogen was invaluable as it could be used for large-scale phenomena.

makes them that makes them feel real. Life is not predictable, it's random, beautiful, and analogue. We wanted those qualities to shine through in the visual effects.

One of the simplest things we used was glitter swizzled inside a beaker—that provided sparkles for the transporter and the food replicators. Another thing we used in almost every episode of *Star Trek* was a Mylar cheerleader's pom-pom I stumbled upon in a fabric store. I could see straight away that we could use its random energetic reflected light for all sorts of things.

We set up a mirror at a 45-degree angle. I shook the pom-pom above it while Gary Hutzel shot the reflections in the mirror. Because the movement was so frenetic, it looked like pure energy. Different filters allowed some glints of light stand out more. We used the pom-pom for a variety of energy patterns. The force field protecting the *Enterprise* and Deep Space 9 was the pom-pom wrapped around a transparent virtual sphere. The pom-pom's sizzling quality made it useful for phaser hit points on spaceships, combined with an animated phaser beam. In the final episode of *The Next Generation*'s Season 1, we used a blurred single frame of the pom-pom composited into a star field as a nebula.

For a small energy creature I attached a smaller pom-pom to a

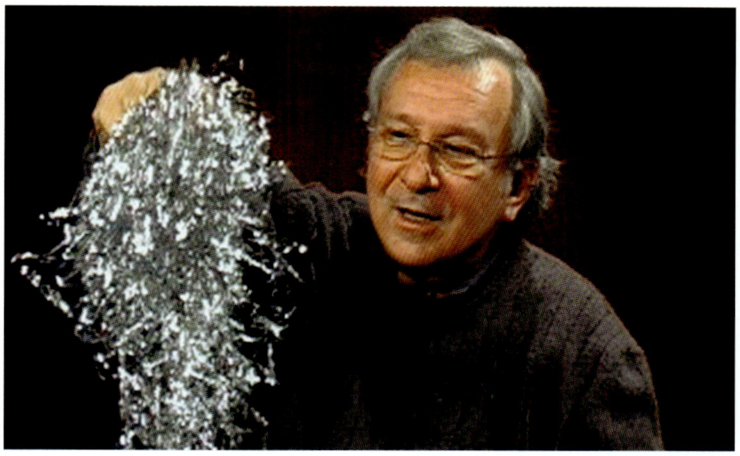

ABOVE: Dan showing pom pom used as *Enterprise* and DS9 force fields, phaser hits, and other elements.

RIGHT: Liquid nitrogen and CO^2 vapors make all sorts of interesting and unexpected kinetic patterns.

BELOW: Ron is pleased with our vat of liquid nitrogen on the stage at Image G.

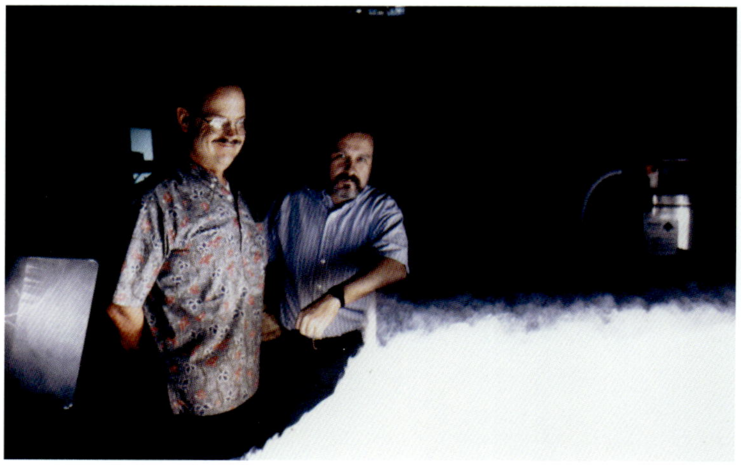

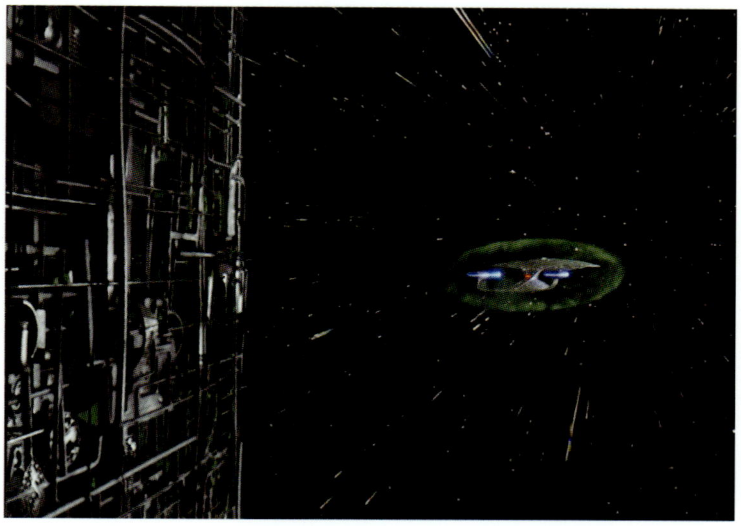

ABOVE: The *Enterprise*'s protective force field was made by wrapping the sparkles from a Mylar cheerleader's pom-pom around a virtual lozenge shape and tracked with the ship.

long rod covered with black velvet. I dressed in black, stood in front of a black curtain and, using sword fighting motions, waved it around while watching a monitor so I could match the live-action scenes. In compositing we took the luma-keyed elements, threw them out of focus, and printed them in lightly for a background glow. Then we layered it in again in sharp focus with a hotter exposure as a hot core to make a very serviceable small energy creature.

I was always looking for things that had interesting energy patterns, or things that would take on a completely different existence if scaled up or down or put in a different context. Creating visual effects changes the way you see the world. You're always thinking, "What could I use that for and what else could it be?"

Water is a great source of elements. A random wave pattern never repeats itself, so it doesn't look like you're running a computer procedural that cycles. If you put high-contrast water highlights on a non-level plane, or in a different context, it doesn't look like liquid, it looks like energy. When someone was locked in

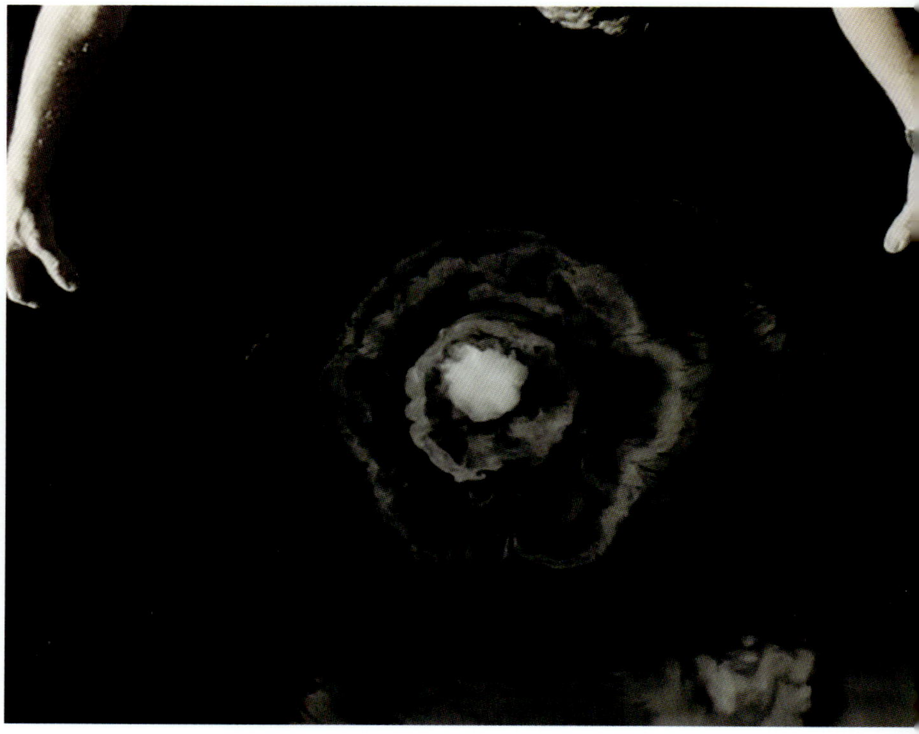

LEFT: Element for bottom layer of solar surface made from dry oatmeal on a light table, made to 'sizzle' by vibrations from an electric motor and colorized in compositing.

the *Enterprise* brig, a sparkling force field would flash across the doorway. That was created using water in a shallow black plastic tub. While we were shooting it, Gary Hutzel touched the tub with a little electric motor. Its vibrations generated micro ripples that appeared as highly kinetic white dots over a black background. We could colorize the ripples, add glows, and fit them into the doorway on set as a force field sealing the portal.

One time I was visiting a hotel in Palm Springs that had a pool that was semi-indoors. The way the light hit the surface of the water made it look like it was either black or white. I had my video camera with me, balanced it on the edge of the balcony, and photographed the water at an angle. We used that for the holographic Doctor's materialization on *Voyager*. We split the video right down the middle and flopped one side horizontally to get a symmetrical mirror image to line up with the center of the Doctor's body. We created a shimmer in the air by displacing the background within its kinetic pattern. Then we printed the Doctor out of focus. His feet came into focus first. We would start mixing him through the high-contrast water ripples so he looked as if he was forming in the air. He would come into focus feet first as the water element dissipated and he became more solid.

Energy patterns are everywhere if you look for them. Once, we filmed liquid detergent in a wire coat hanger. We just dipped the hanger in a bucket of soap, like kids blowing bubbles, producing a sheet of beautiful iridescent patterns. We used that element for energy fields, auroras, and lighting effects.

For one episode we needed to create the surface of a sun. I looked at astronomy books, and I noticed that that there were little cells on the solar surface, with darker spaces between them and vapors that rose up. It occurred to me that the best way to recreate that was to sprinkle dry oatmeal on a light table. The oatmeal was just the

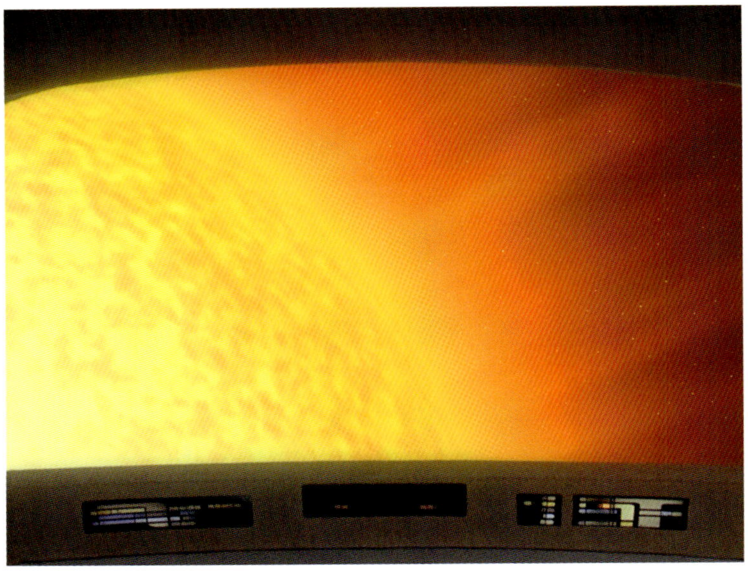

LEFT: On the main viewer—composite sun with elements including dry oatmeal, liquid nitrogen, and bounced lasers wrapped onto a virtual sphere.

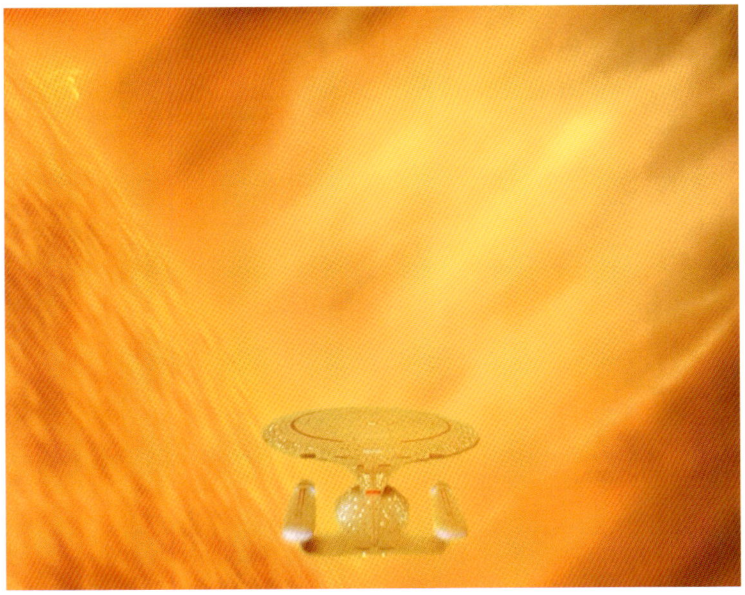

ABOVE: Motion-control *Enterprise*-D model enters an orbit dangerously close to a star.

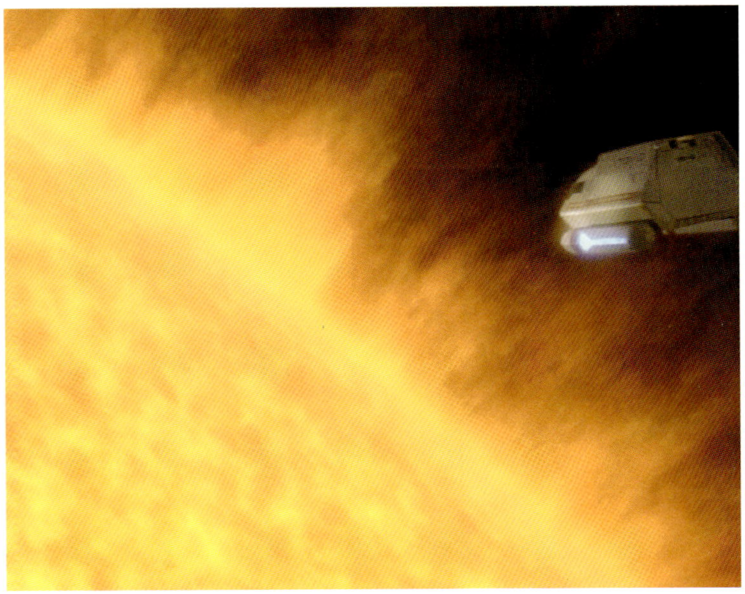

ABOVE: *Enterprise* Type 6 shuttle enters close solar orbit.

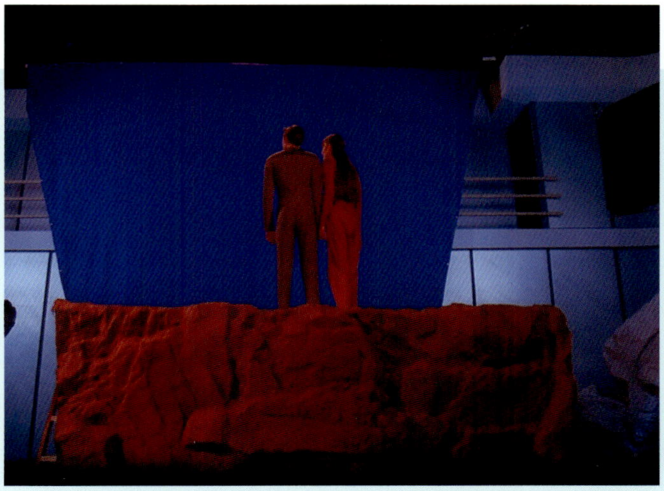

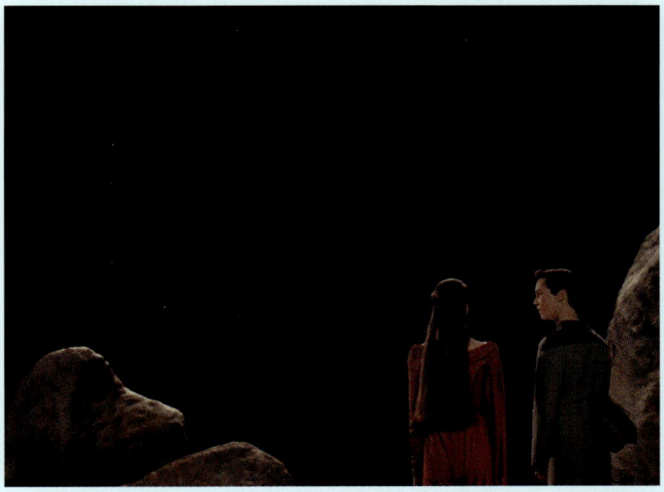

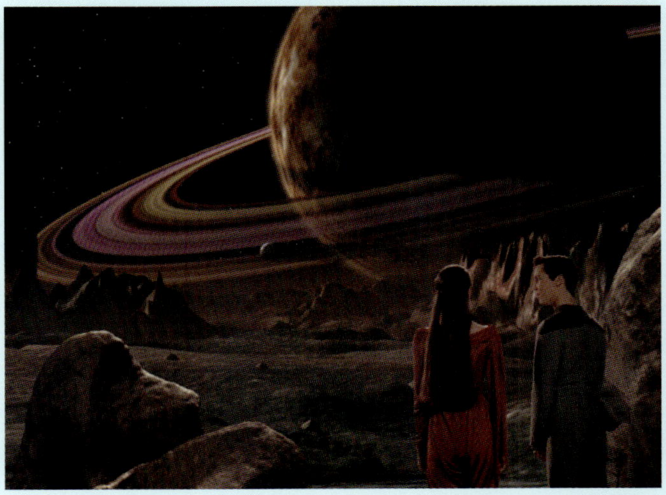

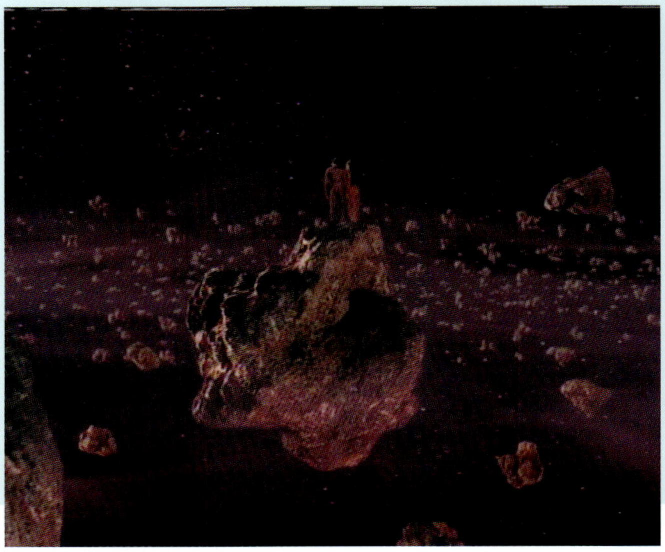

INSIDE STORY

ASTEROID FIELD

We had to make an asteroid field for *TNG*'s 'The Dauphin.' There's a romantic scene where Wesley takes an alien princess into the holodeck to experience drifting on an asteroid. We used tiny little rocks. I remember buying them in a building supply place. There was an area where they had lava rocks in a big bin. Because they had such crusty surfaces, they looked like they might have been bombarded by particles when they'd been drifting through space for eons. I was very careful selecting individual rocks, because I wanted to make sure there were no flat edges or clean breaks. One of the workers came up to me and said, "Hey man, I never seen anybody so particular about rocks like you!"

I wanted to use smaller rocks for the background. It was easier to take photographs and stick them on cardboard; that way you could get the mattes, because it would have taken too long to shoot every one of those rocks without a matte. So I pasted up the asteroids on a piece of black card, and then I traced them with cartoon paint on clear acetate. That gave me the matte for the asteroids. We did the same camera move on both elements so they would register. I learned that trick on *Buck Rogers* from David Stipes, where we had giant icebergs floating in space. We had no time to build models, so we just took photographs of icebergs and put them on glass and moved them with an electric motor.

THIS PAGE: These pictures show how we layered images up to create the final shot. I still have the lava rock they are standing on in my garden.

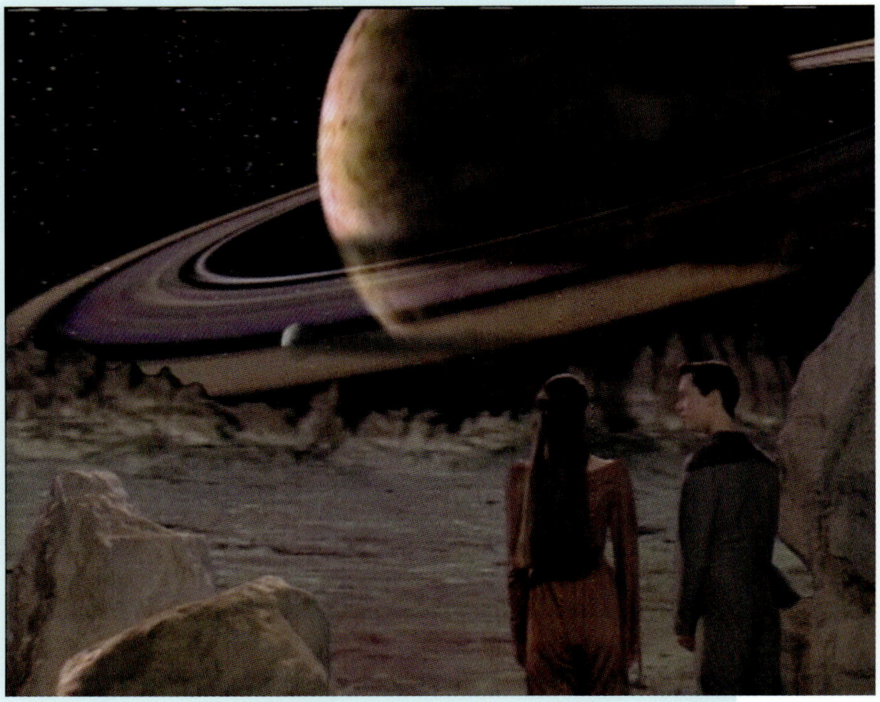

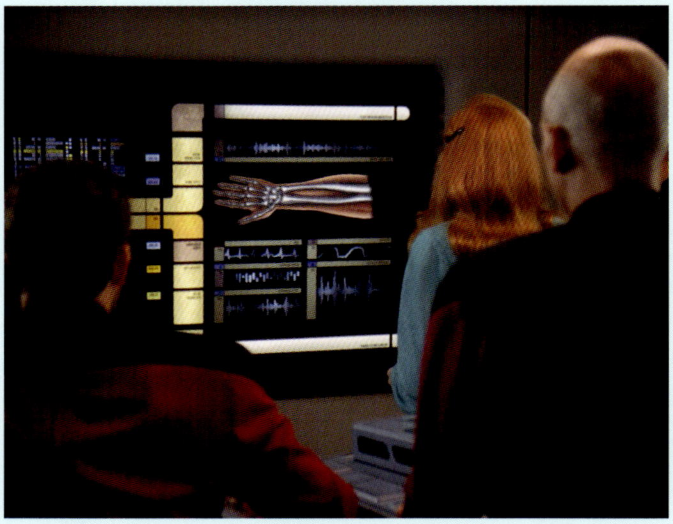

ABOVE: It only appears on screen for a second or two, but the graphic showing Riker's arm involved hours of work and adding color to the original black and white image.

INSIDE STORY

RIKER'S ARM

Not all of our elements were low-tech. We had an episode where they were scanning Riker's arm layer by layer in the medical facility. Of course, we didn't have a means of doing that easily, as CG hadn't yet come along. We would have had to build several different models of Jonathan's arm and combine them all, which would have been very time-consuming and therefore expensive. A distinguished medical researcher at a prominent university did us a favor. He took a cadaver's arm and shaved it layer by layer using a microtome with the help of one of his grad students, who took photographs for us. So when you see that scan in the show, you are seeing layer upon layer within a real arm, even though it isn't Jonathan's.

INSIDE STORY

SALT FLARE

There was a shot in *TNG* where the *Enterprise* was flying by a sun. We wanted solar ejecta to hit the shields around the *Enterprise*, so I came up with the idea of mounting a black bowling ball on a stand, and dropping a few pounds of salt on it—straight down. Because the salt physically went around the spherical ball, it looked like the solar ejecta was going around the invisible force field that protects the *Enterprise*.

When we composited the footage of the salt, we rotated it so it appeared to be coming from the lower corner of frame, and squeezed it from top to bottom so that the spherical bowling ball looked more like the M&M-shaped force field bubble that surrounded the *Enterprise*. We then layered the salt over the pom-pom wrapped around the virtual force field 3D shape.

Baking soda thrown against a black background and photographed at very high speed is another great element for creating solar plumes. The high frame rate slows down time, and makes the baking soda toss, which only lasts a fraction of a second in real time, look like a huge astronomical event.

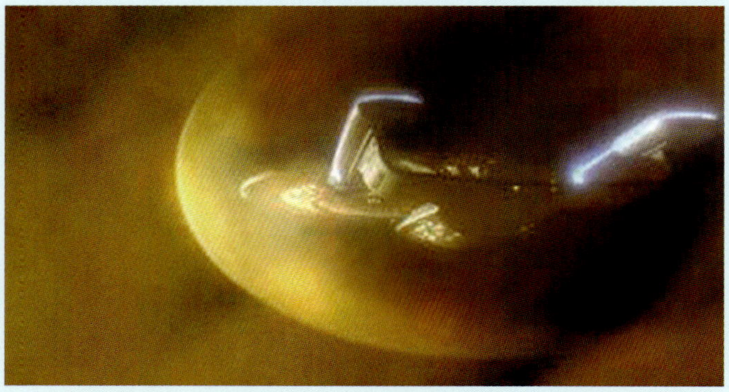

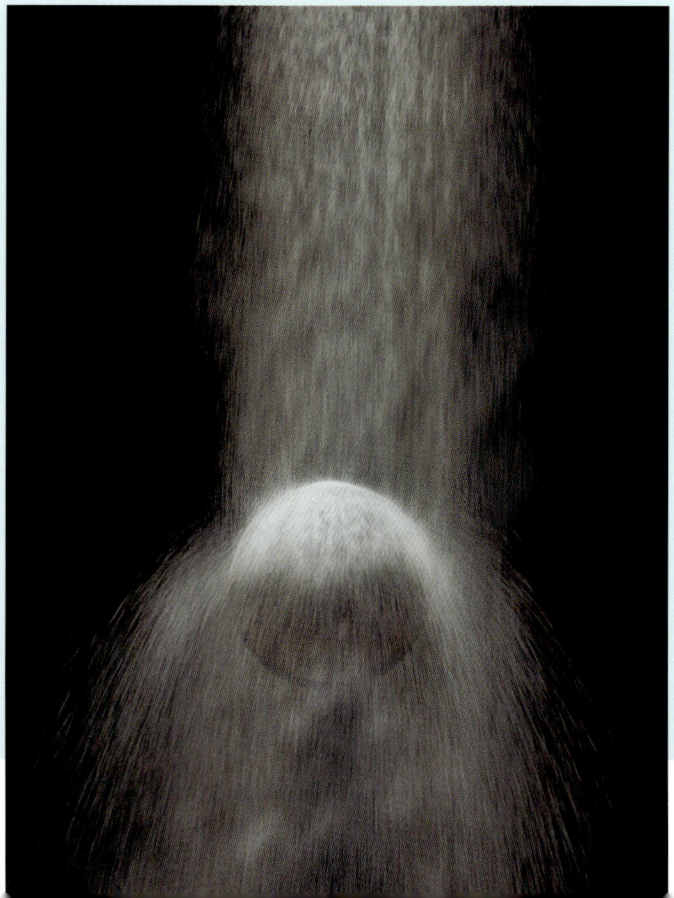

ABOVE RIGHT: Once we had the film, we took it into the edit bay where we rotated the image about 70° clockwise, squeezed it north-south into an oval to match the force field around the ship, and colored it up to match the sun.

RIGHT: We created the impact of solar ejecta hitting the force field by pouring salt over a bowling ball and shooting at a high frame rate to slow it down.

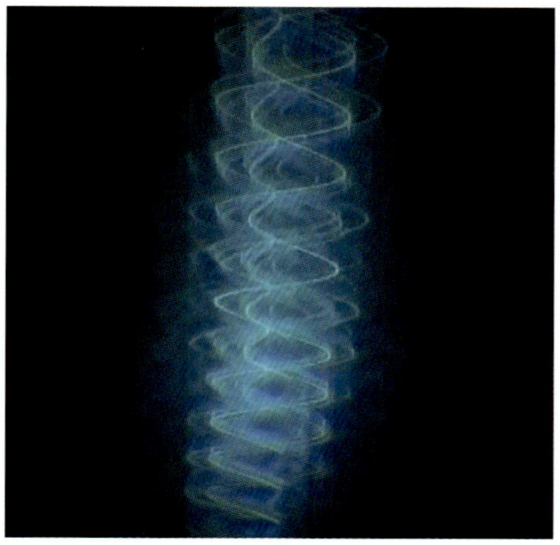

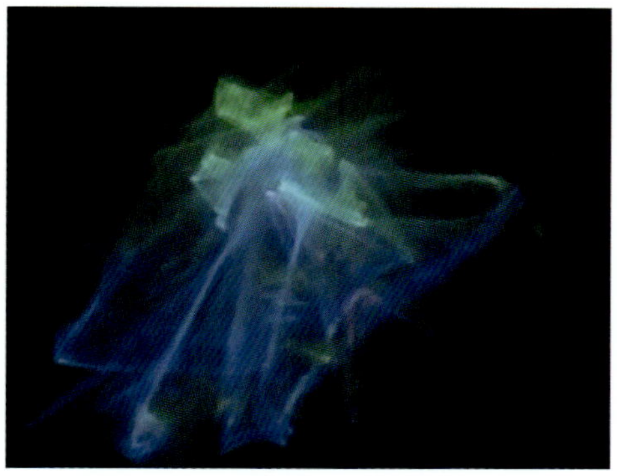

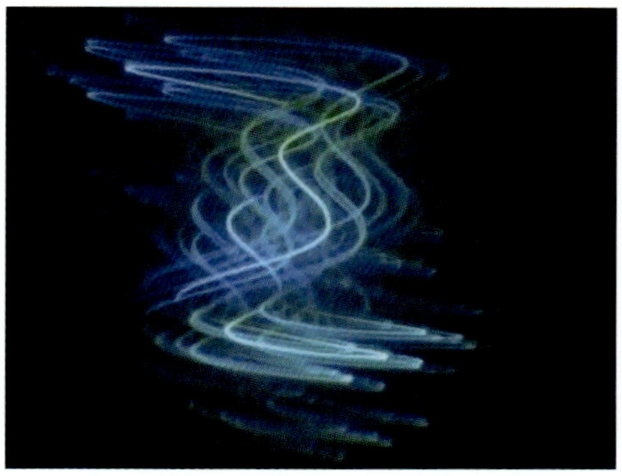

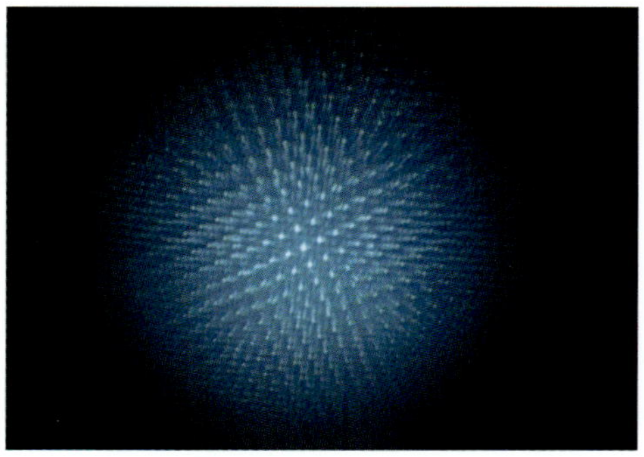

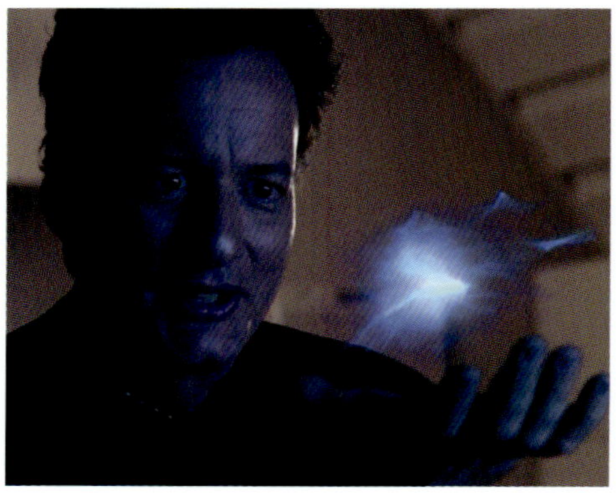

right scale. I spread it out evenly, and put an electric motor next to the light table to make it vibrate. That made the oatmeal look like the solar cells sizzling. We added a little liquid nitrogen vapor in compositing for heat, then digitally wrapped all of it around a virtual sphere, creating a reasonable facsimile of a roiling sun. We made solar flare ejecta by photographing tossed baking soda at 360 frames per second.

Sometimes, unexpected opportunities to capture elements would come up. One day I met a guy who had a super industrial light show laser system. It had a variety of laser generators with mounts for putting prisms and light-diffracting materials in front of the laser projector. We went to his garage for a day; I brought an old Mitchell rackover camera with me. We put a big piece of white matte board on the wall, and started shooting. We fired lasers through all the different prisms he had, but also bounced them off—or through—different objects. It didn't have to be high-tech, sometimes it was just a plastic bag, sometimes a lens, or a bicycle reflector. I crumpled aluminum foil, scrunched a beer can, and tried whatever we could think of, just throwing it in front of the laser and shooting 20 seconds of what was happening on the white cardboard screen.

When you shoot potential elements like that you don't necessarily know what you are going to use them for. There's a lot of experimentation—we might shoot 20 takes and only use one—but it adds to our library to fall back on. As new VFX challenges come up, you think back; "Oh, we can use that for this."

We wound up using various lasers filmed that afternoon many times as force fields, static on monitors, or alien transporters. The tractor beams used by the Borg and *Enterprise*-D were projections of a laser bounced off a beer can and through a melted piece of plastic. If you took the

LEFT: We didn't use all of the shots of bounced lasers, but many were invaluable for everything from force fields and tractor beams to life forms.

BELOW: One of the things those lasers were used for was the kinetic Borg tractor beam that grabs the *Enterprise* in 'Q Who?'

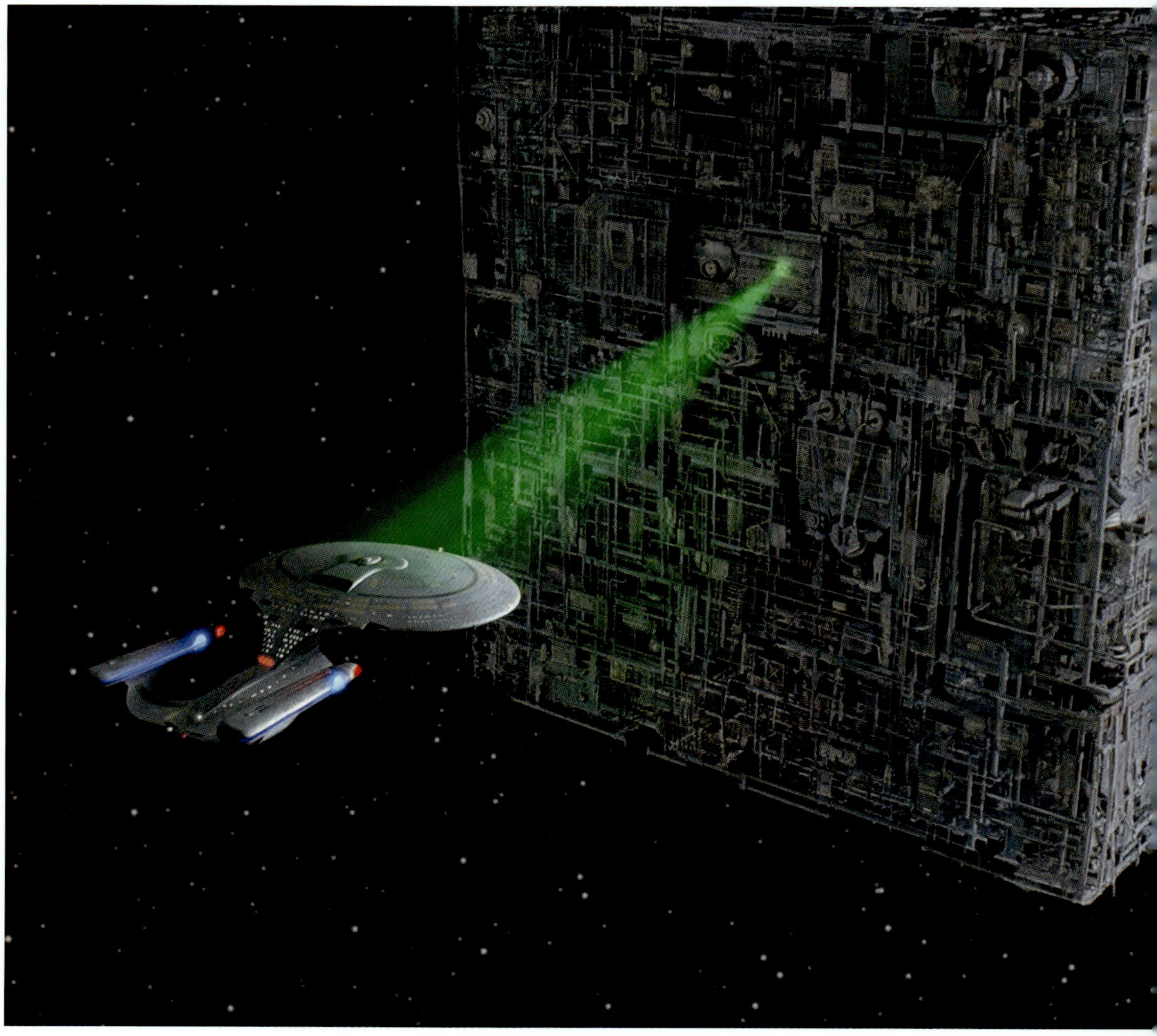

INSIDE STORY

THE PLANET CLEANER

We won our first visual-effects Emmy for 'A Matter of Time.' The key sequence involved sucking the poisoned atmosphere from the surface of a planet, and ejecting it into space. We created the necessary visuals using liquid nitrogen elements that we filmed on the stage at Image G working with Eric Nash and Dennis Hoerter.

I wanted to make it look as if the atmosphere was swirling around, and then being sucked up in a plume and dispersed into space by the *Enterprise*. Ron Moore and I set up a vat of liquid nitrogen vapors lined with black velvet, and started to look for ways of making it move. We discovered that if we swatted the pool of nitrogen vapors with cardboard, or shot a quick blast of air from a compressor into it, the heavier-than-air vapor would billow out, and then fall back on itself in waves that would look like atmospheric tsunamis. We could also force the nitrogen clouds up through a hole in black matte board to create concentric circles radiating outward. If we used a vacuum cleaner to suck the vapors up out of the vat, it created a spectacular plume before being drawn back by the forces of gravity. We experimented with a range of techniques, and selected the elements we thought would work best.

We transferred the film to video at Composite Image Systems in Hollywood with Don Lee. In the edit bay at The Post Group, working with Peter Sternlicht, we 'wrapped' the images shot at Image G around a virtual sphere to literally build the planet in layers from the ground up, starting with the surface. We played the radiating circles of vapor coming out of the hole in black cardboard in reverse to make it look as if they were drawn toward the center rather than expanding outward. Appropriately, the shot with the vacuum cleaner was used for the shot when the *Enterprise* sucked the cloudy toxic atmosphere away from the planet. Liquid nitrogen vapor is white, so I airbrushed some fields of random subtle colors to mix with the liquid nitrogen to give it a natural iridescence.

This is a sequence that really sticks in my memory. It made creative use of materials and techniques, and it was great fun to experiment and discover unique solutions to the challenges presented by the script. We were proud to be recognized by the Academy of Television Arts & Sciences with our first Primetime Emmy. One thing about the Emmys is they can only list a few names, but in reality the award was for all the visual-effects artists who contributed to 'A Matter of Time.'

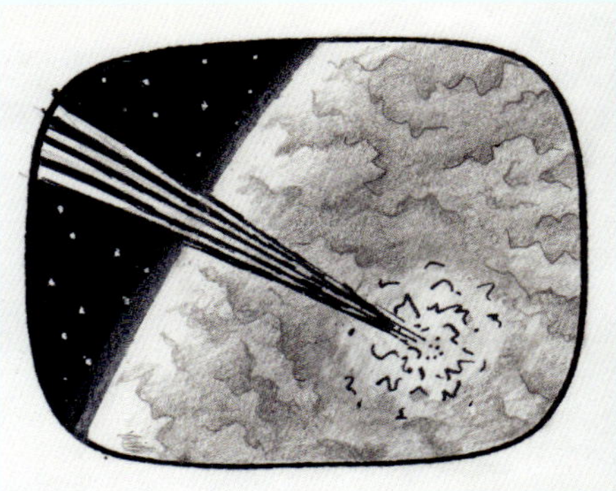
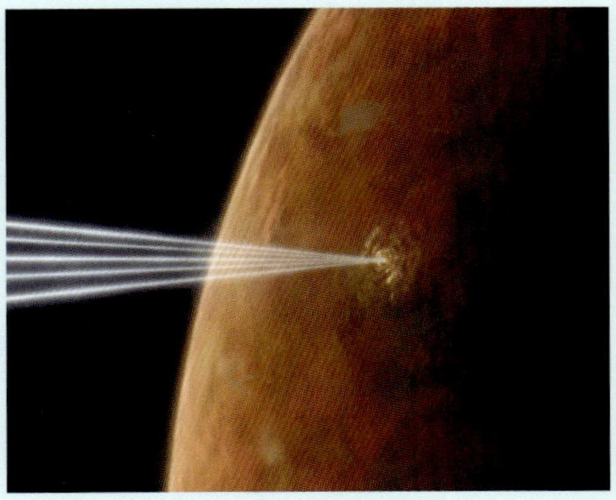
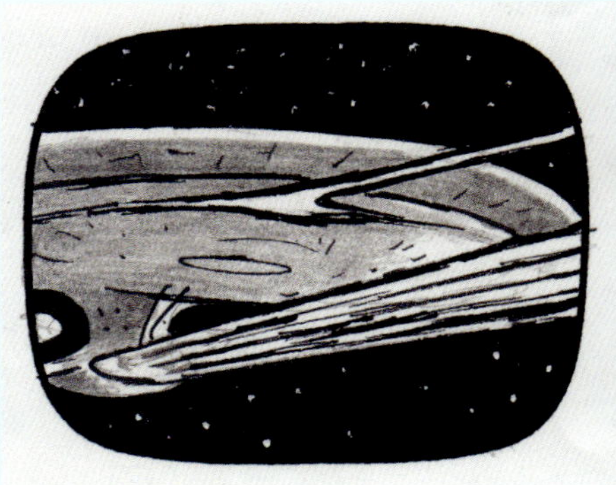
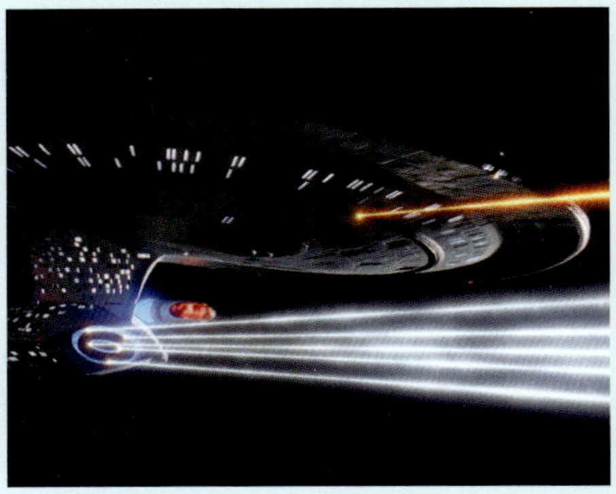
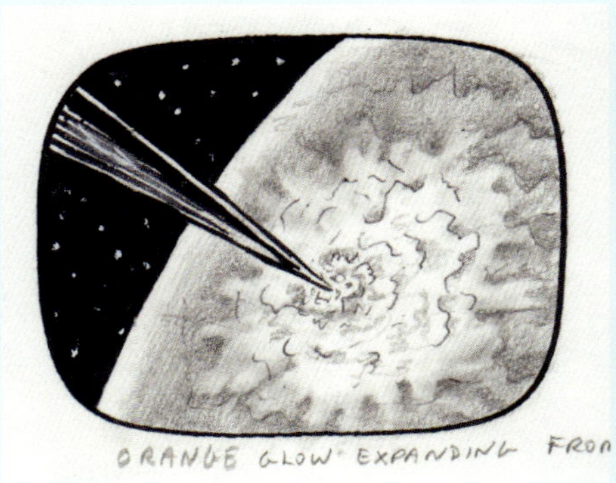

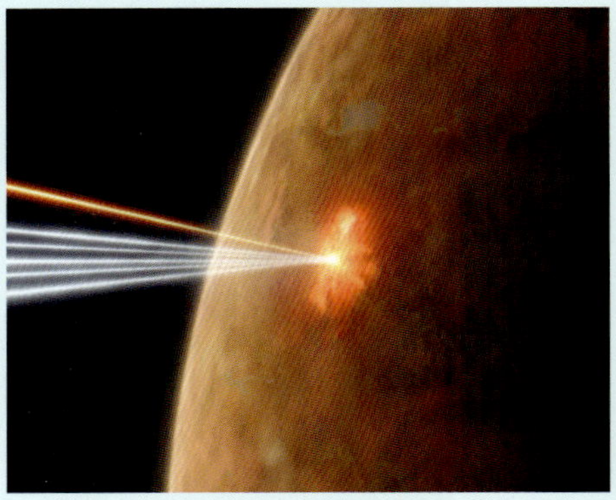
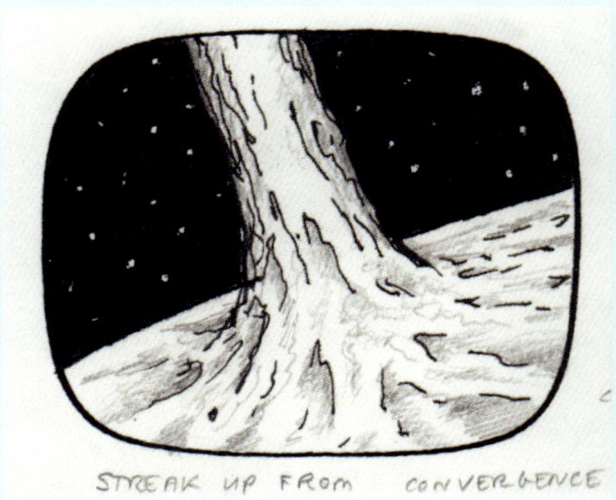

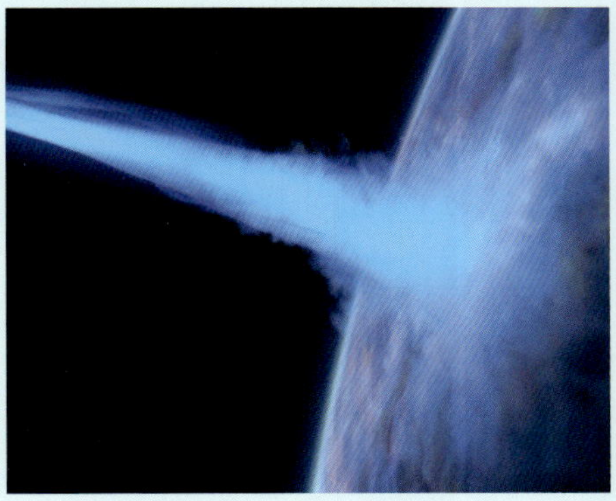

ABOVE: Storyboards help conceptualize a flow of images that will tell the story. When you create the final shots, the real ties of angle, continuity, and other factors inevitably result in changes.

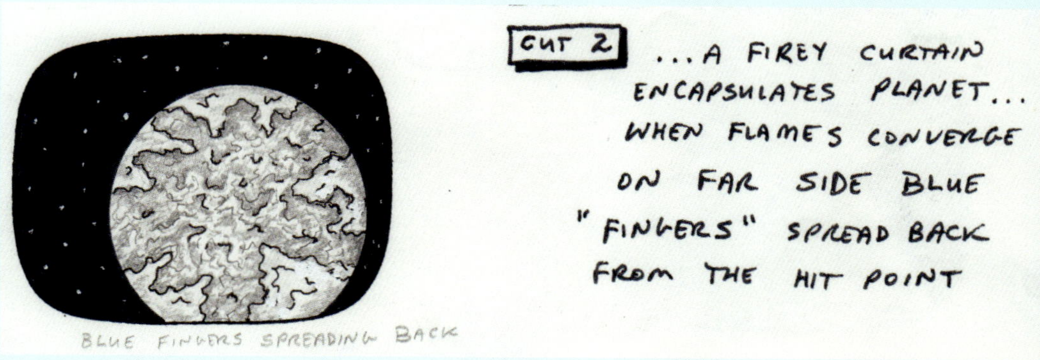

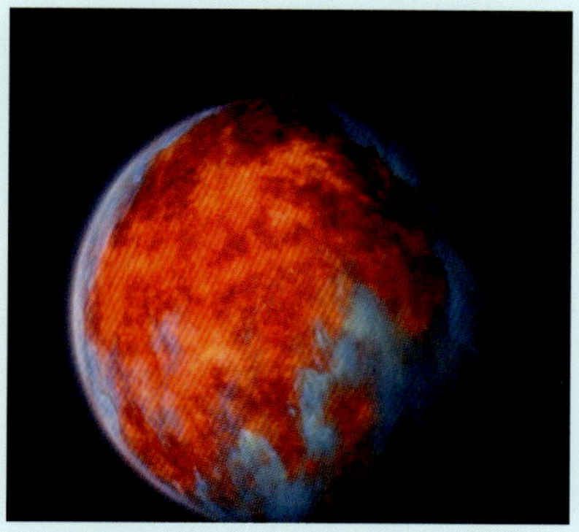

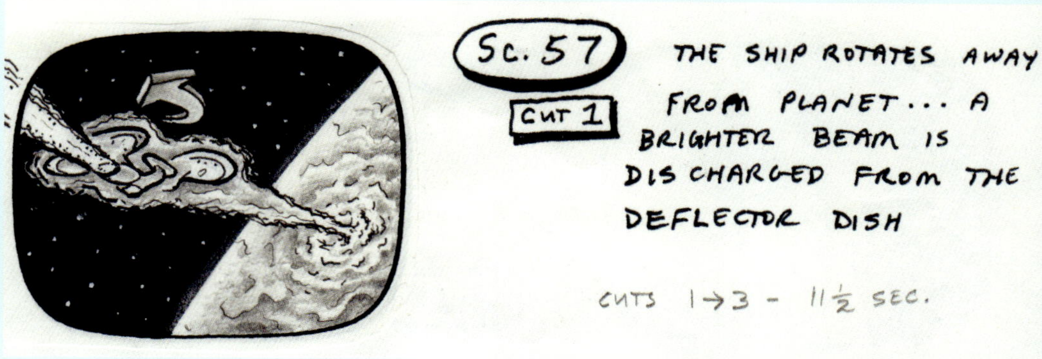

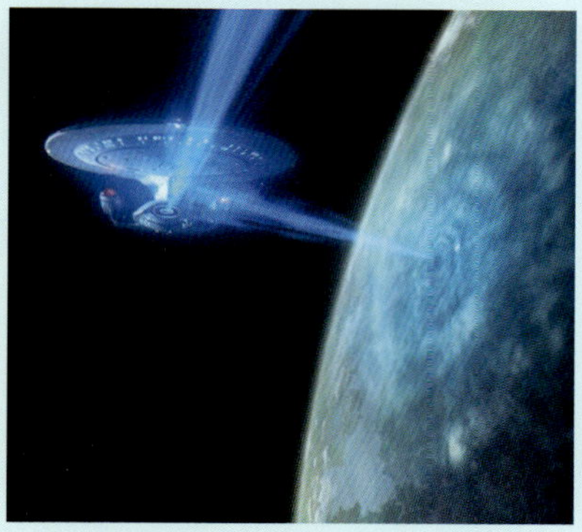

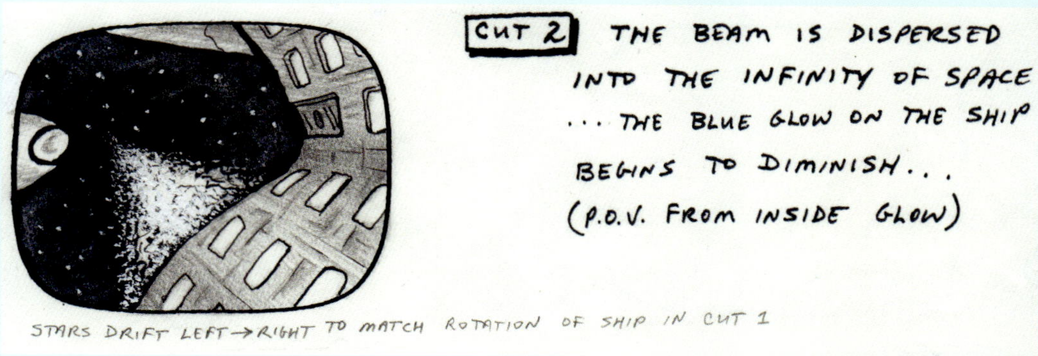

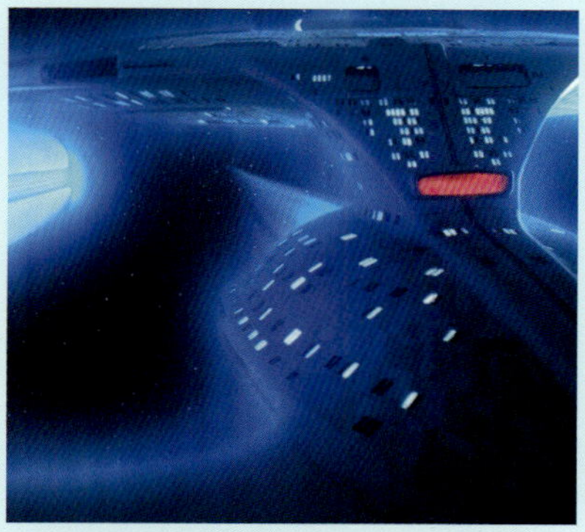

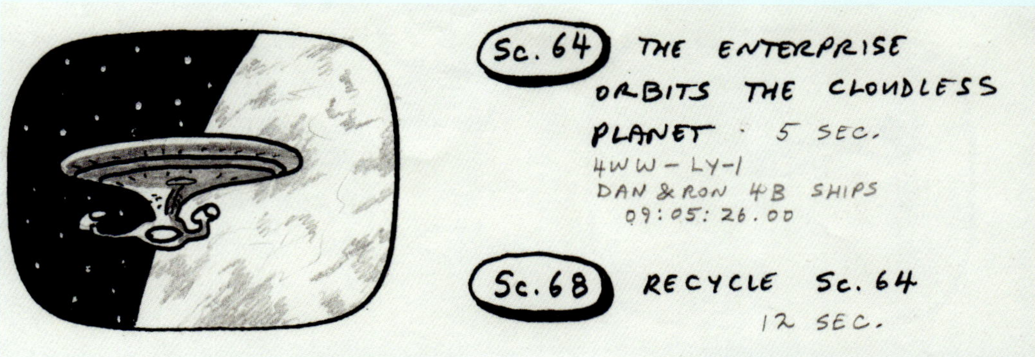

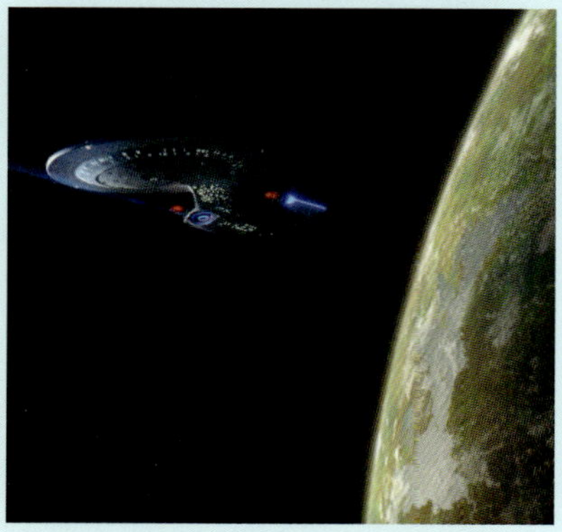

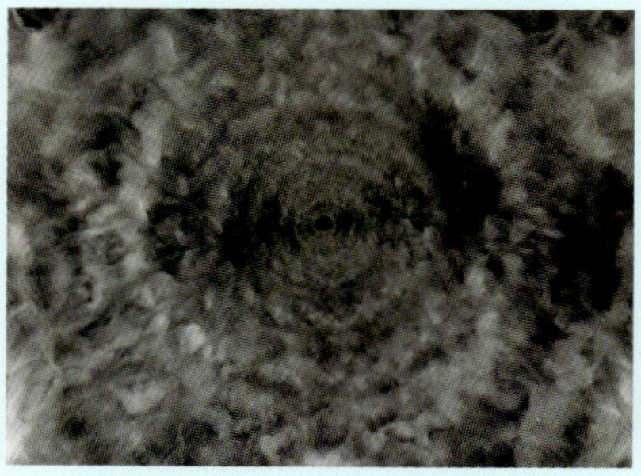

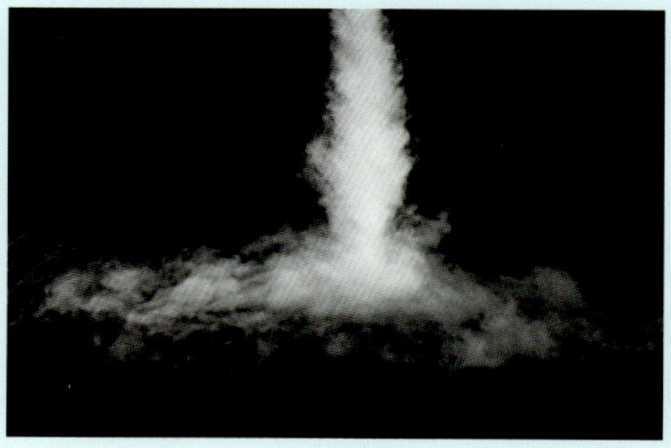

THIS PAGE: The challenge with this episode was getting the liquid nitrogen elements to perform correctly to tell the story and work convincingly with the mo-co *Enterprise*. Our peers at the Academy of Television Arts & Sciences recognized this episode with a Primetime Emmy.

INSIDE STORY

DOG DOO PLANET

One *TNG* episode called for a "brown mottled mining planet." In the edit bay at the time we were using a Sony System G, by today's standards a primitive device, that enabled wrapping a 2D image around a virtual sphere. We had a library of images we could use as planet surfaces. These included satellite images from NASA, macro shots of rocks in my garden, and paintings from the art department or by me. We were reviewing images already 'wrapped' looking for an ideal texture. None of them had the right look. A colleague, who shall remain anonymous, went into the machine room and threaded up a piece of negative he had with him. Seeing it as a planet on our monitor it was brown, had a mottled texture, and I realized if we added a weather system with moving clouds above the surface it would serve our purpose. I asked my colleague where he had gotten the image. He was reluctant to say, so I asked our VFX editor to unwrap the image to get a good look at it. I noticed little spikes such as one might get from pressing toothpaste and then pulling up one's hand, and perceived what appeared to be undigested kernels of corn. The final evidence was the impression of a Nike logo from the sole of a sneaker. My colleague confessed that a few days earlier he was getting out of his car and planted his foot in a substance that a day earlier had been a meal for a canine. In an attempt to turn a bad situation into good, my colleague grabbed a still camera that happened to have a macro lens and took some extreme close-ups of the organic smear for possible future use.

Recognizing that visual effects is the art of creating illusion by making one thing look like another, I figured it was no different than using salt dumped on a bowling ball for solar ejecta. The original source material was irrelevant; what it finally looked like was the issue. Overlaying a weather system on the planet made it impossible for audiences to determine where the texture came from, so we used it. It was used in seven other episodes as either a planet or moon, and was dubbed "Fecus Canis." At the end of the session my droll colleague remarked, "Can't say we didn't do s#*t today."

With the pressures of work I thought no more about it until some time later my mother called and said, "That wasn't very nice." I had no idea what she was talking about, and someone came to her door and she had to go before she could explain. Later, we were having a production meeting and began to discuss a rift in the space-time continuum that the script called for. The director asked how we were going to accomplish the effect. I started to think of a way to do it when executive producer Rick Berman interrupted saying, "Don't tell us... don't tell anyone!" Everyone around the table had a good laugh, but it was clear I had no idea why the hilarity. Without a word, Rick slid a copy of *TV Guide* (a national magazine with articles and schedule listings) over to me. I opened it to the page with a bookmark, and was shocked to see a photo of myself attached to an article featuring the story of Fecus Canis. Someone had leaked the story to one of the magazine's writers.

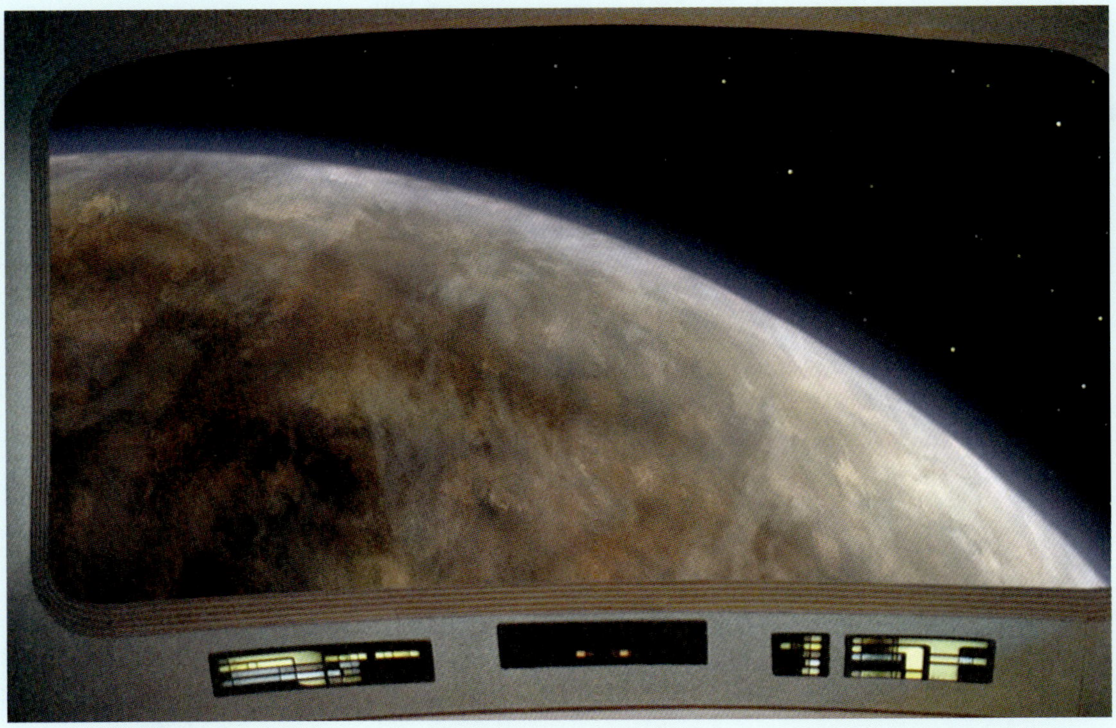

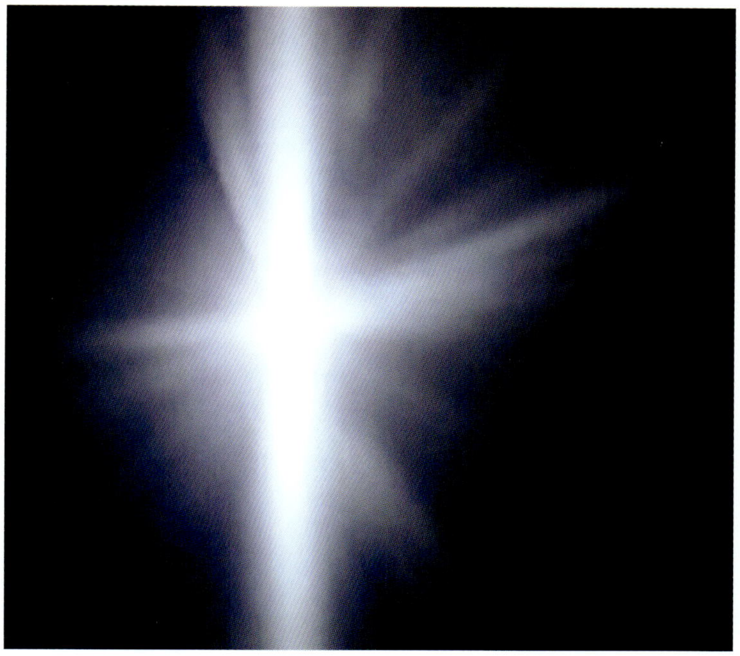

ABOVE: The 'flash to warp' effect was made by shooting a light bulb through a piece of acetate that had been scratched with steel wool to diffract light into rays. We just ramped the light up and down with a dimmer.

laser patterns and blurred them so they were out of focus, they made good nebulae. Another laser pattern served as the Calamarain energy creature for the episode 'Deja Q.' Years later, on *Enterprise*, we were still using the laser elements for the temporal chamber, where characters had a cone of light fluxing around them.

Sometimes, solutions were quite simple. In the fifth season of *The Next Generation* there was an episode called 'Power Play' that featured what we affectionately call 'lightbulb entities.' They were little sentient globs of light that entered our characters and took control of them. We could have done that with animation, but it would have been complicated, taken a long time, and overwhelmed our budget. Instead, I asked the wardrobe department to make me a DayGlo green mitten. I put on a black sweat suit, stood in front of a black drape, and wiggled my fingers inside the green mitten, creating undulating shapes that I could make go wherever I wanted to. We took the 'mitten puppets' into the edit bay, and played around with them until they looked like glowing entities.

Other times, solutions would be as simple as filming a light through something that distorted it. For example, when the *Enterprise* goes to warp there is a star flash when the ship attains warp speed. That was made by taking a piece of clear acetate and rub it in different directions with steel wool to get random organic flares. We photographed a lightbulb through it, turning it up and down quickly with a hardware store dimmer. The acetate would function like a star filter, but one that would spread the light out in directions we chose rather than in a perfect geometric pattern. The same technique was used for Q flashes whenever John De Lancie's character appeared and disappeared.

Another element we used often was liquid nitrogen. Its vapors are heavier than air. There were various ways we could make that move with a reasonable modicum of control. We used it to create cloud patterns, energy patterns, and even the illusion of fire.

At Image G we set up a four-foot-square, six-inch-deep vat lined with black velvet so we had a background that would contrast with the white liquid nitrogen vapors and could be separated in the edit bay with a luminance key. The heavier-than-air vapor stayed in the vat. If somebody tapped the side of the vat, the vapors would form waves. When I swatted it with a piece of cardboard, the tuft of air made the liquid nitrogen spread out and then collapse in on itself in an interesting cloudy wave. We won an Emmy using that for an episode where the *Enterprise* cleaned the atmosphere of a planet. Years later, Ron and I reused it on Michael Jackson's 'Black or White' video; there's a scene where Michael is on a treadmill singing in front of a blue screen and pushes his arms in a swimming motion to reveal new realities. You never see the actual liquid nitrogen element, as it is used as an organic wiping edge to reveal a new background.

There were other ways to move liquid nitrogen. If it bubbled up through a hole in a flat plane, waves would radiate out. Using a vacuum cleaner created interesting vortex tendrils by sucking the vapor up. We did one episode where we had a giant 'space string' that was a cleft into another dimension. For that we covered two large parallel cardboard tubes with black velvet, and put lights and

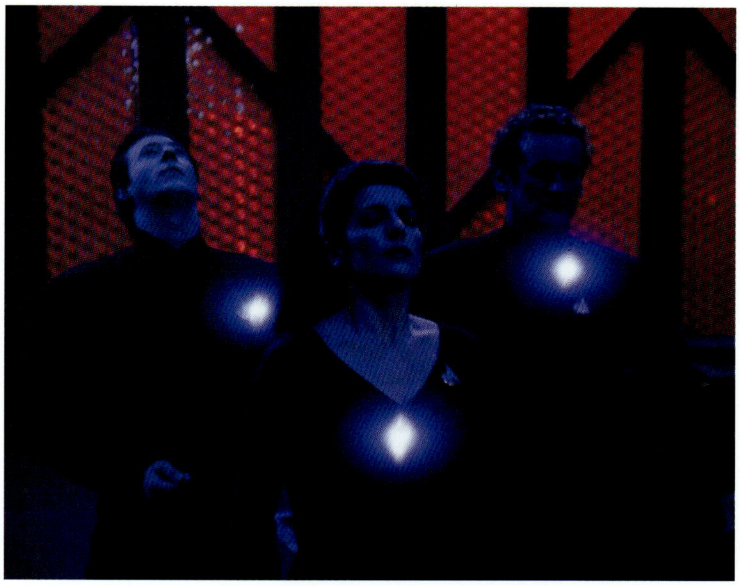

ABOVE: These energy entities were actually day-glo green mittens. I dressed in black in front of a black drape, and animated the lights by moving my arms and wiggling my fingers.

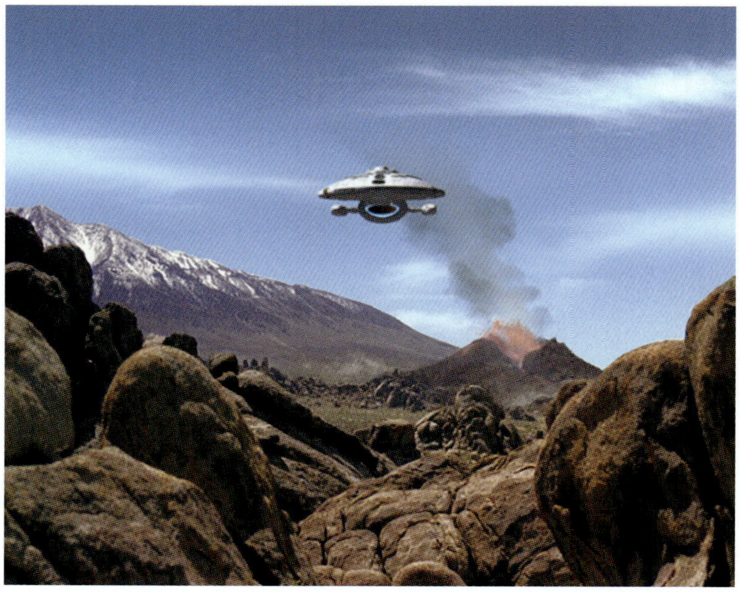

ABOVE: The smoke from the volcano was made by liquid nitrogen vapors. The lava was puffs of baking soda tossed up through a hole in a table, shot at a high frame rate to stretch time.

INSIDE STORY

USING GRAVITY

In the *TNG* episode 'Disaster,' Geordi and Dr Crusher are trapped in the shuttlebay, which is slowly being poisoned by radiation from a plasma fire. To make matters worse, there are containers of unstable fuel that will explode if the fire reaches them. The plan they come up with is to open the shuttlebay door so the containers fly off into space and the fire will go out because it is deprived of oxygen.

Greg Jein built some small models of cargo bay containers, and a model of the cargo bay floor. We set up a platform with a green screen below. Then we turned the model of the floor through 90 degrees so it was a vertical plane rather than horizontal. We fixed the model containers to it with little pins. We put the camera above it pointed straight down, so it looked as if the floor was horizontal. When we pulled the pins out, gravity took over and the containers fell onto the green screen. Then we just combined them with the real cargo bay door when compositing.

I wanted to show Geordi and Dr Crusher being sucked out into space too. Again, the idea was to use gravity and the position of the camera to make it look as if LeVar and Gates were pulled sideways while they were actually hanging vertically. My plan was to film them hanging from a ladder against a blue screen. The perspective of the camera above them would create the illusion that they were being pulled off the ground when we added them to the footage of the set. I can't remember why we didn't do it, I suspect we just ran out of time.

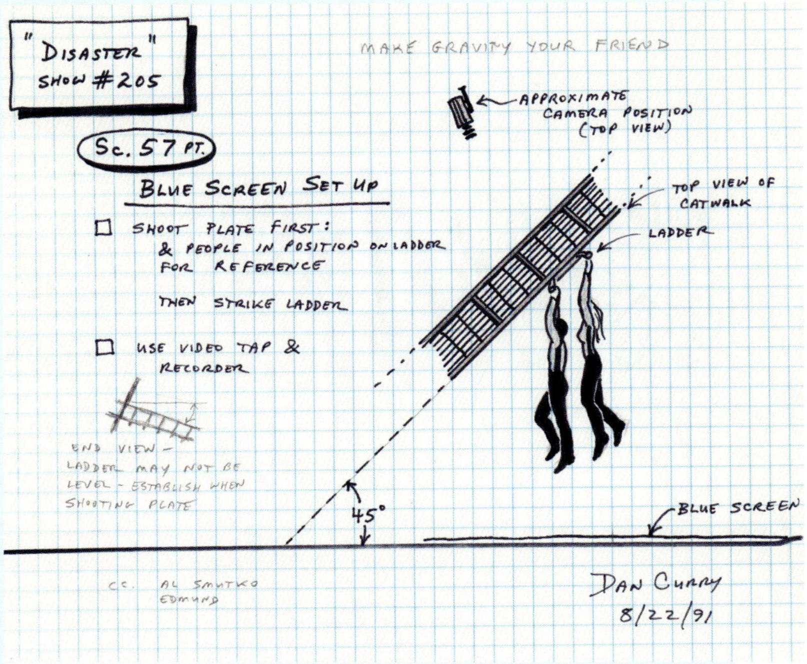

ABOVE: I had the idea to film the actors hanging from a ladder. By aiming the camera down at them, we could make it look as if the bodies were being pulled out the cargo bay door.

LEFT: Storyboards explained how the shot would look, and what we'd need to film to achieve the illusion.

BELOW: A miniature floor was set up vertically. When pins holding Greg Jein's miniature containers were pulled, the barrels dropped onto a green screen. In the final shot (bottom) it appears that the containers are flying up off a horizontal floor.

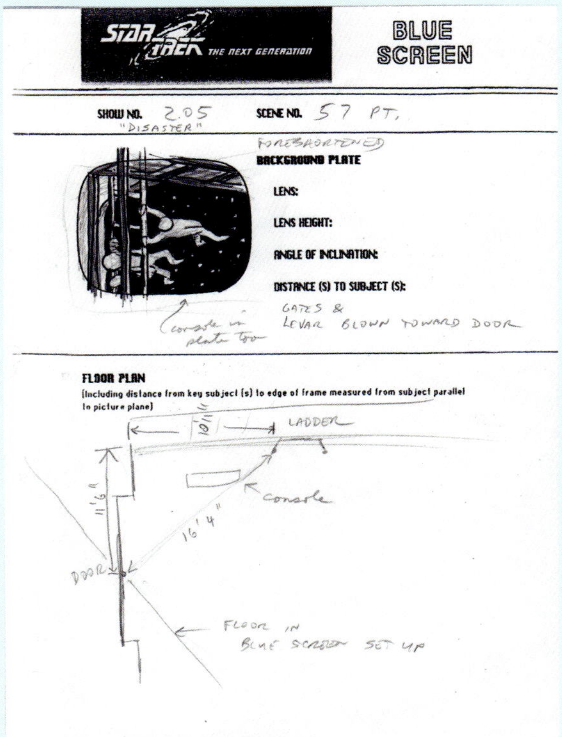

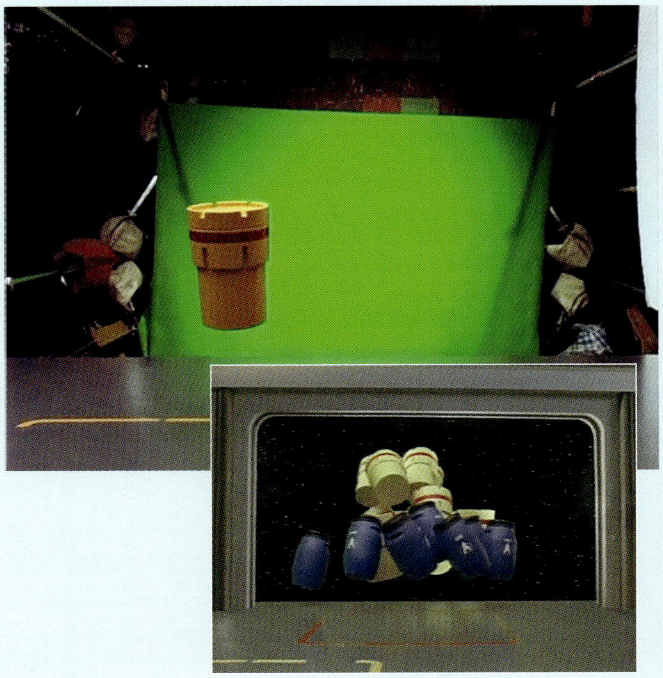

vacuum cleaners underneath. The light made it look like it was lit from behind, and the vacuum cleaners made the vapor churn and boil as it was sucked into the narrow space between the tubes. Printed in reverse, it gave us a convincing sense of a trans-dimensional rift leaking energy into our universe from another region of the space-time continuum.

By experimenting, we discovered that liquid nitrogen was a substance we could use in a variety of ways. "This looks cool, we'll just shoot it and save it for when a use comes up." Liquid nitrogen was the best thing for making scale flames spew out of a model spacecraft. I cut a jagged hole in the side of a black cardboard box, pumped the vapors inside, then used a jet of air to make it stream out. Tinted orange in compositing, it looked like flames cascading out of a hole in the ship. We ended up using liquid nitrogen in *Voyager*'s 'Basics' for volcano fumes, and steam rising off hot lava.

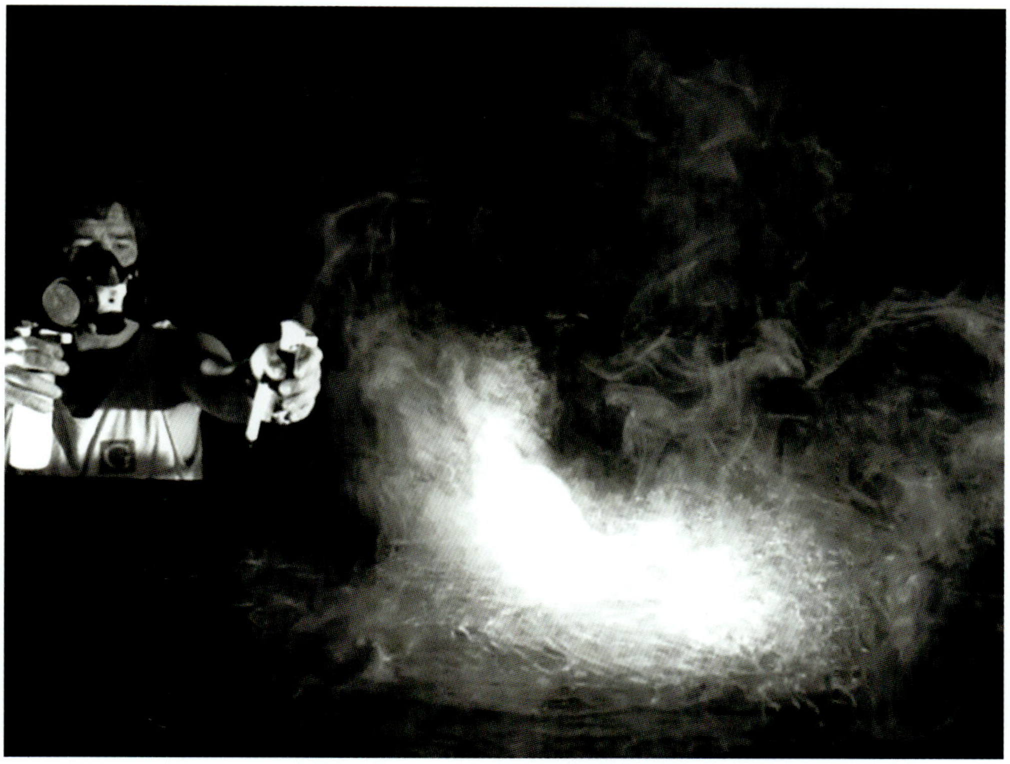

ABOVE: Denis Hoerter spraying two-part A-B smoke (now banned) to create a rift in the time/space continuum.

A *TNG* episode required seeing distant fires sweeping across the horizon. We built a big sloping table, covered with black velvet. We put a trough at the top, filled with liquid nitrogen. The heavier-than-air vapors flowed out of the trough and rolled down the slope of the giant table. We stood at the bottom and blew it back with air hoses. The turbidity of the air jets whipped the liquid nitrogen into flame-like patterns. Then we would key real flames shot separately into it to make it look like distant wildfires. Liquid nitrogen also served as vast nebulosity and other space phenomena.

There was another *TNG* episode where we needed plasma fire on the *Enterprise*. For that I took a glass baking tray, put hot water

INSIDE STORY

VULCAN TEAR

In an episode of *TNG*, Spock's father, Sarek, comes aboard the *Enterprise*. He's suffering from a disease that makes him emotional, which is horrifying for a Vulcan. We discover his affliction when, listening to a concert, to everyone's amazement, he starts to cry. For some reason, Marc Lenard, who played Sarek, just couldn't bring himself to lacrimate. The director didn't like the look of silicone tears, so we wound up doing the tear later as a visual effect.

The tear was just a little milk dribbled out of a straw onto the cover of a vinyl notebook. We used milk because it is opaque white and the notebook was black, which allowed us to pull a contrast matte, or luminance key. The surface of the notebook cover had a similar texture to skin, so it dribbled very naturally. We used the milk tear as a matte to diffract Sarek's cheek digitally. It's probably one of the most subtle and invisible effects we ever did.

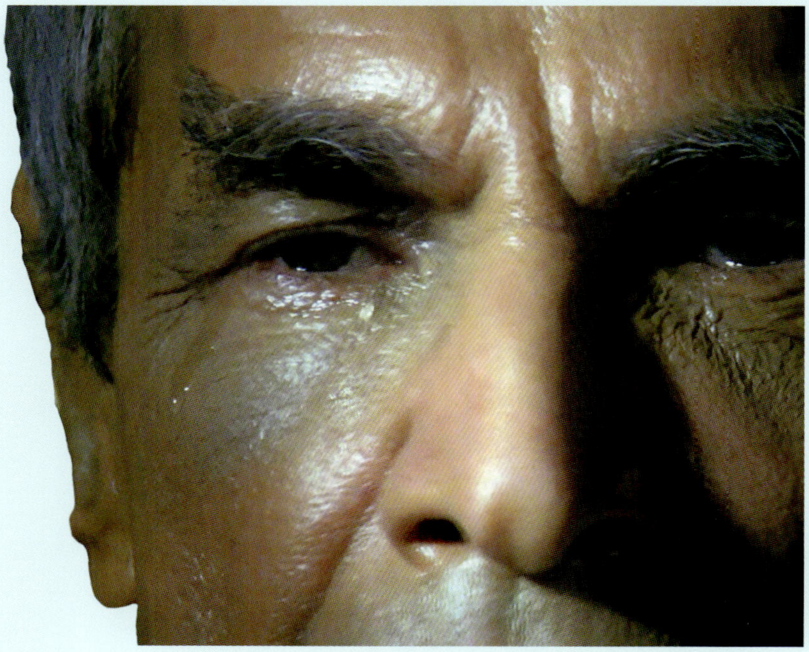

in it, and a light underneath it. Then I sprinkled tiny particles of dry ice into it. When they hit the water, it bubbled and churned. When we tinted that green in compositing, it looked like a weird, creepy energy.

Fire was something that turned up a lot. We didn't always fake it exactly, sometimes we'd use the real thing. In the *TNG* episode 'Interface,' Geordi thinks he's meeting his mother, but she is really a fire creature. Our special-effects supervisor Dick Brownfield and his crew cut rough human shapes out of flash paper (a type of paper embedded with chemicals so that it burns up instantly). We shot the burning flash paper against a black background. In compositing, we distorted the fiery images into the specific shapes needed for the scenes. We used those same fire elements again in the finale of *Deep Space Nine* when Kai Opaka gets incinerated by the Pah-wraiths.

Another material we used to create radiating fire from an energy blast was steel wool. If we wanted a hit from an alien weapon on the *Enterprise*, we would wrap heavy-gauge aluminum foil over the hull of the *Enterprise* model to protect it. Then we spread steel wool thinly over it. There's enough oil coating the steel wool that it burns. You apply fire where you want the beam to hit. The fire spreads out in waves from the ignition point. When it's composited with the footage of the model, there's a beautiful interaction of energy from the blast spreading across the *Enterprise* hull.

After a while, we had so many elements that we couldn't keep track of them. VFX associate David Takemura was the first to realize how much time was wasted in the edit bay looking for elements, so he came up with the idea of making a printed directory that he called 'The Elementary Yellow Pages,' which made it easy for us to find things. Even when CG came along we carried on using our library of elements because there's something about organic elements that you can't replicate in a computer, something beautiful and unexpected.

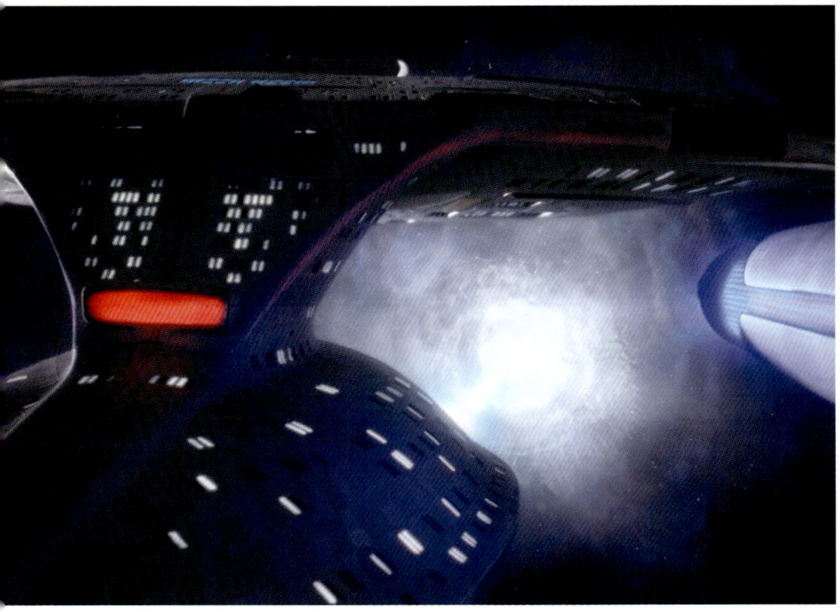

ABOVE: The *Enterprise* scans the anomaly (a liquid nitrogen element) with an inverse tachyon pulse beam.

INSIDE STORY

PRIMORDIAL EARTH LAVA FIELDS

The finale of *The Next Generation* was an emotional experience for every member of the cast and crew, as we all knew that once the episode was wrapped our lives and relationships would never be the same again. Every individual wanted to do better than our best—we owed it to the fans, and we owed it to each other.

Ronald D. Moore and Brannon Braga's script called for Q to take Picard to a primordial Earth, billions of years ago, where an anomaly is threatening to stop life on Earth ever beginning. Working with the eminently resourceful VFX supervisor David Stipes, we hired model builder Tony Dublin to construct a miniature landscape, and set it up at Image G to work with cinematographer Eric Nash and rigger Dennis Hoerter. The rock formations were made of heavy-gauge aluminum foil, coated with foam and other materials to create a rock-like texture that matched the full-scale rock formations on set. We planned to put a primordial ocean beyond the rock formation that had lots of tidal pools, and an area of sky big enough to feature the anomaly. Hot lava must glow from within, so we put our primordial rocks on a large slanted Plexiglas tabletop that was lit from below. The lava itself was created using gallons of methocel, a clear, viscous substance that purveyors of fast food use to thicken milkshakes. We added yellow/orange coloring and shone the lights through orange gel under the Plexiglas for more intense color. The outer crust of the lava was a combination of vermiculite, dry powdered paint, and crumbled burnt cork. The slant of the table made our synthetic lava flow.

David and I drove to Laguna Beach, where we knew a series of rocky tidal pools were ideal for our purposes, and shot a background plate pointing out to sea. For the anomaly, we shot liquid nitrogen vapors bubbling up through a hole radiating out across black velvet. Production designer Herman Zimmerman's crew built a partial cave set at Paramount, where Winrich Kolbe filmed Picard and Q's dialogue scenes. We shot wide locked-off shots with Patrick Stewart and John de Lancie that we could blend into the miniature rock formations for the wide matte shots. We transferred all the film to video at CIS, and took it to master VFX compositor Scott Rader at Digital Magic. Putting all the elements together was a very painterly experience; Scott was super patient with my pushing and tweaking the elements, and accommodating my last-minute visual inspirations. Digital technology allowed us to make all sorts of adjustments in scale, color, and tone until we had a satisfactory final image.

Those shots only last a few seconds on screen, but considering all the people involved these were among the most complex and costly shots done for the series.

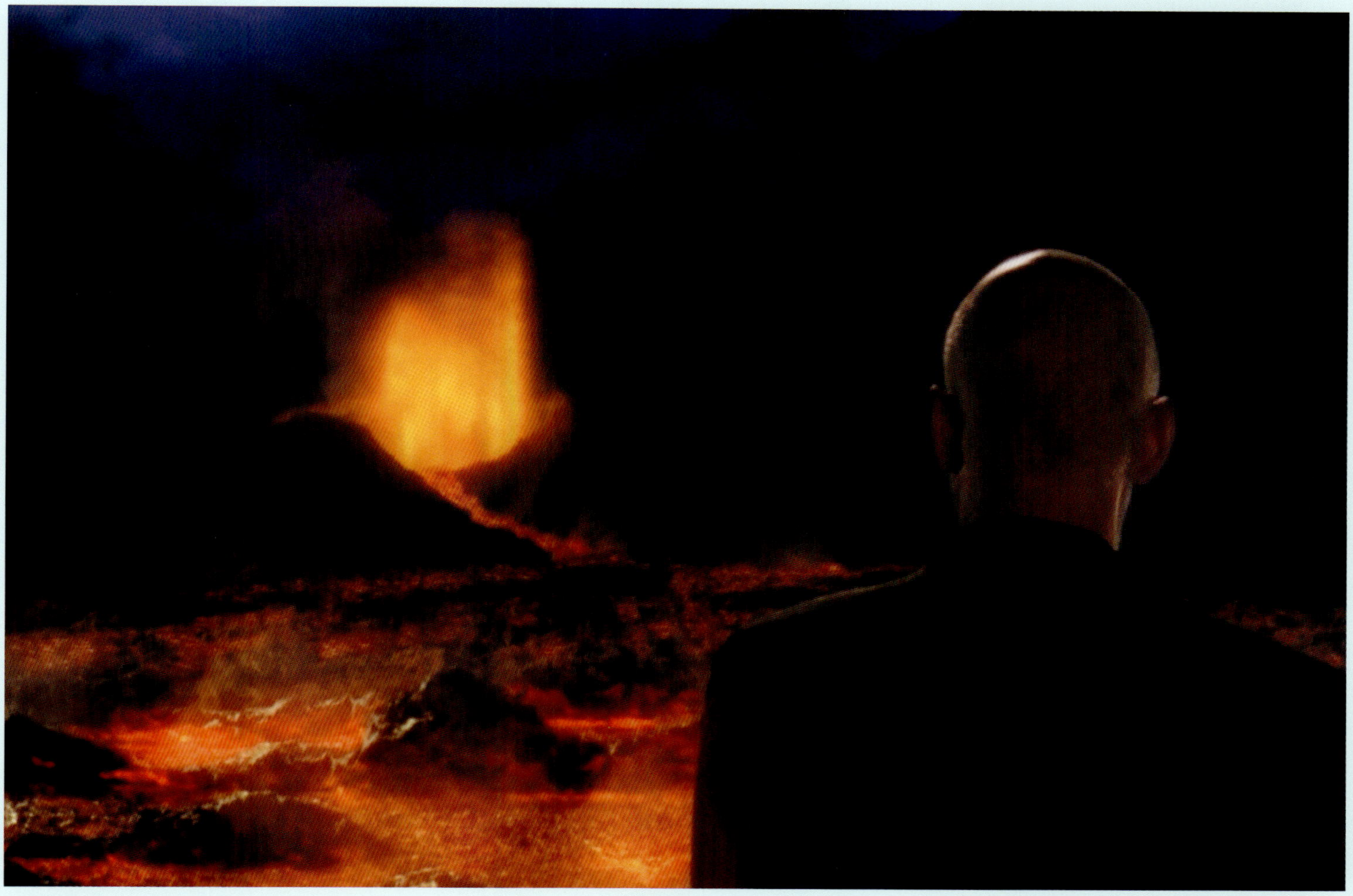

ABOVE: Final composite of Picard in the lava fields.

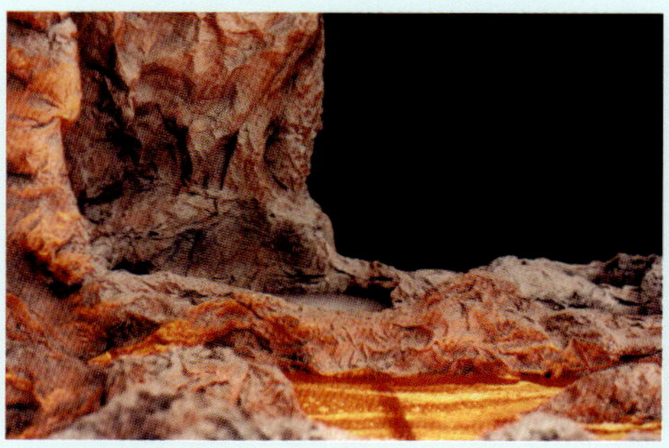

ABOVE: Tony Dublin's large-scale model of primordial Earth rock formations and lava beds.

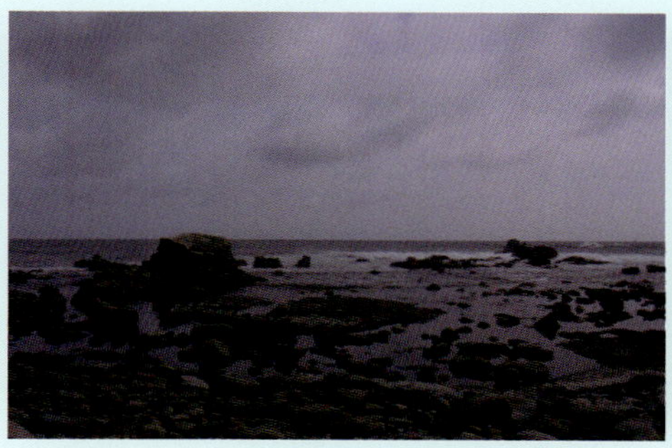

ABOVE: Background 'plate' of ocean at Laguna Beach.

ABOVE: Liquid nitrogen element shot on black velvet, composited with the Laguna Beach plate for the spatial anomaly.

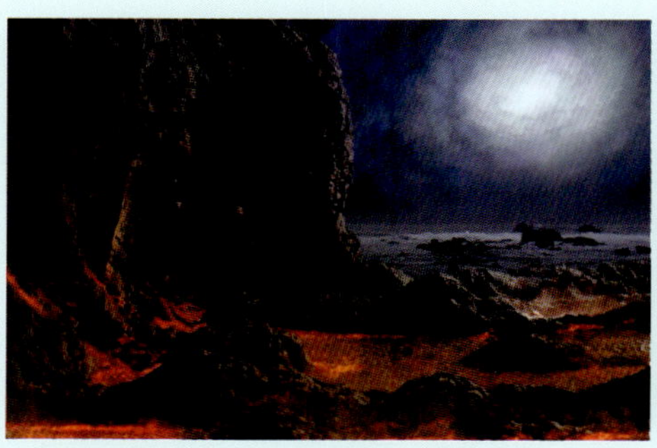

ABOVE: Miniature rock formations with bottom-lit moving lava added to the foreground.

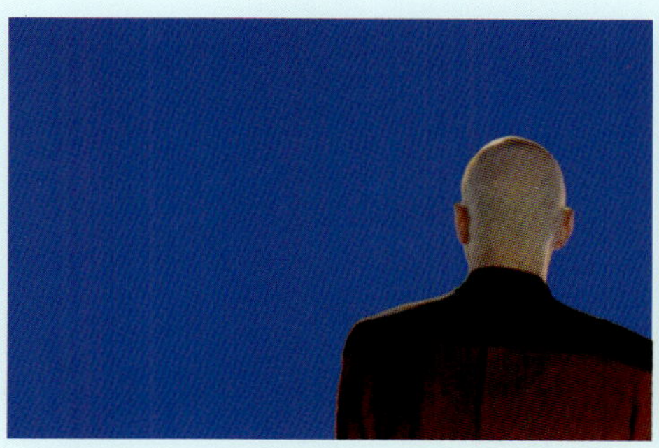

ABOVE: Patrick Stewart as Captain Picard on blue screen for compositing over the other elements.

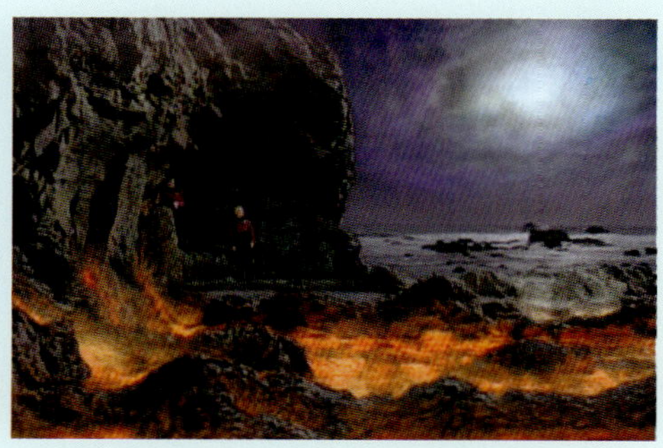

ABOVE: Final comp with Q and Picard, who were shot separately on a partial set, blended in.

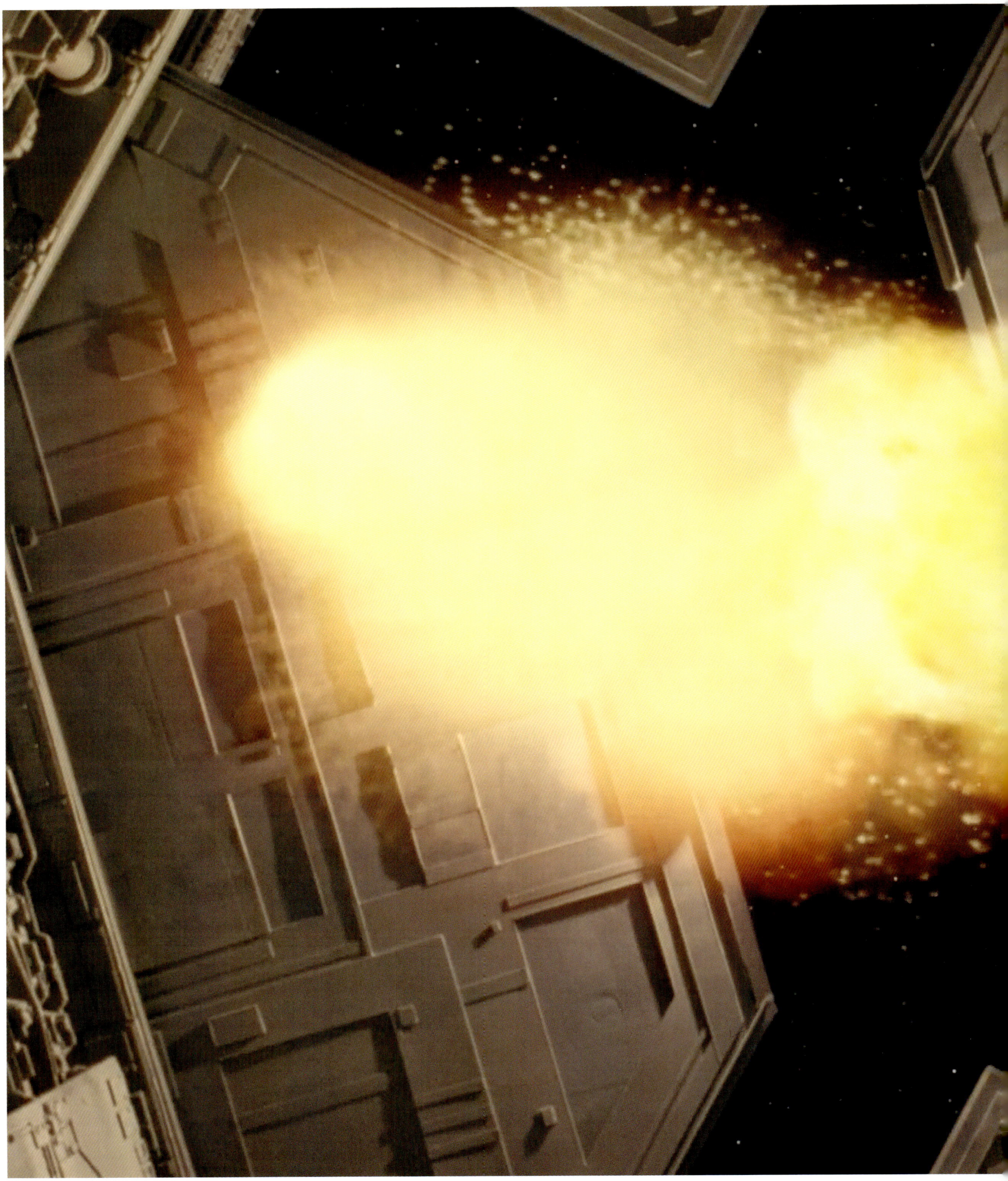

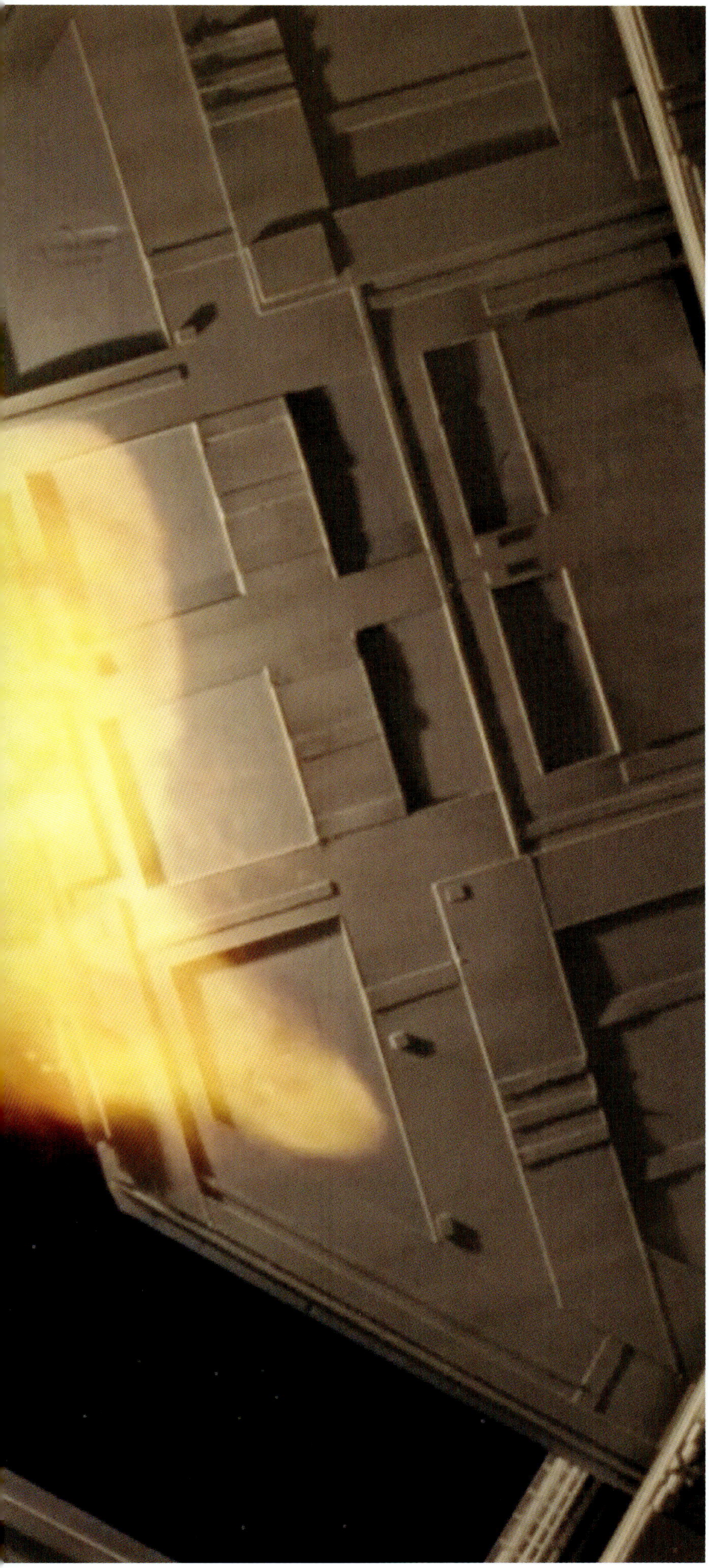

EXPLOSIONS

BLOWING THINGS UP IN EVER MORE CREATIVE WAYS

Legally, only licensed pyrotechnicians are allowed to blow things up or set fire to them. Anything with explosives would be under the supervision of the special-effects department. There's actually a law that if you have any open flame—even a candle or a match—you must have a fireman on set. Paramount had a small LA Fire Department house with a couple of trucks right on the lot.

Star Trek was fortunate to have excellent special-effects supervisors. On *TNG* and *Voyager*, Dick Brownfield led the special-effects team. On *DS9*, we had Gary Monack. *Enterprise*'s SPFX team was led by Rich Ratliff. The value of their knowledge, collaboration, and support for our visual-effects teams cannot be overstated. Time after time they came up with incredible rigs and creative solutions to daunting challenges. Elements for VFX compositing that the SPFX teams worked with us to obtain were indispensable. On *TNG*, we often needed to create explosions, working closely with Dick Brownfield and his crew, who loved to help us blow things up. It was really fun. The spirit of the crew was always great. Imagine a huge sound stage with a giant fireproof black cloth stretched on the ceiling, a mechanized scissor lift that can go up 30 feet, a huge, rarely seen high-speed film Photosonics camera, and a crew

LEFT: A gasoline explosion comped into the mechanical gates of the Dyson sphere built by Greg Jein.

of skilled people running around preparing for the big moment. That's what happened when we blew up model ships. When the explosion finally happens it is over in an instant, but thanks to the camera's high frame rate stretching time, on screen the explosion appears huge, revealing details invisible in real time and lasting a long time. When we needed something special on a large scale, Dick would bring in the best pyro specialists from among his many contacts in the industry.

Star Trek featured lots of spaceships getting blown up in battle. The hero models like the *Enterprise* and the Klingon bird-of-prey were expensive, so we didn't want to actually blow them up. When model kits of *Star Trek* ships became available, we would pack them with explosives, rig to match the position of the hero model, and explode them. When no exact model was available, we would blow up bags of chemicals and debris to get different looks and add them to our growing library of stock explosions. In compositing, we would do a 'jump cut' and pop off the detailed hero model, and in the next frame replace it with an explosion. To the human eye it looked like the spacecraft blew up. The audience would see a ship flying along, and then an explosion made the ship disappear.

When it was an important story point, we would build a special model. For the finale of *The Next Generation*, 'All Good Things...,' the *Enterprise* would be required to explode. Greg Jein built three 4-ft *Enterprise* models using the same molds as the original. Greg painted them to match the exterior of the hero model, but did not install the various lighting circuits and metal reinforcements. The *Enterprise* model wasn't an easy thing to blow up—it was fiberglass and very strong—so Greg cut score lines inside the hull so that it would shatter appropriately.

Shots from our library of explosions became so familiar we gave them nicknames; one was 'Sparky,' a fireball we used when explosions were coming down a corridor. There was 'Fireball 1' that had a dark center, and 'Phosphorous 3' because the chemical yields radiating white sparks when it explodes. Those nicknames helped speed communications along in the edit bay. Because we had already rented the expensive Photosonics camera package for the day, and already gotten the special-effects team to work with us, after shooting the episode-specific material we would spend the rest of the day shooting extra explosions for stock as time allowed.

We had several basic kinds of explosions: phosphorus, the white

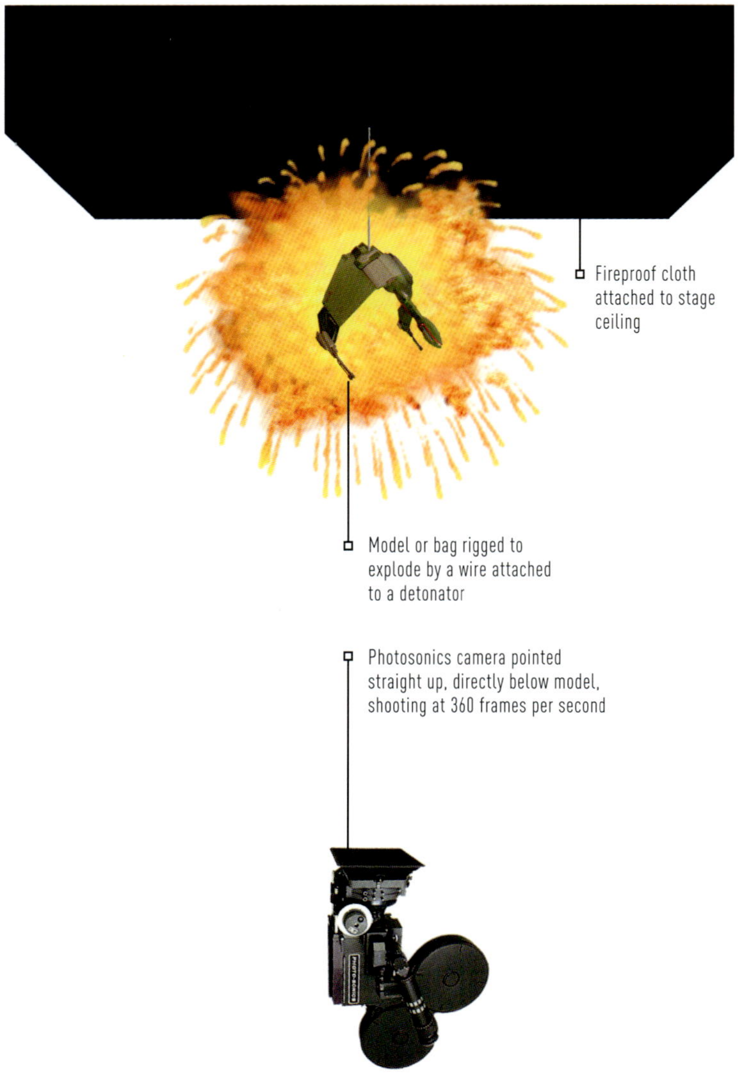

sparkly ones with little hot pellets of light radiating out from the center; and gasoline, which are fiery. These were mixed together with black powder and other chemicals to produce different looks.

When we filmed a space explosion the crew would rig a huge fireproof black cloth on the ceiling. Below it, the special-effects technicians would rig a model or explosive package hanging

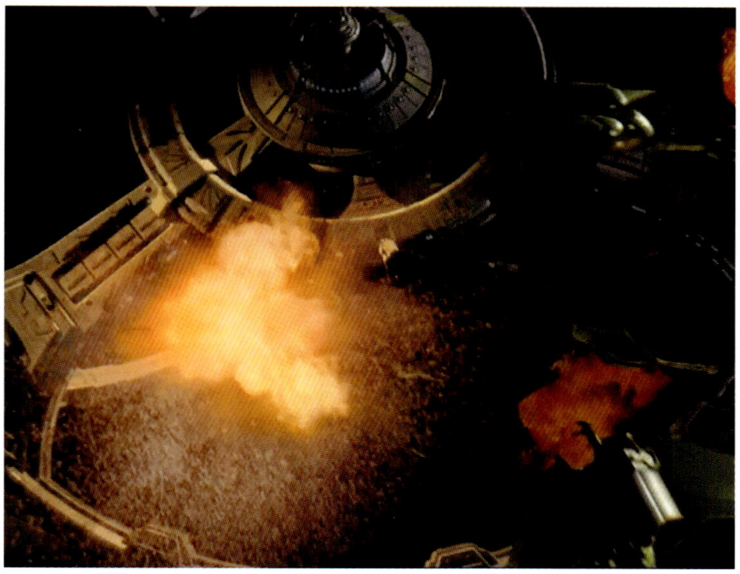

ABOVE: Gasoline explosion composited near Deep Space 9.

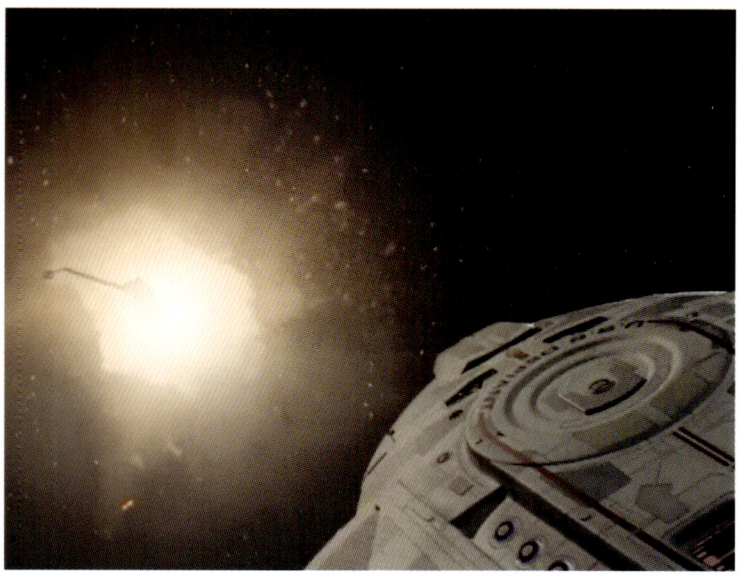

ABOVE: The *Defiant* destroys a Klingon bird-of-prey with a phosphorous-and-gasoline explosion.

VISUAL AND SPECIAL EFFECTS

A lot of people call all film effects 'special effects.' In the past, terms like 'special photographic effects' and 'technical effects' were also used. The studios preferred to keep the terminology vague, as they believed that audiences shouldn't know that anything was 'faked,' since that would interfere with their suspension of disbelief. Given earlier film technology, the endeavors of those creating practical effects on set and those creating elements that would be composited later overlapped considerably, so the blanket term 'special effects' was appropriate. As film technology evolved and divisions of labor became more specialized, separate terms became necessary.

Now, there is a strict distinction between special effects and visual effects. A visual effect, what my department does, implies using elements that are photographed separately or created on a computer, and combining them into a new cinematic reality. Special effects are practical or mechanical effects that are generally filmed on stage. These include wire pulls and hanging actors from arbors, fire and pyro shots, flying weapons, special uses of water, magnets, and so forth. Even simple things like opening and closing the doors on the *Enterprise* were handled by the special-effects department; one of the special-effects crew would actually be standing on the other side of the door, and would pull a rope by hand that would open and close the doors (mostly, but not always, in time with the actors). Will Thoms was pretty good at it.

Special effects and visual effects often work in close partnership. Sometimes, VFX needs the pyro skills of SPFX for explosions and the like. At other times, VFX can help SPFX with rig removal, element blending, and set extensions to make their job easier. The respect and appreciation for all the special-effects artists I encountered in my career cannot be overstated. No production can function without them.

down on a wire. The wire ran to a detonator a safe distance away controlled by the special-effects supervisor. The high-speed Photosonics camera would be positioned directly below, pointing straight up, with shielding overhead to protect it. To achieve the illusion that the explosion was taking place in zero gravity, the blast must radiate out from its epicenter. If an explosion is photographed horizontally, gravity would pull debris and sparks downward, and you would know it was taking place in a planet's atmosphere.

When we did the Badlands for *Voyager*'s pilot, we wanted to create some fire vortices, 'firenadoes.' At the time, one of the attractions at the Universal Studios park was a *Backdraft* demonstration, where they showed how they did all those different things with fire for the movie. Through a friend of a friend we were invited to go over and look at how they created their tornadoes of fire practically. We went early, before the park was open. The guys that did the fire effects for the feature film *Backdraft* were great, they took us in and showed us exactly how to do what was needed, so we were able to shoot elements back on our stage. They did not have to share their hard-earned knowledge with us. Their help was an example of great professional courtesy in our industry, even though we were working at rival studios.

There were two *Star Trek* explosions I will always remember. One was in a *Voyager* episode, 'The Killing Game.' The story took place on the holodeck, where *Voyager*'s crew was trapped in WWII-era France under Nazi occupation. On Universal backlot's 'European' location we shot a night exterior scene around a distinctive medieval-looking tower. When it was time in the story for the tower to explode, the grips rigged a blue screen in front of the tower. DP Marvin Rush directed his lighting crew to rig special lights that would flash on to simulate interactive light from an explosion. Kate Mulgrew and Jeri Ryan as Captain Janeway and Seven of Nine ran toward camera with the blue screen behind them as Marvin's interactive light flashed, letting the actors know when to react to the explosion. Thane Morris, one of Hollywood's most respected pyro masters, added his special expertise. Under Herman's supervision, the crew built a 15-ft-tall tower that matched the full-sized building on Universal's backlot. Thane and his crew lined it with primer cord, bags of gasoline, bags of black powder, and blew it up in a corner of Paramount's backlot. Building parts and debris flew in all directions. We used high-speed cameras matching the angles and positioning from the blue screen shot done at Universal. When we

BELOW: This explosion is a combination of gasoline and other chemicals to give it textural complexity.

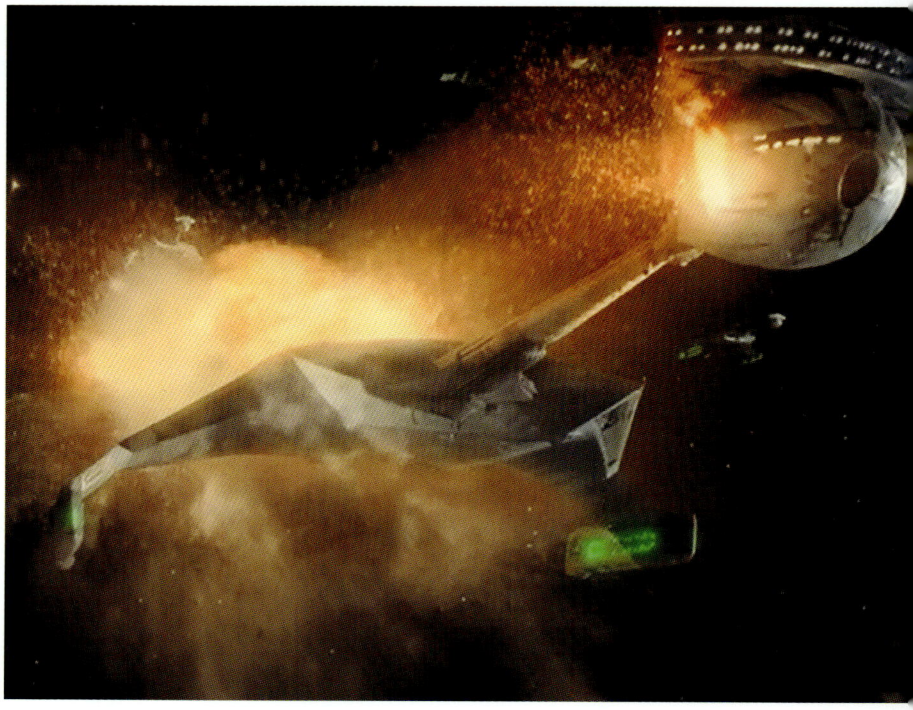

INSIDE STORY

CAPTAIN PROTON ON FIRE!

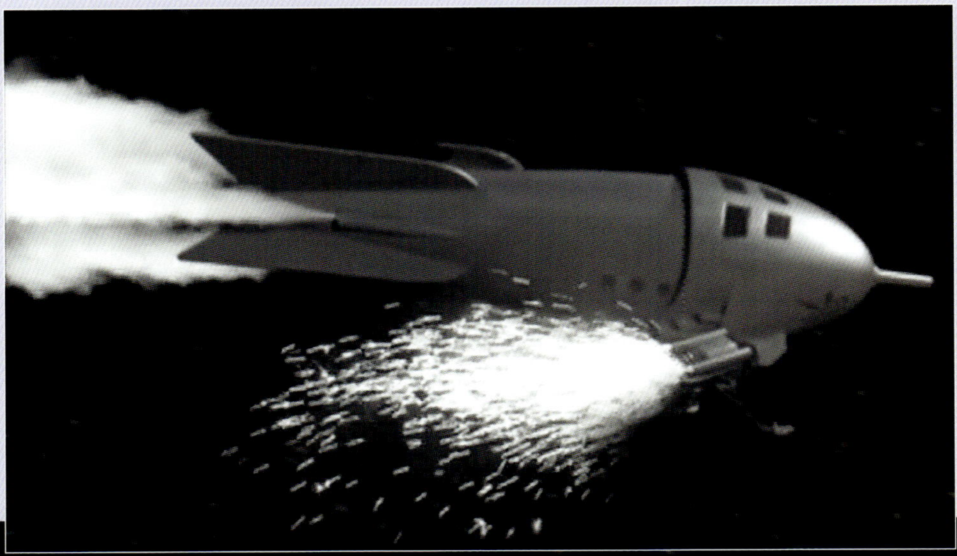

LEFT AND BELOW: It's rare for things to go wrong, but this shot of Robbie flying alongside Proton's rocket ship caused a few problems when the massive sparklers in the jetpack started a fire in his pants.

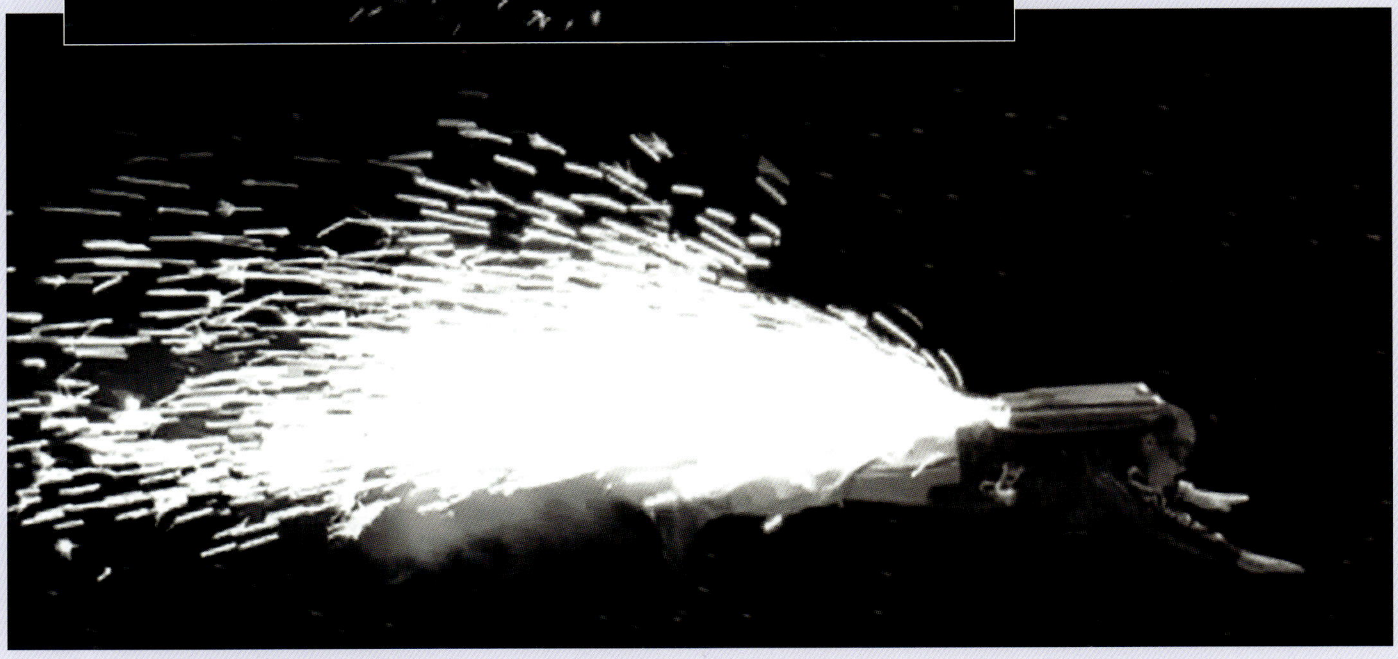

On *Voyager*, we filmed several sequences for the recurring *Captain Proton* holo-novel, which was an homage to the 1930s Republic serials like *Flash Gordon*. I directed a scene in second unit where Robert Duncan McNeill, as Tom Paris playing Captain Proton, was supposed to be using a jetpack to fly after his ship. Amazingly, we got the original jetpack from the serial *Commando Cody and the Lost Planet Airmen*, which was like a holy relic for several crew members. A little historical note: Leonard Nimoy appeared in one of the later *Commando Cody* episodes, 'Zombies of the Stratosphere.'

Dick Brownfield, our wonderful special-effects supervisor, had obtained industrial sparklers that were about 14 inches long. Cody's jetpack was made of polished steel, so we could put the sparklers in there. Robbie was mounted on a form-fitting fiberglass support on a rig like a big see-saw, in front of a blue screen, so he looked as if he was flying. Luckily, Dick also took the precaution of dressing Robbie in a racing car driver's fireproof underwear under his costume. Robbie was in his usual good spirits as Dick ignited the sparklers, and we started filming. It looked terrific—there were huge sparks flying out the back. Then I noticed that Robbie's butt was on fire! We all ran in with fire extinguishers and put out the fire. Thanks to the fireproof underwear, Robbie wasn't hurt.

It showed the measure of Robbie as a man that he took it in really good spirits, recognizing that it was just an unfortunate occurrence. I always respected Robbie, but my respect took a quantum leap forward when I saw how graciously he handled the situation.

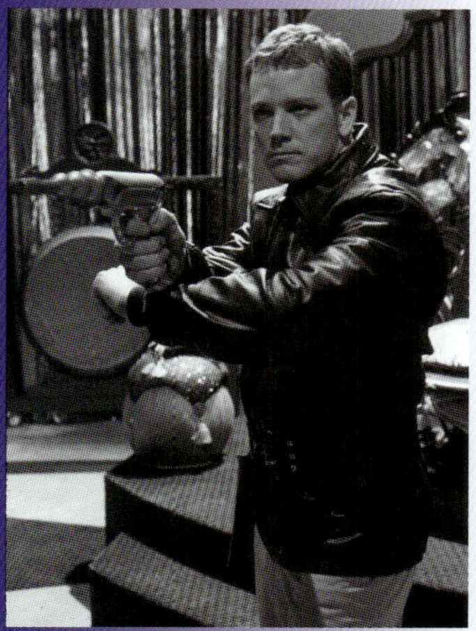

I won't hold Dan personally responsible for my ass getting set on fire. I was laid out on this see-saw, as if I were flying through space. I was strapped in, so when my pants caught on fire and I felt what was happening I couldn't do anything about it. There was nothing to do but yell out and hope they got me down and got the fire extinguishers on me in time. Now it's funny, but at the time it wasn't. It was a little shocking. It could have been much worse, but I ended up being fine. It ended up in the show too. The moments before I turned and said, 'My pants are on fire!' are used in the episode.

Robert Duncan McNeill

composited the two shots together in the edit bay it looked like Janeway and Seven of Nine barely escaped with their lives from a massive explosion. The successful illusion was the result of great acting and the collaborative efforts of a great many people with a wide range of skills.

The biggest explosion we did was on the pilot of *Enterprise*, 'Broken Bow.' This event was incredibly well planned by the producers. We made advance arrangements with a farmer in Bakersfield to plant a cornfield so the crop would reach the perfect height when we were ready to shoot the scene months later. Working closely with director James Conway, we did careful storyboards to help make the shoot day as efficient as possible. Herman Zimmerman's crew built a full-sized grain silo for the express purpose of blowing it up. When special-effects supervisor Rich Ratliff and his team were rigging the interior of the silo, I stuck my head in and saw coils and coils of primer cord, bags of gasoline and black powder, and some items I didn't recognize—all ready to explode. This was going to be a big one.

Jim Conway and Marvin Rush directed their crew to place cameras in various positions around the silo, from very close to very far away, because we knew we could only blow it up once. Armored cameras designed for military use were placed very close. We positioned one camera in a special spot for use later as background for a blue-screen shot of a Klingon warrior leaping out of the way.

When the explosion went off I was with a camera crew on a tower about 400 yards from the silo. My Corvette was parked right behind us on the ground. When the explosion went off we were amazed to see shockwaves radiating across the cornfield like ripples on a pond. When it hit the tower, we felt the structure lurch. I looked down and saw my car pop up about a foot and a half into the air as the alarm went off. Mine wasn't the only one. Crew members raced to turn theirs off.

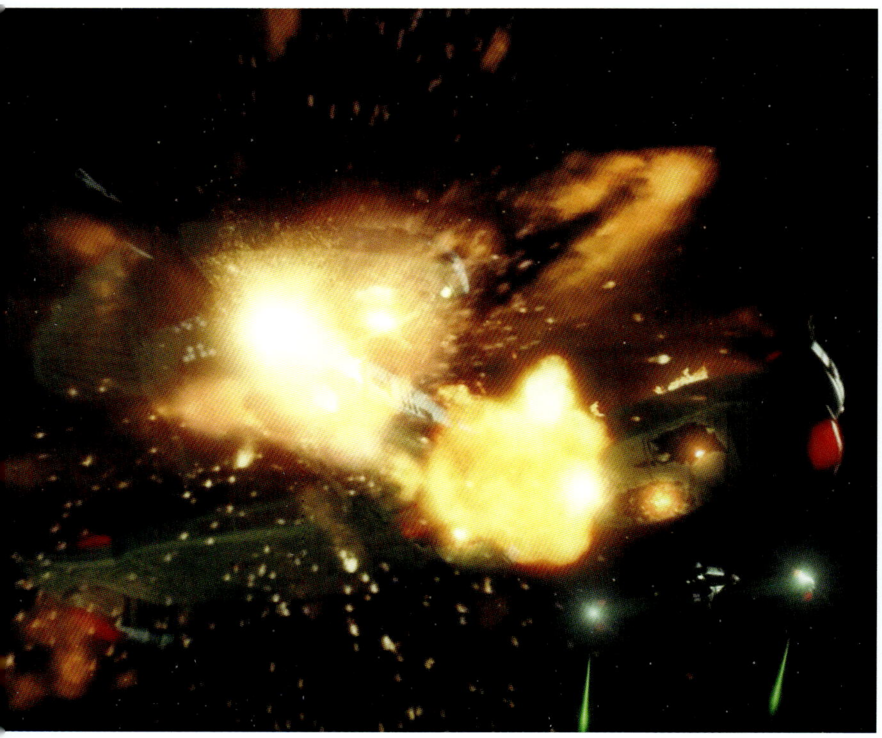

LEFT: The special-effects team was always eager to work with us blowing up ships with spectacular results, like this exploding Klingon warship.

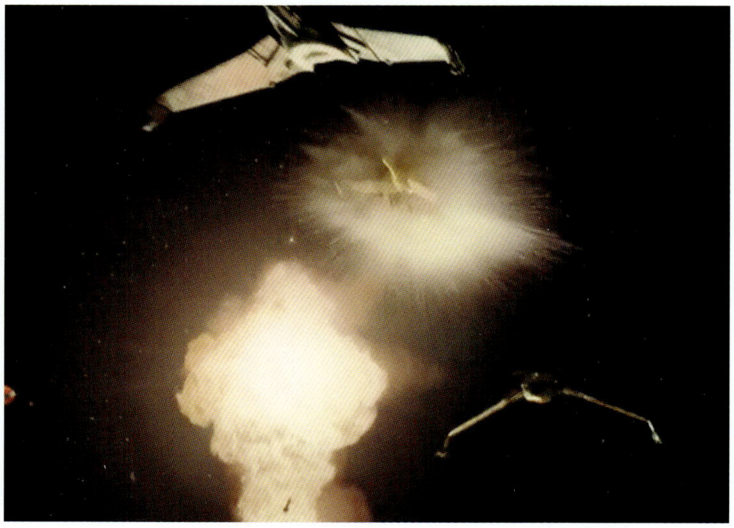

ABOVE: Dick Brownfield's team made different mixes of chemicals to give exploding vessels unique looks.

INSIDE STORY

BLOWING UP REMMICK

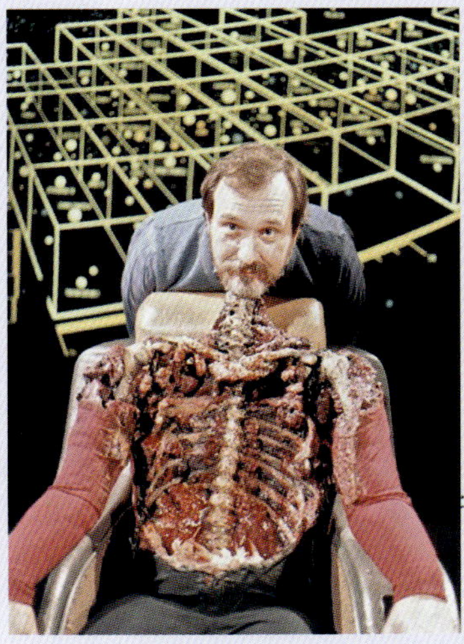

ABOVE: Having a little fun on the set.

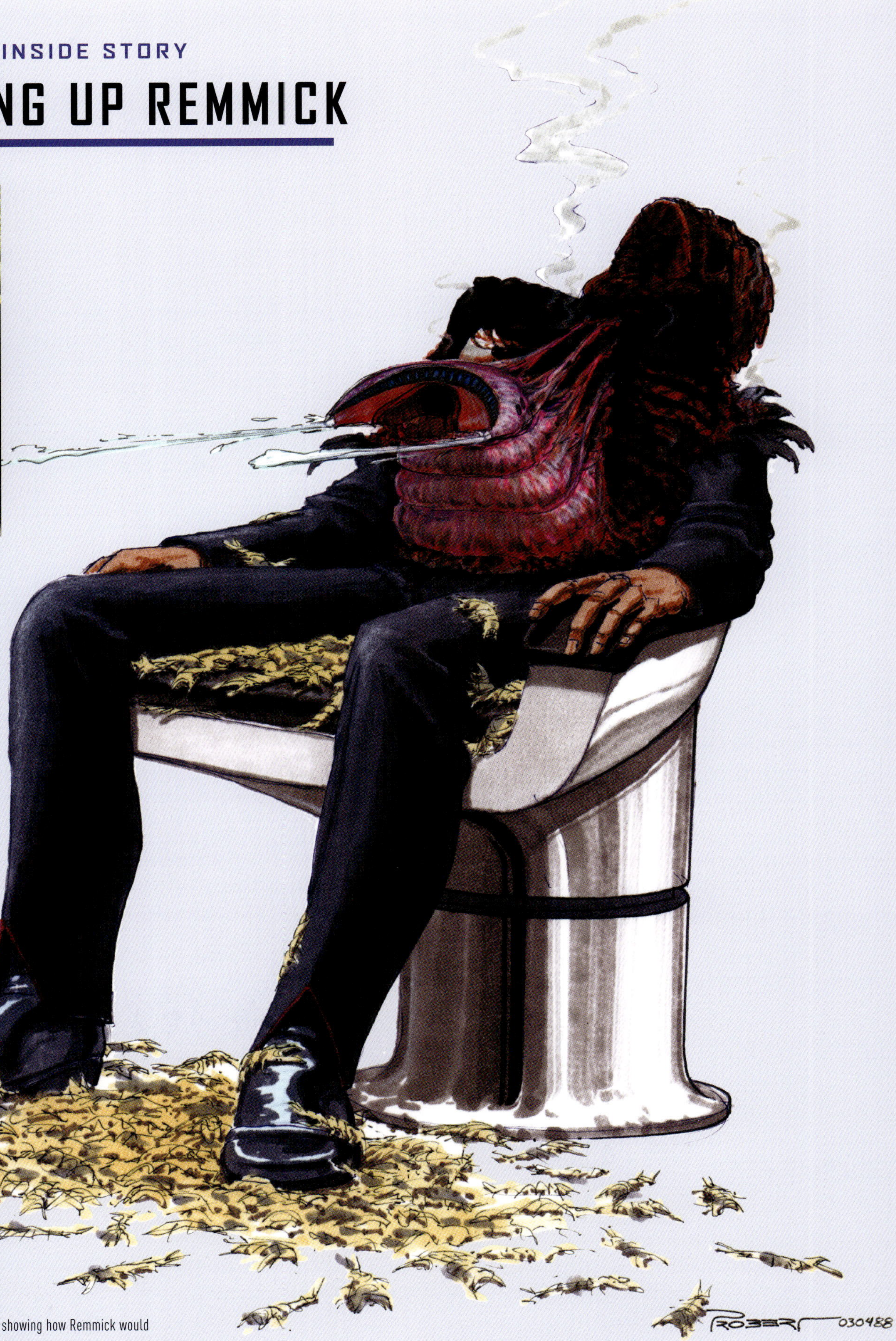

ABOVE: Andy Probert produced some artwork showing how Remmick would look after the mother alien had burst through his chest.

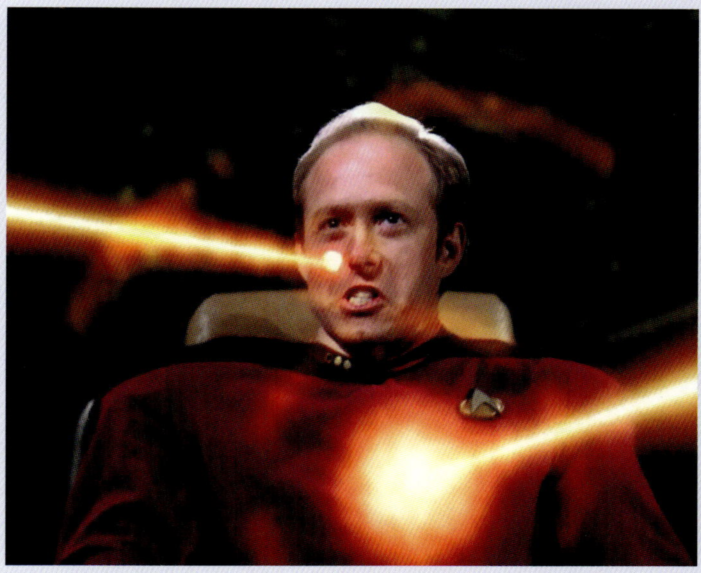

ABOVE: In part of the sequence, Riker and Picard turn their phasers on Remmick.

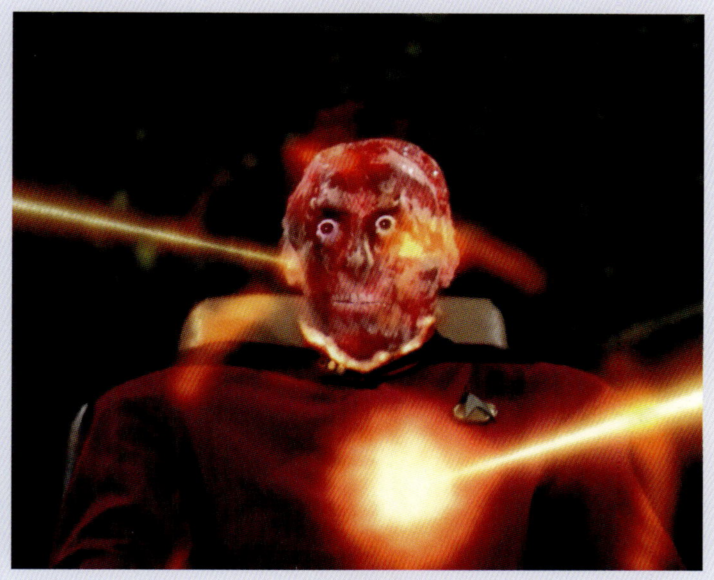

ABOVE: Phaser blasts burn away Remmick's face, and cut a gaping hole in his chest.

In 'Conspiracy,' Riker and Picard discover that another Starfleet officer, Dexter Remmick, has been infected by an alien parasite that is poised to take control of Starfleet Command, so they turn their phasers on him. We got to blow up Remmick's head and chest. Once that happens, a mother alien appears through his broken ribs.

This sequence involved several departments: visual effects, special effects, props, makeup, and camera. The shots of Patrick, Jonathan and Remmick, played by Robert Schenkkan, were filmed by the first unit, directed by Cliff Bole.

The sequence starts with Riker and Picard watching a five-inch alien parasite scuttle across the floor and climb up on Remmick. This was a latex puppet with a wire armature, which David Stipes filmed using stop-motion animation. In second unit, I directed the shots showing Picard and Riker's point of view of Remmick's demise. We put a hollow version of the parasite's tail that we placed over Robert's tongue so he could appear to swallow it. Legendary makeup supervisor Mike Westmore knelt behind Remmick's chair and blew through a series of plastic tubes attached to air bladders under a latex neck sleeve that Mike had put around Remmick's neck. This gave the illusion that the parasite was moving under Remmick's skin while Robert delivered his dialogue.

The next job was to blow up Remmick's head. We packed raw meat into a mold of a head that we found somewhere in the bowels of Paramount storage (I was told that the mold had been made from Paul Newman's head). Dick Brownfield and his special-effects crew added explosives. We mounted the head on a dummy torso, and Dick blew it up for us, spraying raw meat all over. We shot at high speed so that when we played it back at normal speed the explosion would appear to take a lot longer. In compositing, animator Steve Price layered the actor's face over the meat head, and hand-animated the phaser blast that burned away the skin before the head exploded. The 2D compositing was done by Fred Raimondi.

We had a special chair made by Makeup Effects Lab (headed by Alan Apone), based on a design by Andy Probert. The dummy in the chair was missing a head, and had a hollow, burnt-out torso. Water spritzers were strategically placed inside, and the interior was packed with cotton candy and lots of plastic parasites. Prop master Alan Sims was positioned below the chair with a hand puppet of the mother alien sculpted by Patrick Toutopolos from a Rick Sternbach sketch. The spritzers were turned on, and the cotton candy turned into a disgusting sticky goo that doused Alan as he thrust the mother alien upward to be disintegrated by Picard and Riker.

Looking at the dailies, I wanted more parasites spilling out from the torso in the final shot. So I stood in front of a black drape, dressed in black with a pile of parasite models held in a black cloth, and just dumped them out. In compositing, we were able to separate out the parasites from the black background and add them to the spill of baby parasites as the mother alien was meeting her end.

The element used for burning the hole in Remmick's chest was created using black Styrofoam. I splashed acetone on the Styrofoam, which was immediately eaten away, making a rough-edged glowing hollow. We shone light through it in a smoke-filled tent to create 'god rays.' In compositing, we layered the chest from Remmick's costume over the dummy's hollow torso so that the Styrofoam element would appear to reveal a glowing hole in the chest.

Rick Berman and Peter Lauritson were a little concerned: "This might be a little harsh," they said to me. "How old is your son?" Devin was five or six at the time. "Would you mind him

(continued overleaf)

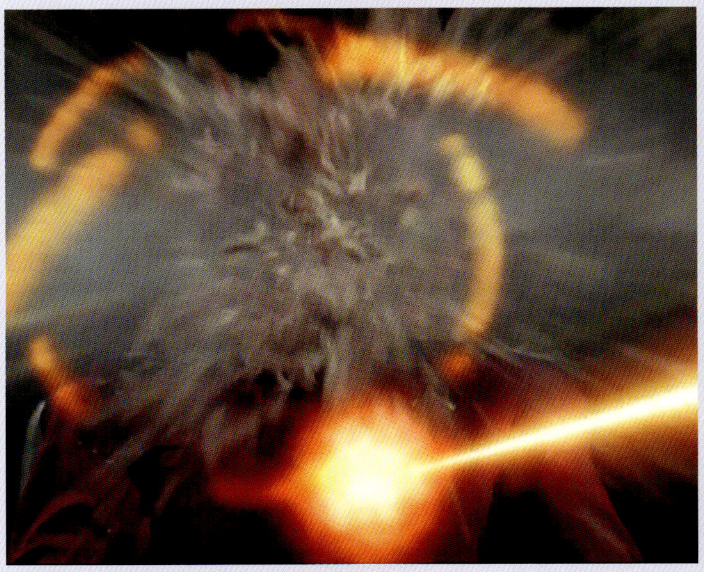

ABOVE: We exploded a head molded from raw meat, rigged on the dummy where the actor's head from the live-action footage would have been.

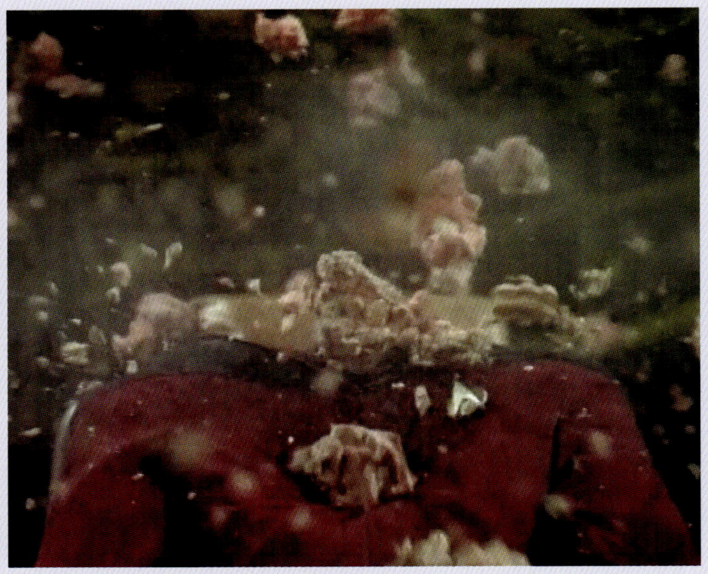

ABOVE: We shot the explosion at high speed to stretch time and make the scattering chunks of meat more discernible.

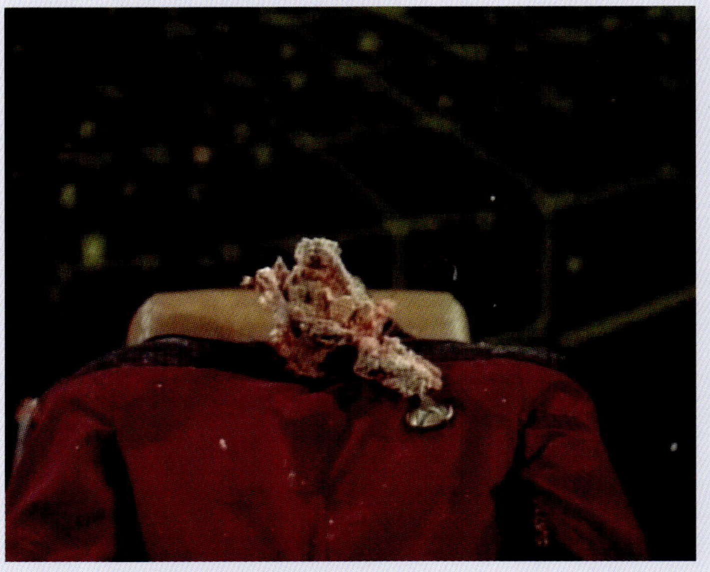

ABOVE: Following the explosion, only a stump of spine and a little soft tissue remained.

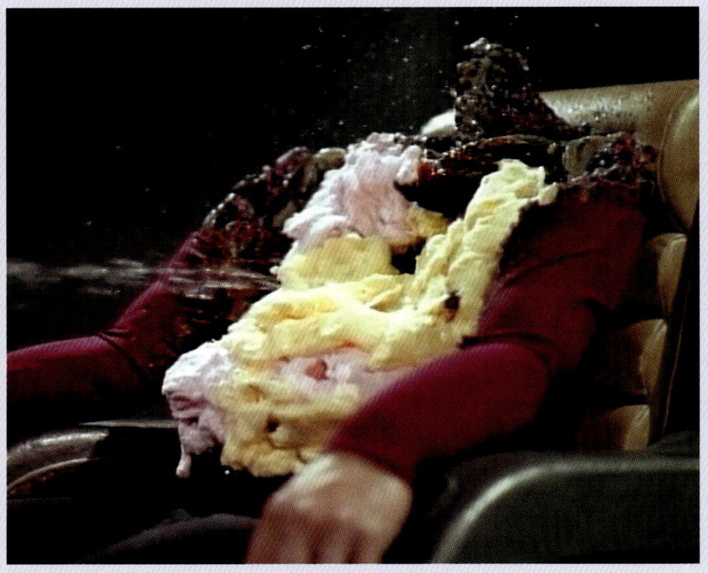

ABOVE: The hollow torso was filled with plastic alien parasites and cotton candy, to be turned to viscous goo by hidden water spritzers.

taking a look at this?" I said "Okay." I brought Devin into the room where they were doing the sound mix, watching the episode on a big monitor. When Remmick's death scene came up, Rick and Peter turned and looked at Devin as he calmly watched the action. When it was over, they asked, "What do you think of that?" Devin said, "I think you should make a Remmick action figure with a button. You press it, and his head blows up!" Rick and Peter thought, "Well, he's a little kid, and he did not have much of a reaction. Let's go with it." What I neglected to tell them was that Devin was with me when I was checking progress over a weekend at Makeup Effects Lab, so he had already seen the headless torso with the open chest cavity and heard how we were planning to use it, so he was not shocked at all, just curious to see how it turned out.

In the show's first airing in Great Britain in 1991, Remmick's death scene was cut out. Canada's sci-fi network added a 'viewer discretion warning' prior to airing—the only *TNG* episode to ever be so honored. I was genuinely surprised at the amount of mail we received from viewers outraged by what they considered to be graphic violence. To this day, 'Conspiracy' remains one of my favorite episodes.

RIGHT: The little alien that clambers into Remmick's mouth was a stop-motion puppet designed by Andy Probert and animated by David Stipes.

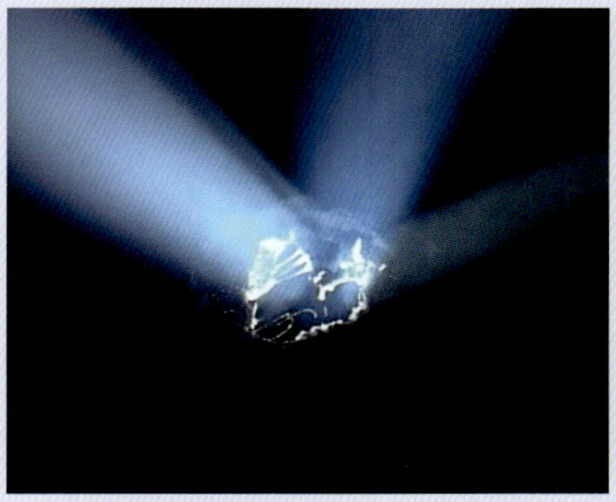

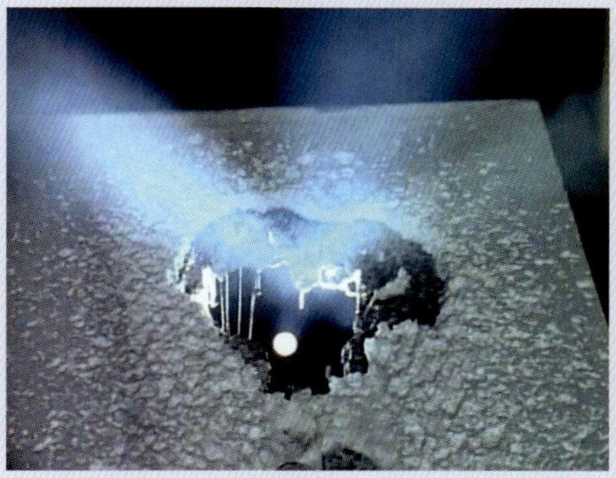

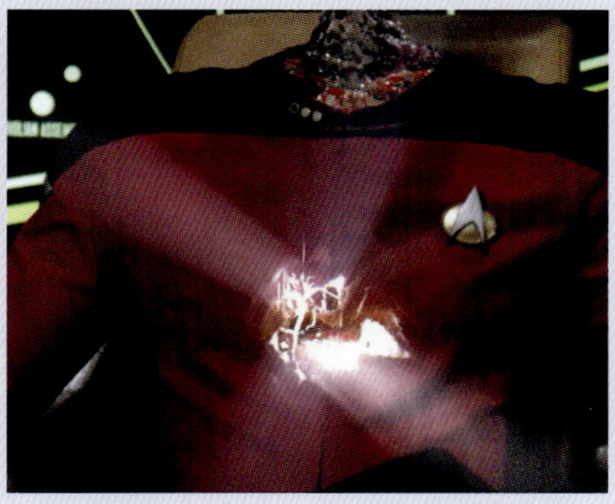

ABOVE: To create the illusion that Remmick's chest was dissolving, we poured acetone to eat away the Styrofoam. We filmed the 'god rays' in a smoke tent, shining lights through black Styrofoam melted with acetone. Once we had the light and Styrofoam elements, we combined them with the live-action footage.

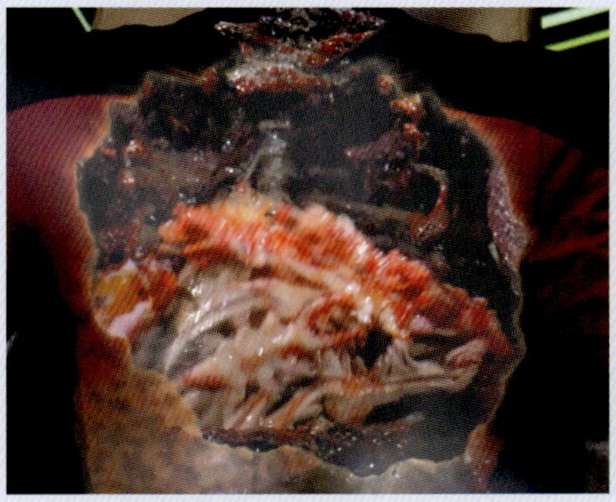

ABOVE: As Remmick's chest disappears and the cotton candy goo dribbles away, we see the mother alien rise.

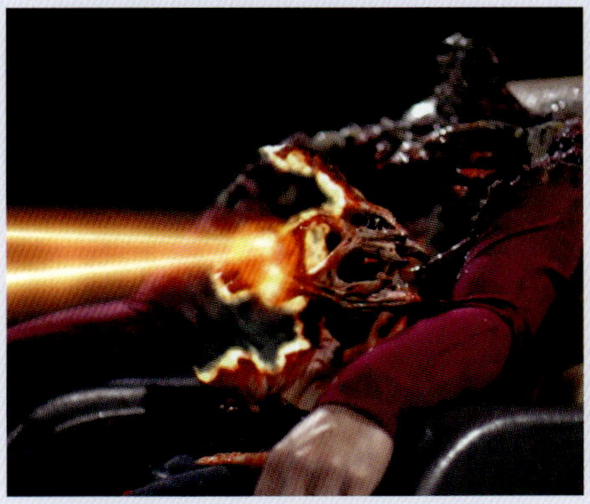

ABOVE: We added a phaser blast, and animated the mother's body disintegrating.

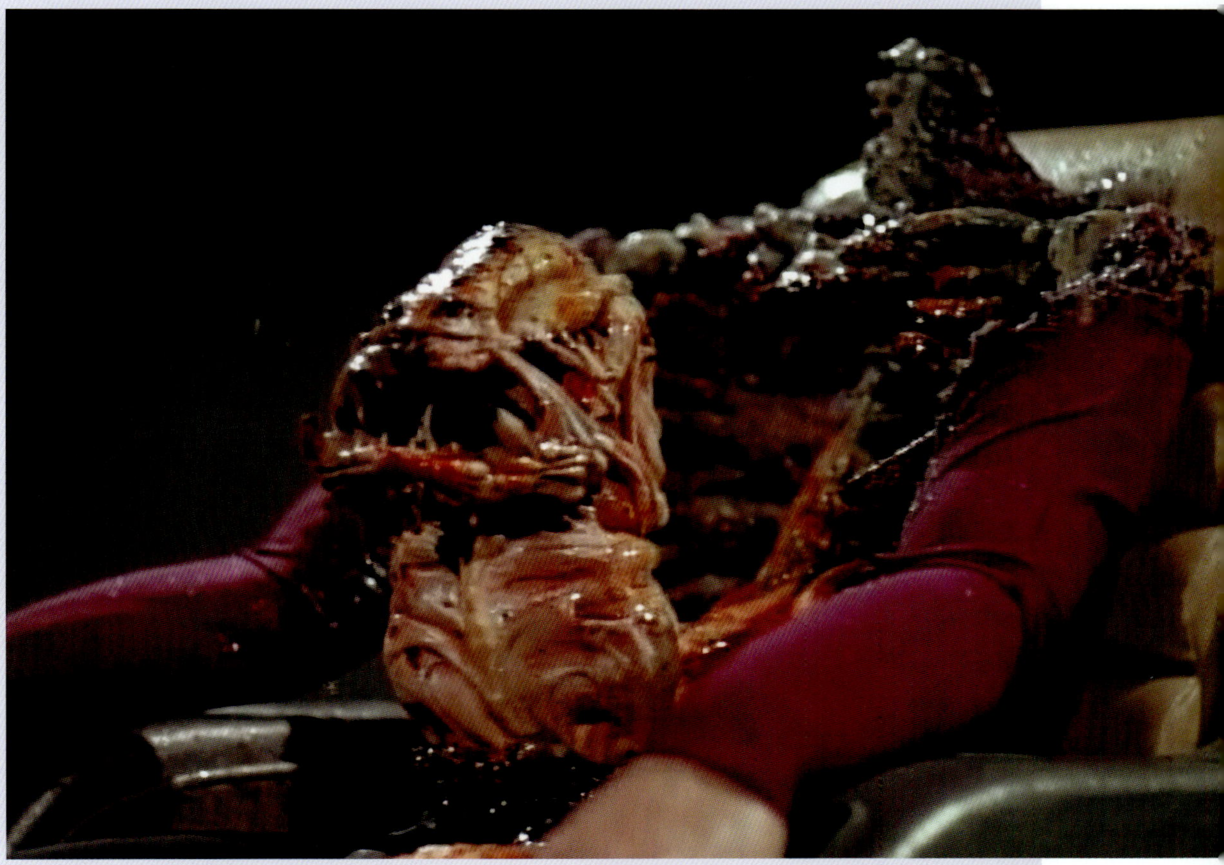

ABOVE: The mother alien glove puppet was controlled through a hole in the bottom of the chair.

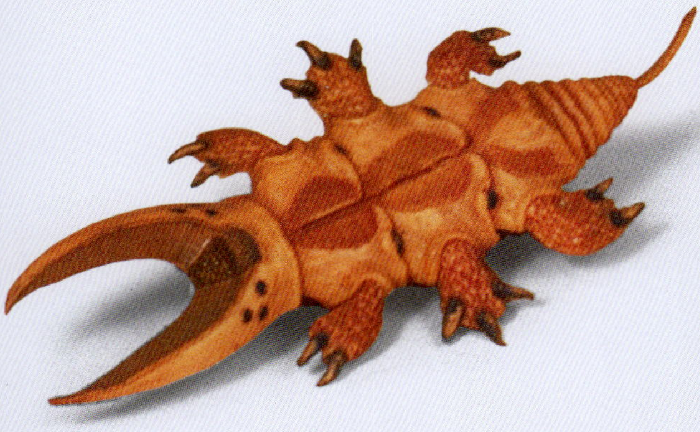

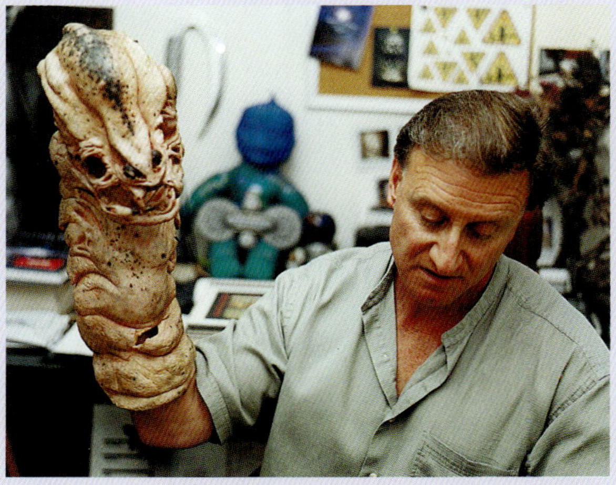

RIGHT: Prop master Alan Sims operated the puppet lying under the chair with his arm thrust up through a hole in the dummy corpse. He got covered with sticky goo as the cotton candy dissolved.

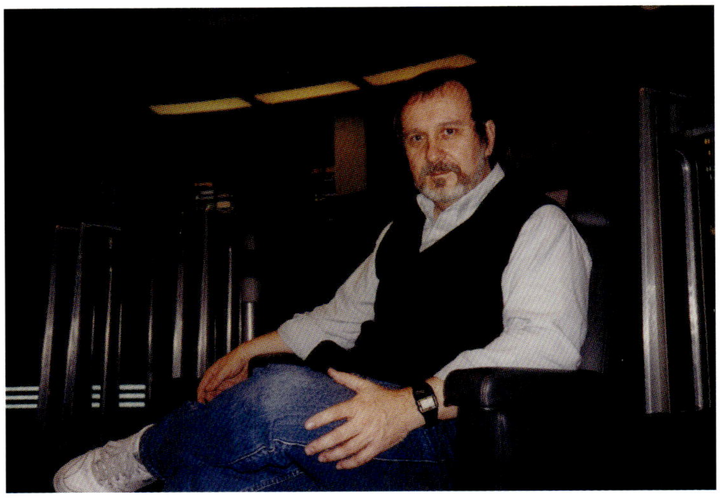

DIRECTING SECOND UNIT

GETTING BEHIND THE CAMERA TO FILL IN THE GAPS

In TV, you are always in a race against the clock. On *Star Trek* we shot an episode—the equivalent of half a feature—every seven working days. The schedules were daunting so we had to be efficient. The first unit is for principal photography. They film most of the dramatic dialogue scenes with the actors. It was a race to get the day's work completed without getting into expensive overtime. The main purpose of second unit was to maximize the use of time on first unit, so anything they didn't have to do themselves would be handed over to us.

Every week or two there would be a second-unit day. The assistant directors scheduled things so first unit would be shooting on one sound stage while second unit used another. Second-unit days frequently involved complex visual effects, stunts, special effects, or scenes that do not require principle cast members. There were also full dialogue scenes that were either not covered on first unit because they ran out of time, or were rewritten after the producers reviewed an edit and decided to make changes or add scenes. As a member of the Directors Guild of America, I had the opportunity to direct all the cast members at one time or another, and learned to appreciate their dedication and artistry. We were always very careful to match first-unit lighting, tone of the scene, and actor performances so the moments we photographed cut seamlessly into the final edited episode.

Second unit also shot 'inserts.' These are shots requested by the editors that are needed to clarify a moment in a scene, or are skipped during principle photography so that the director and crew can concentrate on dialogue scenes. Inserts included hands pushing buttons, animal scenes like working with Data's cat Spot or Archer's beagle Porthos, close-ups of Data's mechanical brains, machines doing things, close-ups of hands holding a device that would later have a moving image composited in, a hand grabbing a phaser, cutting a cake...details that enhance the unfolding of a story.

For example, if Captain Picard was operating a control panel, an editor would request a tight close-up of the captain's hand hitting precise buttons and possibly see a reaction on a monitor. You didn't actually need Patrick for the shot, because the audience would not know if the hand was really his. Central casting would get us a double who looked more or less like the actor from behind so we could shoot over the shoulder, maybe showing a little bit of a character's head. Sometimes the people in central casting would not know exactly what we needed the photo double to do, however, and occasionally that caused problems. One time they hired a double for Captain Picard to press buttons on a console, but the actor's finger had been broken in a past injury. It just hung

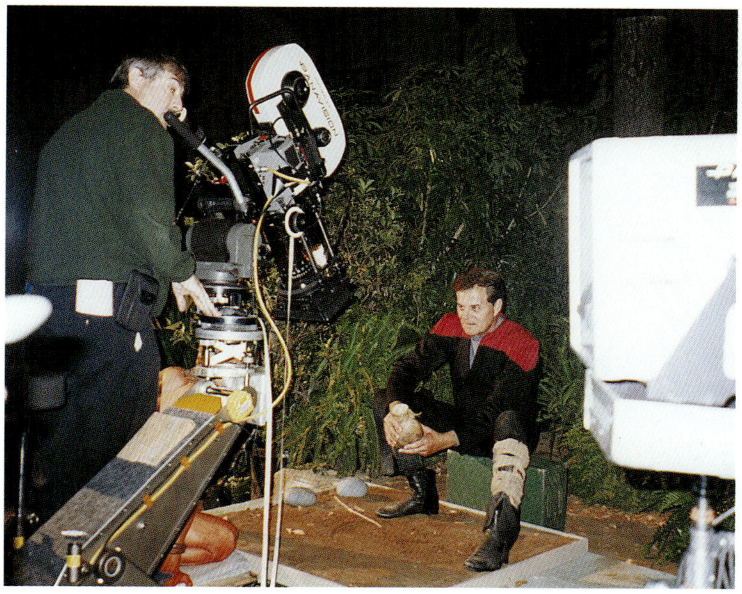

ABOVE: The principal actors' time is too valuable to use when you are only showing someone's hand or leg. Here, second-unit DP Doug Knapp sets up a close-up with Riker stand-in Richard Sarstedt.

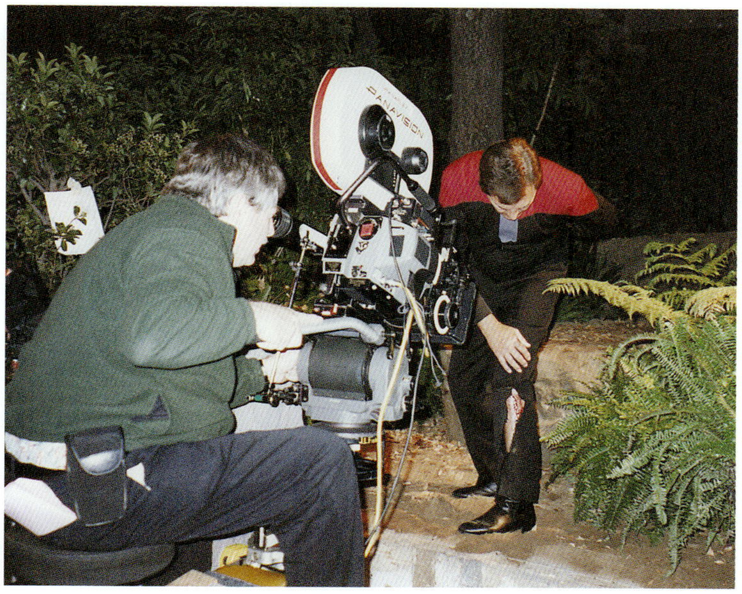

ABOVE: Most episodes involved filming at least one day with the second unit. We were a close-knit team, and worked well together. Over the years we became very fast and efficient.

there limply. We had to do something. I took a piece of welding rod, taped it to the guy's arm, ran it up under his hand, and put a little dab of superglue on his fingertip to hold this finger against the rod. When shooting, we made sure the rig could not be seen by the camera. Now the photo double could hold his finger straight to press buttons.

Another time we had to shoot a close-up of a guest character's ear to reveal a special earring that had hidden technology crucial for the story. Central casting sent a woman who was physically a good match for our guest star. When we finally set up for the close-up of the photo double and she pulled her hair back to show the earring, Kris Krosskove, operating the camera, gave me a concerned look. The woman's ear had been damaged in an accident, and was deformed. I whispered to Kris to just shoot a couple of takes so as to not embarrass the woman, and we reshot the insert the following week.

We did a lot of shots where we had to add video to a device like a PADD or a computer monitor. Those shots are known as 'burn-ins' as a new image is layered into the scene. In the early days, before there was tracking software, if someone was holding a PADD we had to make sure it stayed perfectly still, so we would fix it to a lighting stand and then the actor would pretend to hold it.

We also did shots of the main viewscreen. On the main bridge set, the viewscreen was just a big opening, and we'd composite whatever appeared on it in the edit bay. By necessity, characters on the screen and the crew on the bridge would be shot separately. The audience wouldn't think about it, but we had to make sure that they were looking directly at one another. Usually, first unit would shoot the principal cast on the bridge first. Whenever they were shooting anything that entailed visual effects, however simple, someone from the visual-effects department would be there to record camera angles and various measurements needed to film the additional elements we'd film later to complete the shot. Before we shot what would appear in the viewscreen, I would trace the 'A-side' (the scene shot on the *Enterprise* bridge) onto a piece of gel I got from the lighting department. I'd mount the gel on a piece of foam core with a hole cut in to show the opening of the viewscreen, and put it in front of the camera. We'd look through the traced drawing and then put markers with red X's on the stage where we were filming the actors on the alien bridge. That way, the actors knew where to look when they were talking to the characters on the *Enterprise* bridge.

Scenes that were technically elaborate could take all day. First unit couldn't spare the time, so we would shoot those on second unit. These usually entailed shots when we were adding another element—say a CG character—or where we have two of somebody (say two Rikers or two Picards). Time-consuming sequences, like when we blew up Remmick for *TNG*'s 'Conspiracy,' or when Riker levitated through a trans-dimensional sphincter-like portal, were done in second unit.

I had the opportunity to direct action sequences too, working with our excellent stunt coordinators Dennis Mada one and Vince Deadrick Jr., with their stunt teams and the actors. Fight and action sequences can take a lot of time to choreograph and shoot. It was essential that nobody got hurt, so safety and proper rigging were top priorities.

The time it can take to get performances from animals can be unpredictable, so animal shots were relegated to second unit. Especially working with cats can take forever. I grew up with cats, so I got along with Data's cat, Spot, but even with his capable trainers it could take an hour to get the cat to do what was needed. Captain Archer's beagle, Porthos, was much more cooperative. For one episode we had a falcon that was supposed to be released on set. It was touted as a wonderfully trained bird that could do all sorts of things, but sure enough, as soon as they let it out of the cage, it flew up into the lighting grids and catwalks at the top of the sound stage, and disappeared. We learned that some time later the trainer was able to coax it down.

In another episode, Counselor Troi has visions of her sister, who died when she was a child. The sister was played by a pre-teen Kirsten Dunst. There was a dream sequence where the younger sister walked through the passageways of the *Enterprise* followed by a wolf. This was another shot that would take hours and thus was relegated to me and second unit. We actually had the wolves from *Dances With Wolves*, along with their trainer. We first did a lock-off camera angle with Kirsten walking down the corridor and then, when she was safely off stage, shot the wolf loping along. In compositing, we ran a traveling split screen to make it appear that

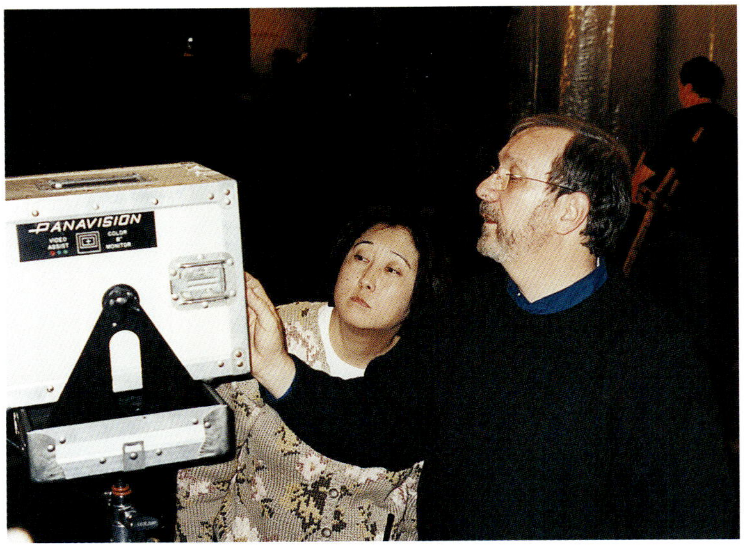

ABOVE: Discussing a shot with assistant director Arlene Fukai.

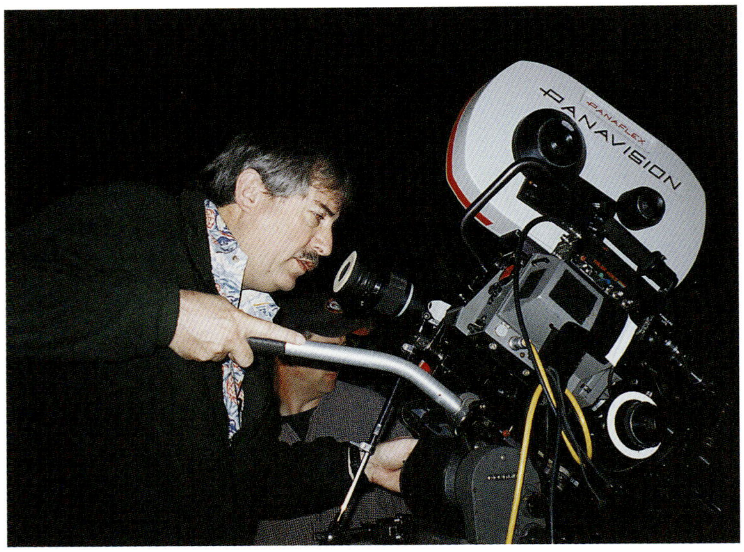

ABOVE: Douglas Knapp, SOC was first-unit A-Camera operator, and a terrific second-unit director of photography.

Troi's younger sister and the wolf were moving close together.

We also needed a close-up shot of the wolf growling into camera. Our DP/camera operator was Tom DeNove. The trainer assured us it was easy—he attached a big bolt to the stage floor, and connected it to a chain around the wolf's waist. The wolf was really amicable, kinda cool, just hanging out. We rolled the camera dolly close to the wolf because we wanted the wolf's face to fill frame, but needed to use a wide-angle lens to exaggerate perspective. Then the trainer broke out a great big cow bone with a little raw meat still on it, and put it on the floor. The wolf thought this was great, and chomped away. The trainer asked, "You want to see him growl? Watch this." He then put a box on top of the bone to hide it, and pulled it away. The wolf goes berserk. Standing safely back behind the camera, I was thinking "this is great." But Tom was operating the camera, and was only a few uncomfortable inches from the angry wolf. After a minute, he turned and looked at me and said, "Isn't that enough?!"

We shot sequences with kids, too. There's an episode where Picard and some children are trapped in a turbolift, and they climb into the shaft before the lift falls away. The shaft and the turbolift car were models that Brick Price and his crew at Wonderworks built for us. The model was only about 12 inches in diameter at most. In the final shot, the boy would see the turbolift plummeting many levels below him. We shot the young actor against a blue screen laid on the floor. As director, I wanted him to just look down, grab the ladder and pull himself in. We were shooting on a 12-ft-tall platform. I was on the platform, looking straight down at the child actor. Every time we did the rehearsal, the kid was really good and would do exactly what I wanted, but as soon as we started rolling he would mug it up. Before each take I said, "Please do it like we did in the rehearsal." But as soon as we turned the camera on he started over-acting again.

I told the director of photography, "Just pretend to shoot this one while I check something." I walked to the back of the platform, and discovered that the boy's mother was standing underneath, miming what she thought he should be doing. So I climbed down the ladder and explained to her that a set isn't a democracy, and that there was only one director. I invited her to have another doughnut and sat her on the side of the stage, out of the boy's sightline. After that, he was just perfect.

The most rewarding second-unit shoots were when we would have complete dramatic scenes to do. Sometimes there would be a big scene that they didn't have time to finish on first unit. For example, in the *Voyager* episode 'The Raven,' Seven of Nine and Tuvok escape from the crumbling ship that Seven was on as a child. The episode was directed by LeVar Burton, but he didn't have enough time to finish every scene. LeVar and I spoke briefly about it. He said, "Just do something cool." I appreciated LeVar's trust, and directed the scene as if it was my own episode. After scrambling through practical debris in the ship's interior, they jump out of a hatch on a fully CG exterior. Then they beam out from a matte painting I did using elements I photographed in the Alabama Hills when we were shooting 'Basics.' The actors were shot against bluescreen and comped later.

Sometimes the editors discovered that an episode was running short, or the producers wanted to replace a scene. We would get new scripts and shoot those in second unit, as first unit was already working on a new episode. Kate Mulgrew was always wonderful to work with. There was one added scene where Captain Janeway has just come from a contentious meeting and encounters Neelix, who was supposed to improve her mood. It had been several weeks since the previous scene was shot. I had studied the cut episode and knew how the new scene should fit in. The first take or two didn't have what I felt was the right emotional arc—it seemed too light-hearted at the beginning. I mentioned to director of photography Doug Knapp, "I've got to talk to Kate about that." Doug was a little concerned, "*You're* going to tell Kate how to give a performance?!" I said, "She's an actor, and she's a wonderful person. I'm not going to *tell* her anything, just ask a few questions about context." So I asked Kate, "Wasn't Captain Janeway angry when she came out of that meeting? How would Janeway's mood evolve during the scene as a result of encountering Neelix?" Kate responded with a gracious "thank you." When Kate and Ethan did the scene again, Kate's performance, as usual, was perfect.

One of the reasons second unit was so enjoyable was that we usually had the same crew, all with the indispensable support of assistant directors like David Trotti, Mike Demeritt, and Arlene Fukai, who helped keep things moving along on schedule. We came to be a special branch of the production family. Frequently the A-Camera operator from first unit would direct photography for second unit, taking advantage of his familiarity of how things had been lit and shot originally. Doug Knapp, Joe Chess, Kris Krosskove, and Gary Tachell made thing go efficiently. If they weren't available, directors

THE SECOND-UNIT CREW

For each second-unit shoot day, crew members were conscripted from the main unit as available, depending on what was to be shot and what special skills were needed. Schedules were planned by assistant directors like Arlene Fukai, David Trotti, and Mike DeMeritt. Representatives from all departments: actors, photo doubles, background artists, camera, lighting, grip, electrical, sound, props, wardrobe, visual effects, special effects, stunts, art department, construction, craft service and security were all needed to accomplish a day's work. We frequently had to rebuild parts of sets that had already been struck to use as backgrounds for the scenes we were shooting. On days when we had technically complex VFX shots we had time for only a few scenes. On other days we had to complete over fifty set-ups. Though our schedules were as daunting as principal photography, everyone enjoyed some time away from the pressures of first unit and work in a more relaxed atmosphere. Every individual was a consummate professional. I was proud to work with all of them.

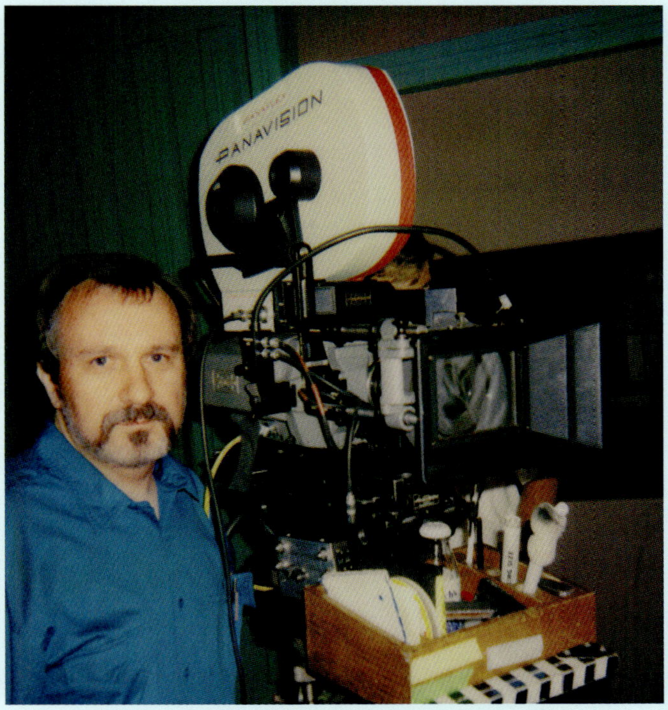

RIGHT: On set with the trusty Panaflex Gold 35mm film camera.

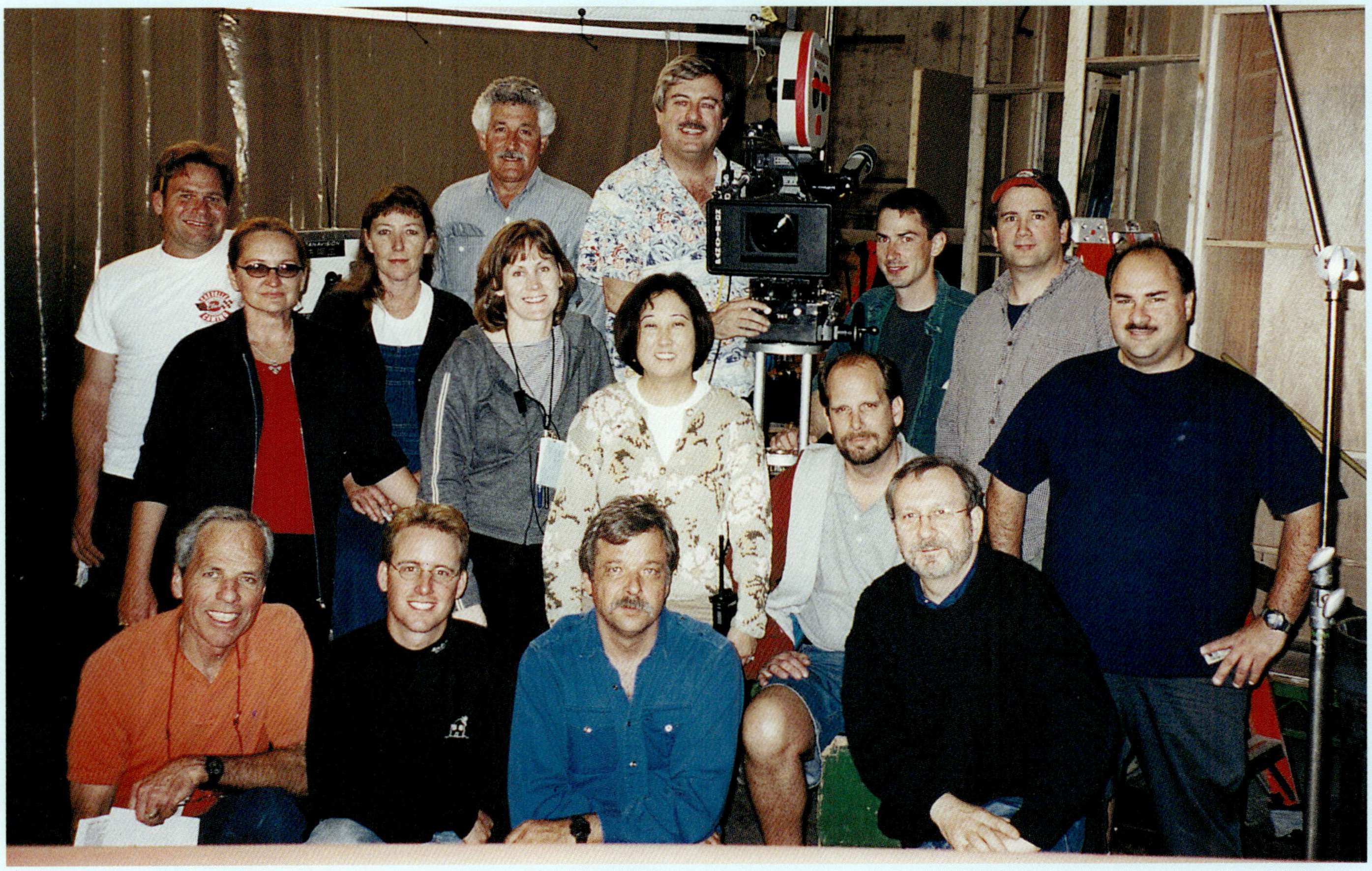

ABOVE: The terrific second-unit crew. Each individual was a valued part of the team and made the work fun.

of photography familiar with the show were brought in. We were happy to welcome Jerry Finnerman, director of photography on the original series, and hear great stories from his lengthy career. We also worked with Tom DeNove, Lowell Peterson, and others.

I always looked forward to the second-unit days. Any time you get to direct anything, it's a great privilege working in our species' most powerful art form. I loved working with all the cast members. Second unit was always a little more relaxed, and I like to think the actors enjoyed some time away from the intense pressures of principle photography.

BELOW: Directing a group of background artists for a second-unit blue-screen visual-effects shot.

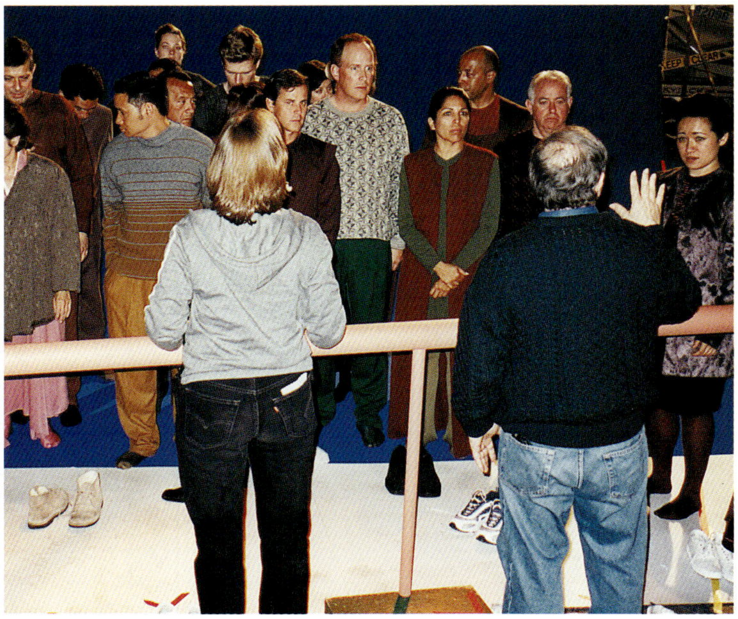

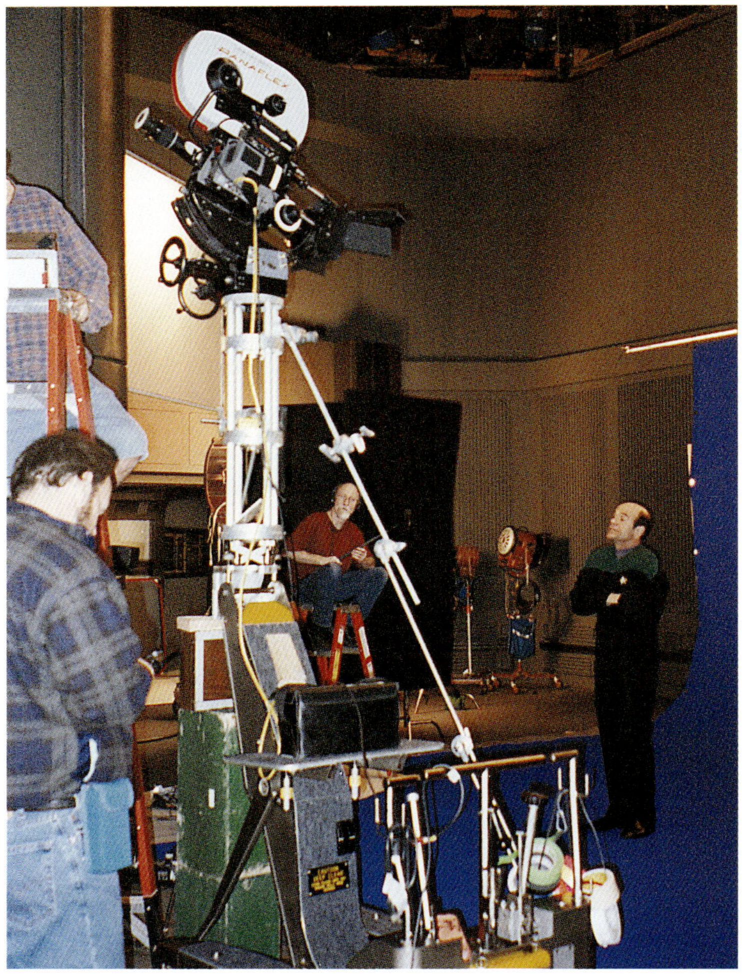

ABOVE: Setting up a visual-effects blue-screen shot with The Doctor, played by the great Robert Picardo.

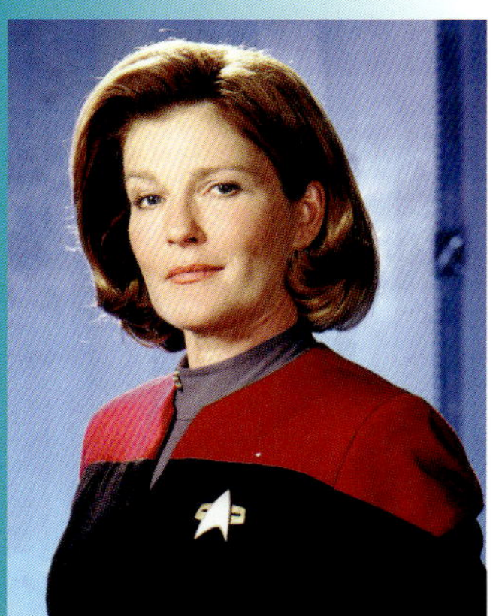

"I must have met Dan Curry very early on, but it was only as time went on that I realised he was the covert genius behind the entire thing. Everybody would sort of quiet down when Dan entered the sound stage. I remember saying to somebody, 'Why does everybody whisper around Dan?' and they said, 'Because he's the bona fide genius behind this whole thing. Go ask Rick Berman how important Dan Curry is.' Then I started to watch the visual effects with a new eye, and I understood it was true. Roddenberry was, of course, the great spirit behind Star Trek*, but I think that without Dan's extraordinary talents it would have never risen to the heights it did.*

I remember his presence as being very easy, very warm. I would say to him, 'What do you mean, it's an alien? It's a tennis ball on a pole!' He would do his level best to explain it, but it was like a giant talking to a tiny idiot. He was always kind and patient. I truly appreciated that, given the extent of what he was thinking about and what he encompassed in that big brain of his."

Kate Mulgrew on Dan

INSIDE STORY

BREAKING THE LANGUAGE BARRIER

Veteran director Rick Kolbe was shooting a scene in Engineering on one occasion. One of our background artists regularly seen as a crewman in Engineering was from Thailand; his English was not that fluent, and Rick spoke with a German accent, which added to the cast member's difficulty understanding what Rick was asking for. There were visual effects in the scene, so I was standing next to Rick. A non-corporeal energy creature was to fly out of one of the consoles, and the engineering crewman was supposed to watch it move past him. It was apparent that the actor didn't understand Rick's direction, so I asked Rick if I could help. I repeated Rick's direction in Thai, and described what the creature would look like—until that moment, no-one on set knew I spoke Thai. The actor was pleasantly surprised, and relieved that he now understood what was required to nail his performance. When I turned back to Rick and the crew, they somehow looked less surprised than I expected.

INSIDE STORY

LOOKING IN THE RIGHT PLACE

On the *Enterprise* bridge set, the viewscreen was just a big opening and we'd add whatever appeared on it later by compositing in the edit bay. The characters on the screen and the cast on the bridge had to be shot separately, but we had to make sure that they were looking at one another with the right eyelines.

When preparing to shoot characters who would appear on the viewscreen, I would trace the 'A-side' (the scene shot on the *Enterprise* bridge) onto a piece of gel and mount it on a piece of foam core with a hole cut for the opening of the viewscreen, and mount it in front of the camera. We had to make sure that the characters on the screen were looking at the characters on the bridge they were talking to. Viewing through the traced drawing enabled us to place markers on set so the actors on the viewscreen knew where to look for each character from the A-side of the shot.

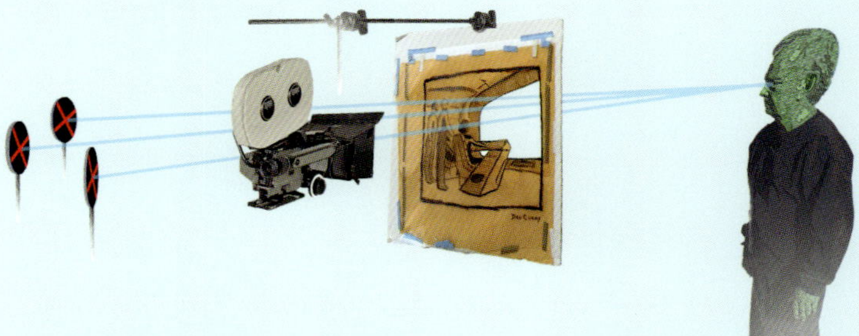

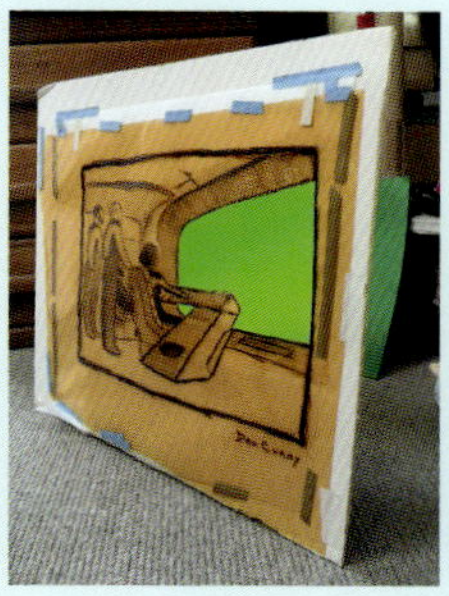

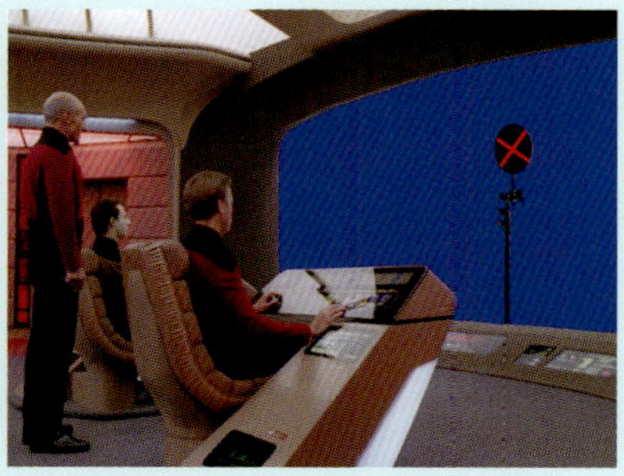

ABOVE: We put the drawing in front of the camera and lined the edges of the frames up so they matched. Then we put dots for the eye lines to show where the bridge characters would be. Once the alignment was established the drawing was removed and we filmed the scene.

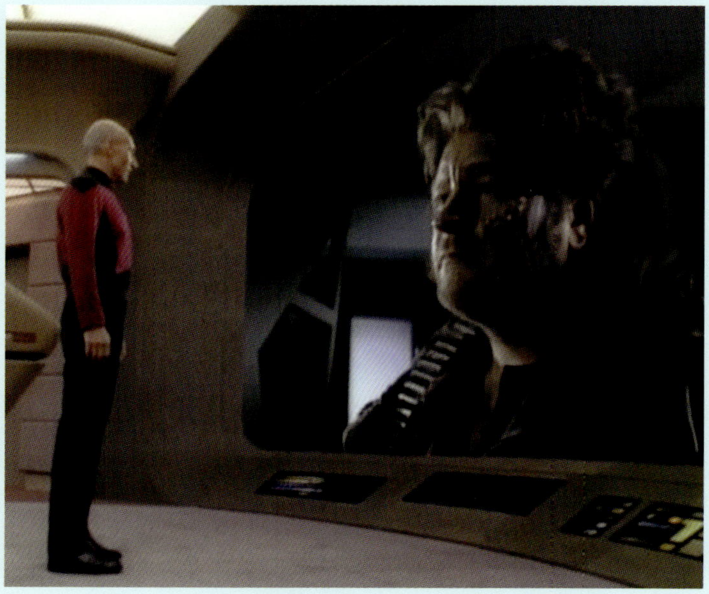

ABOVE: Finished shot of Captain Picard talking with an alien on the main viewer.

INSIDE STORY

LEVITATING Q

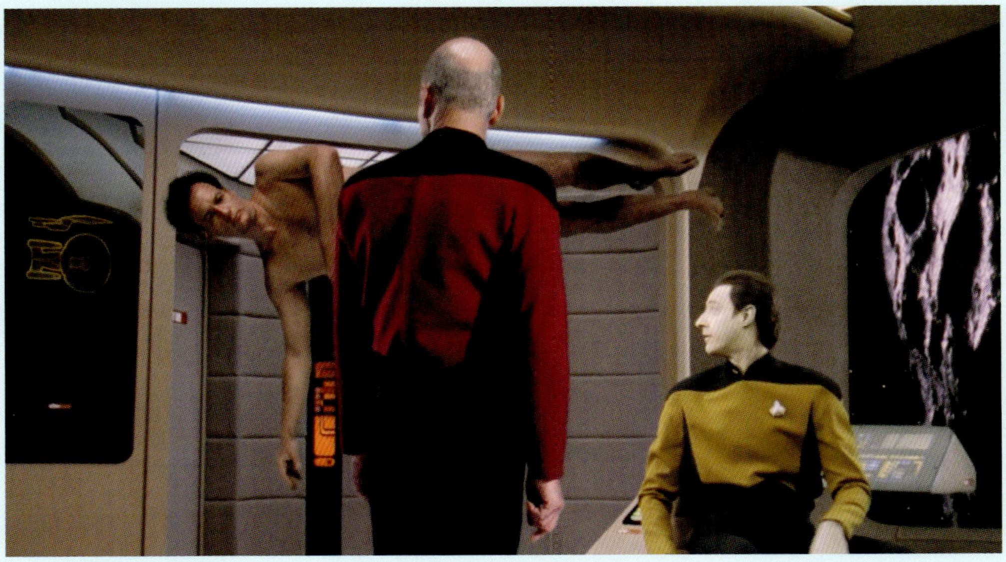

BELOW: Filming this shot involved careful planning in order to preserve John de Lancie's modesty.

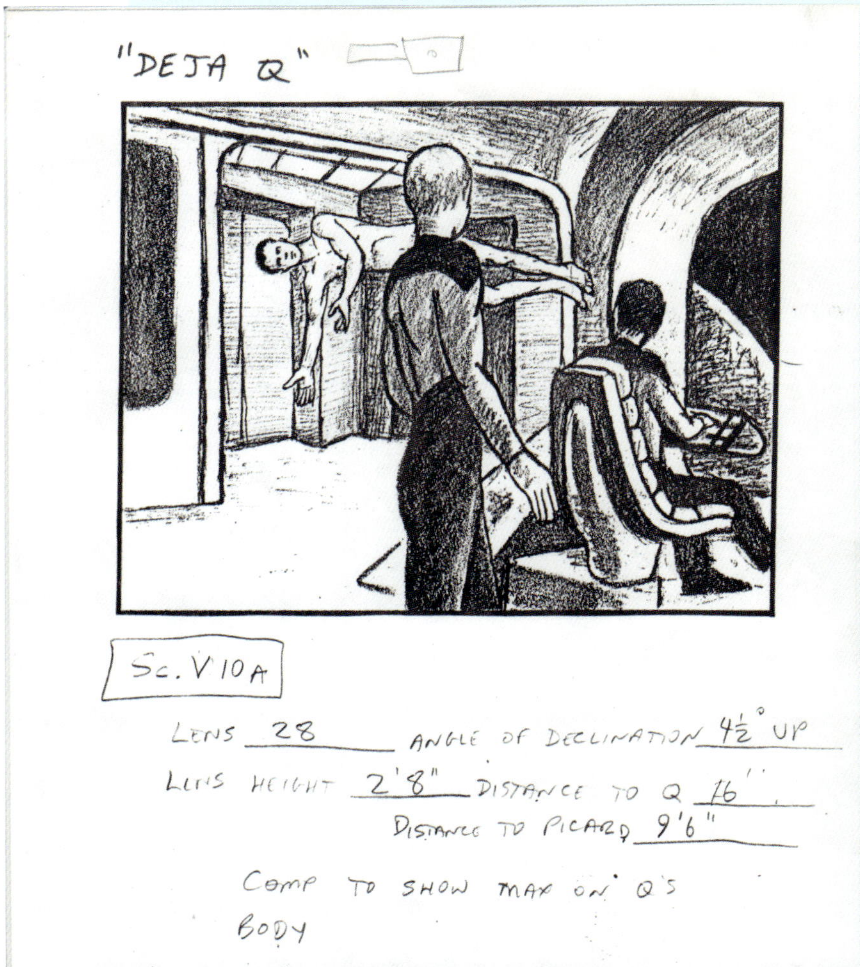

In 'Deja Q,' the inimitable John de Lancie as Q appears stark naked on the bridge, suspended in mid-air. Somehow we had to hide Q's private parts. I went to the bridge set and selected an angle for the shot. I did a storyboard showing Patrick juxtaposed for propriety, making sure there were no subliminal erotic undertones. As we were setting up the over-the-shoulder shot, John, dedicated to his craft, walked in, took off his bathrobe, and there he was as described in the script. I remember assistant director Merri Howard saying, "Let's get you a Speedo." John was not only a wonderful actor, but also a good sport. Now, with Speedo, we moved on with the scene.

Later in the episode there's a scene where the alien Calamarain, non-corporeal energy beings, surround Q with a kinetic energy cocoon that lifts him into the air. To do that, we photographed John in front of a blue screen to composite over a background plate of Engineering. We wanted a camera pan to follow Q's movement, but the shot had to be locked down for the VFX work. We achieved the pan by shooting with an anamorphic Cinemascope lens. The proportions of Cinemascope film are wider than those used for TV. The illusion of a pan was created in a process called 'pan and scan' by moving the narrower TV frame inside the wider C-scope image. This was before the advent of tracking technology, which makes matching camera moves easy.

For the energy cocoon, I had the idea of breaking up Q's silhouette using random microprisms. I took several feet of clear film leader, and dabbed on artist's clear acrylic gel with a scrap of plastic bag, knowing it would dry into transparent tiny peaks that would refract light. I enlisted the help of Bob Bailey, an excellent optical printer operator. Using color separation filters, he obtained a matte of John's silhouette on black and white hi-con film. We duped that through the clear leader with the gel 'prisms,' giving us a randomly kinetic shape changing from frame to frame. In compositing we used this to create the frenetic energy cocoon surrounding Q.

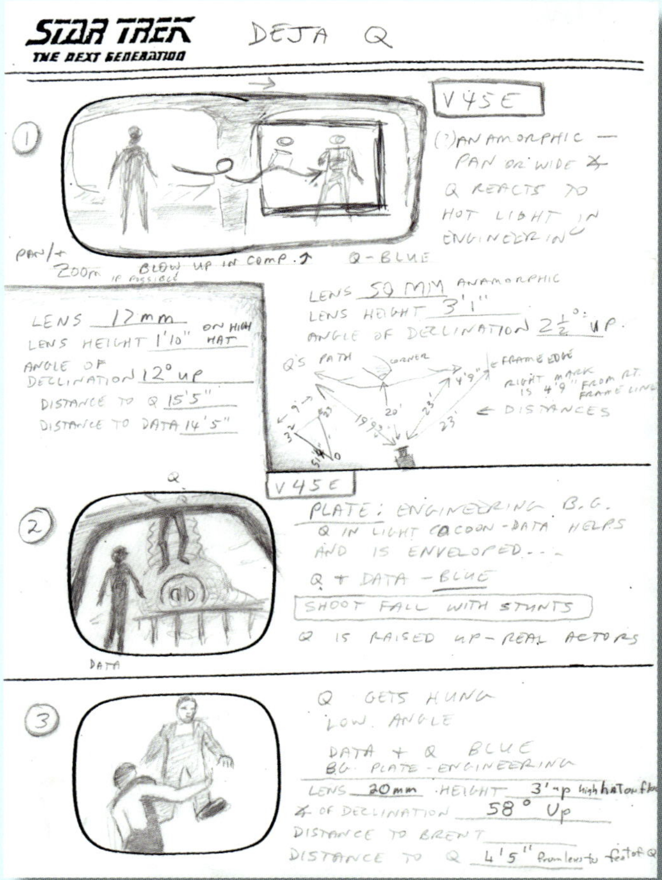

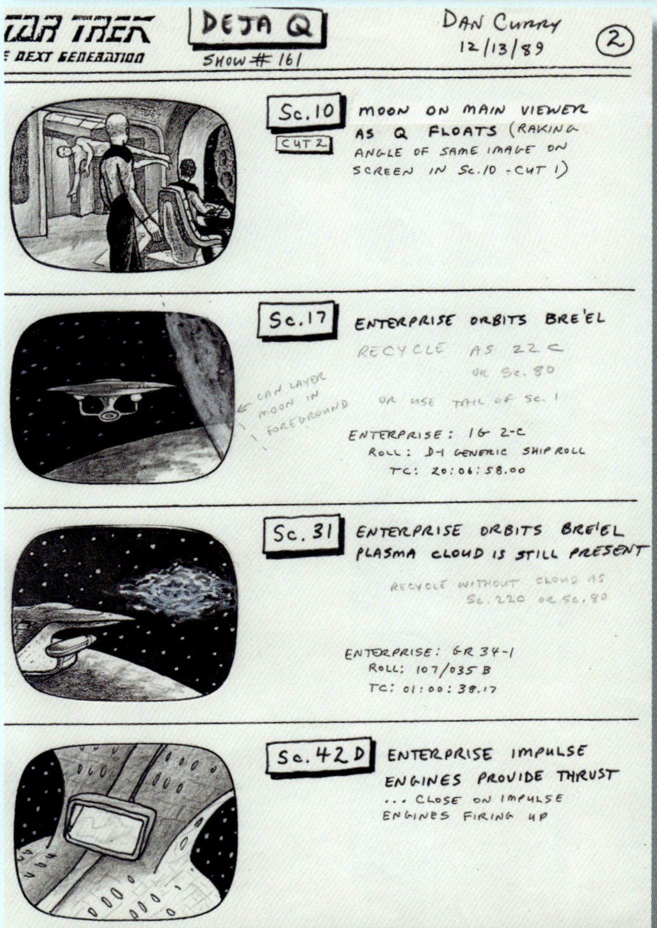

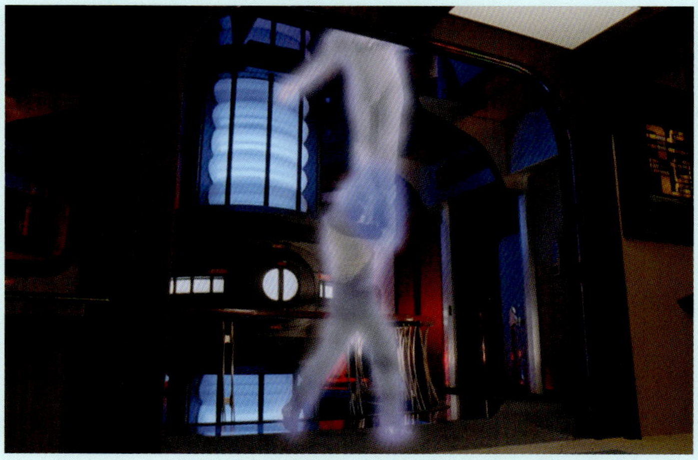

ABOVE: The energy cocoon was made by re-photographing footage of a hi-con silhouette of Q through microprisms on a length of clear film leader, using an optical printer operated by Robert Bailey at Pacific Title and Art Studio.

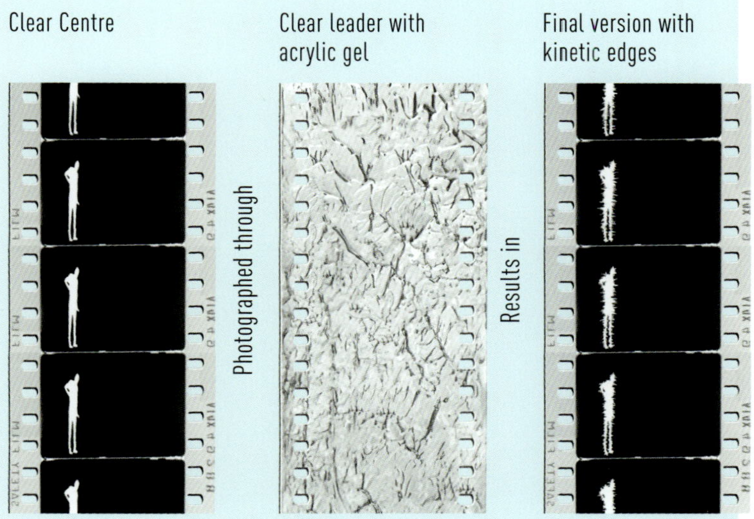

LEFT: Storyboards of VFX shots from 'Deja Q'. The Calamarain energy creature in Scene 31 was another use of one of our laser elements.

BELOW: An eliptical anamorphic Cinemascope lens squeezes a wider view onto a standard 4.33:1 frame. When stretched back out to its 2.35:1 aspect ratio there is room for a standard frame to move horizontally within it and, say, follow an actor as he crosses frame, giving the illusion of a pan.

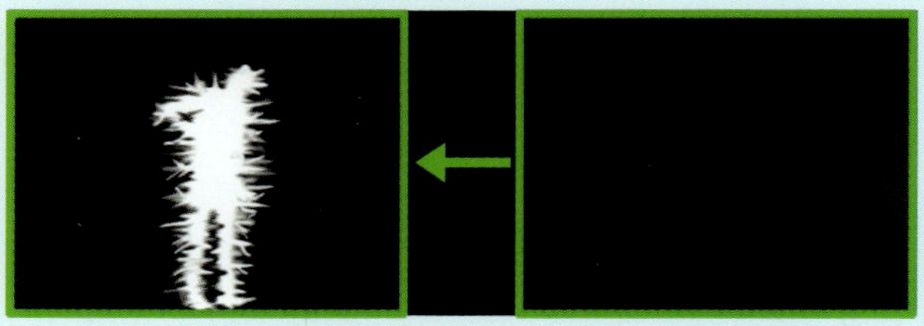

INSIDE STORY

LEVITATING RIKER

In the episode 'Schisms,' aliens abduct the sleeping Commander Riker and pull him into another dimension. He levitates off his bed and floats through a portal we nicknamed the 'interdimensional sphincter.'

I didn't want to use wires to lift Riker because it can look unnatural. To design the shot I brought a piece of two by four to the set cut to Jonathan Frakes' height. I used it to determine how much room we needed to move Riker's body through the portal, and the best camera angle and lens. We shot an empty background plate in Riker's quarters. After consulting with stunt coordinator Dennis Madalone, I asked Jonathan's stunt double, Tommy Morga, to jump from a high platform in front of a blue screen. He landed on a pile of empty cardboard boxes that Dennis determined was a safe landing pad. With a matching lens on a Photo-Sonics camera, we shot at 360 frames per second so that when we played it back at normal speed the movement would appear very slow. We rotated the camera so that instead of falling, it looked as if Riker was rising slowly across the room. Ron B. Moore and I created the portal by draining milk through a randomly shaped modelling clay funnel that we combined with liquid nitrogen elements in compositing.

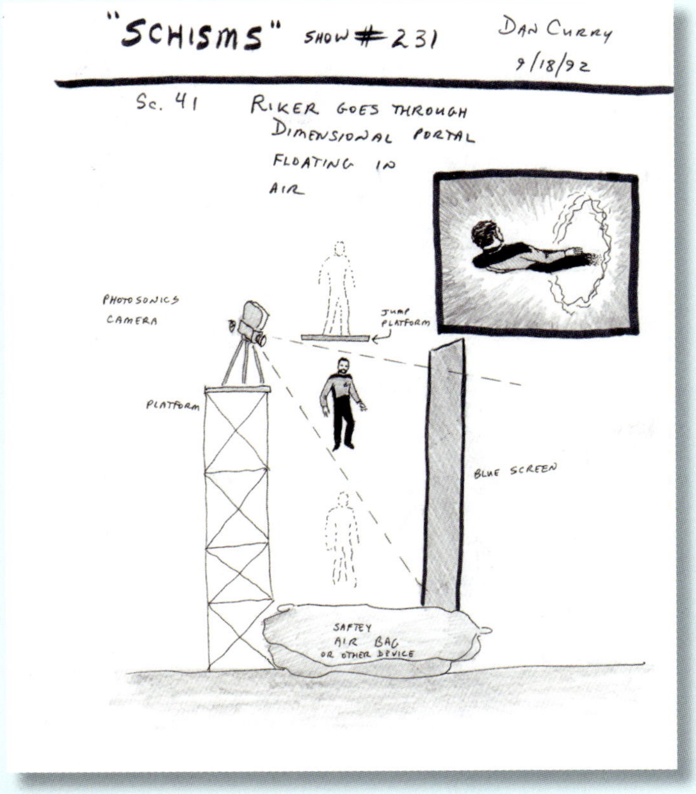

ABOVE: We skewed the camera around to make it look as if Tommy Morga was moving up and across the screen instead of falling.

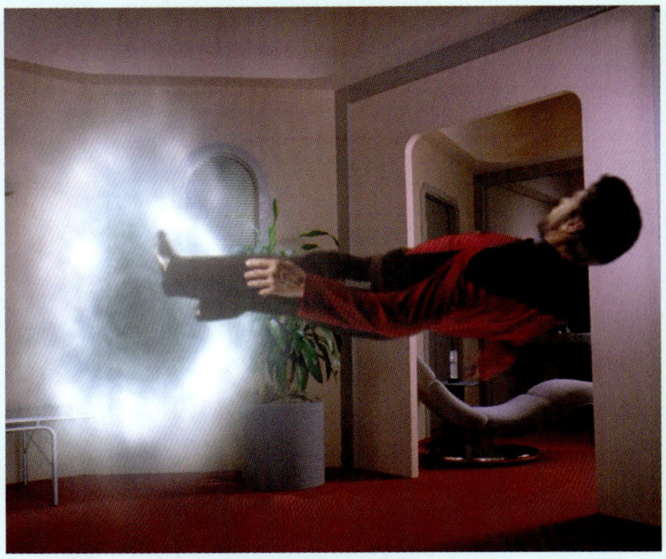

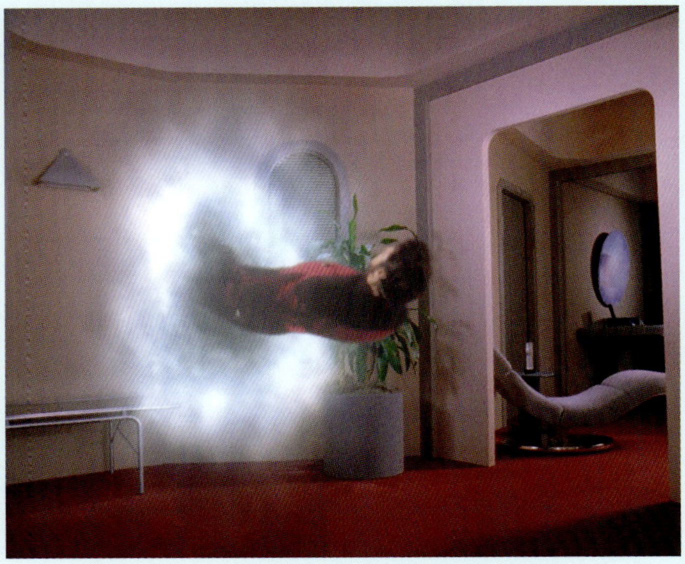

ABOVE: The sequence called for Riker to levitate from his bed, move across the compartment, and be pulled through a portal into another dimension.

ABOVE RIGHT: We filmed stunt double Tommy Morga from an angle that didn't show his face, so viewers believed it was Jonathan. His body was softly erased a frame at a time to create the illusion that he was disappearing inside the portal.

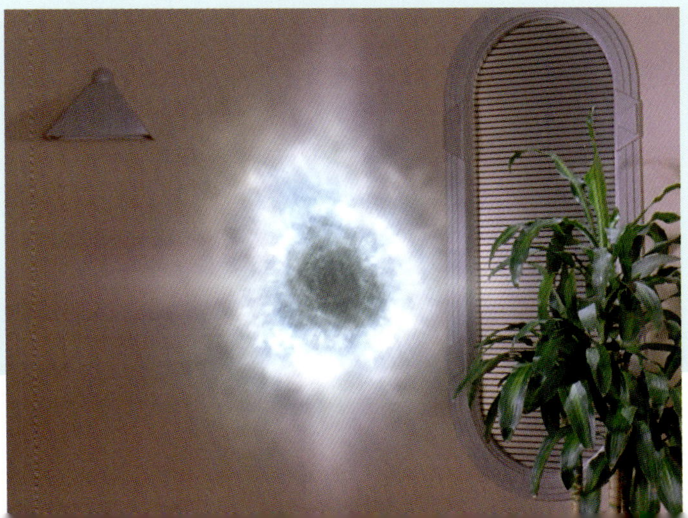

RIGHT: The 'dimensional sphincter' was a separate element we made with milk and liquid nitrogen.

INSIDE STORY

PAINTING 'THE VISIBLE KLINGON'

When I was a child there were two anatomical model kits that were of great interest: The Visible Man and The Visible Woman. The outer surface was clear plastic, and all the bones and internal organs were crafted in bright colors. I was always interested in trying to draw accurately, and I realized that knowing the inner workings of the human body would help.

When I first came back from overseas, I did a brief stint in New York as a biomedical illustrator, improving my knowledge and skills. This came in handy years later, when I was working on *Star Trek*. Conversations with brilliant makeup supervisor Mike Westmore, who designed the Klingon prosthetics, led to discussions of how their internal anatomy would differ from humans. I thought it would be fun to come up with something.

An occasional script would mention an internal feature, such as two hearts and redundant organs, and building upon this I injected my own ideas. One script mentioned that Klingons had 23 ribs; I realized that to squeeze that many in a parallel structure like human ribs would not fit, so I invented a lattice ribcage. I added extra bones in upper appendages, an armored larynx and clavicle, and the hearts would be stacked two-deep so only one would be seen in the illustration. The challenge was fitting all this inside the body of a human actor and having enough similarities to justify the possibility of interbreeding. Drawing inspiration from the work of great portrait artist John Singer Sargent and Renaissance anatomist Andreas Vesalius, I decided on a style for the painting. As I was working on it I casually mentioned it to Rod Roddenberry, who suggested doing an edition of posters through his merchandising company to make it available to fans.

When *Enterprise* had an episode featuring a Klingon medical facility, I suggested that the art department use the piece as part of a medical chart. Brilliant as always, they came up with call-outs in Klingon on a shape that echoed the geometry of a Klingon viewscreen.

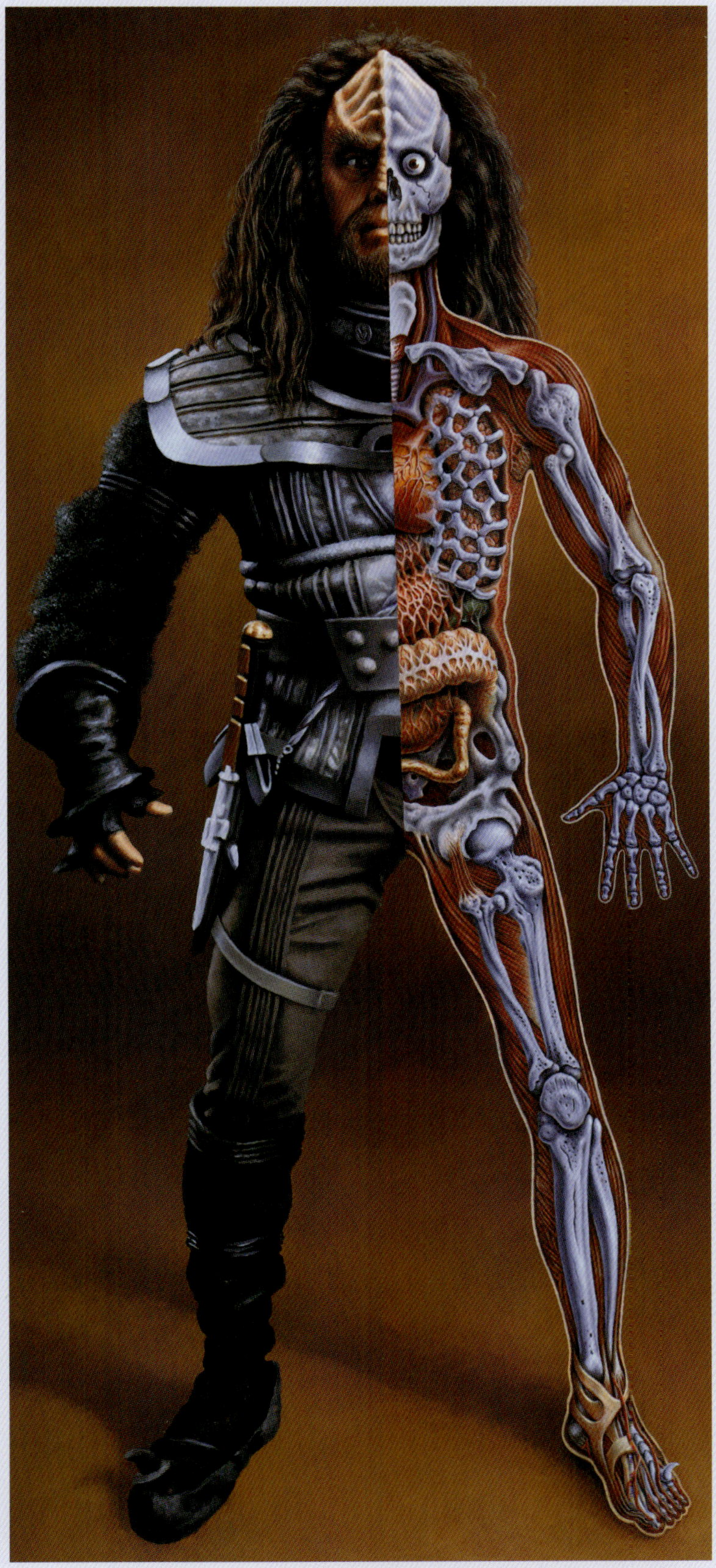

RIGHT: Oil paint, 18" x 24", on gator board, a nice surface to paint on with a texture like egg shell. It was fun squeezing in alien anatomical structures inside a human silhouette.

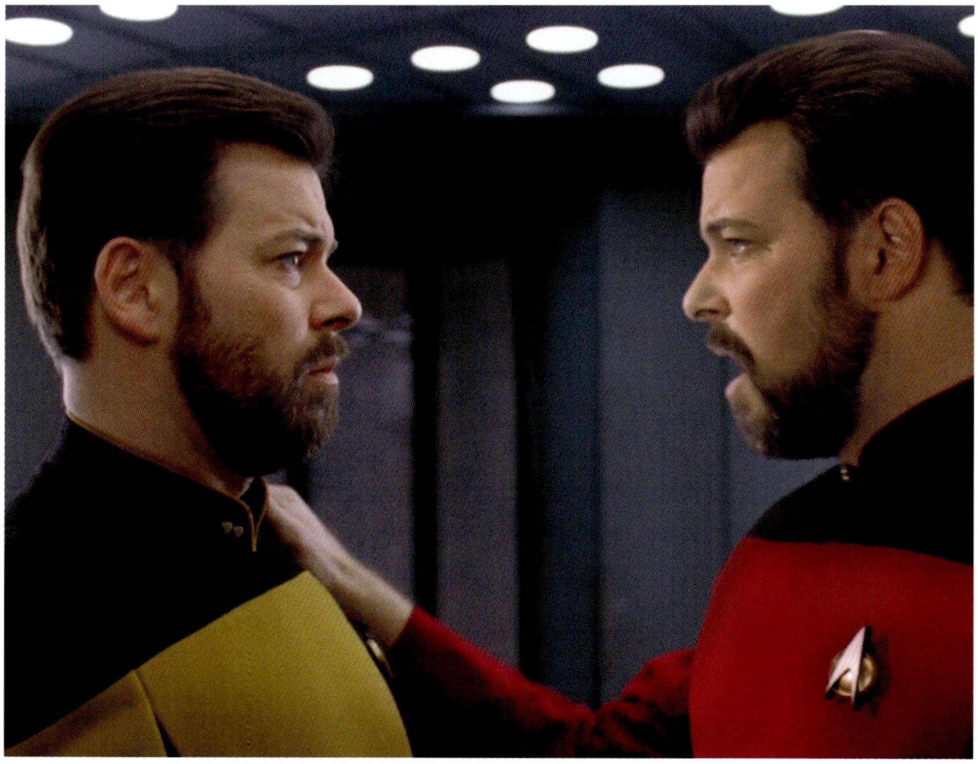

CREATING BODY DOUBLES

THE CHALLENGE OF DUPLICATING ACTORS IN A SCENE

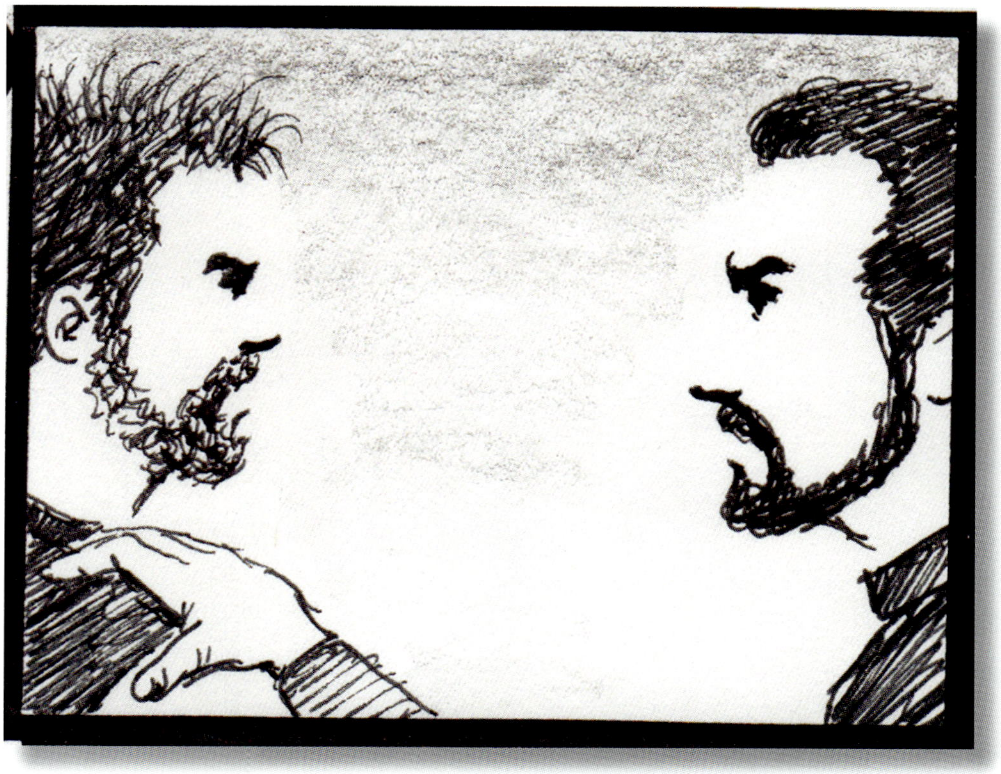

ABOVE: Viewers should never realise that in this shot Riker's arm actually belongs to a body double who has been covered up by the image of Jonathan Frakes.

On *Star Trek*, we often had to create scenes where the same actor appeared in a shot more than once, say if there were two Rikers, or two Picards, or 80 Doctors. The traditional method, called a 'split screen,' was to lock the camera down so that it couldn't move, and then photograph the actor on one side of frame, with the script supervisor reading the doppelganger's lines. Next, the actor would change wardrobe and makeup, and portray the other character in a separate take. Then the two takes are combined in post production. This technique was creatively limited: the camera has to be absolutely static so you can combine both halves of the shot seamlessly and the actor could not pass in front of or behind him or herself.

Throughout the series, we did lots of split-screen shots using the traditional lock-down method, only we did our compositing on video rather than an optical printer. We came up with creative solutions when actors needed to touch their duplicates or hand objects to them. When we wanted one Riker to reach out and touch the shoulder of the other one, we'd film a body double reaching out to touch Jonathan's shoulder. Then in another take we'd position Jonathan so we cover the double's body when we did the compositing, and it would look as if it was his arm. In the final shot there would be two versions of Jonathan Frakes, and a third actor's arm.

If we wanted a character to pass something to a duplicate, we set up a small stand between the actors that we could remove in compositing. In the first take of the shot, the actor put the object on the stand. In a second take the actor, now on the other side of the frame, picked it up. We'd remove the stand and adjust the

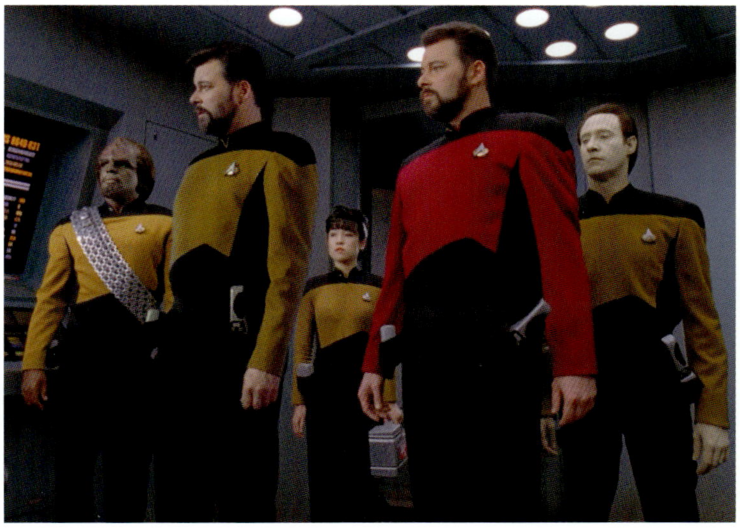

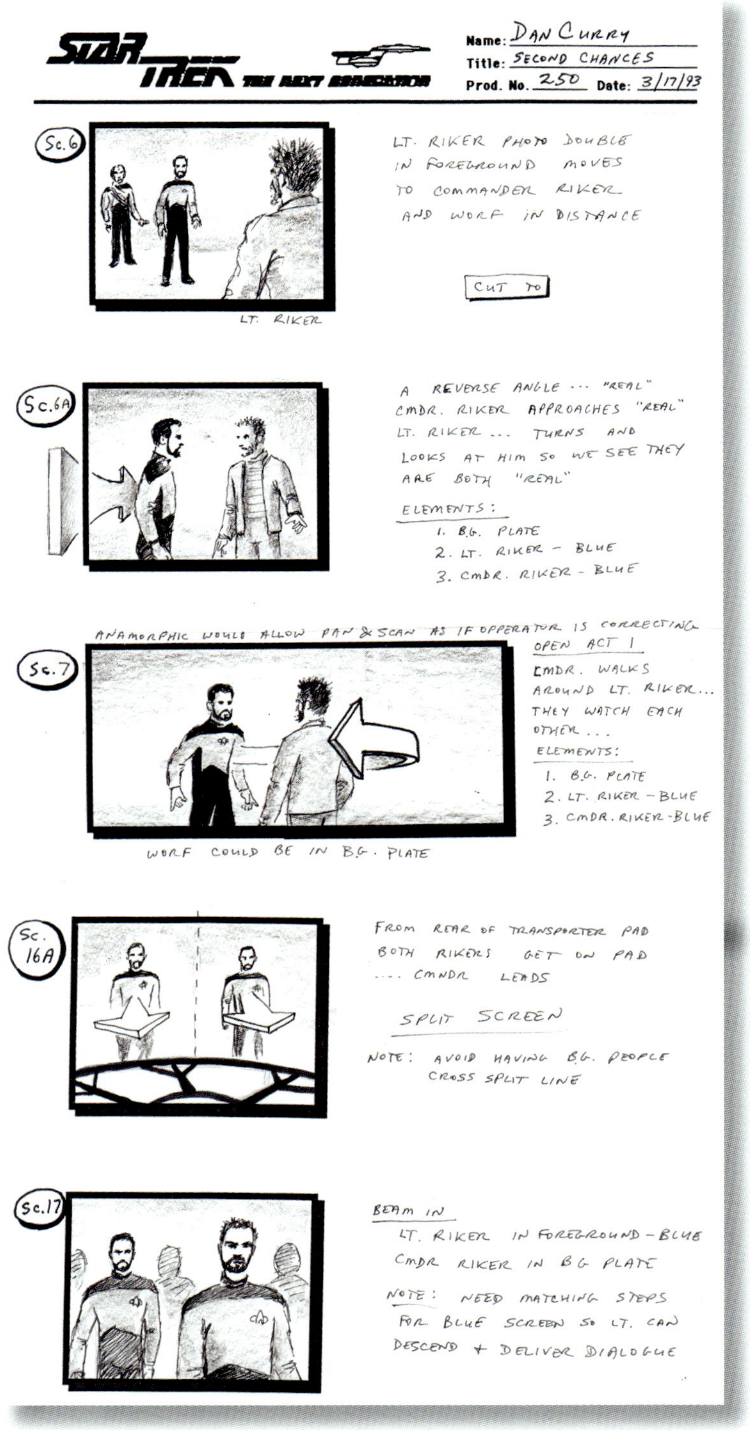

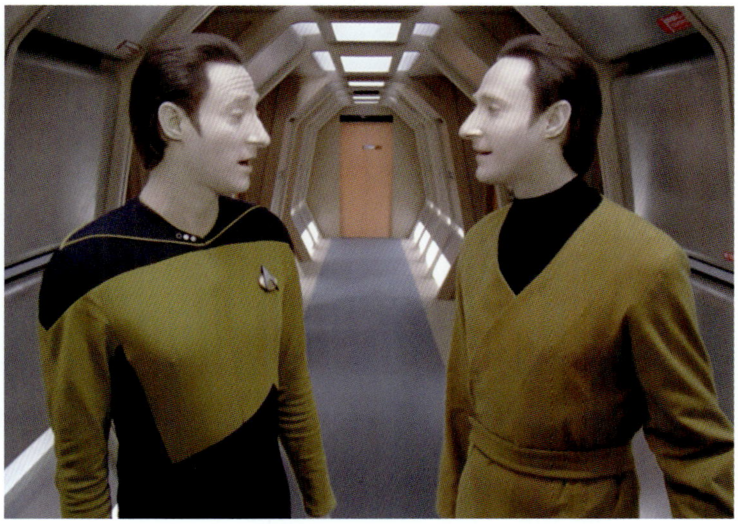

ABOVE: The repeatability of motion control makes it possible to add almost anything, such as a second version of an actor to a moving shot.

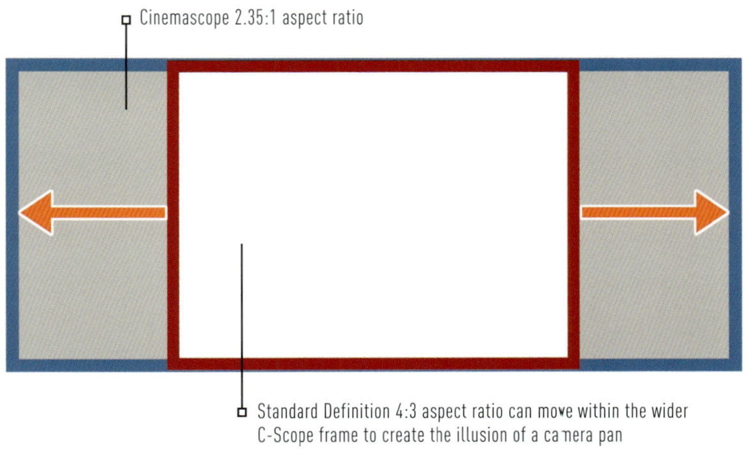

timing so it looked as if they were passing the object to themselves.

You could still create the illusion of a camera move when the camera was locked off if you filmed in in widescrceen. A 2.35:1 image was wider than TV's 1.33:1. In the edit bay, we could move the framing back and forth within the widescreen image, 'pan-and-scan', making it look as if the camera was moving. When the camera had to move, we brought a portable motion-control system onto the set. This gave us the ability to stage more elaborate choreography. We always filmed the background without any actors (a 'clean plate') to use if part of the background was needed to hide things we didn't want you to see.

If a shot needed to show duplicates walking around each other, we filmed them in front of a blue or a green screen so we could cut out each actor as a separate layer that we could combine in editing. The key to making a shot like that look natural is making sure that the double casts a shadow on 'themselves.' We used a framed black cloth 'flag' or a stand-in actor to pass in front of the light source at the right moment. I remember we had Riker doing that in 'Second Chances.'

There were also situations where we didn't have time, or it was just impractical to use a blue or green screen on set, so we just separated the actor out by rotoscoping, a technique where an actor or object is traced frame by frame to derive a matte or alpha channel to use as a separate element in compositing.

LEFT: Making multiples of an actor appear in the same shot involves careful thought and planning.

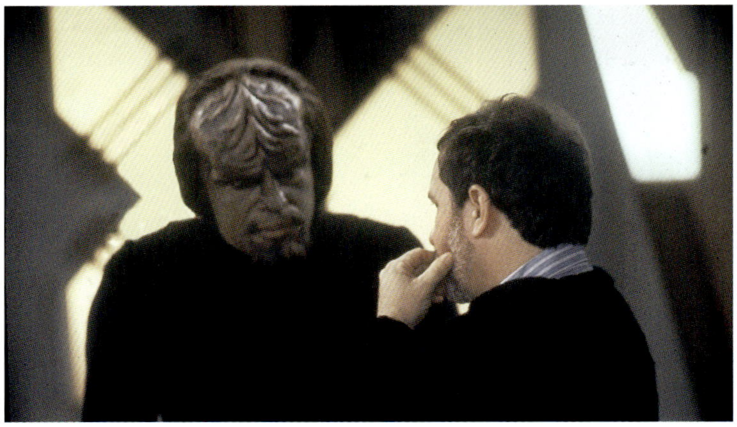

ABOVE: Discussing the nuances of a scene with the excellent Michael Dorn.

DIRECTING 'BIRTHRIGHT, PART II'

CALLING THE SHOTS ON SET IN AN ALL-NEW EXPERIENCE

I had been directing second unit for five years before I got a chance to direct a complete episode. The producers were reluctant to let me direct, because they wanted to make sure that the visual effects were running smoothly, and directing basically took me off-line. I had to make it clear to them that I deserved a shot, and that this was necessary to keep me on the show.

I think I expected them to give me an episode that had a lot of space battles so I could use my VFX skills, but it turned out to be a character show. The episode I directed is 'Birthright, Part II.' It's about Worf looking for his father but actually finding a planet where the Romulans have been keeping a group of Klingons prisoner. According to all the rules of honor, the Klingons should have killed themselves, but instead they've become friendly with the Romulans, and even intermarried and had kids. Worf tries to show them the 'error' of their ways, and at the same time he starts to fall in love with a beautiful young Klingon, and has to come to terms with his own prejudices when he discovers that she's half Romulan. The core of the story was about Worf overcoming his intolerance fomented by generations of hatred between Klingons and Romulans. That's what *Star Trek* does brilliantly—by seemingly

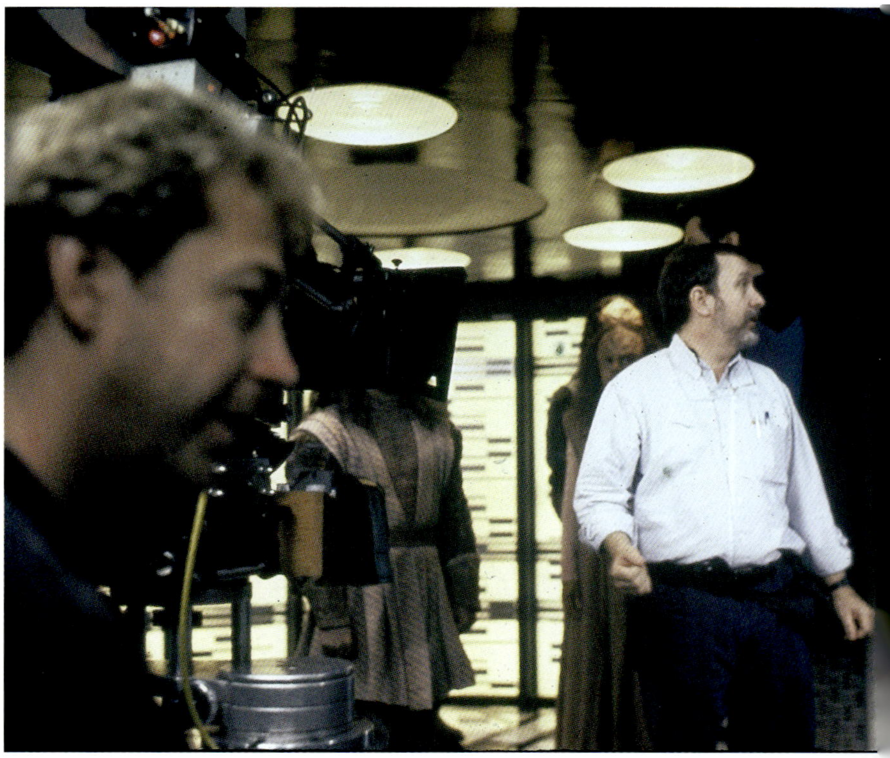

RIGHT: A-camera operator Kris Krosskove watches rehearsal of a scene in the transporter bay.

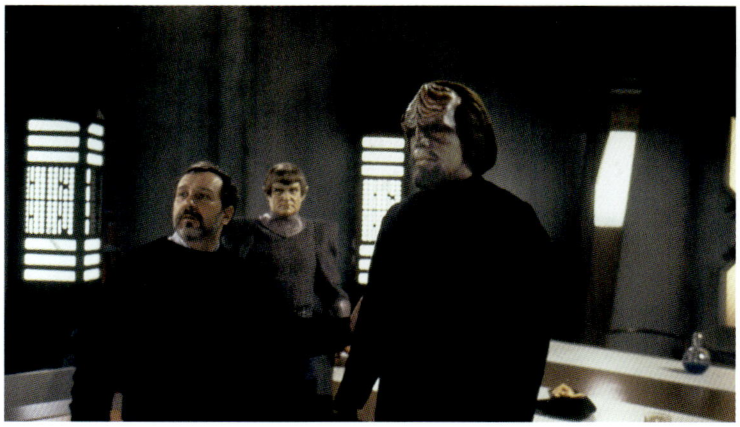

ABOVE: Working out a scene with Michael Dorn and Alan Scarfe.

telling a story about aliens, the episode examines human foibles from a distance. The audience may think, "Why do these Klingons and Romulans hate each other so much? It's ridiculous," but if that's the case, why do we have so many cultural conflicts on Earth that are meaningless in the grander scheme of things?

I'd directed a lot of live theater in grad school, but that's very different. With live theater you have considerable rehearsal time, time to evolve the characters, and time to experiment with blocking. Television is a fast-moving machine—you have to make decisions and live with them. It's basically show up on set, and work and work and work. Every member of the crew, from craft service people to the camera crew, works incredibly hard, focused on their individual responsibilities.

We had a lot to do on this episode. You got seven working days and sometimes a second-unit day to shoot an episode. Normally, you have 55 pages of script. We had 66 pages. That means that instead of shooting eight pages a day, we had to shoot nearly ten. So we were really under the gun, and I couldn't spend as much time on staging scenes as I would have liked.

You don't get a lot of time to prepare. Normally a director gets a tone meeting, where the producers and the writers sit down and make the director aware of their vision for the episode, subtexts, and overall tone, but for some reason that never happened. I think it was because 'Birthright' was a two-part story, and they had already had the tone meeting with veteran director Rick Kolbe, who was helming part one. But as a result, I didn't really know what the writers and producers had in mind. Later on, I learned that Michael Piller intended it to be more like *The Bridge on the River Kwai*; had I understood that, I would have approached directing the episode somewhat differently.

On *Star Trek* there was no time for read-throughs with the actors. The regular cast members know their characters so well they can always be trusted to deliver. As director, you can block the scene and guide the actors, and discuss the intensity of a scene and the emotional arcs, but, as they should, the actors own their characters and their performances. I was fortunate that 'Birthright, Part II' was a Worf show. Worf is a character I have great affinity for, and Michael Dorn was always wonderful to work with. He placed great trust in me, and respected my vision for how the various scenes would unfold. Michael really dug into coming to grips with Worf's intolerance and overcoming it, while not losing his core being. Above all else, Worf is a warrior for whom honor is the highest virtue.

Directors have more influence over the performances of the guest stars, because they don't have an established character. We had an excellent guest cast—Alan Scarfe, who played Tokath, the Romulan commander of the camp, and Richard Herd, who played the older Klingon, L'Kor, were both wonderful, very Shakespearean with great voices. Sterling Macer as Toq did a really good job too. Christine Rose, who played the Klingon mother, gave a powerful performance. Jennifer Gatti as Ba'el exuded the right balance of innocence and sensual curiosity.

I did get a chance to walk around the sets, which were already up before we started because they had been built for part one. That gave me the chance to think about how the scenes would physically play out within the actual spaces where they would occur. I storyboarded the most important scenes, but the important thing about storyboards is one must be willing to throw them away when something unexpected and better comes up on the set. A lot of times an actor will surprise you by doing something unplanned and really wonderful. Serendipity.

I spent a lot of time thinking about the script. What is the point of each scene? How does it advance the story? How can I, through blocking and camera moves, visually support the emotional dynamics? How can I have characters doing something interesting that feels natural when they are delivering expositional dialogue? As the director, you are trying to show what's going on underneath the surface. For example, in the scene where Tokath first encounters Worf in his cell and says, "I have an unusual prison," I didn't want them to just stand there and talk. So I said, "Okay, Michael, let's make up the bed. We'll do a refrigerator shot so that you can have your back to Alan." I thought it was important that Worf had turned his back to be especially insulting and closed off to the Romulan. This turned the simple act of unrolling a blanket into an act of resistance.

The crew was incredibly supportive. Alan Bernard, the sound recorder, had been around forever, his nickname on set being 'Grandfather.' Before we started, he pulled me aside and said, "I'm going to tell you something. When you're doing a group scene, certain actors always want to walk away from the group as if they're thinking about something. The real reason they're doing that is it forces you to give them a single close-up, so be careful. Only let that happen when you want it to." I thought that was interesting. Sure enough, as soon as we began to rehearse a group scene, I saw

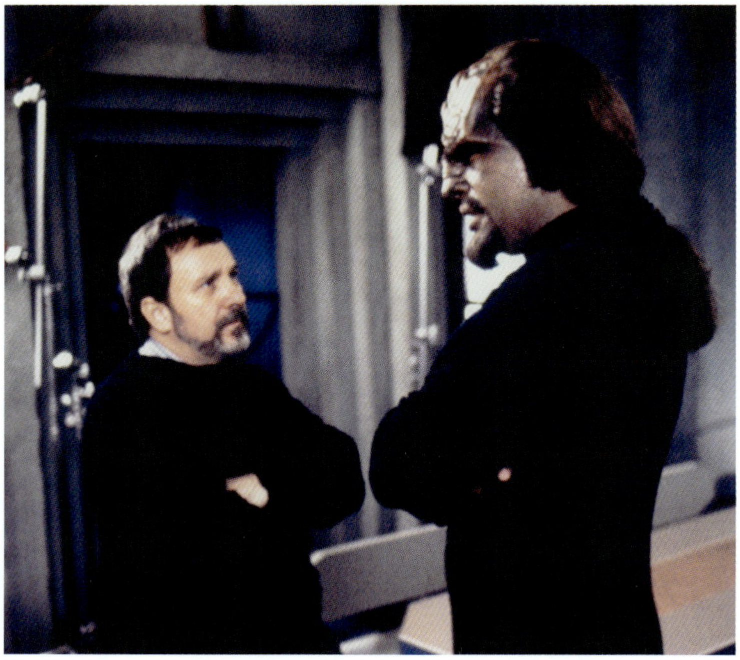

ABOVE: Collaborating with Michael on the interpretation of a scene was immensely rewarding.

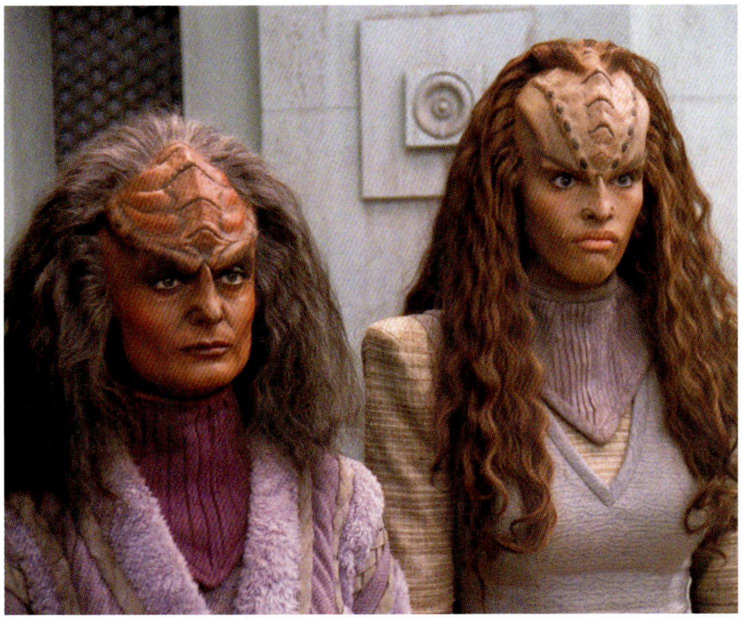

ABOVE: Guest stars Christine Rose and Jennifer Gatti prepare for an emotional scene.

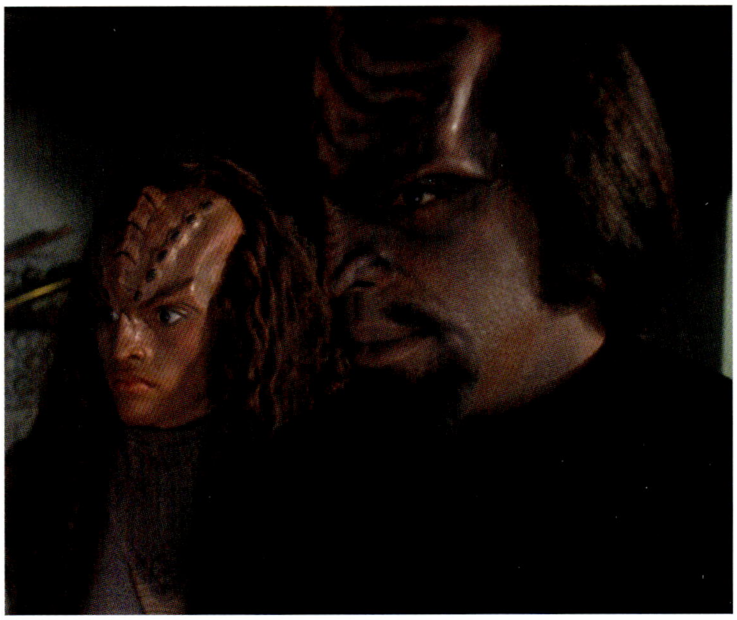

ABOVE: Ba'el and Worf get serious.

that happening. I thought to myself, "Thank you, Alan."

I can't express my appreciation enough to director of photography Jonathan West, who was my great ally, and did everything he could to support me. I have to give him special praise for that. He quietly did me a great favor—when we were rehearsing a scene where Worf comes upon a group of young Klingons playing a game with spears and a hoop, I was looking for the best angle from which to shoot the scene. I noticed Jonathan walked to a different area than where I was, and stood there. I realized he had to have a reason for doing that, so I walked over to where he was, and discovered he had found a better angle. That's why he's the director of photography. Editor Steve Tucker was immensely helpful in cutting the episode together. His talent and experience was instrumental in telling the story.

There are moments in the show where I was very pleased with the artistic use of lighting to reinforce the emotional context of a scene. There's a scene where Worf and the young Klingon woman, Ba'el, meet in a quiet corner of the set. She flirts with him, asking him if Kahless, the legendary Klingon warrior, ever took a mate. They start getting very romantic. They are about to kiss when Worf sees her pointed ears, and realizes that she's half Romulan. Working with Jonathan and his gaffer (chief lighting technician) R. D. Knox, we had one lighting set-up next to another in the same space so that when Worf and Ba'el are being romantic we had very warm, flattering light, but when he notices her ear he steps away from her into the shadows. For the rest of that scene, Worf is primarily a dark, ominous silhouette in the foreground. What I was trying to underscore with lighting was that Worf withdrew into himself, brooding. What he was saying to her wasn't really about her, it was more of an internal battle for Worf as he confronted his own demons. By putting him in the foreground and keeping him confined in shadow, it subliminally showed the audience the dark space his spirit had taken him to.

When I was in grad school I had the incredible honor to host legendary director Frank Capra when he visited campus. One thing he said that always stuck with me was, "The script has no sprocket holes, you can't run it through a projector." The script doesn't tell you everything in detail, it leaves room for the director's creative vision. There was one scene where the description just said, 'they play a game with spears,' so I made up two games. The one that the young Klingons were playing, not really understanding what the hoops and spears were for, and the hunting practice game Worf teaches them that involved throwing a spear through a hoop. Prop master Alan Sims fabricated the hoops and perfectly balanced spears. There's one moment where the spear comes from behind camera and goes straight through the hoop; I did the live spear throwing myself from off camera.

A primary responsibility of the director is to work out how scenes are played, blocking and action choreography. There's a scene when the young Klingon, Toq, puts his hand on Worf's shoulder, interrupting a session where he is teaching *mok'bara*. The script called for Worf to knock him down. Dennis Madalone, our terrific stunt coordinator, wanted to do a very elaborate series of martial arts moves where Worf flips Toq. However, I felt that Worf was so cool and was such a skilled warrior that dealing with Toq would be more like brushing off a fly. So I said, "Let's just have him flip him over his shoulder with one hand." Dennis wasn't sure what I had in mind, so I had him grab me by the shoulder, and demonstrated

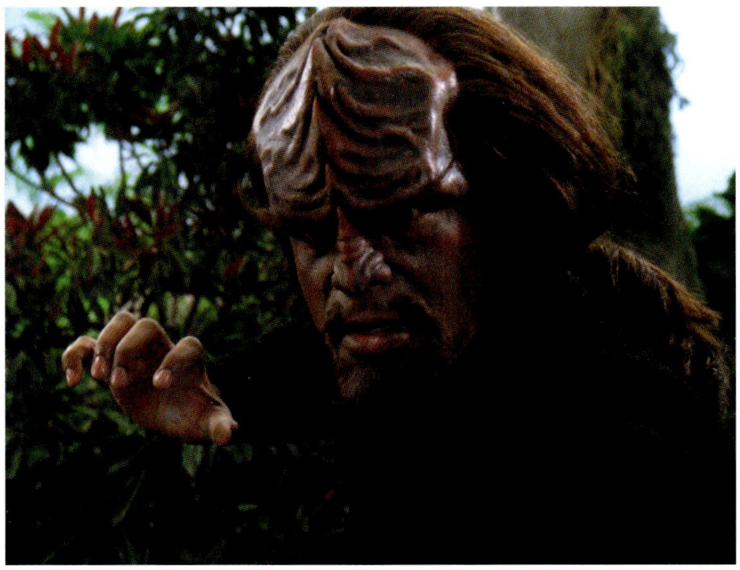

ABOVE: On the jungle set, Worf restrains himself from bashing Toq (off-screen).

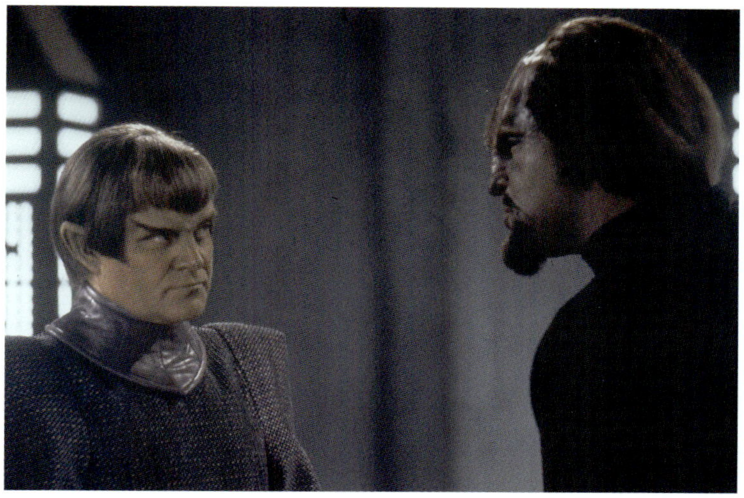

LEFT: Alan and Michael had great chemistry in their intense conflict of wills.

a one-hand wrist twist flip. Michael does that exact same thing to Toq in the finished episode.

I always felt Michael Dorn was trying to do his best for me; I really appreciated that. You can see just how good an actor Michael is in the banquet scene where Toq comes back and throws the carcass of a dead animal on the table (a real sheep carcass). Toq reveals what he has learned about Klingon heritage, and gets really emotional. We cut to Michael. He was just standing there, but he was able to convey very complex emotions with just a look. You could see Worf's triumph from the subtle expressions on Michael's face.

There were also some funny moments while we were filming. There's a scene where a couple of Romulan soldiers are searching for Worf in the jungle. One of the actors was obviously pretending to look for somebody, and wasn't remotely convincing. I asked him what he had with him of value and he gave me his wallet. I hid it in the jungle set and said, "I'm not going to tell you where it is. You're going to have find it while you're doing the scene." After that he was pretty convincing. He found his wallet too.

There are other moments I was proud of as a director. It was late at night, we had been working for many hours and Christine Rose, the veteran actress playing the Klingon mother, was getting very frustrated with the unfamiliar Klingon dialogue. She also wasn't used to working with such heavy prosthetic makeup. There was a moment when she got really upset and had to walk off the set for a while. I wanted to take some pressure off her and give her some time to vent some of the stress, so I told her, "We're ahead of schedule and have plenty of time." This was completely untrue. "It's good that you're feeling so emotionally intense about this because that's the kind of intensity we need for the scene. Just relax, have a drink of water and when you're ready, come back. There's no rush." She just took a couple of minutes and came back and nailed it. Christine's performance was all I could have hoped for, and that next take is the one in the episode.

In retrospect, directing 'Birthright, Part II' was like creating any work of art in any medium in that there are things I would've done differently. There's a scene where Worf is telling stories about Kahless by the fire—I should have shot coverage angles from behind Worf so we would be looking at the people listening and reacting to the story rather than keeping the camera on him. What mattered was the impact of Worf's story on the young people. I think that would've added some strength to the power of that scene.

Another thing I wish I had done wasn't in the script, but if I had been more experienced I would have improvised something and made a bigger moment that revealed Worf's martial-arts mastery. When Worf first encounters Toq digging in a vegetable garden with the *gin'tak* spear, he picks it up and explains, "This is a weapon of war..." I should have had Worf do some impressive spear moves that I could have improvised for Michael—that would have driven home the fact that this spear was not something to dig in the dirt with. And it would have further established Worf's status as a great warrior, and also given us some cool action.

Another change I would've made is the hunting scene. I think I did it too much like real hunting, where hunters remain silent in a blind and wait for the game to come by. It would've been more interesting if they were finding tracks, with more physical action moving through the jungle set. As it was, Worf and Toq share a philosophical moment while waiting in a blind, which lets the audience focus on the mentoring aspect of this scene.

Having worked with most of the crew for years and developed lasting friendships, I was overwhelmed by their support during production. My role as visual-effects supervisor required working closely with everyone in post-production, so I got to have more involvement with the process than most. The editor, Steve Tucker, was super-great working with me, and wanted to do everything he could to make the story powerful. My friend and brilliant musician Jay Chattaway was composing the music for the episode, so I got to collaborate with him more than most directors, who wouldn't hear the score until the show was finished. I wanted a lot of odd, savage percussion in the chase sequence. There were no humans in the show, so I didn't want to have obviously recognizable instruments. I suggested to Jay, "Let's do something that's really weird, like how Chinese and Tibetan music sounds very alien to us." There's a Laotian musical instrument called a *kaan*; it's a reed instrument, and to Western ears it sounds very alien. I brought it in, and Jay sampled it to use on his synthesizer. It can be heard in the score of the show.

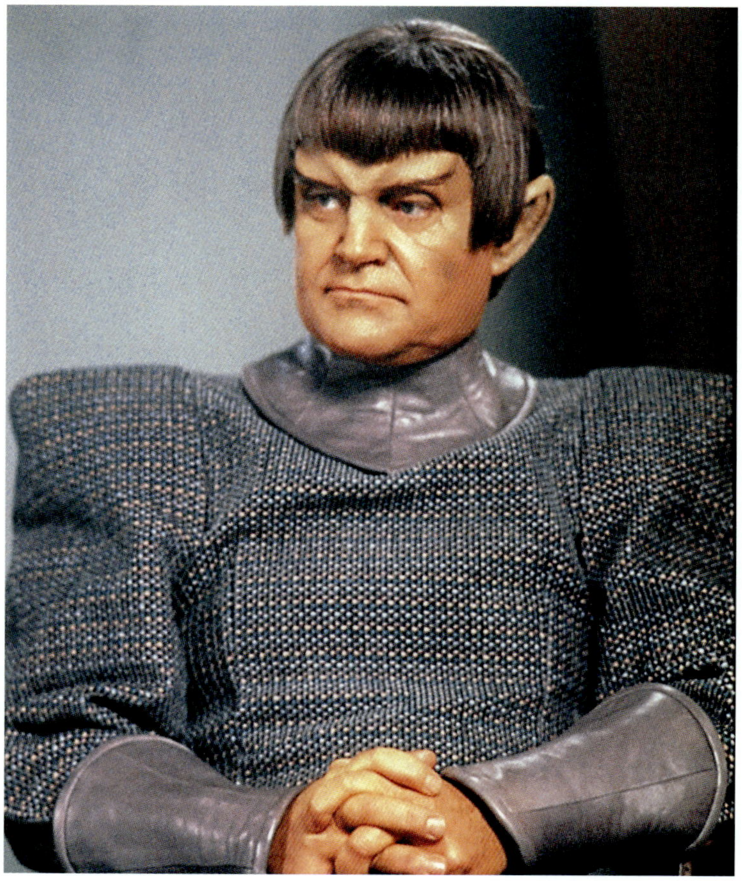

ABOVE: Guest star Alan Scarfe brought great gravitas to his role as Romulan Commander Tokath.

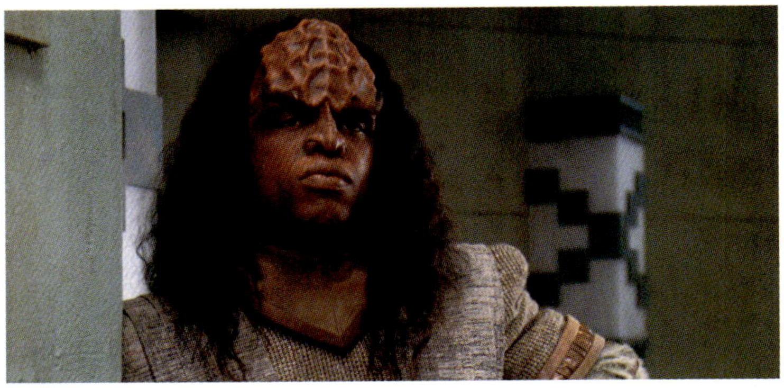

ABOVE: Guest star Stirling Macer Jr.'s character, Toq, discovers the meaning of his Klingon heritage under Worf's influence, and evolves from obedient acceptance to rebellion.

BELOW: Working with veteran actor Richard Herd was a privilege. He portrayed the complex and conflicting emotions of Klingon leader L'Kor masterfully.

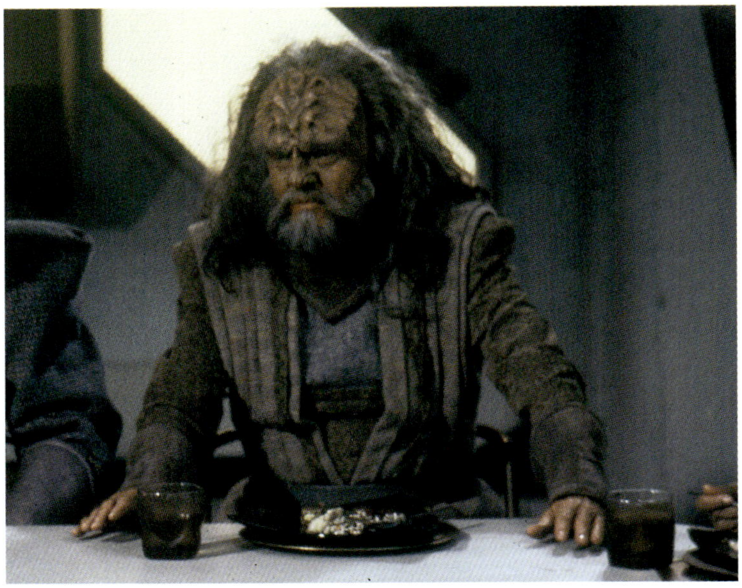

My friend and colleague Ronald B. Moore was of immense help taking on visual-effects responsibilities to allow me to focus on directing. After the episode had been shot and was in editorial, I worked on VFX like I would have done on any other show. On a paint system, I did the matte paintings showing wide exterior views of the Romulan compound. The art department created a miniature that matched the full-size set. We shot the model compound, matching perspective and lighting to still photographs I shot in Laos during the early 70s.

I'm proud of the finished episode, and in particular, thanks to Michel Dorn's performance, of the way Worf's character evolved. The actors and the crew were wonderful, and went out of their ways to make me look good. I enjoyed myself doing the episode, so I was frustrated that the opportunity to direct didn't come up again, but at the same time I could see how much work had to be done running the VFX team. Around that time, Rob Legato left and I took over responsibility for *DS9* and then *Voyager*. That meant dealing with a larger VFX team and more vendor companies, and I had very little time for anything else. But I love directing, which is an opportunity to work in the most powerful art form as yet created by our species, and I loved directing *Star Trek* because it was a chance to work with great actors and a great crew on incredible sets, telling stories that hold meaning for millions of fans.

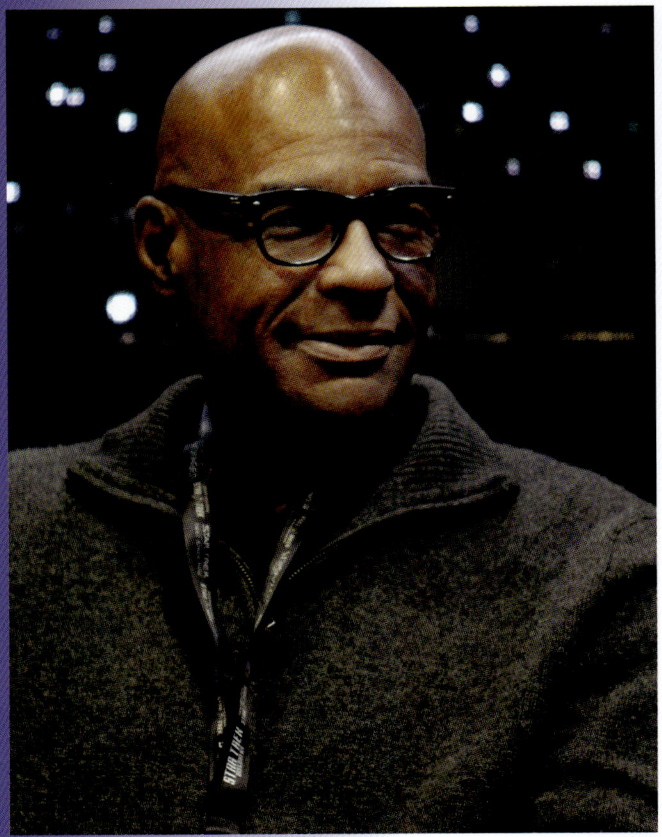

"I got to know Dan at the beginning of* The Next Generation. *He would come down to the set, and show us what to do for the effects. The heavens didn't open up or anything, but it was clear he was a very, very good guy. He's a very humble and very smart person, and he's unassuming. You could always depend on him for real answers, and for real support without any ego. It was only later that I learned more about him, and that had a real influence on how Worf developed.

"In the very first year, I went to Gene Roddenberry because I was concerned that my character was always getting beat up—constantly. So I asked Gene, 'What is this about?' He said, 'Besides Data, Worf is the most powerful person

means these people are very powerful, and it makes a big impression.' I said 'Okay, that makes sense, but he is so animalistic that he's always screaming and yelling, and out of control. I would like to do something different. I really want to do something more in the line of a samurai, martial artist, that type of thing.' Gene said, 'Hey, whatever you like.' He was very open to that stuff.

"The next step was I said, 'We have to make this character more fluid so that he's not just running and jumping and hitting people.' I didn't know this at the time, but Dan is a very good martial artist—he's a master. He is very unassuming, but he could rip out your throat (in a nice way). I love that about him. I've always gravitated toward guys like that—I find them fascinating, and I wanted to emulate him.

"We said 'Why don't we take all the things that Dan knew about martial arts, and add that to the character.' So instead of Worf being out of control, we see him doing Tai Chi, or practicing with a weapon. Whenever there was a scene that had to do with fighting, Dan would come down and we would go through a huge amount of things. That's how the Klingon martial arts started.

"He would say 'These are the Tai Chi moves.' I'd go, 'Okay, what I need to do is flip the guy,' or 'I'm going to punch him' or whatever. Dan would show me what to do. I'm not a martial artist, but I am very athletic, so I can make it look right. One of Worf's favorite punches is with the bottom part of the hand by the wrist. He does it all the time. If you've ever been hit with this part of the hand, you'll know it's a very powerful stroke. That's something that Dan taught me.

"I always made sure that Dan knew when a fight scene was going to happen. He would show up and we would go through it. Our stunt coordinator Dennis Madalone got used to the idea of Dan coming down. We would never encroach upon Dennis's area, but Dan and I would come up with a lot of moves. The stunt people kind of took off from there. It was always collaborative.

"There was still a lot of screaming, but now it was controlled and very focused. They loved that, because it really played into who Worf was. It added a lot, and you saw a real change in not just Worf but in the Klingon culture. They took what we created, all the stuff that I imbued Worf with, and they ran with it.

"There is a very funny story. In the fourth season or so, licensing was everywhere. They were licensing books and recordings and just everything. So Dan and I said, 'Why don't we do a Klingon martial arts video?' We were very excited about the idea. We talked to the licensing people and they were very excited about it, but then we got to Paramount legal and they said, 'There's absolutely no way we are going to license a martial arts video and have kids slicing each other up! It would be the biggest lawsuit you could imagine!'"

Michael Dorn

MARTIAL ARTS AND WEAPONS

DEVELOPING THE ART OF COMBAT IN KLINGON CULTURE

It all started with Kirk Douglas. When I was a little boy growing up in Bellerose, New York, the movie theater was at the end of our block, and I used to go with my brother John. There's a scene in *Gunfight at the O.K. Corral* where Kirk Douglas, as Doc Holliday, is sitting in his hotel room, throwing a pile of switchblades into the door. I thought that was so cool. When we got home, my brother and I set up pieces of wood on the wall in our basement. We started throwing steak knives at them, and actually became quite adept. I still keep a balsa wood target set up in my yard, and practice every morning—a minimum of ten throws per day, just to stay in practice. Errol Flynn played a part too. My favorite film of all time is the unequaled 1938 *The Adventures of Robin Hood*, so of course I became an archer. We had a long driveway that I could shoot arrows down into a target in the yard, and I also did some long-range shooting in the open spaces next to the Belt Parkway that we used to call 'The Hunting Grounds.'

Ever since then I've been interested in weapons, how they are designed and why they work. That interest meant that on *Star Trek* I'd often get to design weapons for whatever alien culture we would see in an upcoming episode. On most shows, custom weapons would be designed by the art department, but because of my special interest and background in martial arts I was trusted to take on this work. Among the variety of weapons I designed for *Star Trek*, the best-known is Worf's 'sword,' the Klingon *bat'leth*. I first had the idea for what would become the *bat'leth* when production designer Michael Riva asked me to be the weapons consultant on *The Golden Child* and help out with Sanskrit graffiti. I suggested that the villains use a Chinese fighting crescent and a special hooked sword used in pairs called a Chinese double axe, which has sharp, crescent-shaped hand guards on the hilt. When I was demonstrating the use of those weapons I started to imagine a weapon that combined different elements from both of them and could be used both like a quarterstaff and a sword. I always liked the idea of the crescent shape. Because it was concave it could block and redirect your opponent's weapon, but I really had no reason to bring the weapon I was imagining into existence.

The *bat'leth* first appeared in the *TNG* third-season episode 'Reunion,' which called for Worf to inherit a special bladed weapon. The art department proposed a sword similar to a pirate cutlass. I felt that the Klingons should have something unique and original that we had not seen before. It was important to me that it was ergonomically sound and had practical fighting utility, as I have never been a fan of over-the-top fantasy movie weapons that were impractical to wield. Even as a child I became annoyed when I saw a weapon, especially a bladed one, that was designed to look cool

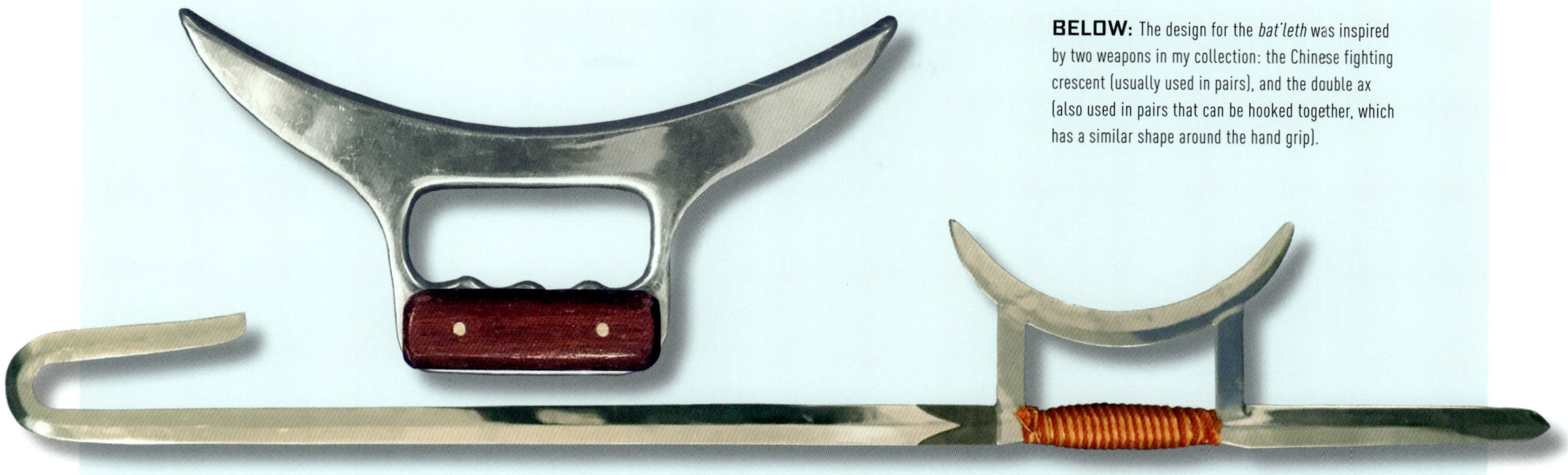

BELOW: The design for the *bat'leth* was inspired by two weapons in my collection: the Chinese fighting crescent (usually used in pairs), and the double ax (also used in pairs that can be hooked together, which has a similar shape around the hand grip).

but obviously had no practical value for fighting. By now I had been thinking about this weapon for years. I made a foam core version with a curved blade, four points and three handholds. I showed it to Rick Berman, demonstrating ritual movements and explaining the purposes behind its design, and promised I could invent a martial-arts style around it.

He said, "If it was 4 inches shorter we could use it." So I just scaled it down by a couple of inches. It didn't matter; it should be proportionate to the user anyway. Rick dubbed it the "*bat'leth*," and it became the iconic blade seen in episodes and features across the franchise.

I drafted a full-sized drawing and gave it to the art department. They had the prop guys make a test one out of thin plywood. For some reason somebody decided to ignore my design and make an asymmetrical version. I was not pleased. "No," I insisted, "it's gotta be symmetrical. The whole point is its symmetry allows all these different fluid movements and keeps it balanced." Then they followed the actual design.

It's all very well designing a weapon, but you have to be able to fight with it. I don't practice other martial arts formally any more, but I still practice tai chi and have been doing so daily for 50 years. I think, like a tiger or any other beast in the wild, humans have

BELOW: Kevin Conway as Kahless.

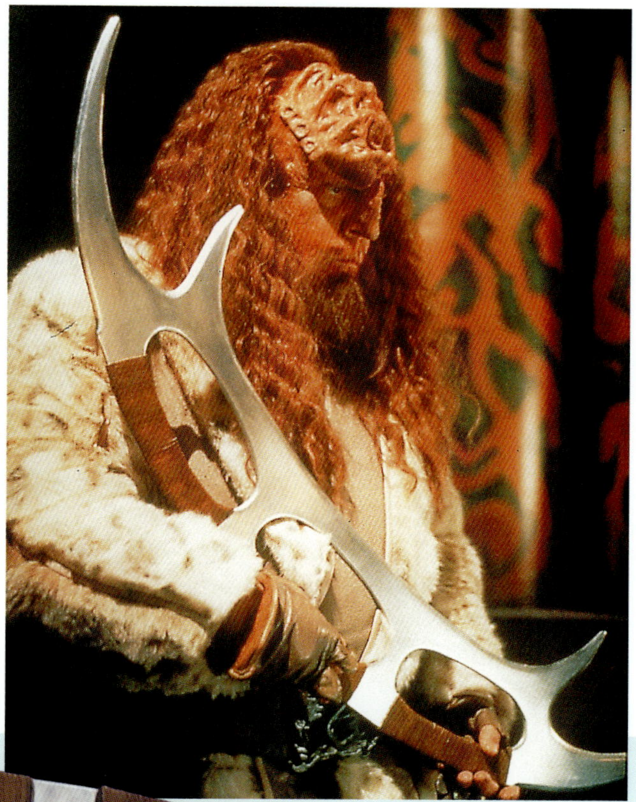

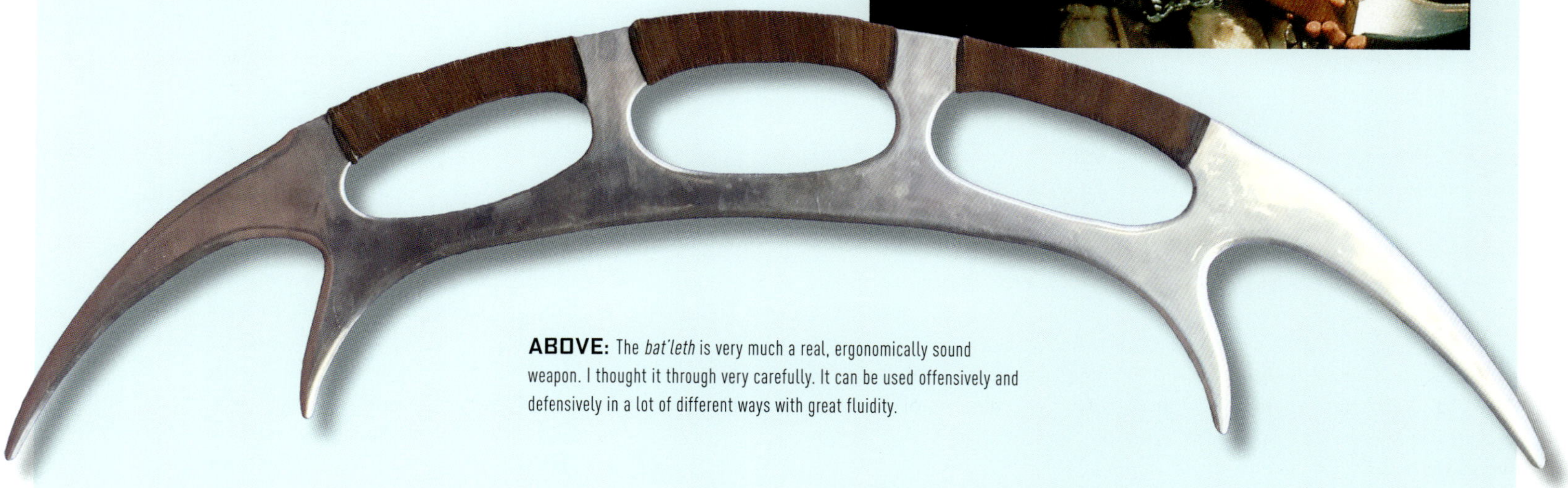

ABOVE: The *bat'leth* is very much a real, ergonomically sound weapon. I thought it through very carefully. It can be used offensively and defensively in a lot of different ways with great fluidity.

the instinctive ability to fight, but because we are 'civilized' we have to get out of our own ways. Tai chi teaches you muscle training, breath control, meditation, and developing an awareness of your own internal energy and how to use it. Amazingly enough, its exquisite slowness teaches you to move your body in a way that enables you to become really fast.

Once I had a physical *bat'leth* I showed it to Dennis Madalone, our stunt coordinator. The first time he saw it, Dennis was very skeptical. I remember he said, "This is worthless. I can't do anything with it." I said, "Check this out, Dennis," and I showed him a lot of the moves I had invented for it. He looked at me and said, "Oh, OK, we can work with that!"

Stuntman Tommy Morga, who doubled for Jonathan Frakes, really got into the *bat'leth*, contributed to its style, and became a true master.

I put all my martial-arts training into thinking about how you would fight with the *bat'leth*. The amount of curvature allowed it to roll behind your back and roll off your shoulders. The three different grips enabled you to do a wide range of things—glissades, parries, thrusts, and chops—as you would do with a saber or a sword, but you can also use it like a staff. You can use it as a twirling object and spin through a crowd like a reaper. The extra flanges give it the double leverage of a can opener. There's a scene where Worf finally kills Gowron. It happens just off screen, but we imagined that Worf would stab underneath the sternum with the longer back blade, and then use the forward blade as a fulcrum and just tear up and out through the chest. Of course, we couldn't show that on camera.

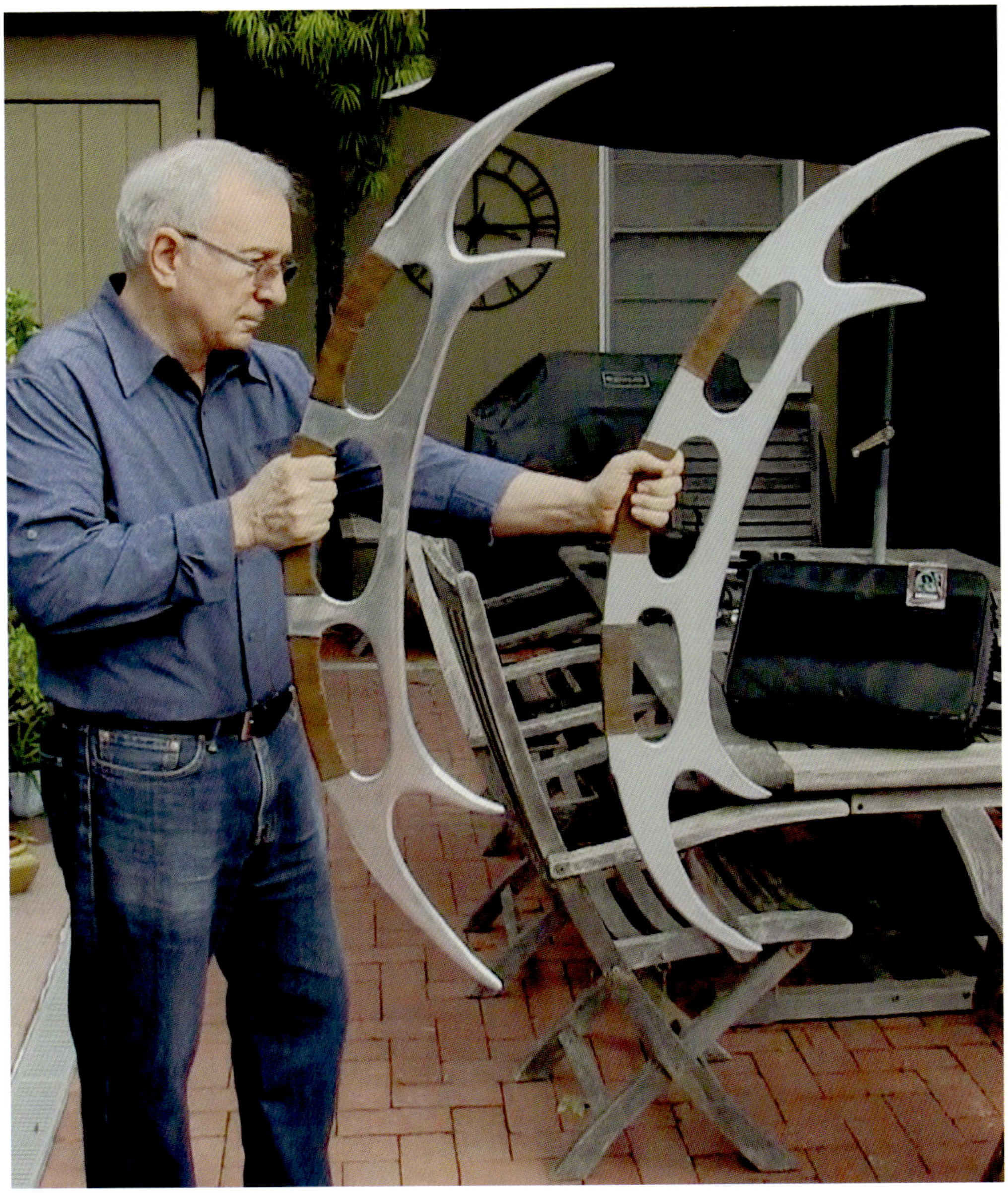

ABOVE: Comparing the hero metal prop bat'leth with the rubberized version used for on-set combat. When we were making *Star Trek*, actors would often come over to learn some moves and get in some practice.

You can also throw a *bat'leth* like a lumberjack's axe if you want to, which we never did on *Star Trek*, but I used to practice doing that with bales of hay in my backyard. You can rest it on your shoulder and kind of roll it off—just be careful not to remove your ear in the process.

Another big influence on me was a book my mother gave me by Edwin Tunis, which I can highly recommend, called *Weapons*. It's a history of weapons from the Neolithic times to the atom bomb, illustrated with the author's beautiful pen-and-ink drawings. It depicted bladed weapons, projectile weapons, medieval siege weapons, and so on. I began to see that no matter what culture, or no matter how strange looking a weapon is, all practical weapons are based on sound ergonomics, and their design serves a combat purpose. I used to look askance at an ancient Egyptian sword, with its odd hooked blade, until I suddenly realized the hook could be used to pull an opponent's shield down, opening up his head and upper torso for a thrust. Then I understood the brilliance of its design.

On *Star Trek* we always wanted to present the audience with new ways of looking at familiar things. One of the ways of doing that was to take inspiration from unfamiliar cultures. My design sensibility has been very influenced by Asian weapons. When I graduated from college in 1968, the Vietnam War was raging. I was more than happy to serve the country, but I didn't want to do it in a way that would require taking people's lives over a political issue that I knew would become irrelevant in 20 years' time, so I volunteered for the Peace Corps. I worked for the Royal Thai Community Development Department designing and supervising construction of small dams and bridges in remote villages in Northeast Thailand. The mighty Mekong River ran between Thailand and Laos, and an atmosphere of ongoing war was all around us. I was blessed to live in villages prior to the arrival of electricity and experience life in a beautiful culture that had been unchanged for centuries among honorable, wise, and gregarious people. I learned so much more than I could possibly give. I discovered that some villages had a martial-arts tradition that went back many generations. There were masters who were kind to the clumsy foreigner, and generously and patiently shared secrets of their indigenous martial arts. As my interest and knowledge grew, I sought out teachers with special skills.

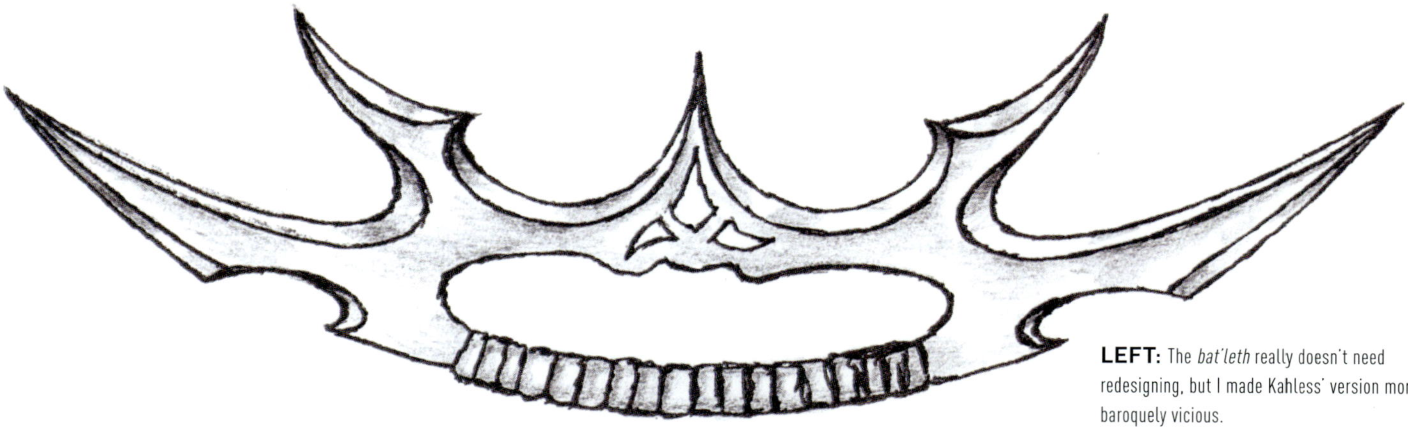

LEFT: The *bat'leth* really doesn't need redesigning, but I made Kahless' version more baroquely vicious.

I split my time between working in villages and living in the town of Khon Kaen, reporting to the head of the Provincial Community Development Department. The movies they showed in the local theaters were Indian musicals, Thai soap operas, or Chinese martial-arts movies. So, of course there was no choice. I became an aficionado of Shaw Brothers sword flicks that further piqued my interest in Asian martial arts, as most were period films and I could see the world contemporary martial arts had evolved from. I realized some of my friends were really good martial artists who had been trained from early childhood and who were willing to introduce me to their world, and I started studying quite seriously.

Hanging around with my friends, their martial-arts subculture just became kind of a part of me. A lot of my studies with those people were very informal. They were friends passing on information to friends, very quietly. I was lucky enough to speak the language, so they gave me a little bit more trust than they might have otherwise.

I got to work with some truly wonderful masters. There was a man named Tang Chang, a poet and an artist. He was a great master of iron palm, sword and dagger. I learned a lot from him. He was one of those individuals who could catch a dagger by the handle as it flew by, and yet he was kind of roly-poly and was an incredibly sensitive artist. You would look at his abstract paintings and get drawn into the universe of his imagination.

Years later, I moved to Bangkok, where I found Kim Myung Su, who was considered one of the top tae kwon do teachers in the world. I studied with him for several years. He was an incredible martial artist, and an amazing man of great dignity. He could break

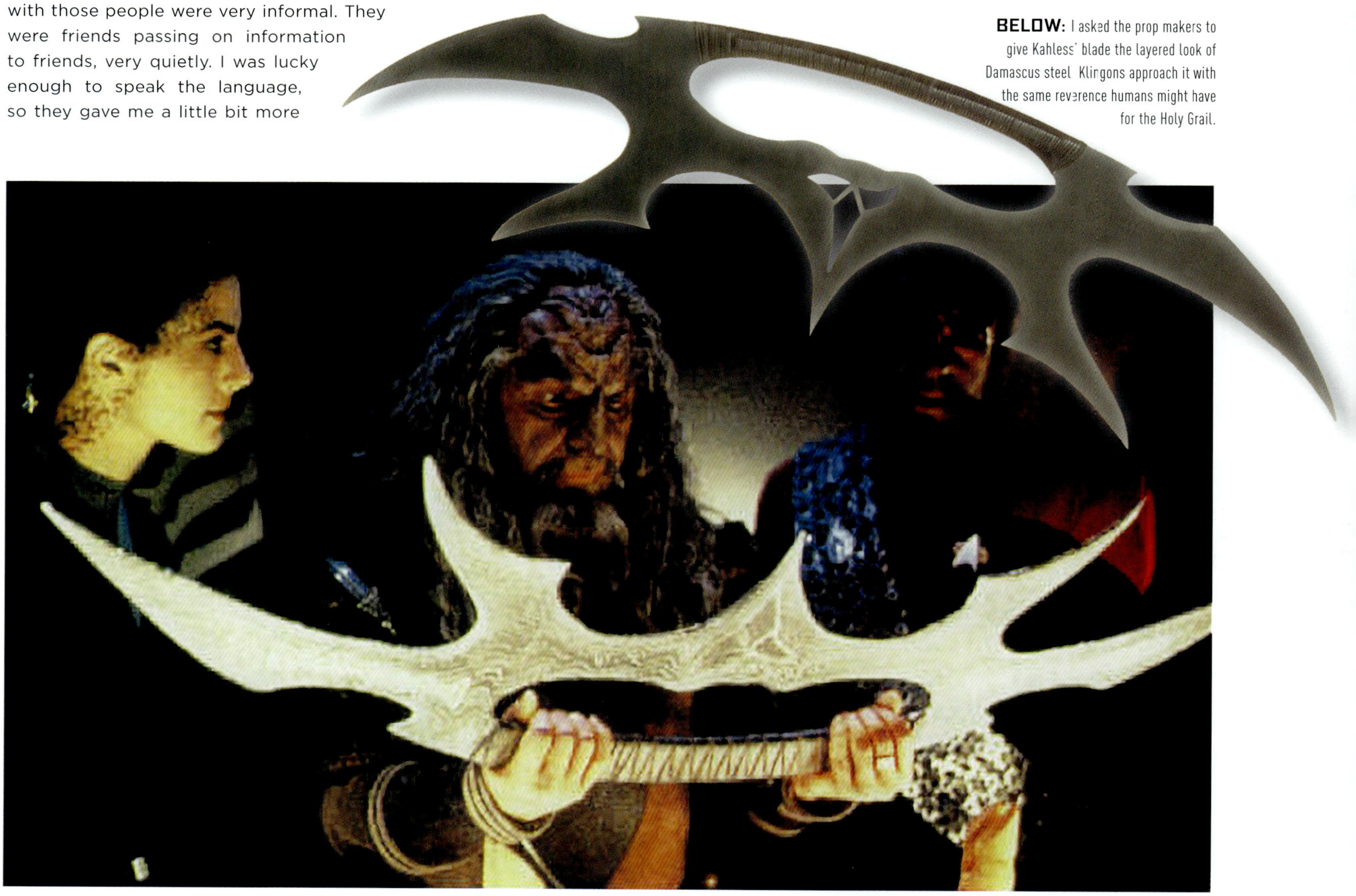

BELOW: I asked the prop makers to give Kahless' blade the layered look of Damascus steel. Klingons approach it with the same reverence humans might have for the Holy Grail.

BATTLE KLINGON STYLE

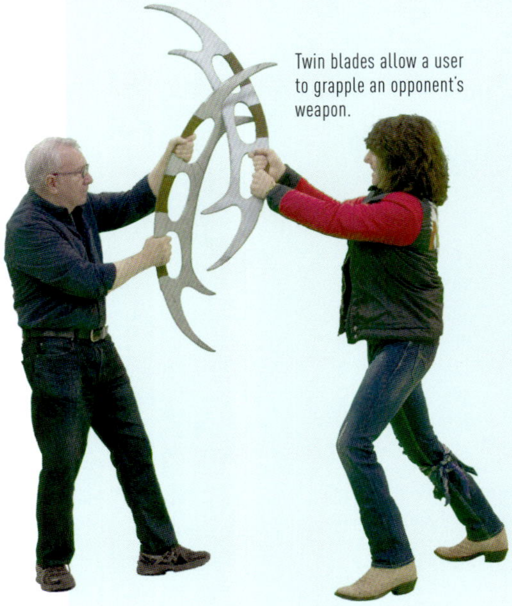

Twin blades allow a user to grapple an opponent's weapon.

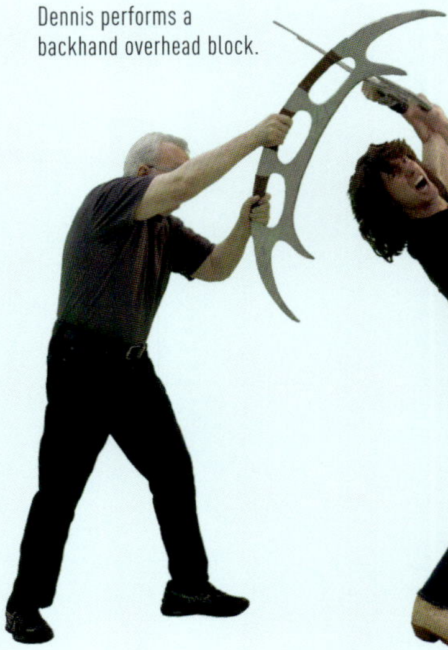

Dennis performs a backhand overhead block.

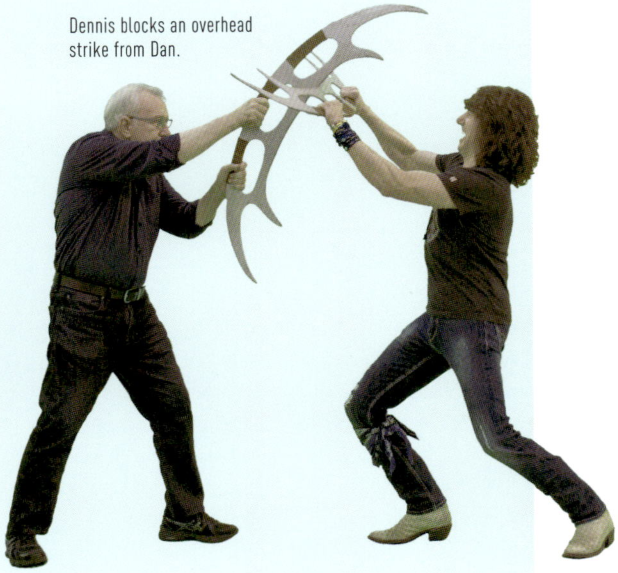

Dennis blocks an overhead strike from Dan.

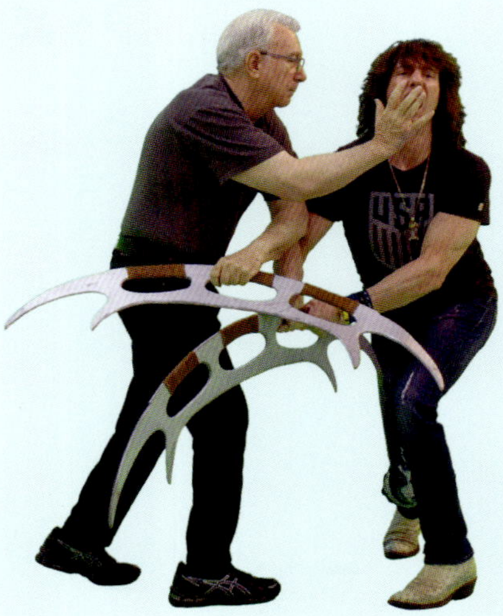

Dan counter-strikes with palm.

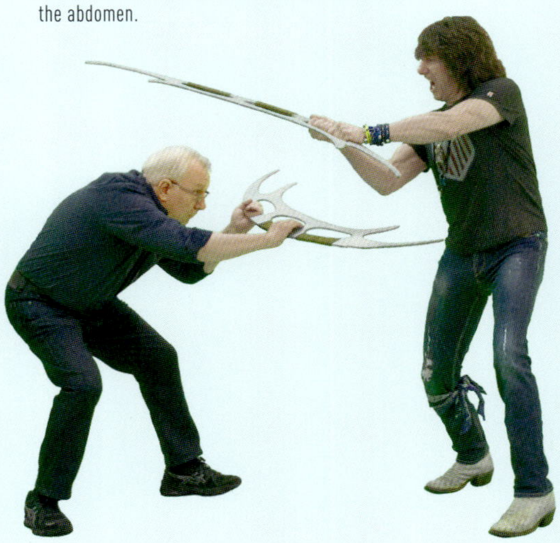

Dan ducks under a slice from Dennis, and goes for the abdomen.

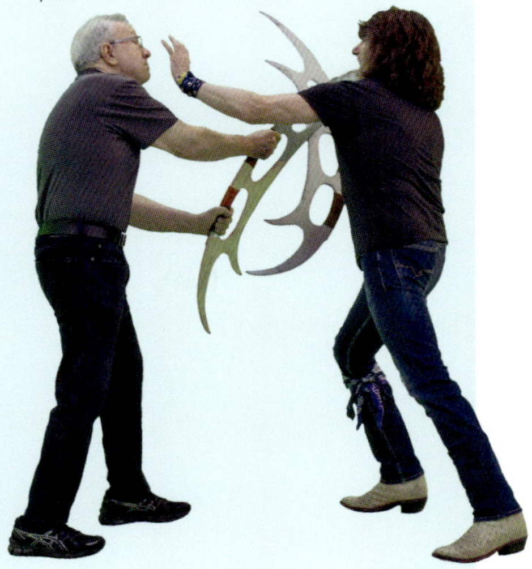

Dennis grapples Dan's bat'leth, and counters with a palm strike.

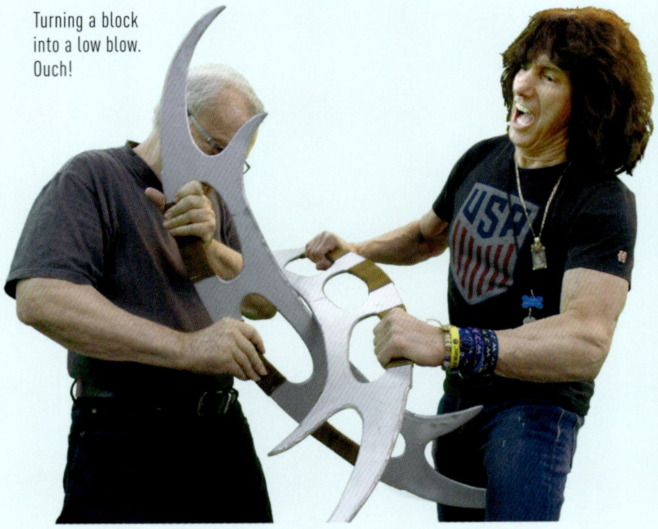

Turning a block into a low blow. Ouch!

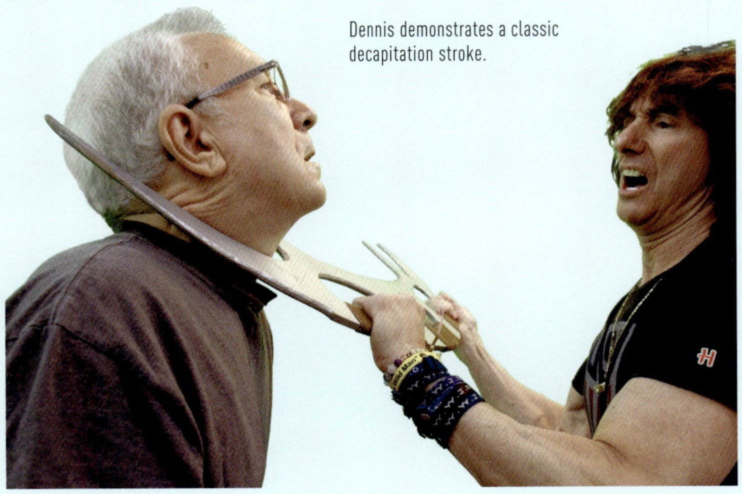

Dennis demonstrates a classic decapitation stroke.

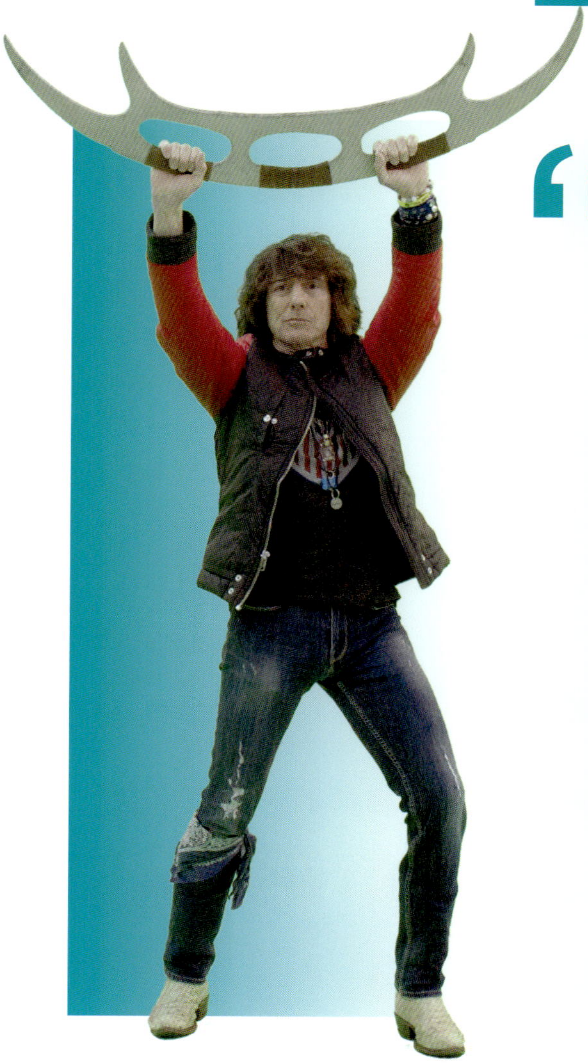

I always tell everyone when I first saw the bat'leth, *I thought, 'Forget about it!' and then I started using it and it ended up being a treasure.*

We were in the production meeting and Dan was showing it to everyone. It looked very awkward and I thought, 'Gosh, how are we gonna fight with this guy?' I didn't say anything during the meeting. I was just thinking, 'This is madness!' After the meeting, I got to touch the bat'leth. *Dan was doing some swings and then I started to ad lib some stuff and, oh my gosh, what a great, fun, crazy weapon he had created.*

I turned out it was one of the greatest things we had to fight with. It is a real working weapon that you could actually use.

Dennis Madalone, Stunt Coordinator

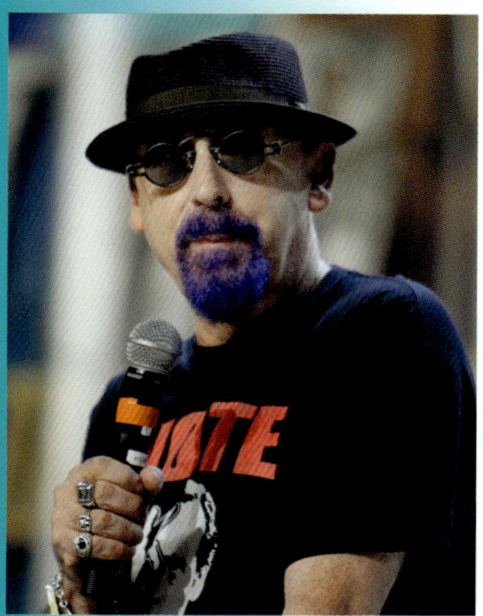

What I find so wondrous about Dan is that it seems every conversation I've ever shared with him ends with talk of self-defense, weapons, and body damage. And yet Dan is one of the sweetest guys I've ever known. He is living proof that each of us contains multitudes.

Ira Steven Behr,
executive producer *Deep Space Nine*

a row of bricks balanced on a student's arm with one swipe.

My studies led me to discover some Asian weapons based on a different logic than of those in the West, and other designs that are universal as form follows function. Each culture has its own sword design and sword fighting style. I started to collect weapons, and mailed a lot of them home in my Peace Corps trunk. Customs officials were so happy there were no illegal substances that they just let the weapons go right through.

My collection of bladed weapons includes various designs from Nepal, Tibet, Thailand, Laos, India, Japan, and China. My best sword is a really beautiful northern Chinese Jian, or in Thai, Dop, a straight, double-edged sword with a blade so flexible that you can whip around your opponent's defenses and nick a blood vessel.

Everything on *Star Trek* was a team effort, and everybody collaborated. In various episodes over the years I got to work with Dennis Madalone a lot with the choreography. There were some moves I would like to do, and some that Dennis suggested. With any heavy weapon you have to feel its momentum and go with it, guiding it. With the *bat'leth* it's all about fluidity—every full extension is the beginning of a withdrawal.

Sometimes I would instruct the actors who took to the *bat'leth* very well. I got to work with Michael Dorn, Roxann Dawson, and

KUT'LUCH DAGGER

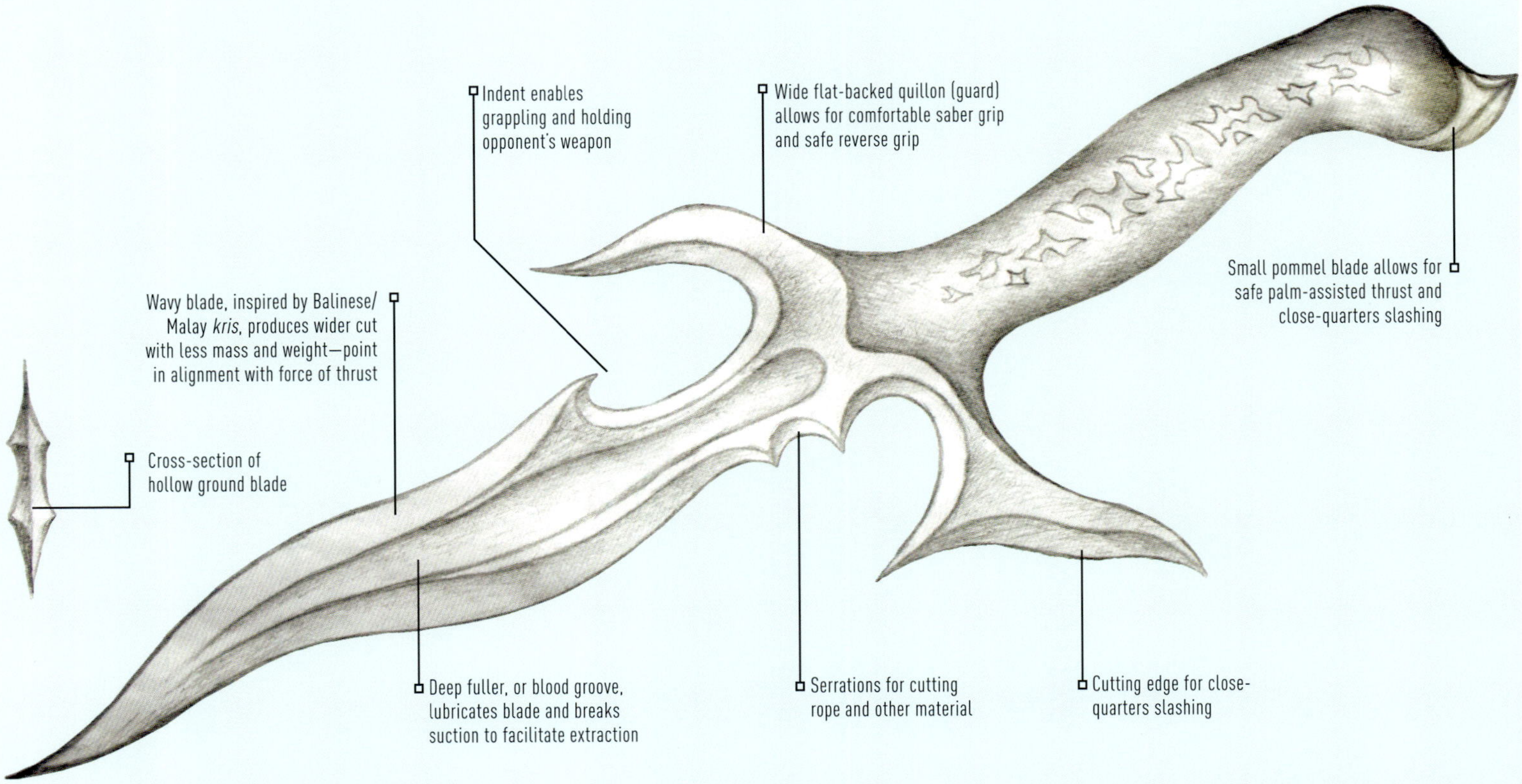

I also designed the *kut'luch* dagger. You didn't see it that often—I always hoped it would see more action in in the show. My thinking was that it was totally ergonomic. It was inspired by a Balinese or Malaysian *kris*, with a wavy blade; that kind of blade means you get a bigger cut with less weight and less metal. It had a fuller (or a blood groove) to lubricate extractions.

I designed it so you could use all the classic grips: the saber grip; the hammer grip, and the palm-assisted thrust. There's also a little blade on the pommel, so if you're at really close quarters you can use the back of the knife as a cutting edge. I designed the quillon (or the guard) so it was quite thick and broad at the top—that way if you wanted to do an underhand block, it would take a blow without the sharp top edge of the weapon cutting your arms.

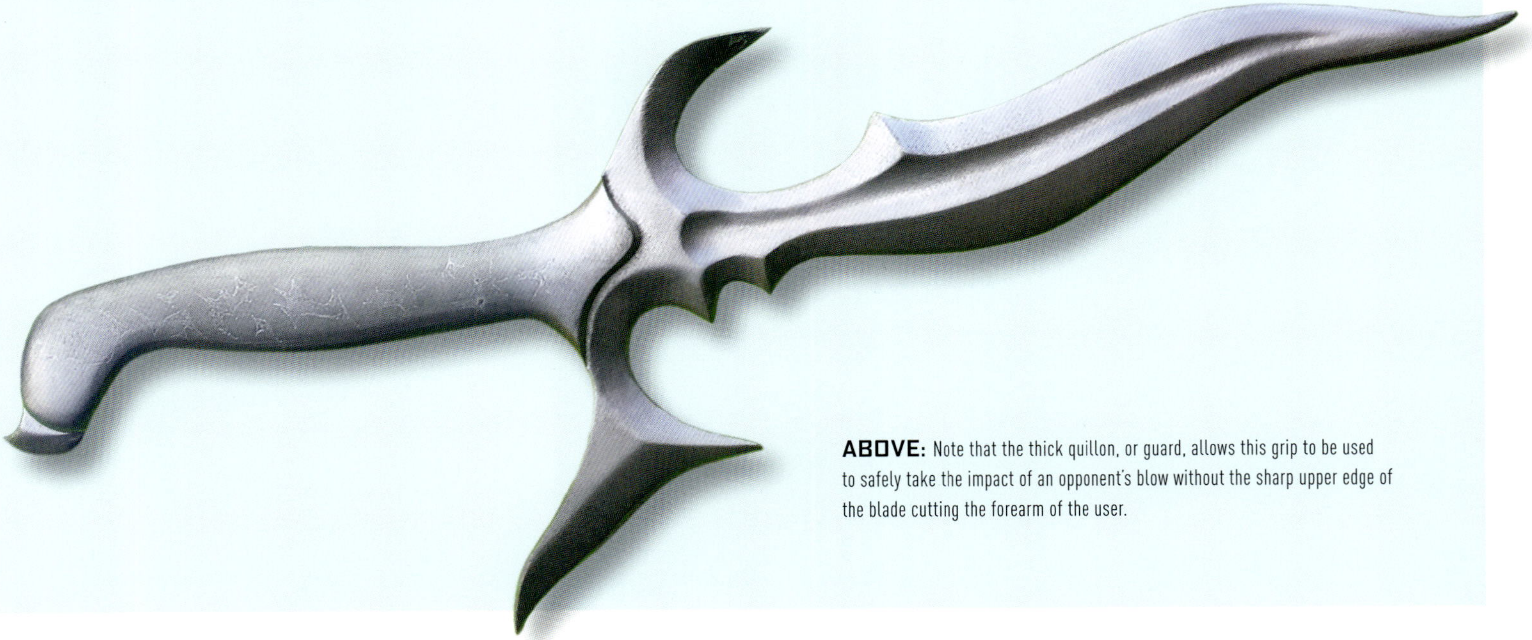

ABOVE: Note that the thick quillon, or guard, allows this grip to be used to safely take the impact of an opponent's blow without the sharp upper edge of the blade cutting the forearm of the user.

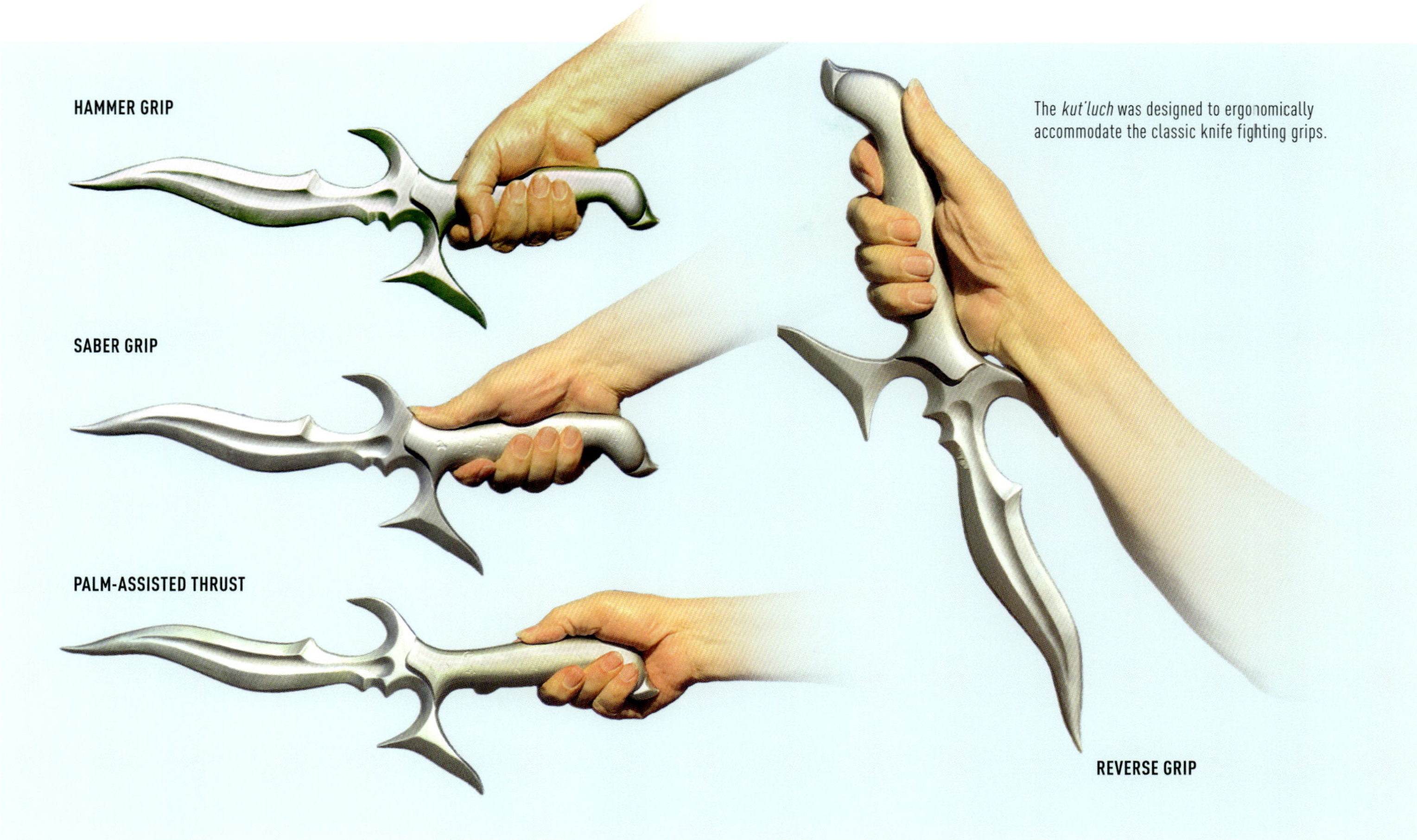

The *kut'luch* was designed to ergonomically accommodate the classic knife fighting grips.

Armin Shimerman. I helped them learn how to use those weapons with finesse. It's funny, but as soon as the actors got this weapon in their hands they became warriors.

The prop department, under prop master Alan Simms, had craftsmen who would fabricate the actual props. The ones used for fighting on set had a thin steel core with rubber exterior coating so that characters could fight with them without the likelihood of inflicting any real harm. There were a lot of the rubber versions.

I kept a metal one and a couple of rubber ones so I could work with actors privately when schedules allowed so when *bat'leth* scenes came up they would look like masters of the weapon. Interestingly enough, when we were doing *Voyager*, Roxann and

HUNTING SPEAR

The Klingon hunting spear was designed by Alan Sims. I liked aspects of it—it was perfectly balanced if you gripped it in the gray area, and it looks like a giant pin. It was a short but heavy spear, which made sense for their hunting style in a tight jungle, because you wouldn't want a really long spear, but its mass would give it great penetration into an animal. The knob on the end makes it easy to do a palm-assisted thrust. The fun thing about this spear is that in the episode the young Klingons were not aware of their warrior history, so they had made a game like bowling, where they would throw the spear through hoops. Worf teaches them that it's a weapon, and he demonstrates how to throw it. I did all the live spear throwing.

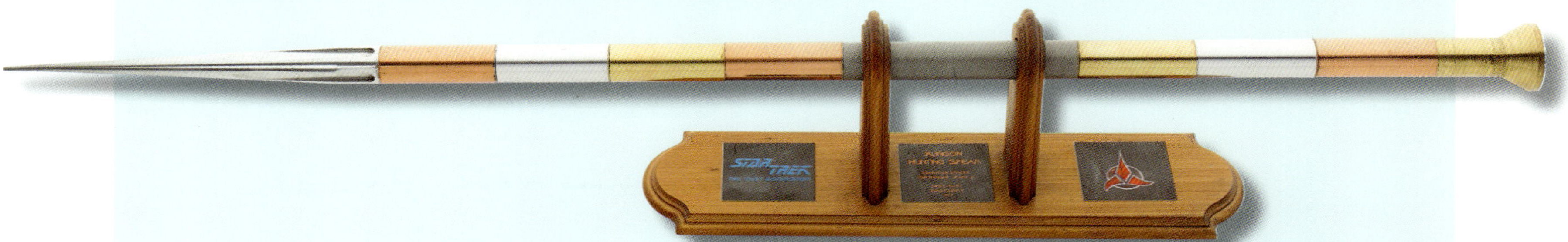

JEM'HADAR KAR'TAKIN

When the opportunity came up to design a pole weapon for the Jem'Hadar on *Deep Space Nine* I wanted sound ergonomics so that Dennis Madalone and his stunt team would have something unique to work with. It had to look alien, but practical; something that could slash and stab, but could also be used effectively for defense.

I decided on hard geometry. The blade had open negative spaces to keep it light, and also serve to protect the forward hand when using the weapon for close-quarters thrusting, like a Zulu *assagai* or a bayonet on a rifle. It can be used for cross-blocking and wide horizontal cuts. Both hands can also be used together, or you can use it one-handed, swinging it from the butt end for extra reach. There is a counterweight on the butt end to provide balance. The pole weapon can also be used underhand for a sweeping strike, like a scythe. When I demonstrated it to Dennis he immediately saw its potential, and was eager to start working with me to devise moves for action sequences.

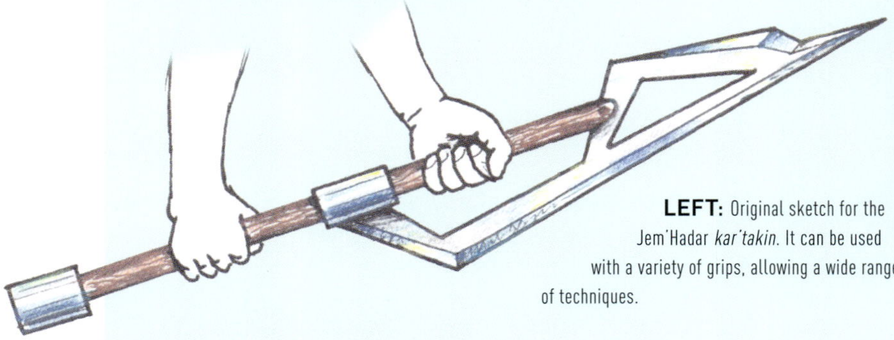

LEFT: Original sketch for the Jem'Hadar *kar'takin*. It can be used with a variety of grips, allowing a wide range of techniques.

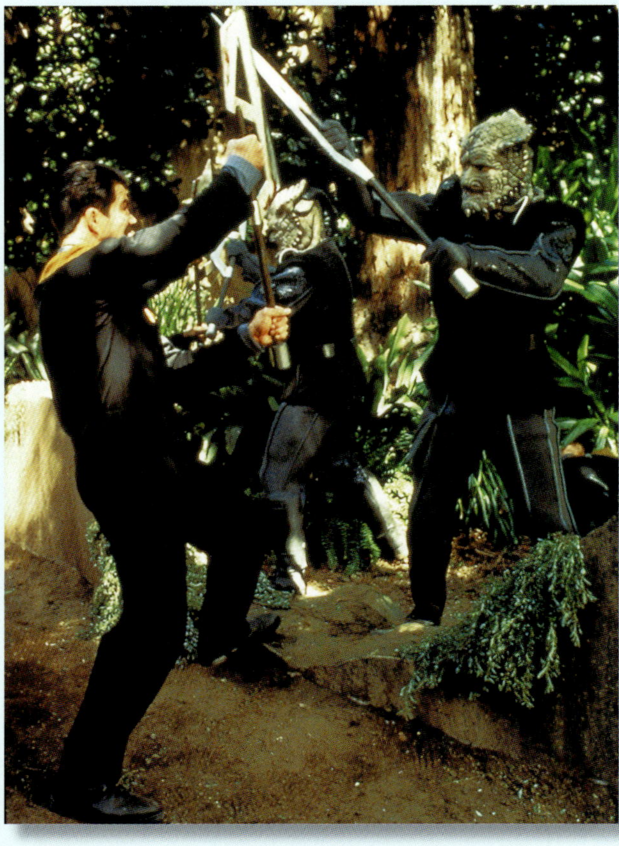

ABOVE: DS9 crew versus Jem'Hadar. Stunt coordinator Dennis Madalone and his team loved the practicality of this weapon and its ease of changing grips.

JEM'HADAR CLEAVERS

The Jem'Hadar fighting cleavers were inspired by Tibetan fighting cleavers. I thought the Jem'Hadar, being reptilian, would want something that hooks, like an extension of their talons.

I take the Charles Darwin approach to designing things: form follows function. I thought about what the Jem'Hadar had evolved from; they would intuitively claw and slash like a Deinonychus. The greatest threat from Deinonychus would be to be disemboweled by its hind claws, so a clawing weapon seemed appropriate. It was fun devising a fighting style with Dennis and his stunt team.

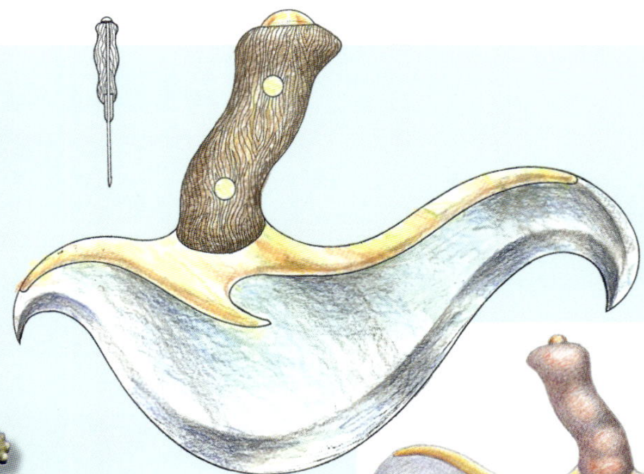

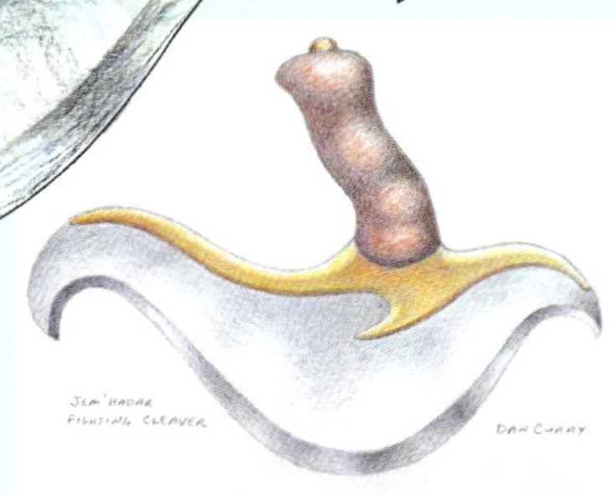

ABOVE: For the Jem'Hadar weapon I modified the Tibetan blade (adding a second curved beak), and gave it a more ergonomic grip.

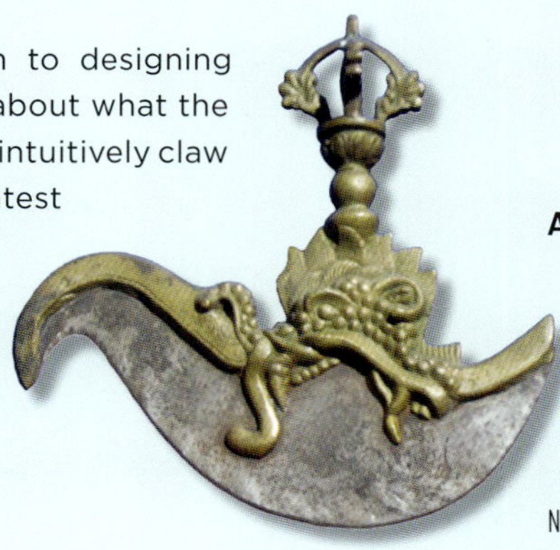

LEFT: Antique, beautifully crafted Tibetan artifact I brought back from Nepal—inspiration for the Jem'Hadar cleaver.

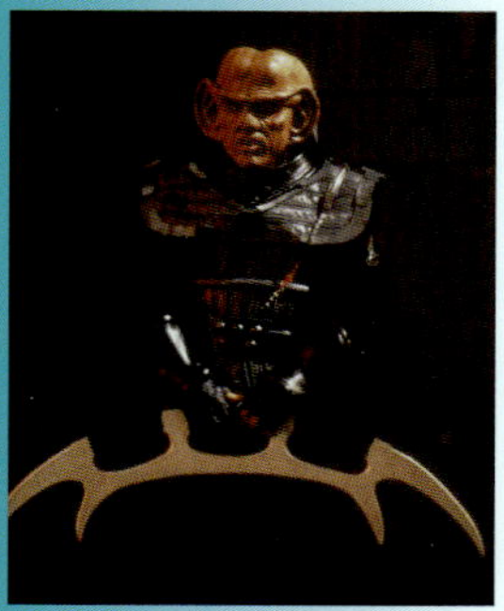

"I consider Dan to be a true friend. He's enormously talented: he's a brilliant artist, he's a musician, he's a renaissance man, he's charismatic. There's more to him than anyone suspects. He is very secretive about elements of his past, and I find that intriguing. He is not only knowledgeable in lots of areas, but has a very creative mind and is eager to find out about things that he's not familiar with. That's what makes him so wonderful—he's not caught up in his own world. He's always kind. He's a little reticent. He's very modest. He's not trying to convince you that he's wonderful. I love his wife Hua and his son Devin. They are just good, good people. He's the sort of person that I aspire to be.

"In 'Looking For Par'Mach In All The Wrong Places' it was required that I fight Worf with a bat'leth. *Dan very nicely spent a lot of time teaching me how to wield this weapon that he had created. I had known about it for years, but I don't think I had ever touched it. He was very kind, very gentle, very helpful, very funny. He was very gracious about giving me time and expertise, and our friendship blossomed. He taught me to respect the weapon and to trust it. Then he showed me how to allow the weight to allow it to do what it needed to do. He said, 'Follow the weapon. Don't try to control it. It will show you where to go.' He gave me some Klingon etiquette for the beginning of the fight. Eventually I did most of the bat'leth fighting myself because Dan made me slightly competent."*

Armin Shimerman

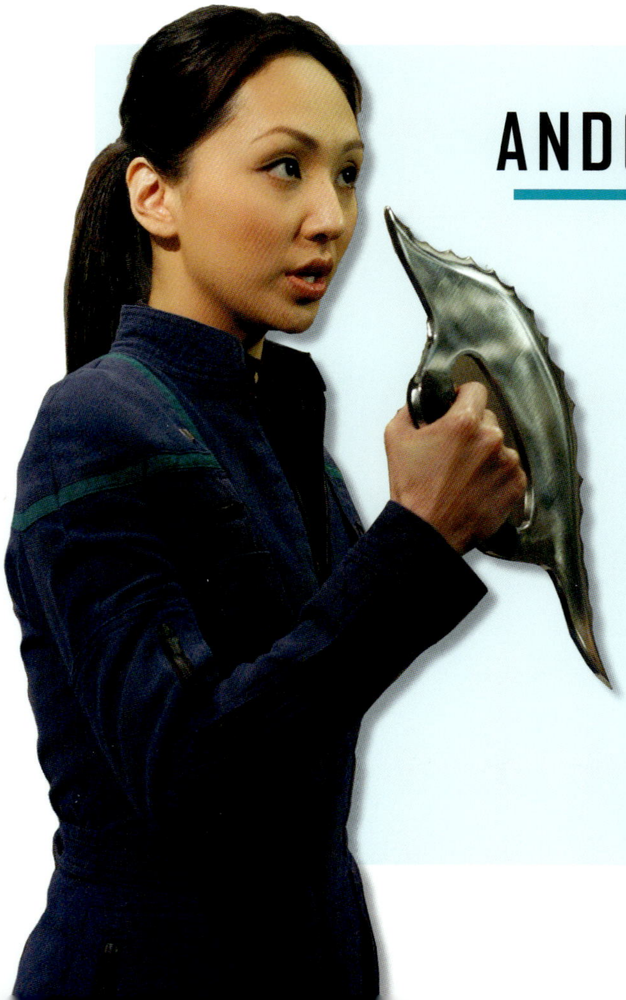

ANDORIAN ICE CUTTERS

Featuring a convex cutting edge similar to a Jem'Hadar cleaver and an Inuit *Ulu*, I designed this weapon to have grips parallel to a cutting edge that had deep serrations capable of slicing blocks of ice on their frozen moon home world, Andor. As well as inflicting vicious wounds on enemies, the long teeth can also grapple and hold an opponent's weapon. Ice cutters are intended to be used in pairs with boxing motions.

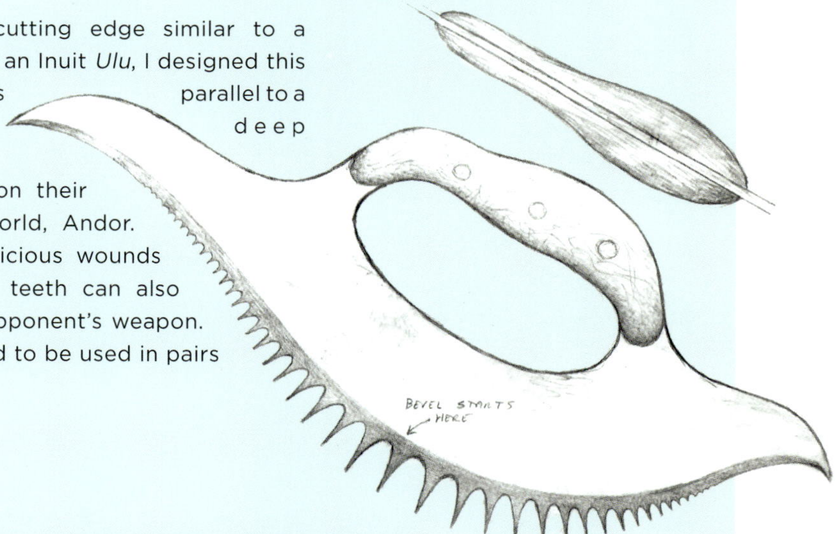

LEFT: *Enterprise*'s Hoshi (Linda Park) wields an Andorian Ushan-Tor. My design evolved from the Jem'Hadar cleaver, but is less curved and has nasty serrations.

THE MEK'LETH

When Michael Dorn signed on to *Deep Space Nine*, I got a phone call from him. It began with his inimitable baritone, "Daniel, I need a new weapon." Michael wanted something unique and original, small enough to hide behind his back, but effective enough to counter an attack from a larger weapon like a *bat'leth*.

Michael came over to the house to see my weapons collection. One of the items I showed him was a Nepali *kora*, a heavy, downward-hooked sword. I said, "Why don't we borrow the front end of the *kora*, but give it a different back?" We both liked the idea of having something that could be used backhand, forehand, could be thrown like a hatchet, and had lots of cutting edges so you could inflict wounds from any grip, and could grapple an opponent's weapon.

Michael and I did some sketches. Finally, I cut a shape out from the side of a cardboard box and reinforced it with popsicle sticks and tape (popsicle sticks have a myriad of uses for an artist). We went out in the backyard, and fooled around with it against a variety of weapons. Michael loved it. We showed it to Rick, who said, "I like it." That's how the *mek'leth* came into existence.

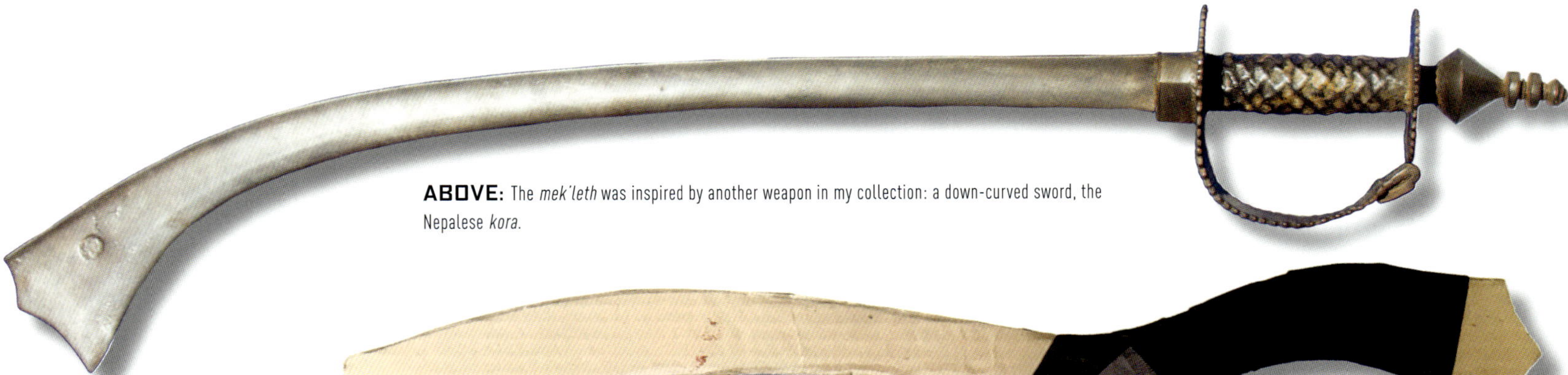

ABOVE: The *mek'leth* was inspired by another weapon in my collection: a down-curved sword, the Nepalese *kora*.

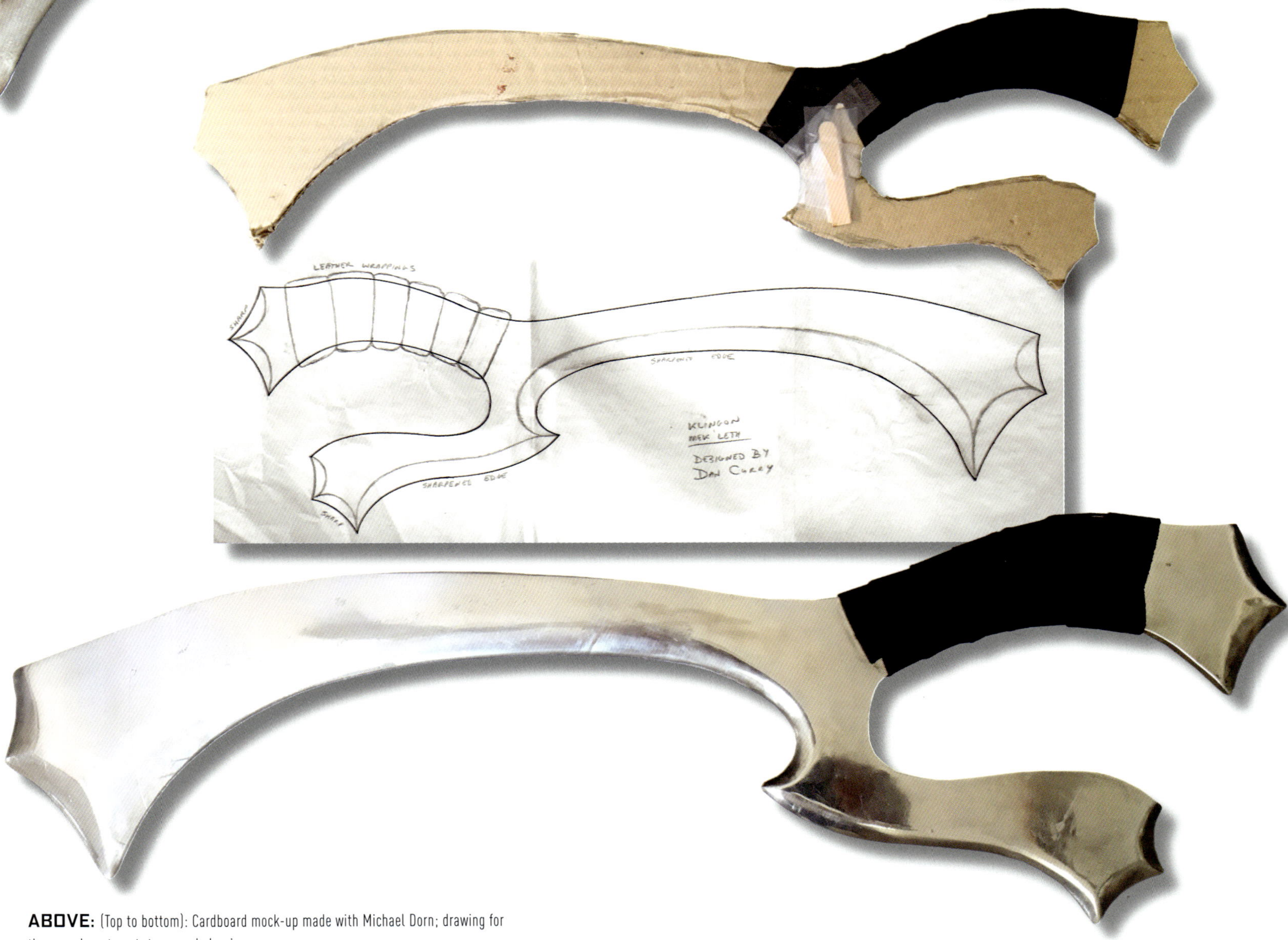

ABOVE: (Top to bottom): Cardboard mock-up made with Michael Dorn; drawing for the prop department; tempered aluminum prop.

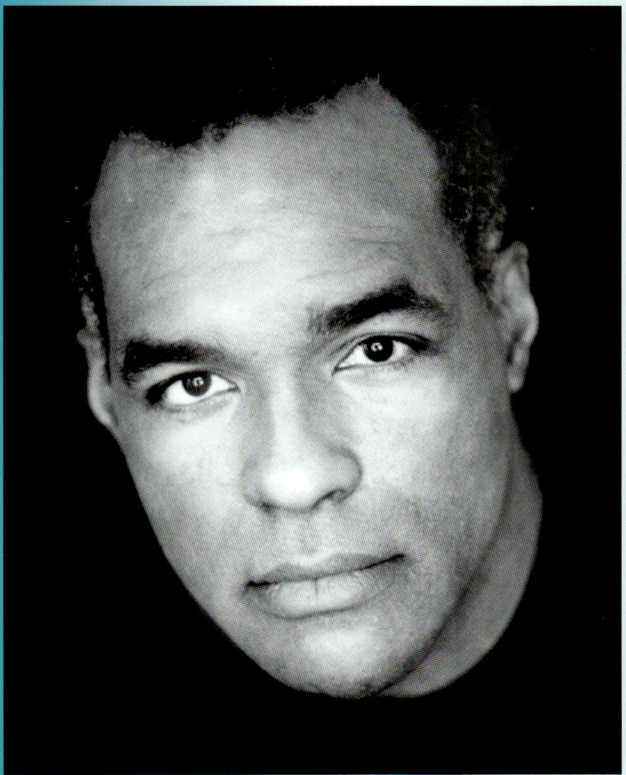

There's a part at the back of the mek'leth *where there's a shape like a hook. Dan said 'There's a good reason for that. It comes into play when you block someone.'*

It worked exactly as advertised. There was one scene where I was fighting Dennis Madalone. He was playing an alien in a full costume with the full mask. I blocked his attack, and his sword slid alongside the mek'leth *until it caught the hooked part at the back, which flicked out and sliced Madalone right across the face! Luckily he was wearing the face mask, but he was blinded for about 10 minutes, so this shit works. It wasn't just some bizarre thing that Dan came up with out of nothing, this was a real weapon.*"

Michael Dorn

"*We wanted Worf to have a new weapon, and we were very involved with each other when we designed it. Dan came up with the design for the* mek'leth*—that's what he does; he is a wonderful artist. Then basically he taught me how to fight with it. He would say, 'This is what it is. This is why we have this. You hold it like this.' I'd say, 'Oh, okay that makes sense.' Then I kind of took over. Whenever we were planning a fight with it I would consult with Dan constantly and ask him, 'How do I do this?'*

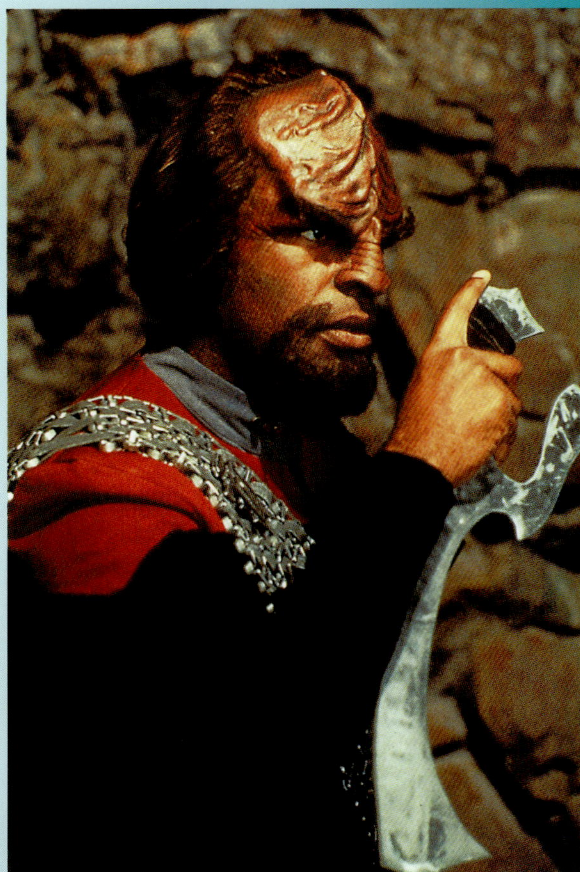

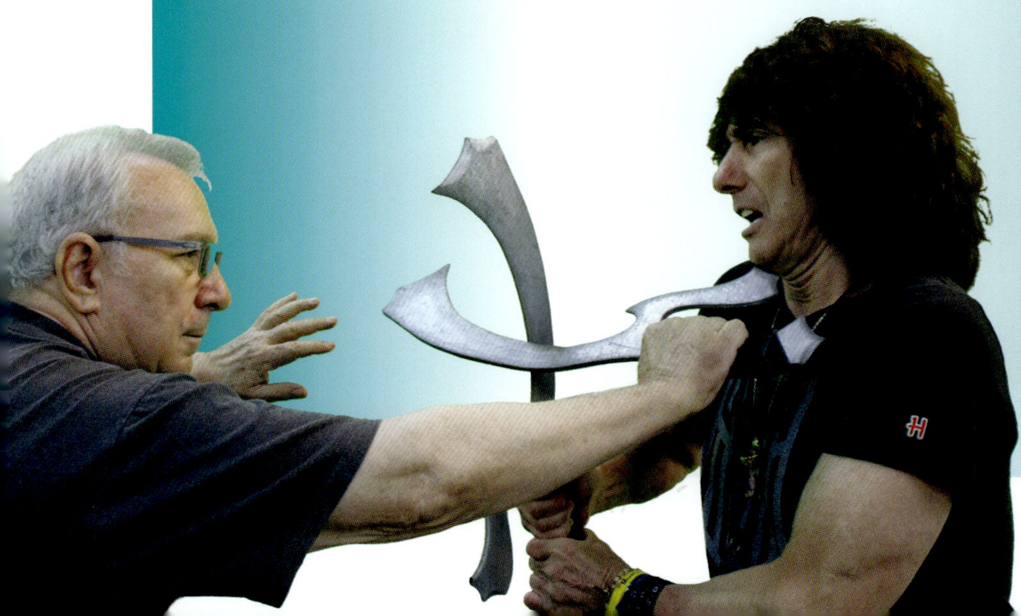

THE GIN'TAK SPEAR

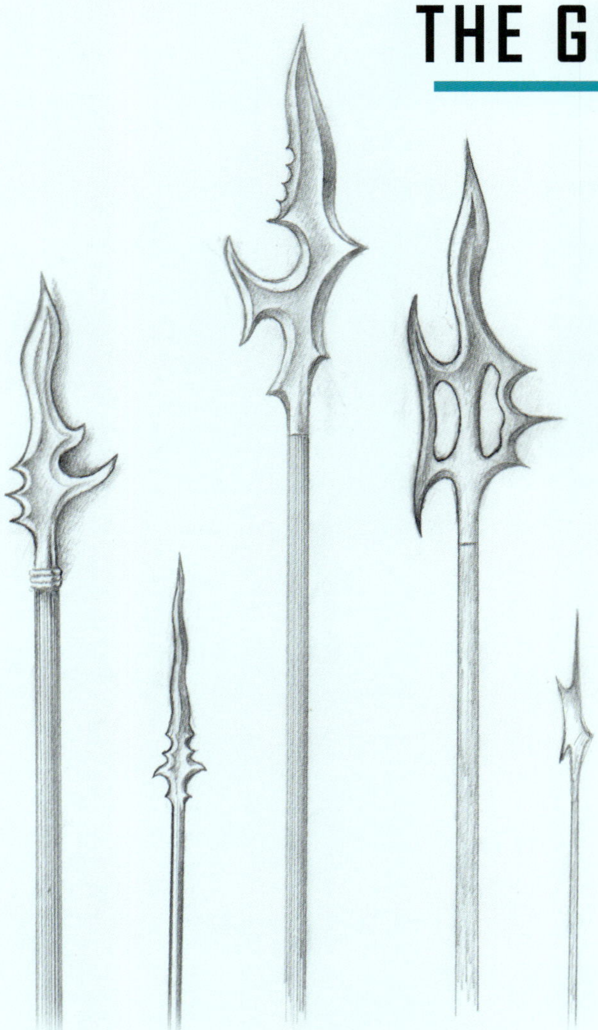

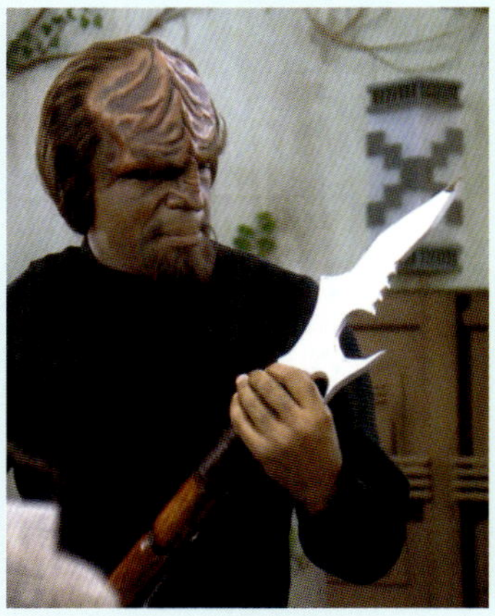

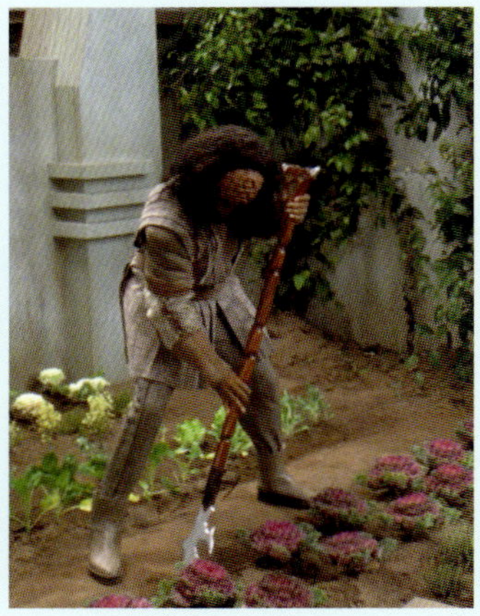

ABOVE: Worf explains the meaning of the spear to Toq, who was unaware of its original purpose.

The *gin'tak* spear was a collaboration between our prop master Alan Sims and myself. I based the spearhead partially on medieval halberds, and partially on what the Wicked Witch of the North's guards carried in *The Wizard of Oz*. You see them walking around with weird pole weapons with a lot of extension blades on them. Alan had the idea of doing a flared butt end with the carvings on it. That appeared in several episodes. In 'Birthright, Part II' Worf comes across Toq, who is digging in a garden with it. Worf tells him it shouldn't be used like that—it's a Klingon *gin'tak* spear!

LEFT: My original sketches for the gin'tak spear were drawn from childhood memories of *The Wizard of Oz*. In the story for 'Birthright, Part II' it symbolised the way the young Klingons had lost touch with their identity as warriors.

XINDI INSECTOID WEAPONS

On *Enterprise* we had the Xindi Insectoids, which were CG creatures built by the brilliant John Teska. I had to design a gun that could be operated by Insectoid hands. It had to look like something that could compete with a phaser.

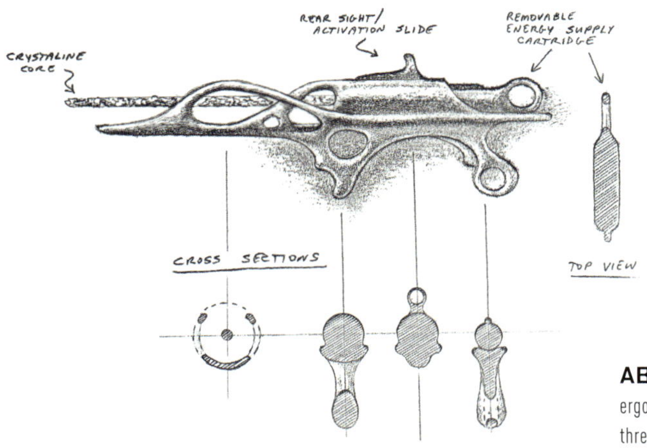

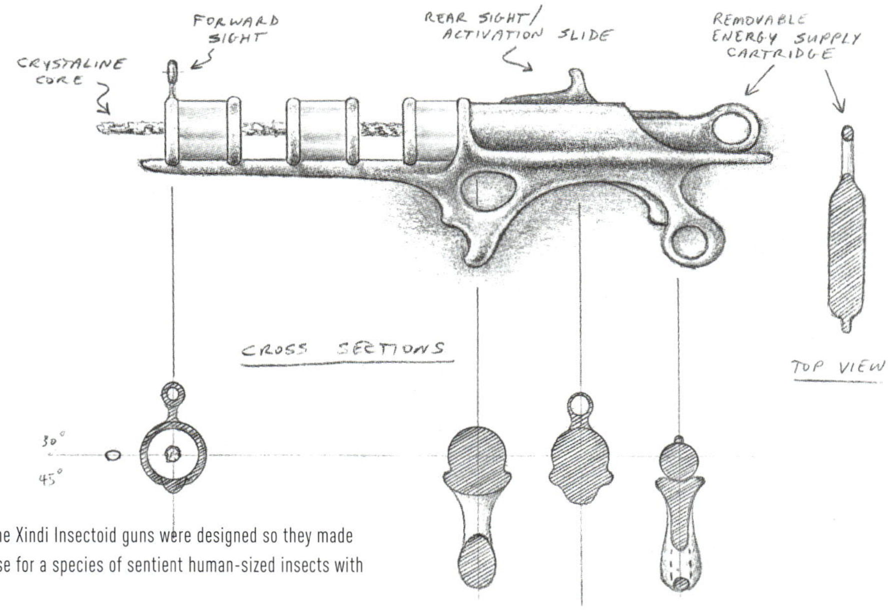

ABOVE: The Xindi Insectoid guns were designed so they made ergonomic sense for a species of sentient human-sized insects with three fingers.

I shared a property line, so sometimes she would come over for a brush up. If we knew a bat'leth scene was coming up, we'd work on some exciting moves. She was a very adept student.

In episodes where Worf was teaching a martial-arts class on the *Enterprise*, Michael Dorn and I would work out the moves in advance. He was a really terrific collaborator, and we came up with some great sequences. When shooting on set, I would be behind the camera doing the exercises so the class could see me and Michael could see me to help remember the moves, like a teleprompter.

Amazingly, The *bat'leth* became an icon of Klingon culture, and I think it has appeared in every version of the show since we came up with it. Interestingly enough, when they were doing one of the features, a crewmember called me up and asked me if I could change it what changes I would make. I said I wouldn't change it, apart from possibly making the handles a little thicker. It's already correct, and if you change it you would be making change for change's sake, and it would be less effective as a weapon. Why would you change a classic Renaissance rapier?

There was one exception: on *Deep Space Nine* we did a show where they are looking for Kahless's *bat'leth*. It's a kind of mythical weapon, a bit like the King Arthur's Excalibur. Kahless was the quintessential Klingon warrior from ancient times. He lived in even more vicious times than the contemporary Klingons, so I thought it would be appropriate to make his *bat'leth* more baroque and more vicious looking. That's why it has that central flange in the middle. I called it the disembowelment flange. It has more indents so you can grapple an opponent's weapon a little bit differently. Instead of having three holes, I was thinking of it being more primitive, so it just has one large handle. Kahless would be so powerful he could wield it in a way unequaled by other Klingons.

I think the *bat'leth* is a cool weapon. I pick it up and work out with it once in a while, just to keep the feel of it.

PRIMITIVE WEAPONS

In the two-part *Voyager* episode 'Basics,' Captain Janeway and her crew are marooned on a primitive planet inhabited by warlike humanoids with a Neolithic level of technology. Their weapons had to be made from readily available materials like wood and stone. Inspired by primitive weapons I have seen on my travels and in museums, as well as the illustrations in Edwin Tunis' beautifully illustrated book, *Weapons*, and adding my own ideas, I came up with this group of weapons to be wielded by the Stone Age inhabitants of the 'Basics' planet.

The stone-tipped club was inspired by an Aztec club, but more primitive and less elegant. The staff sling is actually a medieval European weapon that throws rocks much like a lacrosse stick. It is basically a hand version of the throwing arm of a trebuchet (siege weapon), but could have been made by primitive people. My brother John and I made one as children; on his first attempt to throw a rock, John hit me in the ankle, inducing significant pain that was difficult to explain to our parents.

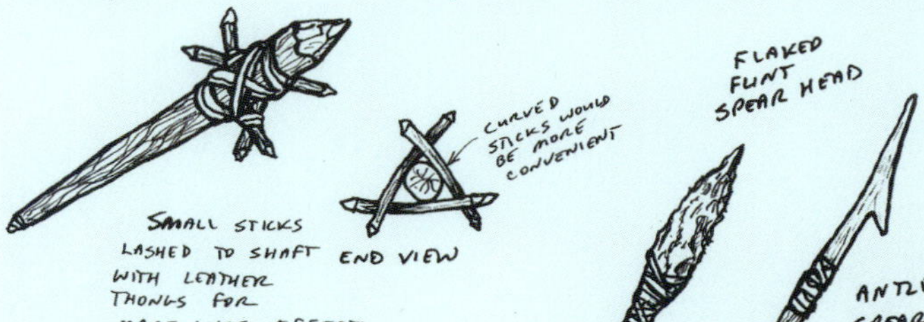

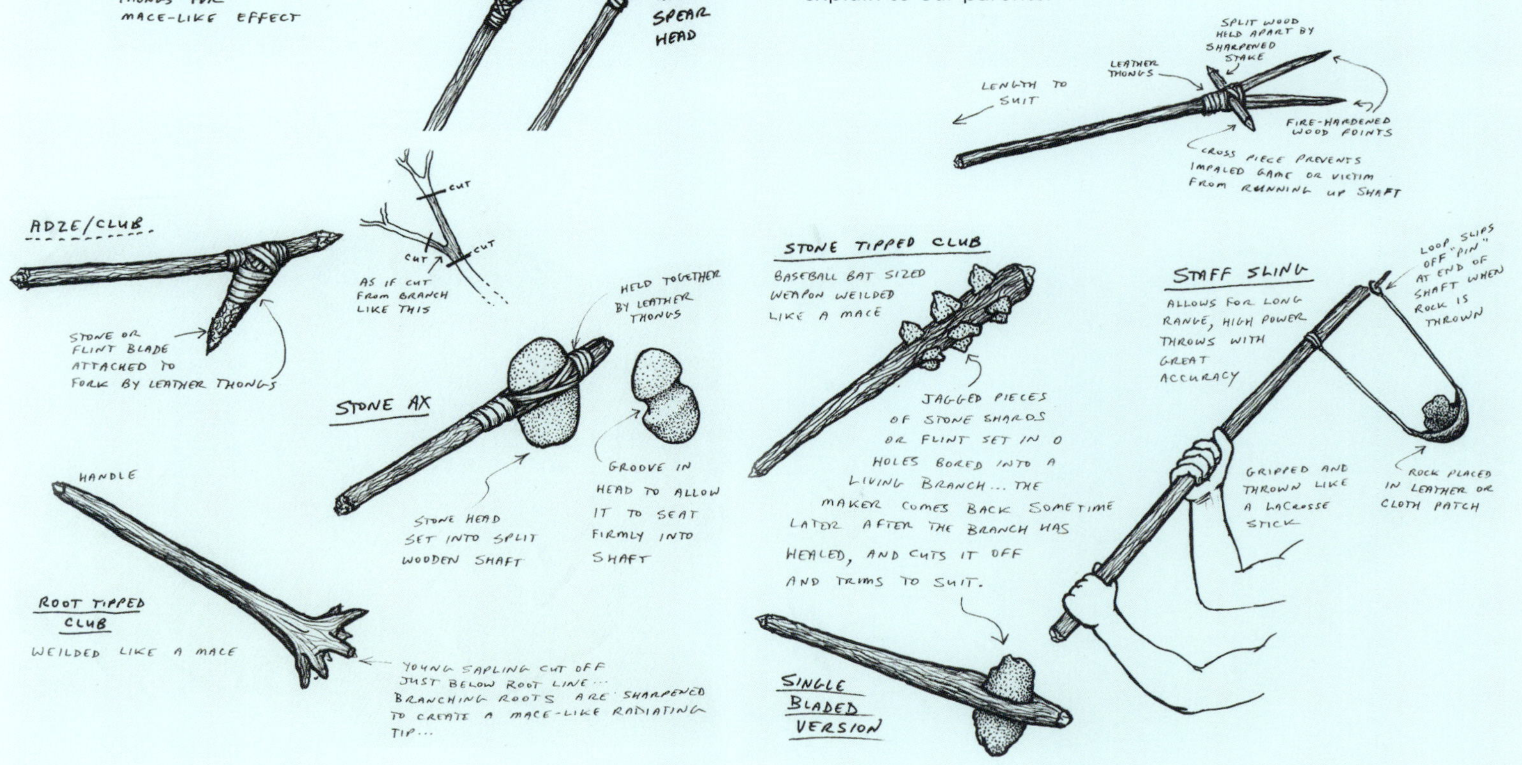

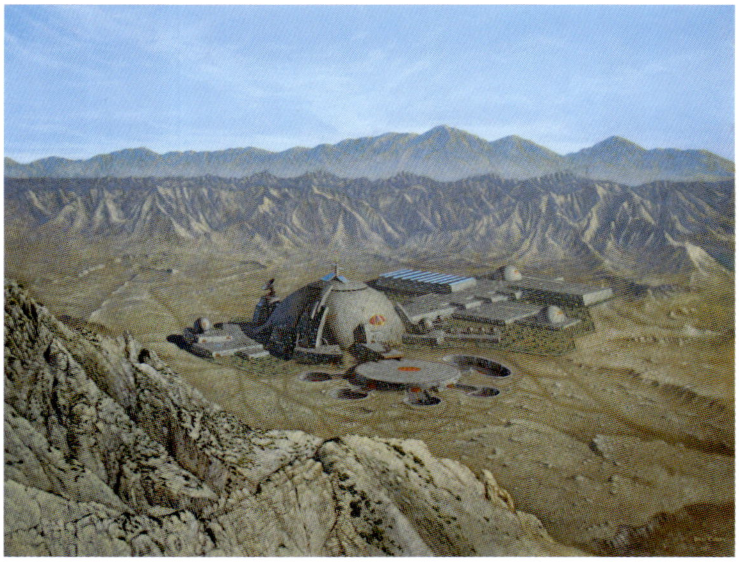

ABOVE: Originally done for *Buck Rogers*, I dug out this matte painting and reworked it for the first season of *TNG*, doing a virtual camera move as if passing over the mountain.

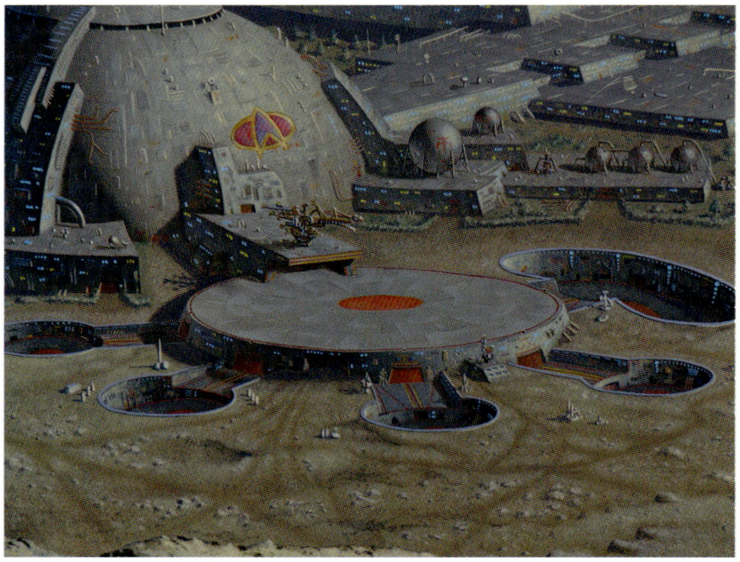

ABOVE: The oil painting was on Masonite, which allowed us to drill holes in it and mount tiny grain-of-wheat light bulbs behind it for a more life-like effect.

MATTE PAINTING

CONJURING UP ALIEN WORLDS USING PAINT, BRUSHES—AND A LOT OF IMAGINATION

I got my start in effects as a matte painter. In the late 1970s I was doing my masters in Film and Theatre when I got the chance to have an exhibition of some of my paintings. One of the people who came to see it was George Lucas's first wife, Marcia. She was a great film editor, who had worked on *Taxi Driver* as well as *Star Wars*. One of the paintings I was showing was something I'd done in Kathmandu while I was in the Peace Corps. Marcia thought it had a lot of the qualities of a good matte painting, and recommended me to Dennis Muren at ILM. He put me on to Peter Anderson, who took me on to do matte painting on *Buck Rogers In The 25th Century*. From there I went on to learn about all the different visual effects.

When I started on *Star Trek*, it was a given that we would use matte paintings to create alien worlds—in 1987 there wasn't really any other way of doing it. They'd used matte paintings on the original series too, when one of my heroes, Albert Whitlock, had created paintings for many of the extraordinary places that Kirk, Spock and McCoy would visit. We were lucky enough to do a lot of work with Syd Dutton, who studied under Al and is a true master of the art. So I would sometimes contribute one, or rework something Syd had done.

The idea behind matte painting has always stayed the same, but the technology has changed almost beyond recognition. It's a

BELOW: I produced original matte paintings for *TNG* using traditional techniques. This one shows the Klingon Lamassary on Boreth.

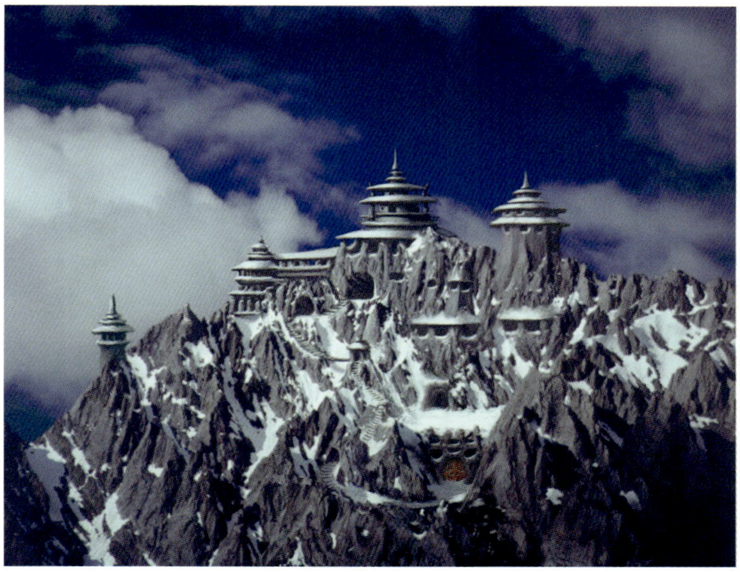

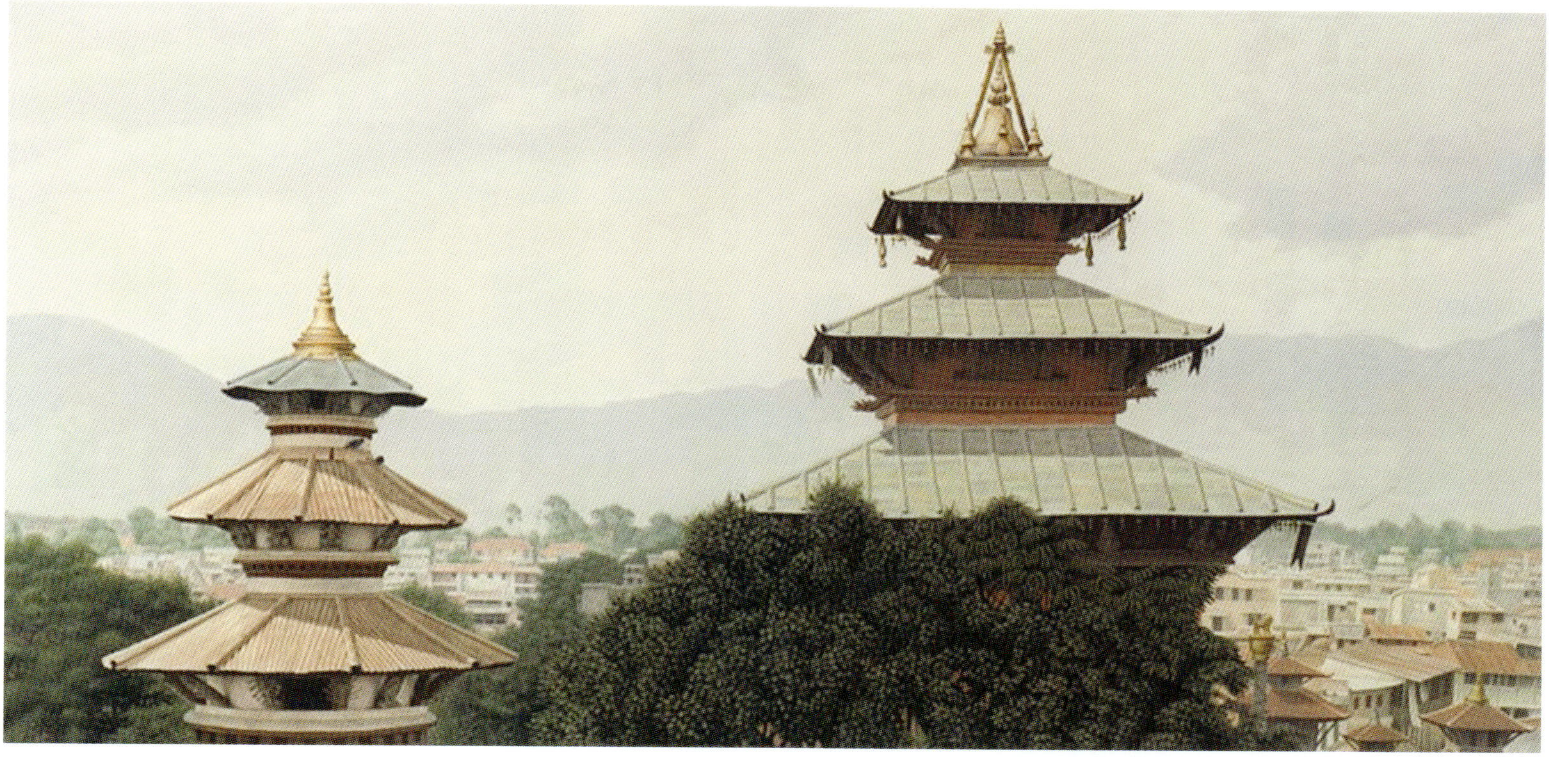

ABOVE: This painting wasn't done for *Star Trek*—it wasn't even a matte painting—but when Marcia Lucas saw it in a student show, she introduced me to Dennis Muren at ILM, whose kind mentoring began my career in VFX.

technique that allows you to use photoreal painting to create the illusion that you have filmed in a place that doesn't exist, and with a little trickery you can make it look as if it has movement. It can be a complete image that fills the screen, or used in conjunction with live-action footage so it looks as if people are standing inside the painting.

When we started on *The Next Generation*, our matte paintings would be done on Masonite or glass. Then, as the various digital paint boxes got more sophisticated, we started to create them using photographs and freehand drawing, and by the time we got to *Voyager* we were able to add CG elements, or even create them entirely in CG.

Early on, we used Illusion Arts to do most of our matte paintings. They were one of the best traditional matte painting companies in the business. It was founded and run by Syd Dutton and Bill Taylor. We chose them because Syd Dutton is both a brilliant painter and a brilliant designer.

Syd would create large paintings on Masonite that Bill would film for us. The paintings were pretty big—they would be a minimum of 2.5 ft by 4 ft. That's important because if the painting is large, you can move the camera over it to create a sense of motion. That stops the shot from being too static, and makes it look more real. It also means you can get several shots from one painting, since you can photograph different parts of it to create different compositions. When we needed something very detailed, or wanted to do a big move, the paintings could be even bigger. One of the biggest Syd ever did for us was the Borg cube interior for 'Q Who?,' which was about six square feet.

Syd made a huge contribution to the look of *Star Trek*. When you're working with an artist of Syd's caliber, you let him be a

BELOW: By *TNG*'s second season, I had started doing digital matte paintings on an early paint box system. This is one of the earliest—it may even be the first.

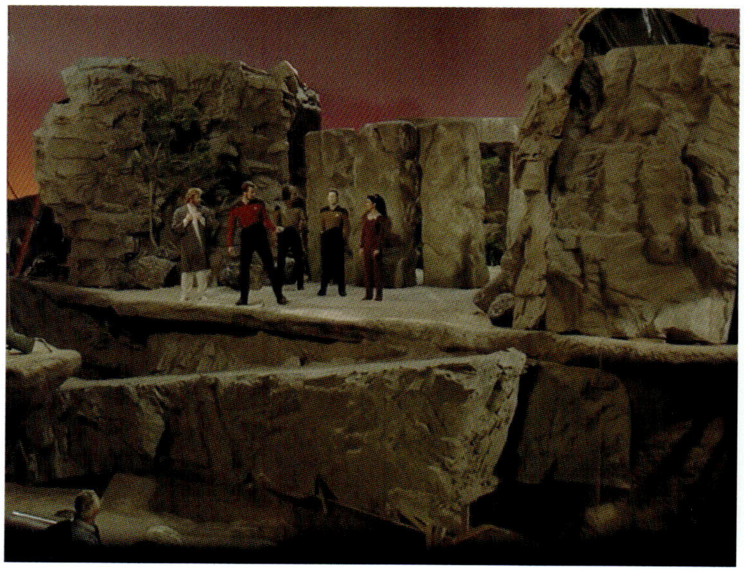

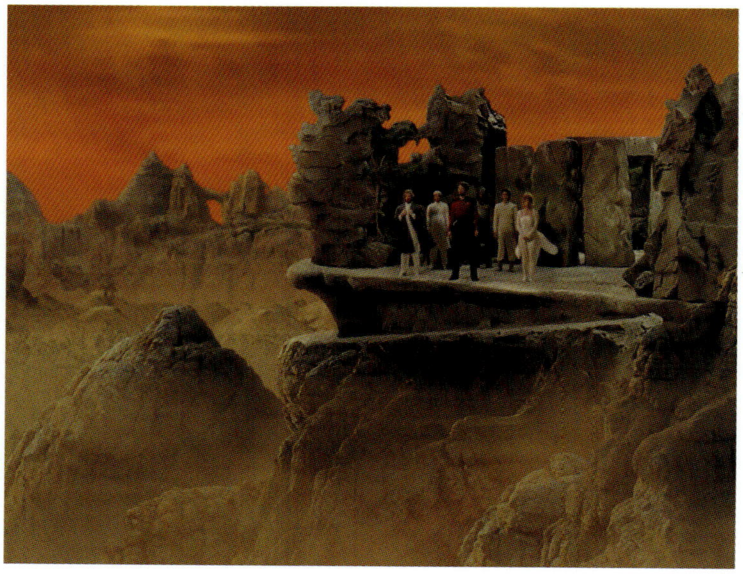

INSIDE STORY

INSIDE THE BORG CUBE

Sometimes we would use rear projection to make it look as if people were moving around inside a matte painting. The pullback in the interior of the Borg Cube for 'Q Who?' was done that way. Our live-action set was quite small, only just enough to provide a physical space for a row of Borg drones and the away team to beam in and move about. The shot was scheduled for the last day of shooting. Everyone was exhausted after a very long day, but, as always, cast and crew were cheerful and professional. The angle was selected, and we locked the camera down. Measurements and angles were recorded, and then director Rob Bowman captured the performances he wanted, and the film went to the lab.

Days later, Bill and Syd projected the full-frame image of the practical set onto a large sheet of Masonite, and established how the perspective worked. We discussed the scope of the interior and the nature of Borg technology and aesthetics before Syd started painting. It was great checking in with Syd to see the progress of the painting, and to be able to comment as it evolved. When it was ready, the painting was mounted at the end of a motion-control track. Bill cut a hole in the painting where the practical set would appear, and mounted a precision-cut piece of rear-screen material. Behind the painting, he set up a projector aimed precisely at the cutout. Because different exposures were required for the painting and the rear projection, the shot had to be done in two passes, thus the necessity of shooting motion control as both camera moves had to match exactly. The first pass was the painting. The area where the rear projection would be was covered with black to prevent that part of the negative from being exposed. Bill stopped the mo-co camera at several distances from the painting so he could build structures made of painted Tonka 'Legions of Power' construction toys—this gave the impression that the camera was moving through a complex three-dimensional system of conduits and machines. Bill then back-wound the camera to frame 1, and synced the rear projector with the mo-co camera's shutter and long exposure. While shooting, the only light in the room was the small projection itself.

Years later, when I supervised visual effects for the Blu-ray re-release of *The Next Generation* Season 2, we realized that Syd's brilliant painting was created for the lower-resolution standard-definition format, and therefore looked a little too painterly for high-def. Working with digital artist Sean Jackson, with great reverence for the original, we recreated the interior of the Borg Cube shot. Newer technology allowed us to build in a lot of kinetic elements that were impossible when the original was done.

BELOW: The only part of the Borg Cube that wasn't a matte painting was a small section of corridor with the actors in. The rest was masterfully painted by Syd Dutton.

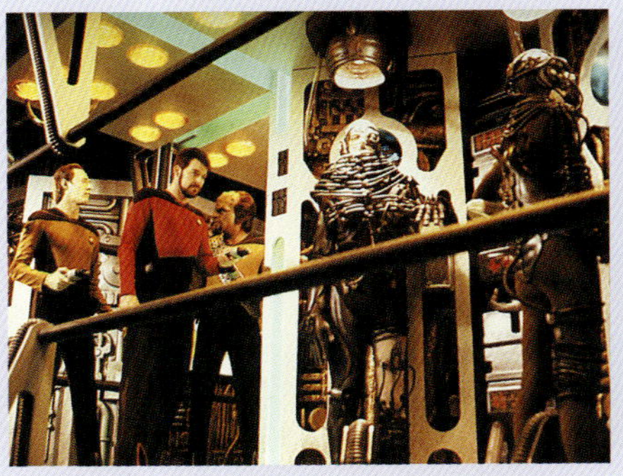

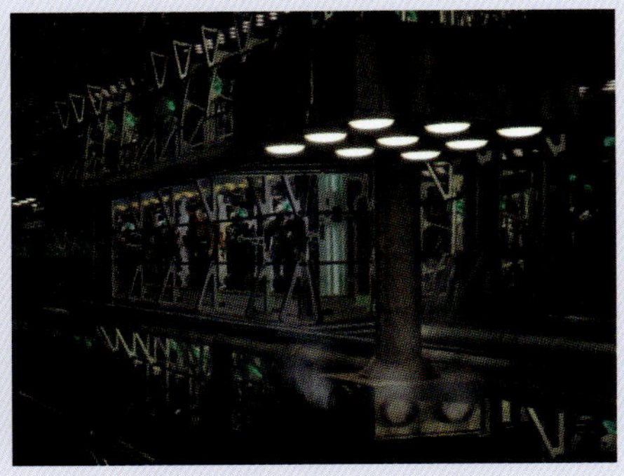
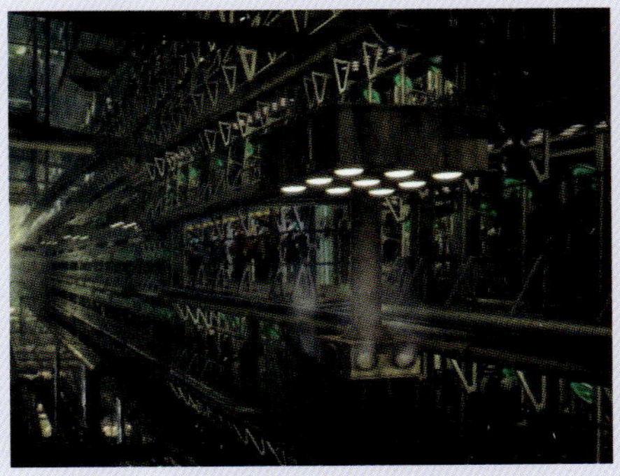
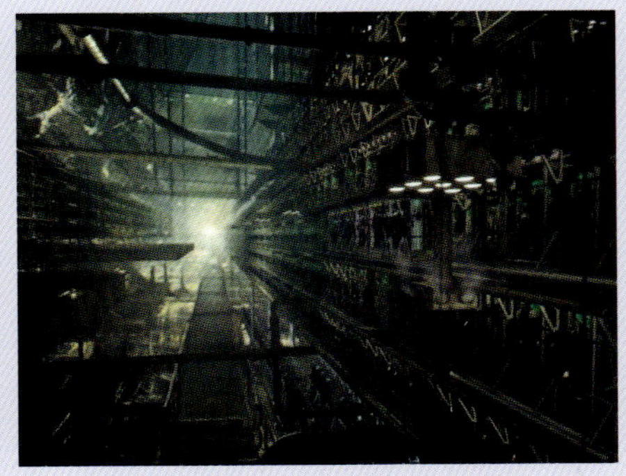
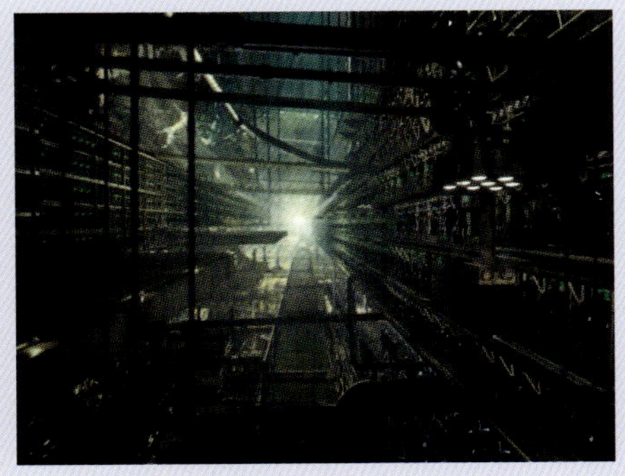

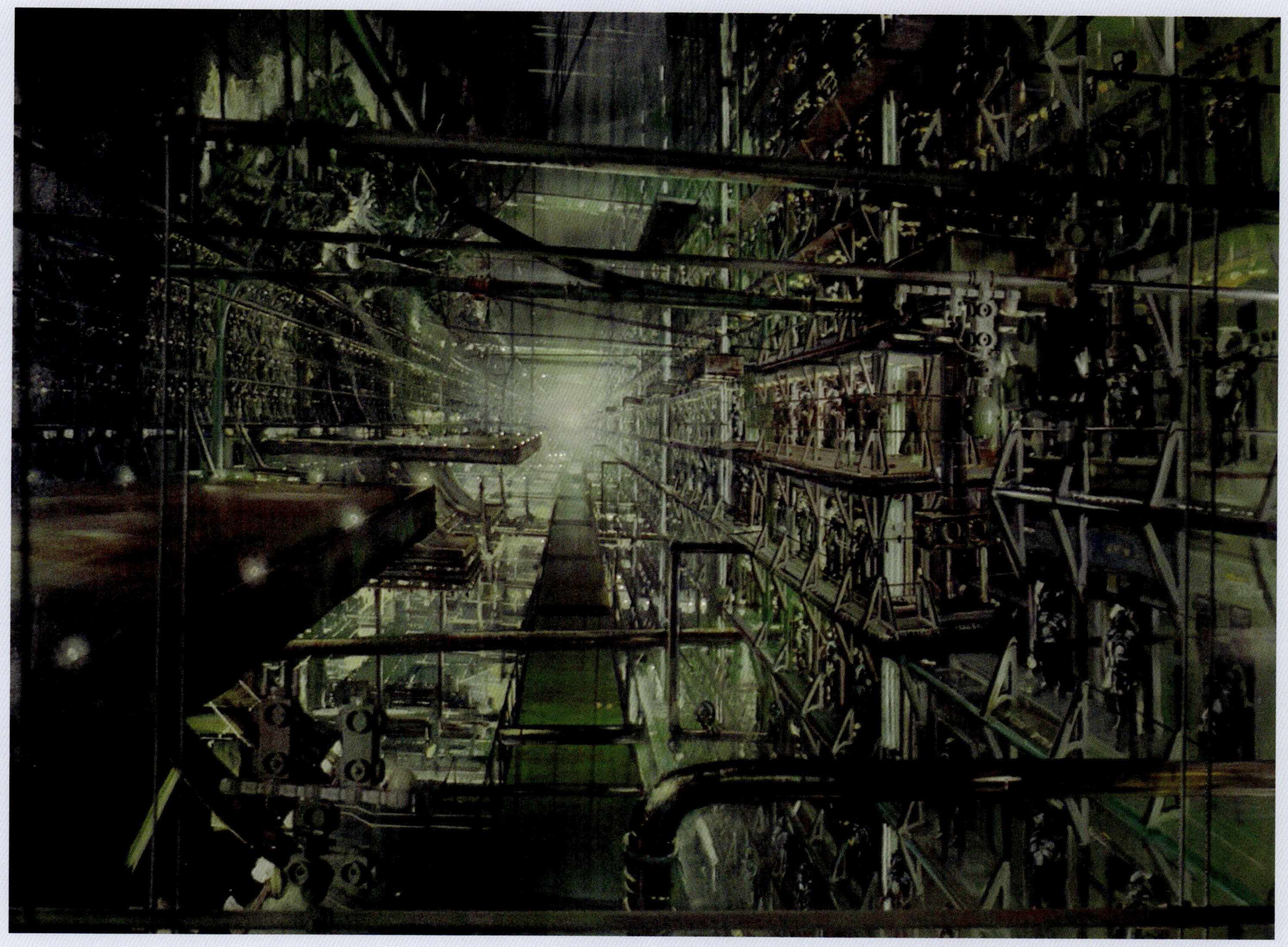

ABOVE: Syd Dutton created the matte painting of the Borg Cube interior. As the camera pulled back, he and his partner Bill Taylor would stop and build more physical parts in the foreground to create an illusion of passing through three-dimensional structures.

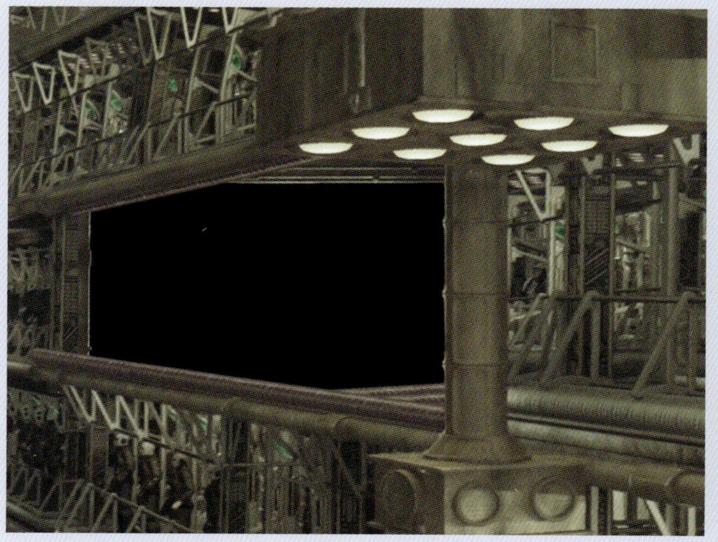

ABOVE: There was a small hole precisely cut out of the matte painting that was covered with rear-projection material.

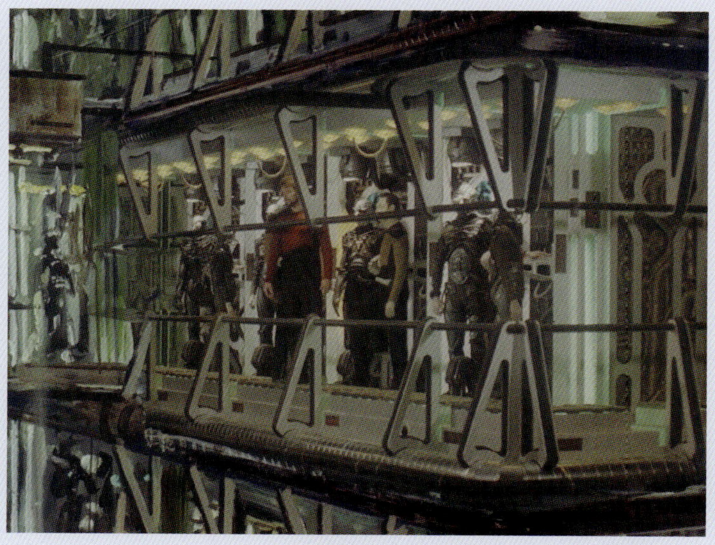

ABOVE: Bill projected the live-action footage into the cutout to match it seamlessly into the painting around it.

INSIDE STORY

SYD DUTTON MATTE PAINTINGS

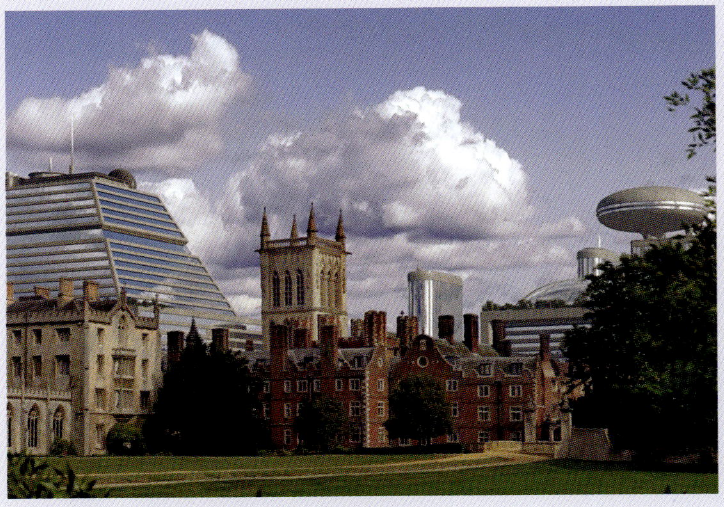

ABOVE: Cambridge University; *TNG*'s 'All Good Things...'.

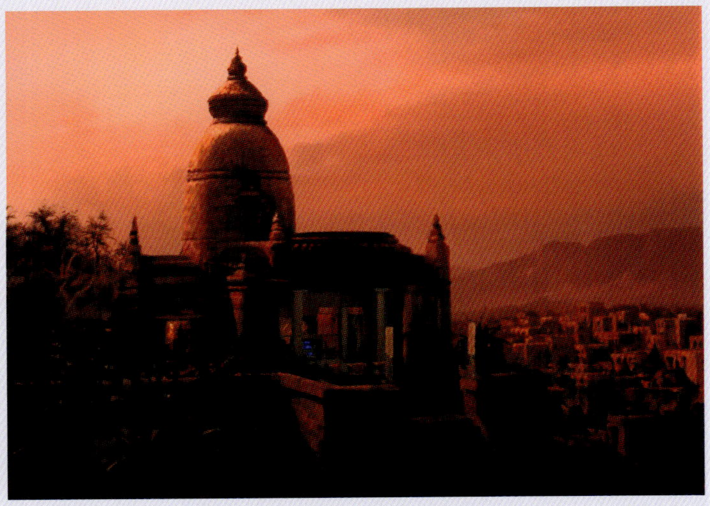

ABOVE: Final composited matte for Ligon III from *TNG*'s 'Code of Honor.'

Syd and I first met at Universal after I was newly inducted into the matte artists union as its fifteenth member when I was working on the original *Battlestar Galactica* and *Buck Rogers*. Syd's mentor, legendary matte artist Albert Whitlock, Syd, and Bill Taylor, ASC, gave me a tour of their department and unselfishly shared decades of experience and insights. That one afternoon saved me years of trial and error in the art of matte painting.

Years later, Syd and Bill formed their own company, Illusion Arts. As VFX supervisor on *Star Trek*, I was delighted to work with them as a client. I had long considered Syd one of the best artists around because of his skill as a photoreal painter and his incredible design sense. I enjoyed collaborating with Syd and having the rare privilege of passing paintbrushes back and forth to tweak details. Syd's iconic alien cities related well to our full-sized sets, and became an important part of the visual universe of *Star Trek*.

My son, Devin, interned at Illusion Arts before starting at USC. He was privileged to learn under the tutelage of such brilliant artists.

BELOW: Syd painted this for himself and let us use it on *Star Trek*—extra wide to allow for a camera pan.

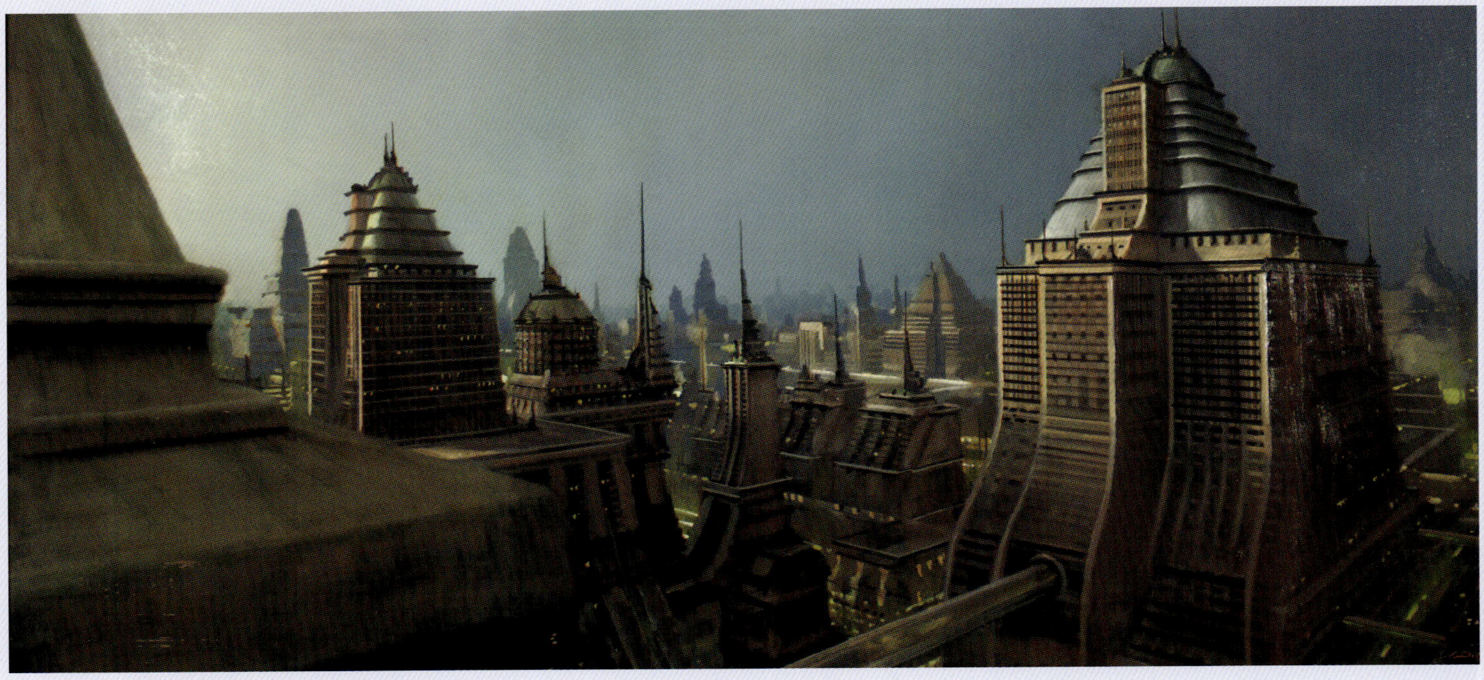

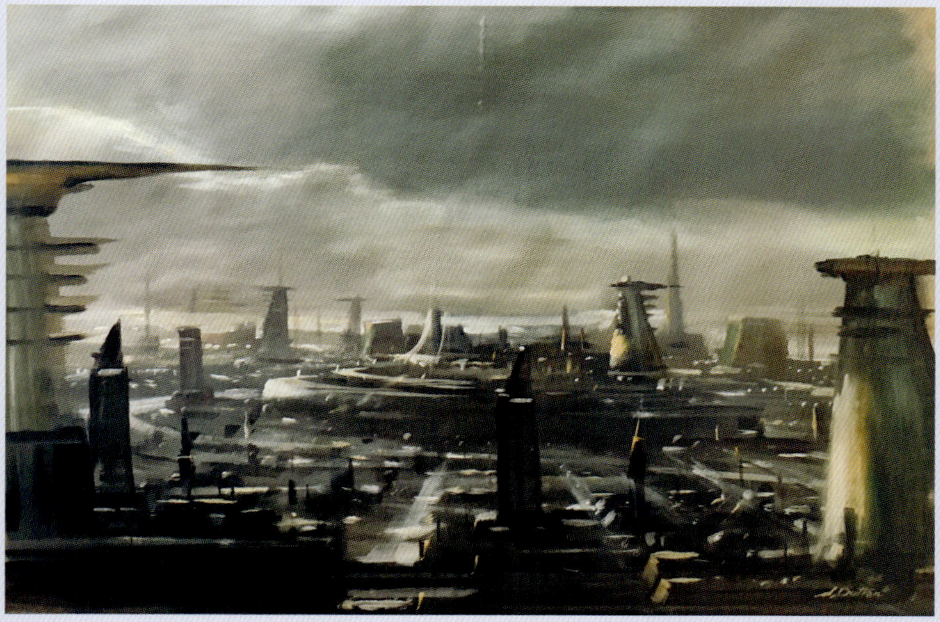

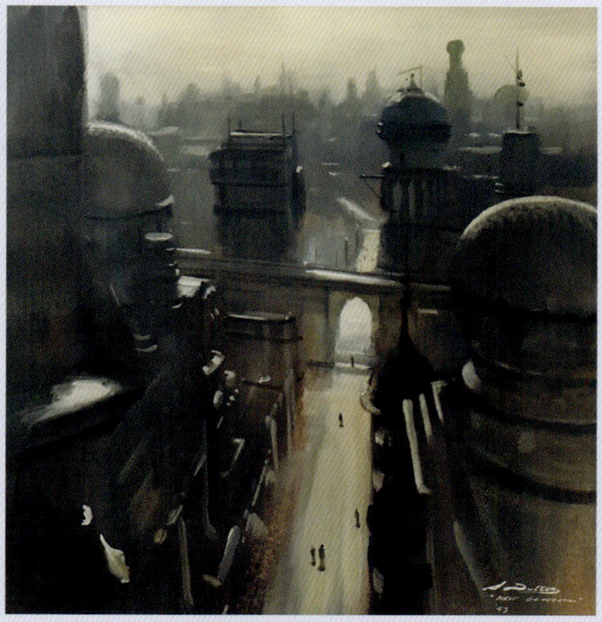

ABOVE: Concept sketch, oil on brown paper; Romulus. City was revised to be more 'Roman.'

ABOVE: Oil sketch; unused concept for alien city.

BELOW: Oil concept sketch; Klingon outpost. I had asked Syd to make it look like it could be in the Himalayas.

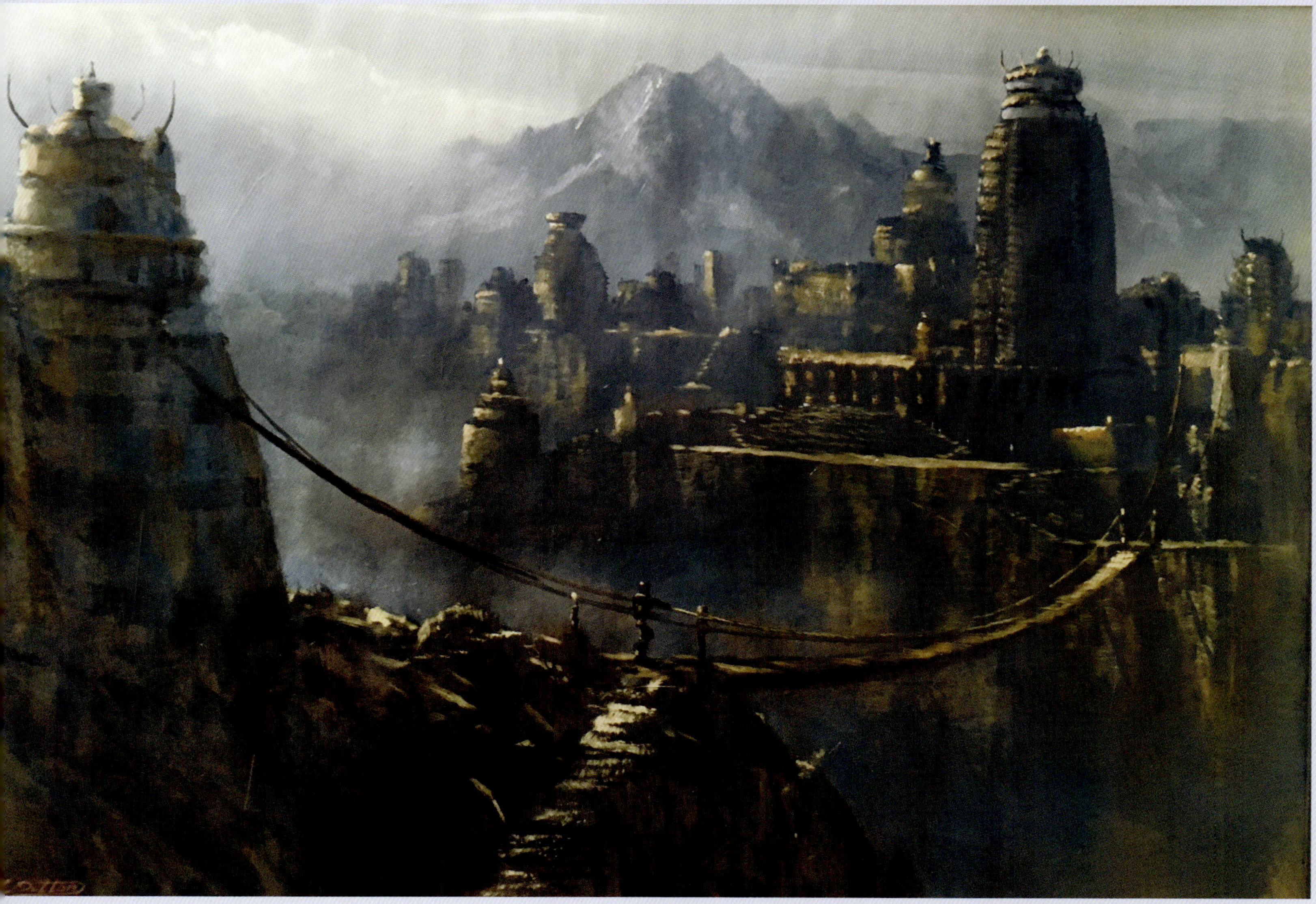

INSIDE STORY

THE BAJORAN FIRE CAVES

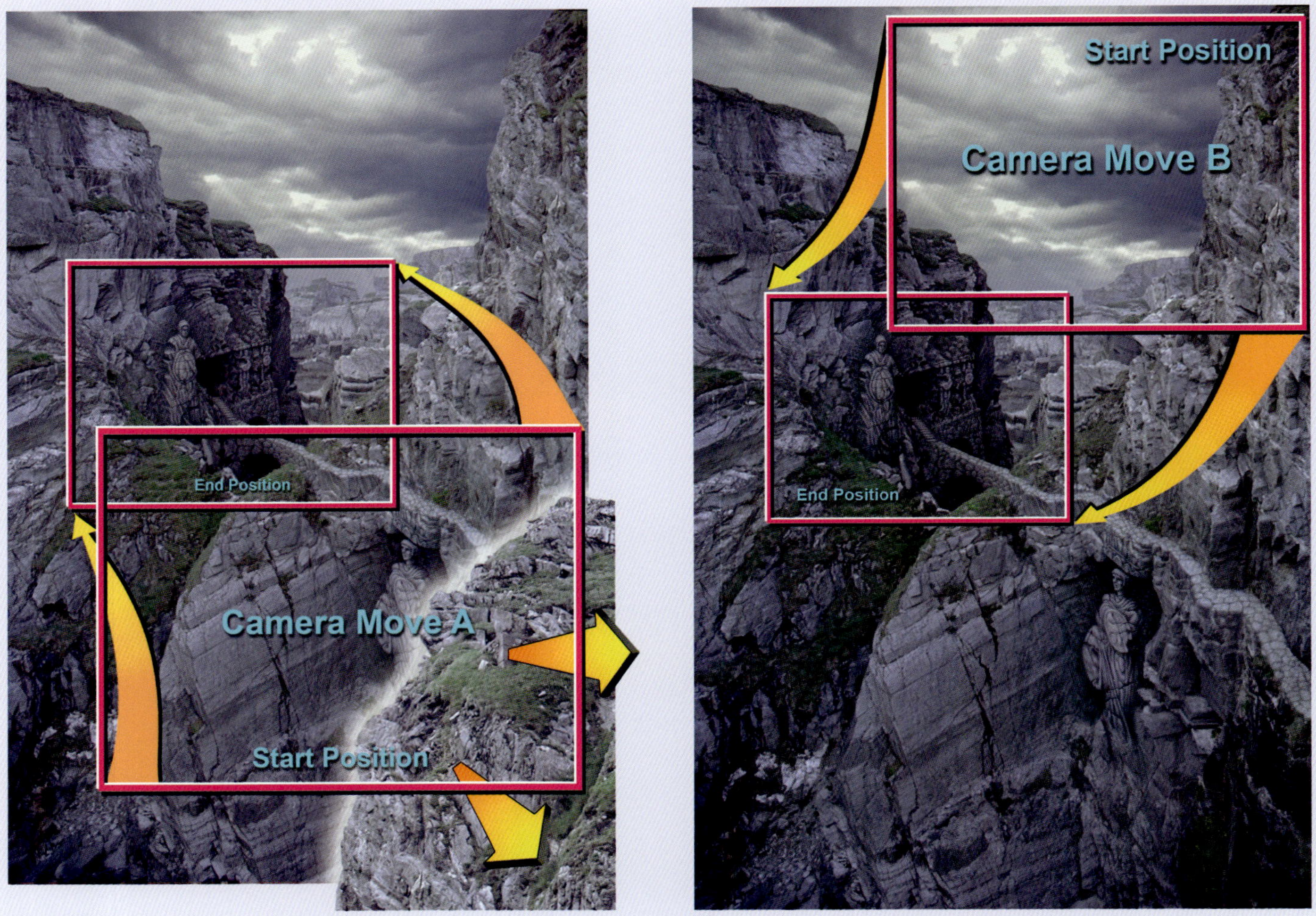

ABOVE: A 2D image with a 'canvas' that is much larger than final broadcast size allows you to 'film' different virtual camera moves on the same digital painting with no image quality loss, and to reveal different aspects of the same location. Zooming over a foreground layer in perspective creates the illusion of passing over a cliff to reveal the statues and cave.

In the script for the *DS9* finale, Kai Winn and Gul Dukat enter the Bajoran Fire Caves, where they summon the ethereal Pah-wraiths and have their final confrontation with Sisko. I remembered some photos I took in Mizen Head, Ireland, which became the basis for the cliffs of the Fire Caves. I imagined a path and giant statues carved into the rocks, with a bridge to a cave.

I made one high-resolution digital painting so that we could move the camera across it to create different moves. I split part of the cliff off and put it on a separate plane that could move independently toward camera, creating the illusion of depth. Painting freehand, I 'carved' the path into the cliff, adding the cave and the ancient statues of Bajoran monks. We put in a more interesting sky from a different photograph. To allow the illusion of movement, we set it as the backmost layer. We locked the bottom to the horizon and expanded the top corners upwards and to the left to create the illusion of changing perspective and moving clouds.

The inside of the caves was a combination of the partial set and a CG environment that was based on some reference photographs of Crag Caves that I took on the same trip to Ireland. When we filmed the actors on the stage, our director of photography Jonathan West knew we had to make fire appear, so he transitioned the set lighting from the cold gray light to firelight. Because I wanted the light to look like it was interacting with the stalactites and the stalagmites inside the cave, they had to be 3D. I did a rough sketch of what I wanted, and gave it to 3D artists at Foundation. Brandon MacDougall did most of the work, with help from Koji Kuramura and John Teska. Most of the fire is CG, but some real fire elements were added. The cave set extension is all CG. The only real part of the scene is the immediate set where they are standing.

Moving Sky

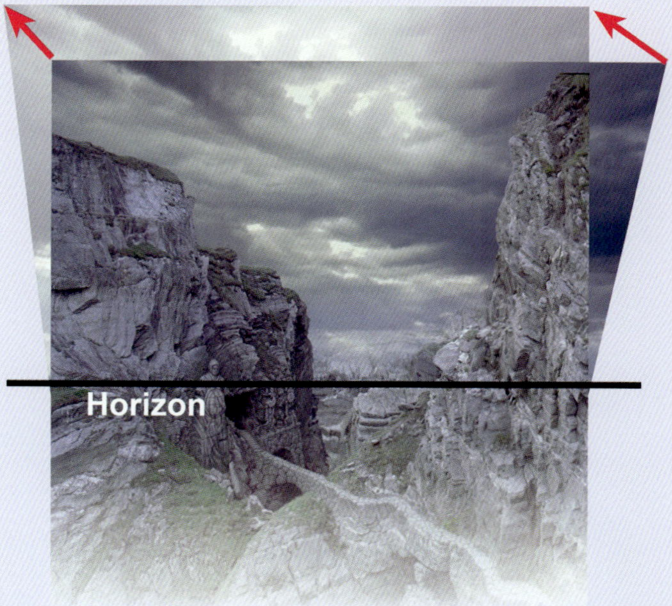

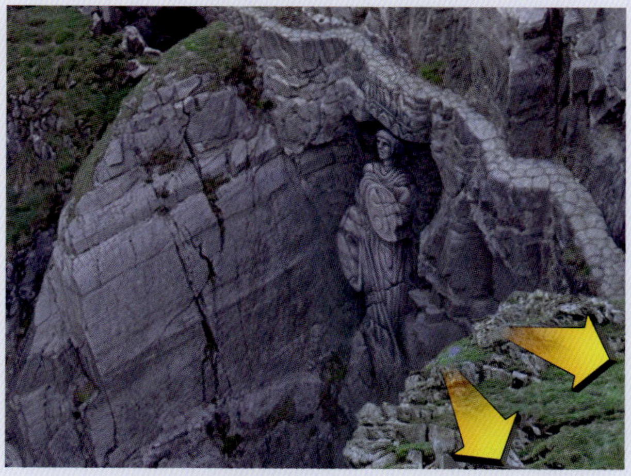

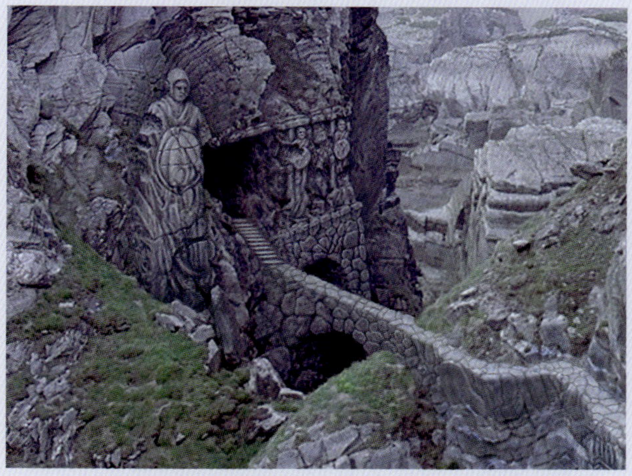

ABOVE: Corner pinning sky to add movement in perspective.

ABOVE RIGHT: Start and end framing for virtual camera move A.

BELOW: Interior fire caves; partial set on sound stage and digital set extension with stages of animated fire.

1

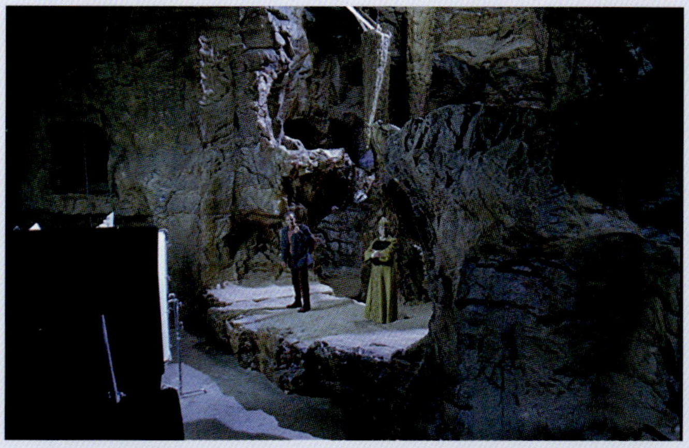

2

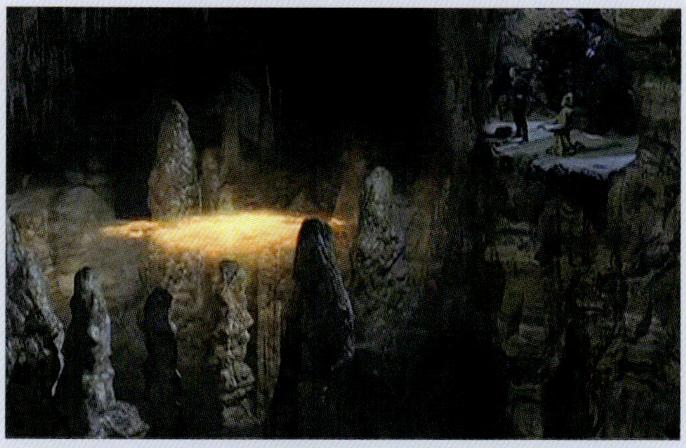

3

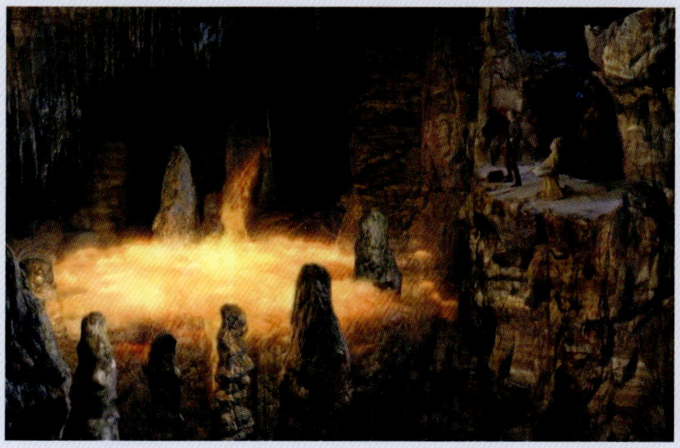

4

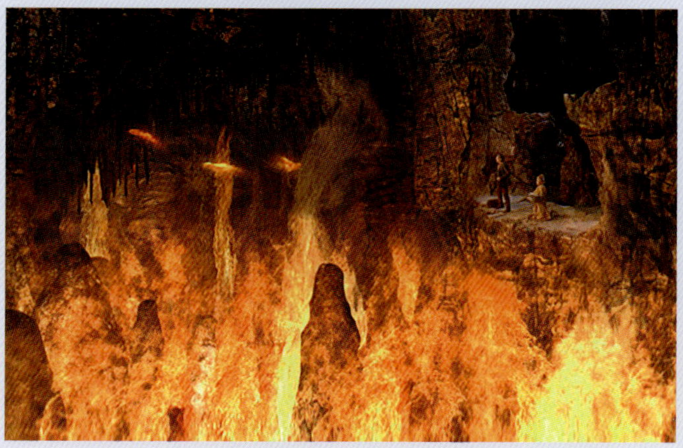

genius. I could give him a general idea and let him run with it. One of the great matte shots he did for us was Starfleet headquarters. There is a very architecturally futuristic water reclamation plant in Van Nuys that has a spectacular garden (luckily the aroma did not translate to the audience); Syd extended those buildings to make it look like a much larger complex, and put San Francisco Bay and the Golden Gate Bridge in the background.

Klingon, Ferengi and Romulan architecture was all Syd's design work. Syd was big on reference—if you look at Klingon buildings, there's a hint of Nepali architecture, along with a hint of Thai Lao architecture. Sometimes we'd have sketches from the art department, but more often than not our production designers Herman Zimmerman and Richard James would just trust us. We would normally start out with mood and reference, and then Syd and I would talk about the culture of the people. Sometimes I would do a loose sketch on the spot, then Syd would do one of his wonderful, really loose paintings on brown paper. I would show it to Rick and Peter and whoever else was involved, but usually the feedback was pretty minimal.

When you get close to a matte painting, it might not be exactly what you expect—it's not totally photorealistic. One of the best pieces of advice I got early on is, 'don't over-paint the details.' If you do, it looks like a miniature. Matte painting is much more impressionistic; I remember seeing a shot that Al did for *Hello, Dolly!* There's an incredibly elaborate staircase with beautiful gold statues at the base of the banisters. They look totally real on screen, but when you see the original painting you realize that they are just squiggles.

There are a lot of gags you can do with matte painting to make them look more realistic, and to create the illusion of movement. One of the things that makes a matte painting more lifelike is a technique called multi-planing, where you have different two-dimensional, partially painted layers stacked in front of one another on glass. Sometimes the full-frame background painting would be on Masonite. As the camera moves forward, the partial paintings

BELOW: Example of multi-plane matte shot (2.5D).

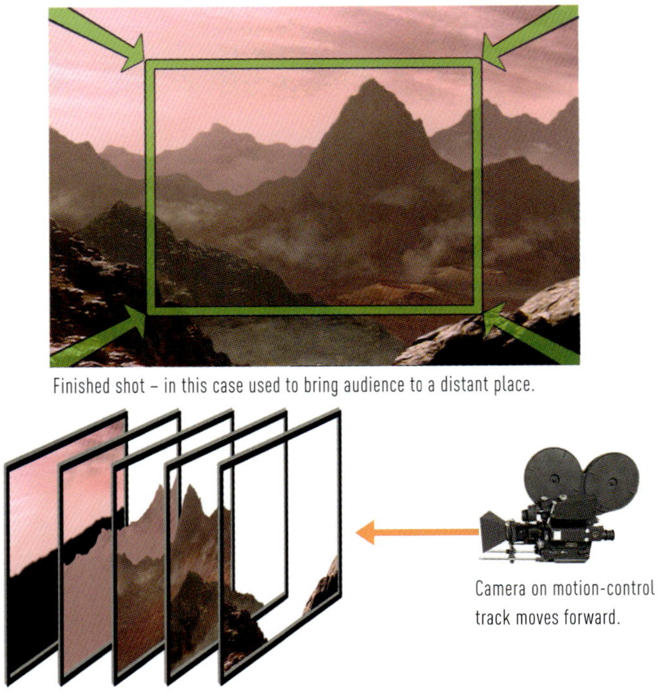

Backmost layer: oil on Masonite. Foreground layers: oil on gessoed glass in wooden frames, spaced so that each layer can be lit.

on the different layers move past the lens, creating the illusion that you are moving through a three-dimensional space. Today, that technique is done digitally and called 'two-and-a-half D.'

Years ago, when I started on Universal's *Buck Rogers In The 25th Century*, I got to know David Stipes, who would later come and work with me on *Star Trek*. Back then, David was the matte camera operator and I was a matte painter. He was always generous with

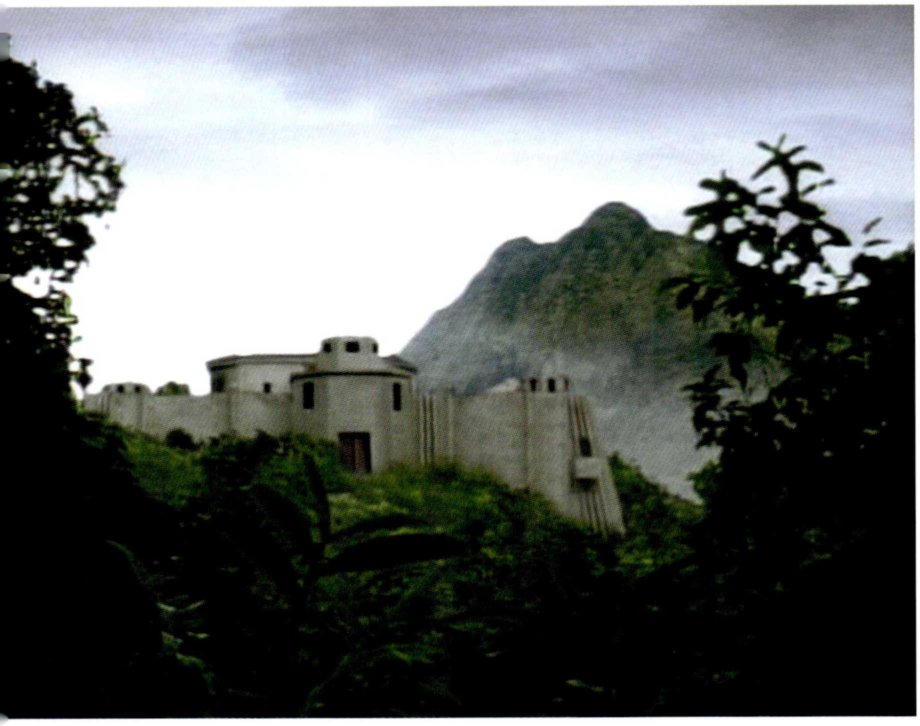

ABOVE: Working with the compositor we created two versions of this matte painting of the prison camp on Carraya IV, one showing it during the day and one at night. It was a relatively easy change to make the lighting change in Photoshop.

INSIDE STORY

PHASER DRILLING

There were times when we designed a physical gag to work with a matte painting. There's a *TNG* episode, 'Legacy,' where we go to Tasha Yar's home planet and see a city in ruins. A phaser blasts down from space and drills a hole in the ground, causing dust to billow out. As VFX supervisor, I commissioned Syd to paint the ruined city. Lynn Ledgerwood at Illusion Arts built the foreground terrain using powdered walnut for sand. He installed a tube underneath the table filled with 'sand' held by a plug a few inches below the surface. When the plug was pulled downwards, the 'sand' above it collapsed. Bill Taylor shot at a high frame rate to stretch time and give it the scale of a full-sized event. The scale dust bursting up through the drill hole was a separate element—baking soda, shot at high speed, tossed up through a hole in black velvet. When we did the compositing at The Post Group, we added the animated phaser beam and some smoke to enhance the power of the blast.

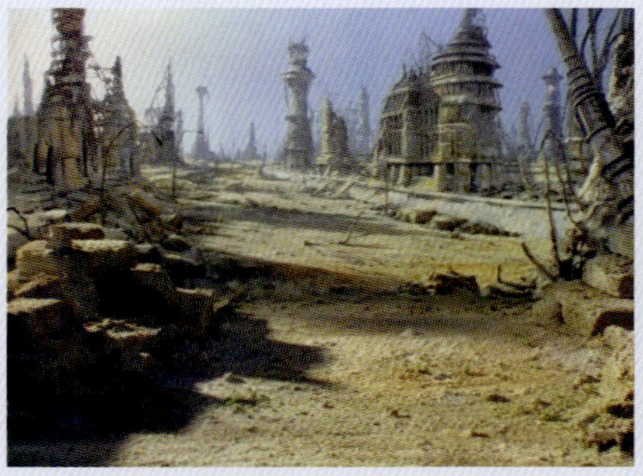

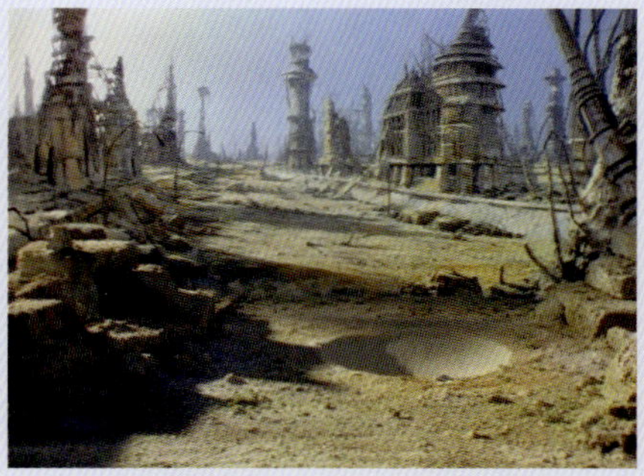

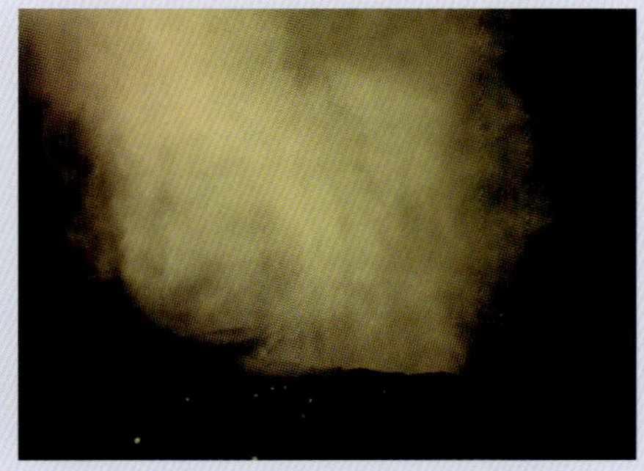

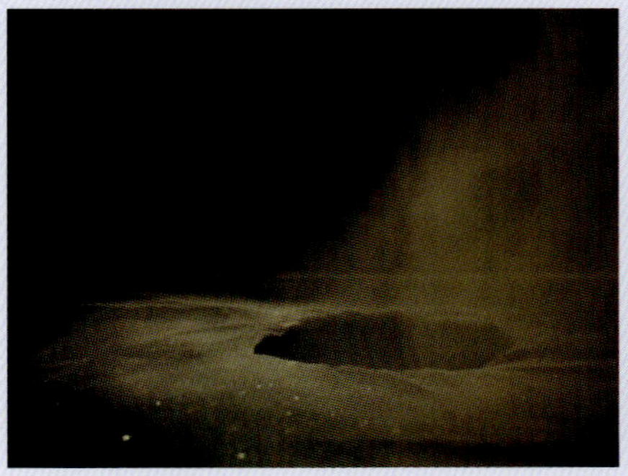

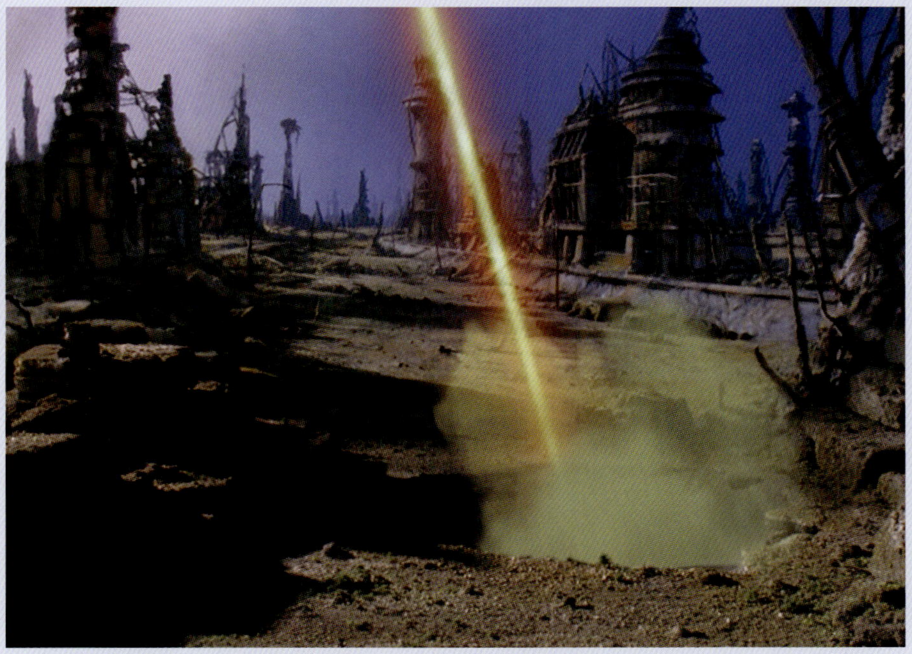

ABOVE AND RIGHT: Some matte paintings involve foreground miniatures that create an even greater sense of depth. In this case, Syd and Bill added an element showing the ground being drilled away.

sharing his wealth of knowledge. One of the techniques he taught me was making the clouds move in a static painting. To accomplish this so it looks natural, you photograph the sky in parallel layers through slots in a frame between the camera and the painting so that only one portion of the painting is exposed at a time. Cloud movement is then achieved by moving successively higher layers a little faster on a rail, using a precise electric motor.

Sometimes in the old days, if you wanted a moving crowd, you would paint the crowd on glass and then you do another painting behind it of small patches of scumbled colors. Then you shave little patches of paint off the foreground glass painting wherever the crowd is depicted. If you move the scumbled painting behind the crowd painting on glass, its motion shows through the patches of clear glass randomly, creating the illusion of rustling in a live crowd. The same trick can be used to create the illusion of moving leaves in static trees.

For the Ferenginar matte shot, Bill Taylor did something with some kind of gooey material. He animated the droplets by hitting this gooey material with a stick, and it made it look like raindrops hitting the surface.

Many times, Bill would create the illusion and then do the composite on an optical printer and send us the finished shot. We would transfer that to video. We found that that was actually a better way for us to work, because Bill and Syd could make sure they were happy with the comp first, and we would always get their best work.

I always liked to work with Syd when schedules allowed, but sometimes I would do matte paintings myself. The Starfleet outpost in 'Coming of Age' was originally a painting that had structures I did for *Buck Rogers*, which I revised for *Star Trek*, changing some of the buildings and signage. In the original one I had a radar screen, and I shot a little rotating ball to cover that up. That was on a 5ft-by-4ft piece of Masonite. We drilled holes in the panel, and put small grain-of-wheat light bulbs behind them so that there could be blinking lights.

Sometimes we mixed physical miniatures with matte paintings. In 'Contagion' there was a scene on a desolated planet where Captain Picard was investigating ruins of an ancient culture. Patrick was on a practical set on stage. We had to create the exterior to establish where he was, but in reality it only existed as words in a script. Herman Zimmerman's art department made a foreground miniature tower out of a swimming pool filter that they painted to look aged and weathered. At Image G we set the miniature tower up on a table, and partially buried it with powdered walnut, an excellent stand-in as miniature-scale sand. We placed a large physical sky painting behind the table at the far edge of the depth of focus so it would be a little blurred. Finally, we added some blowing liquid nitrogen to create the sense of a sandstorm.

There were other times when we designed a physical gag that worked with a matte painting. There's a *TNG* episode called 'Legacy' where we go to Tasha Yar's home planet. We see a city in ruins. Then a phaser comes out from space and drills a hole in the ground, and smoke comes billowing out. Syd painted the ruined city. At Image G we built the foreground terrain, once again using powdered walnut for sand. We installed a tube underneath the table with a plug some inches down from the surface. When the plug was pulled downwards, the sand above it collapsed. Shooting at high speed but playing it back at normal speed made it take longer, and gave it the scale of a full-sized event.

In compositing we combined Syd's painting with the foreground terrain, and added the phaser drilling and some smoke to show a direct reaction. Sand bursting up through the drill hole was actually baking soda, shot at high speed, thrown up through a hole in black velvet.

There were times when I altered Syd's paintings so we could reuse them. I'd make changes to fit a story a little better. When we did 'Angel One,' Syd did a wonderful cityscape with several layers of buildings multi-planed on glass. Later, when we did 'Samaritan Snare' for the Blu-ray release of Season 2, I wanted the city to look a little more sci-fi, so I digitally retouched some of the buildings, adding strange tops and odd windows.

Sometimes, to add verisimilitude, I'd sometimes put footage of a real tree, shot against a blue screen, on top of the matte painting, because we'd filmed a branch of a real tree rather than painted it, and the leaves would move naturally. Live trees against a blue sky are readily keyable, so it was relatively easy to do.

There were times we'd burn video into a matte painting. The most famous example is the matte of Cardassia, where we'd see a character talking on the screen. Syd delivered the painting, and we filmed the actor in matching perspective on set at Paramount and comped him in there.

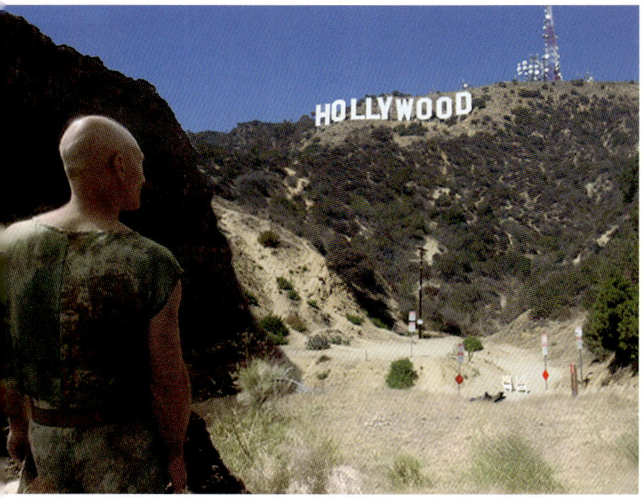

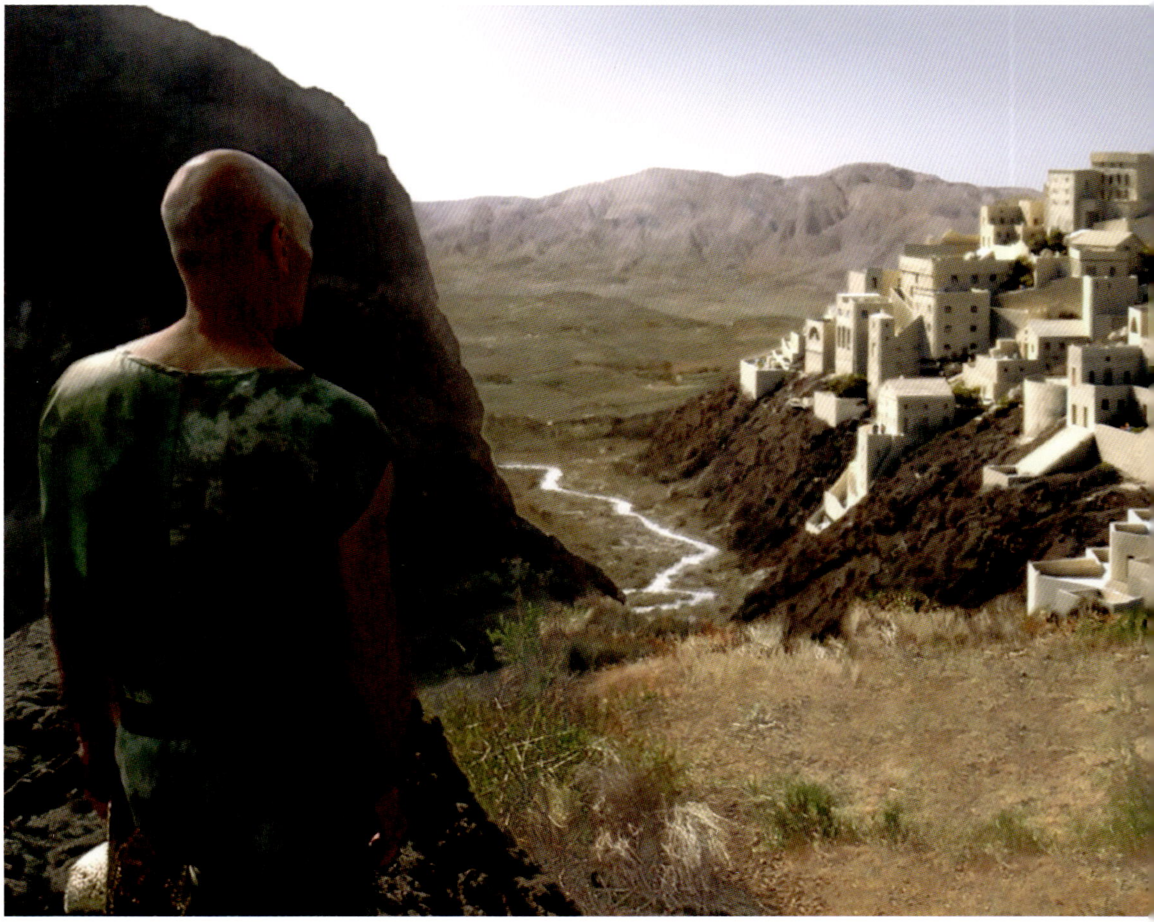

ABOVE AND RIGHT: In 'The Inner Light,' directed by Peter Lauritson, Picard looks out over an alien village. In reality Patrick was on location in Griffith Park's Bronson Canyon, looking at the Hollywood sign (above). This was my first, possibly one of the first, really ambitious digital matte paintings, and it was the beginning of a major change in the way things were done.

INSIDE STORY

WRECK OF THE *RAVEN*

You can see Jeri Ryan and Tim Russ in the foreground. We shot the scene on a partial set on stage, and I knew as long as the actors stayed contained within the foreground rock formation I could rotoscope (trace the silhouette of) the rock to remove the unwanted visual information, and replace it with a digital matte painting and CG wreck of the *Raven*. Later in the episode, Seven of Nine and Tuvok escape the crumbling wrecked ship—I directed that scene in second unit. As they jump out the hatch of the ship, in reality they were on a bluescreen stage, and were composited into a CG ship with 2D elements of rocks based on photos of the Alabama Hills in Lone Pine, California, where we shot the *Voyager* episodes 'Basics, Parts 1 & 2.' For the shot in which Seven of Nine and Tuvok beam out, Jeri and Tim are also on bluescreen, and for the background I pieced together environmental elements from that 'Basics' shoot and craters I photographed in Hawaii's Mauna Loa volcano.

RIGHT AND BELOW: The wrecked ship was a CG model rigged to crumble. The terrain was done in layers in Photoshop. The live action was shot on a soundstage, with the unwanted part cut out. Another layer of foreground rocks done in Photoshop tied everything together. The challenge in shots like this is to make sure the lighting of all the elements matches.

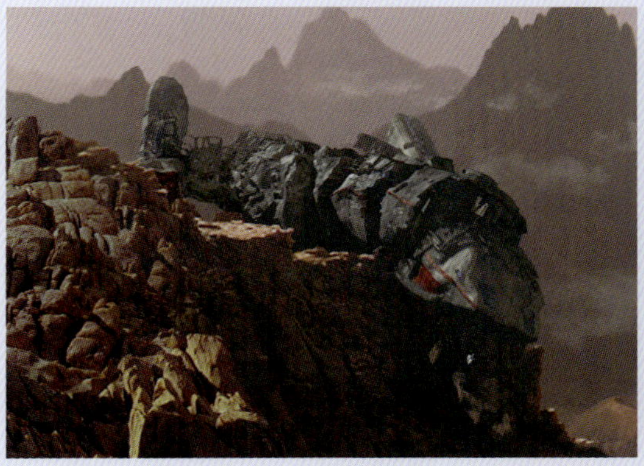

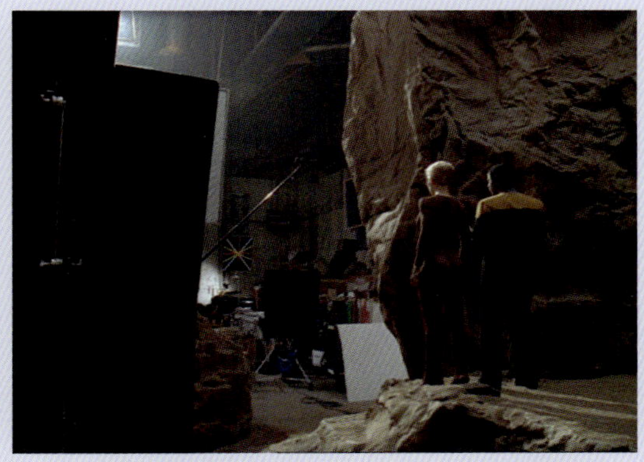

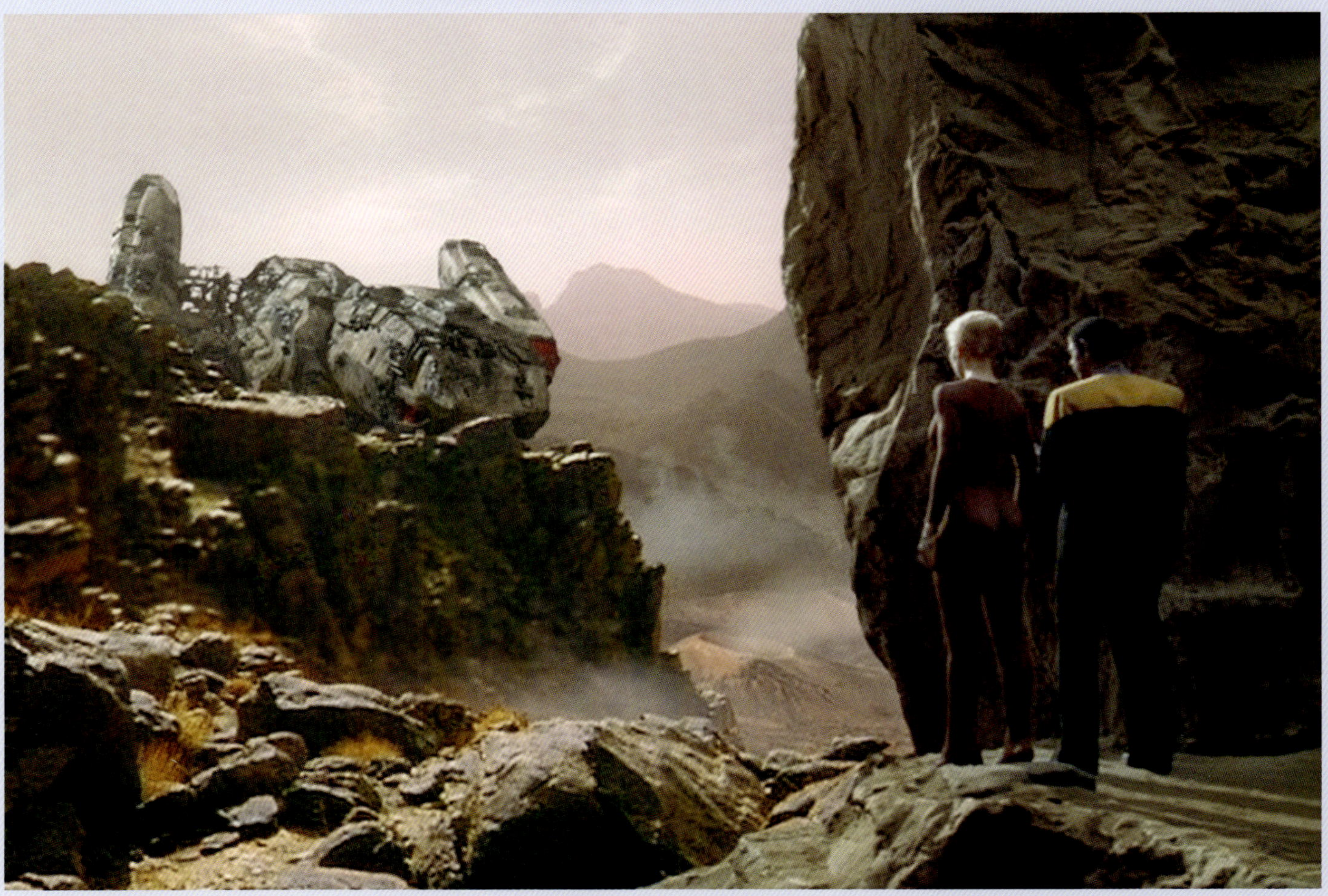

As we were working on *TNG*, video painting software became much more sophisticated. That started to change what we could do. We evolved with the technology, and the technology evolved because people like us were pushing the manufacturers to do more. When we were doing 'Q Who?' the episode required a shot showing Riker and the away team beaming in, but we didn't have the shot of the set without the actors in it (necessary for the characters to materialize in). So I took a frame of the shot of Riker and his away team on the paint box of the day, and painted out the actors and free-handed what the set would be behind them. We got away with that because the audience never really got a good look at the background, which was quickly covered up with transporter sparkles.

Around the same time, paint software got powerful enough to create a matte painting from scratch in the edit bay. The first time I did that was for the *TNG* episode 'Loud As A Whisper.' We had a partial set on stage designed by Herman Zimmerman. It was our job to tie that set into a wider landscape to give the scene scope. I dug out some photos I took on a road trip through the Badlands National Park in South Dakota as reference, rearranging specific natural structures to blend in with Richard James's set. We also added some liquid nitrogen, tinted to match the palette of the scene, as a heavier ground fog-like mist to put some life into the scene.

Paint boxes gave us a new and different kind of freedom; we could take a photograph and change it around using freehand painting to add things to it. It also meant I could do more myself. I couldn't have been working on an oil painting and supervising on set or in the edit bay simultaneously, but since I would spend considerable time in the edit bay working with the compositing editors anyway, I could effectively do two things at once. There was a paint system right where I sat, so I could be kibitzing with the compositing editor and working on a matte painting at the same time. It became really obvious that this was a valuable tool that was fast and therefore relatively inexpensive. That doesn't mean it was simple. I don't think people realize how complicated this stuff is.

When you're combining different elements you have to make them look as if they belong together. That involves a lot of color correction, and a lot of work to blend them together. One of the things that the great matte artist Al Whitlock taught is that we don't really see anything, all we see is the light bouncing off things, moving through air, or the airless vacuum of space, so paint the air and paint the light, and forget the object.

There's an early film version of the Japanese classic story *Chushingura: The 47 Loyal Ronin*. The filmmakers put layers of silk scrim in the interior sets to create the illusion of atmospheric perspective. That inspired me to do that digitally—I would make

BELOW: The only real part of this shot is the cave set and the immediate area around it. The rest is based on photos I took on a glacier in the Canadian Rockies.

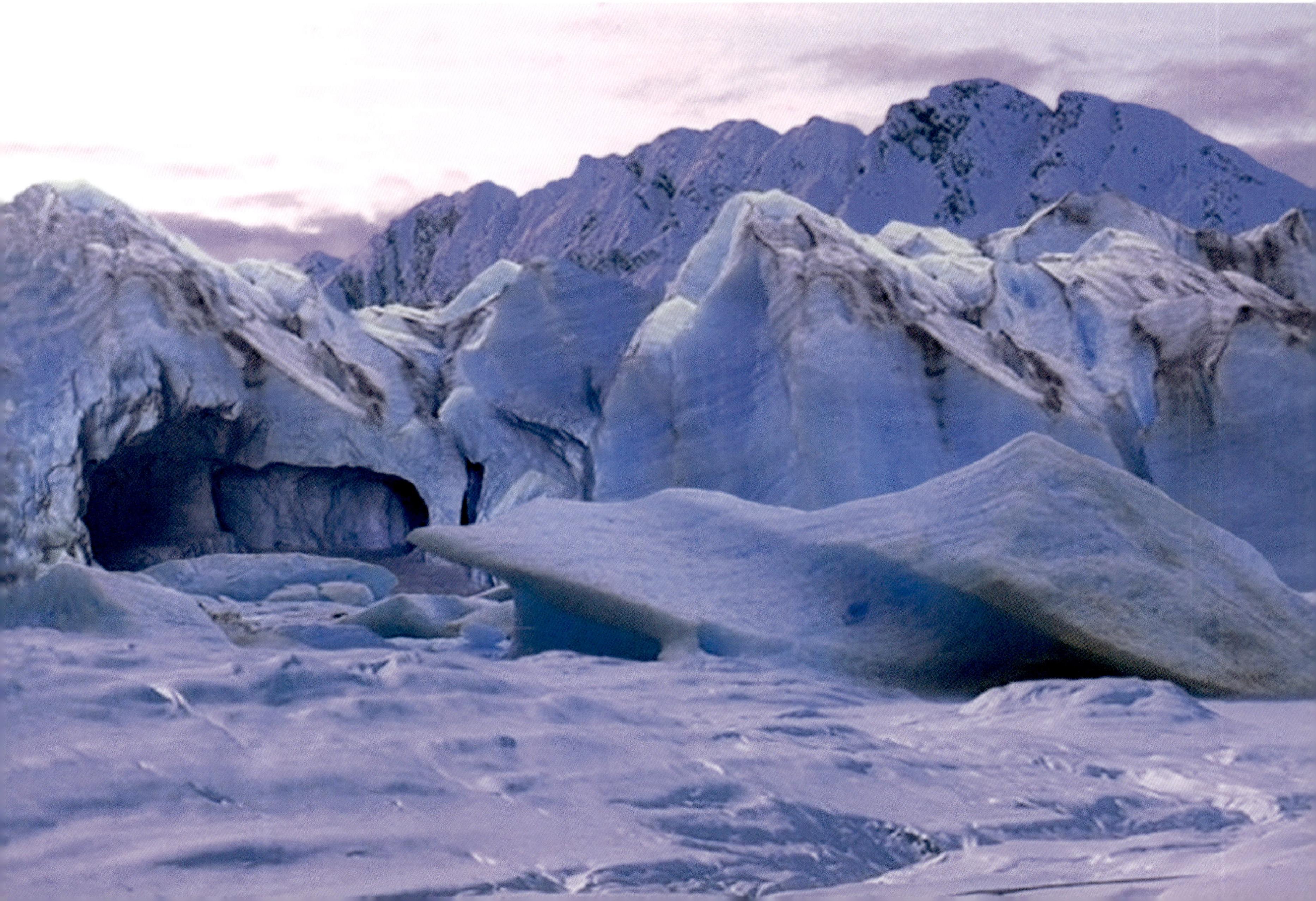

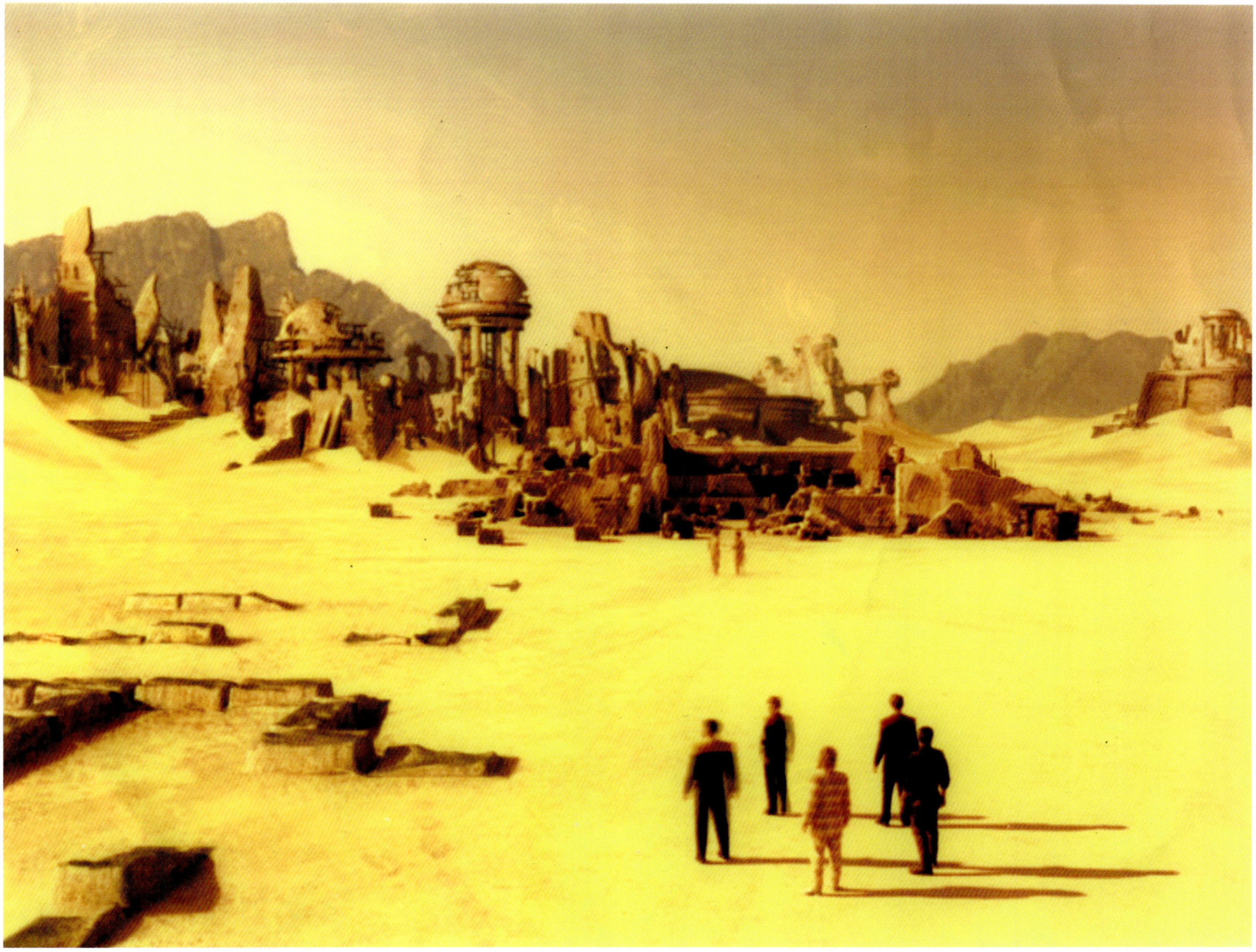

ABOVE: Concept rendering for the *Voyager* pilot. Our crew approaches a ruined city.

layers of 'scrim,' where I'd pick a color from the sky and put that in low opacity as a layer of air, feathered off into where it would hit the ground. Another example: In order to really marry distant mountains with the sky, I put a layer of low-opacity sky color in front of the mountains so that you can 'feel' the air. You can't see the air layer, but people instinctively know when something doesn't conform to their real-world experiences. If the edge of a matte is sharper than the object being depicted then it always looks phony. You have to make sure that the air feels real. The average audience member wouldn't say, "Oh well, those matte edges are too sharp," but they just intuitively sense it.

One of the best mattes I did in the paint box was for 'The Inner Light.' We went up to Bronson Canyon in LA's Griffith Park. I set the camera up on a hillside, and shot over Patrick Stewart's shoulder. In the distance we could see the Hollywood sign. On the edit bay's paint system I painted that out, and replaced it with a Mediterranean village, then I added a landscape with a river and elements like that.

When we started doing matte shots digitally, I'd use elements from photographs I'd taken when traveling around the world. I'd use anything that looked suitably otherworldly. My wife, son and I had taken a trip through the Canadian Rockies, where I photographed glaciers, mountains, and botanical gardens. In 'Rightful Heir' the Klingon monastery was inspired by structures I saw in the Himalayas, and the mountains in that shot were the Canadian Rockies. The ice caves on the Andorian planet are also from that trip.

It got to the point where I started to take photographs when I was traveling, specifically so I could use them in matte shots. The world became reference. I wouldn't know exactly what I was going to use them for, but I'd shoot things that looked interesting. I would always include a shot with somebody in it to enable us to match lighting actors on blue or green screen. Now, thanks to modern SLRs that can shoot 24p hi-def video, I shoot moving footage with natural movement.

One trip was particularly fruitful: photos I took on a family trip to Ireland played prominently in several episodes of *Star Trek*. When my family and I visited a restored fort, I knew it would be a great location for something, so I went around capturing the various angles needed to construct a scene. I also took a lot of photos of the unusual rock formations in the area of Ireland known as The Burrens, kind of white crusty pieces of rock sticking out through clumps of small photosynthetic organisms. When I read the *Voyager* script for 'Blink of

RIGHT: Rough concept digital sketch for the 'Workforce' city.

BELOW: Very rough concept sketch for the exterior of the 'Workforce' city.

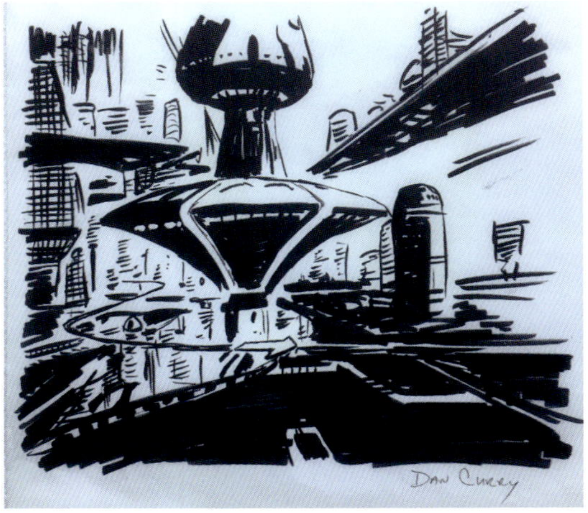

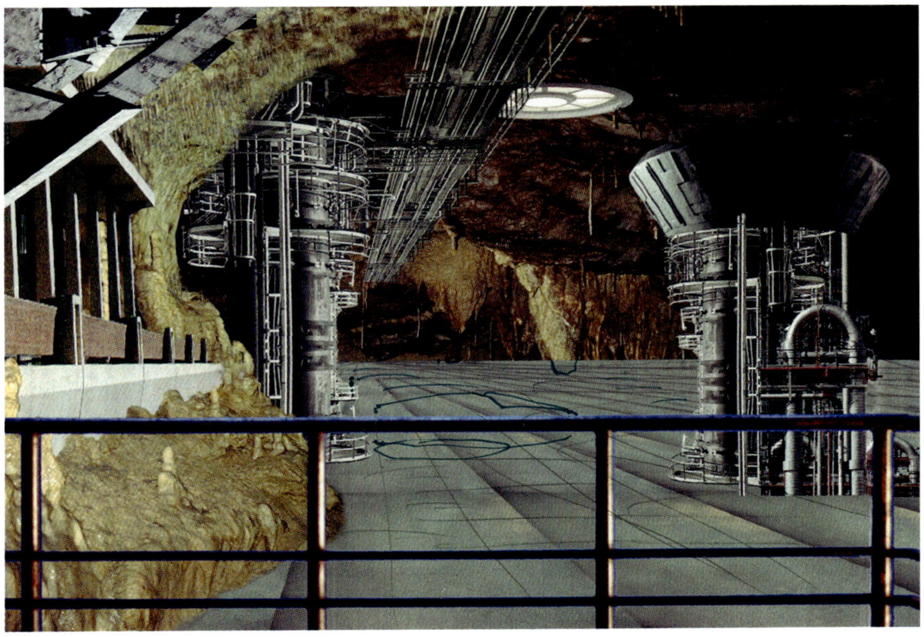

GRETHOR

BELOW: The amazing rock walls in Ireland were the inspiration for the walls of Stovokor.

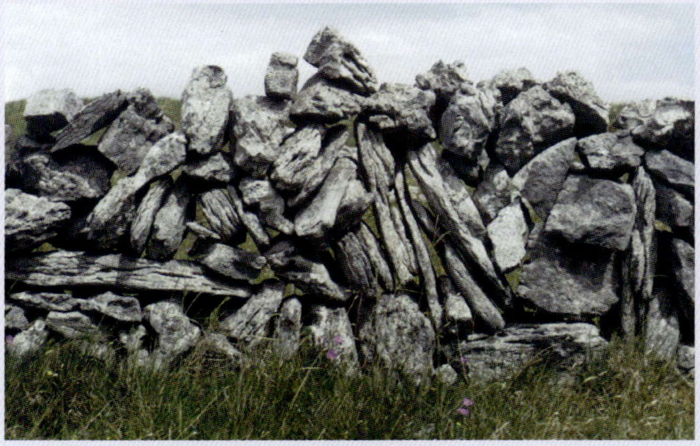

BELOW: The fiery underworld of Klingon Gre'thor was a combination of many elements: fire, liquid nitrogen as fire and smoke, and digital paintings.

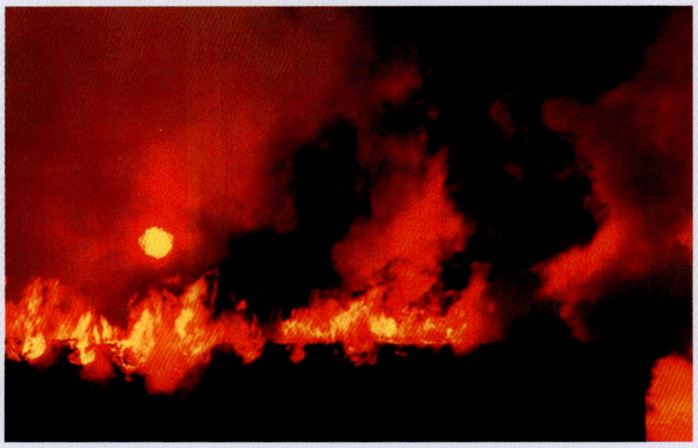

BELOW: The gates of Gre'thor, the Klingon hell, were based on a gate I discovered on the grounds of Ashford Castle in Ireland.

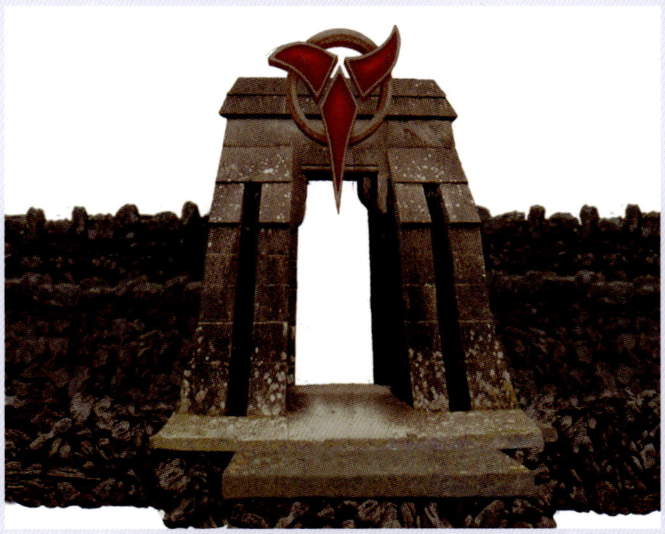

BELOW: The finished shot required a complex composite of many elements with accurate reflections.

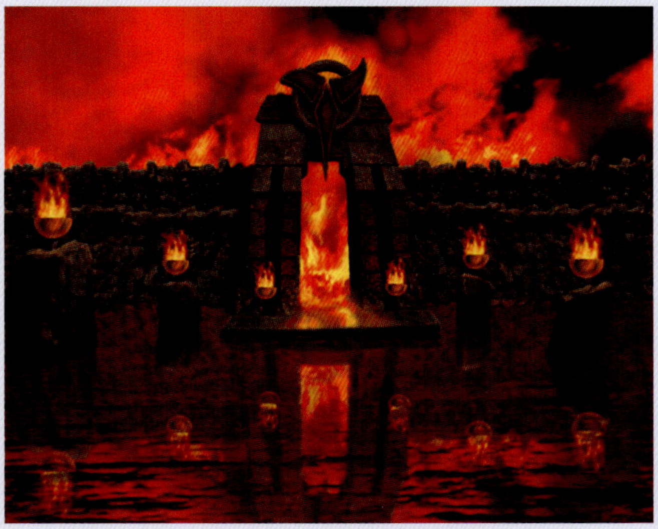

INSIDE STORY

THE JEM'HADAR BEACH

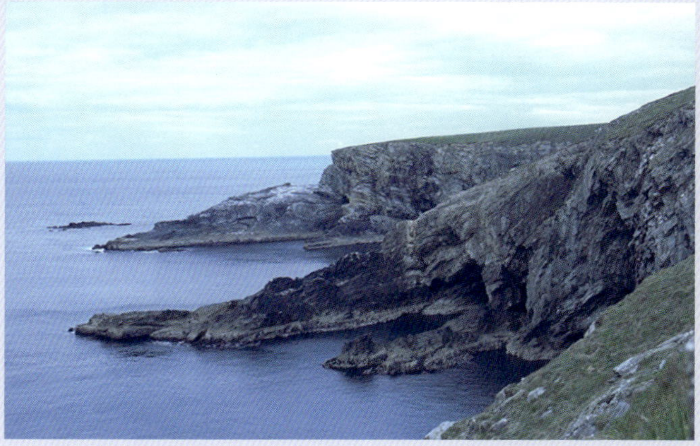

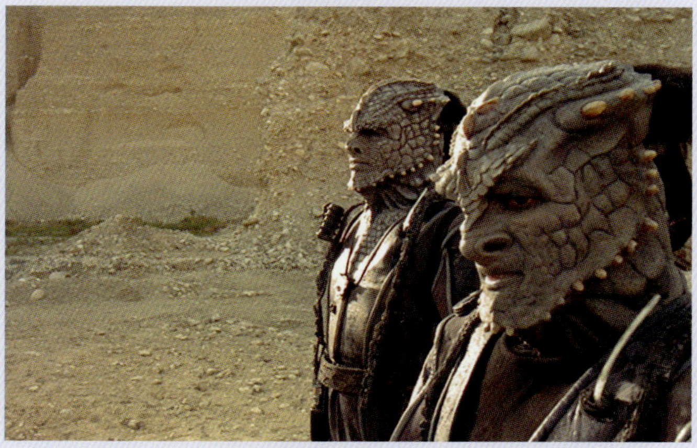

In the *DS9* episode 'Rocks and Shoals' Sisko and his crew crash-land their stolen Jem'Hadar fighter. They aren't the only people on the planet. Another Jem'Hadar ship and crew had crashed there weeks earlier. The episode was shot in Sun Valley. I did two matte paintings that involved combining live-action plates that were shot in a sand quarry with photographs I'd taken on vacation in Ireland, and footage of the ocean at Malibu Beach.

This shot, showing the Jem'Hadar looking out to sea, began with a take showing the actors on location in the sand quarry. I found a good place in the original image to cut away the rocks in front of the actors and replace them with a new background. For the distant vista, I used a photograph I'd taken of the Irish coast. The actual shape of the shoreline wasn't exactly what I had in mind, so we squeezed it east-west to make the terrain more ruggedly vertical, and color-corrected it to match the quarry. The water in the still photograph was static, so in compositing we added live-action footage of the ocean at Malibu in matching perspective. To help make the blend of images more seamless, I painted in more rocks on the cliff.

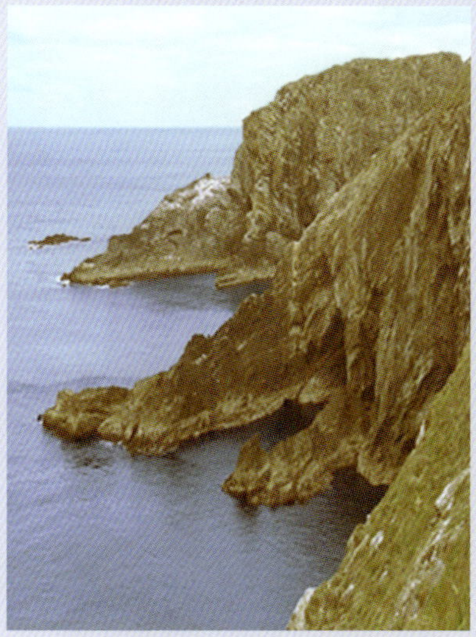

ABOVE: Elements for the shot: The west coast of Ireland; live-action plate in a sand quarry; and the Irish coast colorized and squeezed east-west.

BELOW: I painted the edge of the cliff where it would be in the live-action plate, and we comped in the coastal background.

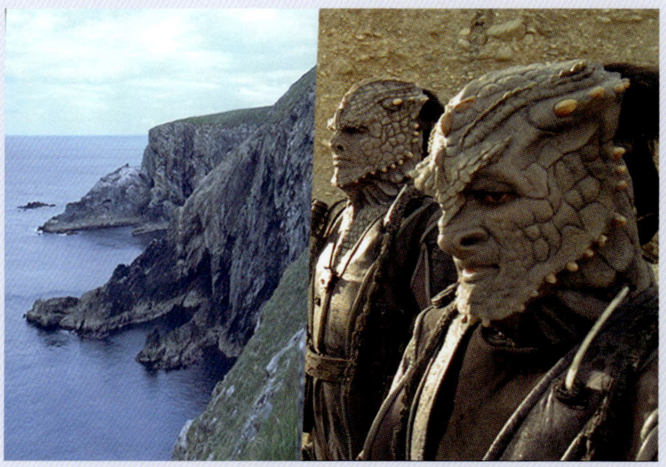

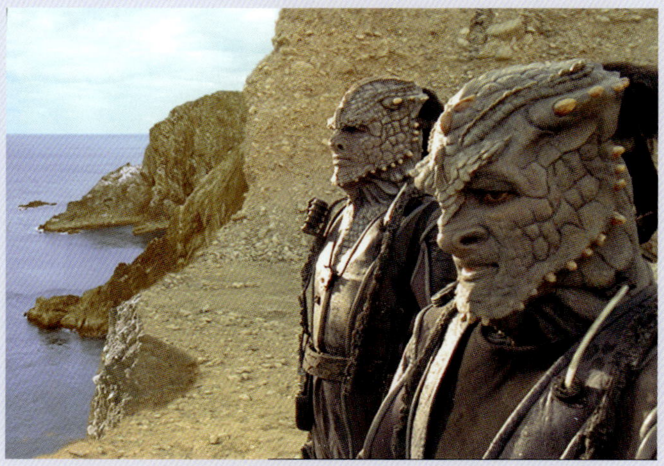

an Eye,' I remembered all the pictures I'd taken in Ireland. I showed the photos to Ron Moore, who was the VFX supervisor on that episode, then I went to Rick, Peter, and Richard James and said, "I've got this wealth of material so let's make the alien environment based on that." That way they get thousands of dollars worth of material for free. They liked the unusual look, so Richard and his team created a practical set that was an amazing match for The Burrens with a large blue screen behind it so we could matte in background hills and other elements.

With a lot of hand painting, incorporation of Irish hills, stone wall textures, actors on blue screen, torch fire, and color timing we were able to create a number of shots at various times of day in different time periods. All these shots were done in 2D on a paint box. That same trip provided a good chunk of the Klingon realm of the afterlife depicted in *Voyager*'s 'Barge of the Dead.' I used textures from Ireland's amazing stone walls to create the walls of Grethor, the Klingon hell, and the main gate was modified from a photograph of a gate on the grounds of Ashford Castle.

By the time we were several seasons into *Voyager*, matte shots were pretty much all done digitally. What had once been time-consuming effects could be accomplished easily and quickly. Work that had taken days and weeks could be done in hours. By that point, 3D/CG technology came in too, so you could add 3D buildings to a matte shot or even create complete 3D environments that the camera could move around and through to give a greater sense of verisimilitude.

CG matte shots and set extensions were more time-consuming and more expensive than 2D ones, but luckily we had some great artists who were really quick. One sequence that stands out to me was in the *Voyager* episode 'Workforce.' Dave Morton did cityscapes for us in 3D using Lightwave software, along with British matte painter Charles Darby. In the story, there was a brainwashed workforce on this planet. On the Paramount lot there's 'the tank' that they use for sequences involving open water. It's where they filmed the sequence in *Star Trek IV* with the Klingon ship crashing in San Francisco Bay and the whales trapped inside. It has a giant sky backdrop that can be painted for the needs of a given scene. Behind the sky is a climate-controlled studio vault building, and a very interesting industrial staircase. I had the idea that we would follow a train or a monorail on its way from a futuristic alien city to the station, where we would land on the exterior industrial staircase and see the brainwashed Captain Janeway and her companions in the crowd as if descending from the train on their way to work.

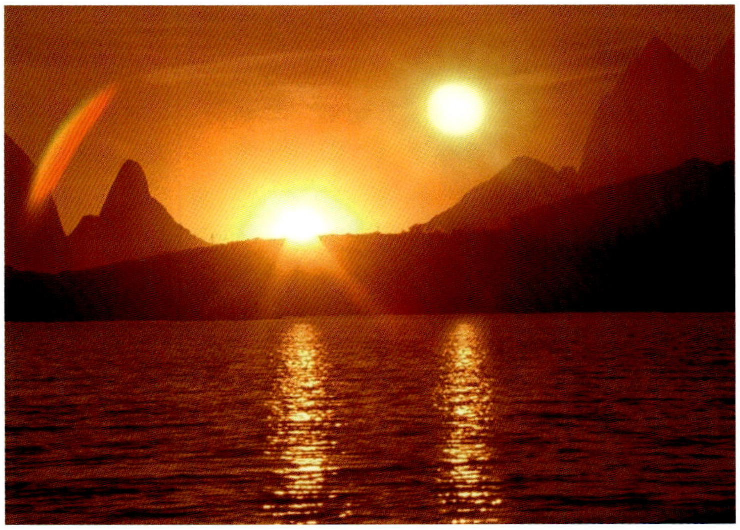

ABOVE: For this shot of Risa I combined 35mm film of Malibu with mountains from Maui and a second sun that I painted in digitally.

INSIDE STORY

ALIEN VACATION

In the *Voyager* episode 'Blink of an Eye' we see a culture evolve over thousands of years. We decided that the best way to depict this was to show the same location changing over time. The culture starts out in the Iron Age and eventually evolves into a technologically advanced civilization. I showed VFX supervisor Ron Moore, our producers and production designer Richard James some photographs I'd taken on vacation in Ireland that I thought could work. Richard designed and built practical sets, perfectly matching the Irish terrain with blue screens behind them. This allowed us to composite actors and sets with my digital matte paintings and photographs to complete the landscapes.

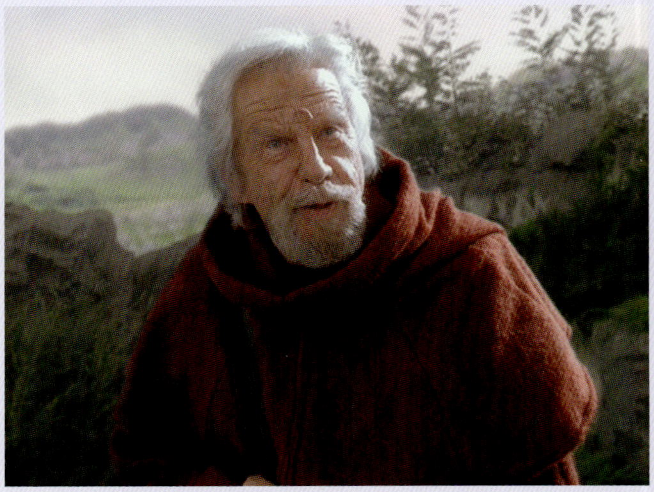

ABOVE: Olaf Pooley as the Cleric, shot on blue screen and comped into a digital matte shot.

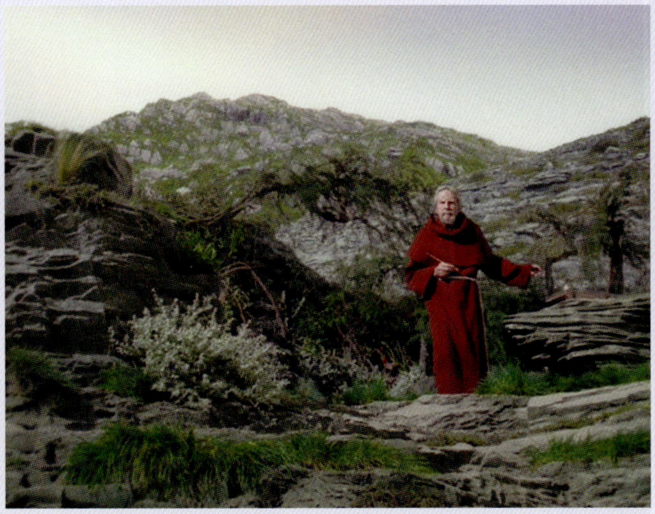

ABOVE: The Cleric on a partial set, built to match the Irish terrain with a matte painting set extension.

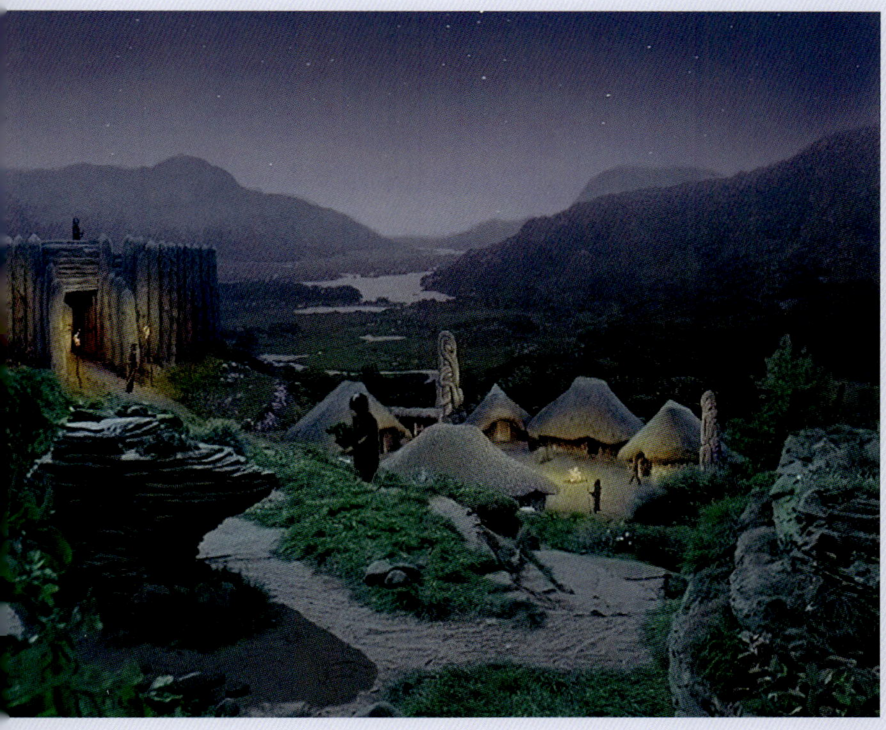

ABOVE: Partial set with digital matte painting of Bronze Age village.

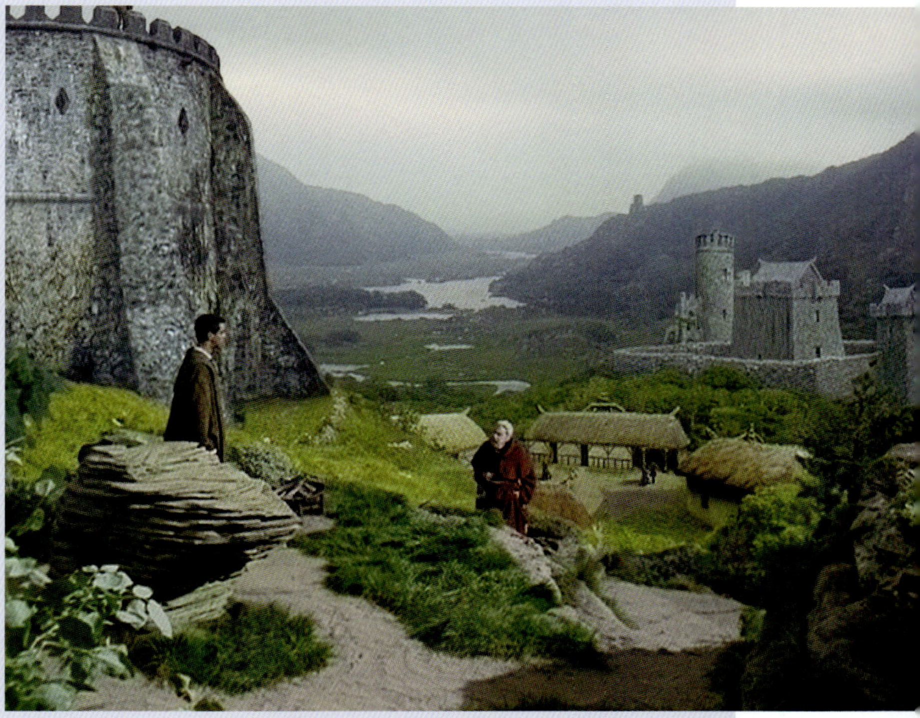

ABOVE: Same foreground partial set, now with medieval structures in the same distant terrain.

BELOW: Same partial set, with Industrial Age structures based on the Mt. Wilson Observatory.

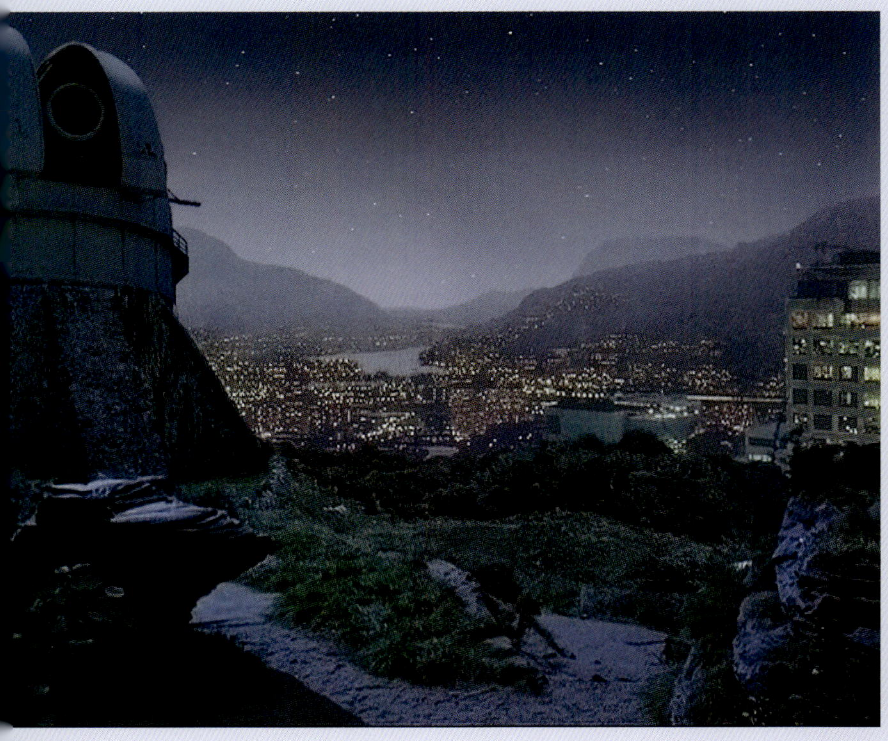

BELOW: Now a futurist time period in the same place. It was great fun working with Ron Moore, and figuring out the evolution of this world.

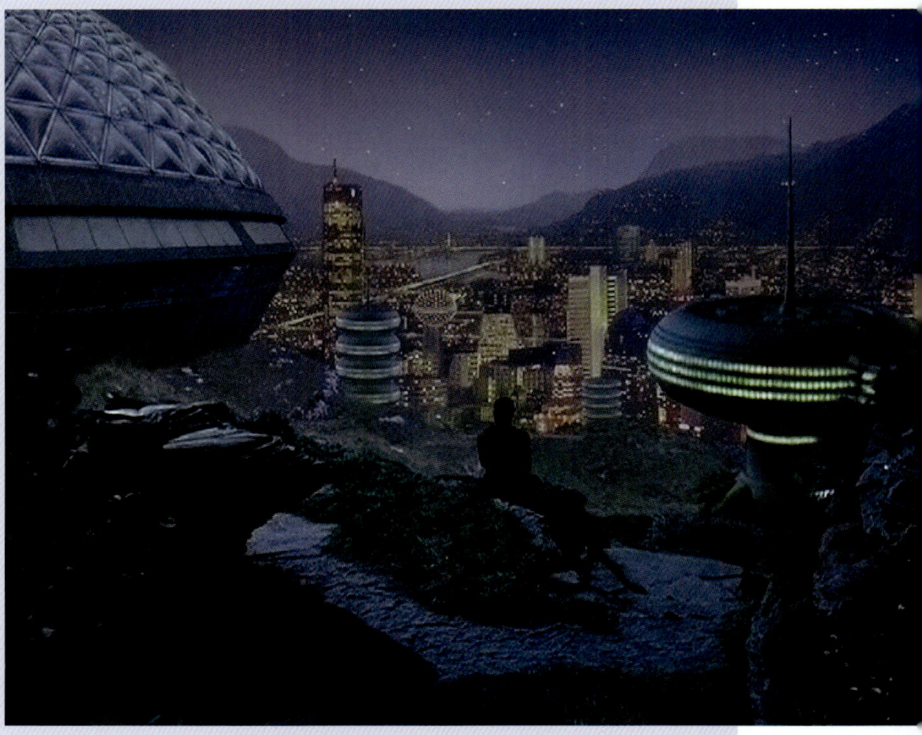

MATTE PAINTING – A HISTORY

Matte painting began in the early days of photography. Victorian photographers posed costumed models in a historic site of Greek or Roman ruins to recreate the ancient world. A skilled artist would do a painting on glass between the camera and the subject to cover parts of the ruins and make the structures look new. In the final photo the models appeared to be in antiquity. That mixture of live action and painting, known as glass shots, initiated the evolution of matte shots in cinema.

Years ago, I did my only glass shot for a McDonald's commercial, depicting an around-the-world scooter race. Shooting from the Greystone Mansion, I transformed Los Angeles into Paris by painting the Eiffel Tower and surroundings on glass, and shooting the characters through it. The problem with glass shots is that natural light constantly changes as the sun moves through the sky. There are only a few minutes when the angle of the light on location matches that in the painting. If the cast and crew are not ready when the light matches, you lose your opportunity and have to revise the painting on the spot.

Gone with the Wind has a famous glass shot. Tara is actually a building in Culver City—the tree-lined road leading up to the O'Hara mansion was painted on glass. Sometimes artists painted on layers of glass. When the camera pushed in ('multi-planing'), an illusion of changing perspective, or parallax, results.

In the pre-digital era, the best image quality was achieved through a technique known as latent image original negative in-camera compositing. This allowed both the painting and the live action to be the same generation on the original negative. The laborious process began on location when you weighed the camera down to immobilize it. Then a black, lightproof tent was erected around the camera, with a wooden frame in front of the lens. Looking through the lens, black matte board was cut precisely to block off the part of the frame where the painted set extension would go, preventing that part of the negative from being exposed. After shooting test footage and a final hero take being approved, the camera loader would put a physical notch on the edge of the film so the hero take could be located by touch in the dark. A couple of feet of test footage would be processed while storing the undeveloped negative in a refrigerator.

In the studio, a camera with a matching lens would be mounted on a stable support, or rostrum. A frame of the test footage would be threaded up, and a prism placed behind the film gate, enabling a lamp house attached to the side to convert the camera into a projector. The image would then be projected onto the surface to be painted (glass or Masonite), and the line separating the live action from the painting, the matte line, would be traced. The area where the live action appears would be painted black to prevent that part of the frame from being exposed when the painting was photographed. Each day, a new piece of undeveloped test footage negative would be put in the camera and the painting photographed to check its progress and the success of the blend between the painted image and the live action. Weeks later, when everything was completed to satisfaction, the unprocessed negative containing the 'latent,' already exposed live action would be threaded up into the camera, hoping the production camera loader's notch was on the correct sprocket, and final shooting would begin. What made this process scary was that there was only one chance to get it right because once you'd exposed both parts of the film it couldn't be done again.

When optical printers came along, the painting and the live action were photographed separately, and put together optically on a new negative. This necessitated using two

BELOW Creating moving clouds from a still image

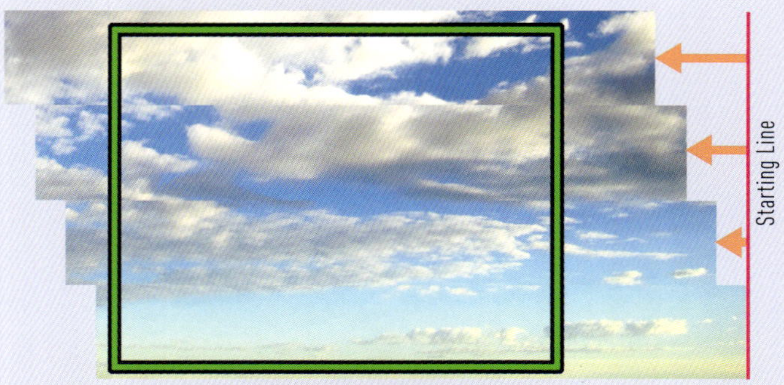

Pre-digital Compositing: Use a wider-than-needed size for the final aspect ratio, and divide into horizontal layers. Shooting with a static camera, photograph the layers one at a time through a foreground matte box. Back-wind the film to frame 1 for each pass so all layers appear on the original negative exposed one layer at a time. Each successive layer will move a little faster than the layer below. The clouds at the top of the frame would be nearer and thus move faster, as they would in natural perspective.

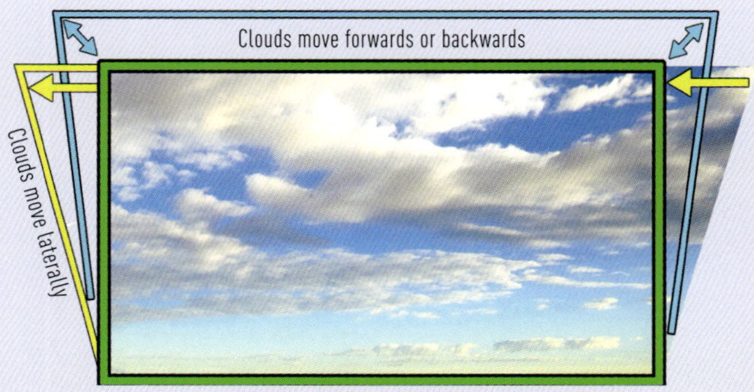

Digital Compositing: The same effect can be achieved with considerably less effort by 'corner pinning' in digital compositing by skewing the image by dragging a top corner out in one direction and shifting it in the opposite direction over the duration of the shot (see yellow arrows above). It is also possible to create the illusion that the clouds are moving forward or away by dragging the upper corners in and out, or in and down (see blue arrows above).

different generations of film images going through the complicated process of making interpositives and high-contrast black and white film for mattes to prevent different areas of the new negative from being exposed. The problem was the duping process created a second film generation—like a photocopy—so the image quality suffered.

PRE-DIGITAL COMPOSITING METHOD SHOOTING ON FILM

Use a painting wider then needed for the final aspect ratio so there is room to accomodate movement.

The rectangle shows what the camera sees (in perspective). The black area indicates where light is being blocked, and the bright rectangle shows the area where the painting is being exposed.

The final image is shot in four passes, backwinding the film to frame 1 for each pass photographed through a foreground matte box that allows layers to be shot seperately on the same negative.

Nearer clouds appear to move faster than the distant clouds.

The horizon level pass does not move. Each successively higher (nearer) layer moves faster than the one below, resulting in an illusion of clouds moving in natural perspective.

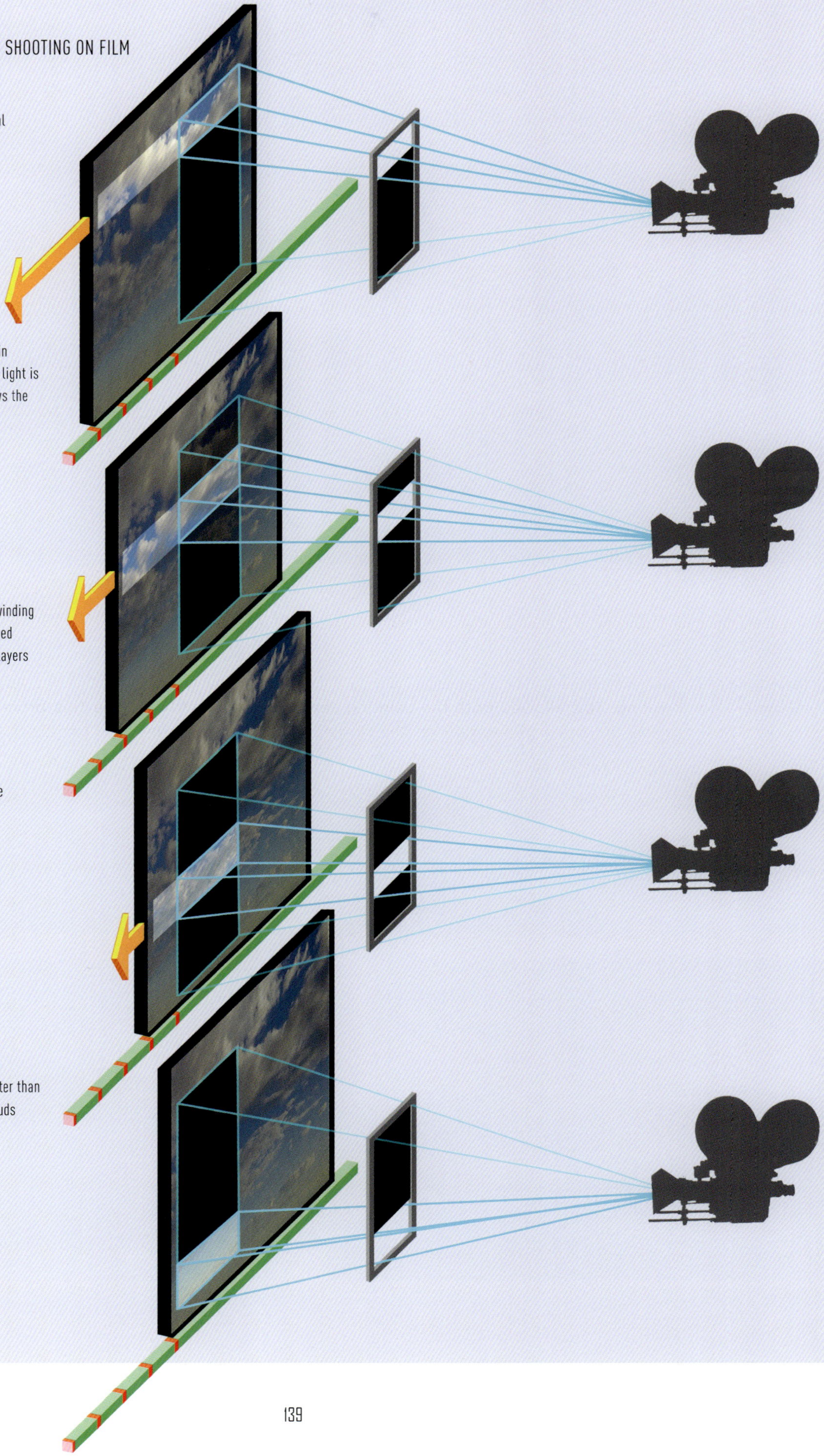

INSIDE STORY

PHYSICAL MINIATURES

Whenever I used to go into the art department, I would notice that they had a number of models of buildings. I'm not even sure exactly why they had built them; one of them was a study model for an earlier version of Deep Space 9. Those kinds of physical models can help to make a matte painting more convincing, so I set up a blue screen outside on the Paramount lot, and shot from a variety of different angles. Then, when we were doing matte paintings, we could add them in to create futuristic cities.

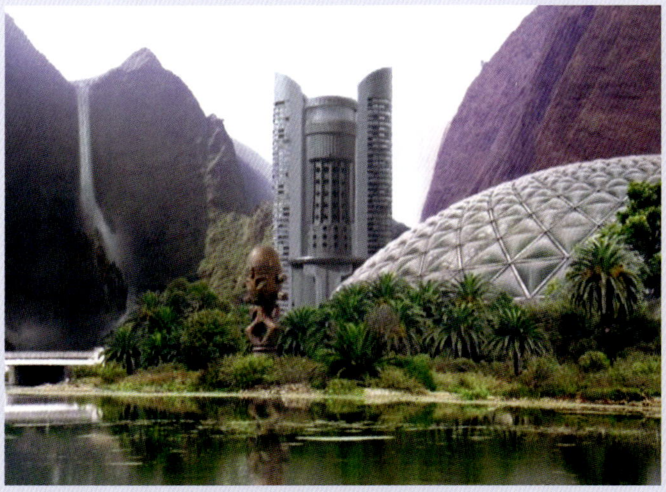

ABOVE: The matte shot of Risa combined models such as the tower and the Horga'hn with other elements I photographed and some freehand painting.

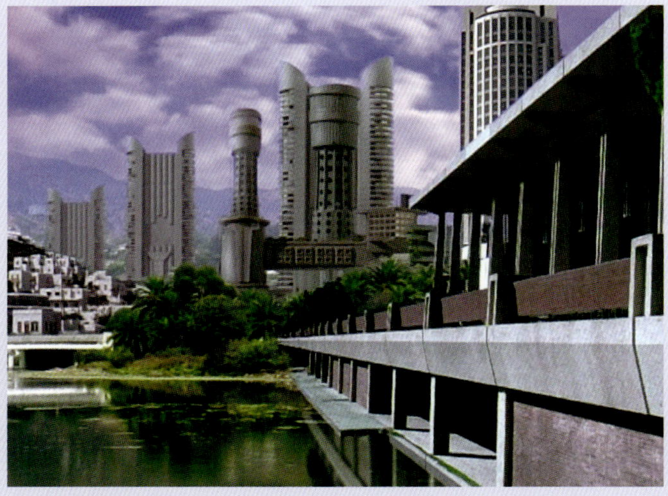

ABOVE: We reused the model of the tower in this matte painting I did for the *Voyager* episode 'Random Thoughts,' which also features the library from Cal State Northridge.

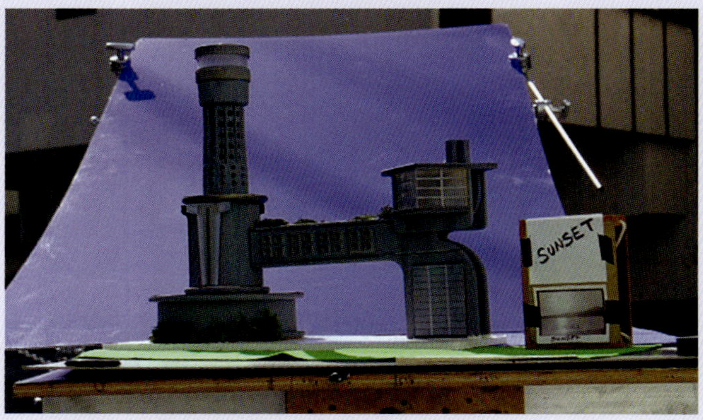

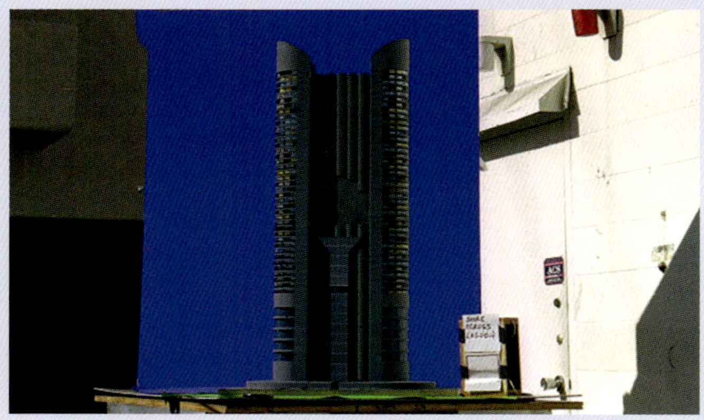

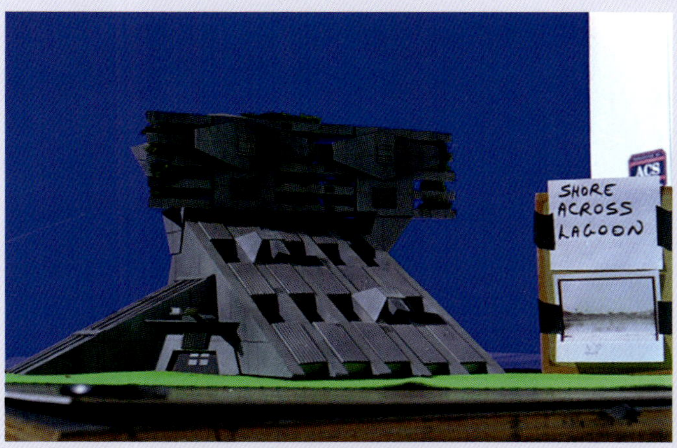

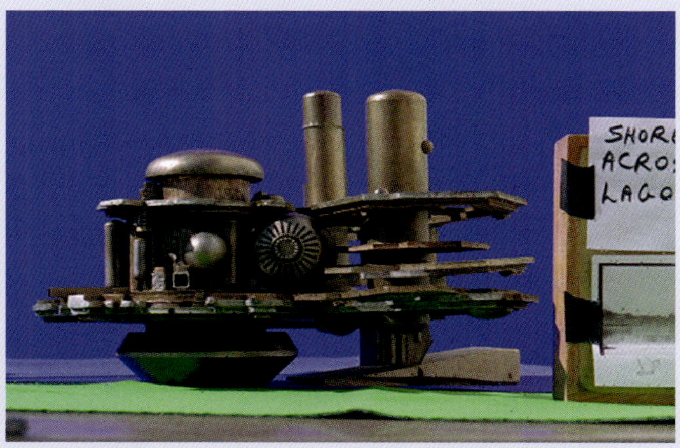

ABOVE: The art department had various models that I photographed on the backlot and comped into different matte paintings. I'm not sure why each one was built, but I do know the bottom-right one was a rejected design for Deep Space 9.

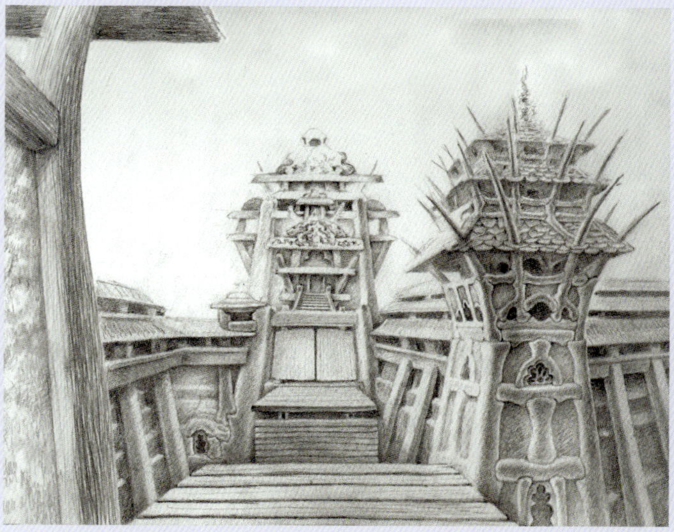

ABOVE: Concept for early Klingon architecture with collapsible bridge.

INSIDE STORY

UNUSED CONCEPTS

When designing architecture for pre-industrial alien cultures, and especially old Klingon structures, I was influenced by my travels in the Himalayas and Southeast Asia and the buildings I saw there. Before presenting concepts to the producers I would sometimes explore various ideas with quick sketches so they would have some choices to react to. Sometimes this would lead to an entirely new concept. Here are examples of concepts that were part of the evolutionary process leading to the final versions that appeared on screen.

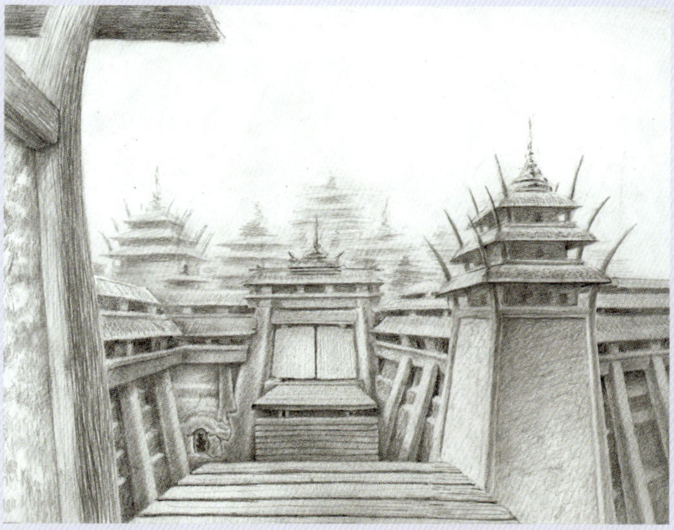

ABOVE: Using a paper overlay to save time, I simplified key architectural elements while preserving the central structures.

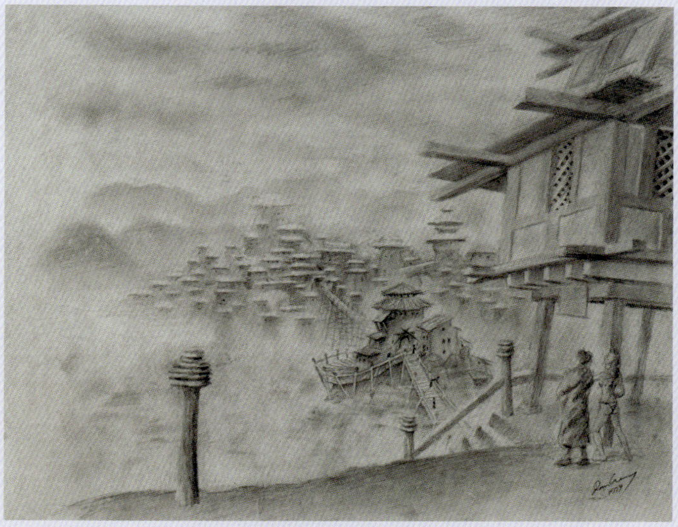

ABOVE: Pencil sketch for a primitive settlement shrouded in mist.

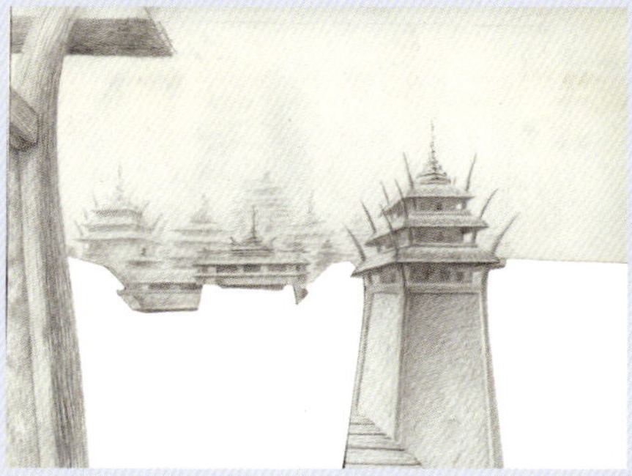

ABOVE: Paper overlay cut to fit precisely over the original sketch to save an element of the original drawing that I wanted to keep.

RIGHT: This rough pastel of a concept for a Klingon outpost was inspired by Mongolian architecture with a hint of Tibetan.

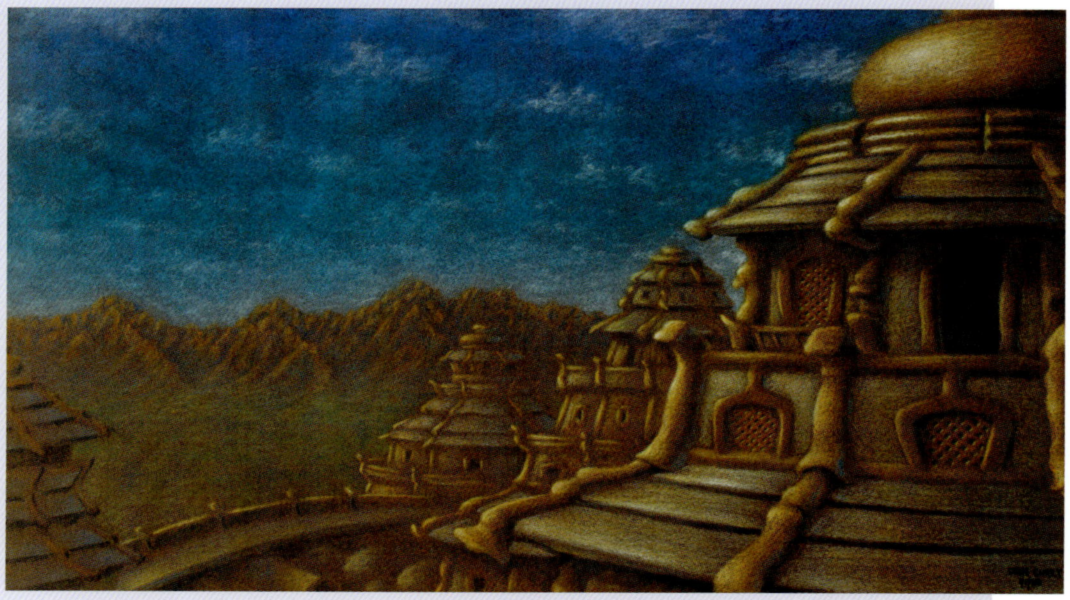

INSIDE STORY

ICONIAN RUINS

In the *TNG* second-season episode 'Contagion,' Captain Picard explores the ruins of the legendary Iconian civilization on a now lifeless planet. The visual effects on this episode were supervised by Rob Legato, but he asked me to do the matte shot depicting the ruins. Years later, I got the chance to revisit it when I supervised VFX for the Blu-ray release of Season 2.

For the original version, Herman's Zimmerman's art department provided a miniature of the main tower with windows matching those on the full-sized interior set where we filmed Sir Patrick. The model tower was built using a swimming-pool filter mounted on a cardboard tube, embellished with model and toy parts. I based the terrain on the desolate landscape of Death Valley; working with the crew at Image G we set up a tabletop, partially burying the art department's model tower in powdered walnut shells (which served as scale miniature sand) in the extreme foreground, and photographed it against a blue screen so we could pull a matte and isolate it for compositing. Using photographic reference from several desert locations, I did an acrylic painting of the terrain, adding distant ruins rising out of the sand. The sky was a separate painting, so it could be independently controlled and moved in compositing. In the edit bay, we added liquid nitrogen vapors to simulate blowing dust and sand.

When we did the hi-def Blu-ray version, I was excited to have the chance to improve shots I wasn't satisfied with the first time around. With visual effects, especially for television, there is only so much time until a shot has to be delivered. Even if you would like to push a shot further or rethink some aspect, you're done. There is an air date that must be met. For the up-res we assembled a team of artists at Illuminate Hollywood to re-transfer the original film negatives to hi-def and recreate the visual effects. Exterior space shots looked great in hi-def as the ship models were shot on film, which has even better resolution than Blu-ray.

Certain shots that had been intended to exist only in standard definition did not up-res as well as others. The Iconian ruins matte shot was one of them, and I wanted to make improvements on the original anyway. The intent of the project was to preserve the flavor of the original visual effects, but with state-of-the art high-definition imagery. I worked closely with *Star Trek* veteran artist Doug Drexler on the digital modeling of the tower, and with compositor and 3D artist Sean 'Coco' Jackson to bring this complex multi-layered matte shot to a Blu-ray incarnation.

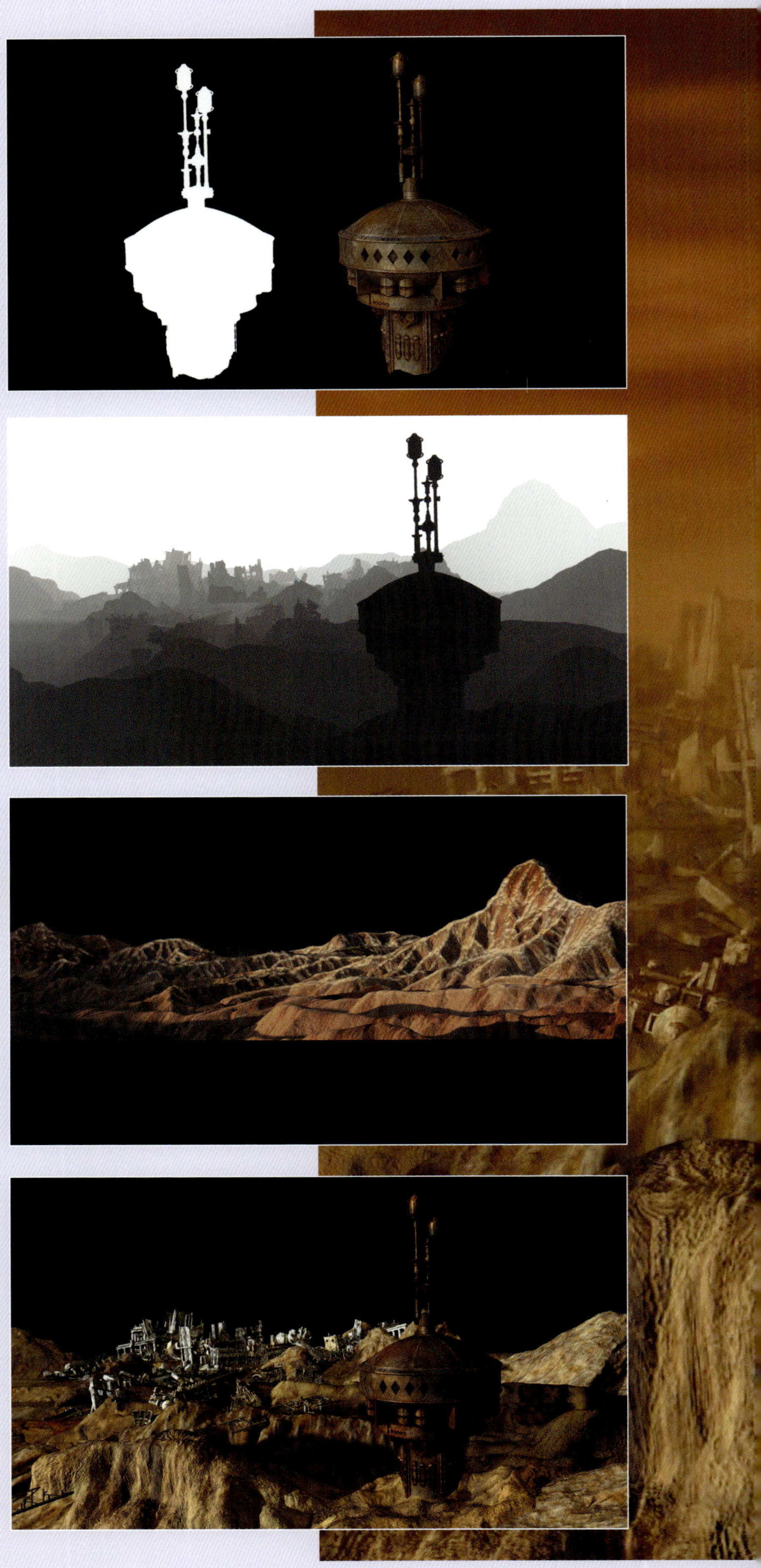

RIGHT: This shot of the ruined Iconian outpost was originally comprised of a foreground miniature made by the art department to which we added paintings, and some footage of liquid nitrogen. This is the revised version using CG elements for the HD release.

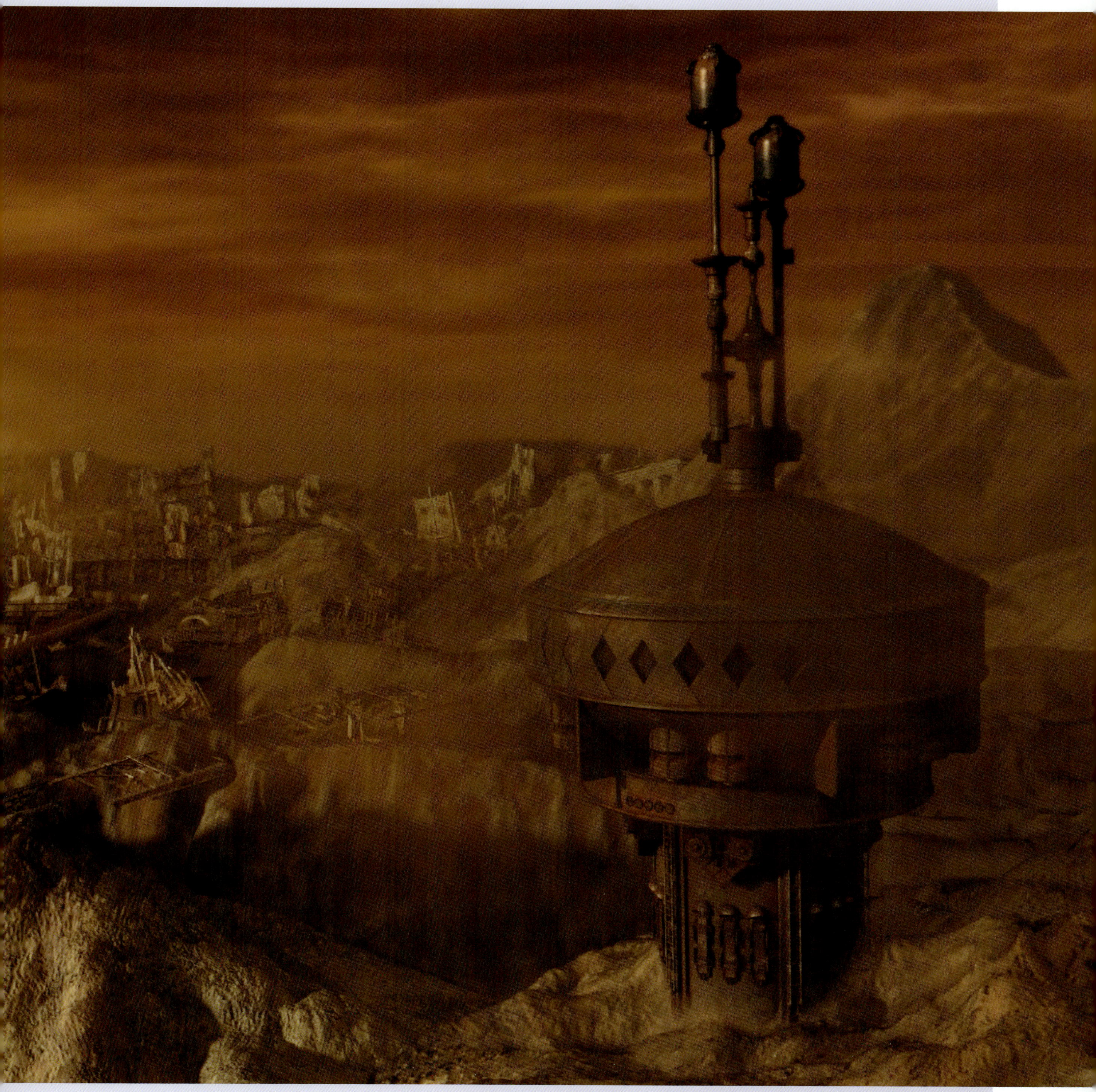

VISUAL-EFFECTS PRODUCER

A NEW ROLE—RUNNING TWO SHOWS SIMULTANEOUSLY

For my first five years on *Star Trek* I shared responsibility for supervising visual effects with Rob Legato; he worked with Gary Hutzel, and I worked with Ron Moore. We would alternate episodes, so one would cover the stage while the other could be shooting motion control, or focus on compositing. In *TNG*'s sixth season work started on *Deep Space Nine*, and Rob and Gary went over to run the effects on the new show while Ron and I stayed with *TNG*. The expanded organization changed the structure of how things were done.

Instead of directly supervising VFX on alternating episodes, Rob and I each took complete responsibility for one series. Supervising producer Peter Lauritson encouraged me to take the visual-effects producer title because I would get better parking, but I wasn't a VFX producer in the traditional sense of the word—I functioned as a senior supervisor, as did Rob. Ron and Gary had proved their worth, and were promoted to supervisor. We brought in two more excellent supervisors—David Stipes to work with me on *TNG*, and Glenn Neufeld to work with Rob on *DS9*—so we still maintained the two alternating teams system. After the first season of *DS9*, however, Rob decided to leave, and I took over responsibility for *DS9* too. I was now overseeing visual effects for two series. Once *TNG* wrapped up, we started *Voyager* so I looked after two series for the next five years until *Deep Space Nine* ended—then it was time to begin *Enterprise*.

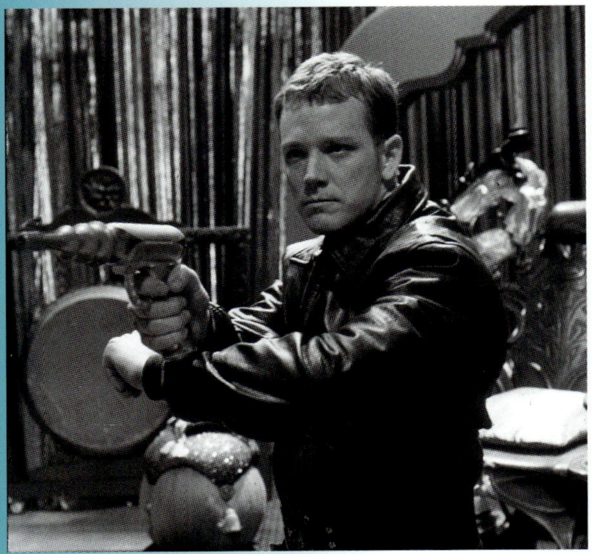

"Dan and I have known each other for 25 years now. He's a lovely man, and a very big part of my career. He is a renaissance man, a philosopher, a musician and a humanitarian. He's a world traveler, and he really has a lot of wonderful stories about his experiences.

"I first met him on* Voyager*; he'd be there to supervise VFX shots and things like that for us. I always found him a magnetic and charming personality. It's slow doing visual effects—the lighting is more precise, and the time between when you're rolling slows down, but Dan always made it fun. I remember in 'Day of Honor' B'Elanna and Tom are floating in space, running out of oxygen, and they finally confess their feelings for each other because they think that they're dying. We were floating in the air in front of a green screen. Those space suits were hot; you'd get warm and sticky, and it would fog up the glass in the helmet, so you couldn't see anything. Dan filled the time with

stories. He talked about being in the Peace Corps in Thailand and Southeast Asia, learning a lot of martial arts, including a lot of very secret and almost ninja-like moves that could kill or incapacitate your opponent with just the pressure of a thumb. Those kind of stories were fun to hear. And he had stories about working with people like Michael Jackson on videos and commercials.

"When we did CG creatures it was always fun to see Dan Curry running across the set with a silver ball on the end of a stick. He would get really animated when he was portraying something we had to look at and react to as if it was some kind of horrifying monster—those were always silly moments.

"I got to know Dan much better when I started directing. I would always talk to him when I was shadowing and observing, he was very helpful. He approached VFX as a real character, and as part of the storytelling rather than as a technical hurdle to overcome. I would listen to him describe ways of doing VFX that could enhance and seamlessly integrate into the emotional beats that the scene was dealing with. He'd talk about it from a story place and from a character place, and how the images could advance that point of view in a good way.

"When I directed my first episode of *Voyager*, which was 'Sacred Ground,' I was very nervous, and he was very patient and helpful during that process of figuring out the shots that I would need to tell the story in the most efficient and creative way.

"Whenever I was directing he was very helpful. The budgets on *Star Trek* were healthy, but not unlimited, so you had to fit the visual-effects components within a budget. That was a big part of your conversation with Dan—how to deal with the technical side of things and be able to tell the story with only two visual-effects shots rather than a dozen. Those two visual-effects shots had to really pack a punch and tell a lot of story, and Dan was very good at maximizing those opportunities.

"He would break things down in a way that was just simple. Because of his art skills, he could draw out an image as you were talking about it. I've always valued that. He would draw and sketch a shot, or a plan, or an idea, so as we were talking about it, we also had something to look at. He's got great skill at that.

"After *Star Trek*, when I started to build a directing career and started producing TV shows, I was able to hire Dan. We've done three or four shows together since *Star Trek*. Dan came on to the series *Chuck*, where he was able to help us travel the world with our nerd spy hero, and we were able to do that from the parking lot of Warner Bros studios. He was a really big part of the way that show was done. Just this last season I was on a show called *The Gifted*, a Marvel X-Men show that Dan was on. I was so happy to be working with him again. "

Robert Duncan McNeill

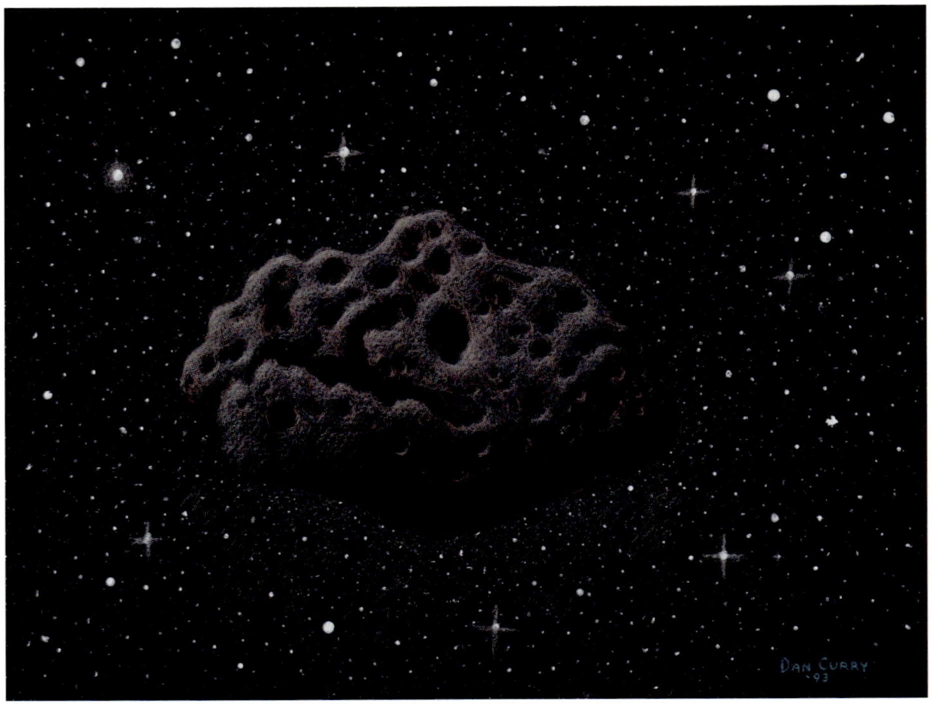

ABOVE: Color pencil concept sketch of asteroid with crevasse.

Unlike many producers, I still did a lot of hands-on work, including matte paintings, storyboards, conceptual design, and working with Ron and David, on-set VFX supervision, and collaboration in the edit bay. All our supervisors were incredibly capable. My involvement was based on the demands of specific episodes, and where my support was needed most.

Whenever we set up a new series we wanted to make things look fresh and different. For example, on *Voyager* we redesigned the transporter effect, and I had a lot of fun figuring out how the holographic Doctor, played by Robert Picardo, would appear and disappear. I especially wanted the effect to include a volumetric shimmer in the air to start or conclude his materialization.

At the beginning, I admit I felt as if I was a bit of a fill-in on *Deep Space Nine*. Rob, Gary, and Glenn had set the look and procedures of a lot of the effects. I started to feel more at home after we had the premiere screening of the *Voyager* pilot in the main theater at Paramount. As we were leaving, Armin Shimerman said to me, "That was great. Now that's over, let's get you back where you belong on *Deep Space Nine*." Armin probably doesn't even remember saying that, but it made a significant change in my attitude, and I started to feel that I was a real part of the *DS9* family. I belonged.

I got on well with showrunner and executive producer Ira Steven Behr, the cast was wonderful, and as I got into the mythos of *DS9* I really started to enjoy myself. The effects weren't technologically that different from what we were doing on the other *Star Trek* series, but they were thematically different. There were so many possibilities for new ways of thinking about things, because the stories were darker and different from the *Voyager* and *TNG* ones. I really enjoyed creating the Bajoran Fire Caves; scenes that took place on the surface of planet Bajor gave us the opportunity to do some epic matte shots. *Voyager* was different again, as Captain Janeway and her crew were lost in a distant quadrant of the Galaxy, and everything they encountered was new.

Over the years, some supervisors left, or moved between the shows. Glenn left after the fourth season of *DS9*, so David Stipes moved over to work on that series, and we brought in Mitch Suskin as a new VFX supervisor on *Voyager*.

As technology progressed, we started to work with different vendors—the workload was so great that it couldn't be completed on schedule by just one or two companies. We also started to use more and more CG, which brought in companies like Digital Muse and Foundation Imaging. We still used CIS for pin registered transfers from film to video, and some 2D compositing with people like Don Lee, Steve Bowen, and Price Pethel. We also forged relationships with other vendor companies for 2D compositing and FX animation. Our relationship with The Post Group changed, and we began to rely on Digital Magic and Pacific Ocean Post, both in Santa Monica. They had great compositing editors like Paul Hill, Steve Fong, and Don Greenberg among others, with a solid support system behind them. For VFX animation including phasers, photon torpedoes, tractor beams, and episode-specific special animation, we began working with artists Helen Davis and Joni Jacobson, and later brought in Steve Scott, Adam Howard, and Greg Rainoff.

The vendors all understood that there was something about *Star Trek* that was more than just turning out a TV show—we were contributing to something that would be seen over and over again for years to come. They were intuitively understanding, and always did the best work possible. There were many talented people who worked there whose names never appeared in the credits, but I always encouraged them to feel as if they were part of the show, which wouldn't have been possible without them.

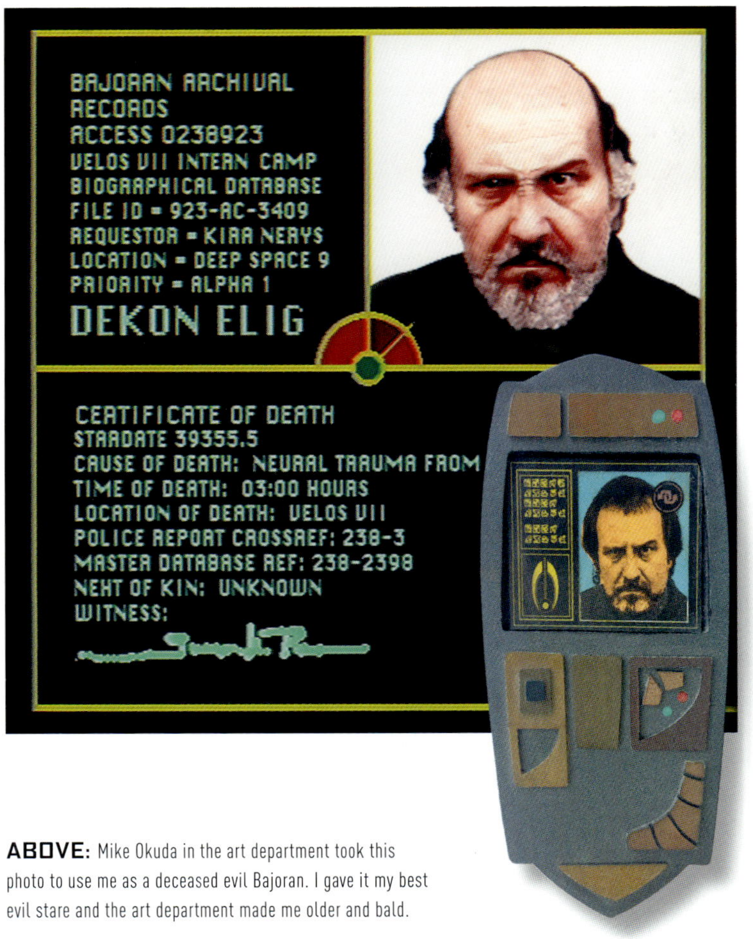

ABOVE: Mike Okuda in the art department took this photo to use me as a deceased evil Bajoran. I gave it my best evil stare and the art department made me older and bald.

INSIDE STORY

DATA'S PAINTING

There were several episodes of *TNG* where we saw Data painting. Obviously the paintings had to come from somewhere, and fortunately, since several members of the crew were serious artists, they would contribute their own paintings. In the episode 'Hero Worship' Data is trying to help a grief-stricken child, and art therapy comes into it.

The painting that Data pretends to paint is one of mine— the original shows the view from our friend's back yard in Hollister, California. For the episode we made a giclée print on canvas, and painted out the railroad tracks. Then Brent simply pretended to paint over it.

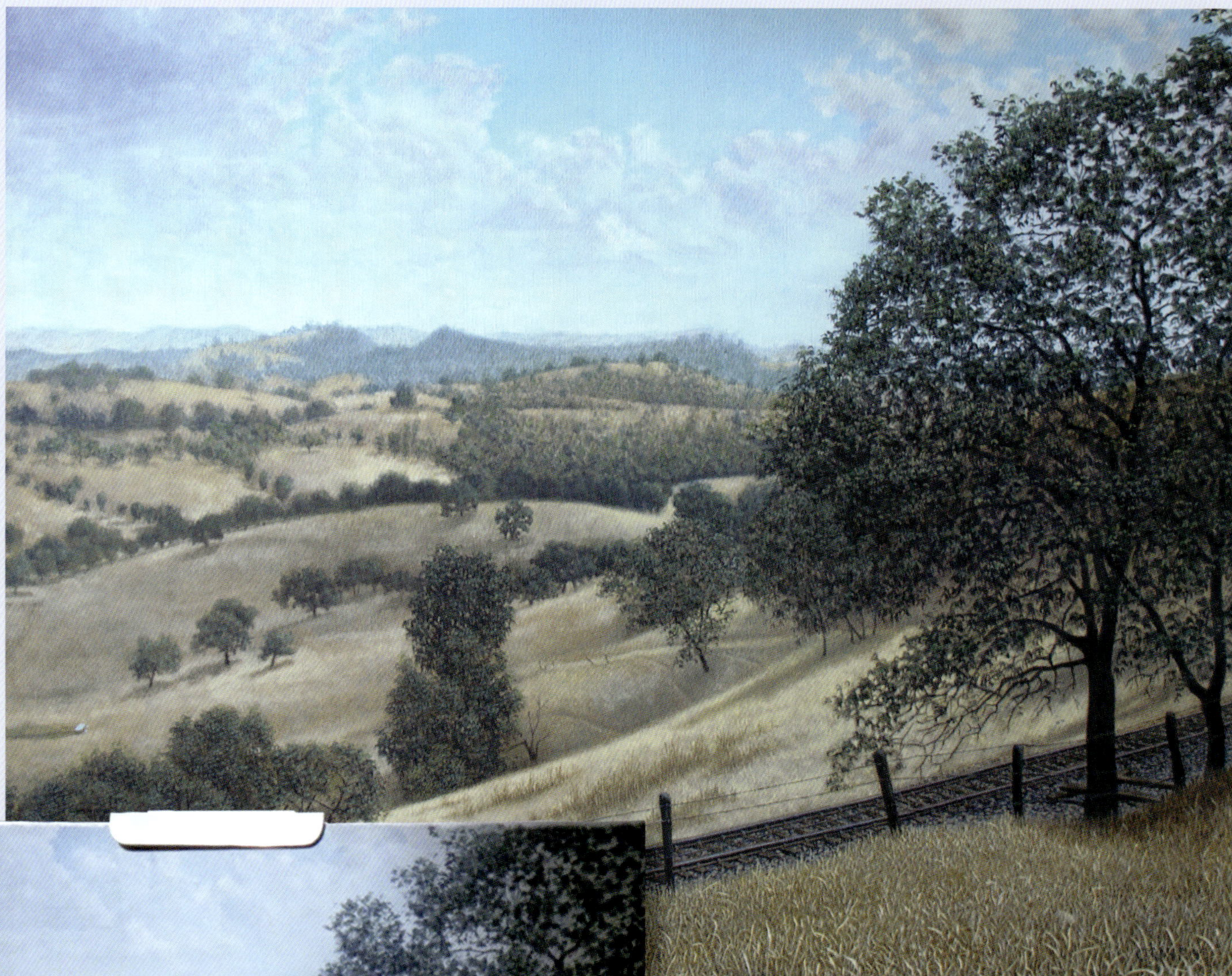

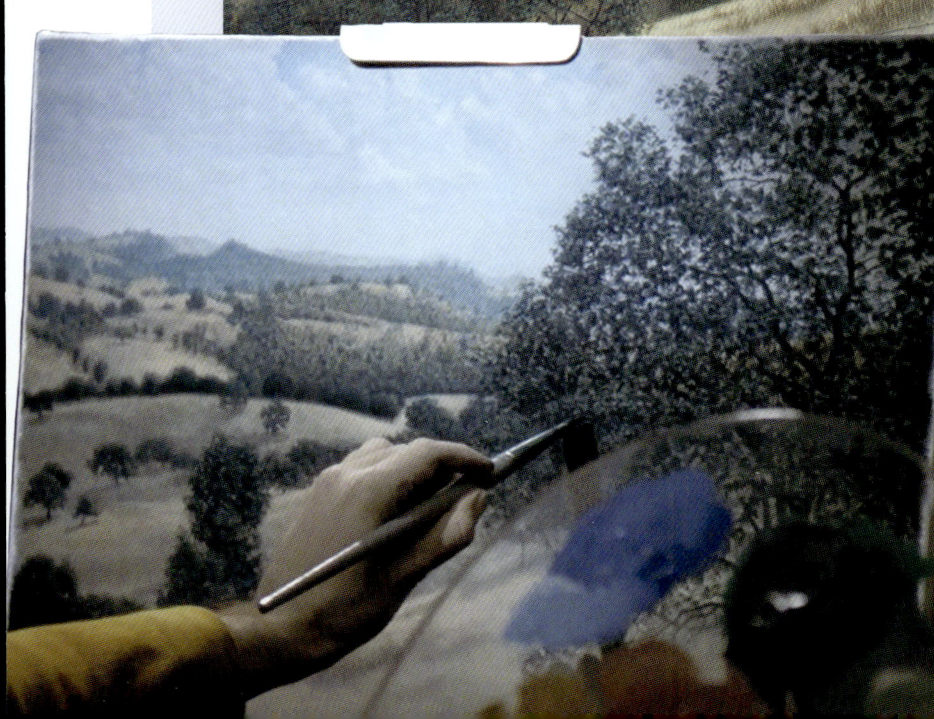

ABOVE: The original "Old Railroad Tracks Through Golden Hills - Hollister, CA" is oil on canvas (28" x 22").

LEFT: When we needed to show Data painting in this shot, we made a copy of one of my original oil paintings (above), removed the twentieth-century train tracks and scumbled in an area where Data could be seen to paint.

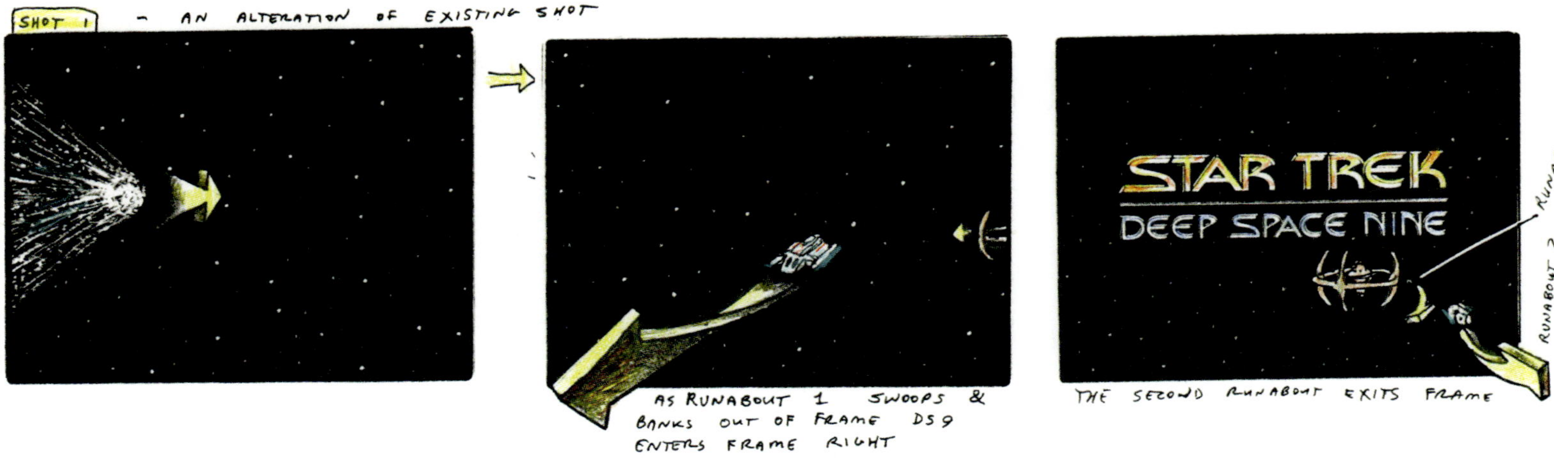

ABOVE: In the original version of the *DS9* titles, the concept was to show that the station was alone in the distant reaches of space. I decided to open with a shot of a comet to suggest remoteness, before discovering the station itself in the distance.

DEEP SPACE NINE TITLE SEQUENCE

AN ELEGANT NEW APPROACH FOR A NEW *STAR TREK* SERIES

The theme for the *DS9* titles was 'We're alone out there.' Rick Berman and Michael Piller wanted me to stress the isolated nature of the station, which was on the edge of known space. Normally I would have started with storyboards, but by this point Tony Meininger had built a plywood mock-up of the station, so I took a home video camera and, with some help from Eddie Williams, I shot a very rough and ready version of the sequence.

What I was looking for was a ballet around the station. Walking around the plywood model inspired me to think about the kind of camera moves we could do. Because I had a physical model, I could see that a particular move would be really elegant, or that if I moved over here I'd be able to frame the wormhole, and so on. And I was able to work out where the credits should fall. Once the video had been approved, I made storyboards based on it, and we shot the final model at Image G.

The sequence starts off with a comet, which we did in CG so that we could use particle animation. Then we get to the title card, which, in complete contrast, was done very old school—I actually airbrushed it by hand on a piece of cardboard. One of the things

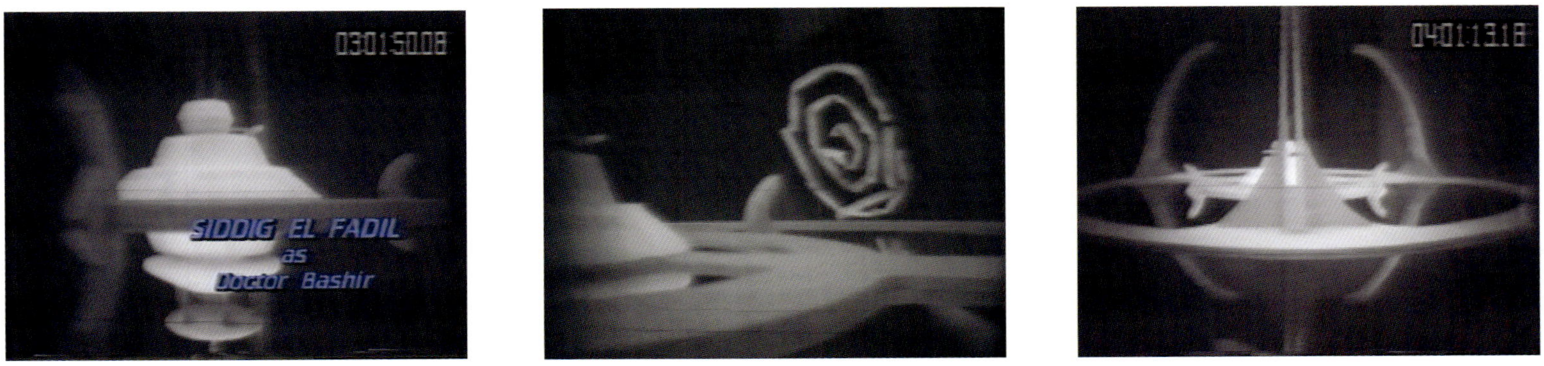

ABOVE: I planned the *DS9* titles out intuitively by filming the plywood study model with a home video camera, assisted by Eddie Williams. That way I could see exactly which moves worked best in a poetic weave of images.

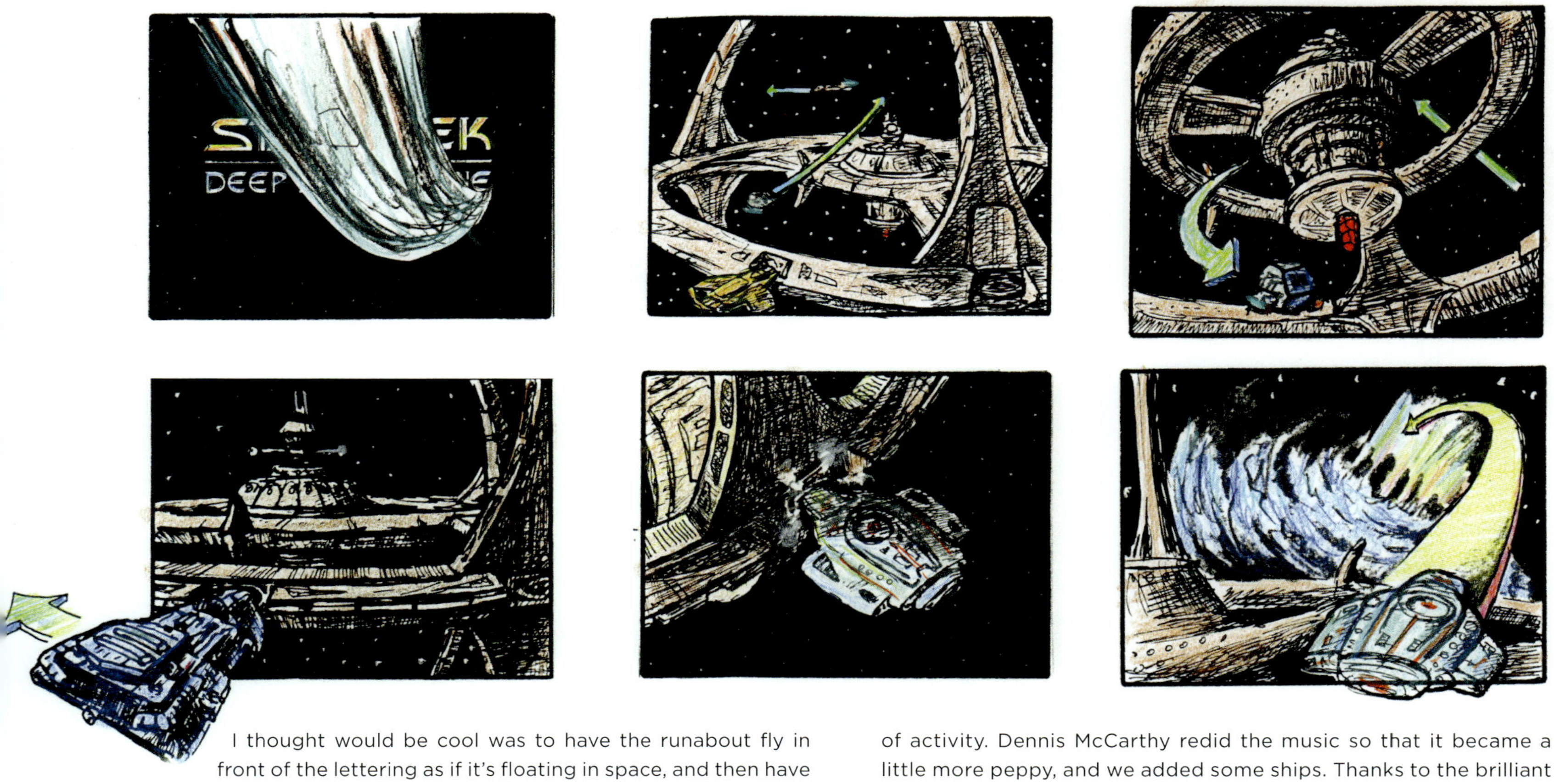

I thought would be cool was to have the runabout fly in front of the lettering as if it's floating in space, and then have its wake wipe the screen blank before we got into the next shot.

Then we have the shots around the station. I wanted the ballet to be dark and mysterious, so everything was backlit so the audience would be able to provide detail that we couldn't really show them. Finally, we get to the wormhole, which was a fully CG effect that Rob Legato designed when he was creating the rest of the effects for the pilot.

By the third season, they'd introduced the *Defiant*, and we wanted to redesign the titles so that the station had become a hub of activity. Dennis McCarthy redid the music so that it became a little more peppy, and we added some ships. Thanks to the brilliant guys at Image G we were able to program in scale moves to add ships that were docked at or flying around the station, because none of the models were the same scale. John Knoll, who is a real pioneer of CG and invented Photoshop with his brother Thomas, created some spacemen for us on his computer at home.

The station was at the heart of both versions of the titles. The model that Tony made was a beautiful work of art, and I felt the audience should appreciate it for what it is. How could you not fall in love with it?

BELOW: We revisited the title sequence in *DS9*'s third season. We added the *Defiant* and several other ships to make it look as if the station was now a hive of activity. Composer Dennis McCarthy revised the theme music to give it more drive.

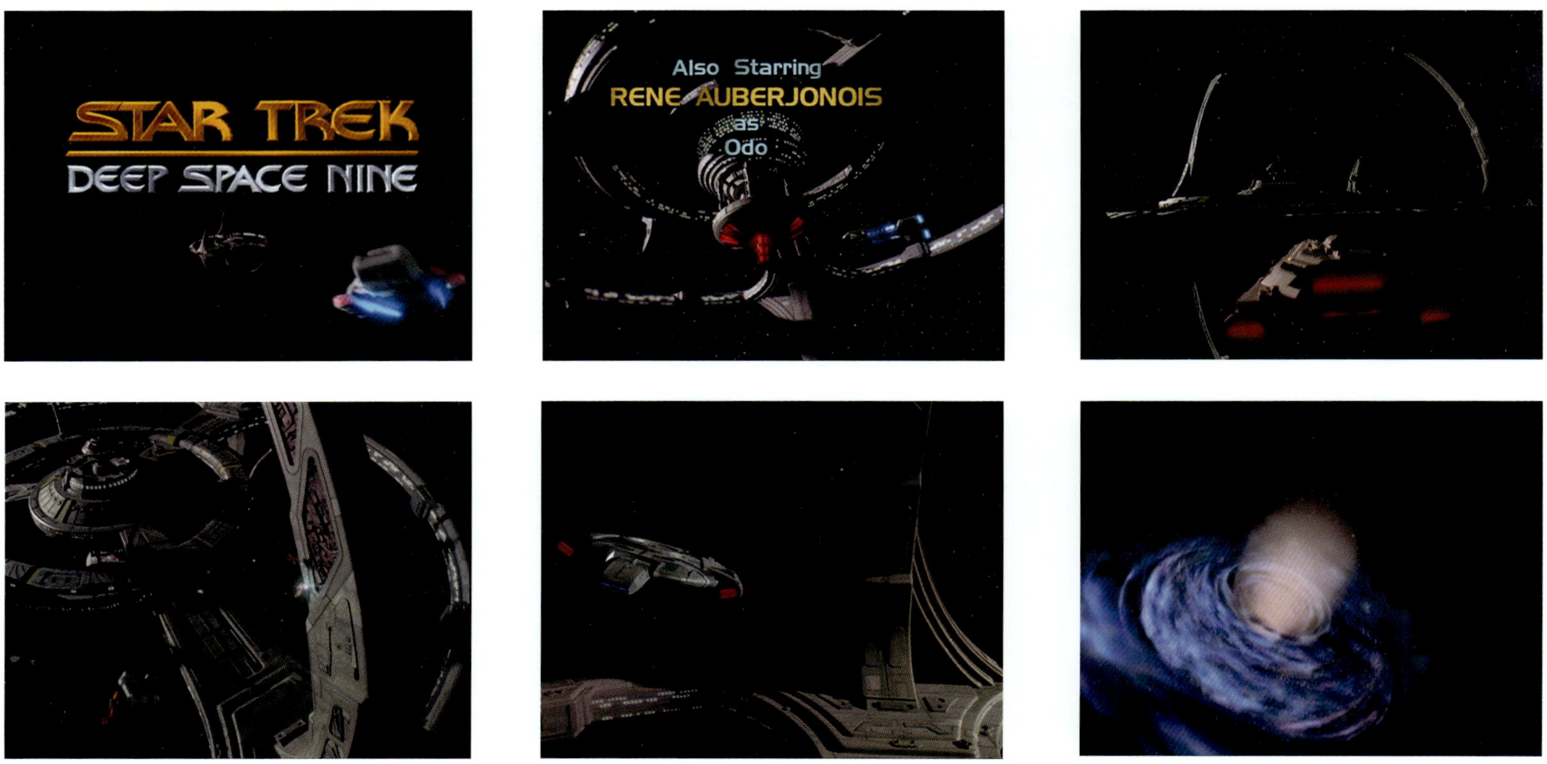

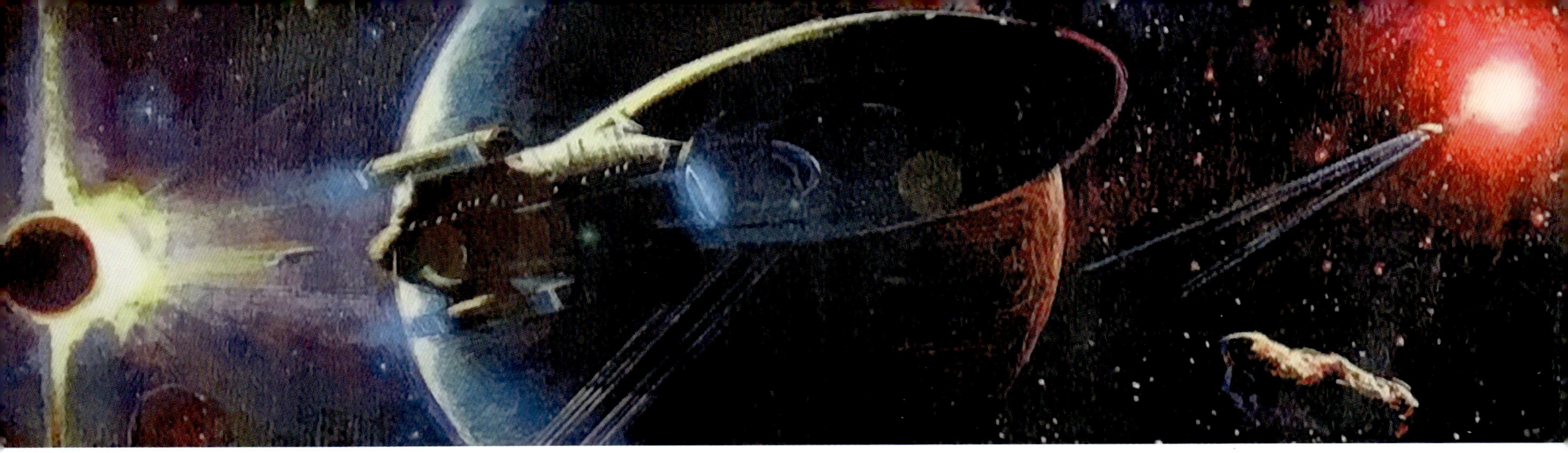

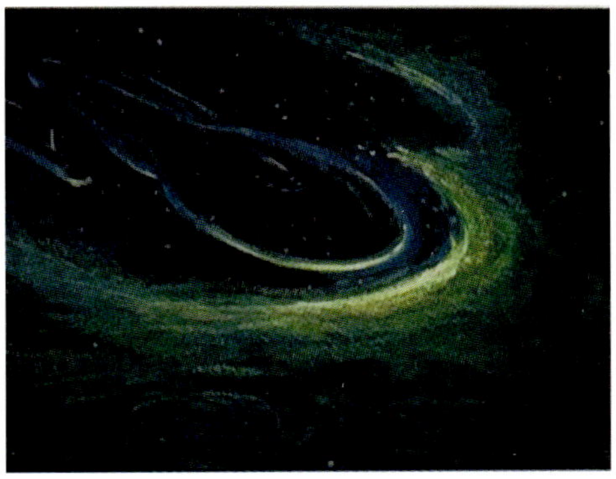

VOYAGER TITLE SEQUENCE

EXPLORING THE OTHER SIDE OF THE GALAXY WITH THE LOST VESSEL

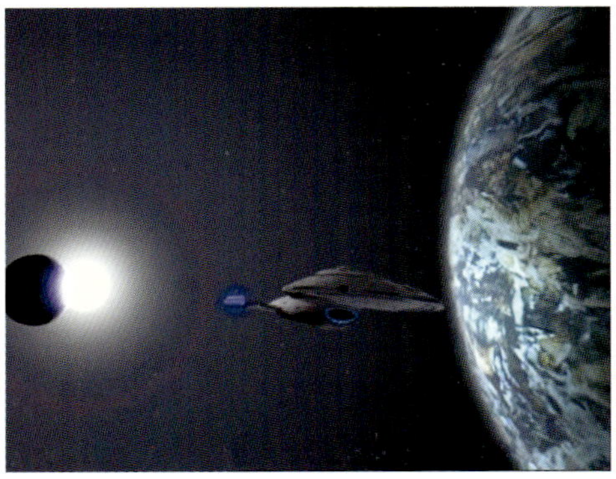

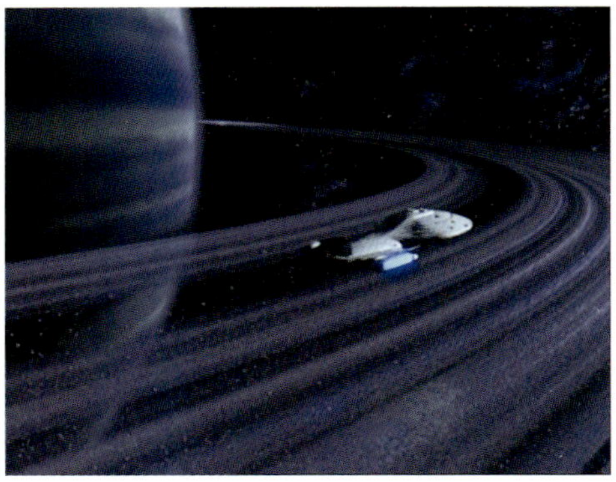

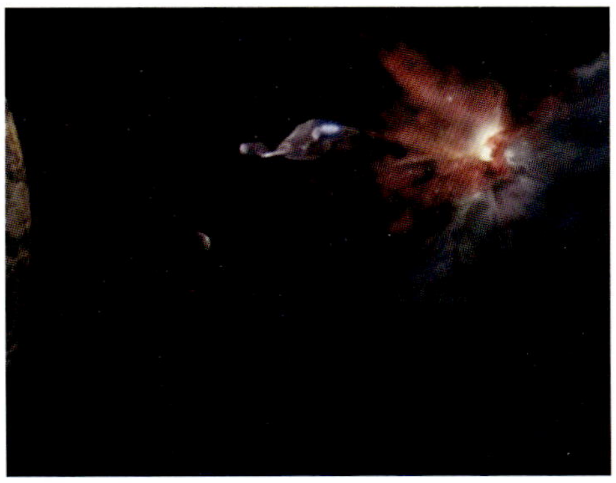

Rick Berman and Peter Lauritson asked me to design the title sequence for *Voyager*. *Star Trek*'s producers were busy running two series and prepping a feature, so they gave me a lot of freedom in the design. I wanted to depict my dream of places I'd like to go and things I'd like to see if I had a starship. I envisioned a flow of images showing *Voyager* encountering spectacular phenomena in unexplored regions of the Delta Quadrant.

First, I designed the main title card using the traditional *Star Trek* font, hand-airbrushed the bevels on the lettering, and determined a color scheme for the rest of the title cards. While some of us were working on the *Voyager* pilot, the rest of the VFX team was still working on *TNG* and *DS9*. *Voyager*'s title sequence benefited from the support and creative collaboration of VFX supervisors David Stipes and Ron Moore, Image G's crew, the compositors at CIS and The Post Group, Amblin Imaging's team, and Santa Barbara Studios' artists. Without their efforts it would never have come into existence.

Santa Barbara Studios had done the visual effects for a documentary depicting a tour around our solar system. They had created some inspiring shots, so I wanted to work with them. One of my favorite shots in the sequence shows the camera sweeping across a planet's rings to catch *Voyager* flying over them. That was inspired by a shot in Santa Barbara's science show.

We decided at the outset that the title sequence would be a hybrid of technologies using motion-control miniatures, traditional painting, and computer animation. For some of the shots we photographed Tony Meininger's exquisite *Voyager* model at Image G. Santa Barbara Studios would be handling the computer-generated images. They provided a terrific storyboard artist, Eric Timiens, whose beautiful color renderings were a significant factor in getting the producers to approve the sequence. This was the first time we had ever built a CG

LEFT: I was incredibly busy with the pilot when we created the *Voyager* title sequence, so I worked with gifted storyboard artist Eric Timiens at Santa Barbara Studios.

model of one of our hero ships. It was done by Amblin Imaging, who made the surface textures on the ship by wrapping photographs of Tony Meininger's physical model around their virtual hull. At the time, miniatures still looked best. For wider shots where the ship was further away we could use the CG ship, but for close-up shots where we would see a lot of detail we used the physical model.

We were always trying to push the boundaries of what was possible. We weighed possibilities and determined the best technical solution for each given shot. VFX supervisor David Stipes and the crew at Image G put in long hours shooting Tony's motion-control *Voyager* as well as other elements, including a 2D planet I painted in oils on a cardboard disk that the ship passes as it leaps to warp. While the mo-co was being shot, Santa Barbara was working on the very complex computer animation. Originally, we planned to do the shot when *Voyager* flies over the ice-covered moon as a normal 2D matte painting. After seeing an early test, Rick Berman asked if the moon could roll towards us, so the CG artists projected our 2D matte painting onto a virtual 3D surface to create the illusion of depth.

A lot of the images in *Voyager*'s title sequence would not have been possible before we had CG. We couldn't have shown *Voyager* reflected in the planet's ice rings, or created the disturbance caused by the ship passing through vapor clouds as easily with traditional techniques. That shot almost didn't make it into the title sequence. An unnamed producer's initial reaction was, "That shot is beyond loathing." Only overwhelmingly positive reactions from others in the office convinced him to change his mind and keep the shot in the sequence.

Voyager flying over the ice rings is a combination of CG and motion-control technology. The planet, chunks of ice in the ring and the reflection are CG, but the ship is the practical model. Some viewers wrote in to criticize the scale of the reflection. They said if it was Saturn the reflection would be so small we wouldn't see it. My response was "It's not Saturn, but a small ringed planetesimal common in the Delta Quadrant." We had to be good at rationalizing on *Star Trek*.

The visuals can't be separated from Jerry Goldsmith's stirring score. Jerry's music lent an uplifting grandeur to the imagery, and conveyed the spirit of human exploration. To this day I still feel a thrill when I hear his beautiful theme.

All of us involved were gratified when the Academy of Television Arts & Sciences honored us with an Emmy nomination for best title sequence.

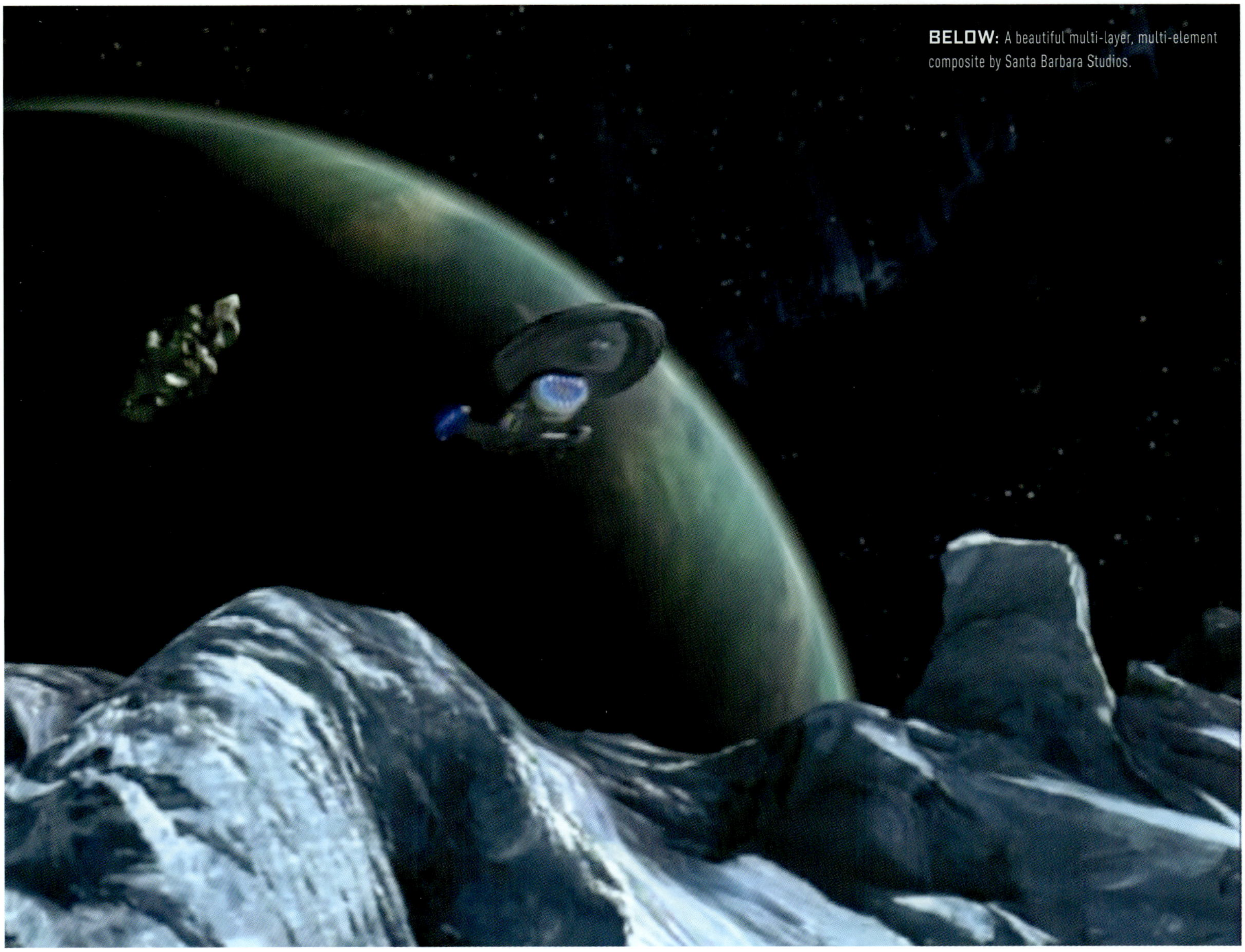

BELOW: A beautiful multi-layer, multi-element composite by Santa Barbara Studios.

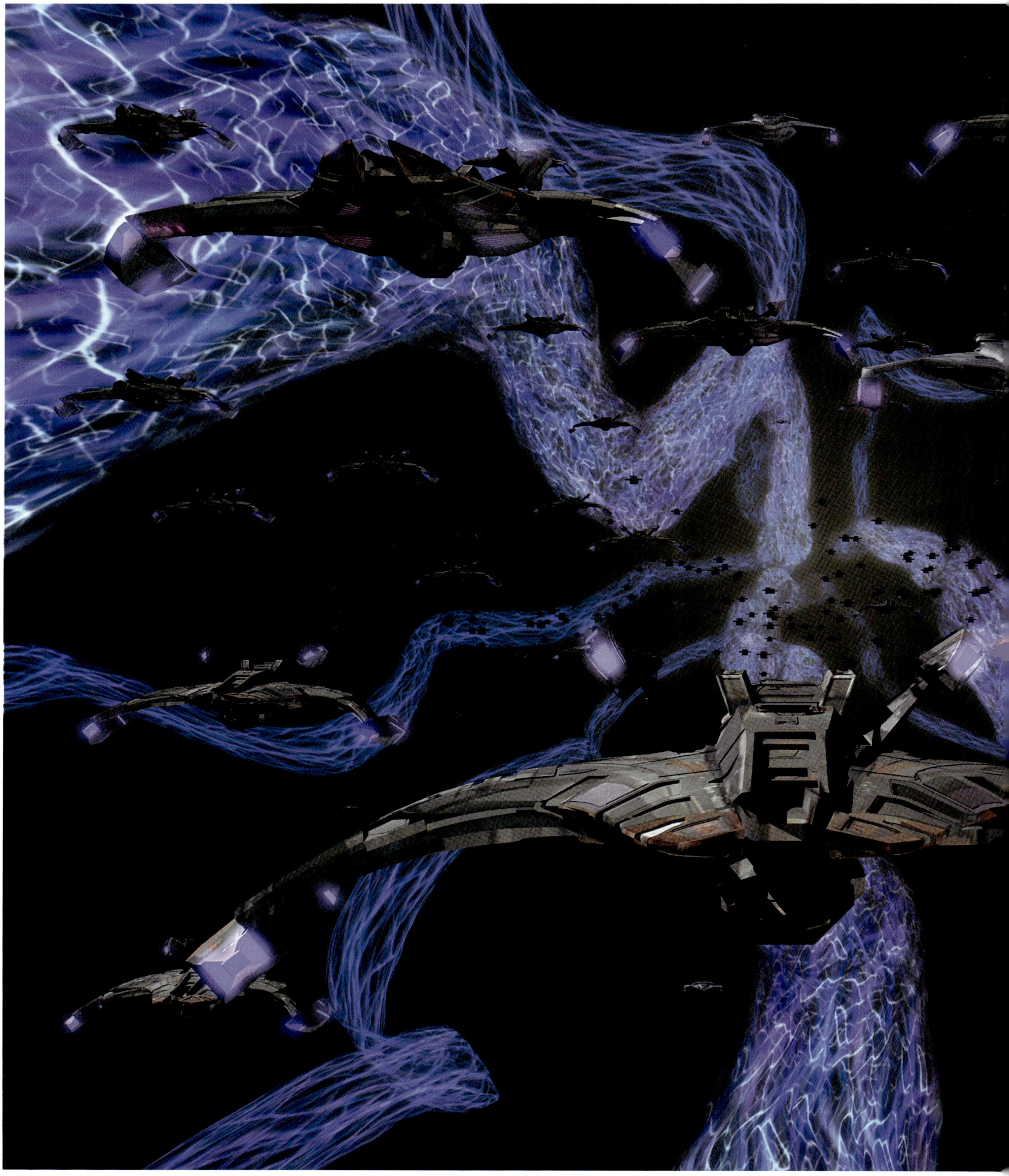

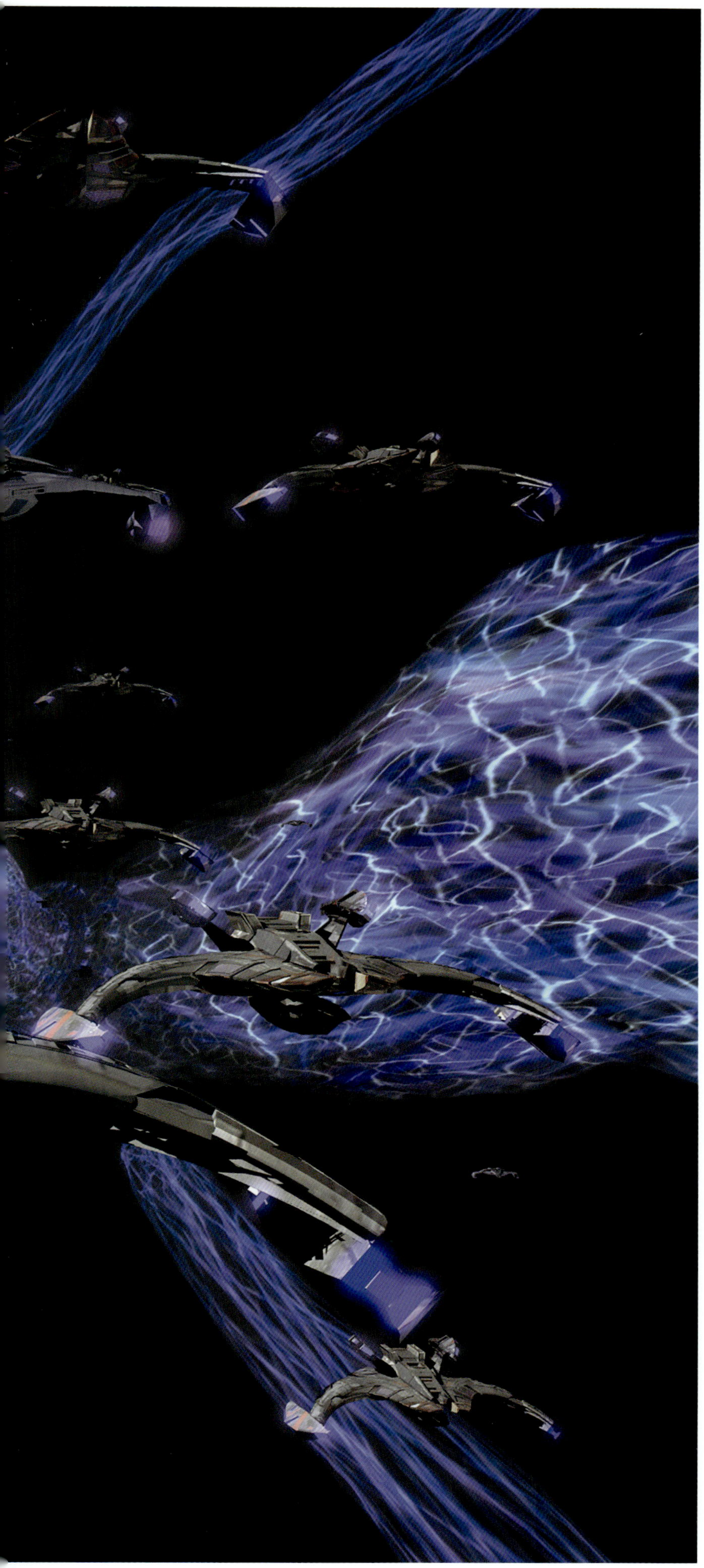

THE MOVE TO CG

NEW TECHNOLOGY COMES INTO ITS OWN AS *STAR TREK* EVOLVES

We had always used CG in *Star Trek*. Even in the first season of *TNG* we used it for the Crystalline Entity; I storyboarded the VFX sequences and Isa Alsop at The Post Group built the virtual model and animated it for us. After that, we used it whenever something appropriate came up; for example, we used it for some shots of Junior in 'Galaxy's Child.' We'd even used it for *Voyager* itself in the title sequence, but it still had problems—for a long time CG didn't look very real, you could see the way the textures were stretched around the shape. So we were very careful when we used it, but it was also a technology that got better and better every year we were working on *Star Trek*. By the time we got to *Enterprise*, we were using it for everything.

The aggressive transition started on *Voyager*. That show in particular gave us the opportunity to go into CG because of the nature of the writing and the images they were looking for. CG was simply a good way to meet the demands of the stories. *Voyager* was in an unexplored quadrant of the Galaxy, humans hadn't been out there, and so the crew encountered new and different phenomena. During the first two seasons we could see that CG was improving to the point where it made sense for us to rely on it. When David Stipes moved over to *DS9*, we needed a new VFX supervisor who understood CG, so I asked the late great Ron

RIGHT: Storyboards helped us depict the flow of images for a complex space battle, and keep track of elements needed.

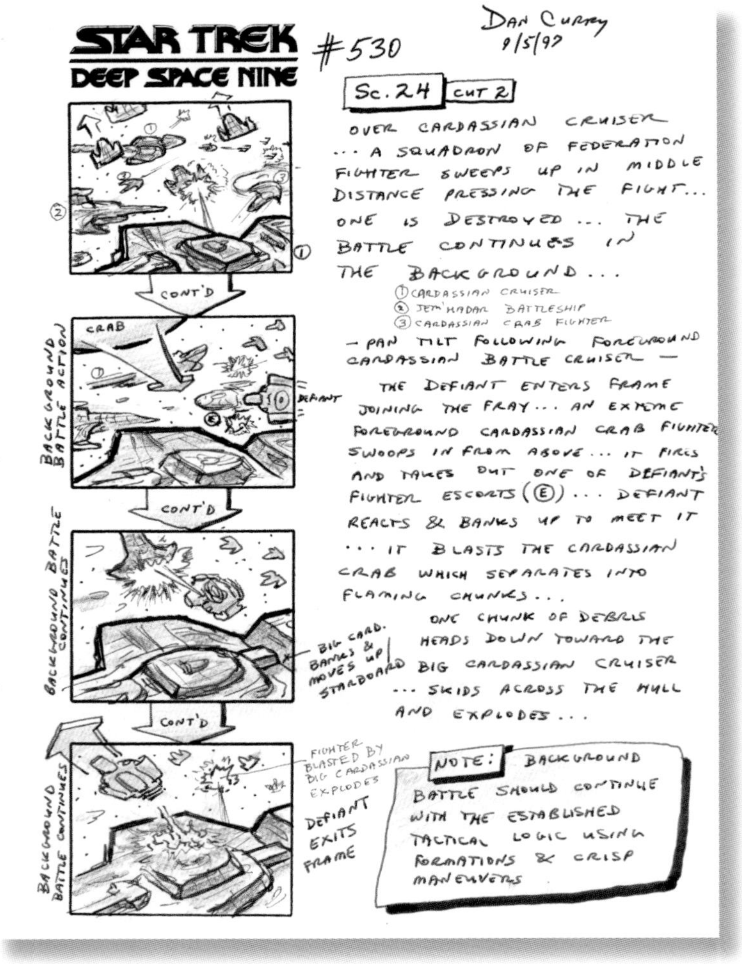

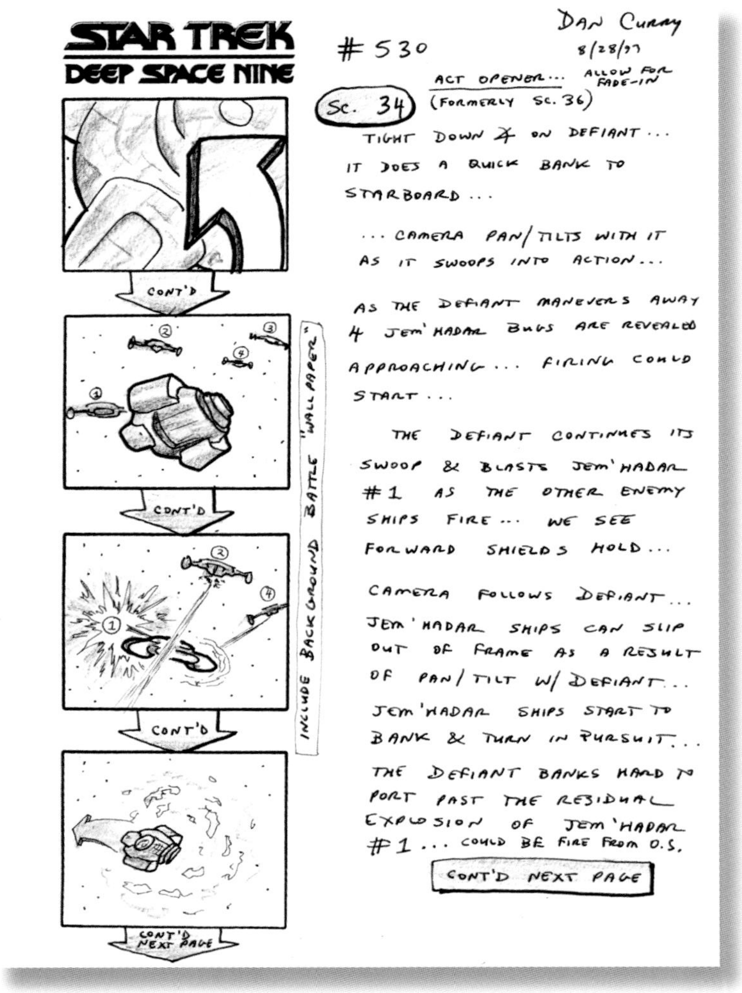

Thornton, a founder of Foundation Imaging, if he could recommend anyone. That's how Mitch Suskin came to join us. Foundation was on the cutting edge of CG, and under Ron's pioneering leadership they were eager to show us what they could do. When they ended their relationship with *Babylon 5*, I was able to give them regular work and bring them into the *Star Trek* family. They started to work for us in earnest during the third season of *Voyager*, doing the cave creature in 'Basics, Part II.' As the season went on we relied on them more and more.

CG is a tool like any other; once the technology reached a certain qualitative level and could technically achieve what we wanted, what mattered was the skill of the artist. I brought a traditional painter's eye to it, along with lots of experience working with physical models. To acquaint new CG artists with how we lit ships on *Star Trek* I would sometimes demonstrate with physical models. One of the things we learned from working with miniatures is that if you back-light you get a dramatic sense of chiaroscuro. You don't have to show everything—in fact, you're better off leaving some things to the audience's imagination. Foundation had some really talented people, such as John Teska, who built the 'Basics' creature and went on to model and animate Species 8472, the "Shroomies," Xindi Insectoids, and other aliens. When I realised how much we could accomplish artistically with CG I pushed for us to use it more often. Foundation Imaging and Digital Muse became great allies.

Not yet completely trusting CG, we still used it for guest ships and the odd creature rather than for the hero ships. That changed when *Deep Space Nine* started to require big space battles. Shots with multiple ships always presented the visual-effects team with a challenge. Executive producer Ira Behr and the rest of the writers wanted to show vast battle sequences with huge numbers of ships fighting one another. That can be accomplished shooting practical models with motion control, but it takes a long time, something we never had on *Star Trek*. VFX demands got to the point where we couldn't shoot the ships fast enough to satisfy the schedule of the show. In 'The Way of the Warrior' the Klingons attack the DS9 station. We had to be inventive using models. Gary Hutzel used toy Klingon birds-of-prey for the background ships. In *DS9*'s sixth season we got the script for 'Sacrifice of Angels.' David Stipes took a look at it and came back saying that if we shot it all with motion control it would take six months and cost well over a million dollars. David was always a big supporter of CG, and suggested that we used it to make the battle possible. Gary and I felt that miniatures looked better, but we thought that if the prominent foreground ships could be practical models then the background ones could be digital, where the less desirable artifacts of CG were less noticeable.

It was clear that there were going to be more multi-ship space battles, so we made a big commitment to CG. We sent our practical models out to our CG companies so they could copy them digitally—Digital Muse handled the Starfleet vessels, while Foundation dealt with the bad guys. We swapped the models between them as needed. We completed the large-scale battles, and even came in under budget. From then on we were regularly using CG vendors on both series. In general, Digital Muse worked on *DS9*, and Foundation worked on *Voyager*, but it wasn't a hard and fast rule. They would work on episodes that involved sequences they were suited to. When

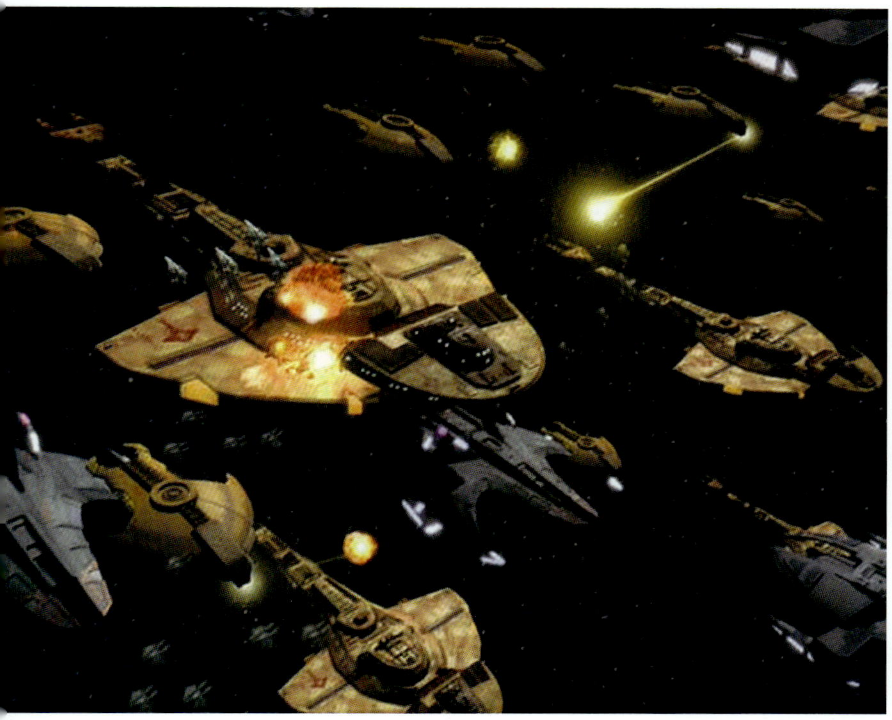

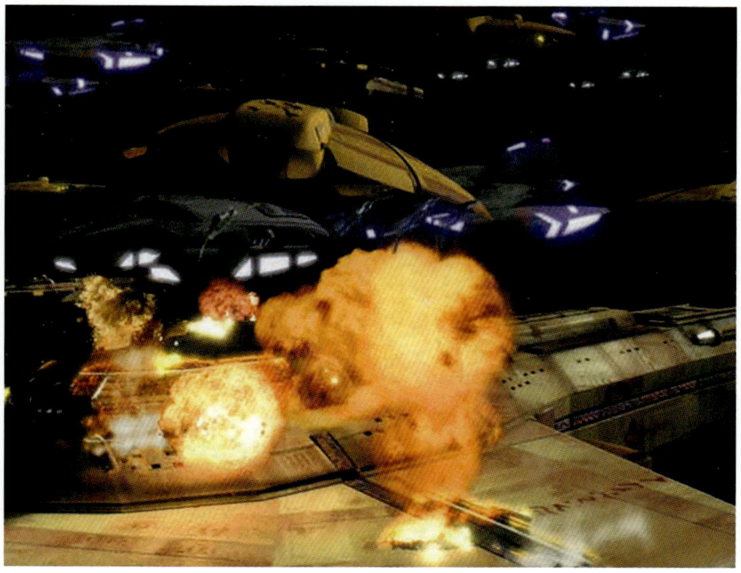

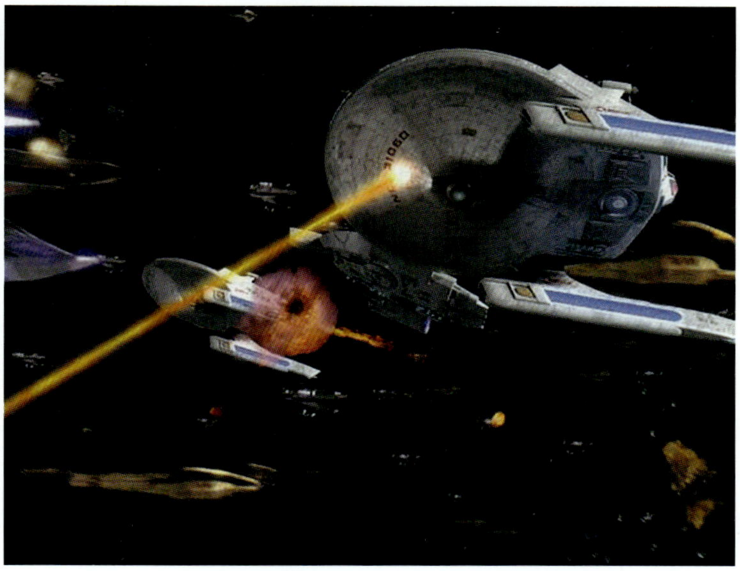

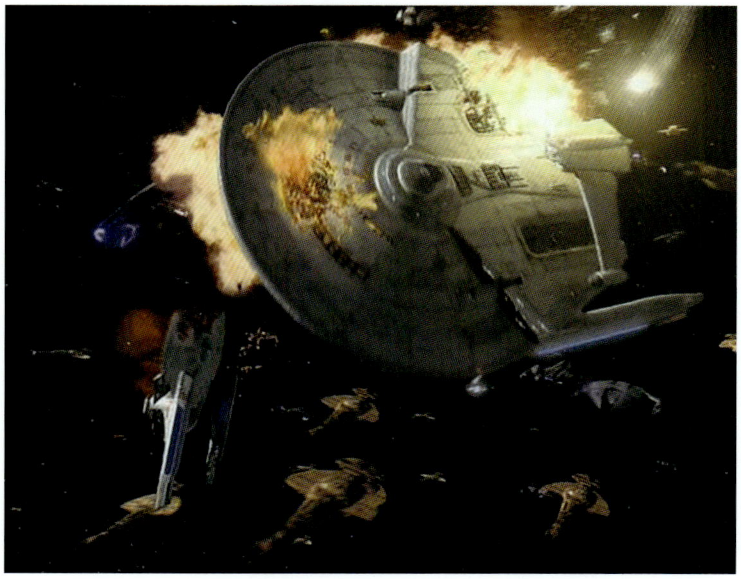

there was a really big show they'd both be involved. Just as we kept a directory listing all the different practical elements we'd shot, we also started a directory of CG models that told us how much scrutiny the model could stand up to, and where it had been used before. If a ship had only appeared briefly in the background, we could easily go in, tweak the shape and recolor it, much the same way we had done modifying Greg and Tony's models, only now digital technology made it faster and cheaper.

Our CG vendors recruited more people, and we benefited from the talents of digital artists like Pierre Drolet, Brandon MacDougall, Rob Bonchine, Dave Morton and Adam Liebowitz. At the same time, computer software improved, and we were able to start doing things like water simulation that would have been impossible just a year or so earlier. We could build vast, complex CG interiors like the inside of the Voth ship in 'Distant Origin.' Because we were working in digital 3D we could include kinetic elements that were previously unthinkable in model ships and traditional matte paintings. We could blow ships up or damage them without having to build another physical model, and we could create creatures that looked truly alien without being limited to human actors in prosthetic makeup.

On *Deep Space Nine* we always continued to use motion control, partly because we already had such excellent hero models, and in most cases they still looked better than CG. We didn't have a CG model of the DS9 station itself until the last shot of the final episode of the series. We had intense loyalty to Image G and their crew for the great work they did for us. But by the time we got to the end of *Voyager*, we were barely using practical elements. Computer imagery completely revolutionised the world of visual effects and changed everything. Anything that can be imagined can be visualized.

ABOVE: Working with my old friend, the amazingly knowledgeable David Stipes, these space battle scenes are hybrids of technology. Foreground ships are physical models shot with motion control, while background ships are CG. We hadn't yet fully embraced CG, but the demand for so many ships in the complex scenes forced us to rely on CG ships to fill out the warring fleets.

ONLY IN CG

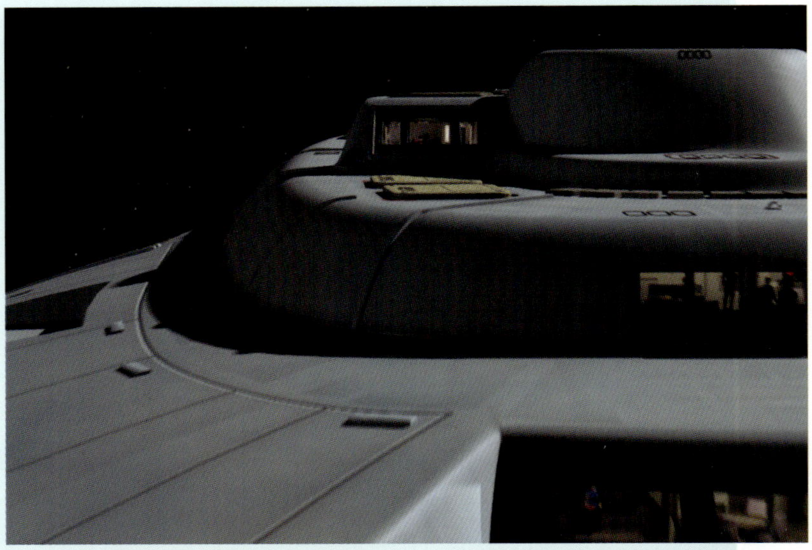

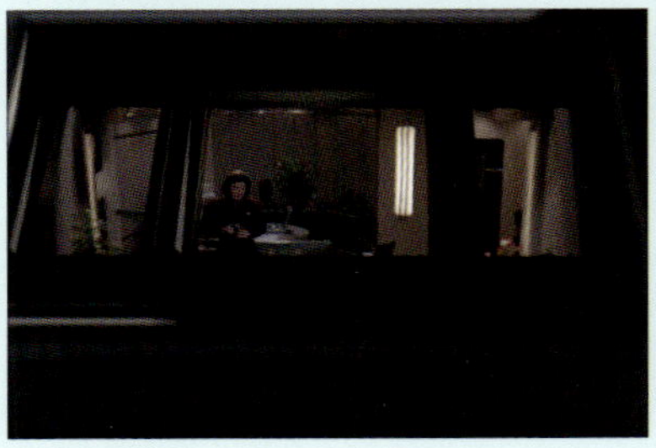

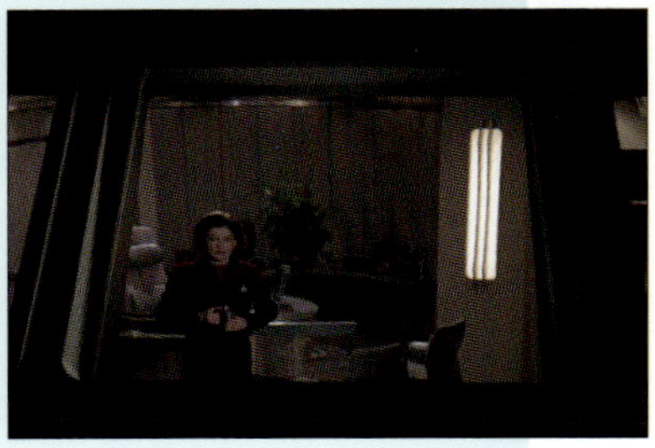

ABOVE: CG allowed us to track in interior shots through windows.

Given enough time and money, you can do anything. But on *Star Trek* we were always working to a budget and, certainly, with limited time. The move to CG opened up several possibilities that hadn't been available to us before. When you were working in motion control you could only show so much of the model in a single shot before the mount would get in the way. With CG there were no mounts, so you could program much more extravagant moves, and because you weren't limited by the physical size of the stage and your motion-control rig, so you could get much further away from the model.

Another thing CG enabled us to do was damage the ship. If we had done that with traditional models we would have to have built a new model for every stage of damage we wanted to show, and each one of those models would have cost tens of thousands of dollars. But in CG we could build different levels of damage into our model of *Voyager*. Then the next week we could switch the damage off, and use our model as if nothing had happened. We could also keep upgrading the model by adding more detail to it, again creating shots that wouldn't have justified creating a whole new model. You could only get so close to a physical model before you would see the grain in the paint. For example, there are two shots in 'Good Shepherd' where we get really close and really far away from the ship.

As we were using CG it continued to get more sophisticated. Water had always been a problem because of the nature of its behaviour—being fluid, it is constantly changing, which makes it impossible to repeat an action so you could film different passes. It's also very difficult to scale water. You see that in the old pirate films, where sometimes the waves look far too big. When they came up with the algorithms to do CG water, it made a significant difference to the VFX industry, and we were able to do the episode 'Thirty Days,' where *Voyager* visited an ocean planet. I looked at it like visiting Atlantis, and I was really excited to do that. You could also put lots of ships in the same shot and render them all in one go. If you had done that with motion control you would have to have filmed each ship individually, and for a big battle sequence that could have taken weeks or even months. So CG brought a lot of things within our reach that would have been prohibitively expensive and time-consuming before.

BELOW: Showing this many ships in a single shot would have taken weeks using physical models and motion control.

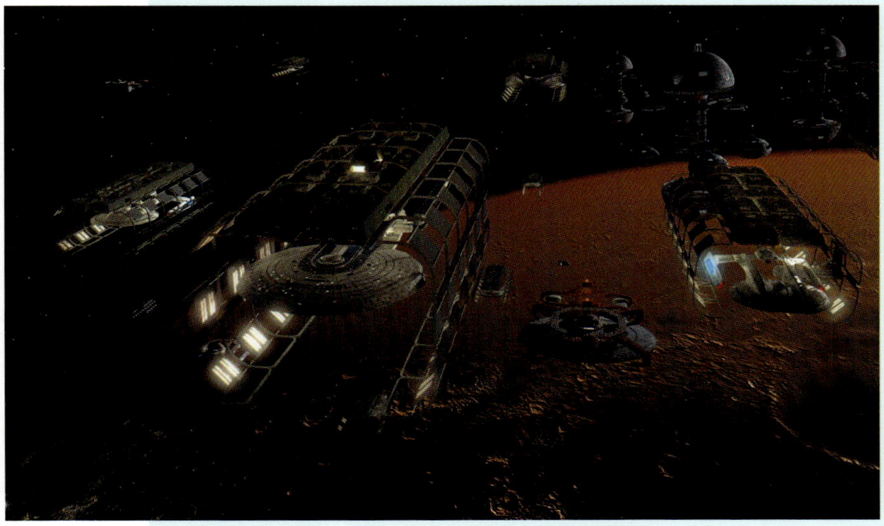

BELOW: If we were using mo-co, damaging a ship like this would have required an expensive separate model.

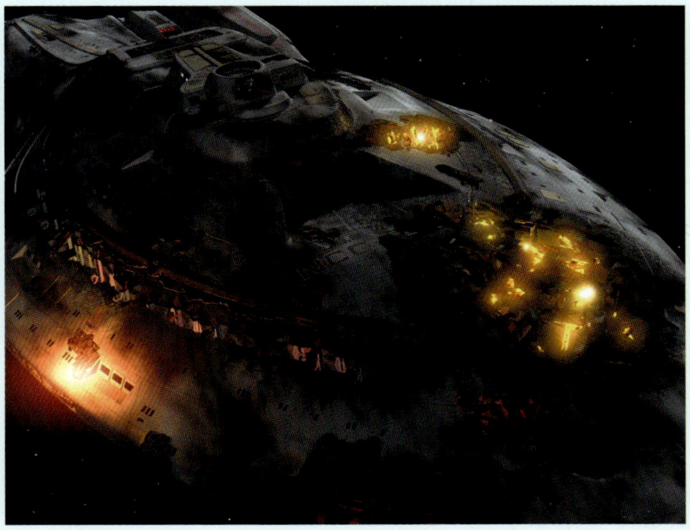

INSIDE STORY

BUILDING AN EXTENSION

Visual effects should not be obvious. After we had shot the scene in *Enterprise* where Archer and his crew watch Admiral Forrest's speech about launching the *Enterprise* NX-01, the producers decided that the event wasn't big enough. Following the lines of perspective, I did a digital painting, expanding the size of the room and reducing the original balcony with Archer and crew to make it appear further away on a higher level. In second unit we shot a new plate against blue screen with background artists applauding and looking where Archer would be, and comped them into the original balcony in front of the NX-01 crew, syncing their performance with the principal photography.

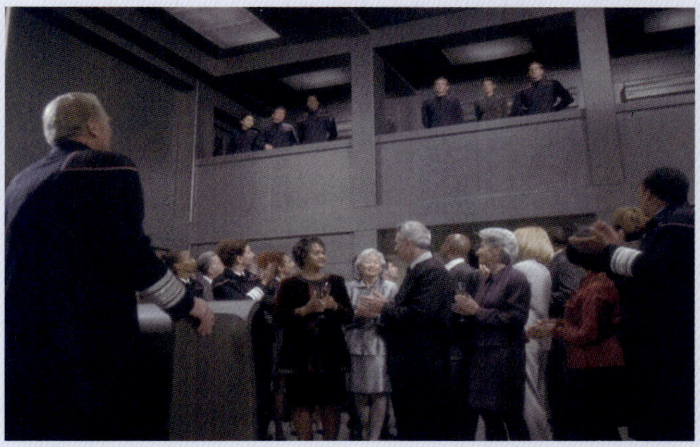

ABOVE: In the original version of the shot, the only people on the upper level were Archer and his crew.

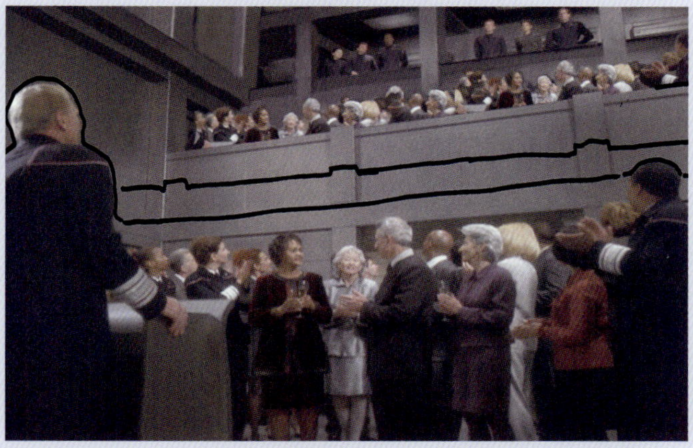

ABOVE: The producers wanted the chamber to look bigger, with more people. The lines show where we could digitally cut away part of the original wall.

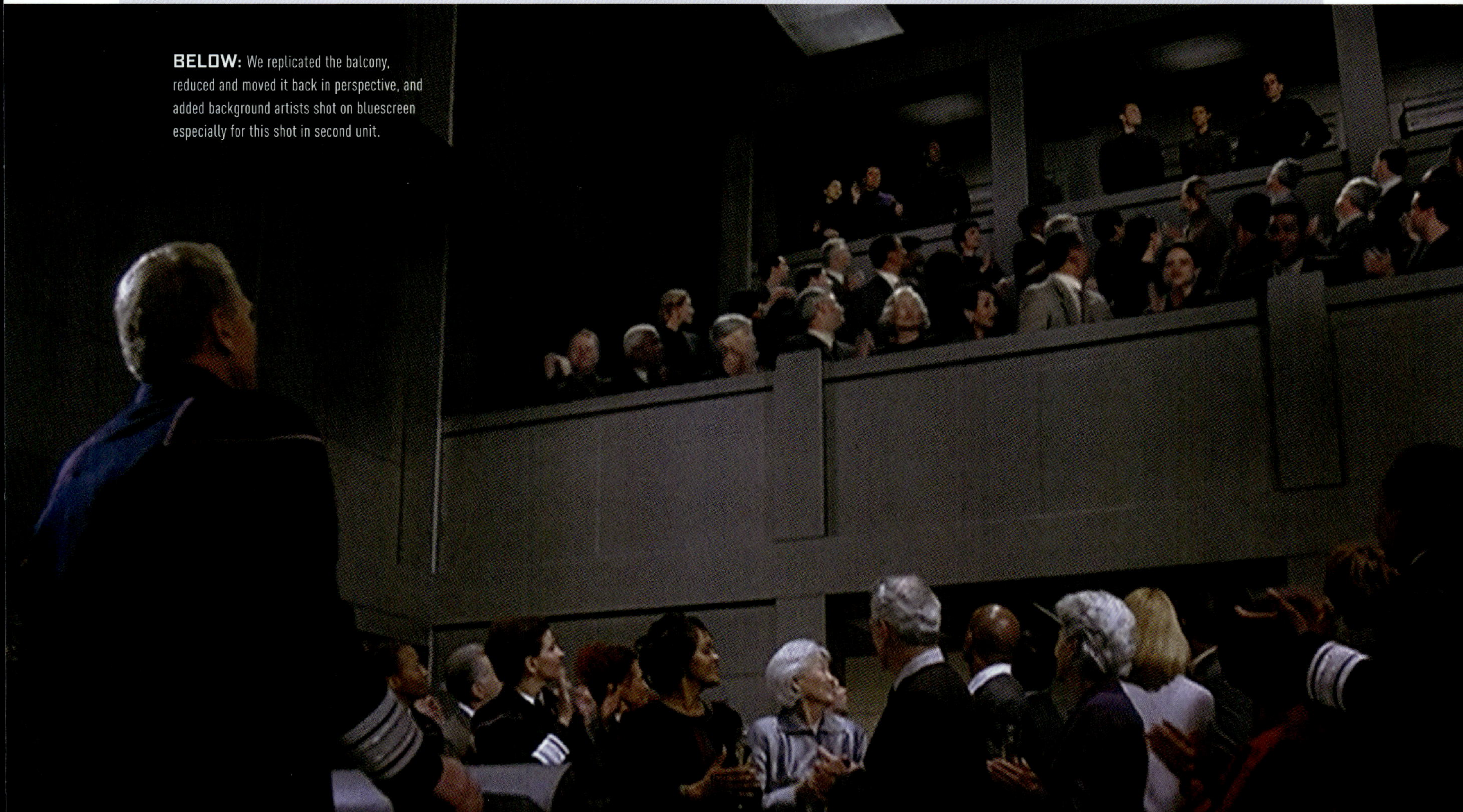

BELOW: We replicated the balcony, reduced and moved it back in perspective, and added background artists shot on bluescreen especially for this shot in second unit.

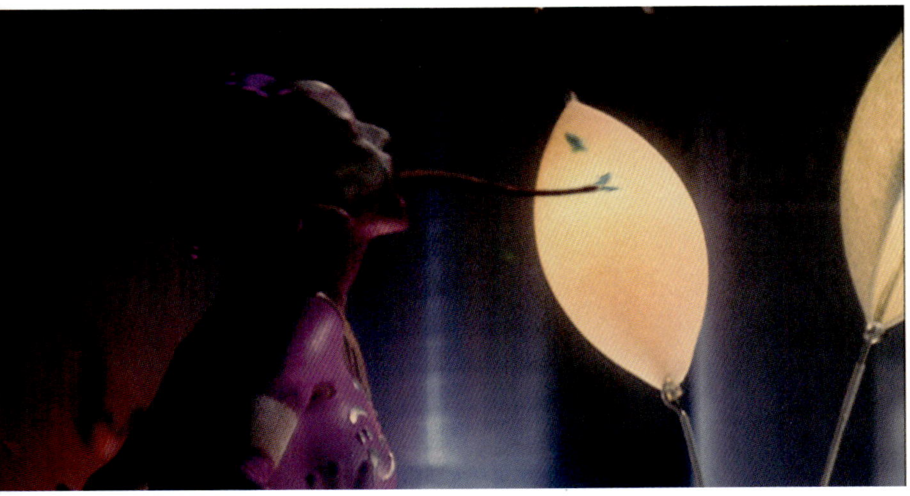

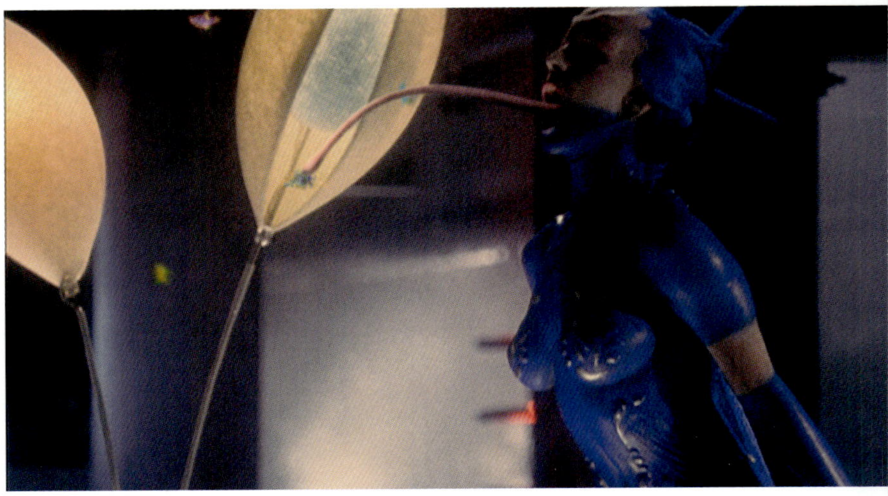

ENTERPRISE: BUILDING A NEW CG UNIVERSE

COMPUTER TECHNOLOGY BECOMES THE DOMINANT FORCE IN *STAR TREK* EFFECTS

By the time we set up *Enterprise*, *Star Trek* was a well-oiled and efficient machine. In contrast to the struggles of the first couple of seasons of *TNG*, everybody knew each other, and after more than a decade, we all knew what we were doing. The VFX team and the way we worked stayed much the same as it had on *Voyager*; Ron and Mitch both came over as supervisors, and David Stipes pitched in to help out on a couple of episodes. We had well-established relationships with our vendor companies too, who were every bit as much a part of *Star Trek* as the actors. We kept the same brilliant compositors and CG artists. We had worked together for so long that we had a creative shorthand with one another. We trusted each other, and had faith in one another's judgement. So the stuff that wasn't broken we didn't fix.

But by that point the nature of the effects industry had changed completely. For the first time ever we were setting a show up that would never need a physical model; instead everything would be created in CG. That wasn't just true for the ships—by now we were making planets in CG, and even routinely replacing actors with CG stunt performers, and we always knew we'd introduce fully CG aliens, just as we had on *Voyager*. Even though our budgets got tighter, we were able to deliver more for the money. At one point almost every episode had a new ship or CG creature, sometimes both.

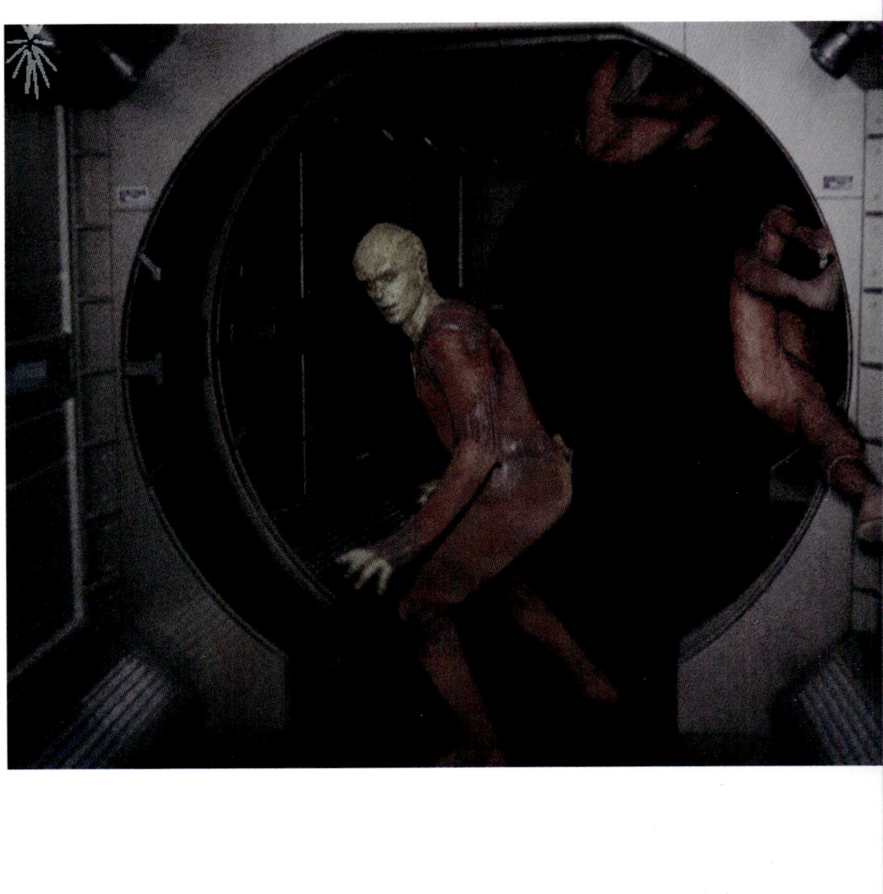

LEFT: CG animation allowed us to add prehensile tongues to the dancing alien twins and the CG butterflies they captured with them. The tongues had to integrate convincingly with Michael Westmore's brilliant and daring make-up design.

We still used some of the practical elements. The energy pattern when you touched a force field was still a water element, and we even used the lasers we had shot in the first season of *TNG* for the temporal chamber. We may have processed them differently, but we still used them because they were randomly organic. Where things were different was in the capabilities of the software. It gave us new tools for creating images, and new tools for storytelling, because we could do stuff that we couldn't do before. That was exciting. The supervisors were always looking for new ways to take advantage of the ever-improving technology of CG. We could do elaborate camera moves with the ships moving through CG structures, and we could have CG characters that could do stuff humans can't do.

Working in CG made things more immediate and painterly in much the same way video compositing had in the beginning of *TNG*. We didn't have to spend days watching a motion-control rig perform passes, and instead of spending hours compositing lights and beauty passes, we could alter the shots and the design of the sequence as we worked on them, exactly the way you would work on a painting. We would do our initial animation design with

SCOTT BAKULA ON DAN

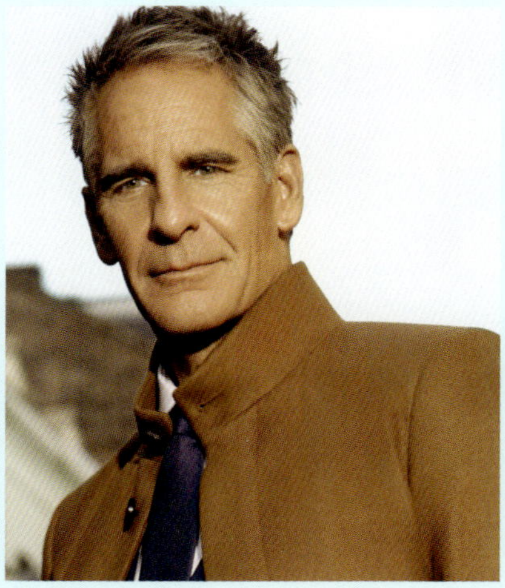

"It was always fun seeing Dan Curry coming, because he'd have an envelope with sketches and pictures. He'd be so excited to show you what he'd come up with, wanting to know what you thought about it. The amount of work and art that he created and would show me was overwhelming, and each one was better than the last, each one unique and special and thought out. He didn't have to spend time showing us that stuff, he could have just said, 'You'll see it when you get there, just look at this green bit of tape on the green screen. It's going to be that tall, so act afraid' or whatever. But he extended himself so much more to all of us.

"He'd bring models too. So here comes a model of the Gorn, and this is what the aquatics are going to be. That's incredibly helpful because as an actor, you're always trying to imagine what something might look like. You're kind of at the mercy of what those folks come up with after you've gone home for the day, but I was never disappointed. It was always just a joy.

"When I was on *Enterprise* I knew that I was working with a lot of masters in their respective areas. It was eye opening. I'd done a bunch of effects work, and I've done a bunch since, but that group was at the forefront of everything, whether it was the latest camera, the latest techniques, or the latest makeup. Everything trickled into each department. It's very collaborative when you're making a show like that, where you have time constraints and budget constraints. You have to be more creative and more clever. They blew my mind all the time, and Dan was at the forefront of it all.

"I was just in awe of these guys. I was so curious about how they did it. You can talk to them, but you can't even begin to learn all the things that they know. You ask, 'How does that work?' or 'How can you do that?' and they explain it to you, but I'm not really a super savvy tech guy, so I kind of nodded my head at times and crossed my fingers. They were all pushing the other guy and gal to do the best we could do, given the opportunity and the budget and constraints that we had. And Dan spearheaded them all.

"Dan is super smart. He is unbelievably creative, and he is kind of non-stop. He is so quick, and really completely devoted to and immersed in whatever world he's creating in that moment. But what I really enjoyed about him was that he really was interested in the story, and pushing it along with the effects. His mind is unlike most people's minds. He just comes up with wild and crazy stuff all the time, and it's unique. Given all of the stuff he's come up with over the course of his career, you would expect that there would be a sense of repetition, but he just keeps blowing up the envelope with new stuff all the time. It's a huge amount of work and thought. It takes up a big portion of your brain to make 25, 26 episodes, and I thought, 'You guys are killing yourselves. It's ridiculous to make this many episodes in a year.' They had just been doing it over and over. I don't know how they did it. I raise my hat to them. It was just crazy, and all the while Dan couldn't be a nicer guy. A low-maintenance guy. You'd think with all that stress and pressure I'd be able to remember a time when he got upset or angry, but I never had any experience of anything other than just that he was delighted to be there and share this great adventure."

LEFT: We didn't use CG for just spaceships, wormholes and morphs. The technology could also be used for giving characters special powers, like Suliban crawling across ceilings. It always helped the sense of verisimilitude when live human actors were also in the shot.

wire frames because they could render so quickly, and you could adjust the move before you did the final version. In that situation what mattered wasn't so much the tools as the people who were using them. Any reasonably intelligent person can learn to use the software, but the way I think of it is that anybody can learn to type, but that doesn't make you a writer. The quality of the CG artists we were working with was extraordinary. They were masters of that art form. They were always striving to be better, and to do better work. They were doing a lot of their own research and development, as were the compositors.

Even though our technology was newer, the series was set in an earlier time than *The Next Generation*. We had to take all that into account when we designed things, but still take advantage of the new image-creating technology we had available to us in order to do something really cool. That was true for every department. I felt that Herman and his art department really outdid themselves; I really like the design of the ship, and the interiors of the NX-01 really made it look like a working ship. We tried to do the same with the effects, designing so they looked as if they belonged in a different era. It was a great artistic challenge, and an exciting time.

Enterprise was also a fun show to work on. A lot of that was as a result of Scott Bakula and his attitude. I don't think that should be underappreciated—he was so wonderful to work with, and an incredibly positive force on set.

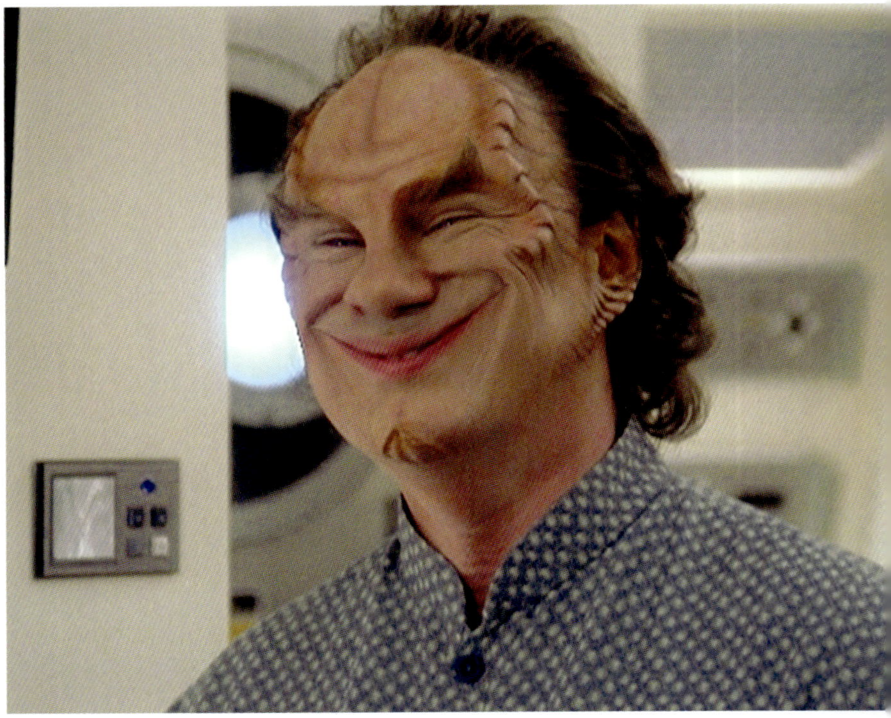

ABOVE: The excellent John Billingsley played alien Dr. Phlox with an ability to smile beyond human capability. This was originally planned to be a CG effect, but John's own smile was so remarkable that it only required a little enhancement in the edit bay.

BELOW: There's also a first in the pilot—we transported Archer while he was running at the end. That's much harder than transporting someone who is standing still. We had to track every element, and rotoscope his matte frame by frame.

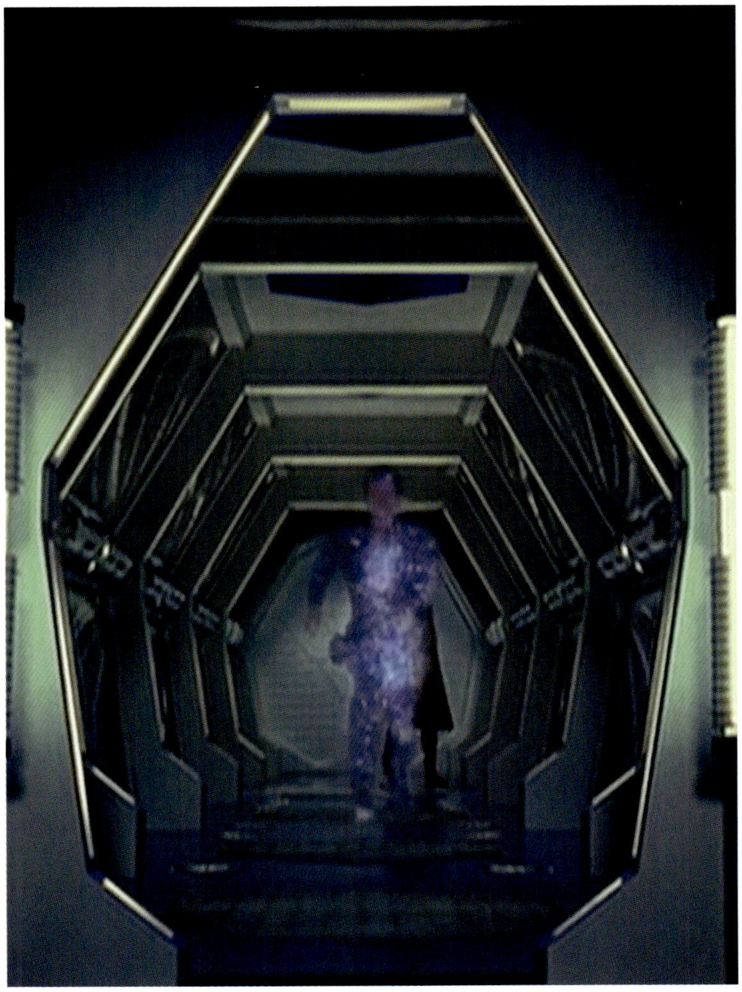

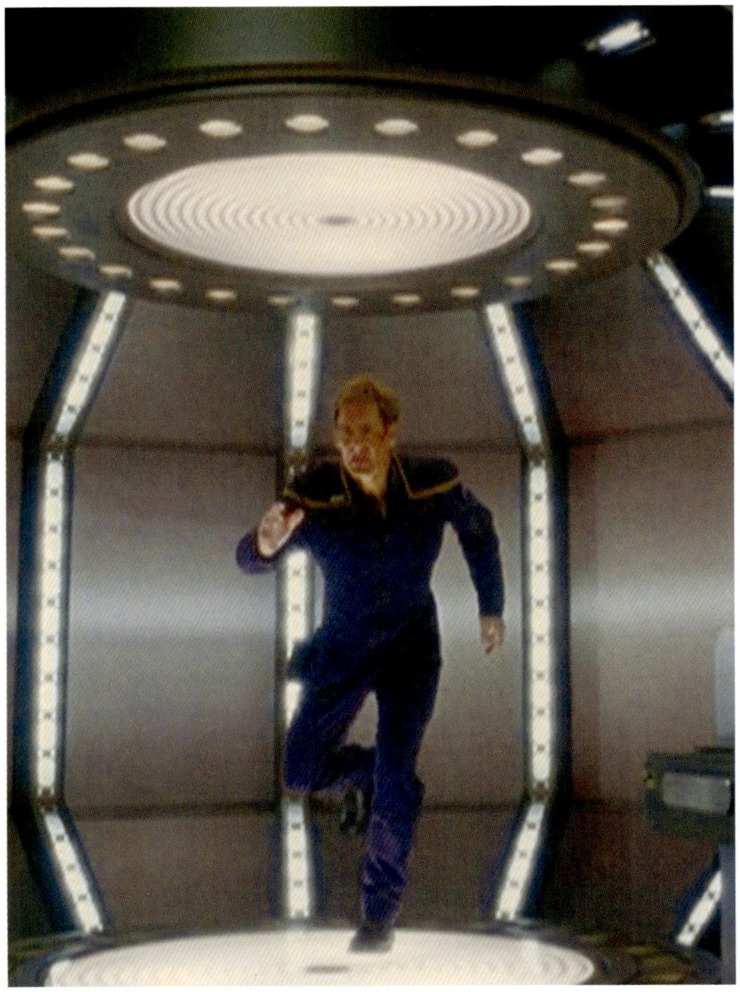

INSIDE STORY

THE SULIBAN HELIX

In 'Broken Bow' the *Enterprise* tracks the Suliban back to their base, where Archer rescues a Klingon. It's a great example of something we could only have done in CG. The *Enterprise* discovers hundreds of Suliban ships hiding in the atmosphere of a gas giant, forming a huge helix that breaks apart. Had we attempted something like that on *TNG* with physical models, it would have been a monumental challenge involving cloud tanks, and mo-co stages full of smoke and liquid nitrogen vapors. We would have struggled to do this in CG even a couple of years before.

I was really wowed by the quality of work delivered by our CG team, especially digital artist Koji Kuramura. There was a remarkable degree of kinetic motion in the clouds and vapors, comprised of layers of semi-transparent elements. The clouds interacted with the ship as it pushed them apart. The complexity of the helix and the way it broke apart was amazing—the Suliban ships were all individual units that were animated separately when the helix disassembled. That would have been impossible with physical models, just because of the sheer number required. It would have taken at least a day to shoot each individual model, and the compositing time would have taken forever. The Emmy-winning episode was remarkable for its time, and still looks great.

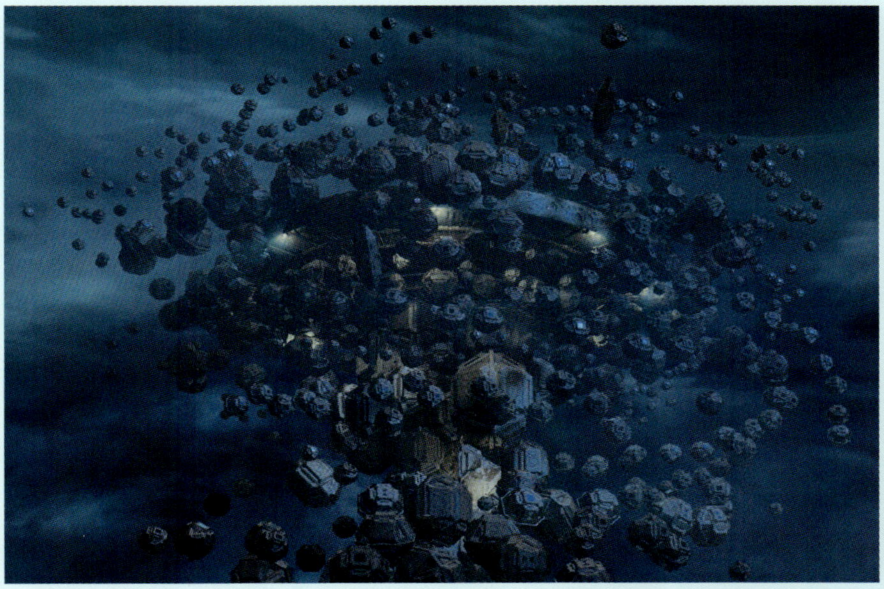

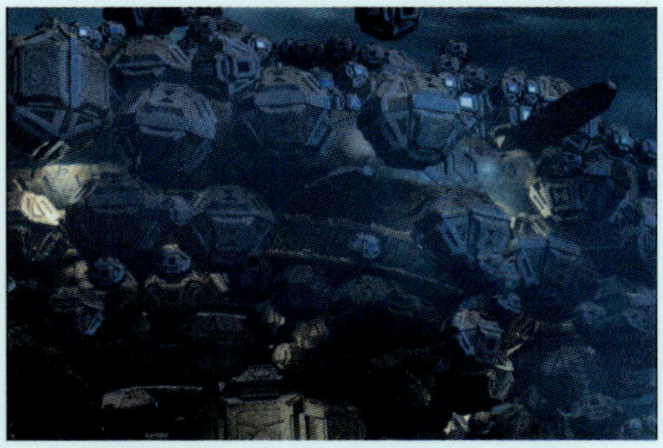

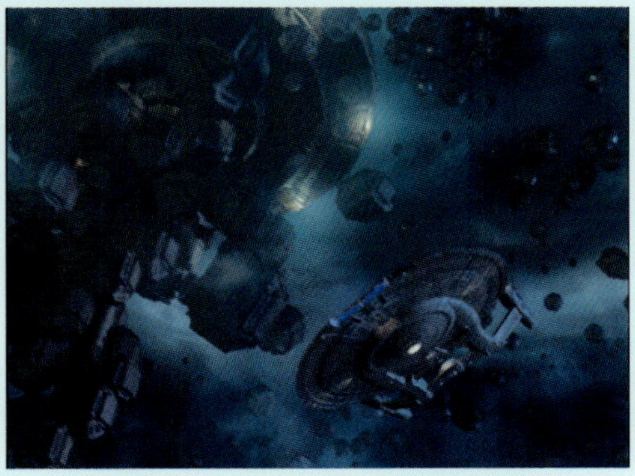

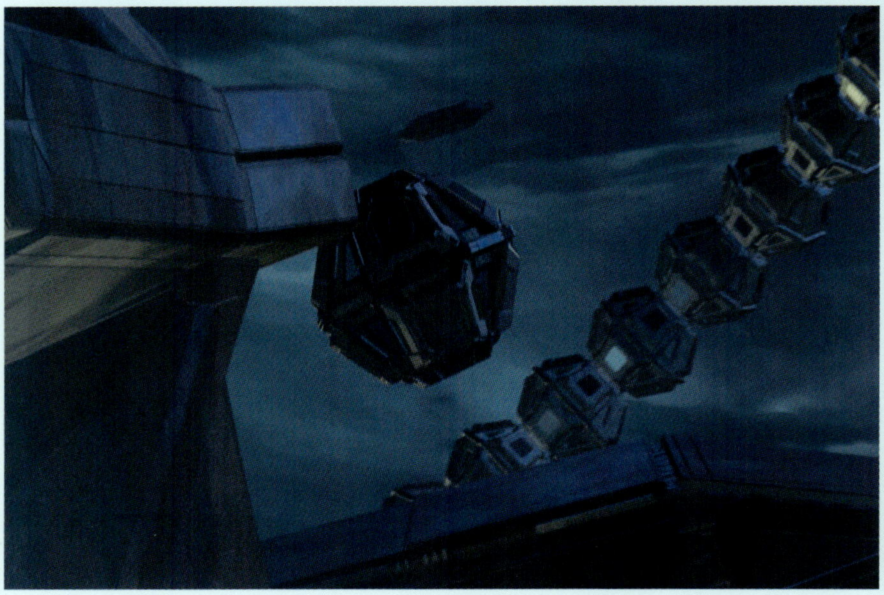

LEFT AND ABOVE: The CG team at Foundation Imaging did an incredible job creating the exceptionally complex Suliban Helix sequence animated by talented CG artist Koji Kuramura. The number of pods in this constantly roiling gaseous atmosphere made this a significant achievement in art, math, and technology.

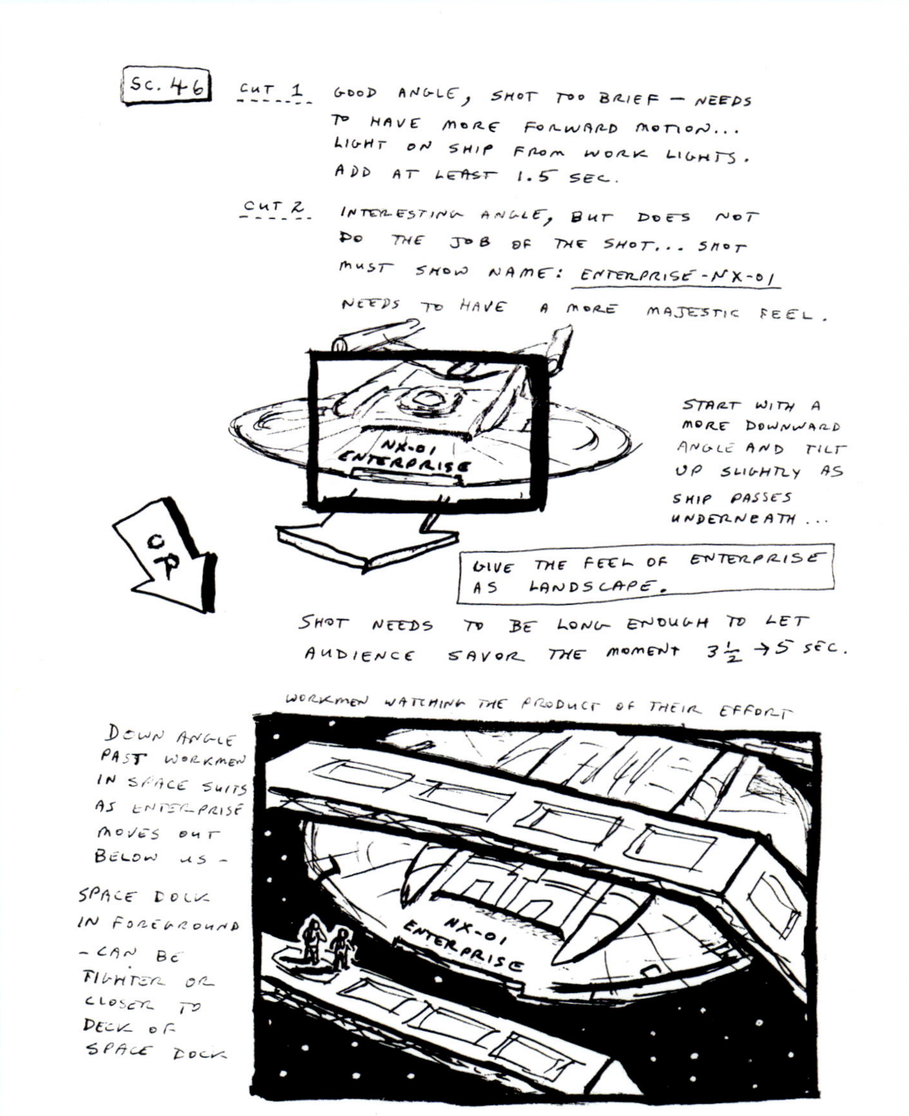

INSIDE STORY

LAUNCHING THE NX-01

The launch of the NX-01 is one of my favorite sequences in *Star Trek*. When I envisioned and storyboarded it I was inspired by the NASA launch footage that I'd seen on TV. I really wanted to include those little spacemen to give that shot a sense of scale, as I was thinking about those old stills you see of construction workers building skyscrapers in the 1930s—seeing a guy standing on a girder gives a sense of how huge everything is. The launch is a testament to the excellence of Foundation Imaging's digital artists who worked on the sequence, especially Pierre Drolet, who built the digital model of the NX-01 and the drydock, which he also designed.

LEFT: Having little time to spare, I did the storyboards hastily, just adequate to communicate what I envisioned to our CG artists.

BELOW: It was important that the scenes flowed progressively, and smoothly inter-cut with director James Conway's live-action scenes shot on the bridge of the NX-01. All VFX shots were there to serve the story.

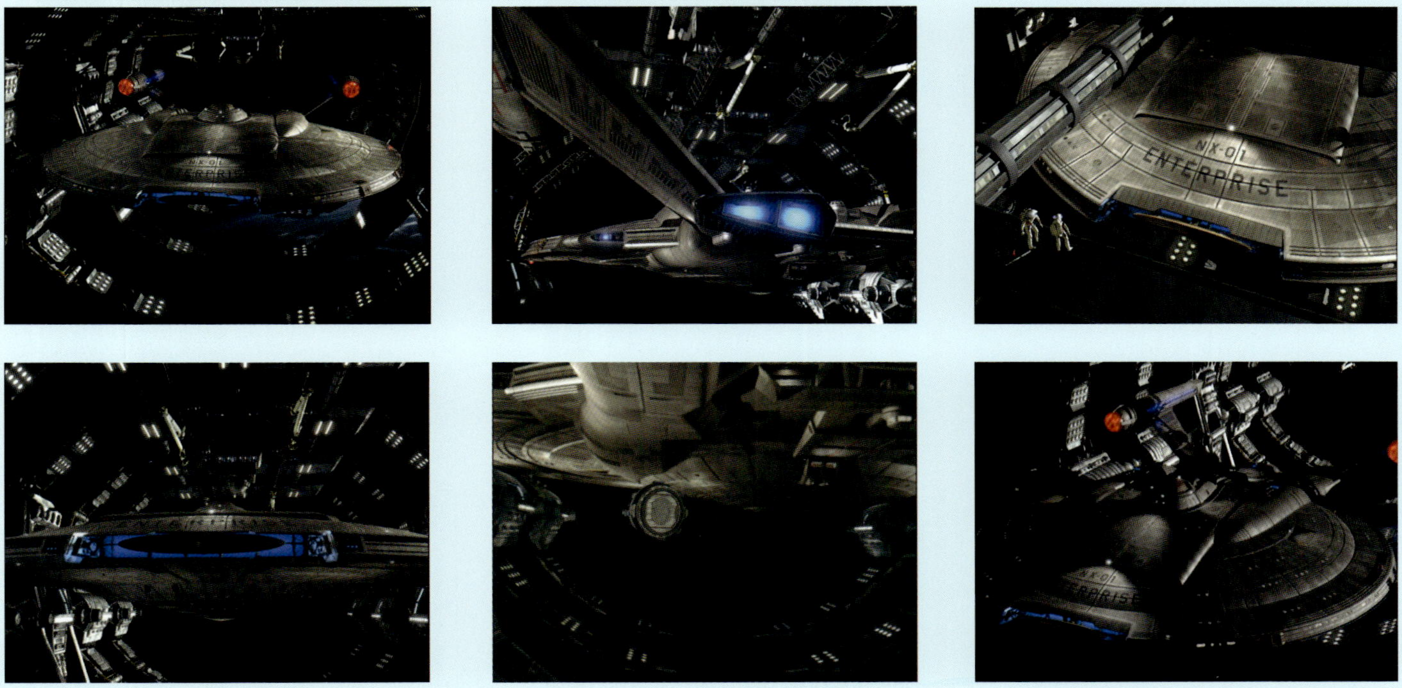

INSIDE STORY

THE DIGITAL NX-01

We wanted a super-high-resolution model of our hero ship so we could get really close to it on screen. When we first started building CG ships, the models were nowhere near as convincing as the physical models made by Tony Meininger and Greg Jein. But now CG technology had advanced. Texturing had improved, making a huge difference in believability. The processing power of computers had increased exponentially, so models could be more detailed, and rendering would be faster.

Collaborating with production designer Herman Zimmerman, Doug Drexler designed the *Enterprise* NX-01 and prepared a CG study model for the producers to review. We brought the design to Foundation Imaging's Pierre Drolet, who created an absolutely brilliant digital model of the starship. Pierre added personal touches like coved seams and other details to Doug's design. Pierre's meticulous modeling allowed us to choreograph shots that brought the virtual camera very close to the hull for 'paint scraper' fly-bys.

Even so, we could still only get so close to the NX-01 before image quality became unacceptable. There were only so many pixels on the model. When we needed to show shuttles launching, grapplers shooting out, or anything else in close-up, Pierre modeled separate high-resolution detailed sections for specific scenes.

RIGHT: The CG version of the ship allowed us to have moving parts and close-up sections for special scenes.

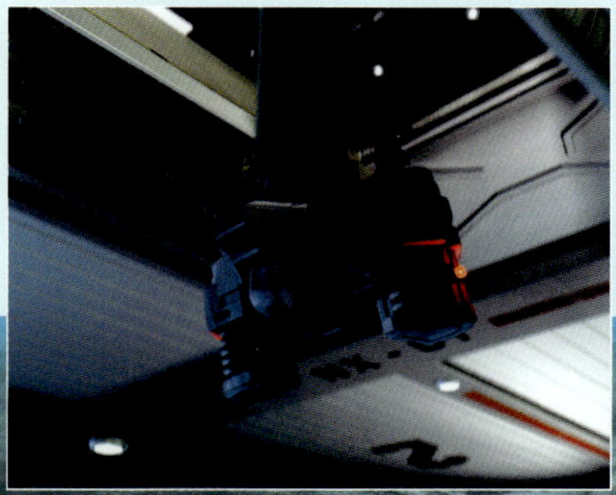

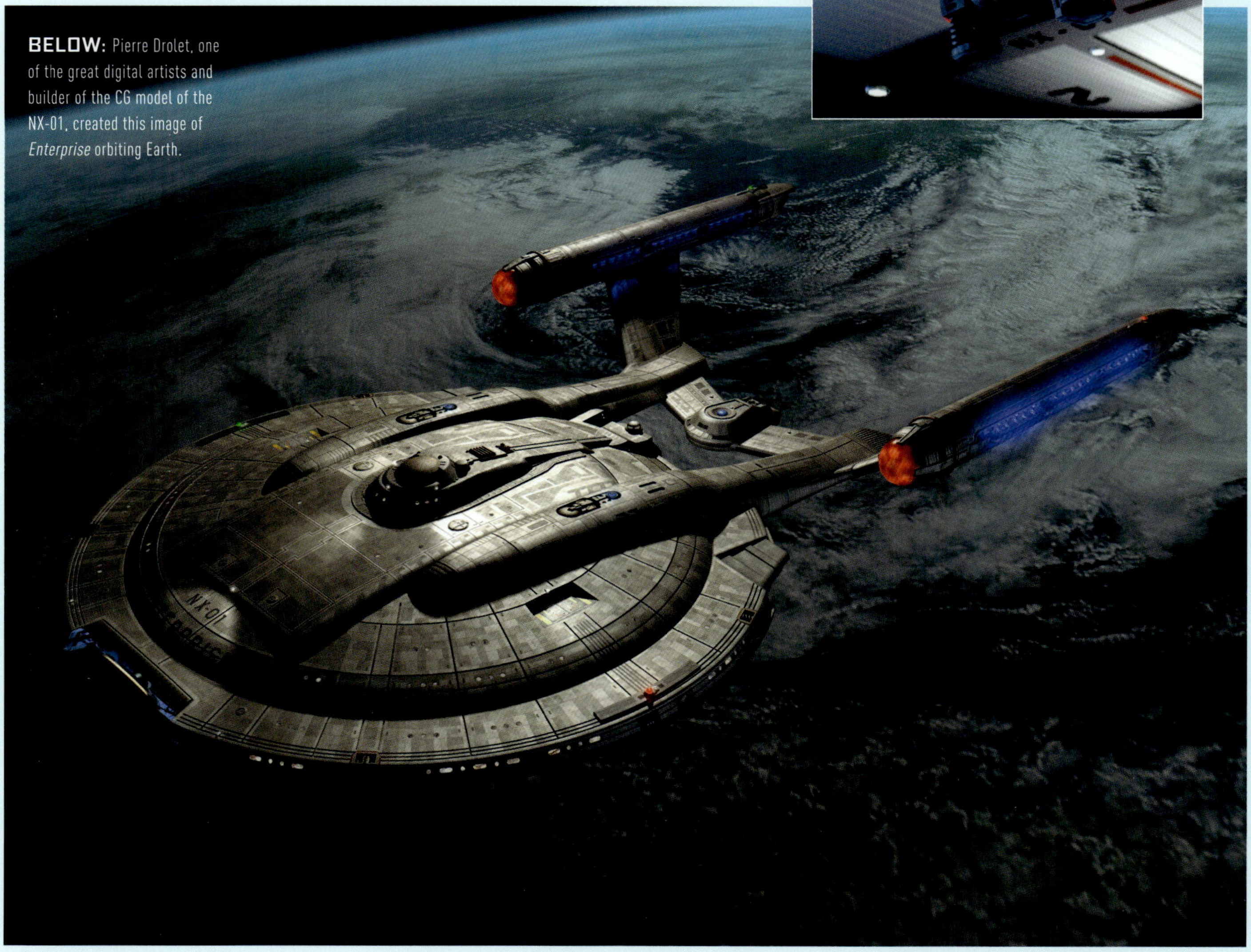

BELOW: Pierre Drolet, one of the great digital artists and builder of the CG model of the NX-01, created this image of *Enterprise* orbiting Earth.

Image by Pierre Drolet

INSIDE STORY

THE PHYSICAL NX-01

We always say that there was never a physical model of the NX-01. That's not exactly true. When we were shooting 'Broken Bow' there's a sequence when Trip and Captain Archer are in a pod, inspecting the NX-01. We had a full-sized version of the pod that was adapted from the nose cone of Zefram Cochrane's ship, the *Phoenix,* from *First Contact*. Scott and Connor were sitting in the pod, and they are supposed to be looking at the underside of the saucer. Scott asked, "Where am I? I need a sense of the geography." So I went over to the craft service table, and picked up two paper plates. Fortunately, there was a plan view of the ship on the stage, so I looked at that, and cut out the body of the ship from a piece of foam core, slid it between the paper plates, taped it all together, and folded the nacelles up. That was the first physical model of the NX-01. I held it up to Scott and Connor, and showed them where they were supposed to be. It made a big difference to them. I gave Scott that model. Then Doug Drexler and Mike Okuda in the art department made me a better foam core one that I used as reference for doing storyboards.

BELOW: The foam core model made for me by the art department was invaluable for helping me visualize shots when storyboarding.

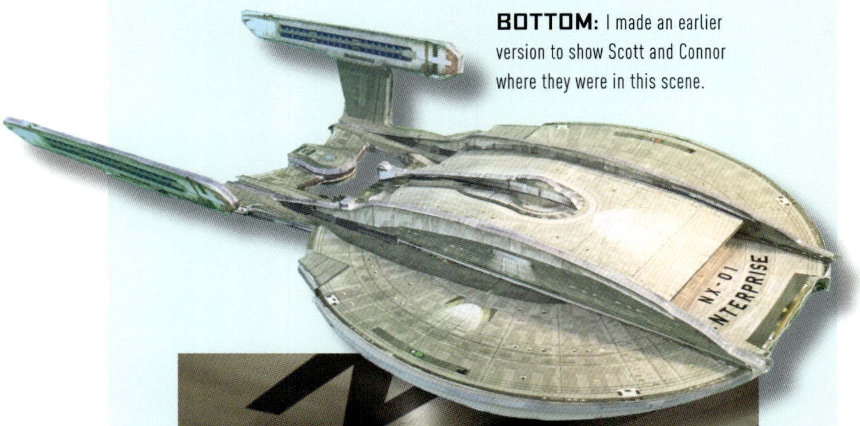

BOTTOM: I made an earlier version to show Scott and Connor where they were in this scene.

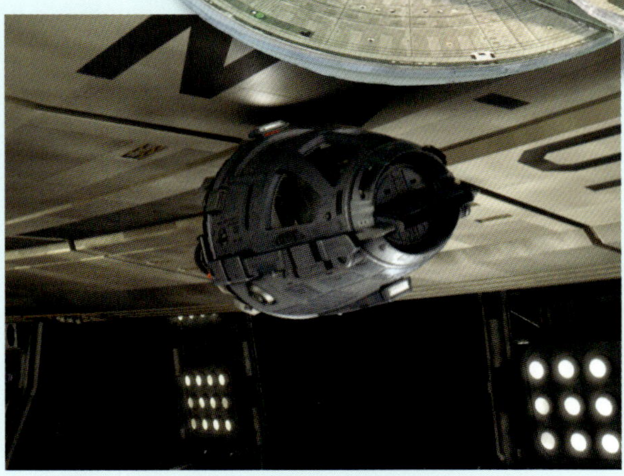

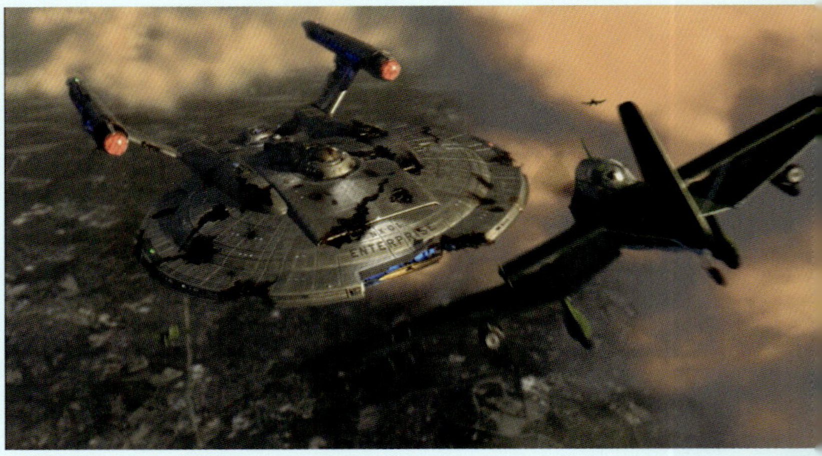

ABOVE: Alien-enhanced Stukas attack the NX-01 over 1940s-era New York City.

In our final season, *Enterprise* won the international Visual Effects Society award for Best Broadcast Visual Effects (especially meaningful for me since I co-designed the statuette). The winning episode was 'Storm Front, Part II,' a story where the crew traveled back in time to an Earth where the Nazis, with alien help, have won World War II and occupied the US. I think we won because there was such a wide range of effects in it. It's an episode that VFX supervisor Ron Moore, coordinator David Takemura, the VFX team and I are especially proud of.

It opens with a newsreel showing Hitler in New York. We intended to make it look like an authentic 1940s newsreel shot on grainy 16mm film. We found a newsreel of Hitler in Paris, and replaced the Eiffel Tower with the Statue of Liberty, using old 16mm film with matching grain. Then we showed Hitler on the observation deck of the Empire State Building. We looked through stock images, but couldn't find a perfect angle from the 1940s, so in Photoshop I took a photo from the 50s, made it black and white, painted out all the people and any buildings that were built after 1939, and added in the binocular stands. Then I eyeballed the angle we needed to shoot the Nazis on green screen to match scale and perspective for compositing into the shot.

The big sequence was a fight over Manhattan between the NX-01 and alien enhanced Stukas. Collaborating with director David Straiton, I prepared detailed storyboards for the terrific CG artists at EdenFX. Led by in-house supervisor Fred Pienkos, Eden's team included Pierre Drolet, eddie Robinson, and Sean Scott. They built a digital 3D model of Manhattan. We evolved the CG animation with wireframes as they require little rendering time and adjustments are quick and easy. At that stage all you are looking for is choreography. Once finalized, Eden's artists

INSIDE STORY

STORM FRONT

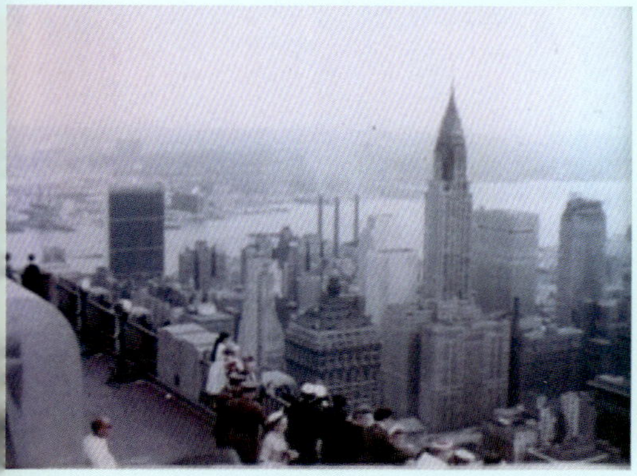

ABOVE: Original 1950s photo of the Empire State Building's Observation Deck.

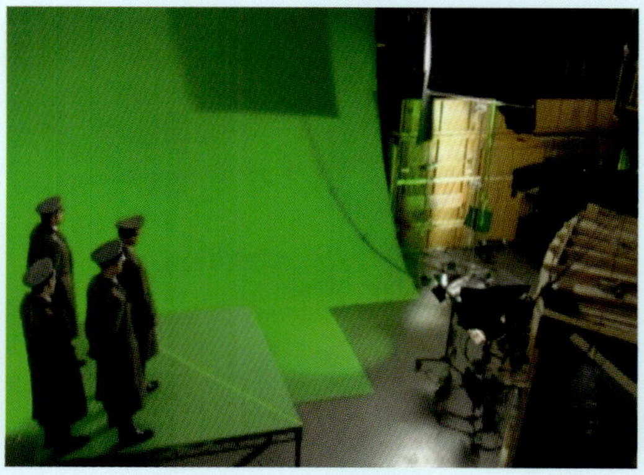

ABOVE: Actors playing the Nazis are filmed on green-screen in 'eyeballed' matching perspective.

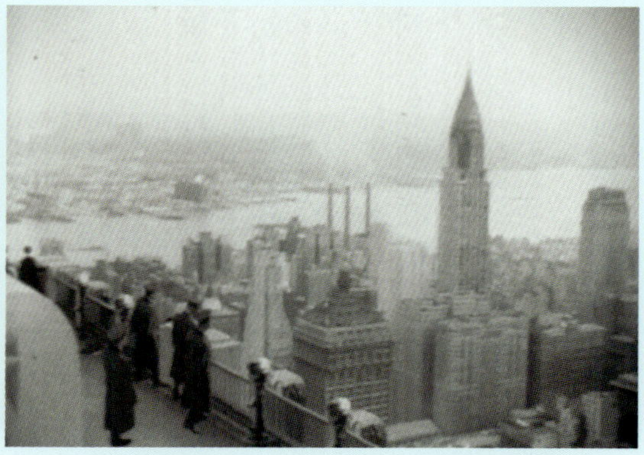

ABOVE: Composite of actors on Observation Deck with original people and newer buildings painted out and binocular stands painted in.

prepared a 'smooth shade' that the editors could cut in. We put in text balloons showing where explosions would occur so the sound designers could start their work. We added a squadron of planes to a shot we filmed outside a sound stage after removing parts of the building and awning so we could see more sky. 2D compositing and effects animation were done by Paul Hill and Greg Rainoff at Technicolor Creative Services.

Finally, we created a unique ethereal effect for a sequence where Captain Archer is outside the normal time/space continuum. That kind of variety was typical for us, and showed the range of skills of the VFX team. The award we won was in recognition of everyone who worked on the show; a chain is only as strong as its weakest link.

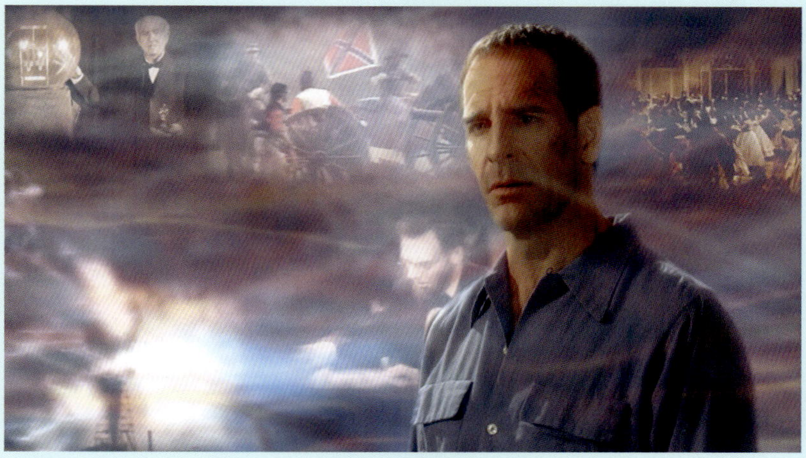

ABOVE: Scott Bakula as Captain Archer outside the normal space-time continuum, seeing history unfold around him. Scott was photographed on green-screen and the background imagery was created in the edit bay.

BELOW: Wire frames are used to plot out CG animated sequences because adjustments can be made quickly.

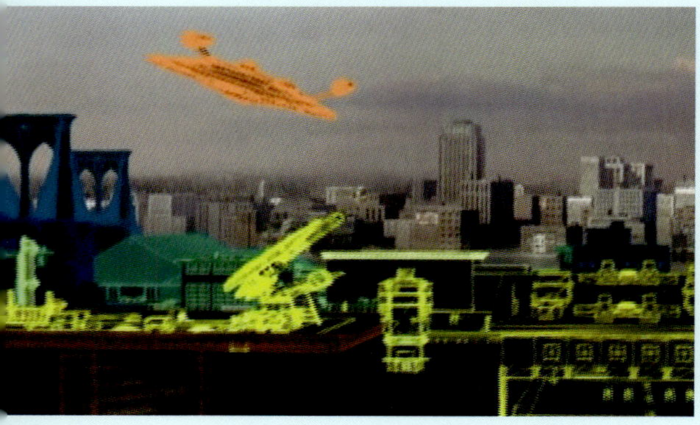

BELOW: A quickly rendered smooth shade is done for the editors and sound department.

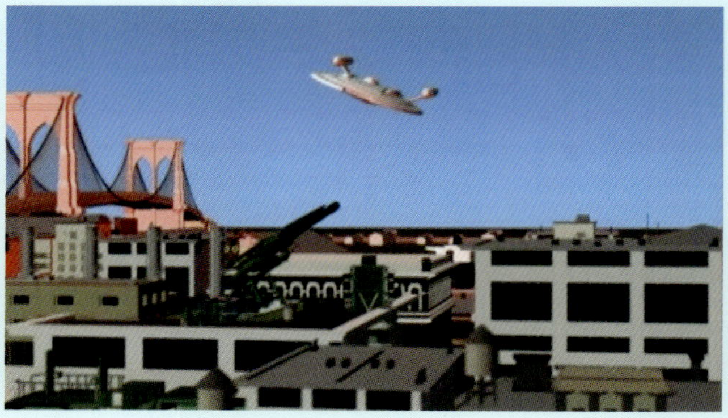

BELOW: The fully rendered composite is time consuming, so we don't want people to wait for it.

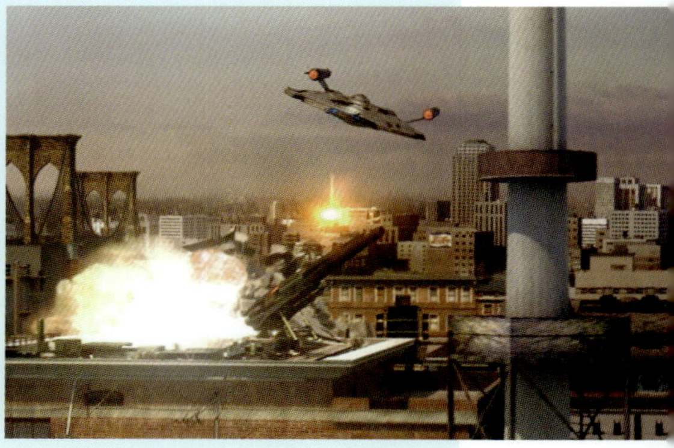

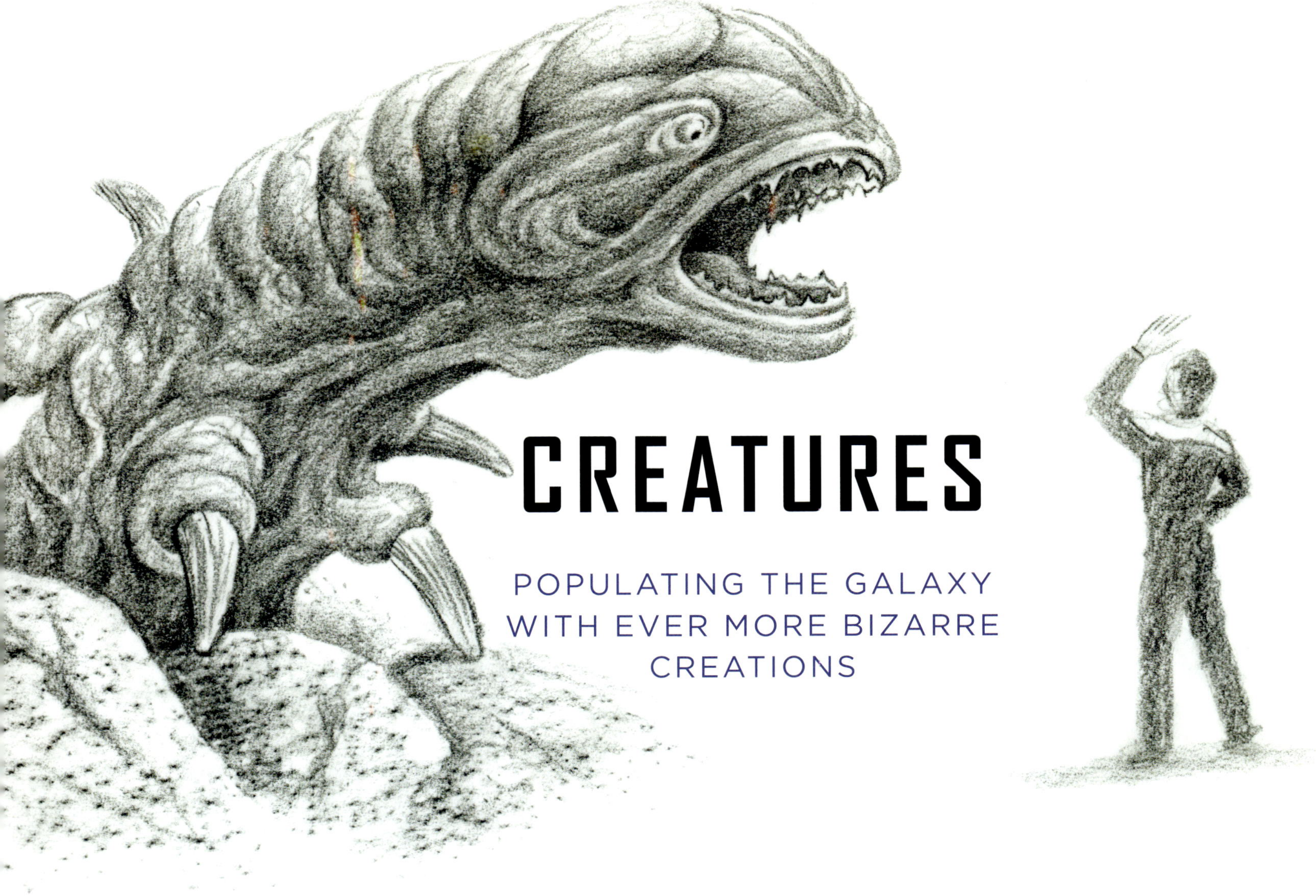

CREATURES

POPULATING THE GALAXY WITH EVER MORE BIZARRE CREATIONS

Charles Darwin was exploring an island in the South Pacific when he came across a unique kind of flower that he had never seen before. He started to think about what a bird would look like if it had evolved to feed on this flower, and he did a sketch of this imaginary bird. A few days later they found a bird that looked exactly like the drawing.

I thought about that whenever I was designing a creature for *Star Trek*. Once you imagine the environment that something lives in, you can start to think about what it would need to survive, what kind of food source it would need, and what it would do for energy. Things are much more convincing when they make evolutionary sense.

For example, in the *Voyager* episode 'Basics,' the crew is marooned on a planet where they encounter a massive worm-like creature living in a cave. I thought it would be cool if it was kind of snakelike so it could slither through narrow passages. That meant that it would need a way to propel itself, so I gave it a radially symmetrical series of clawed appendages that it could use to move itself along. We never had a need to feature it in the show, but I also gave it an air bladder that it could expand like a puffer fish. The idea was that if it wanted to hold itself in a vertical shaft, it would just blow itself up and be very comfortable there. Todd Masters sculpted that creature for us based on my sketches.

ABOVE: Pencil sketch showing the final version of the Hanonian land eel's head in scale with a human crewmember.

Most of the alien creatures on *Star Trek* were created by the brilliant Michael Westmore and his makeup department, but every now and again the script would call for something that we did in VFX. I've spent a lifetime watching creature films, and I love designing creatures myself. Creatures, particularly CG ones, can be very complicated, and one of the best things about doing them is that you work with an incredible team of people who have the talent and skills to bring them to life.

In the early days, before we could use CG, if a creature couldn't be made by putting someone in a costume the entity would have to be either a puppet or stop-motion. We did use that technology a few times: at the end of *TNG*'s 'Conspiracy,' when the mother alien burst out of Remmick's chest, that was a hand puppet operated by prop master Alan Sims. In the same episode, David Stipes animated a small stop-motion puppet of an alien parasite that scuttled across the floor and up Remmick's arm. We made another version of the parasite with a hollow tail that fit over the actor's tongue so he could pretend to swallow it.

We also used a hand puppet in 'Realm of Fear' when Barclay

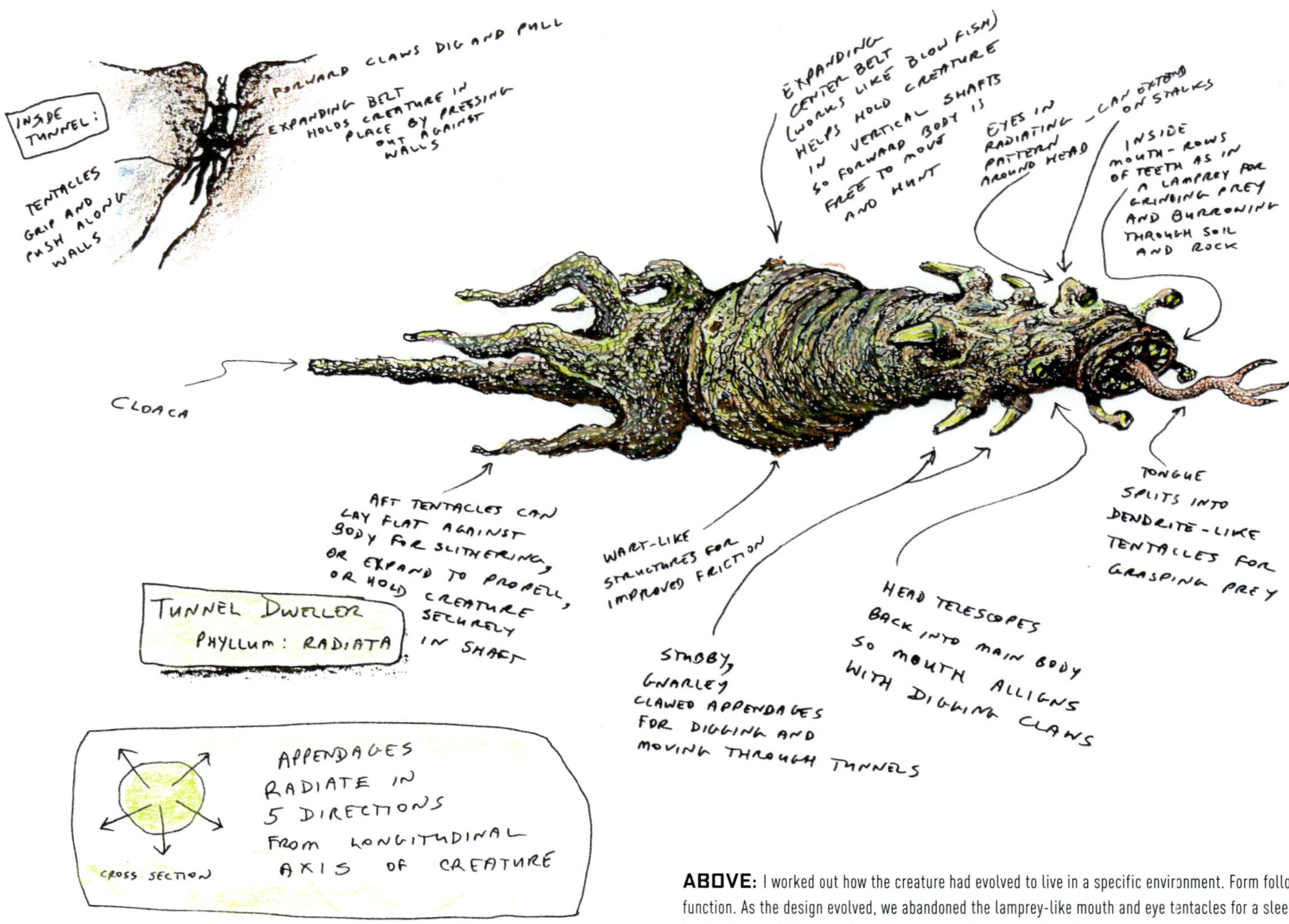

ABOVE: I worked out how the creature had evolved to live in a specific environment. Form follows function. As the design evolved, we abandoned the lamprey-like mouth and eye tentacles for a sleeker head and extendable neck that could more easily squeeze through narrow passages.

RIGHT: Color pencil sketch of the Hanonian land eel grabbing a snack. The equally hungry on-screen version was CG.

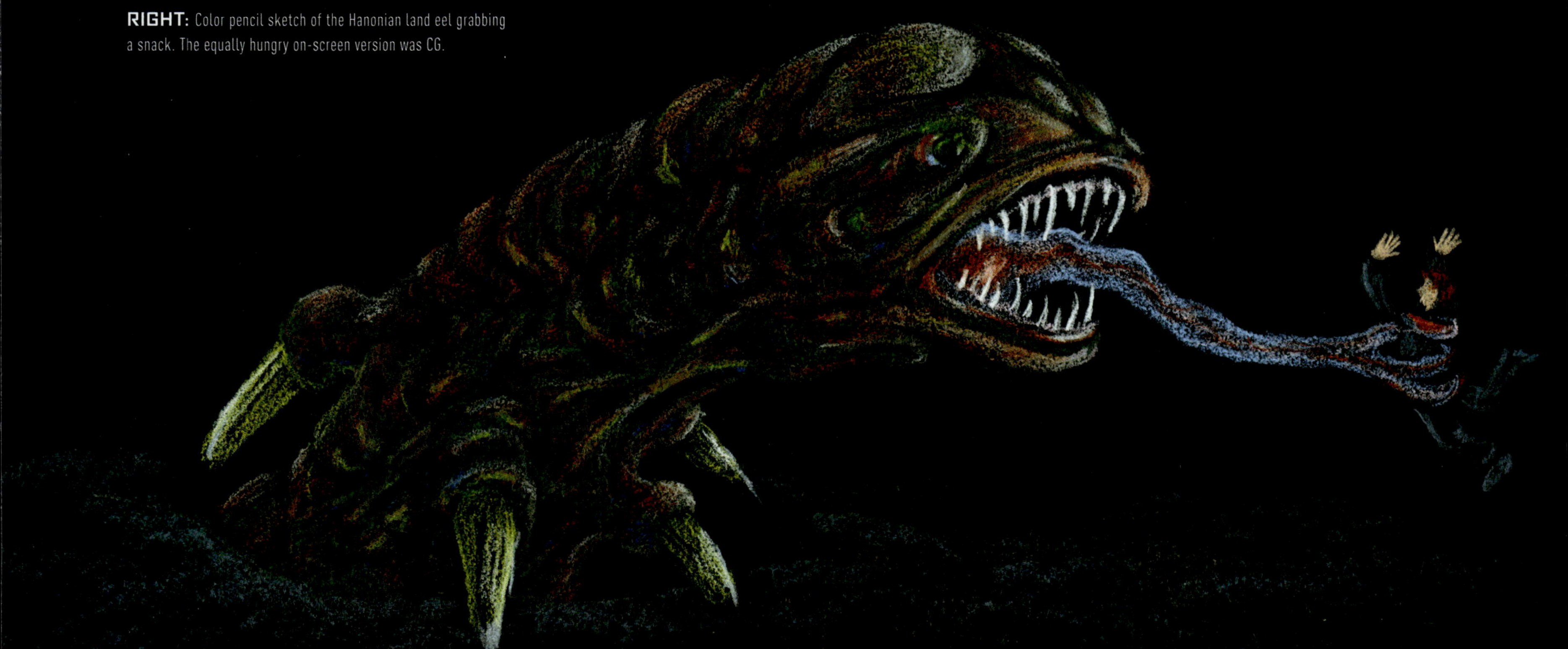

RIGHT: My sketches of dorsal and ventral views of the mother creature that Tony Meininger based his physical model on.

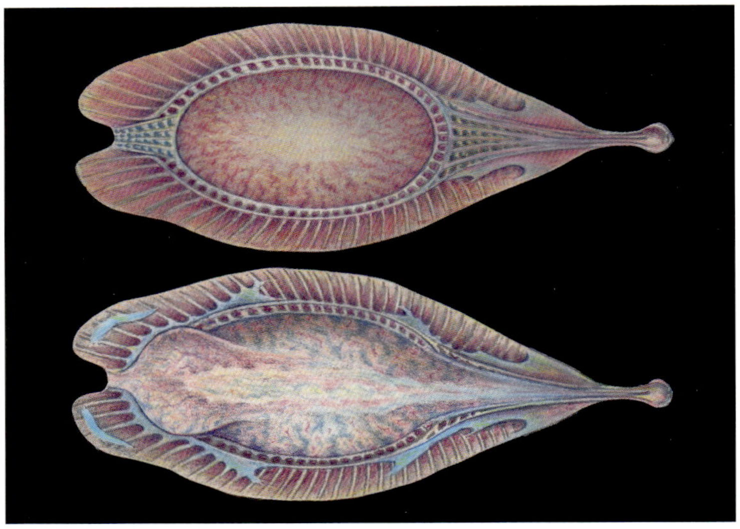

sees misshapen alien creatures in the transporter beam. I sculpted a really rough clay maquette of the creature's head. We commissioned artist Carey Howell to sculpt some more detailed maquettes. The producers picked one, then we made a latex hand puppet. I put on a green suit and stood in front of the green screen, and performed all the motions by hand. Because I'd been doing Tai Chi every day for decades, I was able to make the motion suitably smooth.

But there are limits to what you can do with puppets and stop-motion. Even in the first season of *TNG* we started to experiment with CG. When the crystalline entity attacks the *Enterprise* in 'Datalore' we decided to use CG. It was essential to the script that the entity was made of crystal. Shooting highly reflective and semi-transparent miniatures using motion control is not easy. A physical object would reflect everything around it: the mo-co stage; rig; lights; even us. Not only that, it wouldn't reflect the space and other environments where it was supposed to be because we wouldn't add them until later. Also, the entity's design, much like the branches of a tumbleweed, would be too delicate as a physical model, and it was transparent, which would make it almost impossible to separate from the background. CG was clearly the way to go, since it would allow the entity to reflect whatever virtual environment we put it in.

Where CG came into its own was when we needed to do something that would never have looked as good if we had done it practically. In the *TNG* episode 'Galaxy's Child,' the crew of the *Enterprise* accidentally kills a giant space plankton-like life form and, using phasers, performs a Caesarean procedure to save its unborn offspring. The baby then clamps on to the *Enterprise*, convinced that it's suckling its mother.

We wanted the mother's abdomen and the baby to have a sense of 'blubberiness.' We figured the adults became rigid in maturity. The mother was a physical model built by Tony Meininger, based on a sketch I provided. Tony had installed an inflatable bladder on its abdomen to add a little life, and put tracer lights around its perimeter as if the species propelled itself through the vacuum of space by expelling energy from the rim of its crenelated shell. To evoke empathy, the baby had to be cute and flexible so it could move in an endearing manner. Of course, we could have created an articulated puppet, but by that point the best way to create a cute baby that could move the way we wanted was in CG. It took a little courage on Rick and Peter's part to try what was considered experimental technology, but Rhythm & Hues had been doing some effective CG work, and it was a chance for us to get to work with them. At the time, it was a one-off creature designed to address a specific need in a script.

I designed the species based on Earth ocean plankton, but on a giant scale. I sketched the adult first, and then created the baby by 'Bambi-fying' it, making it cute by giving it a large head on a small flexible body with infant proportions. Then there were two CG models that were made by Rhythm & Hues. One CG model was of the mother's abdomen for the C-section; it had to be blubbery so the baby, which was the other CG model, could emerge from it. Even though the final model was CG, artists at R & H still went

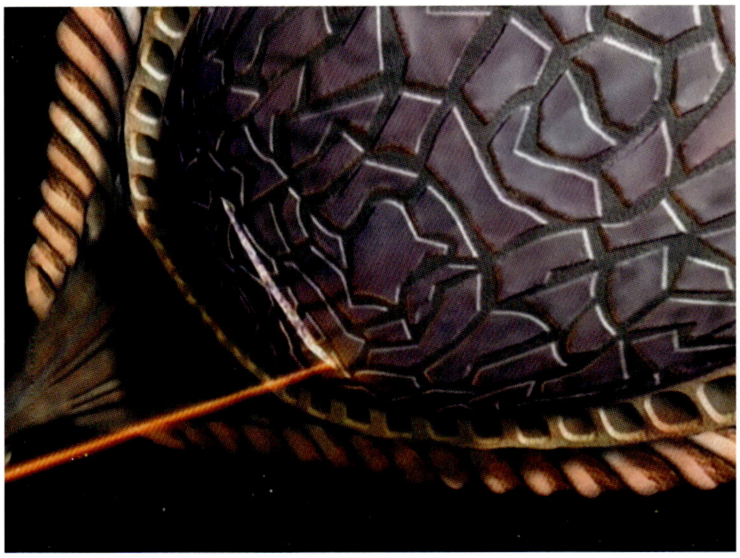

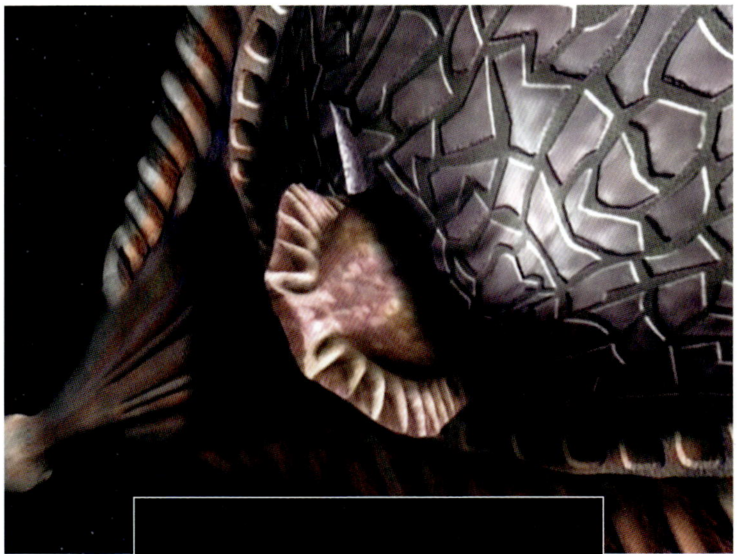

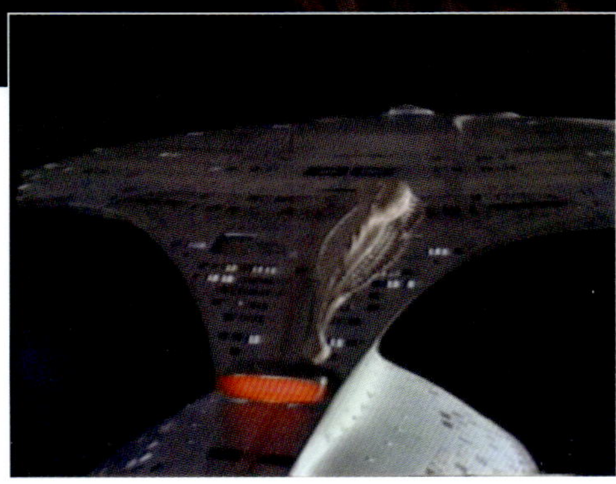

RIGHT: The *Enterprise* performs a Caesarean section on the dead mother creature to save its baby. The infant then attaches itself to the ship, believing it's its mother.

INSIDE STORY

ASSEMBLING THE BORG QUEEN

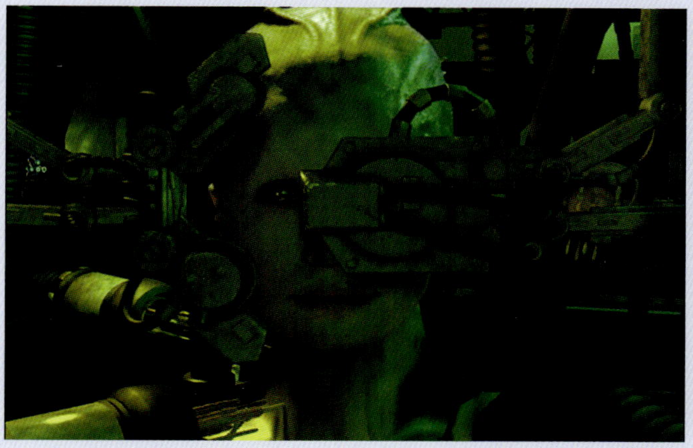

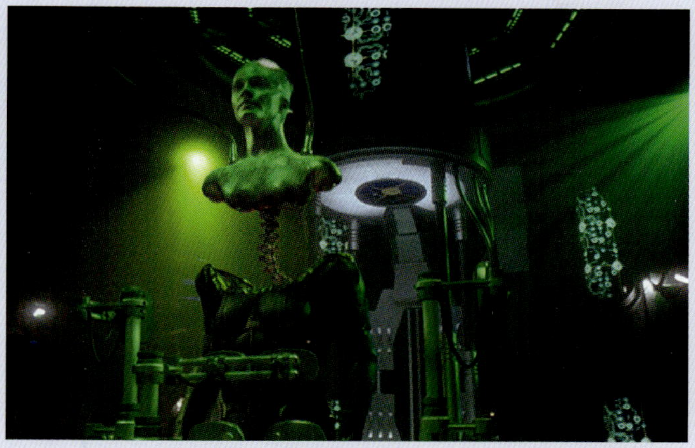

In *First Contact*, ILM's John Knoll created a brilliant sequence where we see the Borg Queen being assembled. Inspired by that, we then did two different versions on *Voyager*, in the episodes 'Dark Frontier' and 'Unimatrix Zero,' both of which were done in CG by John Teska at Foundation Imaging. The first time we did it, writer/producer Brannon Braga said he wanted to see "something new and cool." In the movie, the body is just waiting for her head to drop into it. When I looked at the set, I had the idea to design the sequence to have the floor panels open, and then her body parts would rise from below and be assembled robotically. We filmed Susanna Thompson, who played the Queen in both those episodes, against a blue screen, and separated her head and shoulders so they could be combined with a CG body. At first, I was concerned that the constantly changing light on the set would make it difficult, but the brilliance of John Teska made it work. The CG parts are the assembly mechanism and the floor. The rest of the set is real.

The next time we did the sequence, I wanted to make it different again. This time, I had the idea of seeing her head before the sequence starts, so at the beginning she's in a tiny chamber at the heart of the Borg Cube. She's plugged into the whole ship. She is the ship. Then we see her head travel through corridors before it joins her body.

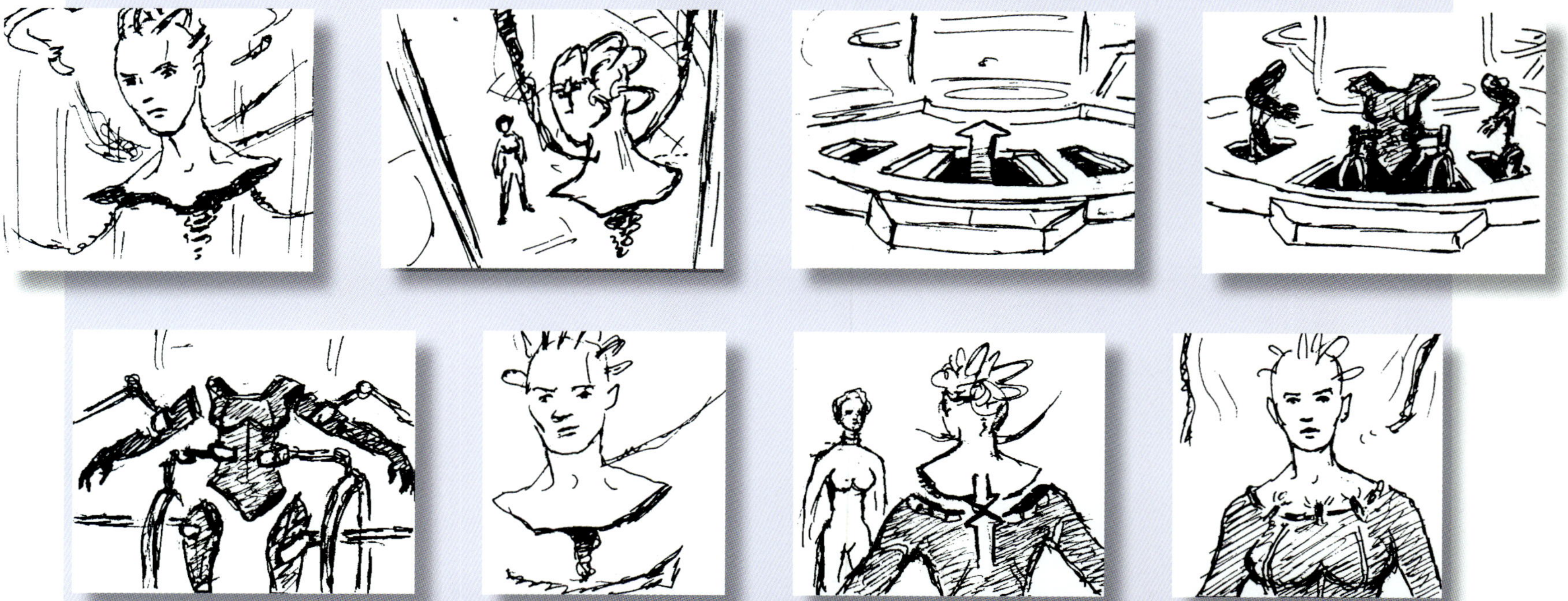

ABOVE: After walking the set I came up with these storyboards for assembling the Borg Queen, beautifully executed by excellent digital artist John Teska, who added his own creative touches.

INSIDE STORY

DISASSEMBLING THE BORG QUEEN

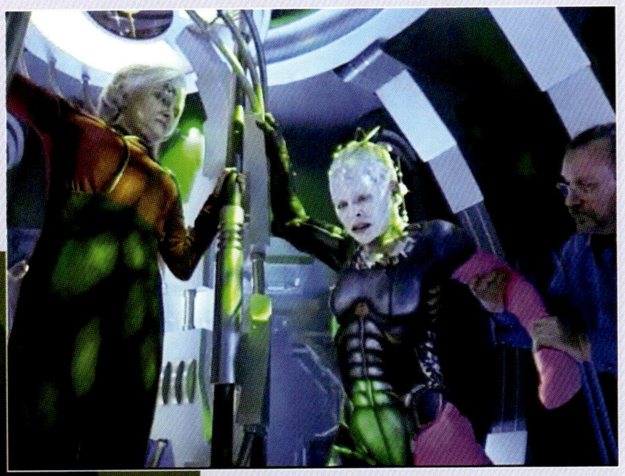

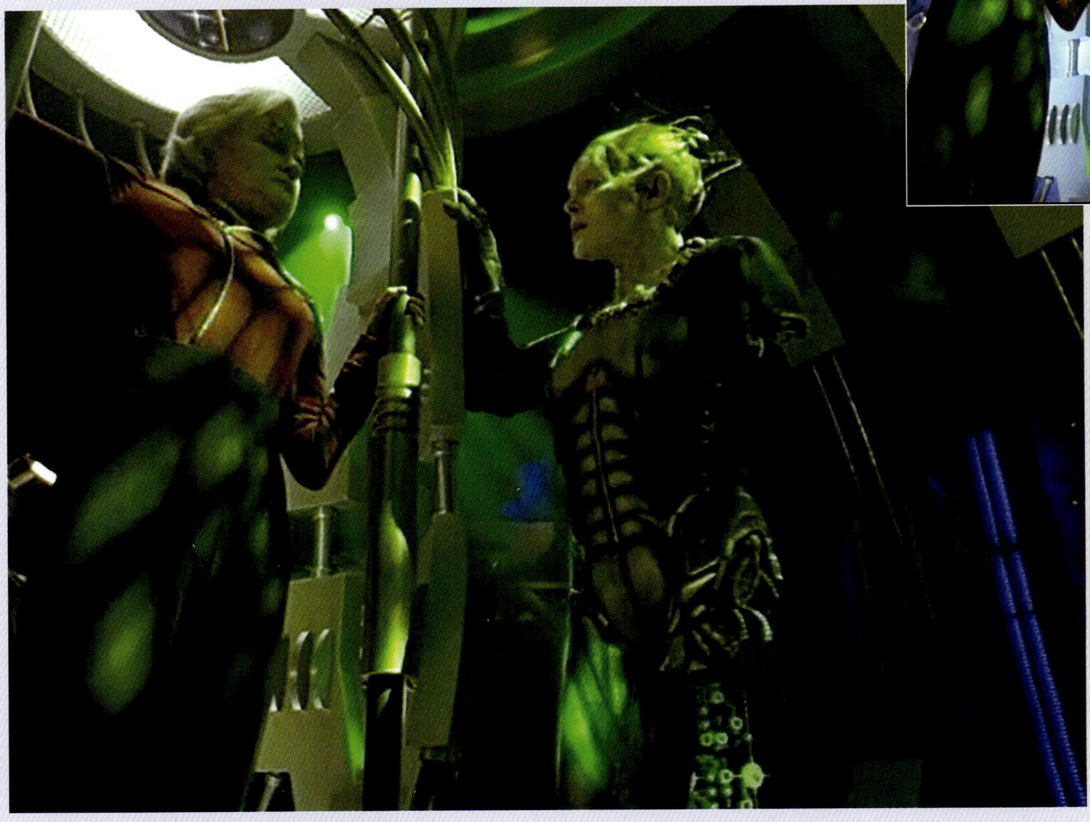

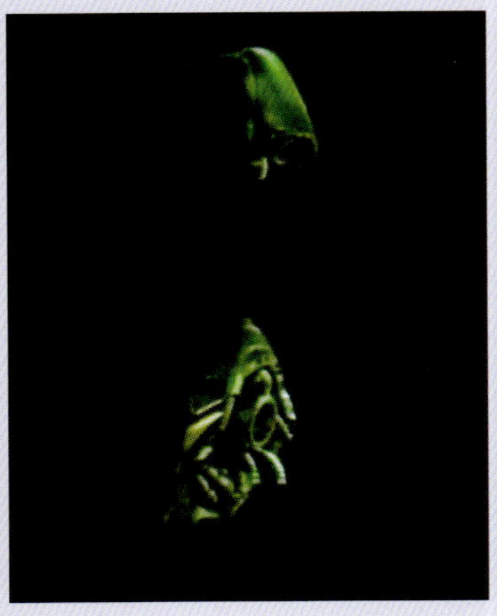

ABOVE: The 3D CG shoulder and hip structures that were tracked onto the Queen's body.

ABOVE: Captain Janeway confronts the Borg Queen. VFX artist John Teska, using the pink cloth as a guide for rotoscoping, removed her arm and leg, and replaced them with CG elements tracked to her movement in 3D.

In the last episode of *Voyager*, Janeway has a final confrontation with the Borg Queen. Thanks to some complicated time travel, an older Janeway from the future allows herself to be assimilated, thus infecting the Borg Queen with a pathogen that disrupts her, and her body starts to come apart. This time, the Borg Queen was played by Alice Krige, who had created the role in *First Contact*. We worked over a 16-hour day to get this done. Kate and Alice were such troopers, enduring long hours in incredibly uncomfortable makeup.

In the sequence, the Queen's arm starts to spark, so she tears it off and throws it to one side. Then she loses her leg before pulling herself up in an alcove to confront Janeway. Finally, she collapses on the floor. We couldn't film Alice against a blue screen because the lighting was too complicated and we would never have been able to replicate it. I put pink cloth over the parts of Alice's body to be removed. The exposure wasn't adequate to isolate that pink to allow us to digitally remove it automatically—there was too much shadow and flashing lights, but the pink showed enough to indicate exactly what area we had to rotoscope out by hand. We brightened the picture so that John Teska could see the edges, making it easier for him to cut them out frame by frame. Then John made 3D pieces that had sockets and sparking cables to cover up the areas where the Queen's limbs had been detached. He digitally attached those pieces to Alice. That couldn't be automated, so every time her body shifted and the perspective changed, John had to adjust the position of the CG pieces by hand.

Mike Westmore made a Borg Queen arm for us that Alice could toss away after she had torn it off, but for the shot showing it on the ground I wanted her hand to move, so we used Alice's real arm and removed the rest of her body. That way we could get the final death spasms of her hand, which looked creepier. John placed the CG socket on the end of the arm where it joined her shoulder.

In one of the last shots, after the Queen has lost her leg, she pulls herself up into a Borg alcove to confront Janeway. Alice had to do that without letting her 'missing' limbs cross in front of her body, as they would have been too

RIGHT: To assemble the Borg Queen, first we had to isolate her head and upper body by shooting remarkable actress Alice Krige against a blue screen.

FAR RIGHT: Next we removed her lower body in preparation for adding her torso stump and metal spine.

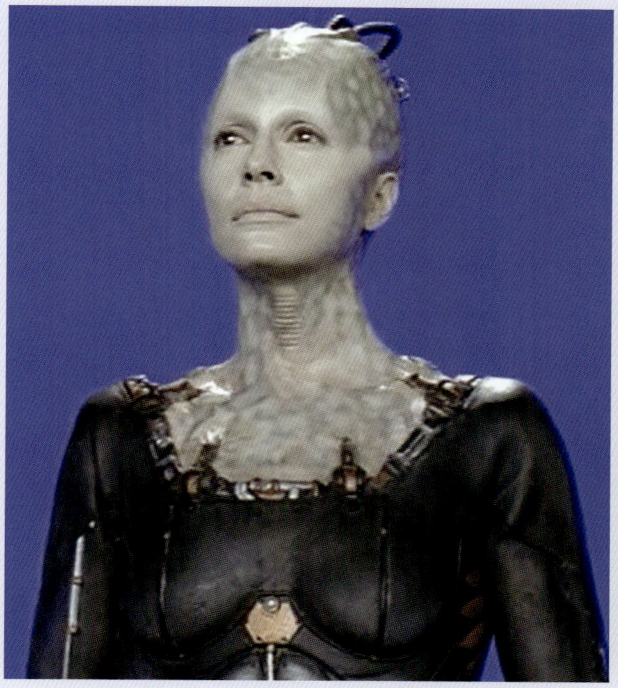

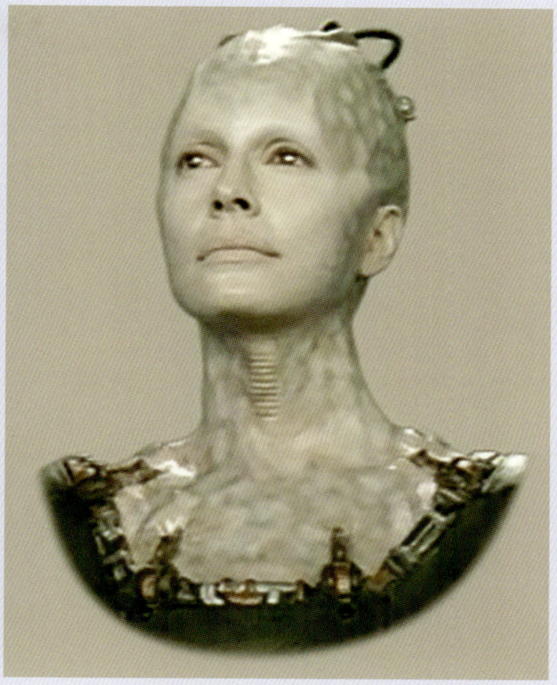

difficult to remove and replace with her torso. That was very arduous for her, so I stepped in and helped her stand. The final sequence is one of the last scenes we shot for *Voyager*, and thanks to Kate's and Alice's performances it's one of the most memorable sequences we did in all seven years.

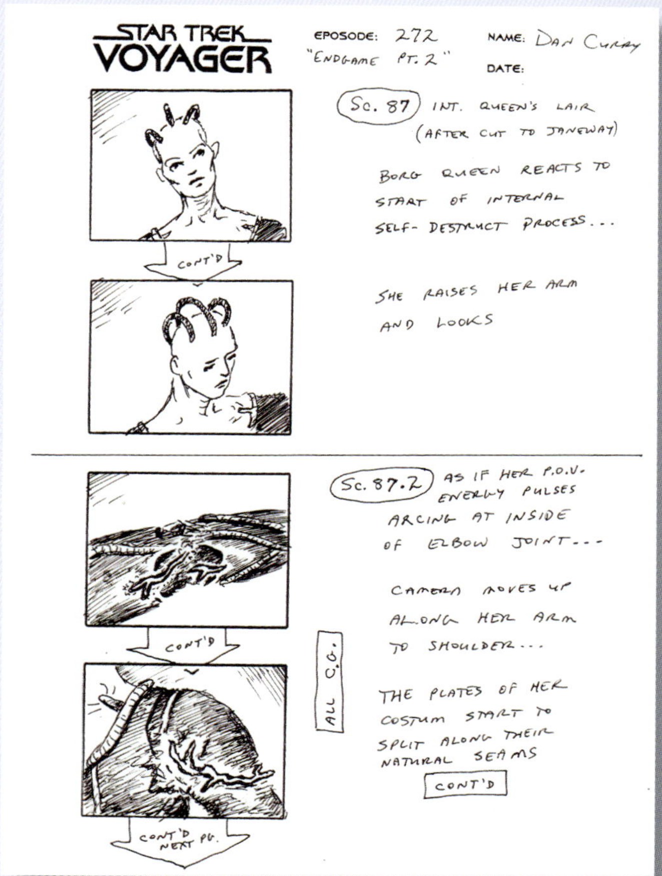

BELOW: We covered the top of the Queen's arm with pink cloth to make it easier for the artist to see and remove body parts by rotoscoping and tracking in CG stumps.

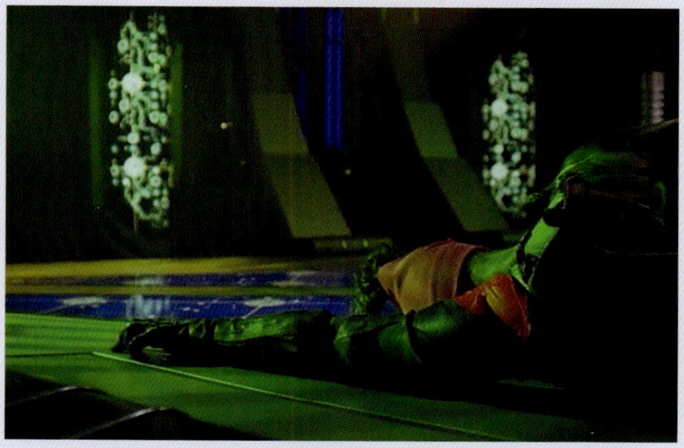

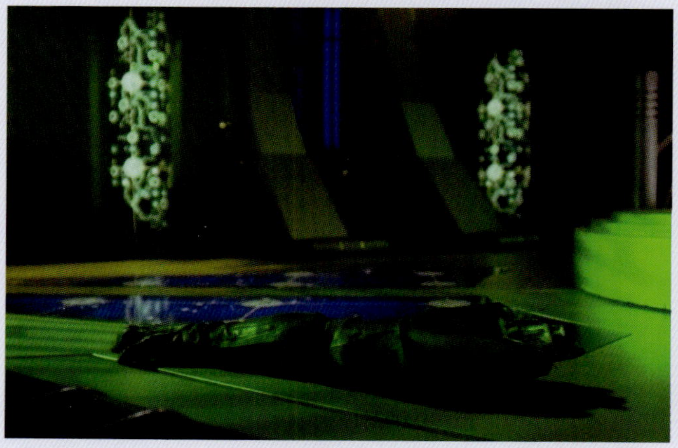

through a physical stage. They had a sculptor there who did a physical model of the right half of the creature. They scanned that, and just flopped the virtual model to make the other half.

The next time we used CG creatures was for the Odo morph effects in *DS9*. That was something that Rob Legato pioneered, and then we all evolved it as episode-specific stories required. CG transmutations were critically important because of the incredible capabilities possessed by the character portrayed by the brilliant Rene Auberjonois.

When we started to use CG for ships on *Voyager*, it was inevitable that we'd end up using it for creatures as well. The writers were aware of the new possibilities presented by using CG because they could see what was happening in features and other productions. They would talk about it when we discussed possibilities for upcoming episodes. Of course, Rick and Peter

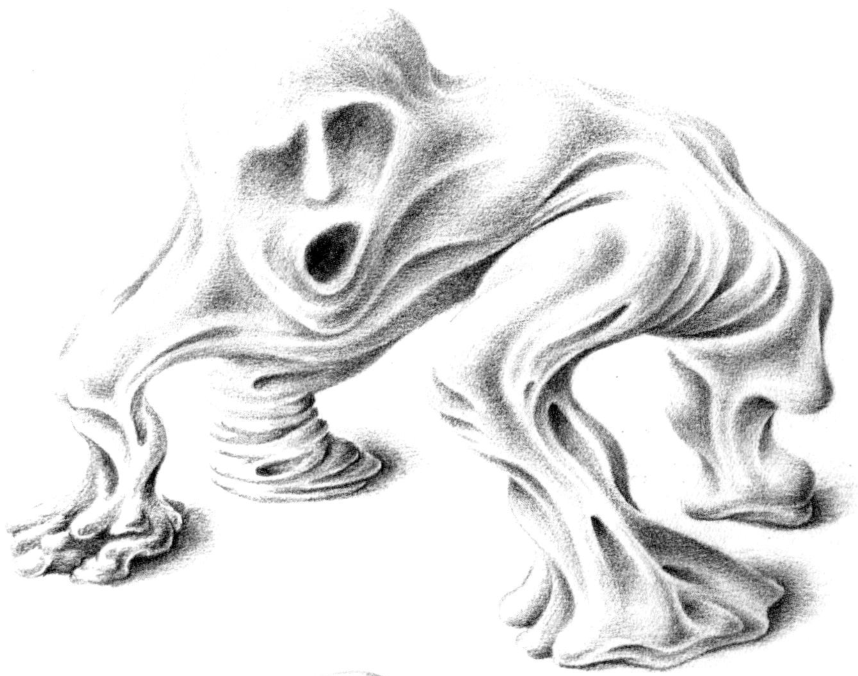

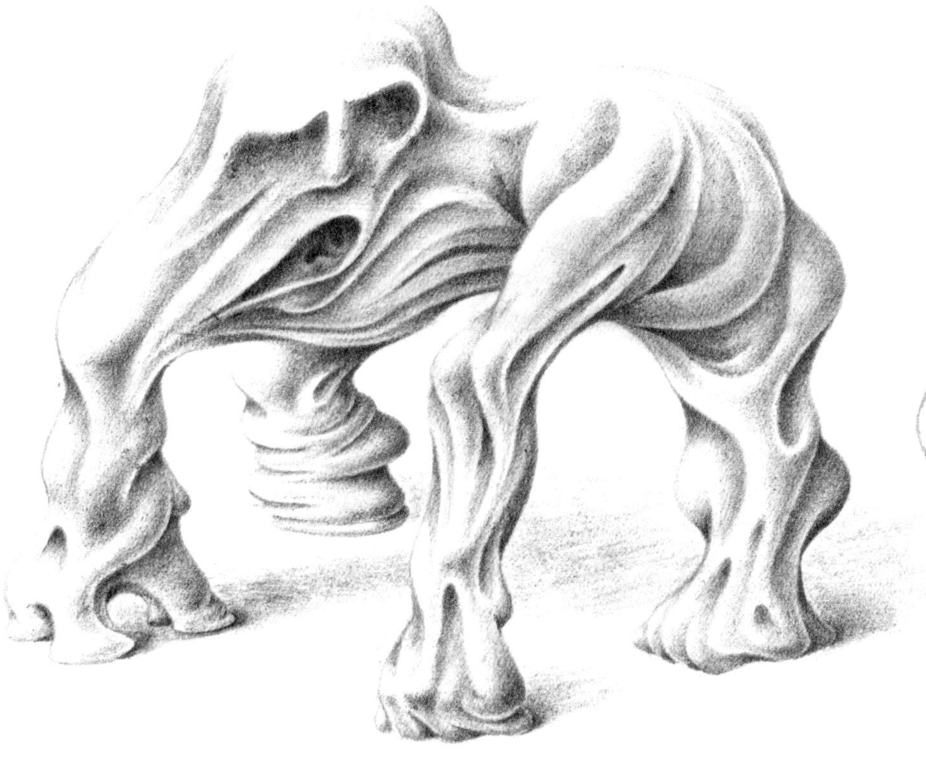

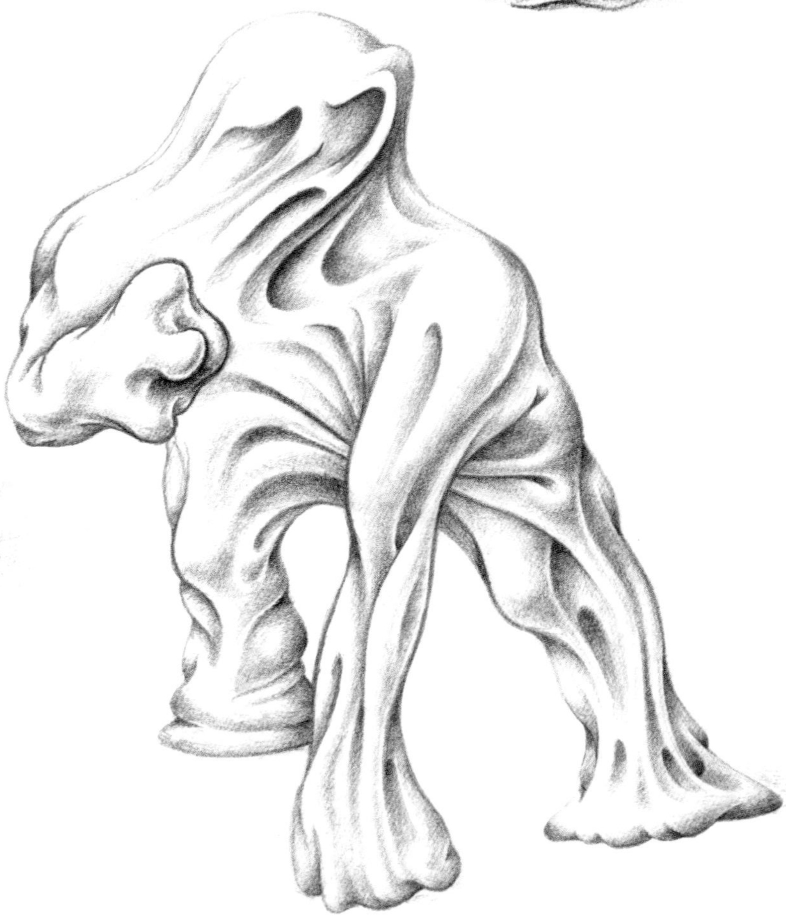

ABOVE: My pencil sketches imagining stages of a Founder morphing from human form into another, nicknamed 'Taffy Man' by my colleagues.

were eager to explore the technology and what it could do for us.

The *Voyager* episode 'Macrocosm' helped to prove that we could put a convincing CG creature in an environment where it interacts with actors. In the story, our crew desperately fends off an attack by a plague of basketball-sized viruses. I designed the macroviruses, loosely based on terrestrial single-celled organisms called diatoms. The CG versions could fly about. For the shots when we needed to show the viruses being destroyed by phasers, the special-effects department made matching corridors, which they painted black. We had large-scale physical models of the viruses, which we packed with explosives and blew up. We lined them up with the CG versions and switched them at the last moment.

Captain Janeway has a close encounter with some viruses. In one scene, Kate had to stab one and leave the knife in the creature as it fluttered to the floor. In order to get the shot, I held a blue Styrofoam ball and used it to menace Kate. Once Kate had stabbed the ball, we removed the part of the picture that I was in, and replaced the ball with a CG macrovirus, so now it looked as if the knife was stuck in the creature rather than a piece of Styrofoam. In another part of the scene, Janeway was on the floor as a virus hovered over her and repeatedly tried to sting her. This also involved me attacking Kate. This time I stood just out of frame, and jabbed at her with a prop

INSIDE STORY

DISMEMBERING THE BORG

At the end of *Voyager*'s third season the crew discovers that there is something even more terrifying than the Borg. Species 8472 is so dangerous that after invading a Borg Cube they tore apart dozens of Borg drones and piled up the pieces in a corridor, creating a powerful and unnerving image. Our production problem was that we didn't have the time or budget to build a full-scale pile of dismembered body parts. We could have done it in CG, but that would have been expensive. I had a much simpler and cheaper solution.

At the time, you could buy highly detailed, excellently sculpted Borg action figure toys. I took a number of these five-inch Borg and cut them up with a Dremmel. Serendipitously, the heat from the friction of the cutting tool partially melted the plastic, giving the dismembered parts the look of strangely desiccated tissue. Since the action figures were already nicely painted, all I had to do was paint the cut sections red to indicate blood. When I had enough pieces, I stacked up the body parts and glued them together.

On set, I described to our director David Livingston and the cast where the pile of dead Borg parts would be, and how much space it would occupy. When they blocked the scene they knew sightlines and not to walk where the Borg bodies would be. Fortunately, Marvin Rush planned to light the set with minimal lights, with lots of artificial smoke for atmosphere. Darkness and diffusion would be our friends. I photographed the miniature pile of bodies against a blue screen, carefully matching Marvin's original lighting, lenses, and camera angles. Then it was a relatively simple matter for our VFX compositing editor to confirm the correct scale, and add them to the scene.

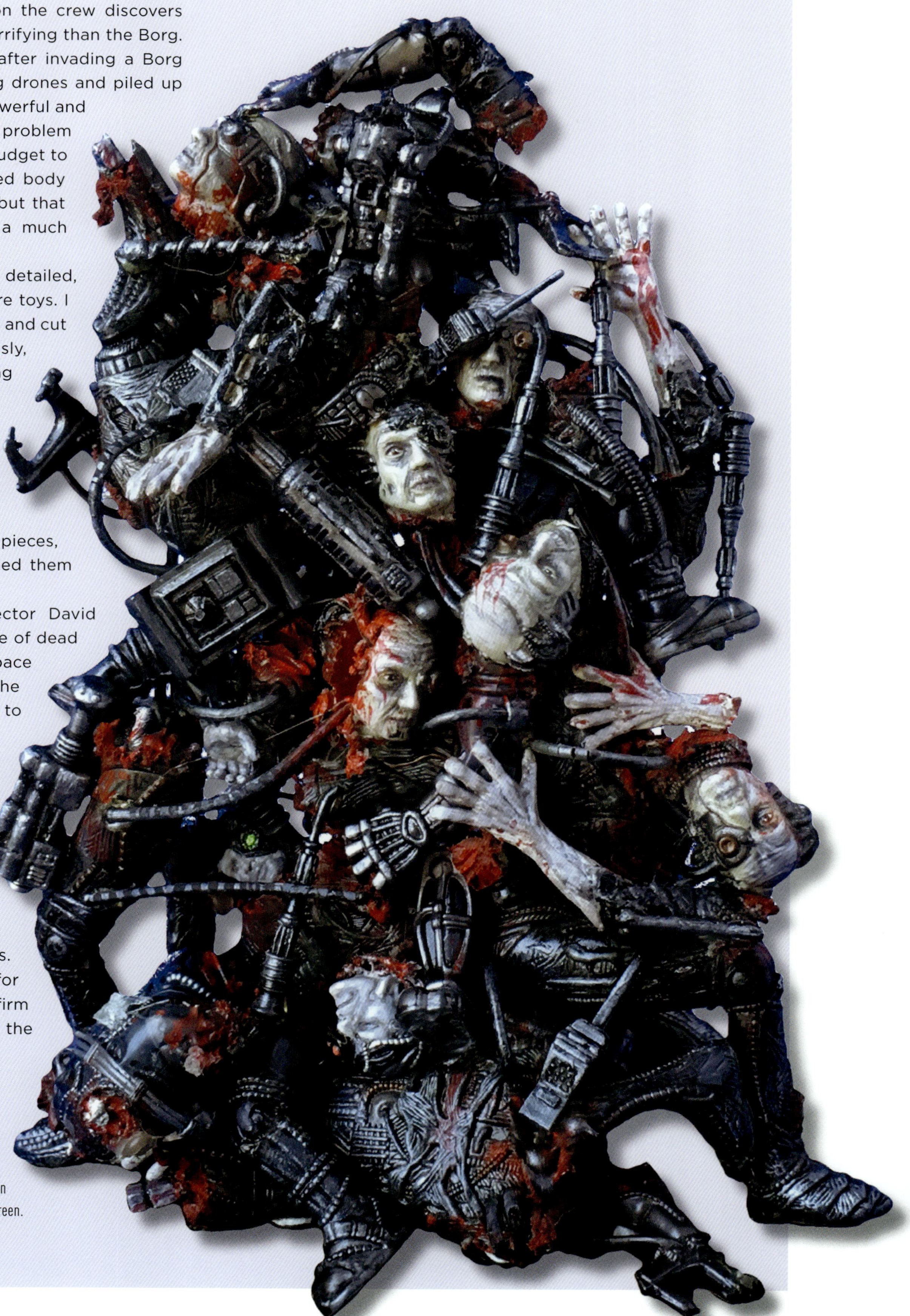

RIGHT: Pile of dead Borg body parts made from toy action figures so beautifully sculpted they looked convincing on screen.

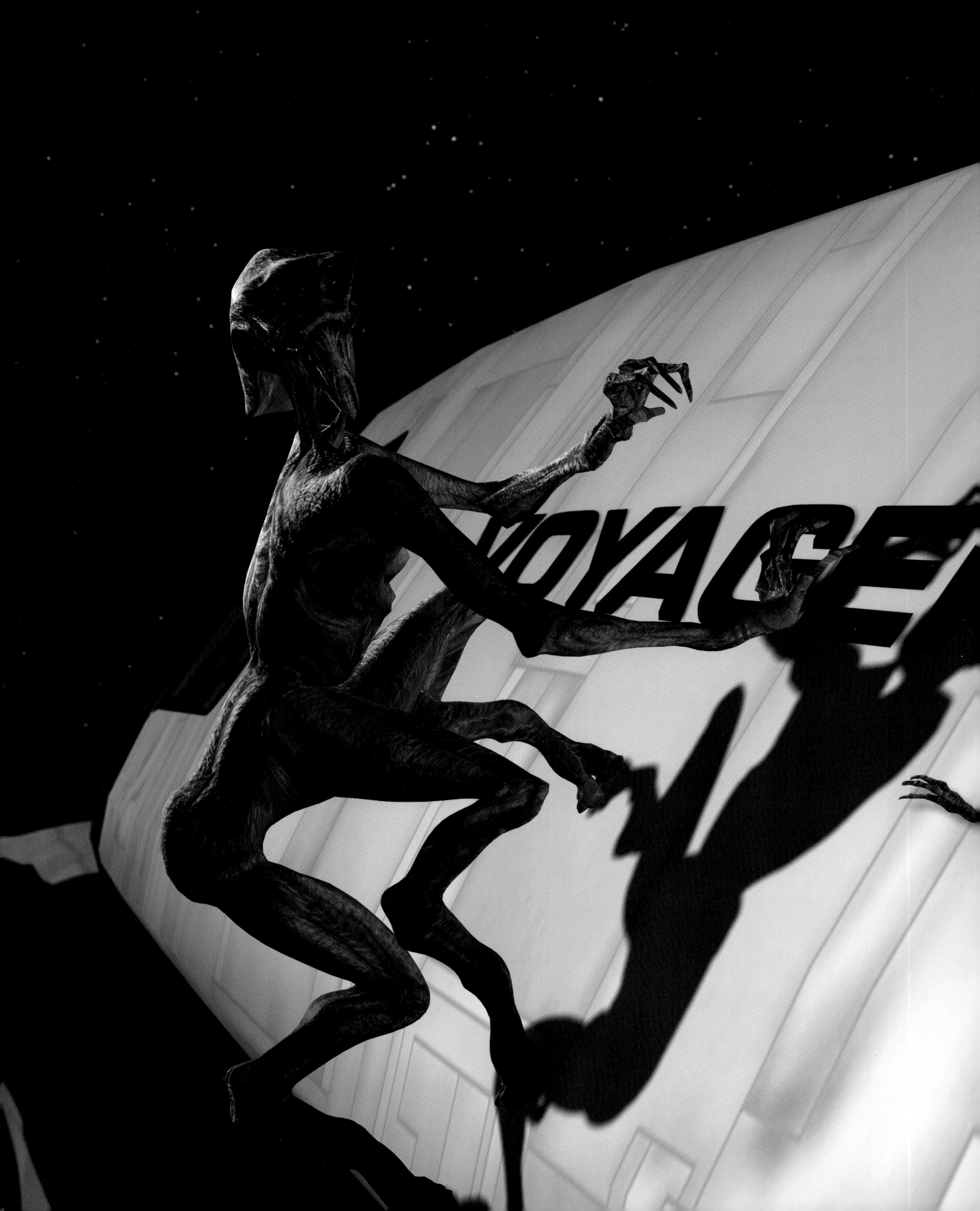

stinger, which she writhed around to avoid. I appreciated the trust Kate gave me to pull that off.

CG characters have no physical limitations, so when the writers came up with Species 8472 I wanted to do something that couldn't be mistaken for a man in a suit. I was intrigued by the idea of a creature with three legs. The original idea came from a play I did in grad school. My theater thesis project, which I wrote, directed, and designed, was a play set in an alien prison. One of the characters was a tripod creature. I thought that was interesting, and would work well for *Star Trek*. I was swamped at the time, so I just had time to do some very rough sketches of some simple ideas that Steve Burg then refined into its final design.

This predatory species was very nasty, so it needed to look powerful and frightening, but also capable of having a technologically advanced culture. I was really happy with Steve's design, there's a lot of beautiful fluidity to it. Digital artist John Teska, a real genius, built it for us at Foundation Imaging, and together we worked out how it would move. A living creature has to convey emotion, give a performance, and have character-driven, species-specific body language.

One of the things about dealing with CG creatures is that you don't have anything on the set. So I made a life-sized slot puppet of Species 8472 that we could stick on the stage so the actors would get a sense of how big the creature was.

By the time we got to *Star Trek: Enterprise*, it was a given that there would be more completely CG characters. For the Insectoid, I had the idea of dressing a stand-in in a suit with a grid on it. The reason we put the grid on the suit was to help our animators understand how the creature needed to move in 3D space. A piece of film or video is actually a 2D image, so when you are putting a virtual 3D object into it you have to calculate exactly how the

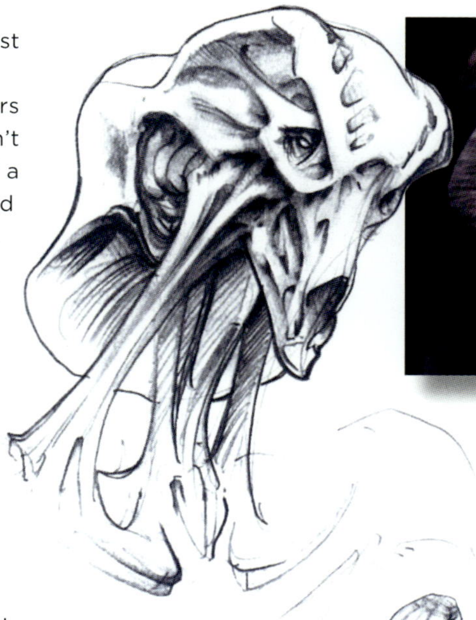

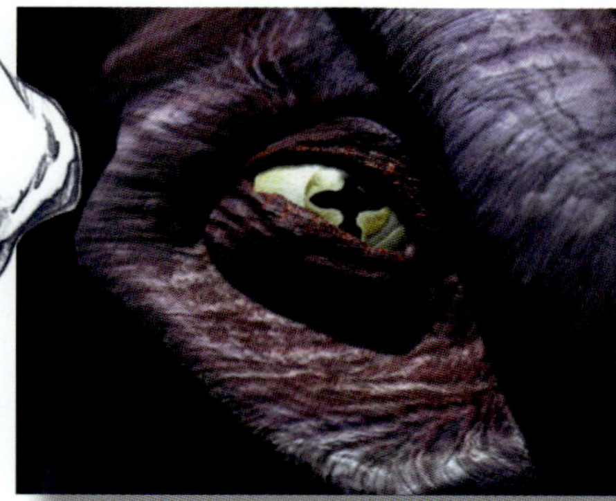

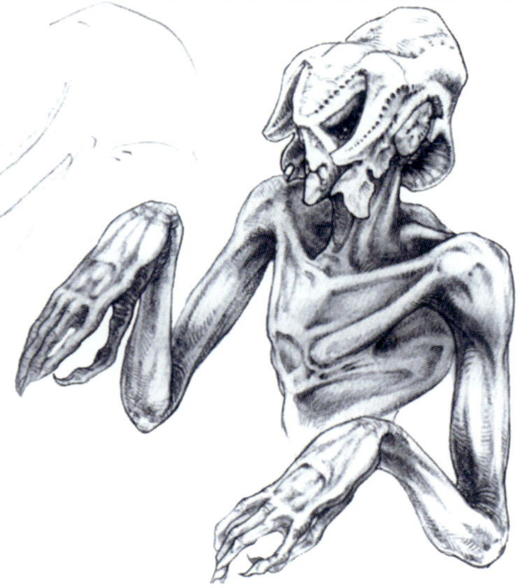

ABOVE AND RIGHT: Steve Burg's brilliant sketches of Species 8472.

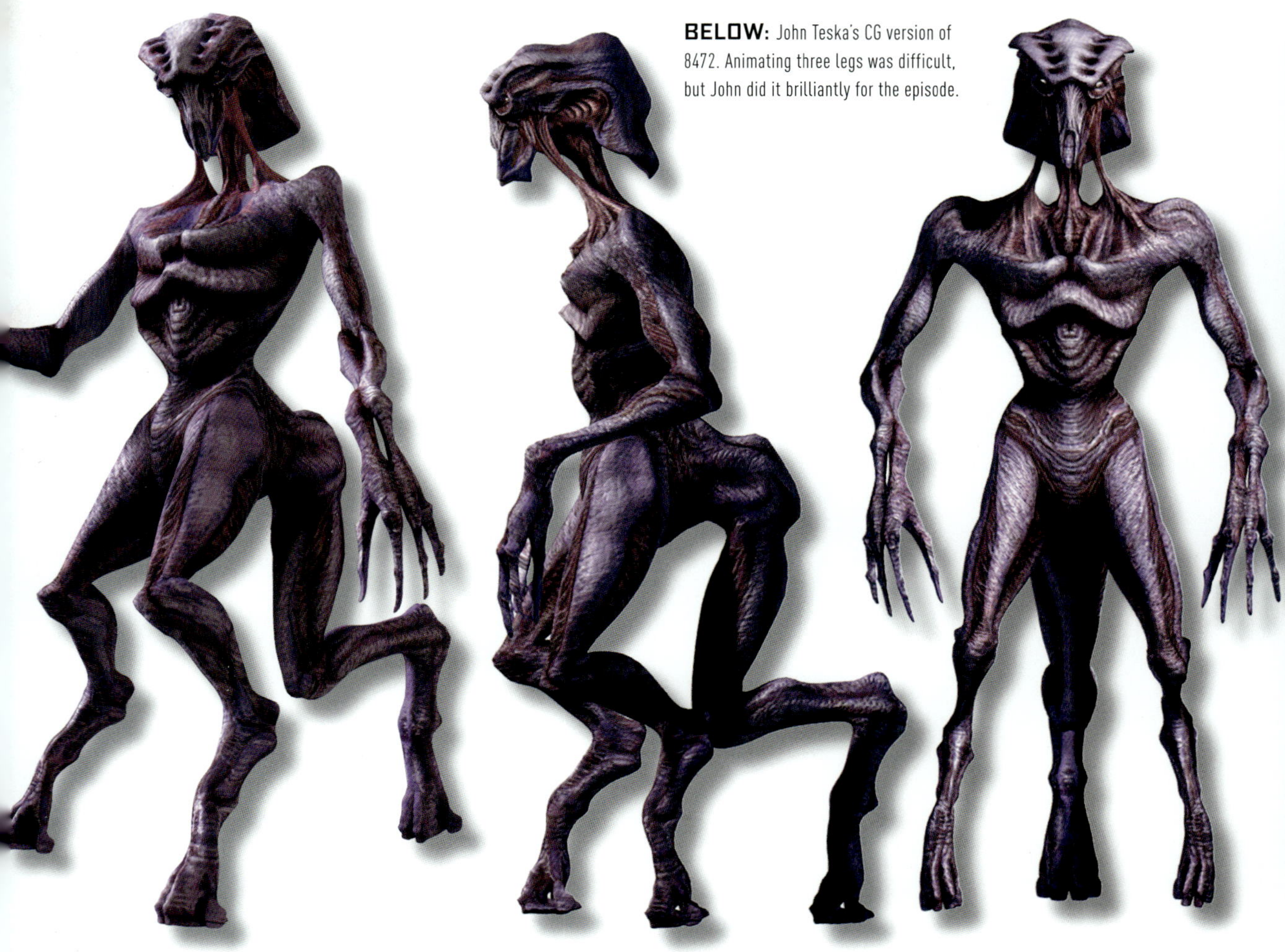

BELOW: John Teska's CG version of 8472. Animating three legs was difficult, but John did it brilliantly for the episode.

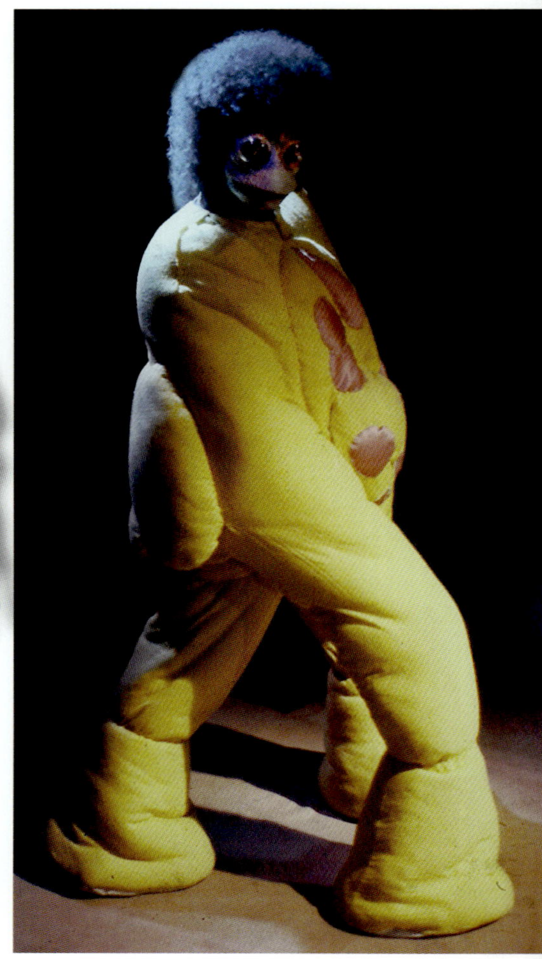

BELOW: A comedic alien from my MFA Theatre thesis project led me to propose having three legs for 8472.

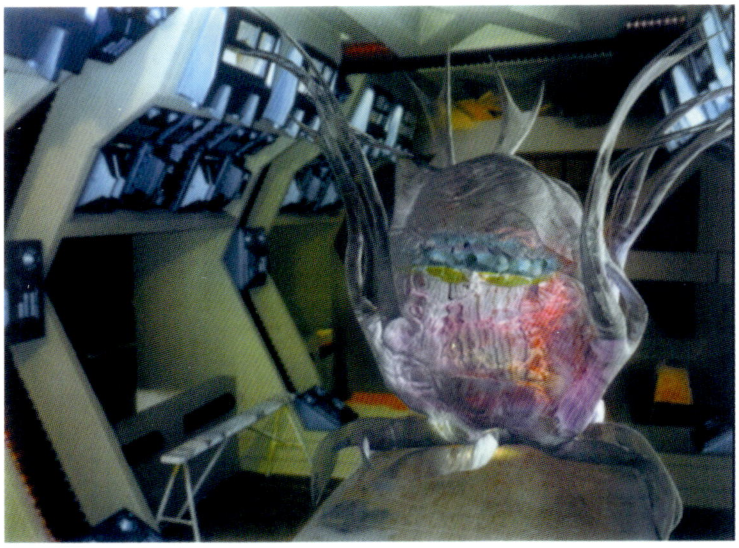

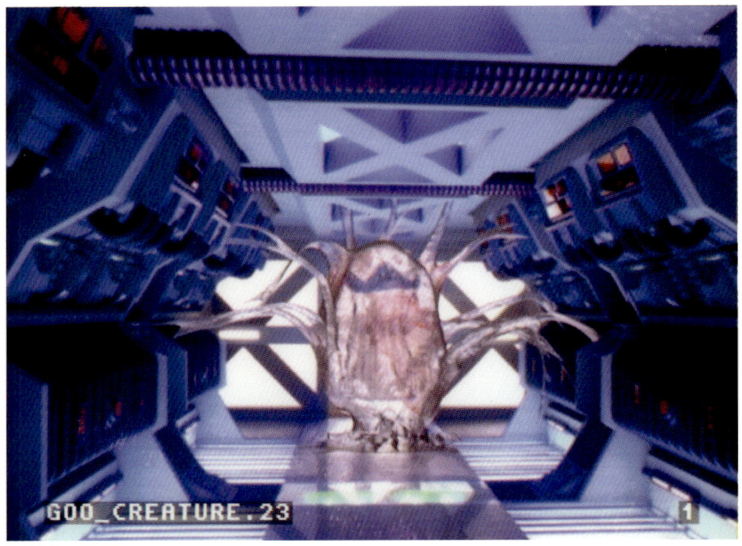

ABOVE: I did several concept paintings of the gelatinous Caretaker creature for the producers to choose from.

LEFT AND BELOW: The macroviruses were loosely based on terrestrial diatoms with added tentacles and a nasty stinger. My concept sketch (below) shows its scale relationship to a human. The on-camera version was CG, except for when they blew up—those were practical models shot at high speed in special black sets so they could be comped into live-action scenes.

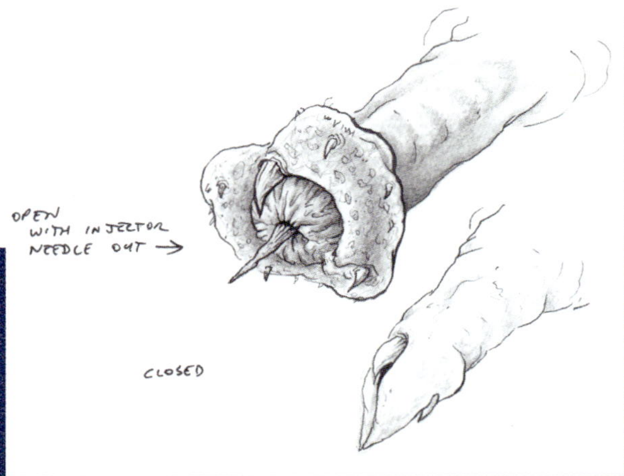

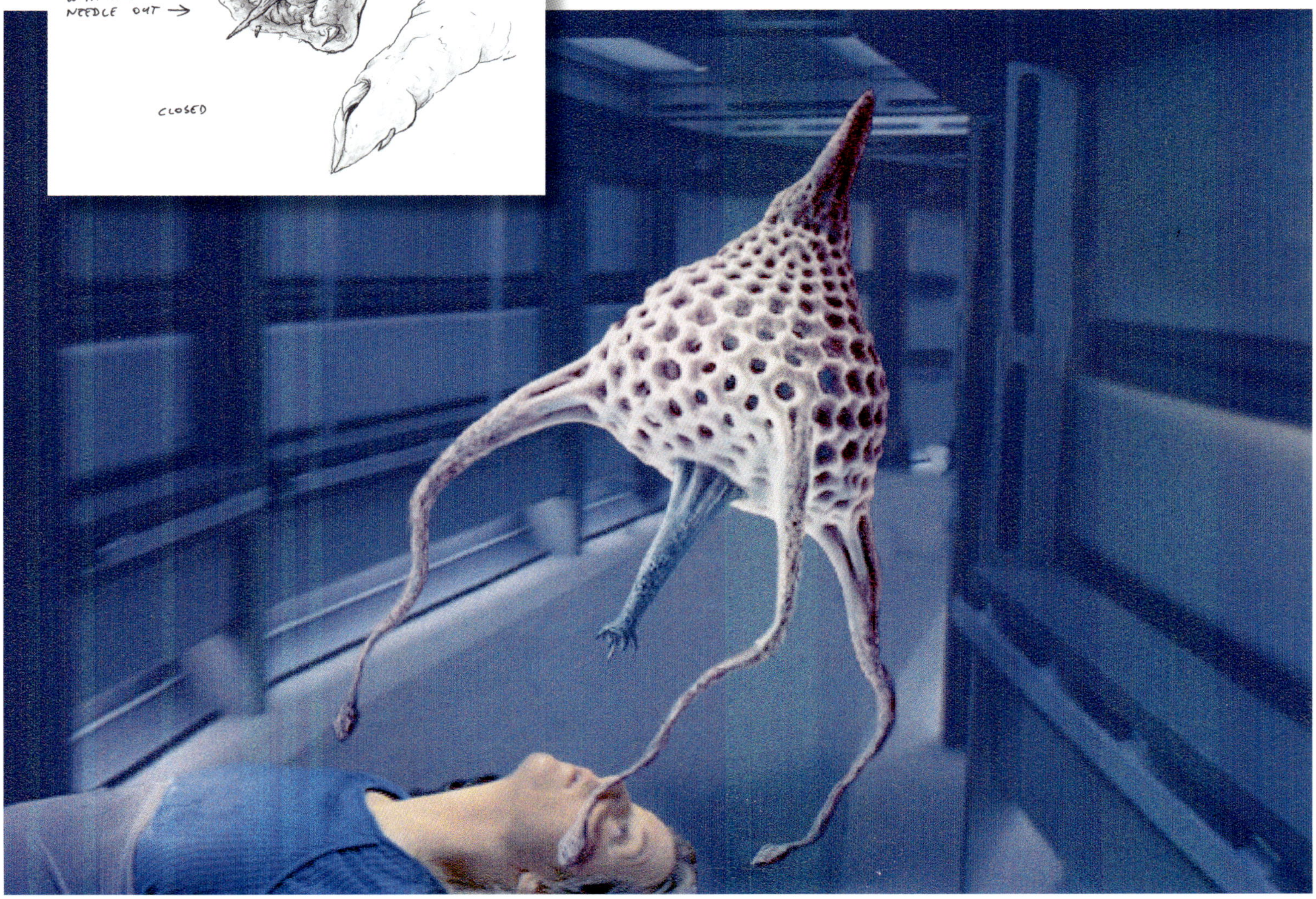

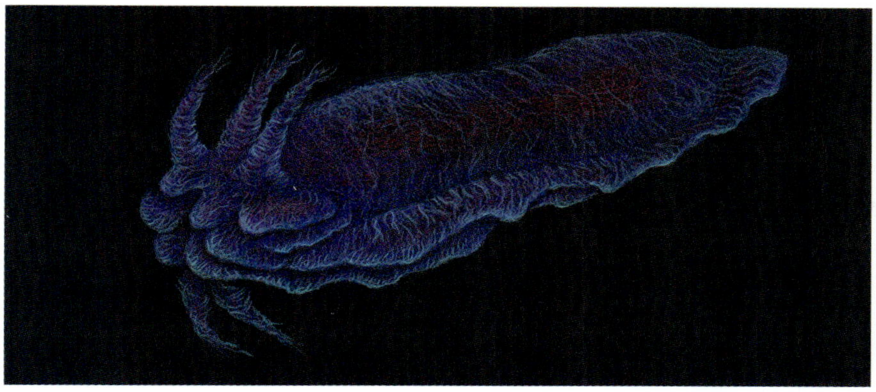

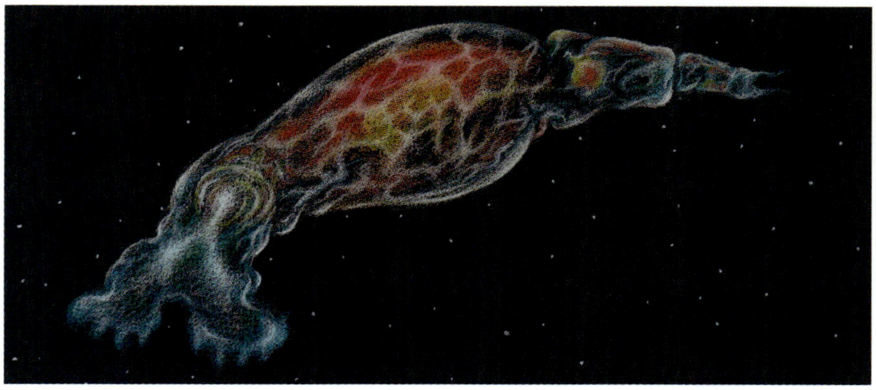

ABOVE: Two color pencil versions of the ephemeral creature from *Voyager*'s 'Elogium.' The producers chose the bottom one, which was done in CG.

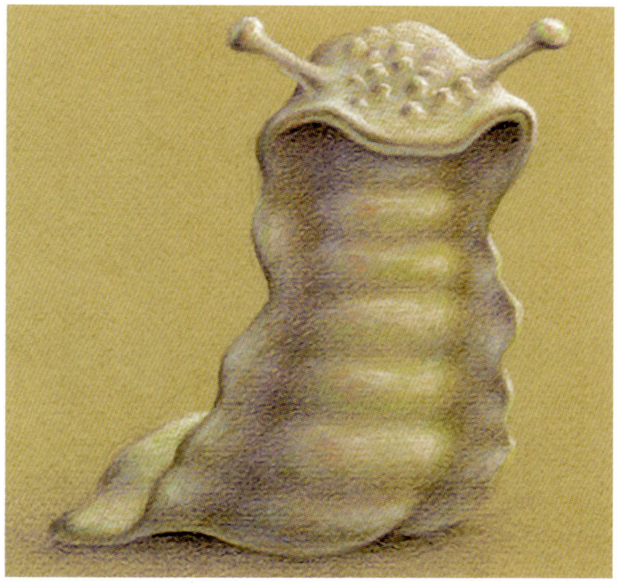

ABOVE: Color pencil concept sketch of the telepathic creature from 'The Shroud.' The final version was CG.

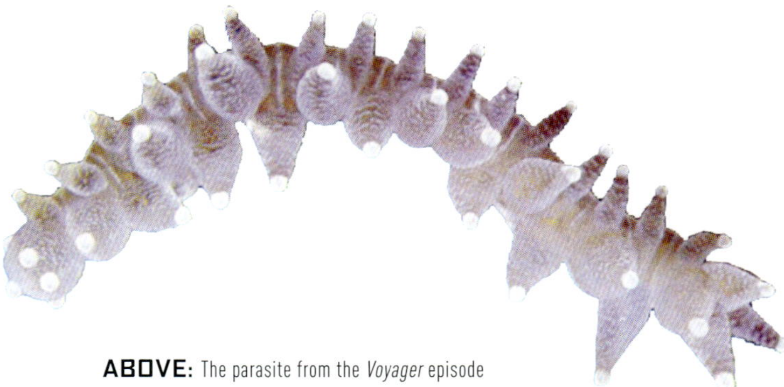

ABOVE: The parasite from the *Voyager* episode 'Good Shepherd' needed to be a believable life form, but also look repulsive.

perspective works. Every time the camera moves, the perspective changes, and you have to take account of the constantly changing angles. By looking at the grid on the suit, the animator could see the perspective of the arms and the body, and that made it a lot easier for them. It was wise to provide the animators with as much reference as possible; one time I made a bounding box out of chopsticks that were hot-glued together. We would put it where a Xindi Insectoid was sitting in a council chamber among live actors. Because the CG artists knew the dimensions of the little bounding box, they would be able to work out the perspective from any angle so when they put their CG creature in, it

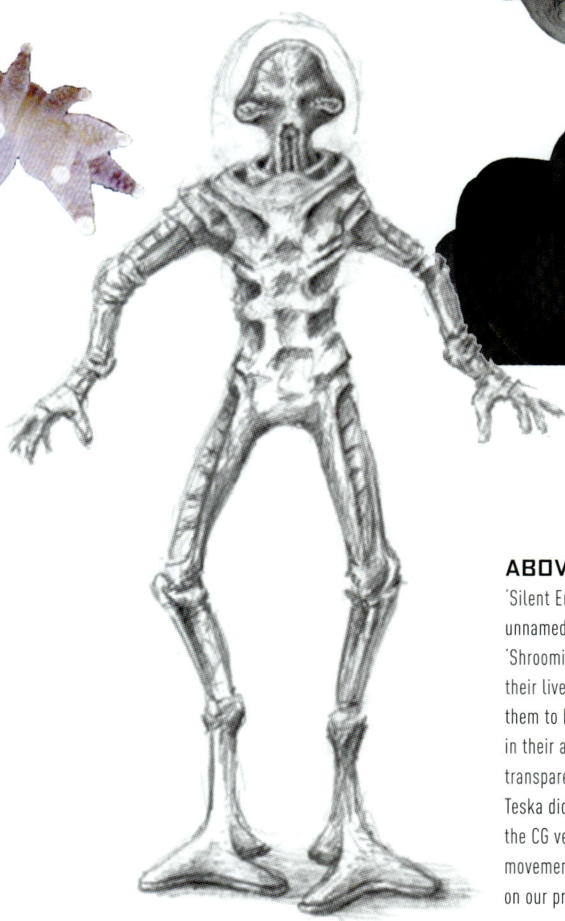

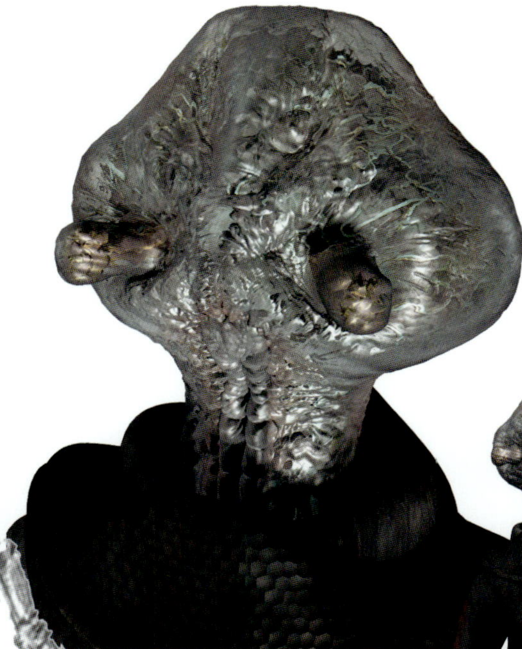

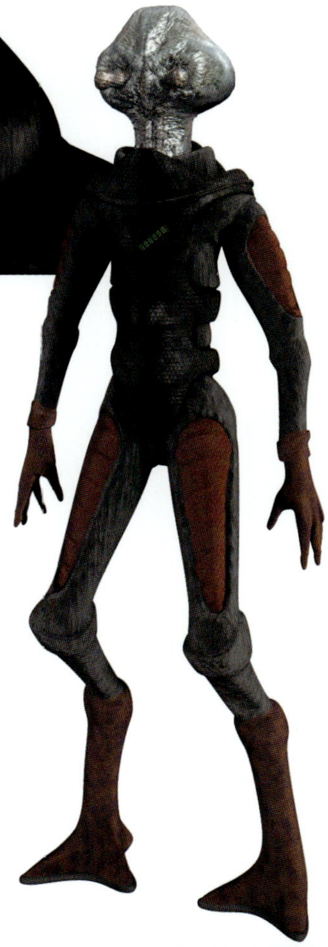

ABOVE: In the *Enterprise* episode 'Silent Enemy' we encounter an unnamed alien species nicknamed 'Shroomies.' As they spend most of their lives in low gravity, I designed them to be spindly with extra joints in their arms and legs, and wearing transparent force field helmets. John Teska did a brilliant job creating the CG version, animating their movements, and matching the lighting on our practical sets.

looked as if it geometrically belonged in the scene.

CG creatures were expensive. They required articulated animation by skilled artists. There would often be notes from the producers, and adjustments in the performance of the CG characters. Our budgets were very tight, and we had to be very diligent in adhering to them, so I would do storyboards so we'd have a sense of how many shots we would be doing and how complicated they were. That was important because filming for CG creatures was more complicated than creating shots with CG spaceships, where everything in the frame could be made in CG. Creatures had to interact with the actors. We would always start by shooting the actors on set first, and then we would add the CG creatures in post-production. Storyboards would give the director, director of photography, and the actors a sense of what was going on in the scene, but they were not locked in stone. The director would frequently change things based on circumstances on set and creative inspiration once the scene was flowing.

In the first season of *Enterprise* we created some CG *targs*, a

BELOW: For 'Hatchery,' the baby Insectoids had to be cute. CG by John Teska.

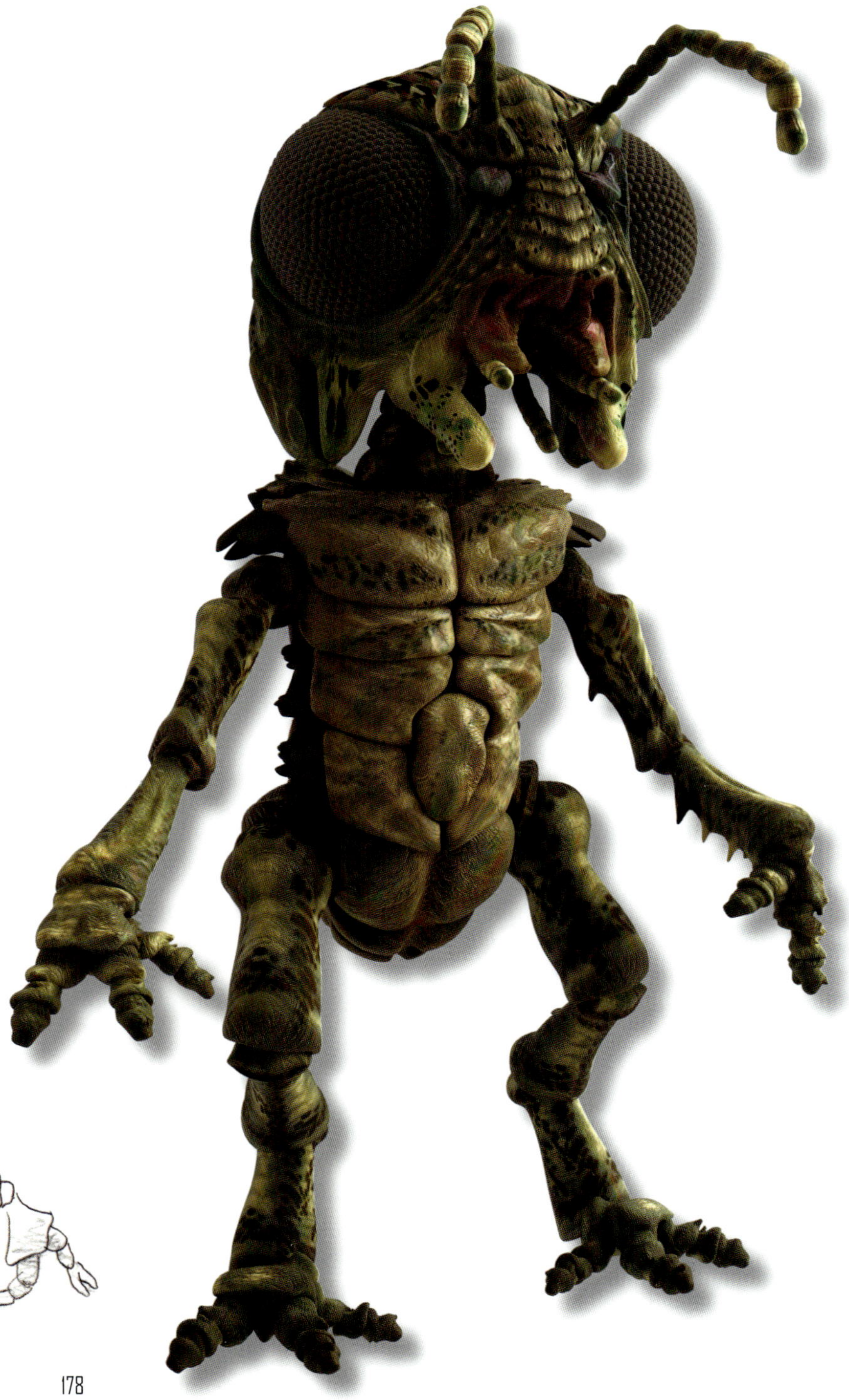

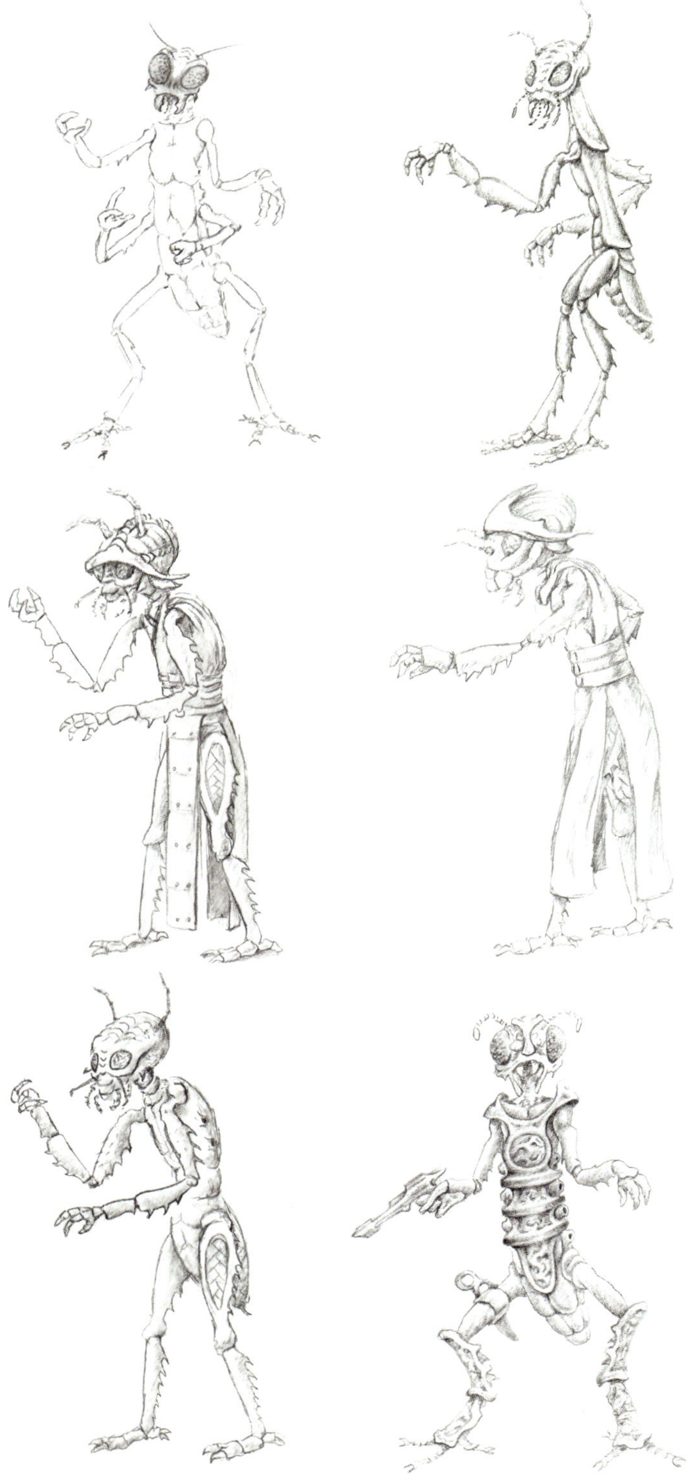

ABOVE: Pencil sketches showing the evolution of the design of the Xindi Insectoids. The bottom-right one is the final version.

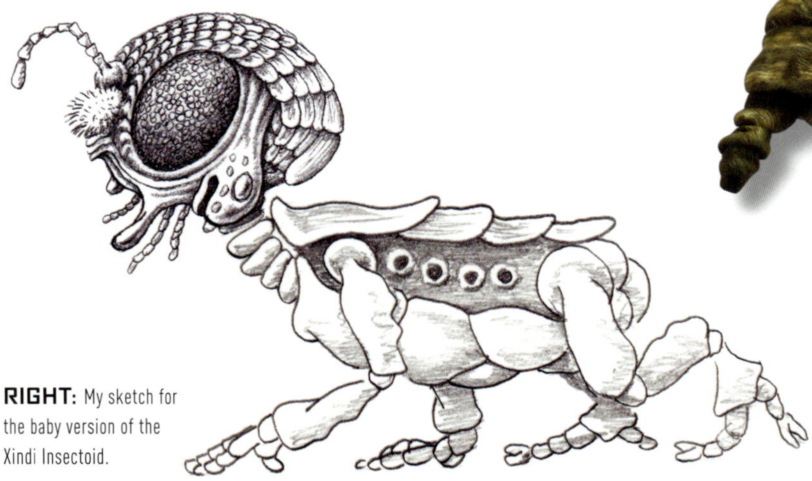

RIGHT: My sketch for the baby version of the Xindi Insectoid.

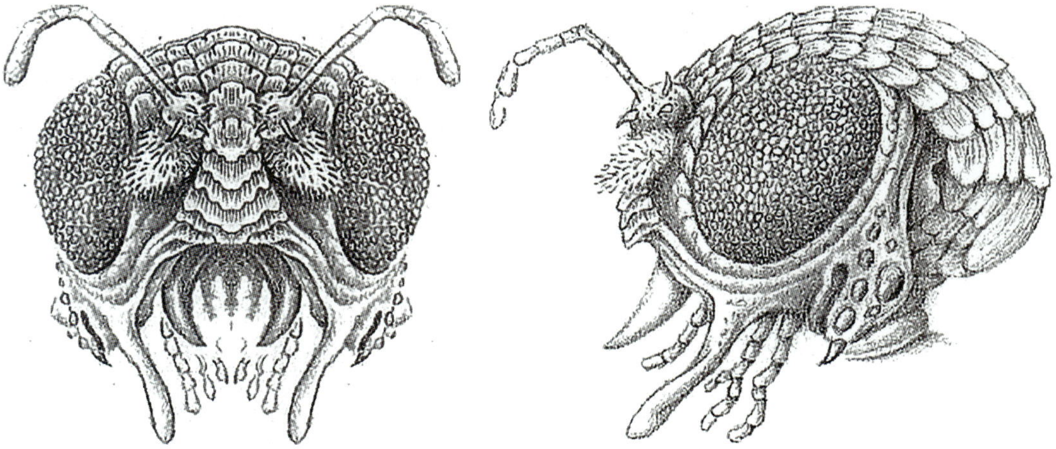

ABOVE: Detailed drawings of an Insectoid head.

BELOW: Stand-ins Evan English and Tarik Ergin (in grid suits) give reference performances for Insectoids that John Teska would match with the CG versions in a 'clean plate' take shot without them.

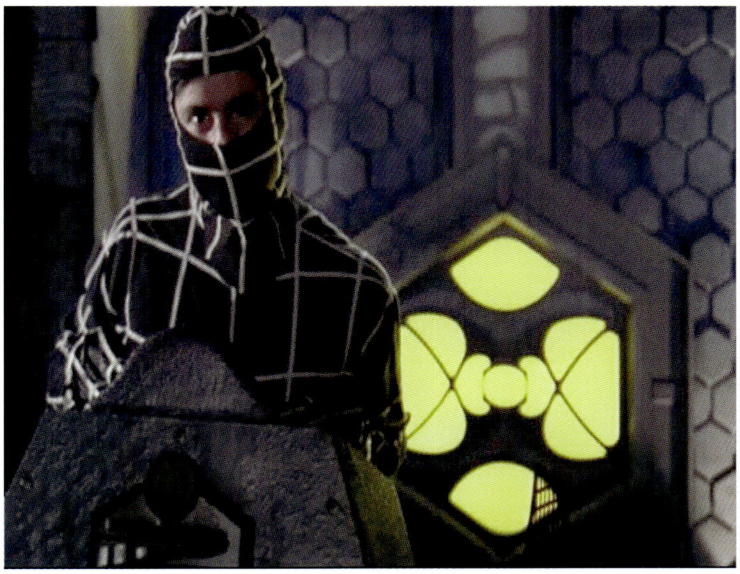

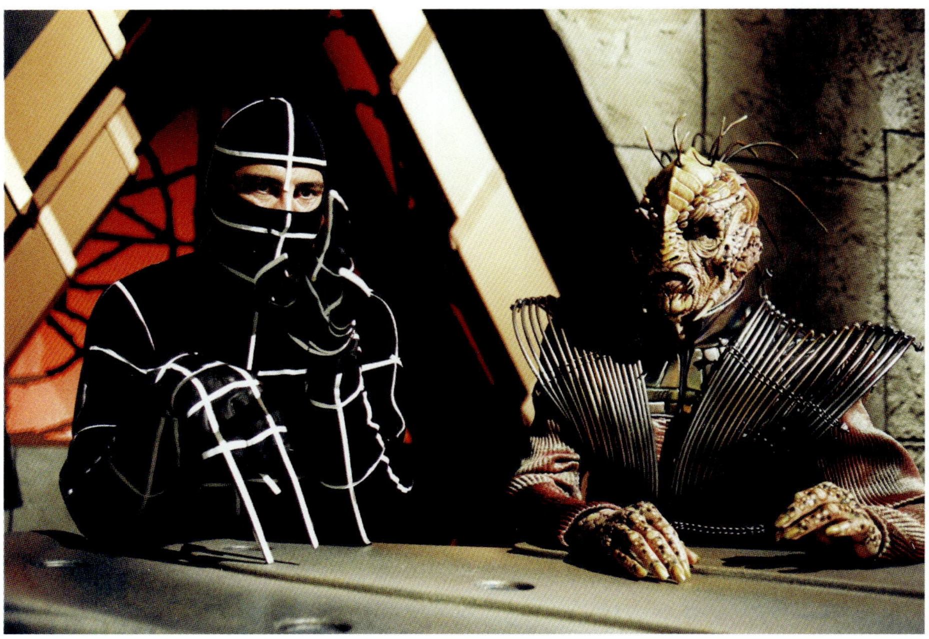

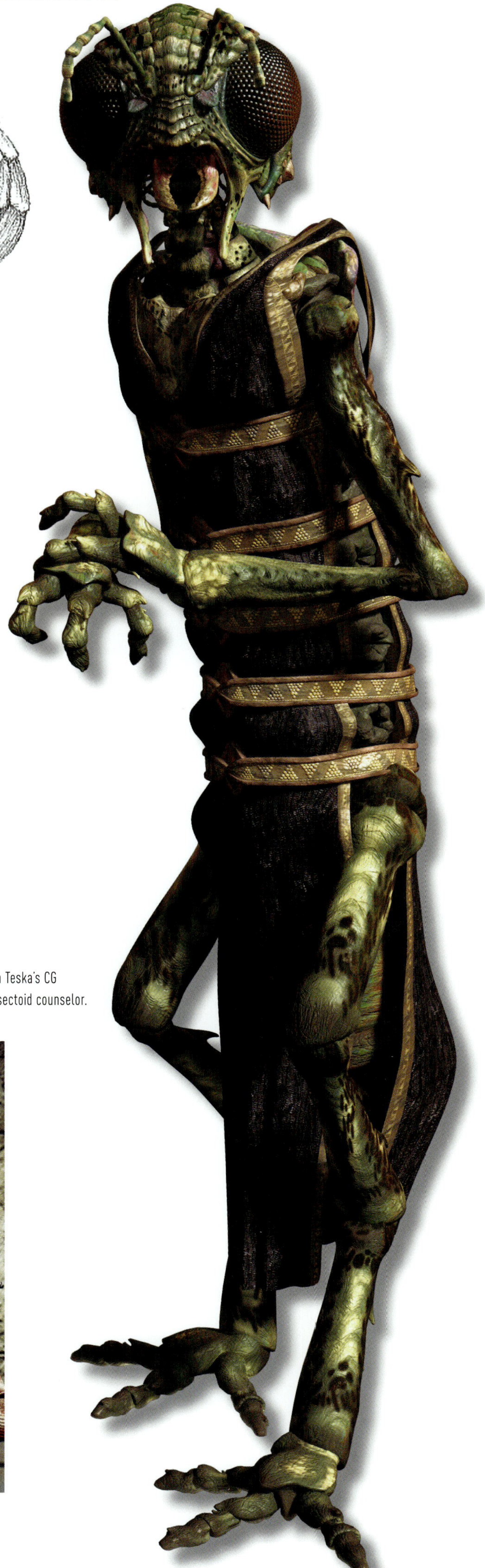

RIGHT: John Teska's CG version of an Insectoid counselor.

RIGHT AND BELOW: Alternate concepts for the Klingon *targ*.

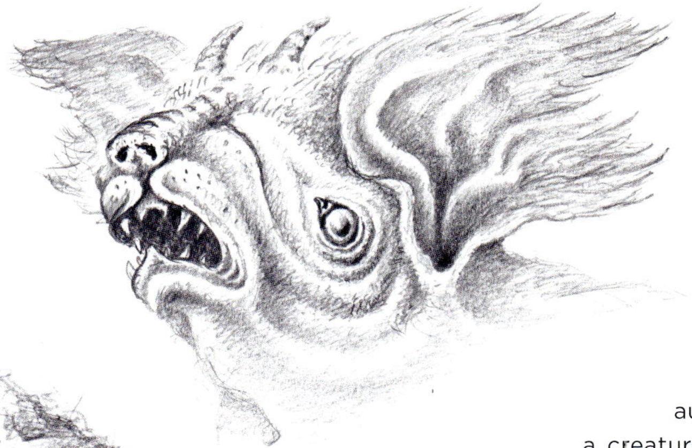

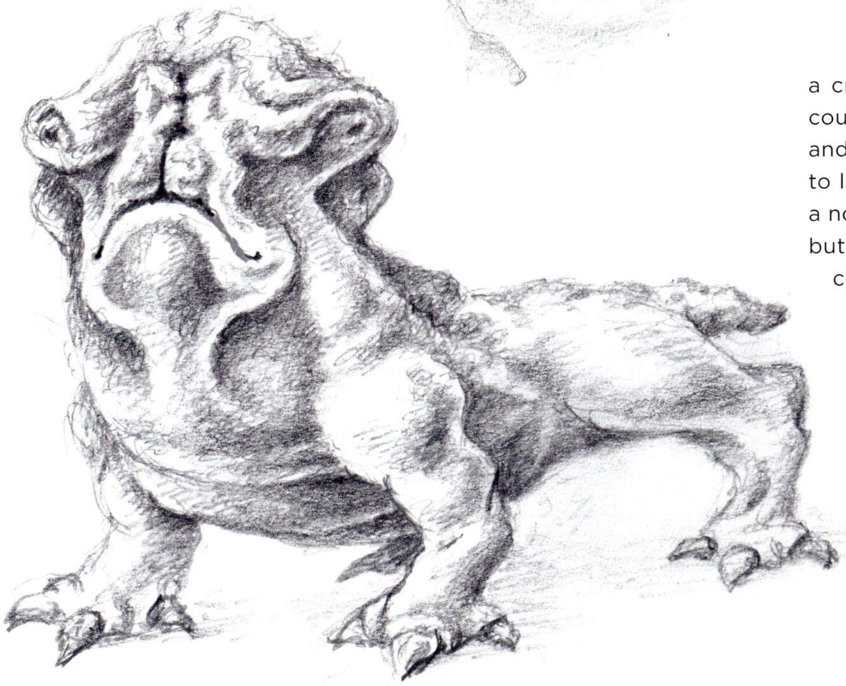

Klingon food source carried live in pens on their ships. They had to have bodies that would look like dead pig carcasses if you slaughtered them and removed their skin, because we were using real pig carcasses to hang on the set and play the slaughtered *targs*.

In Season 3 we had the Xindi, a race with several different sentient species, two of which were completely CG: the Insectoids and the Aquatics. We wanted them to look alien, but they needed to be anthropomorphized enough to have a convincing relationship with the other species, and for the audience to respond to them. For the Insectoids, we wanted a creature that was about the size of a human being so people could look into its face. I looked at macro shots of various insects, and then designed an amalgam of a fly and an ant. I wanted them to look intelligent, so I made the foreheads a little bigger than on a normal insect. Originally, I wanted them to have six appendages, but then it would've made the animation significantly more complex and time consuming, thus too expensive. I designed a special ergonomic gun for the Insectoids that they would be able to hold with their insect hands. What I don't like about some fantasy movie weapons is that they are clearly designed to look cool, but are not practical.

For the Xindi Aquatics, I wanted something that had a kind of prehistoric look, but I conceived of it as mammalian rather than reptilian, although I still gave it gills to breathe underwater. The design was loosely inspired

BELOW: Pastel sketch, final version of a *targ*. The body had to convincingly match the skinned pig carcasses that would be used as props on set.

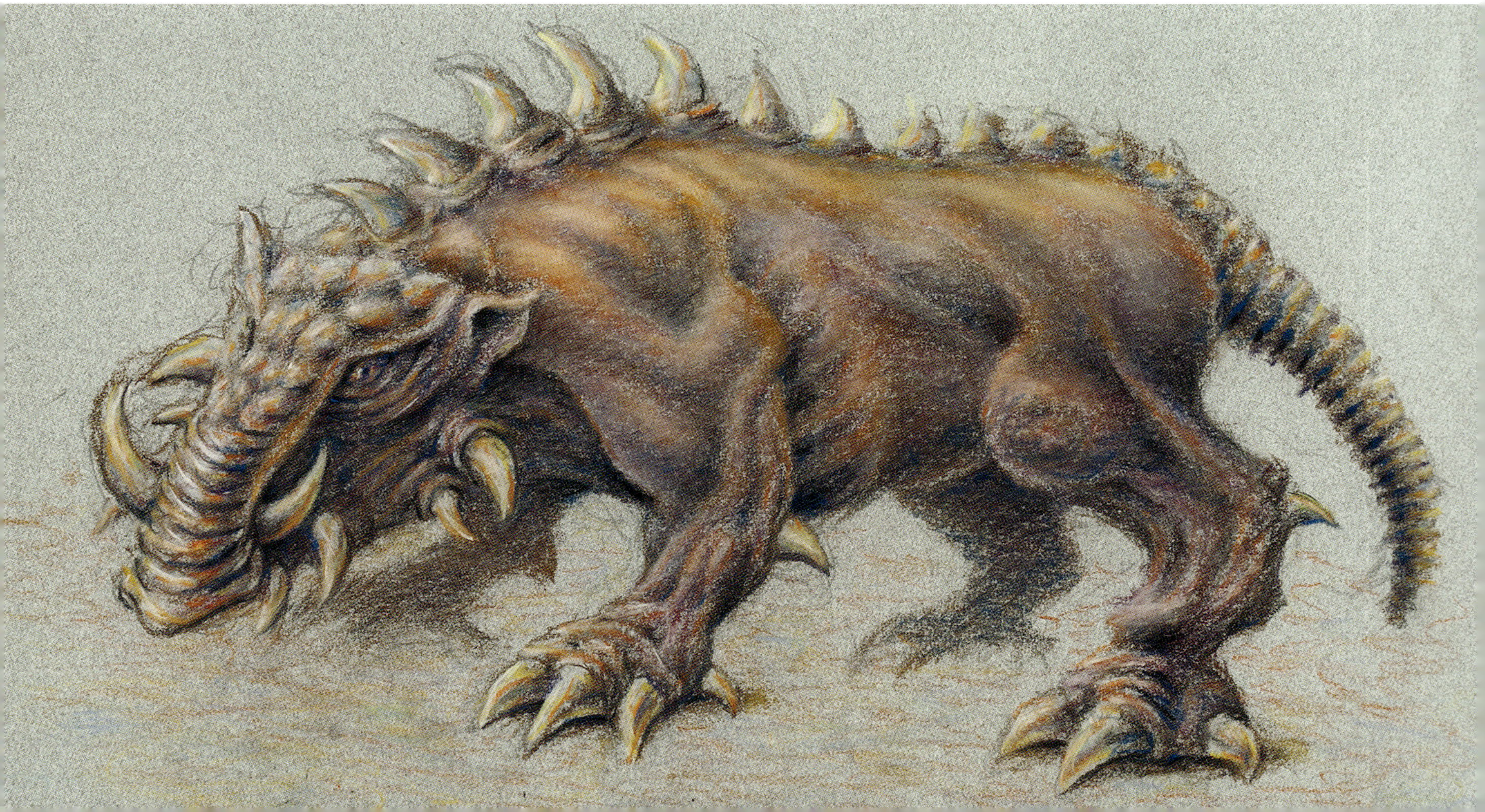

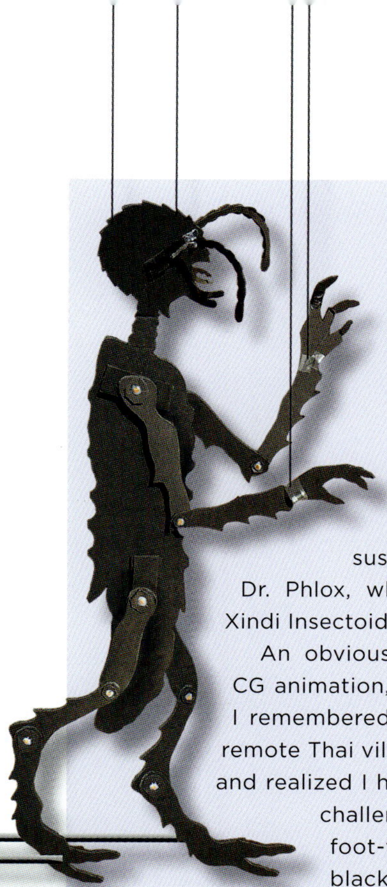

INSIDE STORY

SHADOW OF THE XINDI

Sometimes the best solutions are low tech. In the *Enterprise* episode 'Doctor's Orders,' the crew is in suspended animation except for alien Dr. Phlox, who hallucinates, seeing shadows of Xindi Insectoids.

An obvious way to do this would have been CG animation, but I wanted to avoid the expense. I remembered the shadow puppets I had seen in remote Thai villages when I was in the Peace Corps, and realized I had a cheap and easy solution to the challenge. First, I made a two-and-a-half-foot-tall Insectoid shadow puppet out of black foam core. The hinges were pieces of chopsticks, with clear acetate bushings to minimize friction. Our special-effects supervisor, Gary Monak, donated a pair of small springs to attach the antennae so they would bobble. By placing a strong light on the floor behind the puppet we made it cast huge shadows on the complex surfaces of the NX-01's interior. Since all the shots showed the doctor's point of view, no actors were required to be in the scene, so we did every shot in second unit.

I operated the head and arms using threads like a marionette, while VFX supervisor Mitch Suskin controlled the legs using rods that let him simulate a natural walking action.

So instead of spending a considerable amount of time and money on CG animation, we captured all the shots in one afternoon with real shadows. Nothing is more real than real.

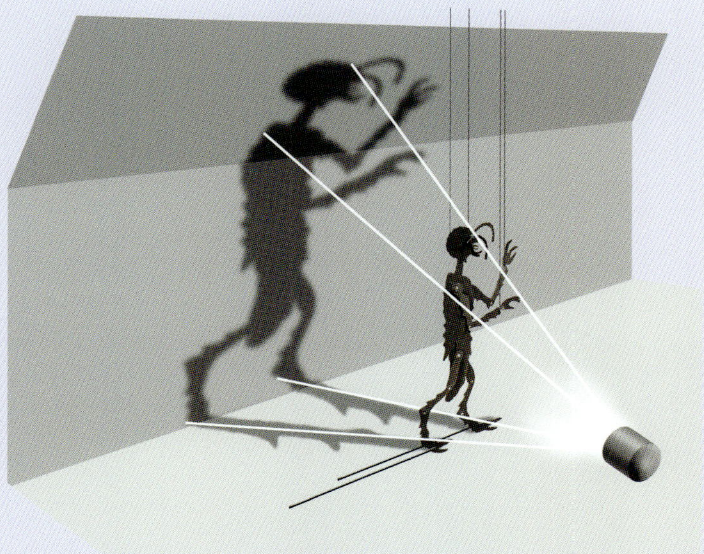

ABOVE: Inspired by traditional Thai shadow puppets, we set up a low-angle light to cast large shadows on the set walls.

BELOW: Production shot of the puppet shadow.

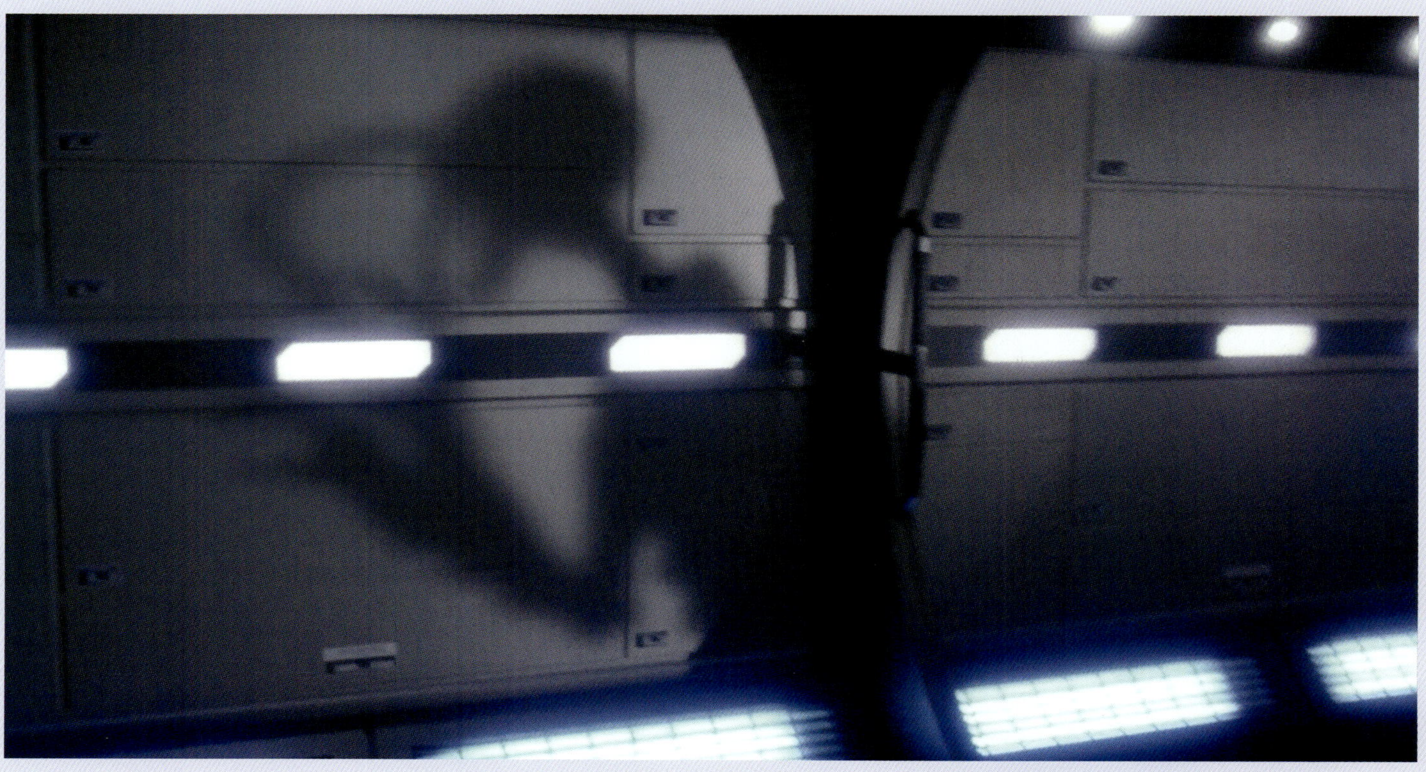

BELOW: Pencil drawing of an unused concept for an extinct sentient Xindi Avian habitat. I was imagining how nest building would evolve into architecture.

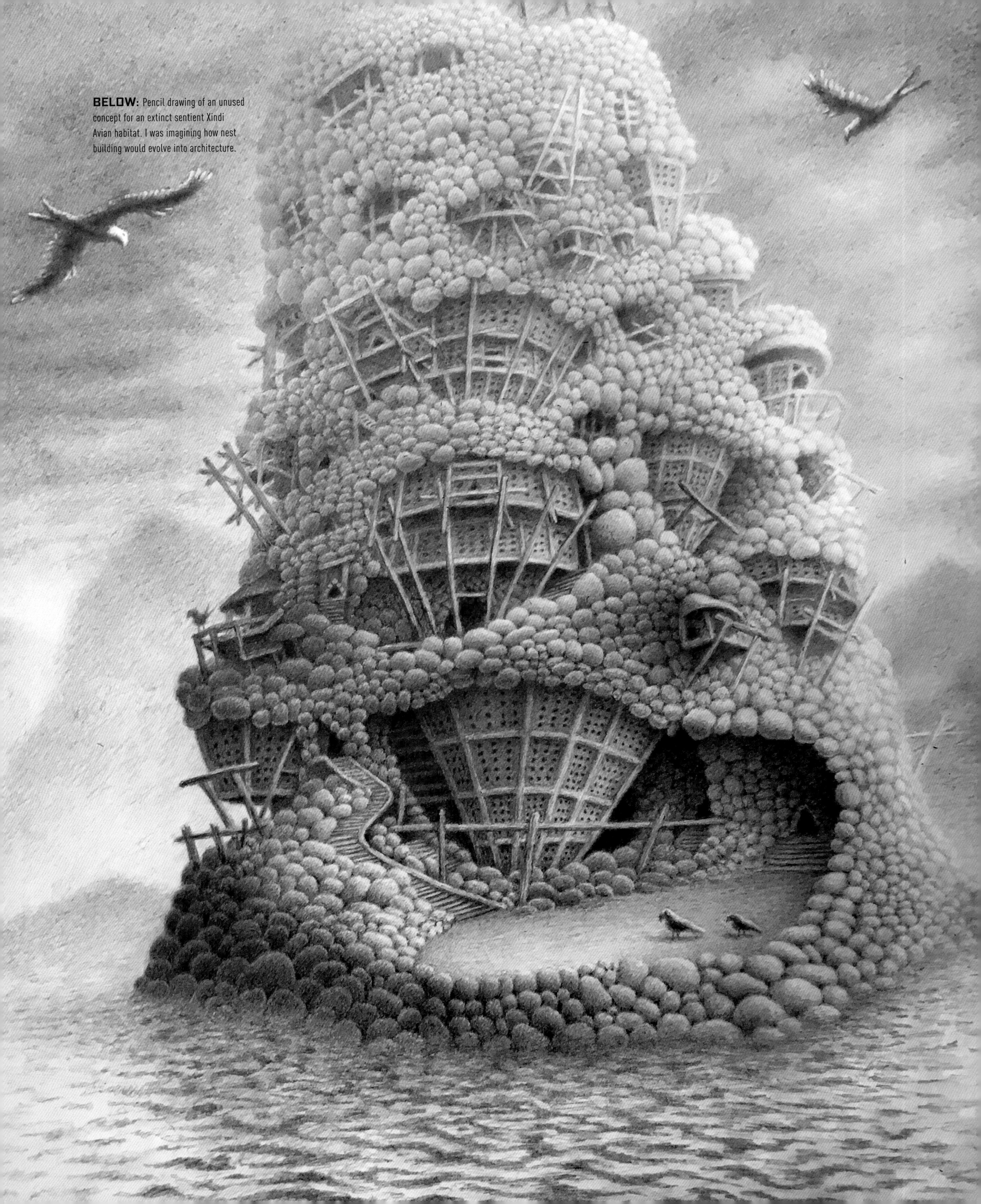

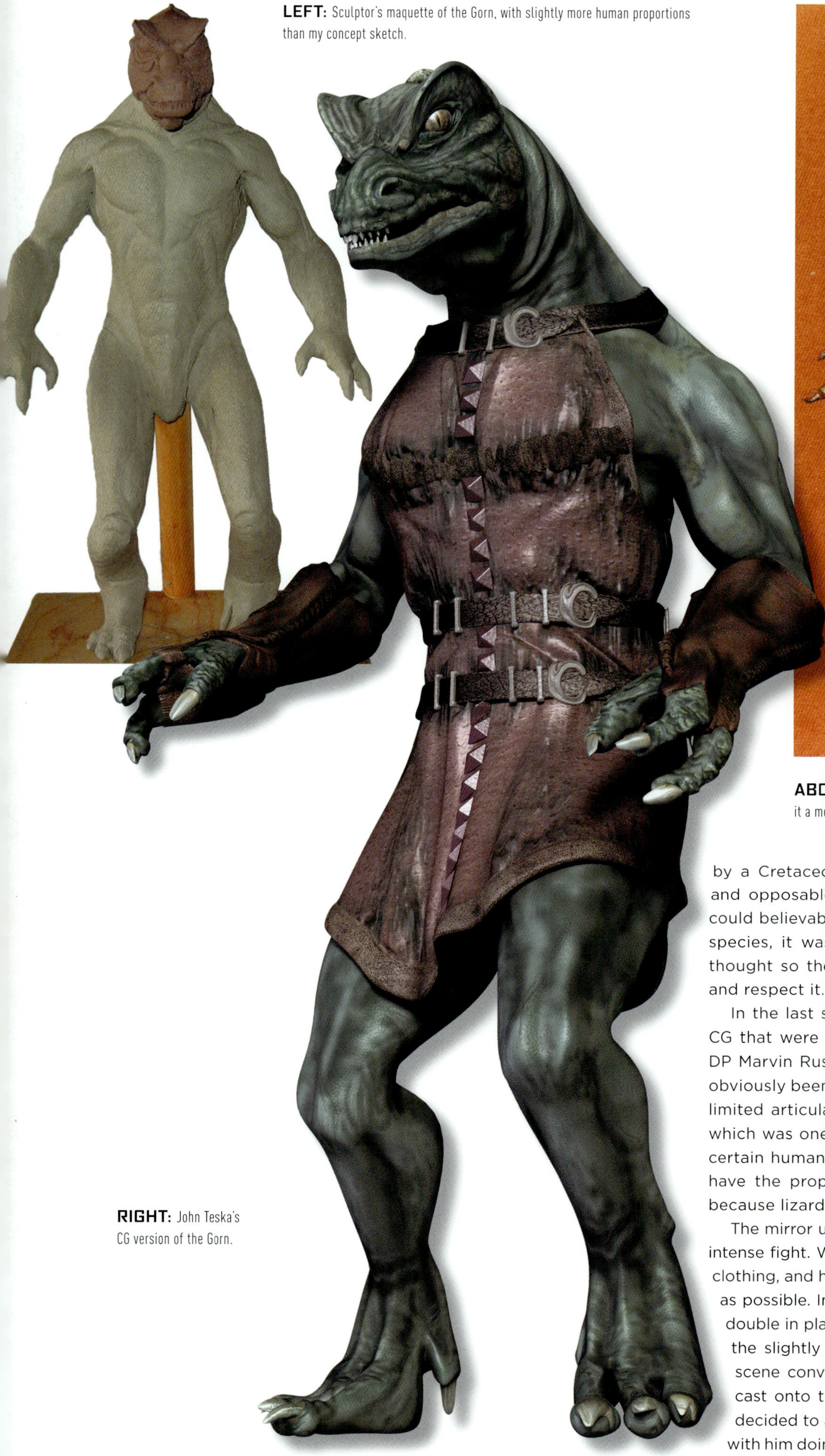

LEFT: Sculptor's maquette of the Gorn, with slightly more human proportions than my concept sketch.

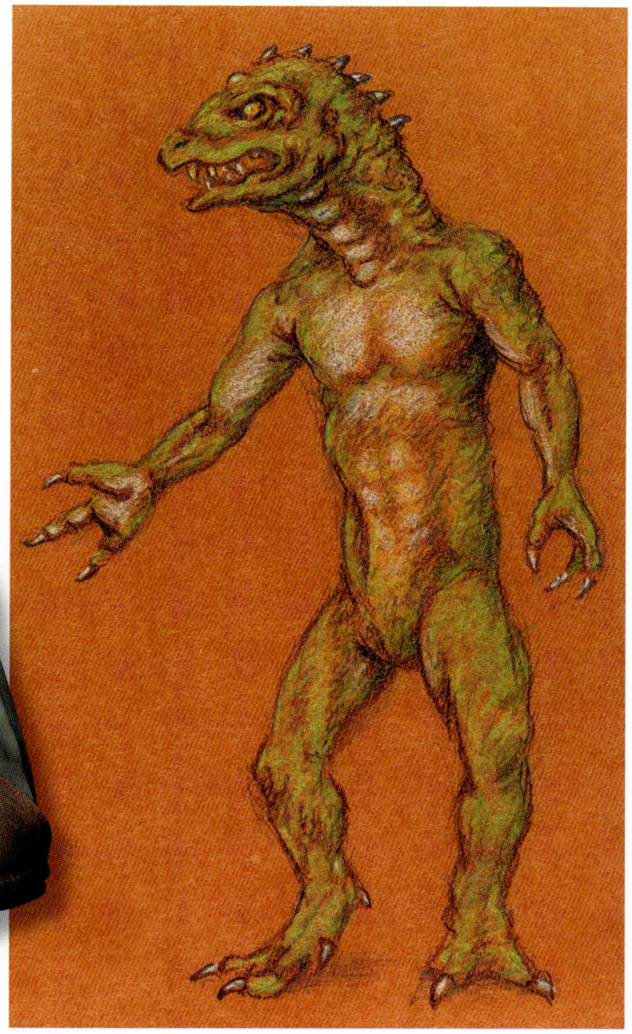

ABOVE: Pencil sketch of the revised Gorn. It would be built in CG so I could give it a more lizard-like body.

RIGHT: John Teska's CG version of the Gorn.

by a Cretaceous Period Mosasaurus, but I felt it needed hands and opposable thumbs, along with a more intelligent face so it could believably have a technological culture. Since it's a sentient species, it was important to me that it looked capable of wise thought so the other Xindi species would be able to relate to it and respect it.

In the last season of *Enterprise* we recreated two creatures in CG that were from the original series. In an episode directed by DP Marvin Rush, the Gorn was brought back. The Gorn had very obviously been a man in a suit, with a stiff prosthetic head that had limited articulation. I had to pay homage to the original version, which was one of *Star Trek*'s most iconic aliens, so it had to have certain human proportions. But I thought it would be cool to not have the proportions be *too* human, so I lengthened the torso because lizards generally have long torsos and shorter legs.

The mirror universe versions of Archer and the Gorn end up in an intense fight. We wanted the way the Gorn interacted with Archer's clothing, and how they grappled with one another, to look as natural as possible. In this we were able to film some shots with the stunt double in place, and our CG artists were able to cover him up with the slightly larger CG Gorn. An important factor in making the scene convincing was making sure the shadows that would be cast onto the Gorn were correct. I was very proud that Marvin decided to ask my son Devin, then a film student at USC, to work with him doing storyboards to help visualize this challenging scene.

Apart from the animated series, the *sehlat* hadn't appeared on screen before, but there were descriptions of it. In 'Journey to Babel' we're told that it's a kind of 'fat teddy bear' with 'six-inch fangs.' The version in the animated series looked like a tiger. I wanted it to look like a viable creature, but something that doesn't exist in our world. I thought it might live in a cold area so I added some elements from a polar bear, but with the teeth from a saber-toothed tiger. I gave it a somewhat armored head like a glyptodon or a pangolin, with a hefty tail to balance its forward motion.

A main factor to selling a CG creature in a live setting is how you light it. If you look at the early work on *The Next Generation* and compare that to the work we did on the later shows, chiaroscuro (or the artful use of deep shadows) became increasingly important. We learned to use strong contrast, making sure everything was lit from the same light source. The trick is to show the audience enough for them to understand what they were seeing, but leaving room for their imagination to provide details beyond what we could show them. The audience's own imagination is the catalyst for the suspension of disbelief. Directors of photography Marvin Rush and Jonathan West were masters of film noir-ish lighting, which they made their own.

We were always racing against the clock when we did CG creatures. CG creatures are much more difficult than CG spaceships because ships are mechanical and move like machines—hard and precise. A living creature is organic, imperfect, has unique individual body language, and most importantly has to give a performance that conveys emotion. The animators would only have a couple of days to work out the performance. I'm really proud and respectful of what the visual-effects team was

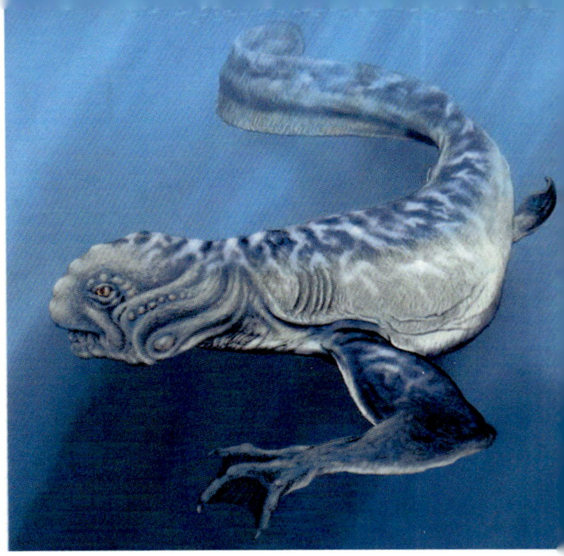

RIGHT: Concept painting for a Xindi Aquatic. I mixed aspects of a Cretaceous-Period Mosasaurus and marine mammals with arms, enabling a technical culture.

BELOW: The CG Xindi Aquatic and the digital sets were created at EdenFX by master digital artist David Morton, with internal rigging by the talented Eric Hance.

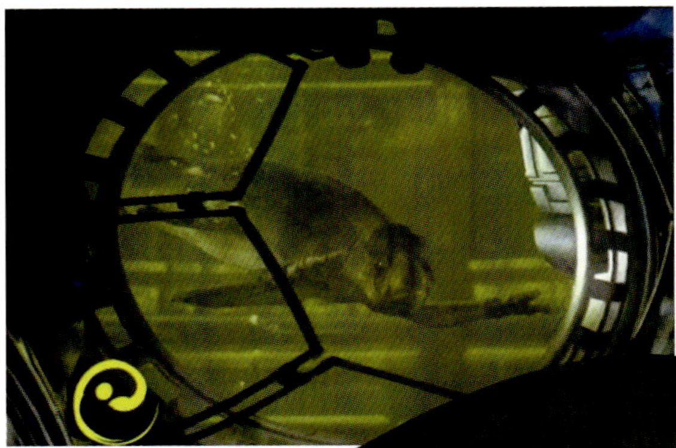

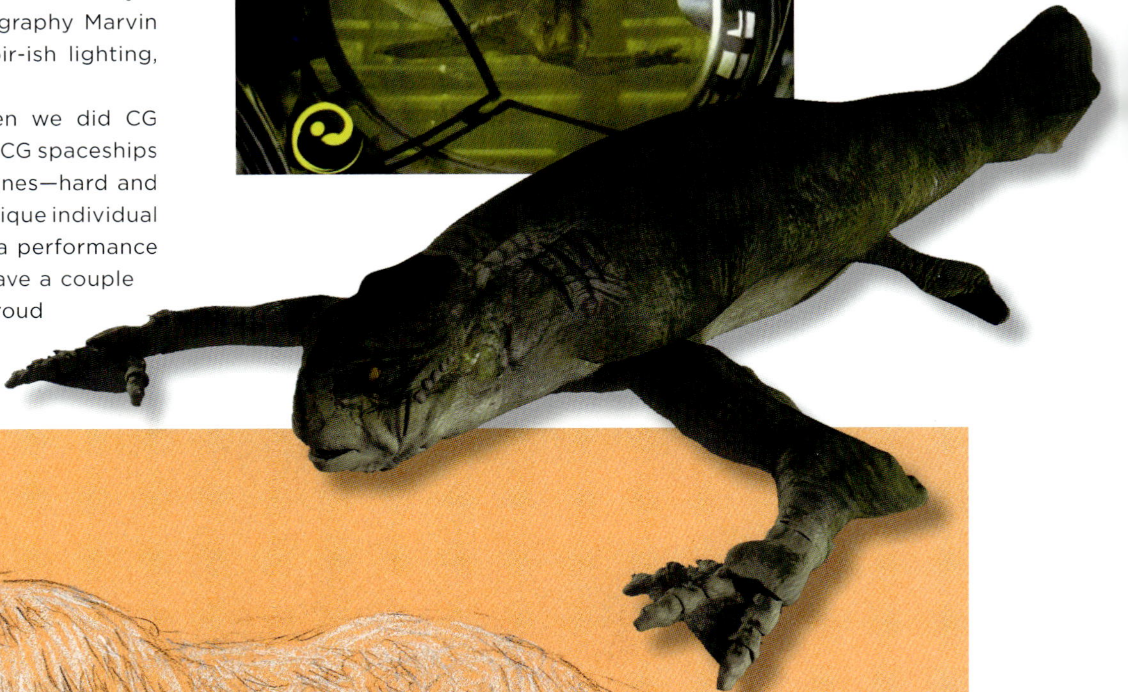

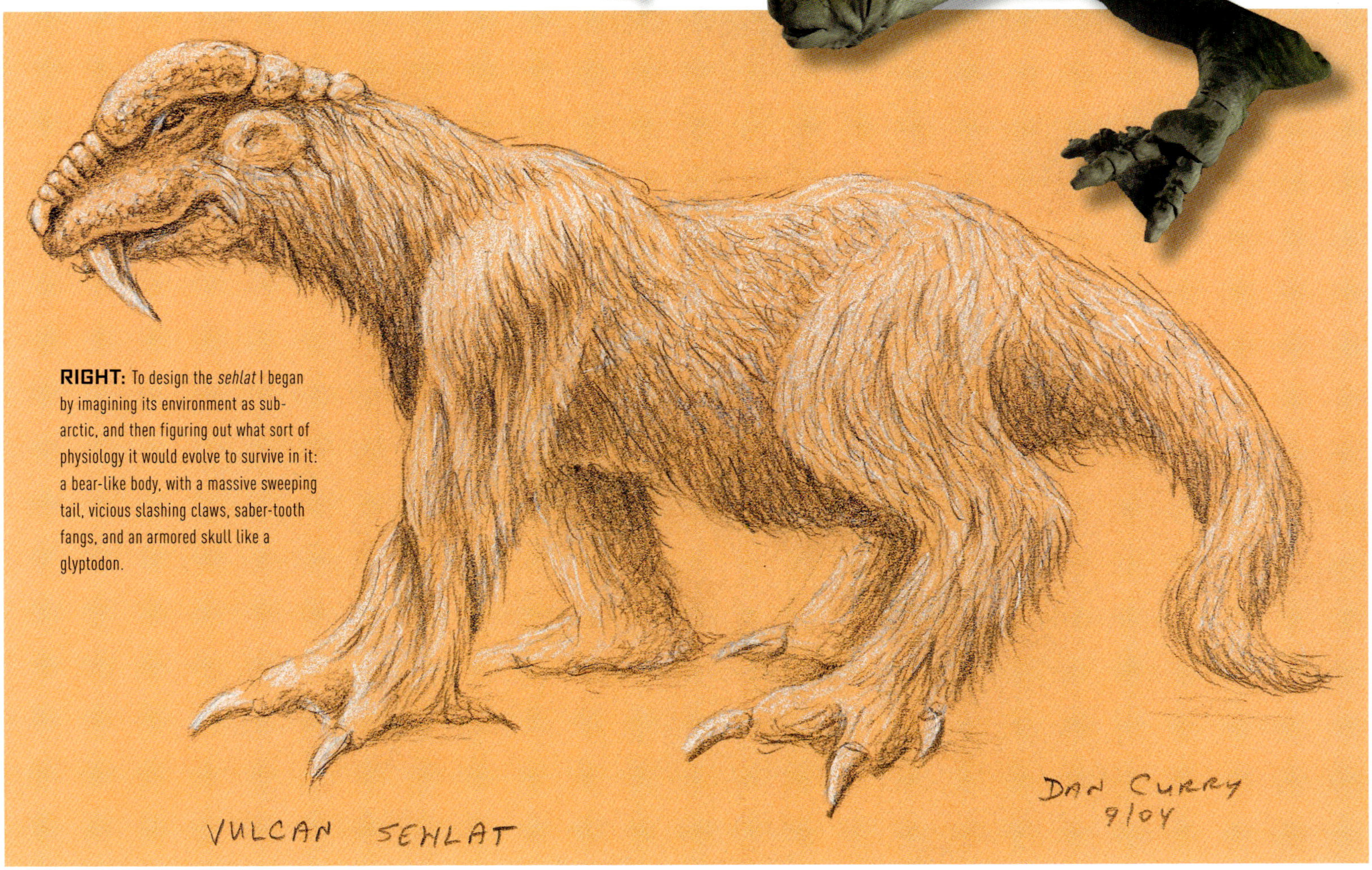

RIGHT: To design the *sehlat* I began by imagining its environment as sub-arctic, and then figuring out what sort of physiology it would evolve to survive in it: a bear-like body, with a massive sweeping tail, vicious slashing claws, saber-tooth fangs, and an armored skull like a glyptodon.

INSIDE STORY

INSIDE THE TRANSPORTER

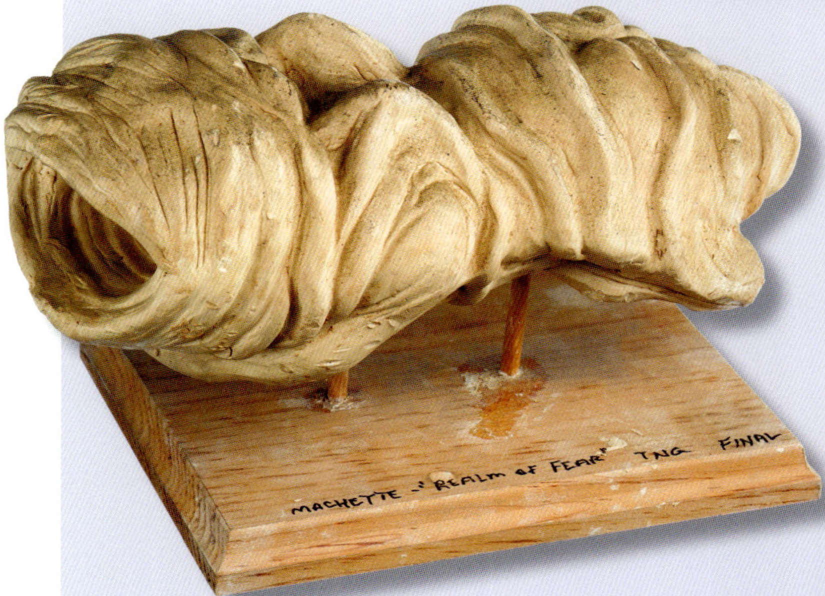

For the *TNG* episode 'Realm of Fear' we were called upon to create the first and only transporter point of view as Lt. Barclay (Dwight Schultz) sees an apparition while transporting. I wanted to give the audience a feel for what someone being transported would experience. We knew we needed sparkles, so we used the pom-pom along with the regular transporter sparkles, but we needed more so we added some weird distortion elements. To obtain these we shot some flapping sheets of heavy clear plastic against light and photographed silver cloth waved in sunlight for high contrast and organic fluidity. We combined those with some shiny elements shot through ripple glass.

During the transport, Barclay's vision of an ephemeral creature was actually a latex hand puppet worn on my forearm with a mouth I could move. I had sculpted a rough clay maquette of the creature's head, then VFX supervisor David Stipes recommended artist Carey Howe to sculpt more detailed maquettes in several configurations. The producers picked one, and then Carey made the final latex hand puppet. I put on a green suit, stood in front of a green screen, and performed all the creature motions by hand—because I'd been doing Tai Chi for decades I was able to make the motion suitably smooth and organic-looking. Working with VFX compositor Janet Muswell, my image and the green screen were removed, leaving only the puppet. Layering that in with the other elements was a very painterly experience, experimenting with the various images and how they affected each other—tweaking color, opacity, and layer order. In the finished shots it looked as if the creatures were swimming within the swirling energy of the transporter beam.

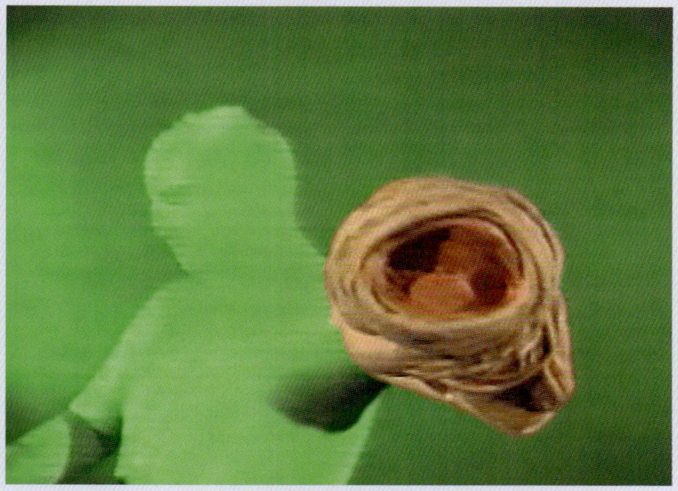

ABOVE: In a green suit in front of a green screen, I am animating the puppet by hand. The green allows the puppet to be isolated for compositing.

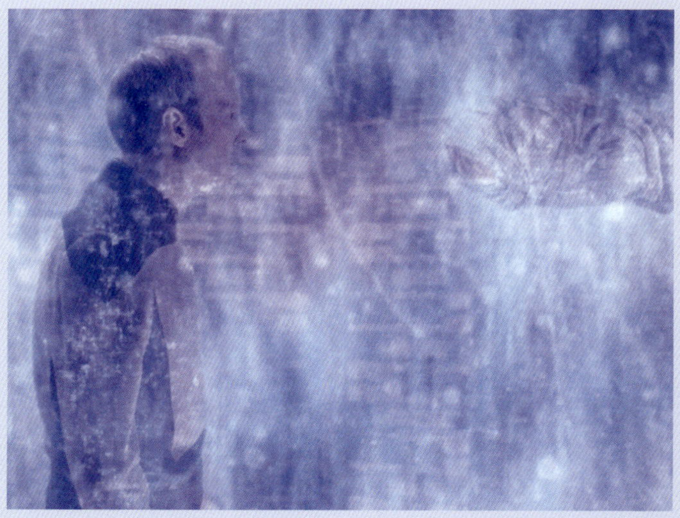

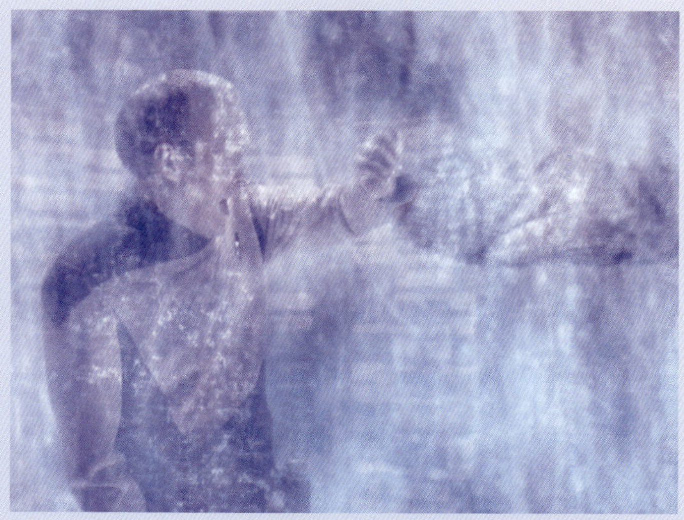

> *I can't forget the first time I worked with Dan Curry, when Foundation Imaging was hired to add visual effects to 'Basics, Part II.' I heard there was a creature that would menace the crew, who were marooned on a desolate planet. Inside a cave, several characters would encounter the large, slithering Hanonian land eel, which would, of course, try to eat them. It was a big deal for our team to get a chance to work on this project, and a meeting was arranged to discuss the creature. Dan's concept artwork was well fleshed out, so it was easy to imagine how it would look. The land eel had a long body and several spiked appendages, so as we discussed how it would move, Dan actually laid down on the floor and moved around to demonstrate. I was quite surprised, since I had not worked with anybody quite like Dan before, and he was not what I was expecting in a client!*
>
> *Only later could I fully appreciate how multi-faceted Dan is. In that first meeting I caught a glimpse of the artist, director, physical performer, and other roles he plays. It was deeply satisfying for a technical artist to collaborate with a person like Dan to bring these fantastic images to life for* Star Trek.
>
> John Teska, visual-effects artist

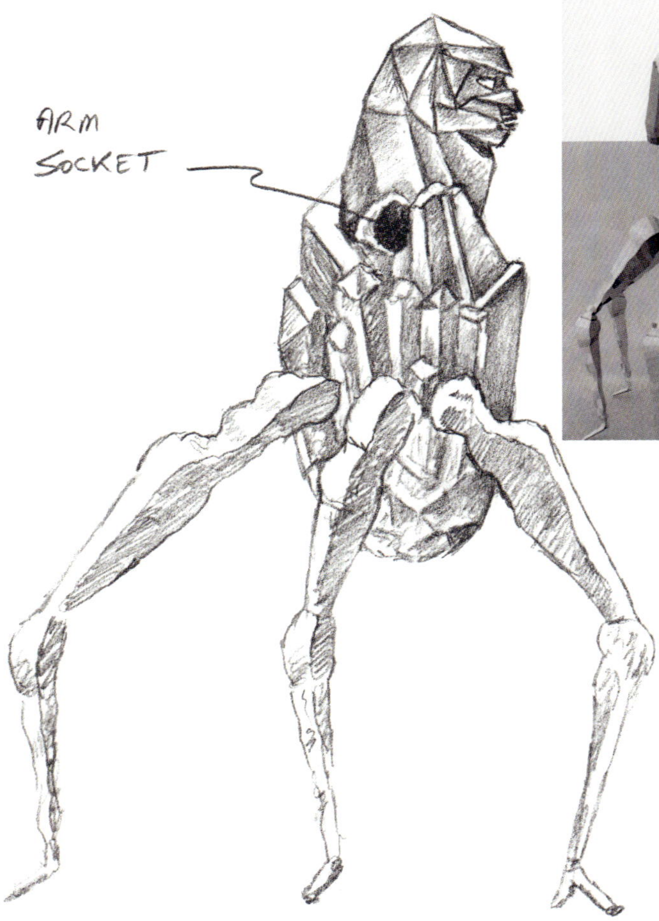

ABOVE: My very rough draft showing the body without arms.

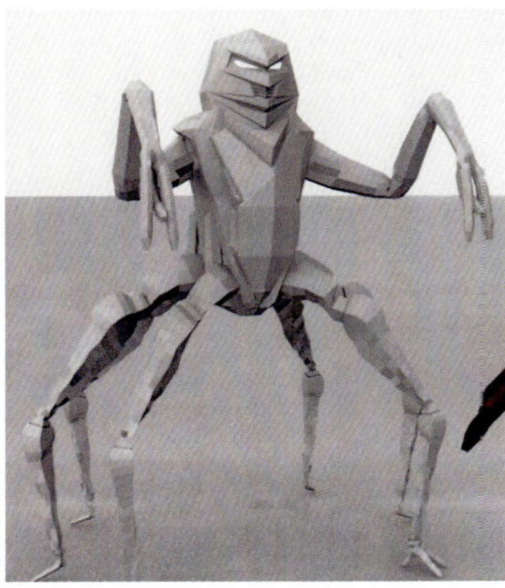

LEFT: CG 'smooth shade,' made with the CG artist's creative input.

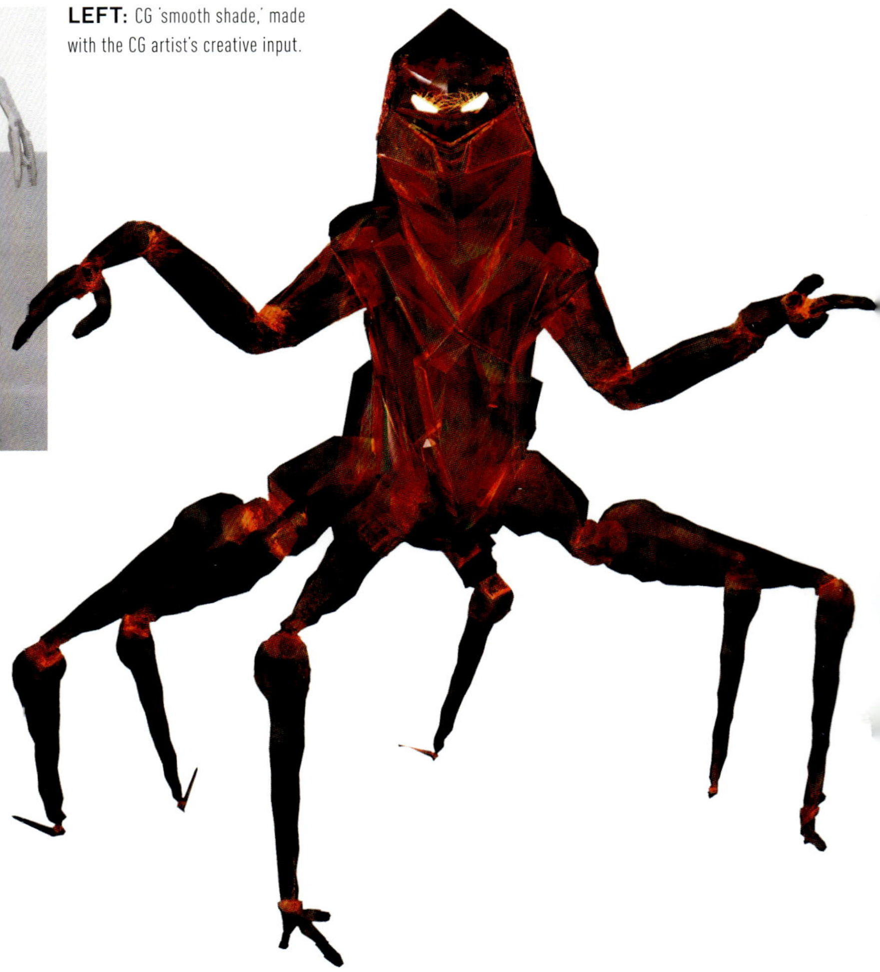

ABOVE: Final CG Tholian by 3D artist John Karner for one of VFX supervisor Ron Moore's favorite epsiodes.

able to accomplish in the daunting schedules we had to contend with. CG creatures are not a one-person effect, there are many heroes at different stages involved in putting them on screen. For example, for the Xindi Aquatics I did the conceptual sketches, Dave Morton did the modelling and animation, and Eric Hance did the rigging of an internal 'skeleton' that allowed the creature to move naturally. Each artist had special skills that cumulatively made the Aquatic possible. We had a great team of dedicated and visionary artists who were capable of delivering more than what we could possibly expect.

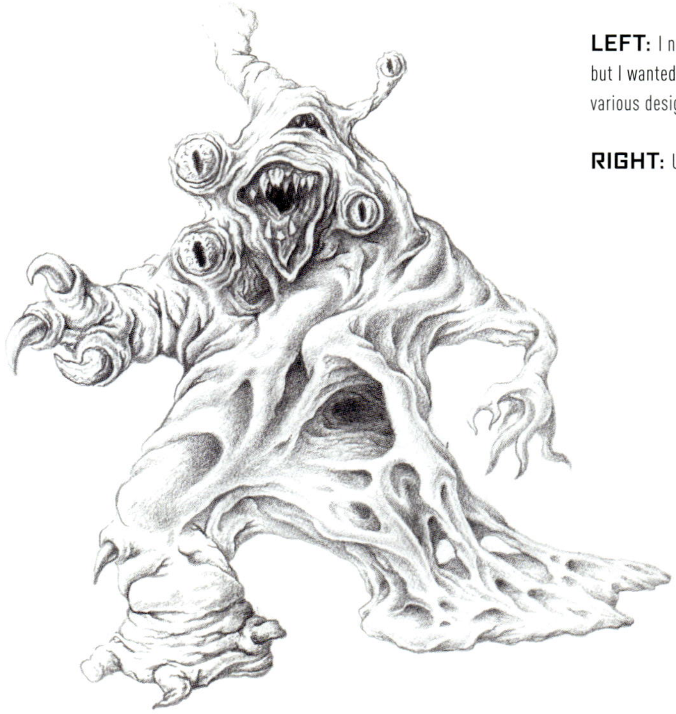

LEFT: I never intended to use this design, but I wanted to get the producers' reactions to various design elements.

RIGHT: Unused rough concept for an alien.

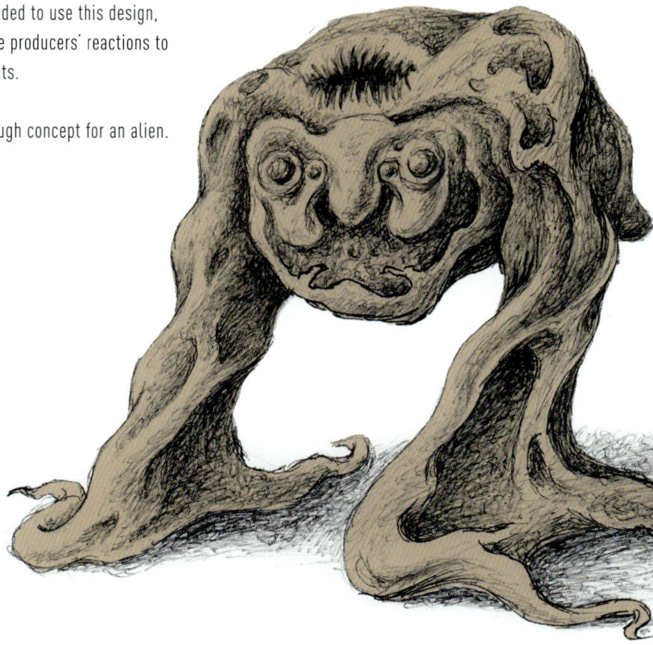

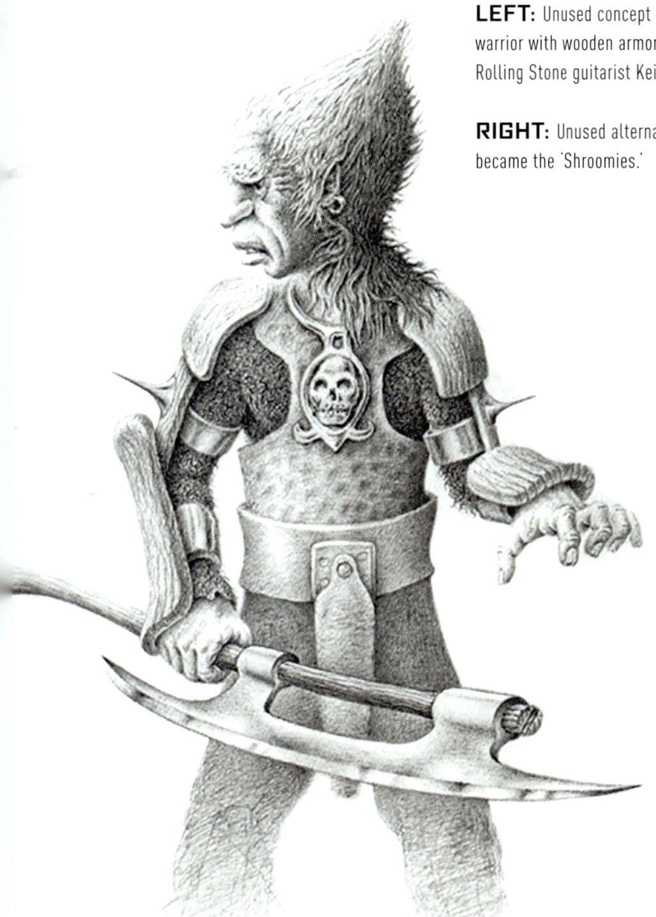

LEFT: Unused concept for a pre-industrial warrior with wooden armor. I was thinking of Rolling Stone guitarist Keith Richards as an orc.

RIGHT: Unused alternate concept for what became the 'Shroomies.'

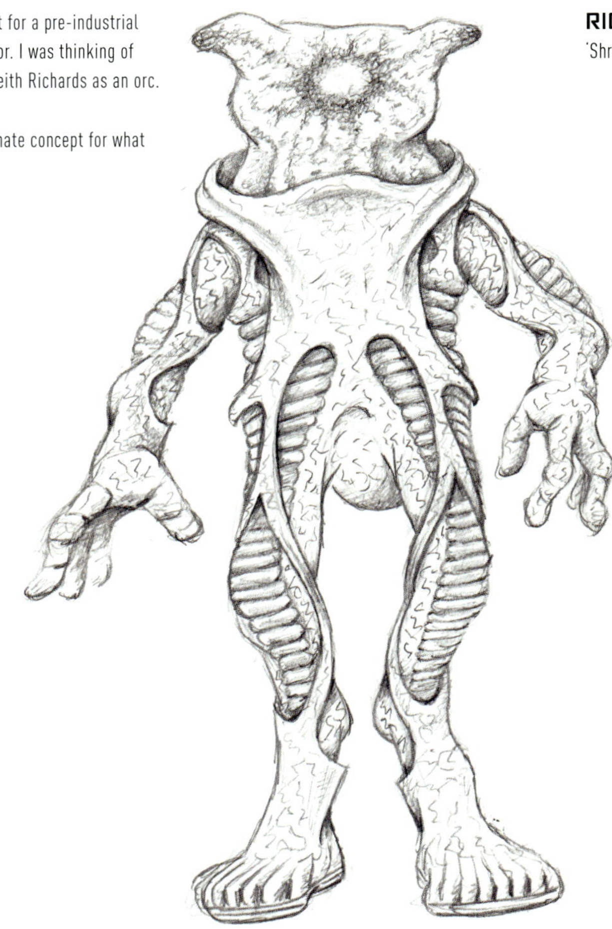

RIGHT: Another alternate 'Shroomie' concept (unused).

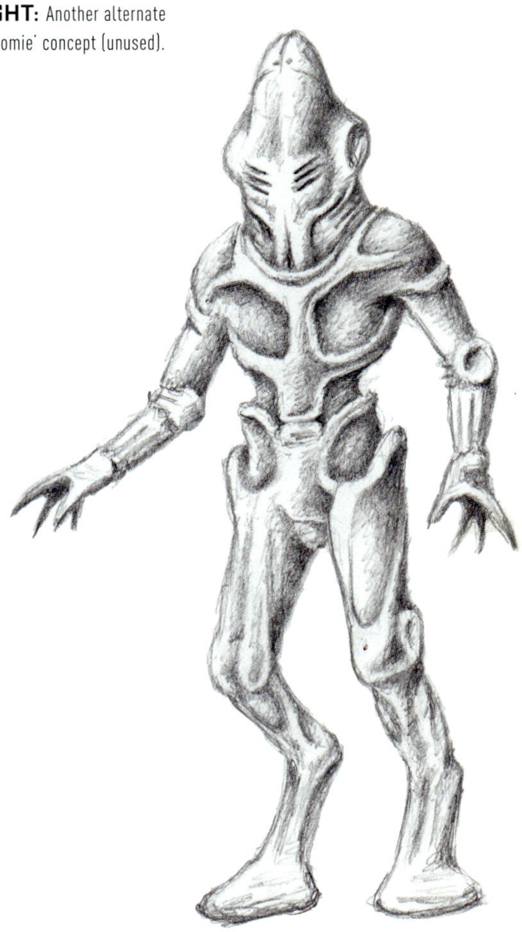

RIGHT: Storyboard pages with the title cards 'Greeked in', expressing the idea of an enigmatic shape revealing itself to be the champagne bottle that christens the new *Enterprise*.

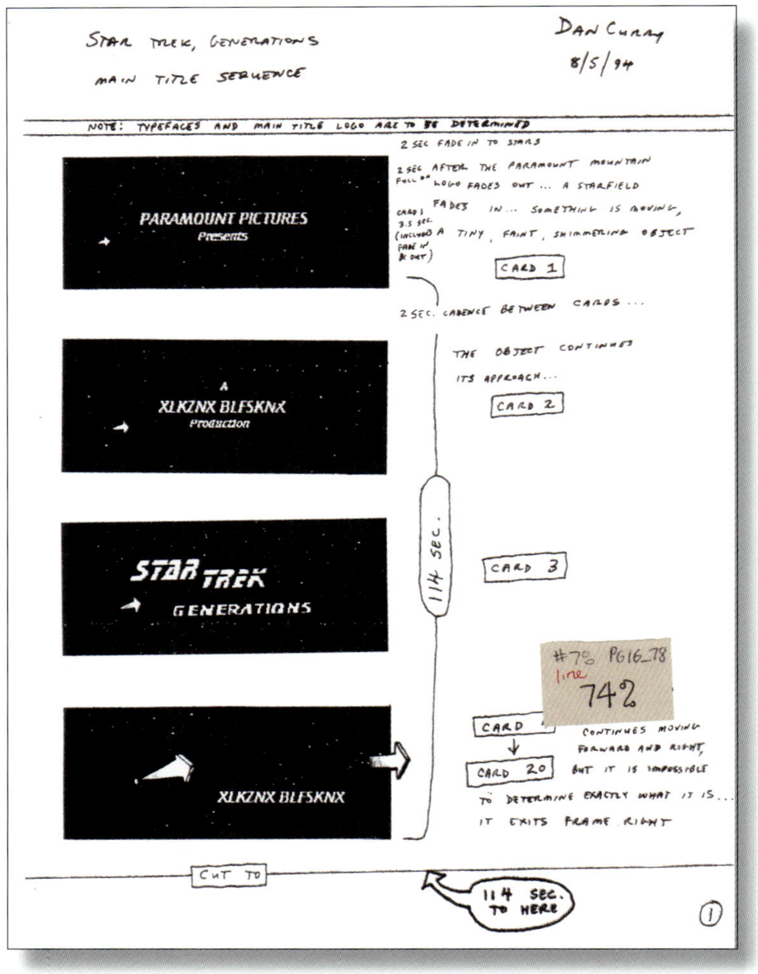

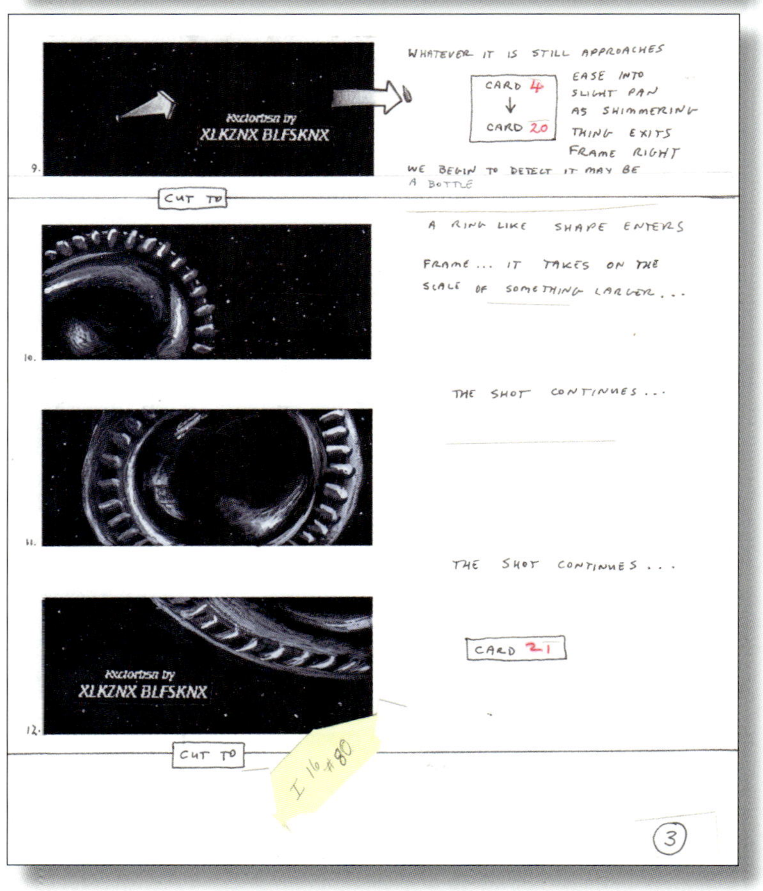

MOVIE TITLE SEQUENCES

DESIGNING *STAR TREK* TITLES FOR THE BIG SCREEN

I designed title sequences for a couple of the *Star Trek* features. The titles for *Star Trek IV: The Voyage Home* were my very first professional involvement with the *Star Trek* franchise, and the first time I met director and legendary actor Leonard Nimoy. This would have been in 1986. I was VP, Director of Creative Services at Cinema Research at the time, where I was supervising visual effects and designing title sequences for all sorts of movies and TV productions. Leonard wanted something really simple. I said, "Let me do something cool with the main title card," and he was happy with that. Working with veteran executive producer Ralph Winter and editor Peter Berger, I came up with a main title logo and a unique transporter effect to reveal it. Then after that everything was super simple—text over black.

I also designed the titles for *Star Trek Generations*, my only involvement with that feature. This time I collaborated closely with director David Carson, exploring his vision for the opening scenes. They already had the shot of the champagne bottle christening the *Enterprise*-B, and we discussed how best to lead into it. We had the idea of seeing something mysterious appear in space. We wouldn't know what it was or how big it was, and the audience wouldn't be able to tell whether it was threatening or benign, so they were introduced to an enigma right away. We recalled the opening of *Star Trek IV*, where a strange alien probe looms out of space, threatening Earth; we wanted our audience to think it might be something like that, but finally we revealed the label and the shape of the bottle, and the potential threat becomes a celebratory moment.

17. 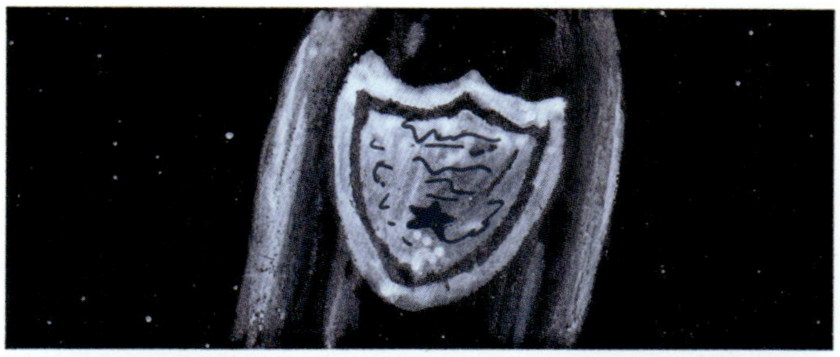

18. 

20. 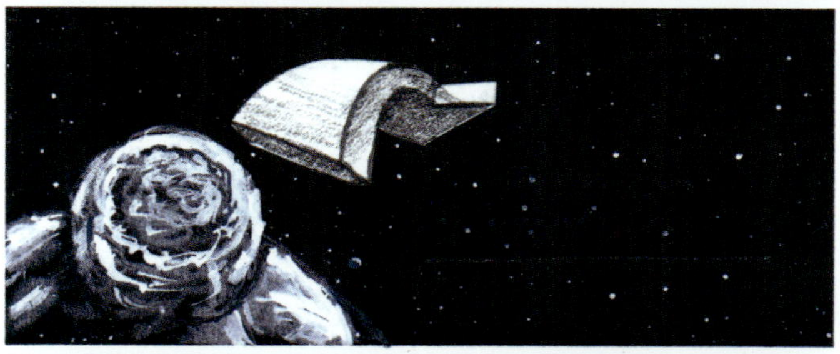

21. 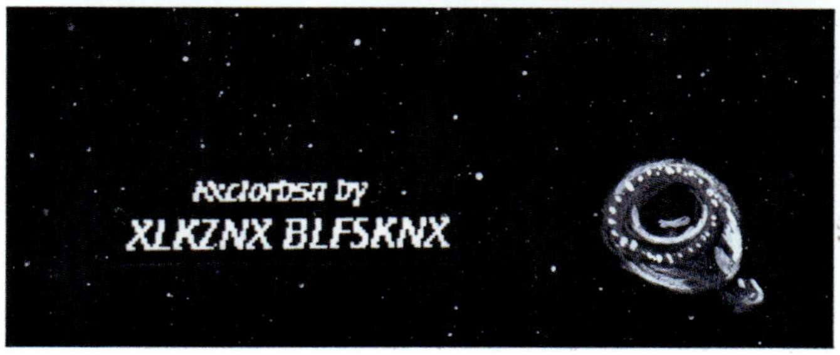

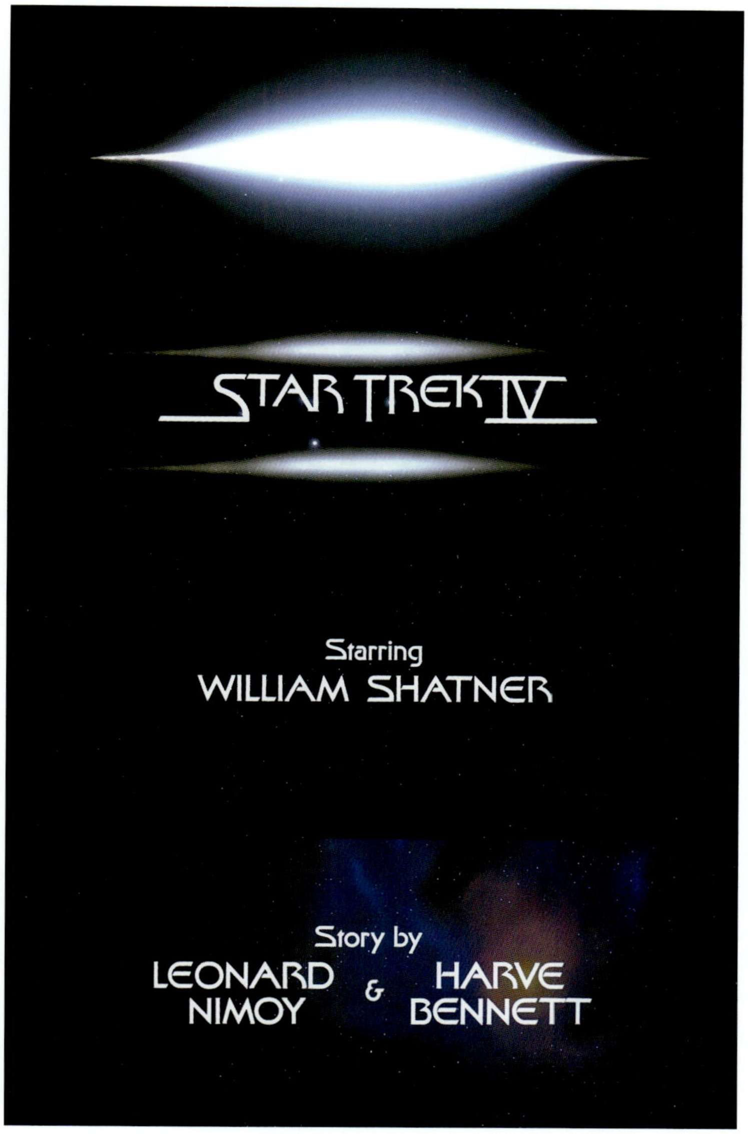

ABOVE: For *Star Trek IV* I suggested having the main title card beam in. Using the classic *Trek* font, I adjusted the proportions of the letters to create the logo.

INSIDE STORY

TNG TITLE CARD

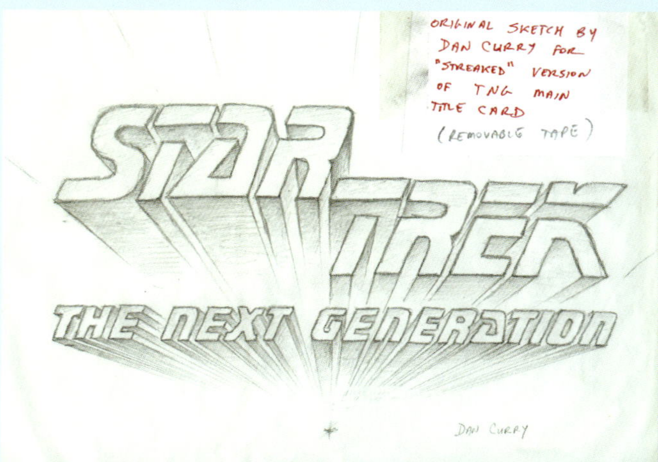

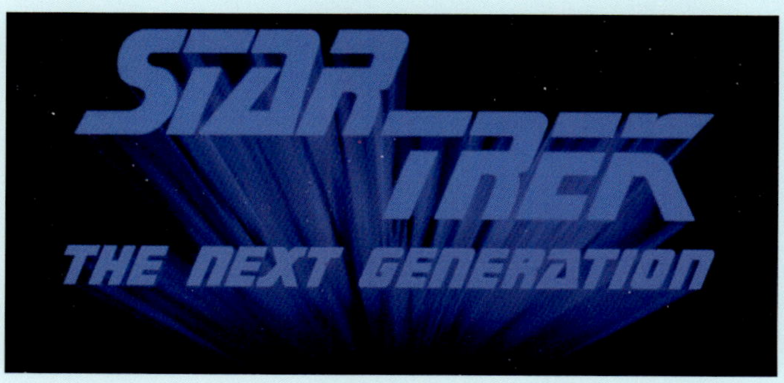

For the fifth season of *TNG*, Rick Berman asked me to redesign the title card so that it streaked like the Superman logo from the movie. We only used it for one year, however, before we went back to the original design.

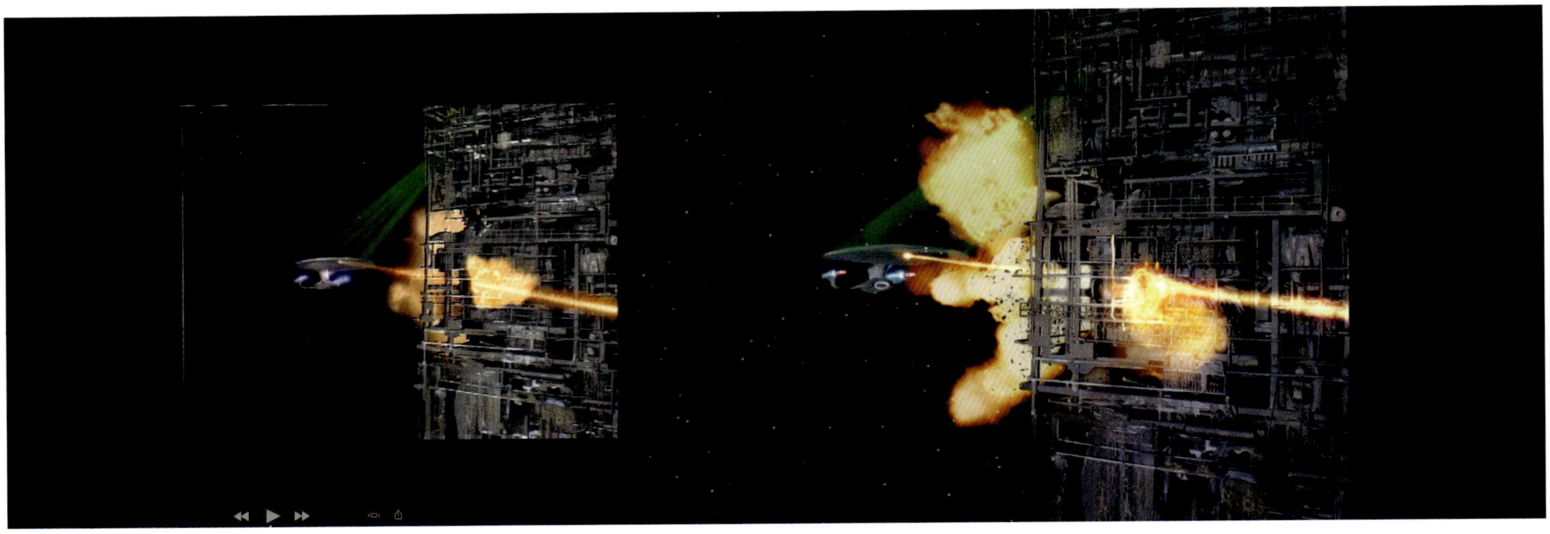

REVISITING *TNG*

AN OPPORTUNITY TO UPDATE SOME EFFECTS FOR THE 21ST CENTURY

Twenty-five years after we started work on *The Next Generation*, the series was re-released in high-definition Blu-ray. The way we had worked in the late 1980s—shooting on film and then transferring the footage to video—had enabled us to produce an unprecedented number of shots on a TV budget and schedule, but it had a disadvantage. The video resolution was never high enough quality for an HD release, and in these days of gargantuan flat-screen televisions, it showed.

However, because we had shot on film, we had the chance to do the transfer process again, this time in HD, recompositing all the motion-control work and all the shots that we'd created in the video editing suites. A company called Illuminate Hollywood won the job, and in 2012 they brought me in to supervise recreating the visual effects for the remastering of *TNG*'s Season 2.

The Blu-ray remastering was spread out among several companies. The entire project was overseen by studio executives Ryan Adams and David Grant, and *Star Trek* art department veterans Mike and Denise Okuda. Their encyclopedic knowledge of all things *Star Trek* was invaluable to preserving the tone of the series. I was able to bring in two *Star Trek* veterans, gifted VFX artist Doug Drexler and super coordinator David Takemura, to join the visual-effects team that also included Michael Davidson, Sean Jackson, Jesse Siglow, and Eric Acsel among others. The younger artists were excited to work on a show they grew up with, and to learn how things were done in the days before CG. I was pleased to take on the project as it would give me the opportunity to review work from decades earlier and to rework shots I was never satisfied with. Back in the day, we often just ran out of time. We called those shots 'CBBs' ('could-be-better'). Other shots that took many hours we called 'AFDs' ('all f*****g day'). Air dates are never to be missed.

It was an amazing feeling to look back on the work our VFX team created. I was delighted to see how well many of the shots held up, but some inevitably suffered from a straight up-res from 720 x 680 pixels to 1920 x 1080 pixels, and had to be significantly re-worked.

One major challenge was retransferring the motion-control ship shots. CIS's pin registered transfer system was no longer available, so the various elements comprising a ship shot—beauty, matte, lights, warp drive, and deflector shields—all had to be hand-tweaked in order to get them lined up perfectly. On the plus side, the ship shots all looked great; the *Enterprise*-D, the Borg Cube, the Klingon bird-of-prey and others revealed levels of detail never seen before, a testament to the skill and artistry of the modelmakers. Every detail of the models was incredibly clear, and had a remarkable level of verisimilitude.

Some shots, although brilliant for the time, had only been designed to be shown in standard definition. One of my all-time

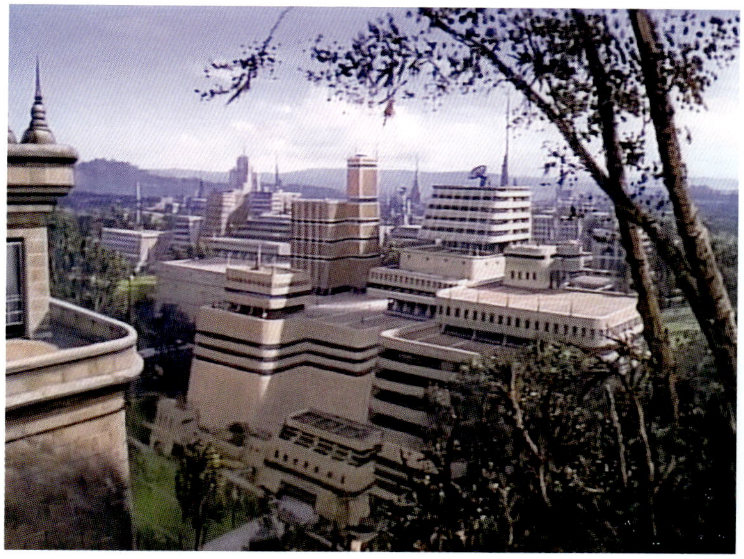

ABOVE: Syd Dutton's original matte painting for Angel One was reused several times.

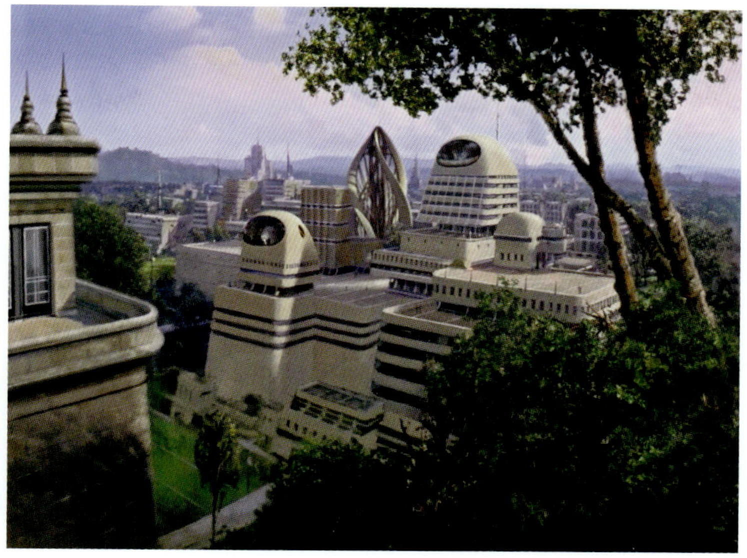

ABOVE: For the Blu-ray release I painted in new details to make the city look more sci-fi.

favorite shots was the interior of the Borg Cube from 'Q Who?,' a large-scale matte painting in oils on Masonite by the great matte artist Syd Dutton, photographed by his partner, Bill Taylor. When Syd did the original painting it was for low-resolution, standard-definition TV. Syd knew just how much detail was required. When we upped the resolution of the shot, the painterly aspects became apparent. I asked digital artist Sean Jackson to take on the task of recreating the Borg Cube interior. With great reverence, Sean recreated Syd's shot digitally, taking advantage of new technology to add kinetic elements like a liquid pool at the bottom, moving Borg in the distance, and the lighting panels in the Borg cubicles.

To make the cityscape in Syd's matte painting for 'Angel One' feel more sci-fi, I took the original into Photoshop and revised some of the buildings. I also broke the architecture up into layers, painting in what would have been behind the foreground elements so that in compositing we could do a multi-plane camera move. There were other original matte shots that needed improvement: the alien ruins from 'Chain of Command,' the badlands shots and disintegration scenes from 'Loud as a Whisper,' Nagilum from 'Where Silence Has Lease.' It was especially fun to recomposite the asteroid sequence in the holodeck and the hand-animated morph scenes from 'The Dauphin,' as well as the exterior space shots of the *Enterprise* facing off with the Borg from 'Q Who?'

Some of the younger compositors had never worked with motion-control miniatures before, and were excited to explore this older technology that produced such pristine images. They enjoyed redoing favorite shots they remembered seeing while growing up. Along with Doug (who won an Oscar for his *Dick Tracy* makeup work) and David T (who is a multiple Emmy winner) we were always asked questions about the surprising ways we did things 'back in the day.'

Between Doug, David T, and myself, we had worked on well over 100 productions. We entertained our younger colleagues, sharing stories of notable moments from our careers. They were talented, dedicated, and seemed to enjoy their adventure into ancient technology, and from the experience gained a new perspective on the art of visual effects. It also gave me a chance to look back. More than anything it reinforced my belief in the beauty of capturing images on film. We discovered crispness of image that we didn't really know was there, and I was proud to see how well the images stood up. In television, visual effects have to be handed over in whatever state they are in on the scheduled 'drop dead' date. I almost always look at every shot thinking there was something that could have been done to make them better.

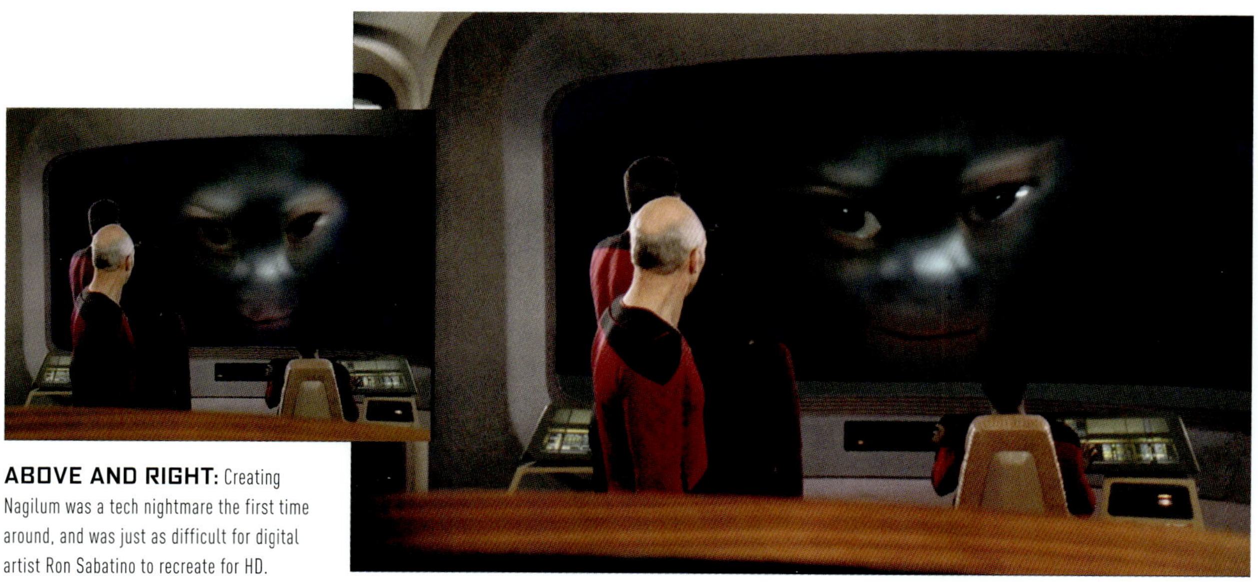

ABOVE AND RIGHT: Creating Nagilum was a tech nightmare the first time around, and was just as difficult for digital artist Ron Sabatino to recreate for HD.

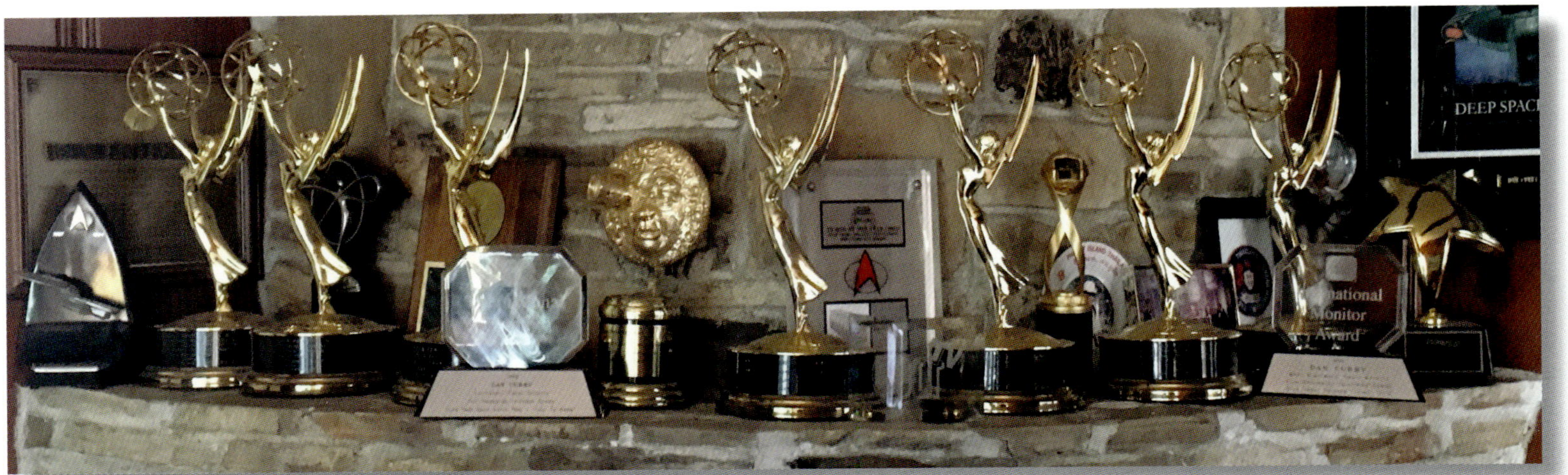

ABOVE: Dan's mantle featuring a selection of awards that were won by the *Star Trek* VFX team.

VFX FAMILY TREE

THE EXTENDED *STAR TREK* FAMILY, THESE COMPANIES PROVIDED INVALUABLE SUPPORT TO THE SHOW

SUPERVISORS, COORDINATORS AND ASSISTANTS

There was a core VFX team of brilliant people on staff at Paramount Pictures who worked directly for the production. When we began *The Next Generation*, Rob Legato and I served as visual-effects supervisors, alternating episodes. Rob was supported by resourceful coordinator Gary Hutzel, and I worked with good friend and coordinator Ronald B. Moore, one of the most organized people in the world. Both teams were supported by visual-effects associate David Takemura, who saw solutions to problems before others were aware that those problems existed.

As the *Star Trek* franchise expanded, adding *Deep Space Nine*, *Voyager*, and *Enterprise*, our department reorganized and grew to meet the visual-effects demands of the series. Rob went to oversee *Deep Space Nine*, and I stayed with *The Next Generation*, with Ron and Gary being promoted to supervisor. A year later Rob left, and I took over responsibility for all the shows. Over the years we were joined by VFX supervisors David Stipes, Mitch Suskin, and Glenn Neufeld, while David Takemura was promoted to coordinator. Michael Bakauskas, Liz Castro, Art Codron, Phil Barberio, Judy Elkins, Joe Bauer, and Adam Buckner joined the team as additional coordinators, and additional associates included Eddie Williams, Laura Lang, Armin Kevorkian, and Eric Alba. When *DS9* and *Voyager* were running simultaneously, supervising producer Peter Lauritson, seeing the need for additional help, promoted David Takemura to supervisor, and Eddie Williams became his coordinator, and they floated back and forth between both series.

CIS

CIS (Composite Image Systems), in Hollywood, played an essential role in *TNG*, *DS9*, and *Voyager*. CIS, led by Joe Mazza, was the only facility in the world at the time that could do pin registered transfers from film to video. This was absolutely necessary for *Star Trek*, as we were shooting motion-control miniatures that required multiple passes. We relied on CIS compositors like Don Lee, Steve Bowen, and Price Pethel to combine those elements into finished space shots, as well as compositing actors shot on blue screen over various backgrounds. CIS animators also did some phasers and VFX animation. Coming from the world of film and optical printers, entering the high-tech world of CIS was like walking onto the bridge of the *Enterprise*. Several years later, corporate changes led us to look for a new home for our artists that had been at The Post Group; CIS adapted two edit bays for the needs of *Star Trek*, and we welcomed them aboard.

I will always be grateful for the welcome extended to me personally by the artists, technicians, and staff at CIS, as well as the support and creative collaboration they gave *Star Trek*.

THE POST GROUP

For the early seasons of *The Next Generation*, The Post Group in Hollywood played a critical role in the creation of visual effects. The *TNG* visual-effects team spent endless hours working with their compositing editors and animators to put together a wide range of visual-effects shots including transporters, phasers, bluescreen, and one-of-a-kind shots. Over the years editors like Fred Raimondi, Peter Moyer, Scott Rader, Don Greenberg, Pat Clancy, David Pincus, and Peter Sternlicht, along with animators like Helen Davis, Steve Scott, Adam Howard, and Joni Jacobson, endured my supervision, shared their knowledge, and dedicated their artistry to making *TNG* visually rich. There was always great music in the edit bays, and fortunately everyone had a great sense of humor, so the long hours were made bearable by the camaraderie. We had a motto: 'Good enough is the enemy of excellence'.

DIGITAL MAGIC

Changes within The Post Group meant that we moved our veteran VFX 2D compositing and animation team to Digital Magic in Santa Monica. They set up two state-of-the-art edit bays specifically for *Star Trek*. First under the leadership of Rich Thorne, then Mark Miller, Digital Magic added compositors Steve Fong and Janet Muswell, along with animators Steve Price, Steve Scott, and Adam Howard. Working with the supervisors and coordinators from Paramount, the *Trek* VFX team at Digital Magic created approximately 3,000 shots per season.

TECHNICOLOR CREATIVE SERVICES (FORMERLY COMPLETE POST)

After two years at CIS, our 2D team sought a new home. We explored several possibilities, but after meeting with Bruce Long, VP at Technicolor Creative Services, who assured us that they would configure edit bays and an animation room to suit *Star Trek*'s specific needs, it became clear that TCS were the right team. Technicolor Creative Services was in Hollywood, convenient to the Paramount lot. Our VFX compositors Paul Hill and Steve Fong, along with animator Greg Rainoff, agreed with our team at Paramount to move to TCS, and together we produced an incredible volume of excellent visual effects that lent reality to the *Star Trek* universe.

PACIFIC OCEAN POST

When *Deep Space Nine* began, the visual-effects compositing demands doubled. Pacific Ocean Post became a particularly important part of *Deep Space Nine*, turning out an incredible number of shots per season. Pacific Ocean Post was in Santa Monica, not too far from Digital Magic, so it was very convenient despite being a little far from Paramount. This was the era when the Flame compositing system was a dominant force in post-production. POP had a great staff; Steve Fong was their brilliant VFX compositor, who was later joined by the resourceful Davy Nethercutt, and digital artist Adam Howard did an excellent job with animation and special shots. POP was a big multi-story building with a large central atrium, and was a pleasant place to work. Owner Alan Koslowski was a terrific guitarist, and had a large collection of unusual guitars in his office. I always enjoyed checking out Alan's museum-like office, and trying out his rare guitars.

FOUNDATION IMAGING

When *Babylon 5* did not renew Foundation Imaging's contract, I realized it was an opportunity for *Star Trek* to expand our CG capability. Led by visionary computer animator Ron Thornton and his partner Paul Bryant, Foundation Imaging was responsible for executing many memorable sequences for *Deep Space Nine*, *Voyager*, and *Enterprise*. *Star Trek* VFX supervisors and I would design sequences and collaborate with terrific CG artists like John Teska, Brandon MacDougall, Rob Bonchune, Adam 'Mojo' Liebowitz, John Allardice, Koji Kuramura, and their talented colleagues to bring them into existence.

Foundation was located in Valencia, north of LA, so we had to plan our visits carefully as the drive time in LA traffic could be considerable. A session working with the artists would keep us away from the studio for hours, but the communication time saved by dealing directly with them, as well as the quality of their work, made it worthwhile.

AMBLIN IMAGING/DIGITAL MUSE/ EDEN FX

Star Trek started working with Amblin Imaging in the final season of *The Next Generation*. Their team of artists delivered an impressive CG sequence at a budget we could live with. I also knew they could play an important part in the upcoming effects-heavy *Voyager* pilot and help us create imagery that would not be possible without CG technology. Because of the huge volume of visual effects needed for *Star Trek*, we split up the bulk of the CG work between Foundation Imaging and Amblin Imaging/Digital Muse. Amblin was founded at Universal Studios to create visual effects for *seaQuest DSV*. When the series was canceled, Universal decided to close up shop, so under the leadership of CG pioneer John Gross, Amblin Imaging reincarnated itself as Digital Muse.

When *Voyager* concluded, John Gross moved again, forming Eden FX, and continued being a part of *Star Trek* until the finale of *Enterprise*. Terrific 3D artists like John Teska, Fred Pienkos, Dave Morton, Pierre Drolet, Sean Scott, Rob Bonchune, Koji Kuramura, Sean Scott, Eric Hance, and many others delivered ship shots, matte paintings, and a range of other visual effects. The crew was great to work with; I was especially appreciative of how beautifully they interpreted my storyboards. They also created some of the best digital models in television. Special recognition must be given to 3D model maker Pierre Drolet, who added his own creative genius to the blueprints provided by *Star Trek*'s art department for *Enterprise* NX-01 and brought into existence one of the most beautifully crafted digital models ever.

VISION ART

Vision Art, led by father-and-son team David and Josh Rose, was conveniently located across the street from Digital Magic, where we did 2D compositing. This made it easy to run back and forth to supervise the work being done in both facilities. Their relationship with *Star Trek* began with *DS9* when Rob Legato developed the wormhole, and stages of the Odo morph. We also relied on them for ship shots.

TREK TANGENTS

OTHER PROJECTS THAT TOUCH THE *STAR TREK* WORLD

RIGHT: Collector's plates are popular among fans. I was commissioned to do a series of paintings based on episodes of *Voyager*.

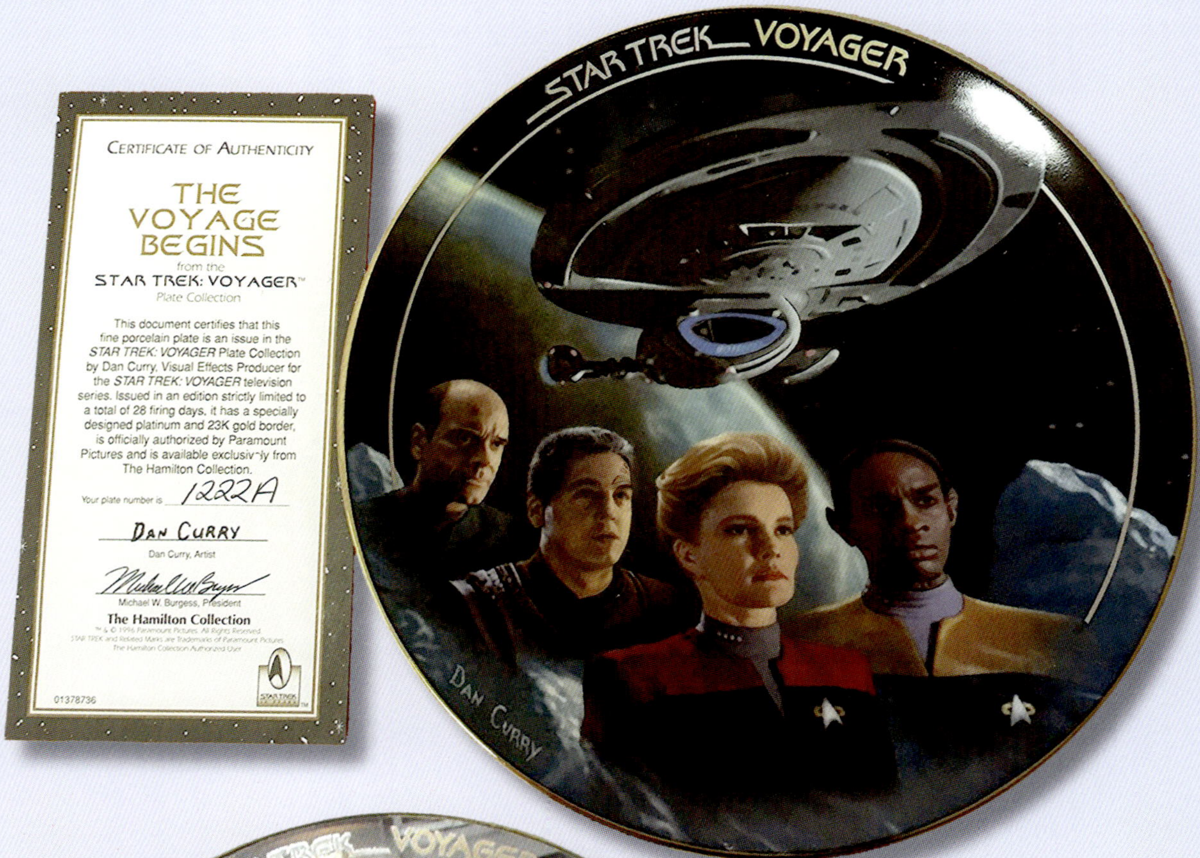

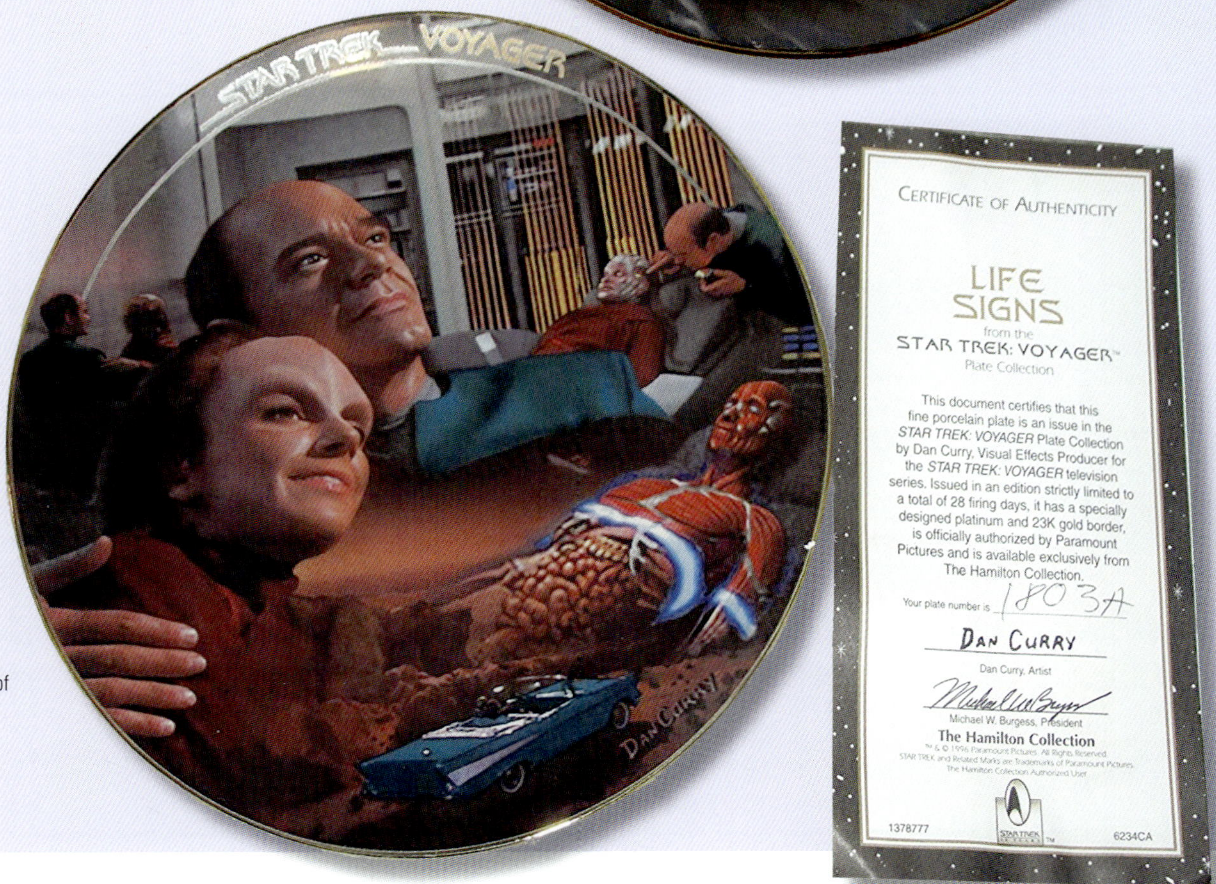

RIGHT: Each plate represents key moments from a given episode that focuses on a particular set of characters.

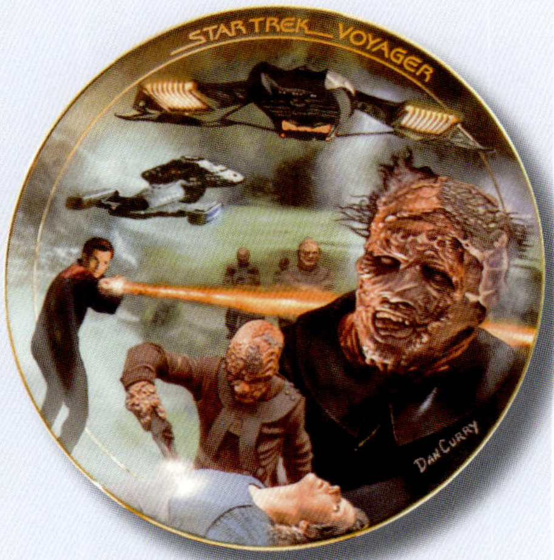

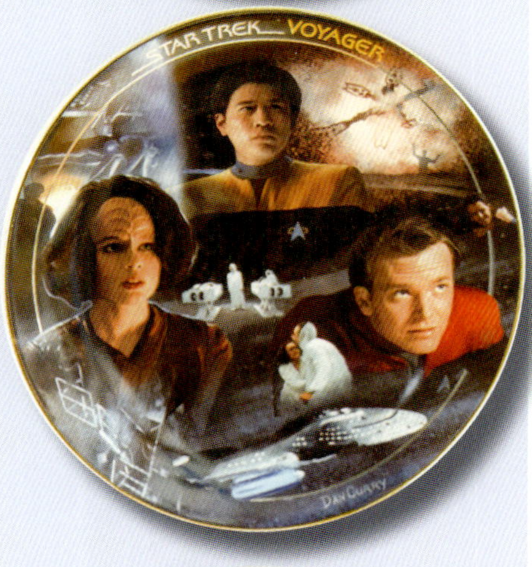

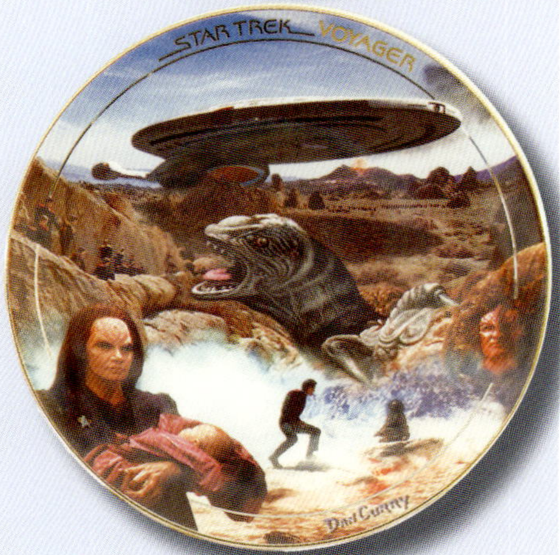

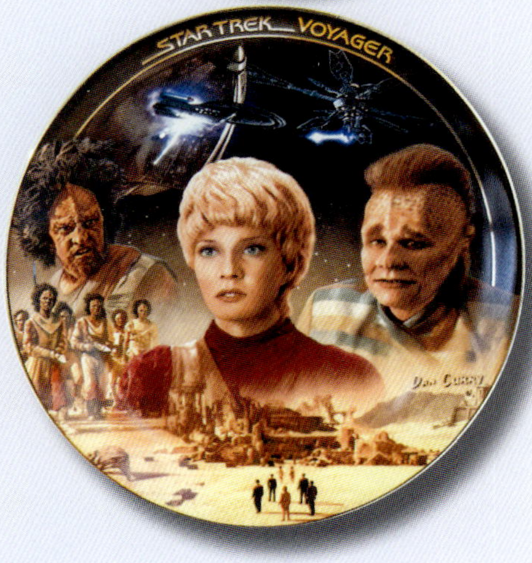

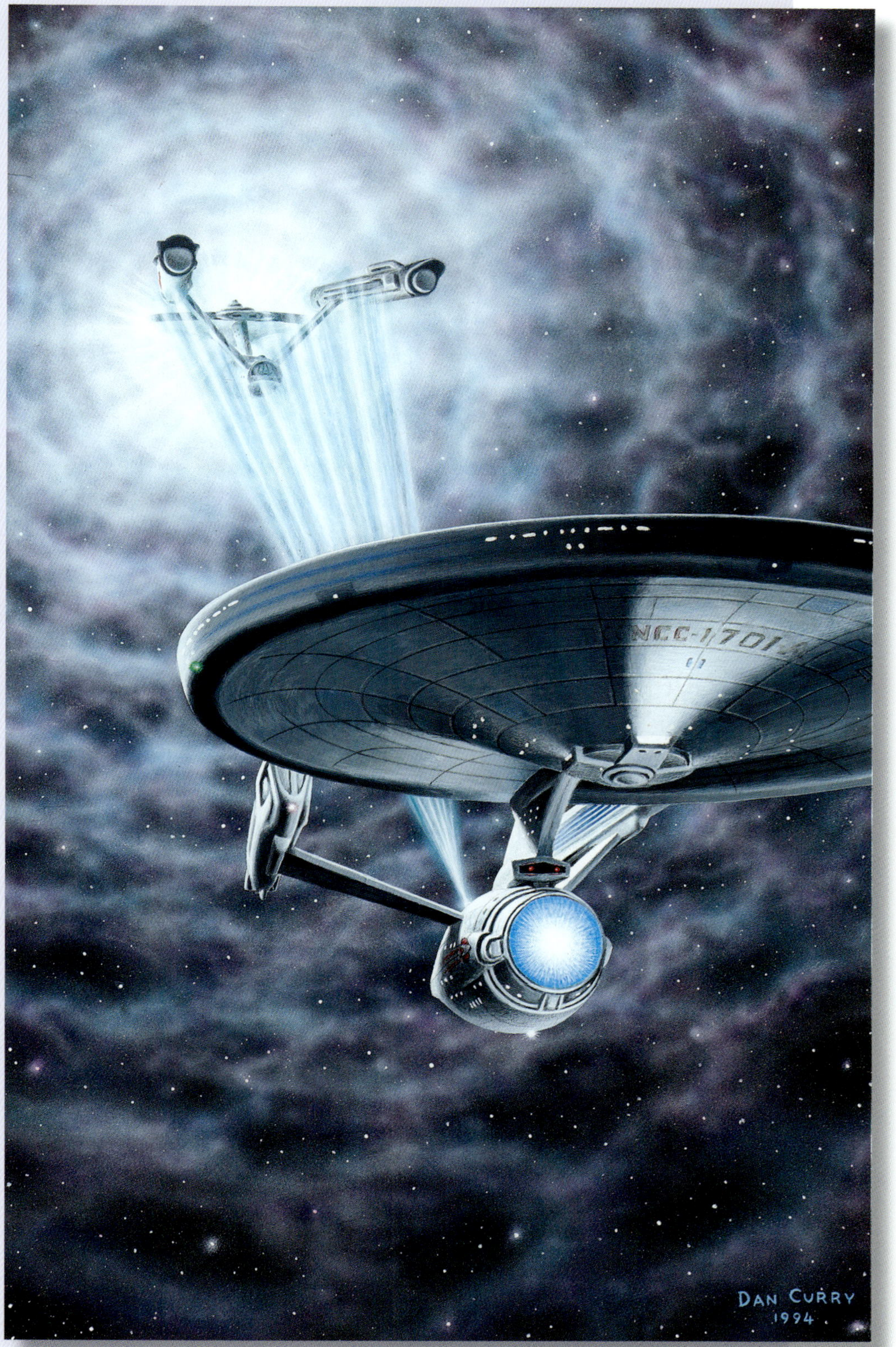

ABOVE: I always wanted to do a comic book cover. In 1996 I had the chance when DC Comics commissioned me to do this one, an acrylic painting on board.

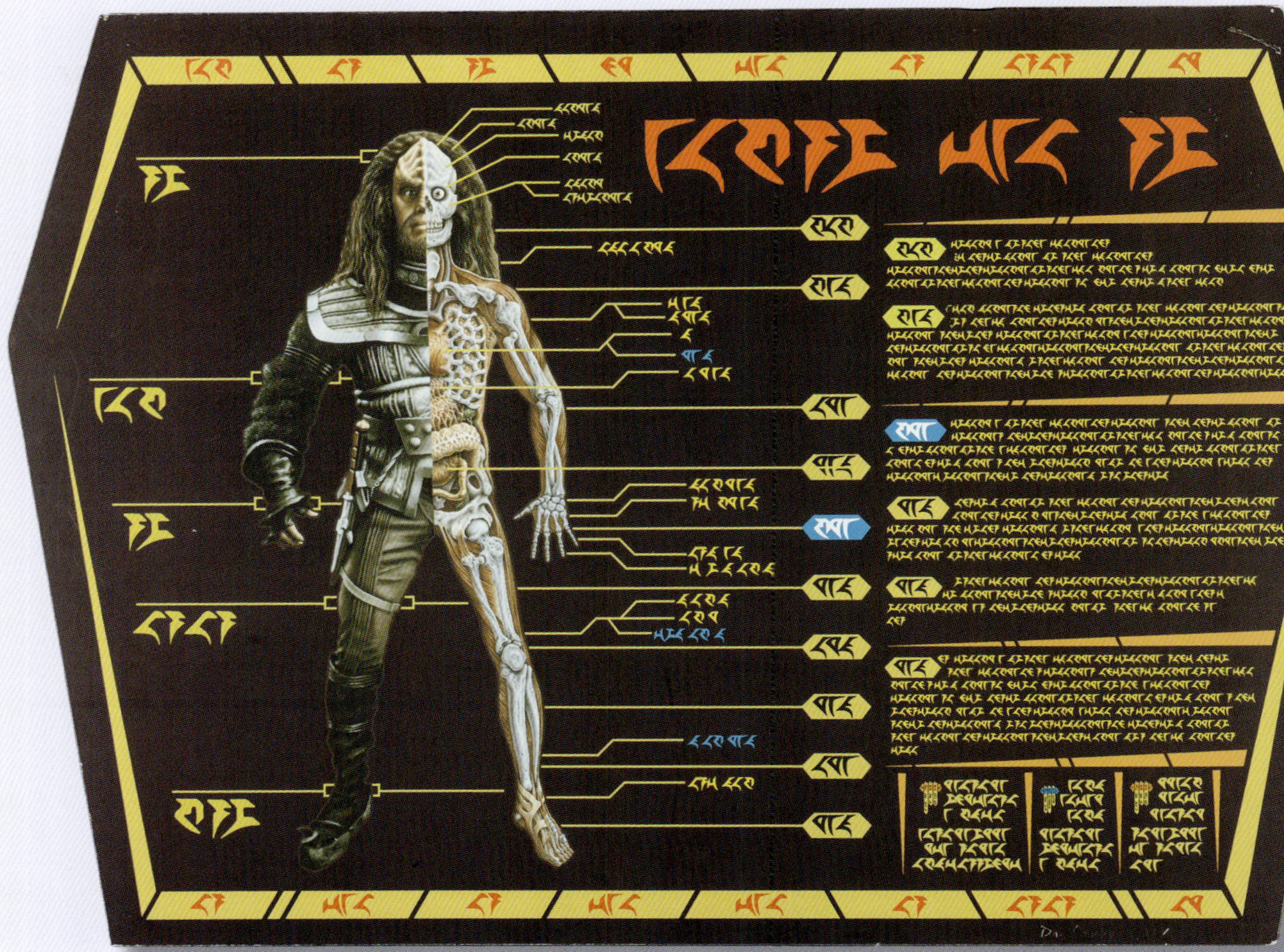

ABOVE: The art department incorporated my 'Visible Klingon' painting into an anatomy chart seen in a Klingon medical lab for *Enterprise*.

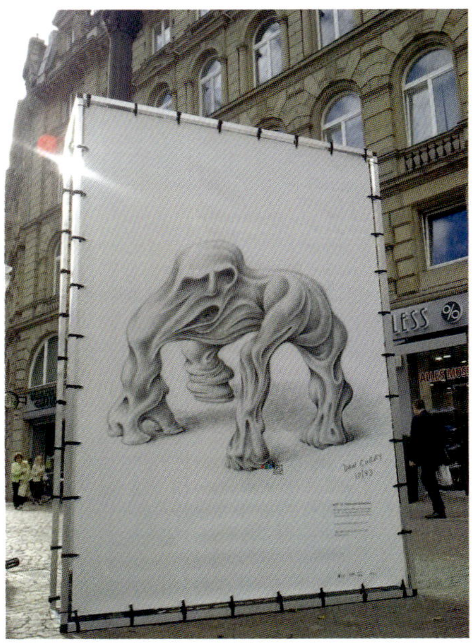

ABOVE: I was amazed when a German museum had an exhibition of movie conceptual art and chose this sketch to blow up (from an original size of 8.5" x 11") for a sidewalk poster.

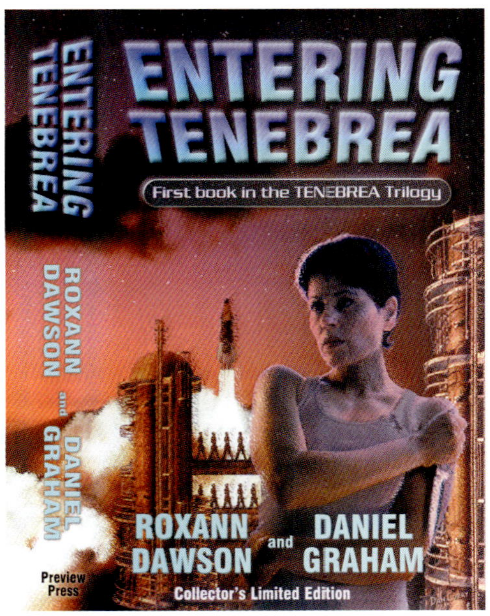

ABOVE: My neighbor Roxann Dawson (Torres) co-wrote a sci-fi trilogy with Daniel Graham and asked me to design a book cover, with herself modeling for the protagonist.

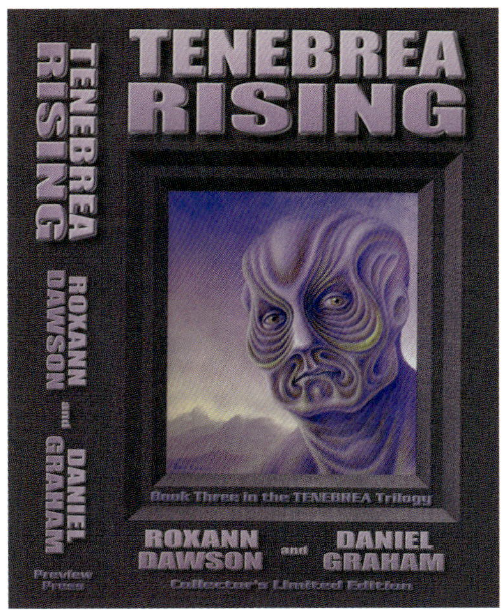

ABOVE: The second book cover featured a wise alien that I painted in oils and combined with the graphic elements in Photoshop.

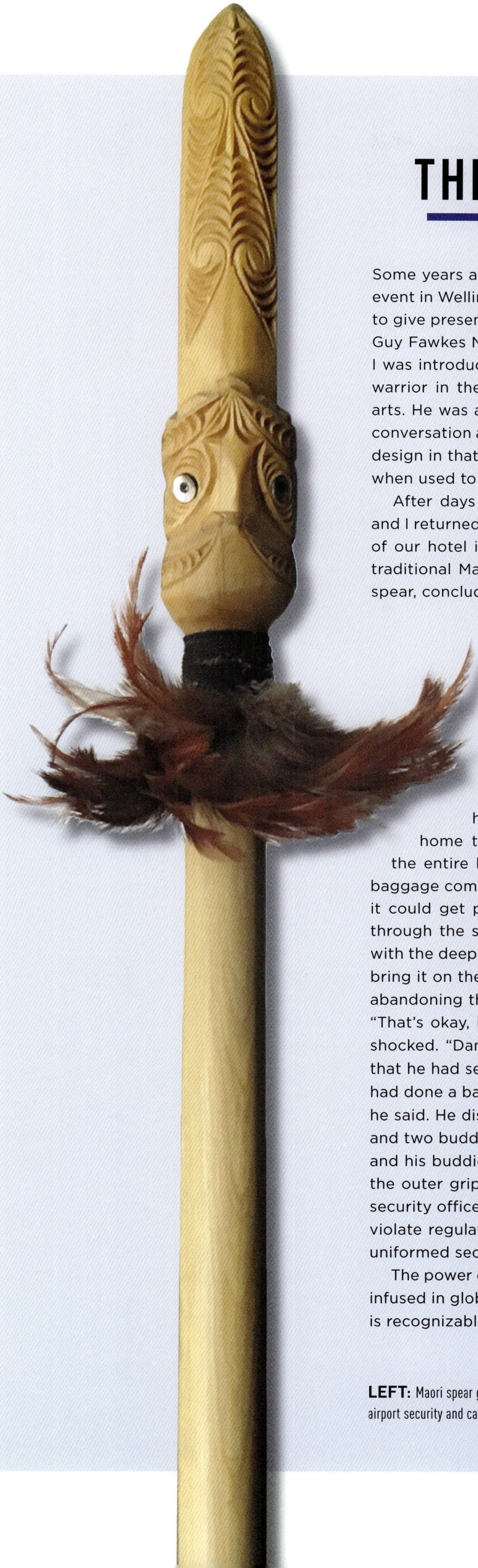

INSIDE STORY

THE POWER OF *STAR TREK*

Some years after I left the *Star Trek* family, the Visual Effects Society sponsored an event in Wellington, New Zealand. A number of visual-effects luminaries were invited to give presentations, and I was honored to be included. Our first night there was on Guy Fawkes Night (November 5th), and there was a huge celebration in the harbor. I was introduced to an incredible Maori traditional martial artist, Toa Waaka, a true warrior in the traditional sense, who ran a school to preserve indigenous martial arts. He was aware of my martial arts contributions to *Star Trek*, and we got into a conversation about spear ergonomics. He explained that Maori spears were unique in design in that they had a flared and flattened butt end that could concentrate force when used to deliver blows, and could even double as an emergency canoe paddle.

After days of lectures, workshops, and presentations, my fellow VES members and I returned from our last engagement at a university. Toa was waiting in the lobby of our hotel in a black suit holding a beautiful ceremonial spear. He performed a traditional Maori presentation ceremony, demonstrating his amazing skill with the spear, concluding with touching foreheads and handing me the spear. Toa asked me to show him something with the spear, so I demonstrated my favorite Chinese disembowelment move, which entails a body shake that draws a perfect ellipse with the blade around an opponent's rectus abdominus plate. We were both chagrined to notice a crowd in the lobby staring at us, but I will always appreciate the generosity of a true warrior, Toa Waaka.

Bringing the wooden spear on a domestic flight thankfully presented no security problem, and the airline staff simply put it in a closet for me. An international flight would have stricter security, however, so I was concerned about how to get the treasured spear home to LA. I found a cardboard tube not quite long enough to protect the entire length of the spear; I feared the ends would get snapped off in the baggage compartment so, since it was just an all-wood ceremonial spear, I assumed it could get put in a closet as on a local flight. Wrong. When the package went through the security x-ray conveyor belt, the security officer, a huge bodybuilder with the deepest voice I have ever heard, told me it was a weapon and that I couldn't bring it on the plane. Begging was of no avail, and I was crushed at the prospect of abandoning the spear, but one of my companions jokingly told the security officer, "That's okay, it's Dan Curry from *Star Trek*. No security threat." The officer looked shocked. "Dan Curry? *Star Trek*? You're the inventor of the *bat'leth*." He explained that he had seen the DVD extra from the Season 6 box set of *TNG* episodes where I had done a bat'leth demonstration. We chatted about the *bat'leth* briefly. "Hold on," he said. He disappeared for a few moments, and came back with a big roll of paper and two buddies. He asked if I would draw out some custom *bat'leths*, sized for him and his buddies. I was happy to do the sketches for them, scaling each one so that the outer grip holes were shoulder-width apart. "I wouldn't ordinarily do this," the security officer explained, "but I'll personally stow the spear on the plane so it won't violate regulations." True to his word, when I got off the plane at LAX there was a uniformed security guard holding the spear and a sign with my name on it.

The power of *Star Trek*. The universe of Gene Roddenberry's imagination has been infused in global culture, and resonates with such intensity that even a specific prop is recognizable on the other side of the world.

LEFT: Maori spear given to me by amazing traditional martial artist Toa Waaka, which miraculously made it through New Zealand airport security and came to LA.

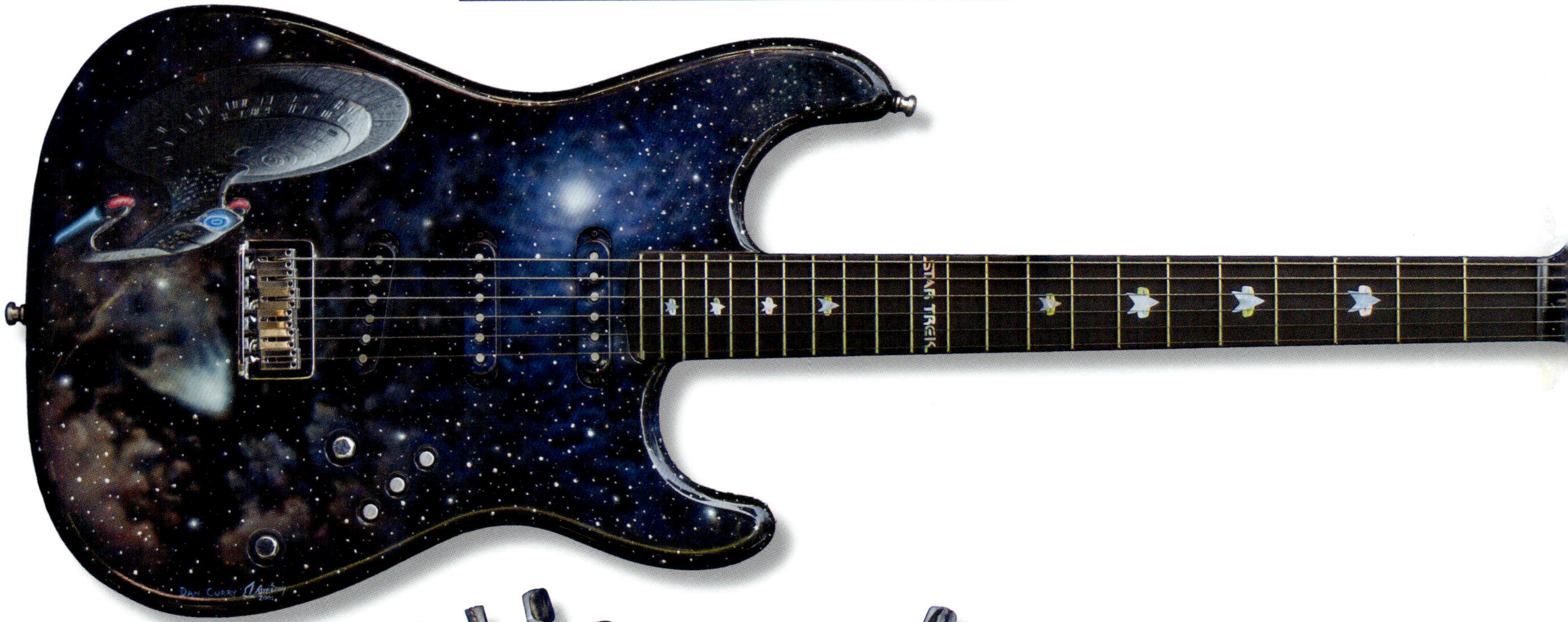

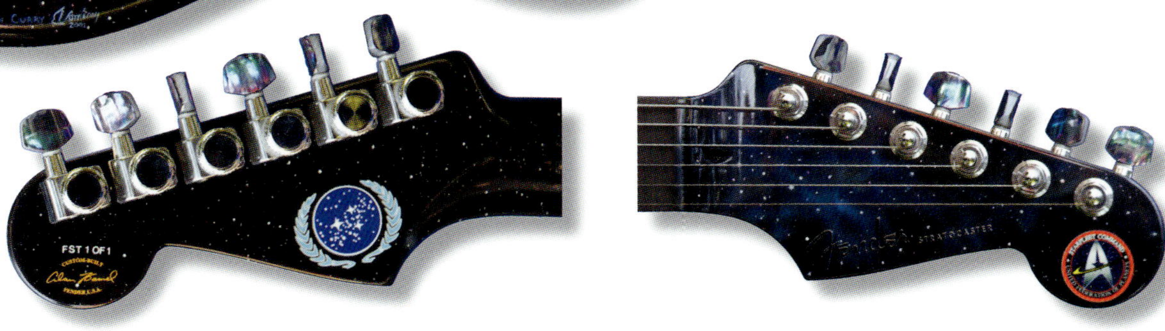

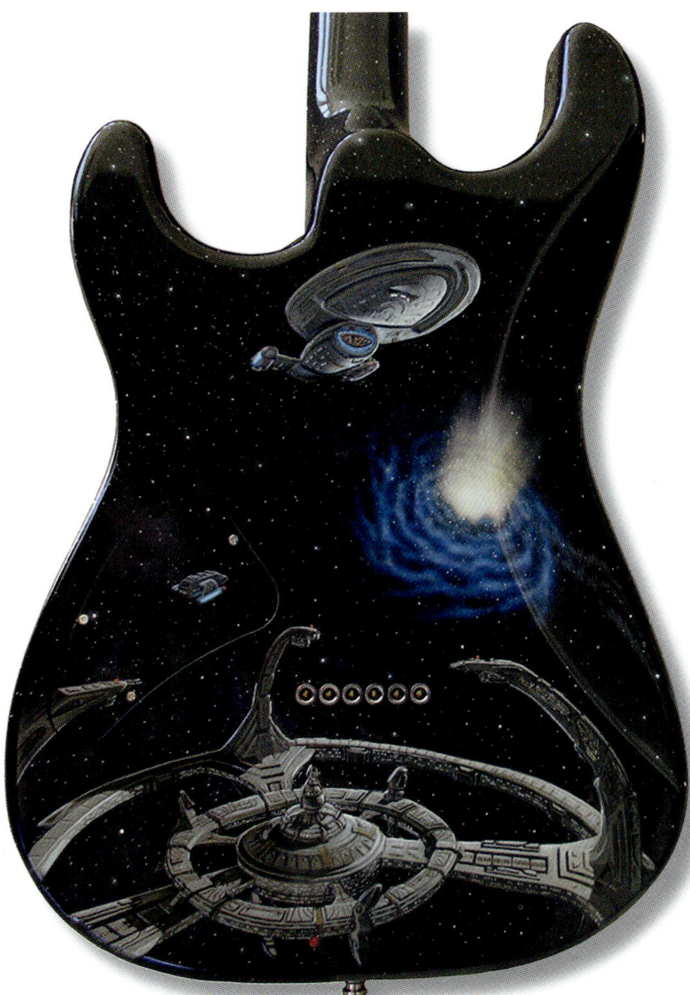

THE *STAR TREK* GUITAR

In 2000 my friend and colleague Ron Moore, who is an excellent guitarist, had an idea. He had friends at legendary guitar maker Fender, and knew that in addition to their regular line of great guitars, Fender also produced specialty 'art guitars.' Ron asked if I was interested in designing a *Star Trek* art guitar. Of course I was, being a guitar player myself, so Ron set up some meetings with Alan Hamel, head of Fender's custom shop in Corona, California, and some of his associates. It was a thrill to visit Fender's incredibly high-tech factory, and after several meetings we came up with a plan to design the *Star Trek* guitar based on Fender's classic solid-body Stratocaster model. The goal was to create a limited-edition line of these guitars, and make them available to fans.

Fender gave me some guitar bodies and necks to experiment with and work out a design. I did some drawings, discussed them with Ron, and finally glued some images on paper onto a blank Stratocaster body, and some scaled printouts of the Starfleet communicator on the neck. The guitar featured the *Enterprise*-D on the front, and Deep Space Nine, the wormhole, and *Voyager* on the back. Ron and I went back to Fender and met with master carver George Amarkay. I wanted a smooth, uninterrupted surface for the front of

LEFT: Ron Moore had the idea of doing a *Star Trek* art guitar with Fender. It was a rewarding collaboration with some amazingly talented people.

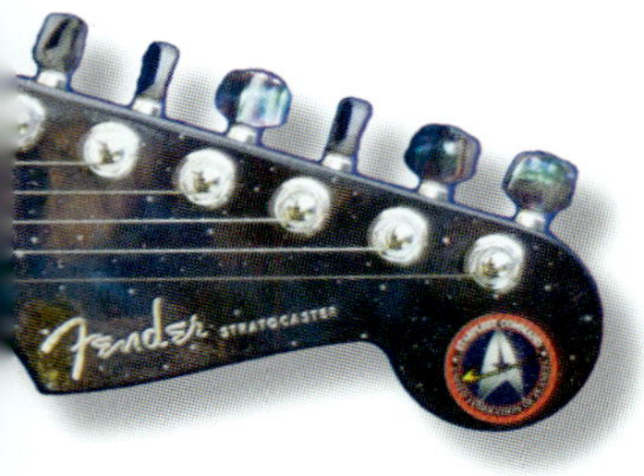

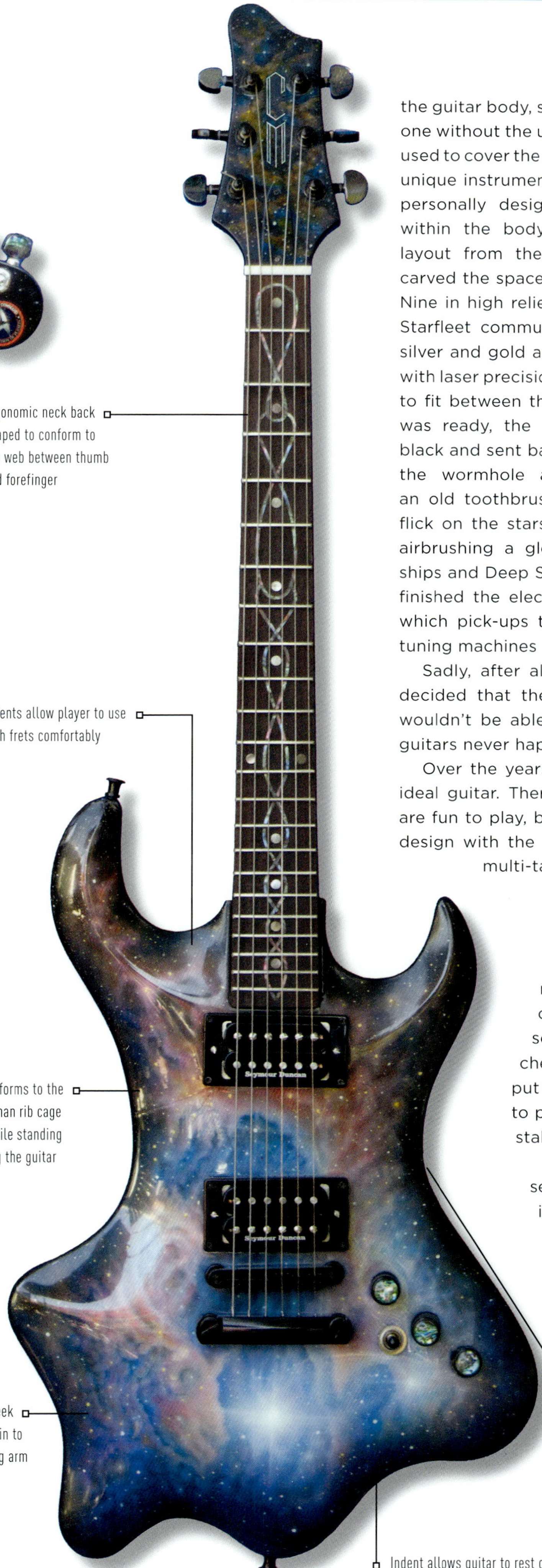

LEFT: The design of the CurMac (Curry/MacDougall) guitar was driven by thoughtful player ergonomics and Brandon's superb sense of craftsmanship.

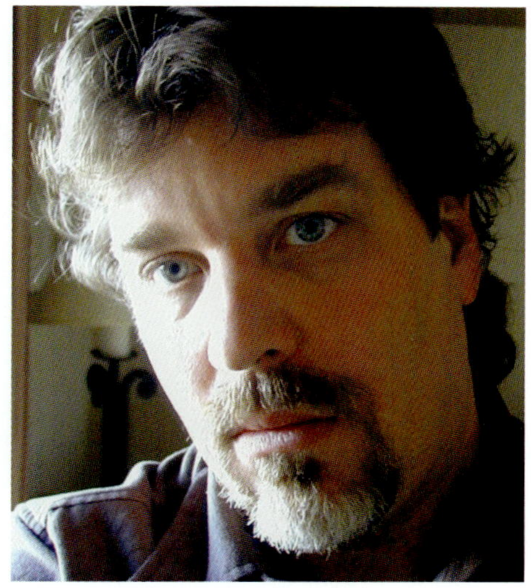

ABOVE: Brandon MacDougall, master digital VFX artist, luthier, violin maker, and guitarist.

the guitar body, so Alan agreed to make one without the usual plastic pick guard used to cover the electronics and made a unique instrument with the electronics, personally designed by Alan, hidden within the body. George copied the layout from the mock-up I did, and carved the spaceships and Deep Space Nine in high relief, like medallions. The Starfleet communicators, crafted from silver and gold abalone, were mounted with laser precision into the neck, scaled to fit between the frets. When George was ready, the guitar was primed in black and sent back to me. I airbrushed the wormhole and nebulosity, used an old toothbrush and white paint to flick on the stars (enhancing some by airbrushing a glow), and painted the ships and Deep Space Nine with small brushes. Fender did the final gloss coat, and finished the electronics with a unique push-button selector system for choosing which pick-ups to activate. Finally, we agreed on mother-of-pearl knobs on the tuning machines to complete the sci-fi look.

Sadly, after all that work, Ron and I were disappointed to learn that Fender decided that the guitars would be too expensive to produce and feared they wouldn't be able to sell them at the price they would need, so these *Star Trek* guitars never happened, leaving only the original '1 of 1.'

Over the years, my personal guitar collection grew as I kept searching for the ideal guitar. There are so many great guitars by different manufacturers, and all are fun to play, but none seemed to fit me perfectly. I began to think about guitar design with the sense of ergonomics I apply to bladed weapons. My friend, the multi-talented Brandon MacDougall, who had been a CG model builder and digital artist at Foundation Imaging and had done a lot of brilliant work for *Star Trek*, was also a master luthier and violin maker. Brandon's electric concert violins are uniquely fluid in design, play beautifully, and sound terrific. Inspired by playing my much-loved Fender Stratocaster, I kept thinking, "What if the upper curve was designed to arc around a human ribcage? What if I added something that would support the playing arm the way a violin's cheek piece allows the player to meld with the instrument? What if I put a concavity in the lower corner of the body for a guitarist wanting to play in seated classical style, allowing the instrument to have great stability?"

I decided to send Brandon sketches of some design ideas, just to see what a great guitarist/master instrument maker thought. Brandon immediately understood the ergonomics, and added his own ideas. We then sent images back and forth until we settled on one design. Brandon has an impressive shop for making instruments, and offered to make a prototype, so we decided to partner together in the guitar project. We both tested the first version, made some design changes that we felt were needed after handling it, and came up with the current version. Brandon and I believe we have come up with one of the most ergonomically comfortable guitars ever: we call it the CurMac Mobius Flux.

A PERSONAL ARTWORK GALLERY

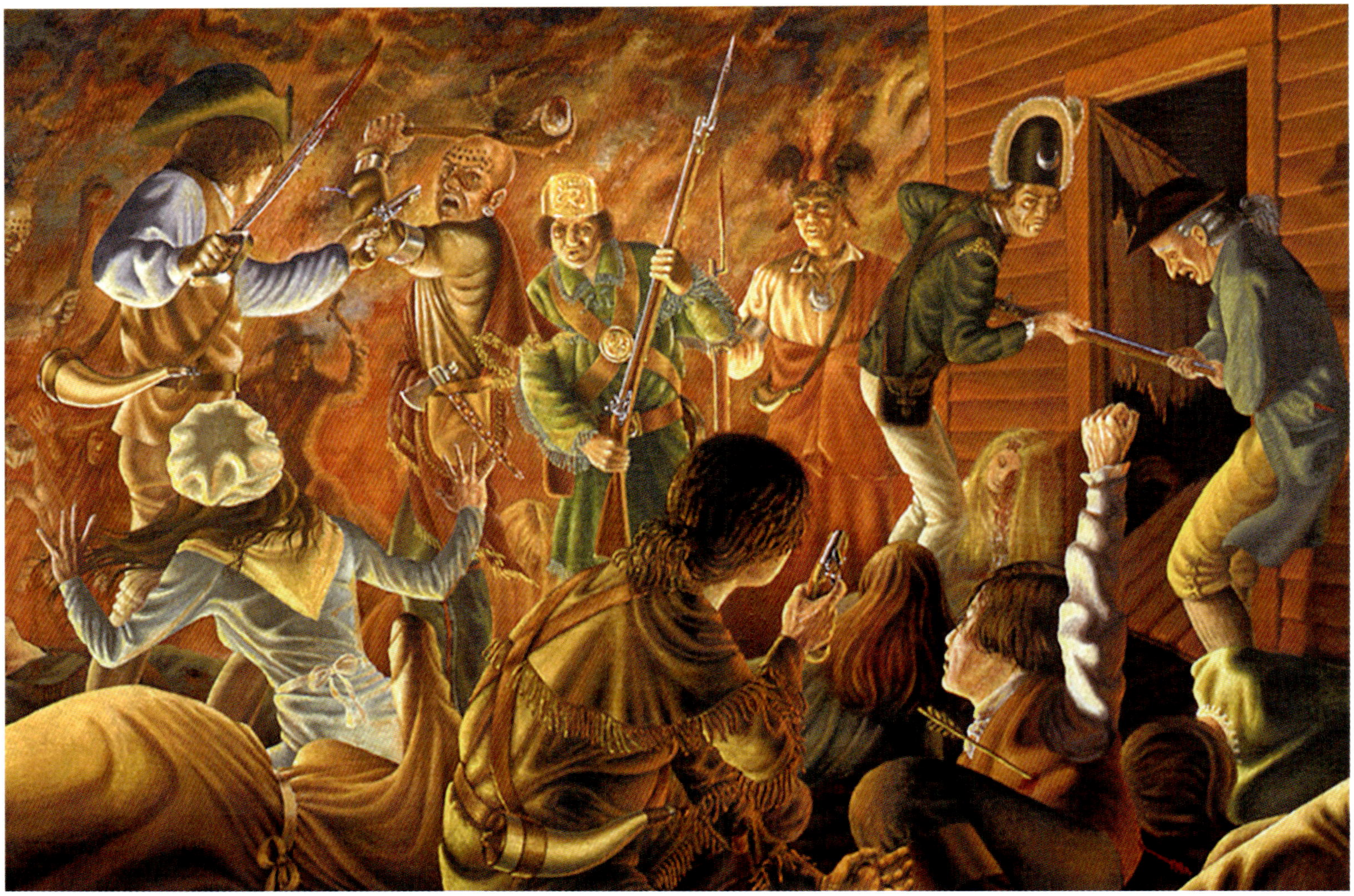

ABOVE: 'Cherry Valley Massacre'; oil on canvas; 24' x 16' (1975). Commissioned by The Heritage Plantation, Cape Cod, MA to commemorate a Revolutionary War battle for the bicentennial.

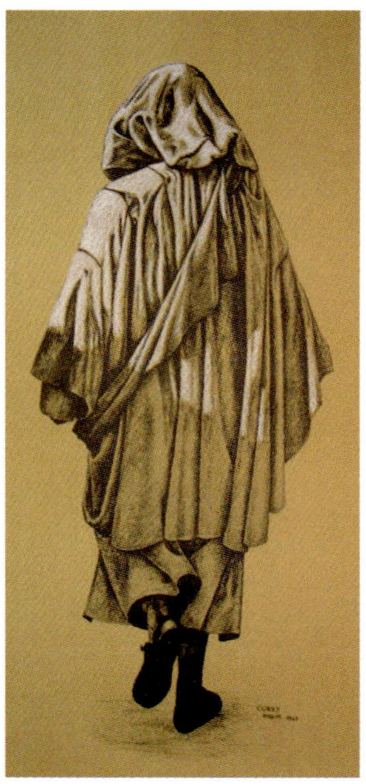

ABOVE: 'Wayfarer'; lithograph from sketch; 12" x 22" (1969).

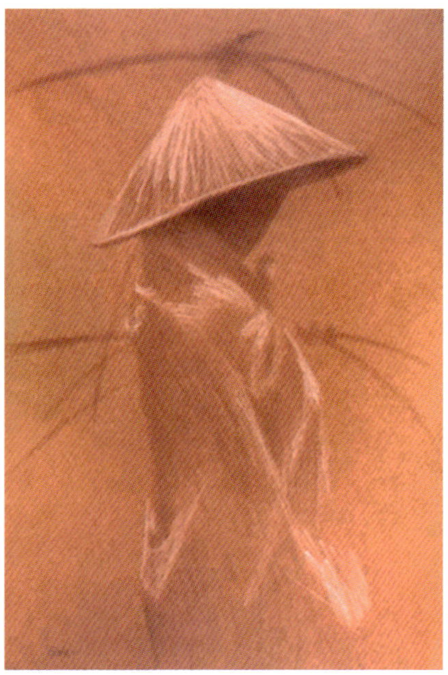

ABOVE: 'Vietnamese Woman Checking Her Nets'; pencil on paper; 12" x 17" (1970).

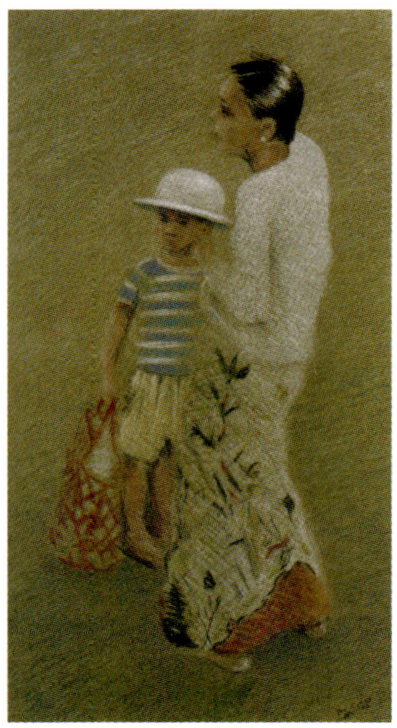

ABOVE: 'Khon Kaen Neighbors'; pastel pencils on paper; 8" x 13" (1972).

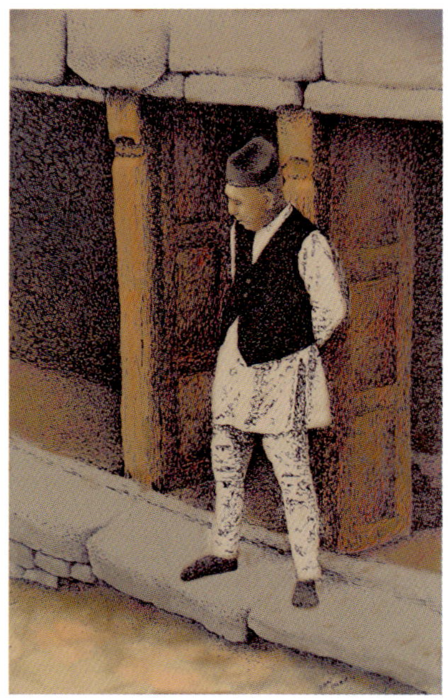

ABOVE: 'Nepali Shopkeeper'; silk screen and pastels; 12" x 18" (1970).

Creating art has been an abiding passion since early childhood, as natural as breathing, always exploring visual expression, trying new ideas and techniques, and applying what I have learned. I enjoy working in a variety of media and styles, sometimes depicting places I've been, and other times delving into the inner world of the imagination in a stream-of-consciousness approach, letting each stroke on an image inspire the next, an expedition into the unknown. These pages are to share with the reader a small sampling of my personal art unrelated to industry endeavors. There is a stress-relieving meditative joy in creating pieces that need approval from no one. They just are.

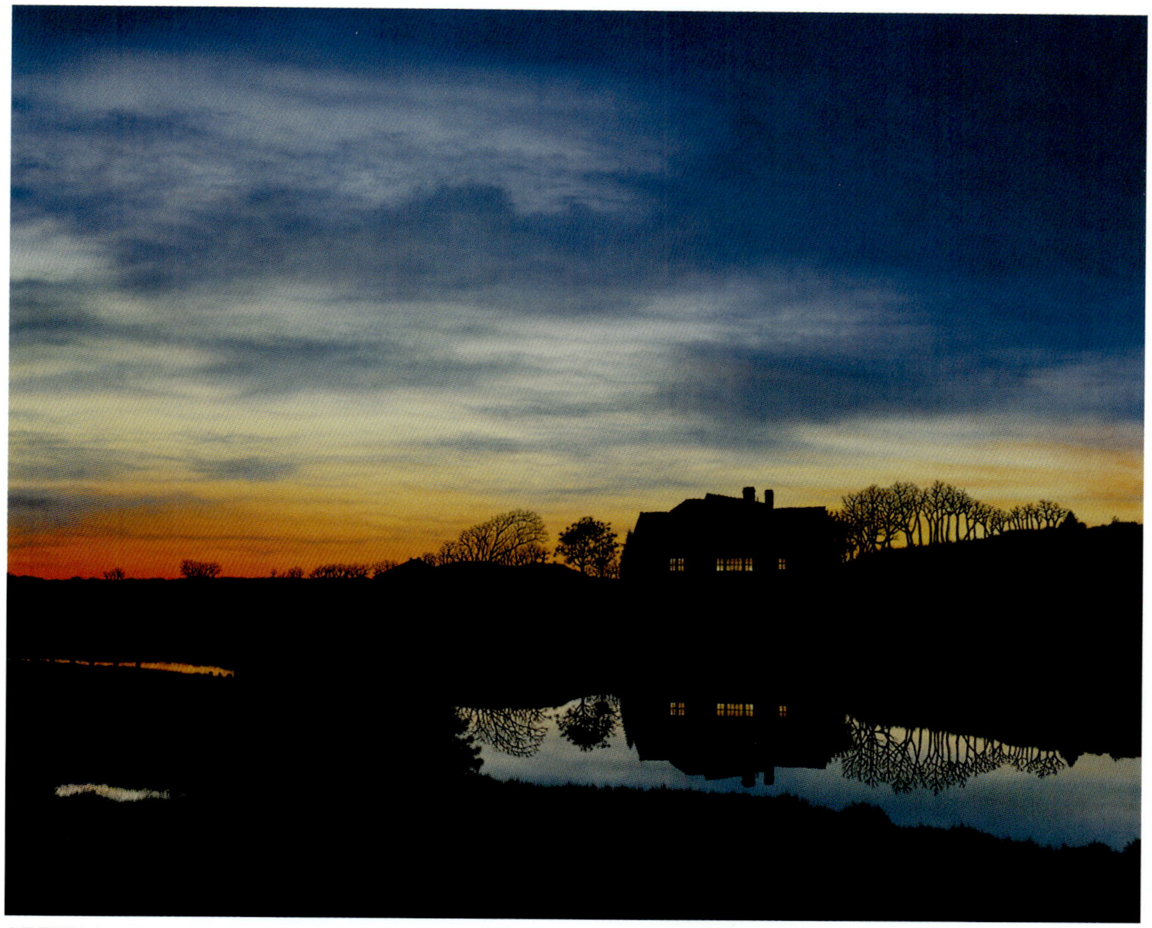

ABOVE: 'Stillness at Last Light, a Late Fall Sunset on Cape Cod'; acrylic on canvas; 72" x 48" (2004).

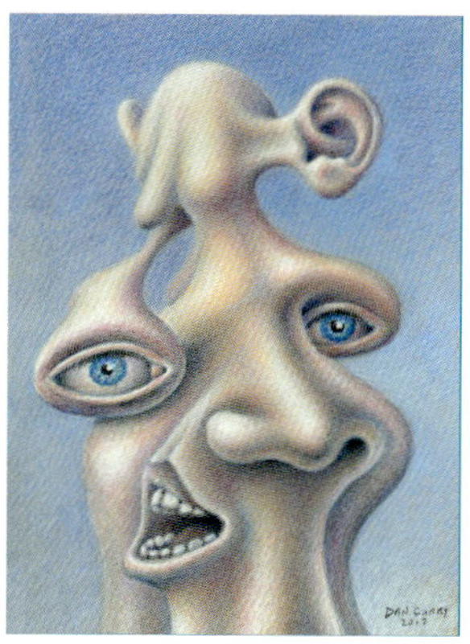

ABOVE: 'Rearrangement'; color pencil on paper; 9" x 16" (2017).

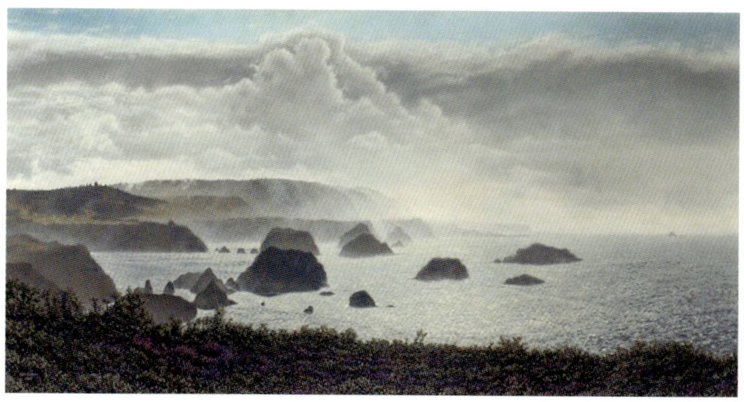

ABOVE: 'Trinidad, California'; oil on canvas; 58" x 30" (1982).

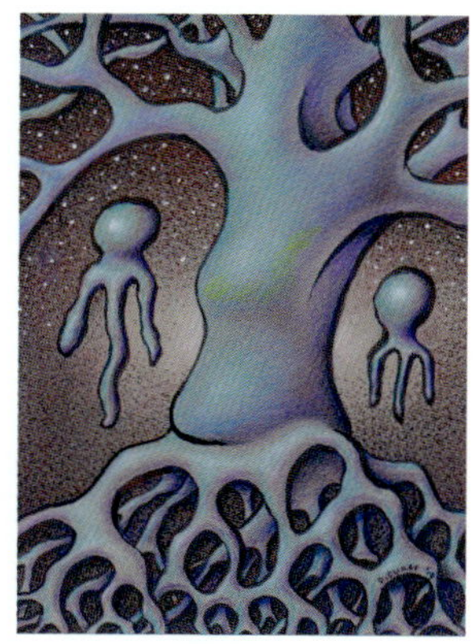

ABOVE: 'Mustache Roots'; pen and ink and color pencil on paper; 9" x 16" (2019).

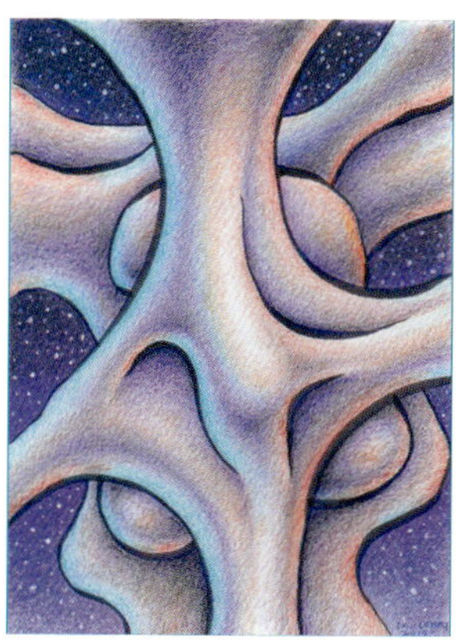

ABOVE Stream of Consciousness sketch.

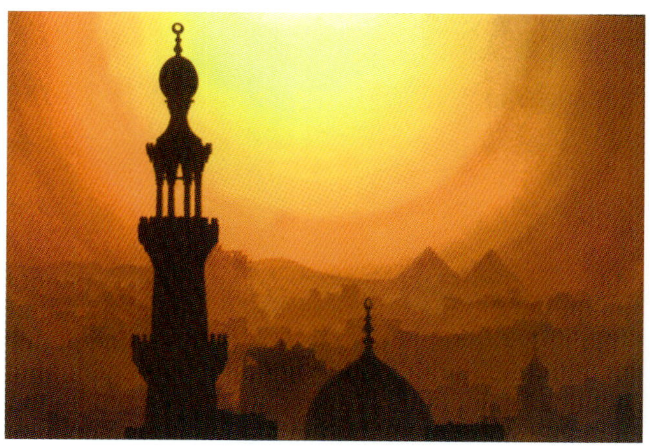

ABOVE: 'The Sun Going Nova As Seen From Ghiza'; oil on Masonite; 36" x 22" (1982).

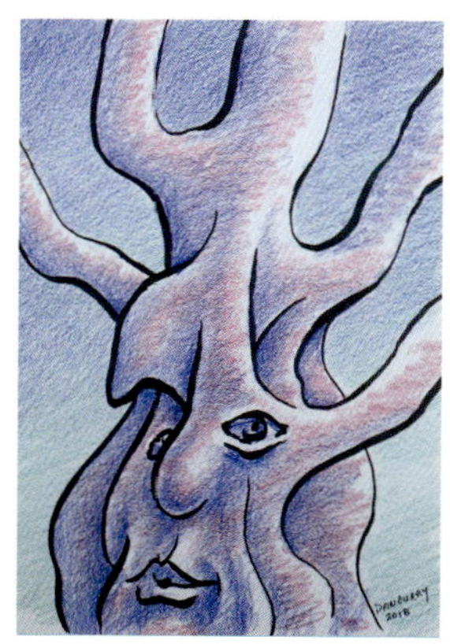

ABOVE: 'Sentient Tree'; pen and ink and color pencil on paper; 9" x 16" (2018).

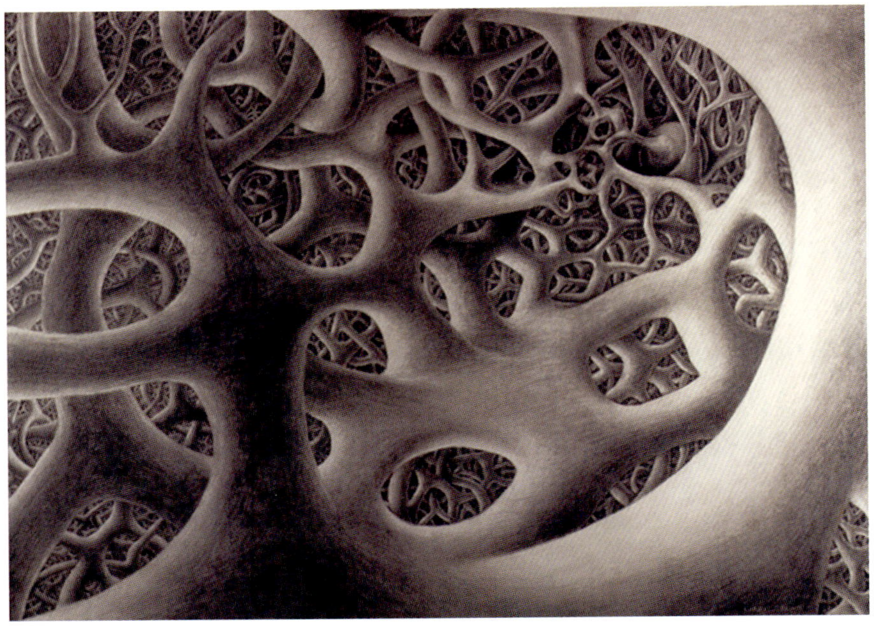

ABOVE: 'Organic Labyrinth'; Crayola on paper; 39" x 28 " (1971). Done in Bangkok, Thailand.

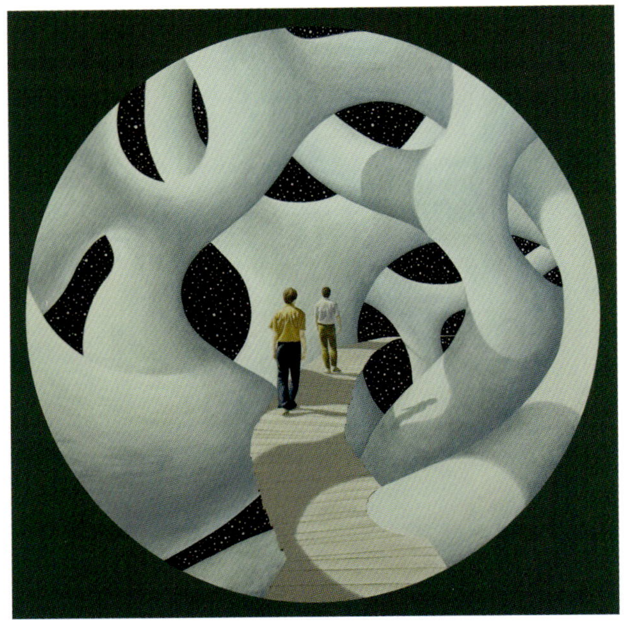

ABOVE: 'Boardwalk'; oil on canvas; 36" x 36" (1974).

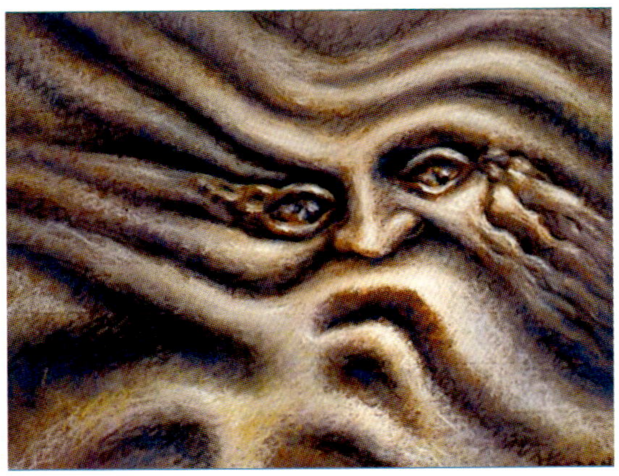

ABOVE: 'Extruded Sneer'; pastel on paper; 11" x 16" (1997).

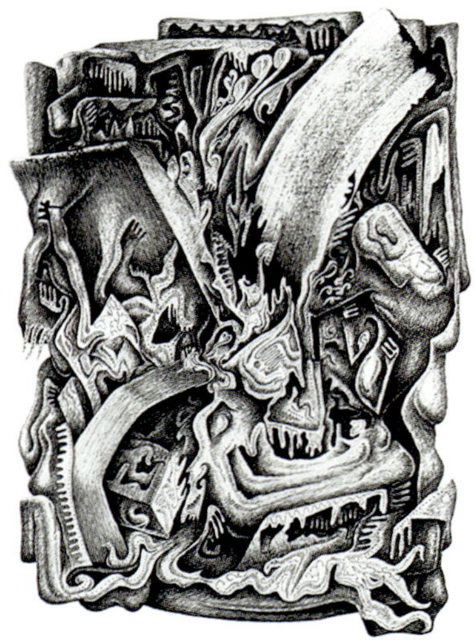

ABOVE: 'Liquid Echoes'; pen and ink; 8" x 11" (1970).

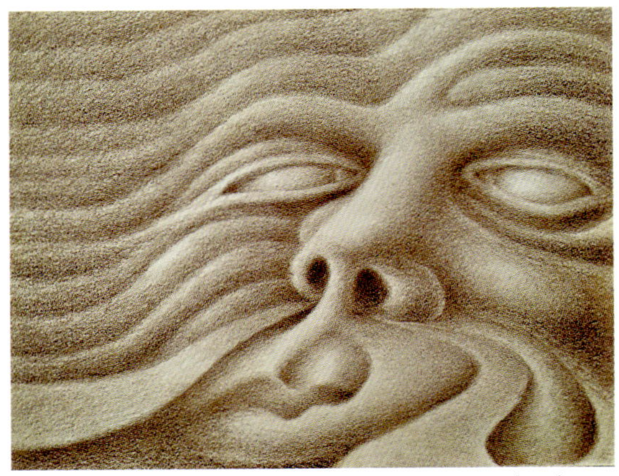

ABOVE: 'Face in the Dunes'; color pencil on paper; 12" x 9" (2016).

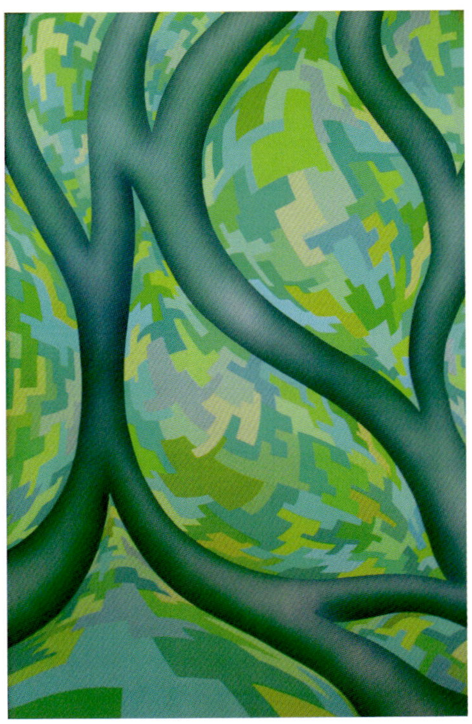

ABOVE: 'Study in Green'; acrylic on canvas; 24" x 36" (1974).

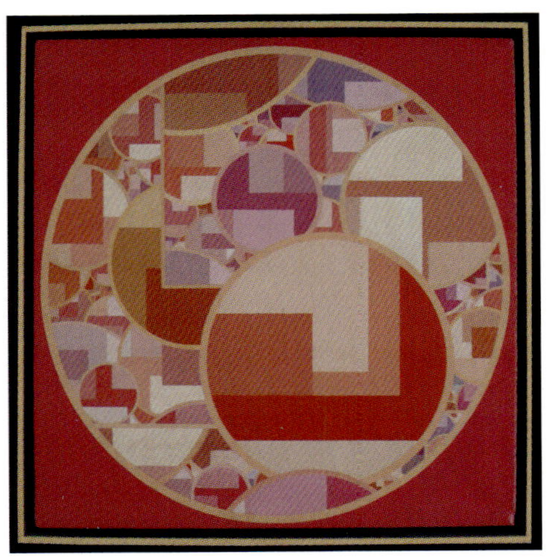

ABOVE: 'Coins'; acrylic on canvas; 18" x 18" (1975).

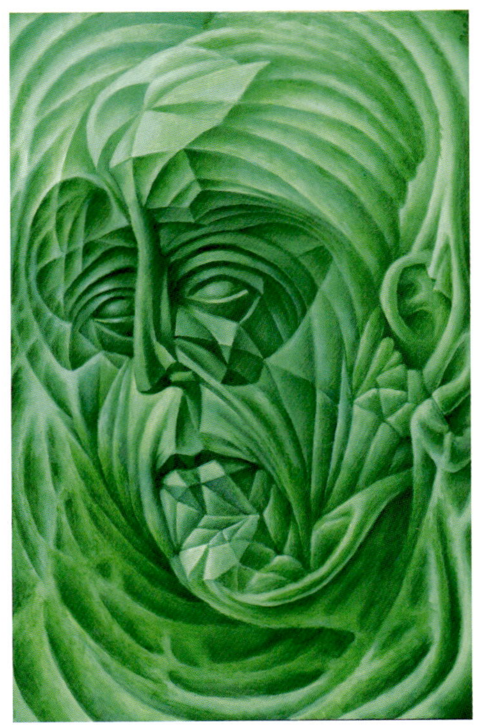

ABOVE: 'Green Prismatic Face'; acrylic on canvas; 24" x 36" (2009).

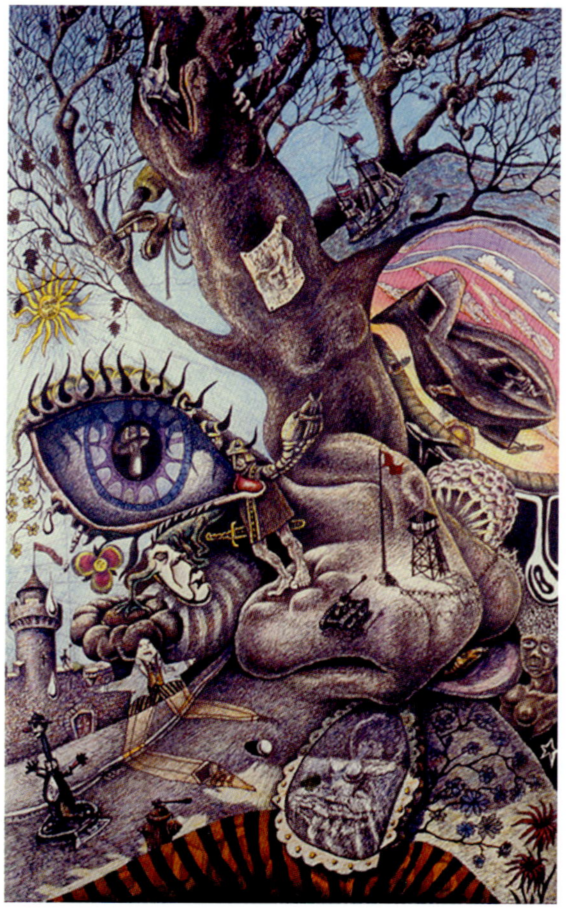

ABOVE: 'Behind the Face'; pen and ink and color pencil; 13" x 20" (1970). Done in Khon Kaen, Thailand.

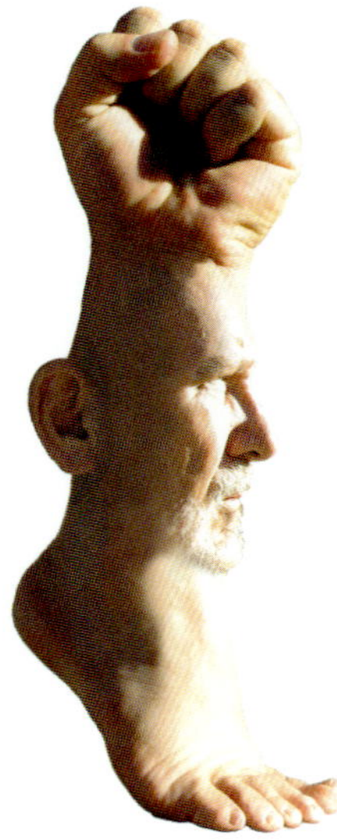

ABOVE: 'Digital Self Portrait'; Photoshop (2007).

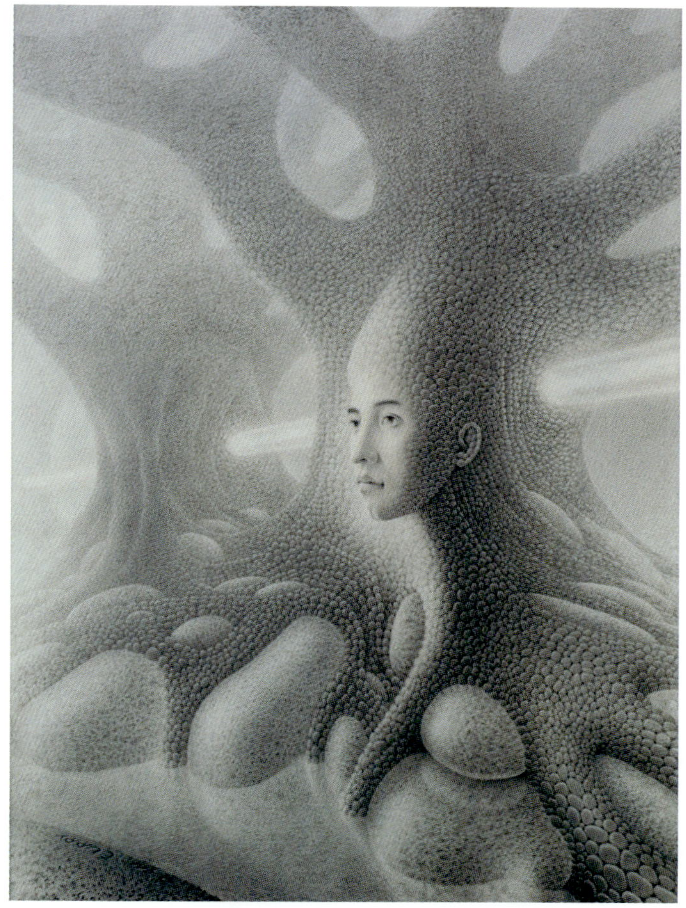

ABOVE: 'Devin Tree'; charcoal on canvas; 36" x 60" (1975). I started with a sketch of my son when he was 15 and followed where the drawing led me.

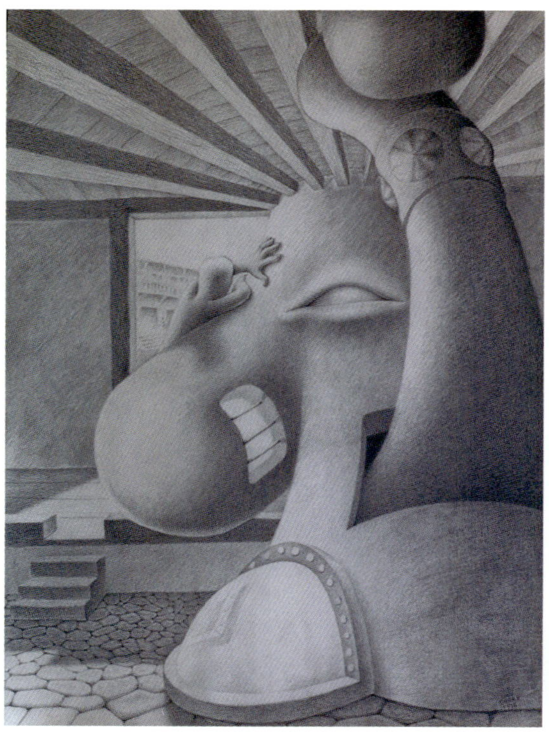

ABOVE: 'The Idolator'; pencil on paper; 18" x 24" (1975).

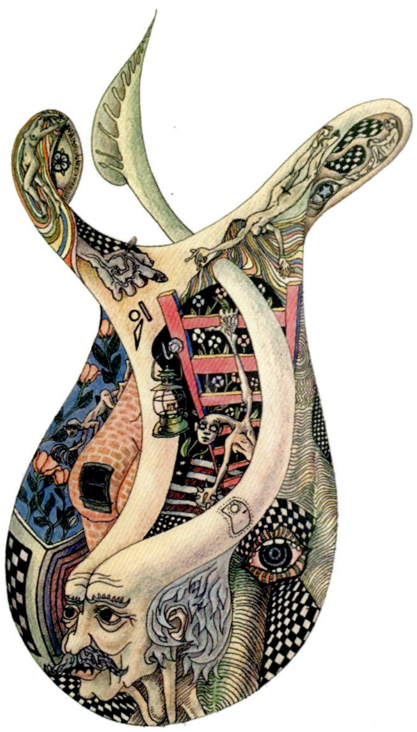

ABOVE: 'Picture Plant'; pen and ink and color pencil; 8" x 11" (1970).

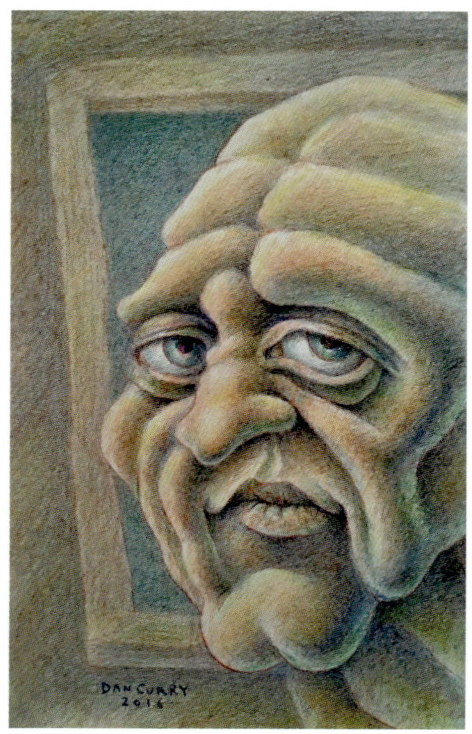

ABOVE: 'Smirking Face'; color pencils; 9" x 16" (2018).

RIGHT: 3D scan of Dan by Gentle Giant.

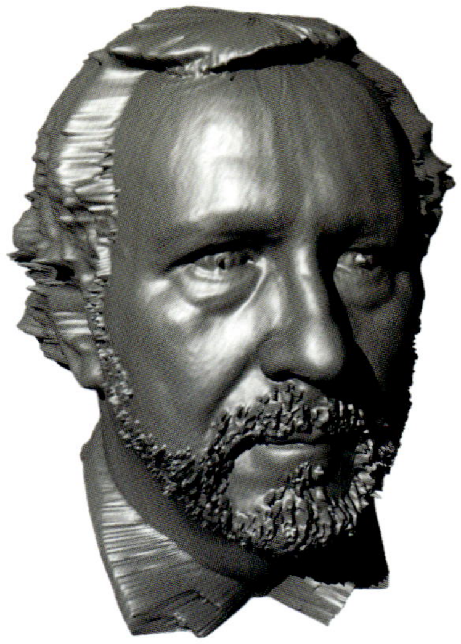

AFTERWORD

A LOOK TO THE FUTURE

Those of us who had the privilege of being part of Gene Roddenberry's enduring creation, *Star Trek*, not only helped to create an inspiring vision of the future, but also played a part in the evolution of image-making technology. We began by relying upon long-established techniques based upon photochemical reactions that, by today's digital standards, may seem Neolithic. Evolving computer technology has given visual storytellers unprecedented tools. Image-capture technology has brought us cameras capable of perfect exposure, from extremely low to extremely high light intensities, making film almost obsolete. Advances in lighting technology provide color temperature precision especially useful for visual-effects applications. Scientists and engineers continue to achieve ever-higher image resolutions, more naturalistic 3D, and create algorithms that can convincingly simulate any imaginable phenomenon.

Future quantum computing, nanoscience, and technologies not yet imagined will empower our species to manipulate massive amounts of data, allowing huge screens to display 3D images without glasses. Ever-improving sound technology will enable great strides in immersive storytelling. Artificial Intelligence and robotics, now in their infancy, will evolve and merge with other technologies to further expand a storyteller's tool kit. Future generations, having grown up with computers and sophisticated interactive games, will redefine the very nature of entertainment. What we create now will come to be viewed as quaint as medieval miracle plays or traditional Thai village shadow puppet theatre. Gene's visionary concept of the holodeck may come to be, with as yet undreamt of technologies to open up new worlds of the imagination to not just satisfy the primordial human need to be told a story, but to virtually live it.

I would like to believe that our work on *Star Trek* will be preserved and enjoyed by future generations, and studied for its visionary storytelling, its place in the evolution of imaging technology, and its positive influence on global culture.

A FINAL NOTE TO THE READER

I believe I can confidently speak for every individual involved in the creation of *Star Trek*'s visual effects in expressing the pride we all had in our team's collective achievement. Although I had the honor of playing a leadership role, I emphasize that there is no single hero of *Trek* VFX. The range of skills and artistry needed to create *Star Trek*'s on-screen images is beyond the capacity of any one human being. Each individual contributed to a whole greater than the sum of its parts. There are too many people involved to mention each important team member by name, but it is to all of them, and to their families that endured the long hours and missed family events, that I express my enduring gratitude and respect. In the grand scheme of the cosmos we all shared a moment in time that seems to have passed in the blink of an eye. Producers, writers, cast, and crew together created a vision of what humanity can be, and shared that vision with audiences around the world.

The majesty, emotional intensity, and excitement brought to visual effects by the music of our brilliant composers like Jay Chattaway, Dennis McCarthy, Ron Jones, and Jerry Goldsmith, along with our team of sound designers, must also be recognized.

Special thanks to the four captains—Patrick, Avery, Kate and Scott—for their leadership on set, and to the rest of the cast for their unwavering support and cooperation with the visual-effects team.

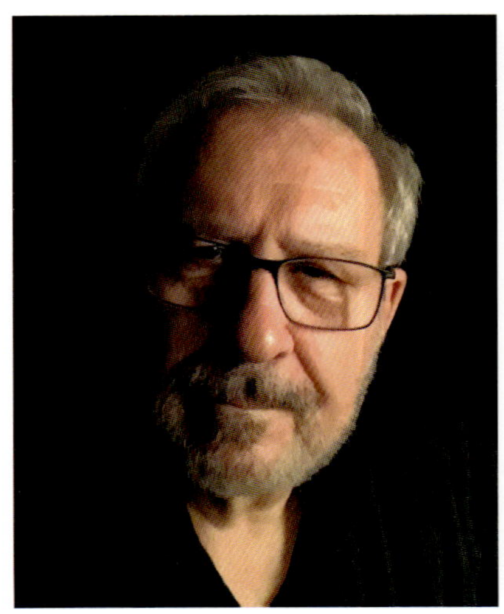

Lastly, a word of appreciation to our audience. Their criticism kept us sharp. Their loyalty and enthusiasm kept us all employed, and reminded us of whom we were really working for.

"That which I should have done I did not do."

Title of painting by Ivan Albright, American artist (1897–1983)

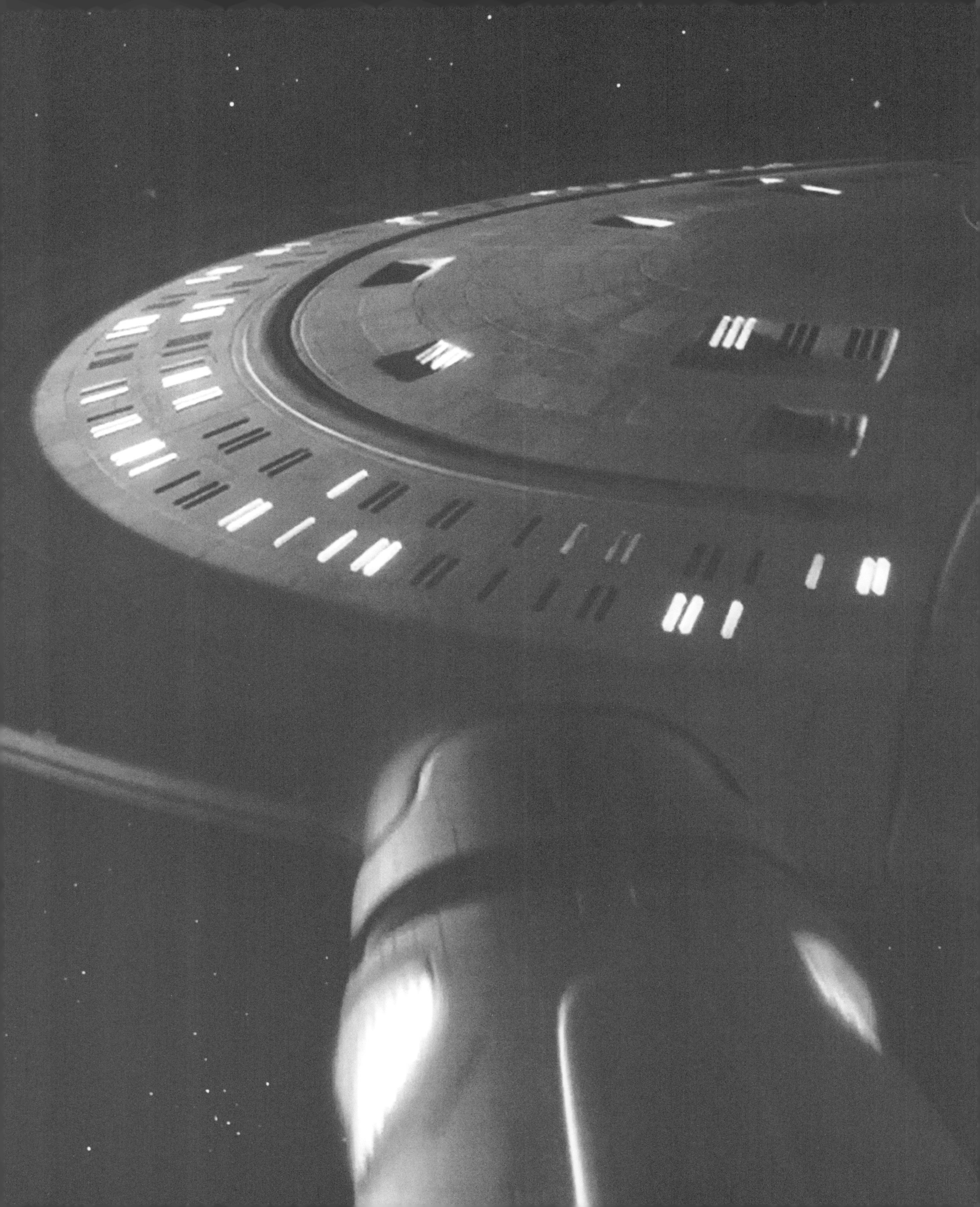